THE LAW OF
LIMITED LIABILITY PARTNERSHIPS

THE LAW OF
LIMITED LIABILITY PARTNERSHIPS

John Whittaker BCL, MA
Barrister, Serle Court

John Machell LLB (Soton)
Barrister, Serle Court

with a tax chapter by Colin Ives ATII, ATT
Professional Practices Director
Smith & Williamson

JORDANS
2004

Published by
Jordan Publishing Limited
21 St Thomas Street
Bristol BS1 6JS

British Library Cataloguing-in-Publication Data

A catalogue record for this book is available from the British Library.

ISBN 0 85308 946 9

Typeset by Jordan Publishing Limited
Printed by Antony Rowe Ltd, Chippenham, Wiltshire

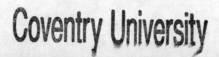

FOREWORD TO THE FIRST EDITION

In response to calls from professional firms faced with the possibility of negligence claims for ever-increasing amounts, the Limited Liability Partnerships Act 2000 ('the Act') has introduced into English law a new corporate entity, the limited liability partnership ('the LLP'). The LLP is not, however, a form of business association available only to professional firms: the owner-managers of any business may decide to adopt it. The LLP can be viewed as 'the third way', an alternative lying midway between the two long-established forms of business association, namely the traditional limited liability company subject to the capital, management and decision-making requirements of the Companies Act 1985, and the traditional partnership with its capital and management flexibility and unlimited liability.

How, and in what circumstances, and with what frequency, LLPs come to be used as vehicles for carrying on a profession or business remains to be seen. But their introduction is a matter of great importance in the development of both corporate law and professional practice in England. No professional and no businessman can afford to be ignorant of the potential and implications of use of an LLP by himself or by those with whom he deals; and no legal adviser can consistently with his duty to his client fail to advise his client on these matters.

The introduction of LLPs warrants a book which sets out to explain the concept of the LLP and membership of it, how to embark upon 'the third way', and what lies ahead for the entity and for its members. The need for a comprehensive text is all the greater because the Act itself is only a framework, and any full consideration of what is involved in entering into an LLP must involve considering both the application to it of common law and equitable principles evolved over the years, and the effect of the extensive modifications made by the Limited Liability Partnerships Regulations 2001 to existing company and insolvency legislation as it is now to apply to LLPs. These Regulations are themselves 100 pages long.

As this book makes clear, the comfort of a limit on liability, together with the convenience of a tailor-made 'LLP agreement', does not come without a price. Professionals will need to face up to the possibility of full (and authorised) disclosure of their accounts and profit figures. Individuals used to minimal outside regulation affecting their current unincorporated business will need to recognise that incorporation brings with it the regulatory rules and disciplines in place to protect creditors. It is to be noted that one of the longest chapters in this book (Chapter 11) is that on the duties and responsibilities of members.

This book considers many of the issues which will be of concern to individual members of an LLP, in particular the continuing possibility of personal liability for one's own negligence, the financial consequences for a person ceasing to be a member, possible liabilities in the event of an insolvent liquidation and taxation.

The Act poses challenges to the judiciary and the legal and accountancy professions. The law relating to LLPs needs to be developed constructively and coherently. Difficult questions of construction of the Act and of its application need to be resolved. This work by two experienced barristers well qualified for the task makes a valuable contribution to the understanding of this area of the law and should enable all who have recourse to it to be able to understand the concepts and legal rules applicable and expound and explain the law with clarity and confidence.

SIR GAVIN LIGHTMAN

PREFACE

The first edition of this book was published in June 2001, shortly after the LLP Act 2000, and the LLP Regulations 2001, had come into force on 6 April 2001. Over the 3½ years since then the use of LLPs as vehicles for carrying on professional practices, and for carrying on other businesses also, has been gathering pace.

As LLPs have been established, whether for new businesses or on the conversion of existing general partnerships, issues have arisen which we, and other professional advisers, have been obliged to consider. At the same time, we have seen areas not covered by the first edition which we think could usefully be covered in this work. And there has, of course, been new legislation, both primary and secondary. In addition, and equally importantly, in May 2002 the SORP for accounting by LLPs was issued by the Consultative Committee of Accountancy Bodies. All these matters have led to us writing this second edition.

The scheme of the chapters essentially follows that of the first edition. There is, however, a new chapter (Chapter 17: Foreign Connections and Oversea LLPs) which discusses issues of jurisdiction over domestic LLPs, and the position of oversea LLPs operating in England. We have also sought in this chapter to provide a resumé of the nature and character of LLPs formed in other jurisdictions, and how they differ from GB LLPs.

The application of new legislation to LLPs is not at all times easy to determine; and we have set out our approach to this general issue in paras **1.14–1.15** of the text. New legislation has had the greatest impact in relation to insolvency, as a result of new provisions introduced by the Insolvency Act 2000 (most of which were not in force at the time of the first edition) and the Enterprise Act 2002. The chapters on insolvency, receivership and winding up reflect these new provisions. New legislation also now permits members of LLPs (like company directors) to have the benefit of Confidentiality Orders, under which the home address of a member may be kept off publicly available documents filed with the registrar of companies. Such orders are considered in Chapter 8.

In order to provide practitioners with the modified text of the Companies Act 1985, the Company Directors Disqualification Act 1986 and the Insolvency Act 1986 as they apply in England and Wales to LLPs, and with other useful material, this edition is published with a CD-ROM. The first edition had as a companion volume the *Limited Liability Partnerships Legislation Handbook*, setting out the modified text of the 1985 and 1986 Acts. As a result of amendments made to these Acts, however, the *Legislation Handbook* (whilst still useful in parts) can no longer be relied upon as a work. The opportunity has been taken to include on the CD-ROM additional material, principally statutory instruments and the EC Council Regulation on insolvency proceedings, but also the SORP for LLPs and material relating to LLPs published by the Inland Revenue, and by Customs & Excise. The inclusion of the full text of the LLP Regulations 2001 (themselves amended by subsequent statutory instrument) will enable the reader to go back to the source to determine for himself (and to compare our interpretation as to) how, in relation to any particular provision of the CA 1985, the CDDA 1986 or the IA 1986, that provision has been modified for LLPs.

There are a number of people to whom we owe debts of gratitude. As with the first edition, our colleagues in Serle Court have been most patient sounding-boards. In particular, David Blayney provided considerable insight on the problems discussed in chapter 5 and Jennifer Haywood produced an invaluable first draft of the new chapter 17. Others who have assisted include David Drake and Hugh Norbury. Outside Serle Court, we wish to thank Claire Harrington of Travers Smith Braithwaite and Jane Feeney of Mayer, Brown, Rowe & Maw LLP for their help. We continue to be grateful to colleagues in the Association of Partnership Practitioners for their thoughts generously contributed. Any errors and omissions are ours alone.

Colin Ives, Professional Practices Director, Smith & Williamson, has again contributed the chapter on taxation (chapter 21), an ever important topic; and we wish to express our thanks to him.

We have sought to state the law as at 20 October 2004.

The publishers have kindly prepared the tables of cases and statutes, and the index; and they have undertaken the core editing of the modified legislation appearing on the CD-ROM. Pat Ashenden in Serle Court has tirelessly typed for us. We are grateful to them all.

John Whittaker
John Machell
Serle Court
Lincoln's Inn

20 October 2004

NOTES ON THE CD-ROM

The scheme of the LLP legislation is that the LLP Act 2000 itself creates the new entity and sets out its core principles, and then regulations made under the Act apply – with modifications – particular parts of the Companies Act 1985, the Company Directors Disqualification Act 1986 and the Insolvency Act 1986 to the entity and its members. As we have mentioned in the Preface, in order to provide practitioners with the modified text of the CA 1985, the CDDA 1986 and the IA 1986 (as they apply to LLPs in England and Wales), and with other useful material, this edition is published with a CD-ROM.

The modifications to the 1985 and 1986 Acts are made principally by the LLP Regulations 2001, SI 2001/1090, which came into force at the same time as the LLP Act 2000 itself on 6 April 2001. There are both general modifications (set out in the LLP Regulations 2001, regs 3, 4(1), 4(2) and 5) as well as specific modifications (set out in the LLP Regulations 2001, Schs 1, 2 and 3, and also in the LLP (No 2) Regulations 2002, SI 2002/913 and in the LLP (Confidentiality Orders) Regulations 2002, SI 2002/915). The most important general modifications are that references to a 'company' shall include references to a 'limited liability partnership', and references to a 'director of a company' shall include references to a 'member of a limited liability partnership'. The phrase 'shall include' is not always easy to apply. In most cases, a simple transposition is required. However, in some places it is not clear whether references to a 'company' are to be read as references to a 'limited liability partnership or company'. Examples are CDDA 1986, s 1 and IA 1986, ss 216 and 217. Inevitably, we have made editorial decisions (for instance, in CA 1985, s 258, defining the expressions 'parent undertaking' and 'subsidiary undertaking'). Where we see a positive lack of clarity as to the effect of the general modification (or it is otherwise helpful to be alert to a point), we have referred to this in a footnote: the reader may wish to consult the relevant Act and the LLP Regulations 2001 in their original form. These Regulations are included in their entirety on the CD-ROM.

The modified legislation is intended to be set out as it stands at 20 October 2004. Perhaps, inevitably, this is a rather arbitrary date. At the time of going to print, the draft Companies Act 1985 (International Accounting Standards and Other Accounting Amendments) Regulations 2004 have been laid before Parliament, with a view to them coming into force on 1 January 2005 as respects companies' financial years which begin on or after 1 January 2005. These Regulations will introduce the option for companies of preparing their accounts in accordance with international accounting standards. We understand that it is intended that the amendments to be made to the CA 1985 by these Regulations should apply to LLPs at the same time as to companies, but with specific modifications for LLPs to be introduced by a further statutory instrument. At the time of writing, no draft of that statutory instrument is available. In the light of this, the modified text of the CA 1985 reproduced on the CD-ROM does not include any prospective amendments by the draft 2004 Regulations. With this caveat (and there are references in the text of the book to prospective amendments), we hope that the CD-ROM proves to be a useful tool. We are grateful to the editorial staff at Jordans for undertaking the core editing.

John Whittaker
John Machell
Serle Court
Lincoln's Inn

20 October 2004

CONTENTS

CONTENTS OF THE ACCOMPANYING CD-ROM

Limited Liability Partnerships Act 2000
Companies Act 1985 (as modified for LLPs)
Insolvency Act 1986 (as modified for LLPs)
Companies Directors Disqualification Act 1986 (as modified for LLPs)
Limited Liability Partnerships Regulations 2001, SI 2001/1090
Limited Liability Partnerships (Fees) (No 2) Regulations 2001 (Sch), SI 2001/969
Limited Liability Partnerships (No 2) Regulations 2002, SI 2002/913
Limited Liability Partnerships (Particulars of Usual Residential Address)
    (Confidentiality Orders) Regulations 2002 (without Sch 2), SI 2002/915
Insolvency Act 2000 (Commencement No 1 and Transitional Provisions)
    Order 2001, SI 2001/766
Insolvency Act 2000 (Commencement No 3 and Transitional Provisions)
    Order 2002, SI 2002/2711
Enterprise Act 2002 (Commencement No 4 and Transitional Provisions
    and Savings) Order 2003, SI 2003/2093
Insolvency Act 1986 Section 72A (Appointed Date) Order 2003, SI 2003/2095
Enterprise Act 2002 (Insolvency) Order 2003, SI 2003/2096
Enterprise Act 2002 (Transitional Provisions)(Insolvency) Order 2003,
    SI 2003/2332
Insolvency Act 1986 (Prescribed Part) Order 2003, SI 2003/2097
EU Insolvency Regulation
LLP SORP
Tax Bulletin No 50 Article on LLPs
Customs & Excise Business Brief 3/2001
Inland Revenue Statement of Practice D 12 revised October 2002

TABLE OF CASES

TABLE OF STATUTES

References are to paragraph numbers.

TABLE OF STATUTORY INSTRUMENTS, STATEMENTS OF PRACTICE ETC

TABLE OF EC AND INTERNATIONAL MATERIALS

References are to paragraph numbers.

TABLE OF ABBREVIATIONS

ASB	Accounting Standards Board
BNA 1985	Business Names Act 1985
CA 1985	Companies Act 1985
CA 1989	Companies Act 1989
CCAB	Consultative Committee of Accountancy Bodies
CDDA 1986	Company Directors Disqualification Act 1986
CGT	Capital Gains Tax
CGTA 1992	Capital Gains Tax Act 1992
CPR	Civil Procedure Rules 1998
CDDA 1986	Company Directors Disqualification Act 1986
DTI	Department of Trade and Industry
FA 1998	Finance Act 1998
FA 2000	Finance Act 2000
FA 2001	Finance Act 2001
FA 2003	Finance Act 2003
FRSSE	Financial Reporting Standard for Smaller Entities
FSA 1986	Financial Services Act 1986
FSMA 2000	Financial Services and Markets Act 2000
IA 1986	Insolvency Act 1986
IA 2000	Insolvency Act 2000
ICTA 1988	Income and Corporation Taxes Act 1988
IHTA 1984	Inheritance Tax Act 1984
IHT	inheritance tax
IR 1986	Insolvency Rules 1986
LLP	limited liability partnerships
LLP Act 2000	Limited Liability Partnerships Act 2000
LLP Regulations 2001	Limited Liability Partnerships Regulations 2001
LLP Regulations 2002	Limited Liability Partnerships Regulations 2002
LPA 1925	Law of Property Act 1925
PAYE	Pay As You Earn
RUPA	US Revised Uniform Partnership Act 1994
SDLT	Stamp duty land tax
SORP	Statement of Recommended Practice
SPD12	Inland Revenue Statement of Practice D12
SSAP	Statements of Standard Accounting Practice
TCGA 1982	Taxation of Capital Gains Act 1982
TCGA 1992	Taxation of Capital Gains Act 1992
TMA 1970	Taxes Management Act 1970
UCTA 1977	Unfair Contract Terms Act 1977
UITF	Urgent Issues Task Force
UK GAAP	UK Generally Accepted Accounting Practice

Chapter 1

OVERVIEW AND INTRODUCTORY MATTERS

A NEW BUSINESS ENTITY

1.1   Section 1(1) of the Limited Liability Partnerships Act 2000 (LLP Act 2000) provides: 'There shall be a new form of legal entity to be known as a limited liability partnership'. The entity (henceforth referred to as an LLP) is brought into existence by two or more persons (the first 'members') incorporating themselves as an LLP. Thereafter, and as in the case of a traditional partnership,[1] members are able to join and leave in accordance with whatever contractual terms they agree.

1.2   The key characteristics of an LLP, set out in s 1 of the LLP Act 2000, are that it is a body corporate and that it has unlimited capacity.[2] The 'limited liability' aspect of an LLP relates to the individual members: their liability to contribute to the funds of the corporate entity, and specifically to a shortfall on a winding-up of the LLP, will be limited to whatever they have agreed with the other members or with the LLP to contribute.[3]

1.3   An LLP is, therefore, a corporate entity with its own legal personality separate from that of its members, and with its own rights and liabilities distinct from those of its members. It is in these respects that an LLP differs from a traditional partnership. A partnership in English law (at least so long as the governing statute is the Partnership Act 1890) has no separate legal personality, but is simply the relationship between a group of persons bound by agreement to each other.[4] The essential characteristic of a partnership is that the business is carried on by each partner acting as agent for all the partners, with the result that each partner is jointly and severally liable for the obligations and actions of any of them.[5] In the case of an LLP, generally speaking, it will be the separate corporate entity (as opposed to its members) which carries on the business; and it will be for this entity that each member will be acting as agent. In the result, and again generally speaking, it will, therefore, be the corporate entity (to the exclusion of the individual members) which is the subject of the duties and liabilities of the business.

---

[1]   Ie a partnership governed by the provisions of the Partnership Act 1890.

[2]   LLP Act 2000, s 1(2) and (3). As to unlimited capacity, see further **3.4–3.5**.

[3]   Ibid, s 1(4) and Insolvency Act 1986 (IA 1986), s 74, on which see further **26.17–26.21**. But this limitation will always be subject to the possible application of the IA 1986, ss 212–214A.

[4]   The draft Partnerships Bill presented to Parliament by the Law Commission in November 2003 (Law Com No 283) provides for partnerships to have a legal personality separate from that of the partners (but the partners would continue to have unlimited personal liability for the partnership's liabilities and obligations).

[5]   Undertaken in the normal course of the partnership's business: Partnership Act 1890, ss 5–12.

1.4 The existence of an LLP serves, therefore (in broad terms), to shield the individual members from personal liability for the acts of another member (or employee) carried out in the course of the business, and from personal liability also for the general commercial obligations of the business. It may also serve to shield an individual member from personal liability for his own acts carried out in the course of the business.[6]

1.5 An LLP differs from the normal company limited by shares in its ability to have a decision-making and profit-sharing structure written uniquely for its business and participants. Whilst an LLP is subject to various provisions of the Companies Act 1985 (CA 1985) (and other legislation) as modified,[7] it will not be subject to any of the CA 1985 provisions relating to share capital,[8] management[9] or meetings and resolutions.[10] Unlike a company, there is no distinction in the internal structure of an LLP between the roles of owners of the business (shareholders) and managers (directors). There are no publicly available articles of association for an LLP. The decision-making structure, and the terms of association of the participants (ie the members), are purely a matter of private agreement amongst the participants. This agreement (which the authors will call 'the LLP agreement'), like a traditional partnership agreement, is not required to be disclosed to the outside world.

1.6 The LLP agreement (subject to certain overriding statutory provisions[11]) will govern the rights and duties of the members as between themselves, and will govern also the rights and duties existing as between the members and the LLP as a separate entity.[12] In addition to the overriding statutory provisions, there are certain 'default rules' which will have effect to govern these mutual rights and duties to the extent that such rules are not written out or varied by the LLP agreement actually made.[13]

DISCLOSURE AND REGULATION

1.7 The bearing of the liabilities of the business by the LLP, and the corresponding limitation of liability on the part of its members, is the key commercial element in LLPs. This protective shield for the members (and corresponding limitation of rights of recourse for those doing business with the LLP) carries with it obligations for the LLP to observe various regulatory requirements, and to provide information about itself for public scrutiny. In particular, it will be obliged (like a company) to file annual accounts (with an

---

6   The possible liabilities of individual members to third parties are discussed in chapter 15.
7   See further **1.13**.
8   CA 1985, ss 58–220, eg allotment of shares, reduction of capital, etc.
9   Ibid, ss 282–347.
10 Ibid, ss 366–383.
11 Ie in the CA 1985 and the IA 1986.
12 LLP Act 2000, s 5(1). The LLP agreement is discussed in chapter 9.
13 The default rules are contained in regs 7 and 8 of the Limited Liability Partnerships Regulations 2001, SI 2001/1090 (the LLP Regulations 2001) referred to at **1.13**.

auditors' report) and an annual return.[14] Additionally, it will need to file notices of any changes in its membership.[15] These (and other) disclosure requirements are part of the price which the members pay for the liabilities of the business being borne by the separate entity, and for their own personal liabilities being limited. The outside world is entitled to know the financial state, and composition, of the limited liability business with which it is dealing. In pursuit of this, the LLP Act 2000 requires that there is always a minimum of two 'designated members', whose essential role is to carry responsibility for the principal regulatory and disclosure requirements being met.[16]

1.8 The other part of the price to be paid for limited liability is that LLPs, and individual members, will be subject to the 'policing' regime of the CA 1985, the Insolvency Act 1986 (IA 1986) and the Company Directors Disqualification Act 1986 (CDDA 1986).[17] LLPs will be subject, like companies, to the power of the Department of Trade and Industry to investigate them, and to the power of the Secretary of State to require information.[18] Members will be subject to the CDDA 1986 in the same way as company directors;[19] and, in the event of the LLP going into liquidation, will be subject to the 'wrongful trading' and similar provisions of the IA 1986.[20]

THE REGISTRAR

1.9 Reference has been made in **1.7** to the obligation on an LLP to file annual accounts, and other information. This filing is with the Registrar of Companies. In broad terms, the Registrar of Companies takes on the same role in relation to LLPs as he has in relation to companies. With certain modifications, CA 1985, Part XXIV,[21] setting out the Registrar's functions, is adopted for LLPs. LLPs are added to the bodies whose names are kept on the Registrar's index of company and corporate names;[22] and the provisions of Part XXIV relating to the delivery to the Registrar of documents in legible form and (if desired) by electronic

---

[14] Annual accounts are discussed in chapter 18. The obligations as to auditing and filing accounts are subject to the same exemptions as for 'small companies'. The annual return is discussed at **4.26– 4.31**.

[15] LLP Act 2000, s 9. The LLP will need to have a registered office, and notice of any change in this will also need to be filed. The registered office is discussed at **2.22–2.23** and **3.12–3.18**.

[16] Designated members are discussed in chapter 10.

[17] 'The concept of limited liability and the sophistication of our corporate law offers great privileges and great opportunities for those who wish to trade under that regime. But the corporate environment carries with it the discipline that those who avail themselves of those privileges must accept the standards laid down and abide by the regulatory rules and disciplines in place to protect creditors and shareholders': Henry LJ in *Re Grayan Building Services Ltd* [1995] Ch 241 at 257 (a director's disqualification case).

[18] This is discussed in chapter 20.

[19] The application of the CDDA 1986 is considered in chapter 32.

[20] Considered in chapter 27.

[21] Sections 704–715A.

[22] CA 1985, s 714(1)(da), added by LLP Act 2000, Sch, para 1.

communication,[23] are applied to LLPs, as are the provisions relating to the supply by the Registrar of documents in non-legible form,[24] and the provisions relating to fees payable to the Registrar.[25] If an LLP defaults in complying with any provision of the CA 1985 or the LLP Act 2000 which requires it to deliver a document to the Registrar, or to give notice to him of any matter, the Registrar may serve a notice on the LLP requiring it to deliver the document or give the notice.[26] If the LLP then fails to do so within 14 days after service of the notice on it, the Registrar may apply to court for an order that the default be remedied.[27]

1.10 Notices of the issue or receipt by the Registrar of any of the following documents will be published by him in the *London Gazette*:[28]

(i)   the certificate of incorporation of the LLP;
(ii)   any document making or evidencing an alteration in the LLP's incorporation document;[29]
(iii)   any notification of a change among the members of the LLP;[30]
(iv)   any accounts and reports delivered by the LLP under CA 1985, s 242(1);
(v)   any notice of a change in the situation of the LLP's registered office;
(vi)   any copy of a winding-up order in respect of the LLP; and
(vii)   any return by a liquidator of the final meeting of the LLP on a winding up.

What is published in the *London Gazette* is not the substance or contents of the document, but notification that the document has been issued (in the case of the certificate of incorporation) or received by the Registrar. Anyone wishing to see the document can inspect it or obtain a copy under CA 1985, s 709 discussed in **1.11**. The purpose of the publication of these notices in the *Gazette* is to enable persons dealing (or considering dealing) with the LLP, and indeed any third parties, to be aware that such events have occurred, and to ascertain the substance of them by inspecting the relevant document.[31]

---

[23]   CA 1985, s 706. 'Legible' means capable of being read with the naked eye: CA 1985, s 715A. The section also specifies requirements in addition to legibility. CA 1985, s 707B permits delivery by electronic communication in a form and manner approved by the Registrar.

[24]   CA 1985, s 710A.

[25]   Ibid, s 708. The Limited Liability Partnerships (Fees) (No 2) Regulations 2001, SI 2001/969, set out the fees to be paid to the Registrar on incorporation of an LLP, delivery of the annual return, notification of change of name and other matters.

[26]   CA 1985, s 713(1). References to 'the Companies Acts' include references to the LLP Act 2000: see reg 4(1)(b) of the LLP Regulations 2001.

[27]   Such an application and order is without prejudice to any penalties contained in the legislation in respect of the default: CA 1985, s 713(3).

[28]   CA 1985, s 711(1).

[29]   As to the alteration of an LLP's incorporation document, see **2.31**.

[30]   As to a change among the members of the LLP, see **8.5–8.7** and **8.33–8.36**.

[31]   See *Official Custodian for Charities v Parway Estates Developments Ltd* [1985] Ch 151 (CA), considering s 9(3) of the European Communities Act 1972, the predecessor of CA 1985, s 711.

'LIMITED LIABILITY PARTNERSHIP SEARCH'

1.11   There are the same rights for any person to carry out an 'LLP search' as there are to carry out a 'company search'. That is to say, any person may inspect any records in relation to an LLP kept by the Registrar for the purposes of the CA 1985 or the LLP Act 2000 and may obtain a copy of any information contained in those records or a certified copy of, or extract from, any such record.[32] As in relation to directors of companies, this right to inspect is, however, subject to any confidentiality order which has been made by the Secretary of State under CA 1985, s 723B in relation to disclosure of a member's usual residential address.[33]

SCHEME OF THE LEGISLATION

1.12   The LLP Act 2000 came into force on 6 April 2001.[34] The Act itself is fairly short (19 sections and a Schedule), and is concerned with setting out the core principles of the new form of legal entity, and creating the framework of legislation by which LLPs are to be governed. Section 1 establishes the form of entity and its key characteristics.[35] Sections 2 and 3 set out the requirements for incorporation.[36] Sections 4 to 9 are concerned with membership, including becoming and ceasing to be a member, the making of an LLP agreement and the position of members as agents of the LLP. Sections 10 to 13 are concerned with taxation of LLPs, mostly by inserting new provisions into existing tax statutes.[37] The broad intention of the tax provisions is that, for tax purposes, the LLP is to be treated as a partnership and the members as partners. For so long as the business of the LLP is being carried on with a view to profit, its existence as an entity separate from its members is ignored: it is 'pass-through' for tax purposes.[38] Section 14 provides that regulations are to be made about the insolvency and winding up of LLPs by applying or incorporating, with such modifications as appear appropriate, Parts I to IV, VI and VII of the IA 1986; and s 15 provides that regulations may be made about LLPs (not being about insolvency or winding up) by applying or incorporating, with such modifications as appear appropriate, inter alia, any law

---

[32]   CA 1985, s 709(1). The right of inspection extends to the original of a document delivered to the Registrar in legible form only where the record kept by the Registrar of the contents of the document is illegible or unavailable: s 709(2).

[33]   The effect of such an order is that documents delivered to the Registrar after the making of the order, and which contain the usual residential address of the relevant member, are not open to inspection. On those documents filed with the Registrar where the relevant member's usual residential address would otherwise require to be given, a 'service address' for him is substituted. The member's usual residential address is still given to the Registrar (at the Secured Register Unit, separate from Companies House) but on separate forms (which, by reason of the confidentiality order, are excluded from public inspection). Confidentiality orders are discussed further at **8.9–8.13**

[34]   Limited Liability Partnerships Act 2000 (Commencement) Order 2000, SI 2000/3316.

[35]   See **1.2**.

[36]   Discussed in chapter 2.

[37]   In relation to income and corporation tax, capital gains tax, inheritance tax and national insurance contributions. Stamp duty is dealt with substantively by provisions in the LLP Act 2000 itself (s 12).

[38]   Taxation of LLPs and their members is dealt with in chapter 21.

relating to companies. Under s 16, regulations may be made to amend or repeal other enactments.[39] All regulations made under the Act are to be made by the Secretary of State by statutory instrument (s 17). Sections 18 and 19 are concerned with definitions, commencement and application. The Schedule contains provisions regulating the name and registered office of an LLP.

1.13 Regulations made under ss 14 and 15 of the LLP Act 2000 are a fundamental part of the LLP legislation. These regulations apply – with modifications – particular parts of the CA 1985 and the IA 1986, and all of the CDDA 1986, to the entity and its members. They also apply certain sections of the FSMA 2000 to LLPs. A grasp of the modified provisions of these other Acts is essential to a full understanding of how LLPs work. The regulations made under ss 14 and 15 of the LLP Act 2000 are the Limited Liability Partnerships Regulations 2001 (the LLP Regulations 2001) and the Limited Liability Partnerships (No 2) Regulations 2002 (the LLP Regulations 2002).[40] The LLP Regulations 2001 apply in particular (but, as mentioned above, with modifications) those provisions of the CA 1985 relating to the preparation and filing of accounts (ss 221 to 250 and supplementary provisions in ss 256 to 262), auditors (ss 384 to 394), identity of corporate status on letterheads and the like (ss 348 to 351), debentures and registration of charges (ss183 to 185, 190 to 196 and 395 to 408), appointment of DTI inspectors (ss 431 to 441), matters subsequent to winding-up (ss 651 to 658) and the role of the Registrar of Companies (ss 704 to 715). The basic technique of the LLP Regulations 2001 in applying these other Acts to LLPs is, generally speaking, to say that (except where the context otherwise requires) references to a company include references to an LLP, references to a director or officer of a company include references to a member of an LLP, and references to the 1985 or 1986 Acts include references to those Acts as they apply to LLPs by virtue of the Regulations.[41] The application of provisions of the CA 1985, the IA 1986 and the CDDA 1986 to LLPs is also stated to be subject to the general modification of 'such further modifications as the context requires for the purpose of giving effect to [those provisions]/[that legislation] as applied by [this Part of] these Regulations.'[42] The LLP Regulations 2002 apply to LLPs (with effect from 2 April 2002) the provisions of the CA 1985 relating to confidentiality orders (ss 723B to 723F), which were inserted into the CA 1985 by the Criminal Justice and Police Act 2001.[43]

---

[39]   Section 16 provides that regulations may make in any enactment such amendments or repeals as appear appropriate in consequence of the LLP Act 2000 or regulations made under it. No amendments or repeals or amendments appear to have been made under this section.

[40]   SI 2001/1090 and SI 2002/913 respectively. Some amendments have been made to Schs 1 and 3 to the LLP Regulations 2001 by the Financial Services and Markets Act 2000 (Consequential Amendments) Order 2004, SI 2004/355.

[41]   This is the approach of regs 3 and 4 of the LLP Regulations 2001, applying the CA 1985 and the CDDA 1986 to LLPs. Regs 5 and 6 of the LLP Regulations 2001, applying to LLPs parts of the IA 1986, and certain sections of the FSMA 2000, differ in this respect and provide that references to the other legislation are to that legislation as it applies to LLPs by virtue of the LLP Act 2000. It is not easy to see the rationale behind this difference in wording between the paragraphs.

[42]   LLP Regulations 2001, regs 3(2)(c), 4(1)(i), 4(2)(i) and 5(2)(g).

[43]   Provisions relating to confidentiality orders are also inserted directly into the LLP Act 2000, and into the CA 1985, by the Limited Liability Partnerships (Particulars of Usual Residential Address)

1.14 References in this work to the CA 1985, the IA 1986, the CDDA 1986 and the FSMA 2000 are references, unless otherwise stated, to those Acts as they subsist for the time being, and as modified to apply to LLPs by the LLP Regulations 2001. This statement requires elaboration. Since the making of the LLP Regulations 2001, a considerable number of amendments have been made to provisions in each of the four Acts which the LLP Regulations 2001 apply to LLPs.[44] There has, however, been no positive reference in the amending legislation (whether statute or statutory instrument) to the provisions in their amended form applying to LLPs; and there have been no new regulations made under the LLP Act 2000 expressly applying the amended provisions. In these circumstances, the issue arises as to whether such later amendments to these Acts apply to LLPs (with the modifications stated in the LLP Regulations 2001) in place of the original provisions referred to in (and applied by) the LLP Regulations 2001. The issue is whether, unless and until further regulations made under the LLP Act 2000 apply the amended versions of the Acts to LLPs, regs 3, 4, 5 and 6 of the LLP Regulations 2001, when providing that certain statutory provisions 'shall apply' to LLPs (with the stated modifications), apply these statutory provisions as they subsist from time to time, or as they stood at the time the Regulations were made.[45] It is suggested that there is nothing in ss 14–17 of the LLP Act 2000 to preclude regulations made under those sections having the effect of applying statutory provisions as they subsist from time to time. The authors have concluded that this is the intention and effect of the LLP Regulations 2001. There are a number of general and specific considerations which lead to this conclusion. Looking at the matter generally, it seems reasonable to suppose, from the framework of the LLP Act 2000, and the LLP Regulations 2001, that the intention of the legislature was that, subject to the stated modifications to the legislation being applied, the statutory governance for the time being of companies was to apply equally to LLPs. It is, for instance, reasonable to assume that Parliament would intend that alterations to the figures for qualification as a small or medium-sized LLP in relation to filing accounts (CA 1985, s247)[46] should be automatically altered for LLPs as they are altered for companies.[47]

(Confidentiality Orders) Regulations 2002, SI 2002/915. Confidentiality orders are discussed at **8.9–8.13**.

[44] For instance, relevant provisions (i) in the CA 1985 have been amended by the Companies Act 1985 (Accounts of Small and Medium-Sized Enterprises and Audit Exemption) (Amendment) Regulations 2004, SI 2004/16, made under CA 1985, s 257; (ii) in the CA 1985 and the CDDA 1986 have been amended by the Financial Services and Markets Act 2000 (Consequential Amendments and Repeals) Order 2001, SI 2001/3649, with effect from 1 December 2001, made under FSMA 2000, ss 426 and 427; (iii) in the IA 1986 have been amended by the Insolvency Act 2000 (with effect from 11 May 2001), and by the Enterprise Act 2002; and (iv) in the FSMA 2000 have been amended by the IA 2000 (with effect from 1 January 2003), and by the Enterprise Act 2002.

[45] For a discussion of the general issue of statutory construction, see, for instance, *Halsbury's Laws* (Butterworths, 4th edn, 1995), vol 44(1), paras 1295 and 1522, and Bennion *Statutory Interpretation* (4th edn, 2002), pp 248–249.

[46] Alterations made by statutory instrument under CA 1985, s 257.

[47] It is clearly the view of the DTI that this is the case: see the Consultation Papers on *'Fair Value Accounting'* (June 2003), para 3.29, and *'Modernisation of Accounting Directives/IAS Infrastructure'* (March 2004), Annex F para 2.15. And see *Halsbury's Laws* (Butterworths, 4th edn), vol 44(1) above, para 1427.

1.15 This general approach is consistent with the state of the Acts which were applied to LLPs at the date of the LLP Regulations 2001 (6 April 2001). Not all of the statutory provisions which were being applied were then in force. Of the sections and sub-sections of the FSMA 2000 which were being applied to LLPs by reg 6 of the LLP Regulations 2001, only one sub-section was in force in April 2001.[48] Another of the sections of the FSMA 2000 (s 356) which, although not yet in force, was applied to LLPs by reg 6 was already going to be replaced by substituted provisions contained in the IA 2000, s 15.[49] Certain provisions in the CA 1985, as applied to LLPs by reg 4(1) of the LLP Regulations 2001, referred to the Financial Services Act 1986 (FSA 1986).[50] It was, however, clear in April 2001 that these provisions of the FSA 1986 would be replaced when the relevant provisions of the FSMA 2000 came into force, and that the provisions of the CA 1985 would need amending accordingly.[51] It seems equally reasonable to assume that Parliament intended that amendments to the CA 1985 consequent upon the envisaged repeal of the FSA 1986 should apply to LLPs. It is against this background of incestuous cross-reference, and the ability to amend one Act by statutory instrument made either under that Act itself or under another Act,[52] that the authors have concluded that the intention of the LLP Regulations 2001 is that the provisions of the CA 1985, the CDDA 1986, the IA 1986 and the FSMA 2000 should apply to LLPs (with the stated modifications) as those provisions subsist for the time being. Parliament has recently acted in a manner consistent with this apparent intention. The statutory instrument which brings into force the new administration regime inserted into the IA 1986 by the Enterprise Act 2002, s 248[53] expressly continues for LLPs (to the exclusion of the new substituted provisions) the former administration provisions of the IA 1986 as applied by the LLP Regulations 2001 reg 5.[54] This express continuation for LLPs of applied legislation without current amendments must proceed on the assumption that, but for such an express exclusion, the new provisions would apply automatically to LLPs. A similar assumption clearly lies behind amendments made in March 2004 to the LLP Regulations 2000, Schs 1 and 3, modifying provisions of the CA 1985 and the IA 1986 as they apply to LLPs.[55]

1.16 There are a number of amendments made by the LLP Regulations 2001 to other Acts. These amendments are set out in Sch 5 to the Regulations. They include (but are not limited to) amendments to the Sex Discrimination Act 1975 and the Race Relations Act 1976 (to make those Acts apply to LLPs as they apply

---

[48] Section 215(6) of the FSMA 2000.
[49] FSMA 2000, s 356 was brought into force as originally enacted on 1 December 2001; and the substituted provisions replacing it were brought into force on 1 January 2003 by the Insolvency Act 2000 (Commencement No 3 and Transitional Provisions) Order 2002, SI 2002/2711, made under IA 2000, s 16.
[50] See, for instance, CA 1985, s 449(1)(c).
[51] As CA 1985, s 449(1)(c) was by reg 22(2) of SI 2001/3649 referred to in footnote 44 above.
[52] See, for instance, FSMA 2000, s 426.
[53] The Enterprise Act 2002 (Commencement No 4 and Transitional Provisions and Savings) Order 2003, SI 2003/2093.
[54] See SI 2003/2093, Art 3(3)(b).
[55] See, for instance, the amendments made by SI 2004/355, arts 8 and 10 in relation to the application to LLPs of CA 1985, s 249B and IA 1986, s 124A.

to partnerships), to certain provisions of the Employment Rights Act 1996[56] and to the Business Names Act 1985.[57]

PARTNERSHIP LAW

1.17 Although the new business entity is called a limited liability partnership, it is not the position that, in default of any other governing provision, partnership law applies. The LLP Act 2000 expressly states that the law relating to partnerships does not apply to an LLP except so far as the LLP Act 2000 itself (or any other Act) provides that it does.[58] Section 15, together with s 17, of the LLP Act 2000 provides that regulations may be made by the Secretary of State, by statutory instrument, about LLPs (not being about insolvency or winding-up) by applying or incorporating, with such modifications as appear appropriate, 'any law relating to partnerships'.[59] This power has been exercised in the LLP Regulations 2001 to incorporate (albeit not by express reference) certain provisions of the Partnership Act 1890 as 'default rules' in an LLP agreement as mentioned in **1.6**.[60] Beyond this specific application, partnership law as such does not apply to LLPs.

PUNISHMENT OF OFFENCES

1.18 Various duties and responsibilities are laid on members, and on the designated members, by the legislation. These are discussed subsequently (in particular, in chapters 10 and 11). Conviction for transgression (or, in some cases, knowingly and wilfully permitting, or failing to take reasonable steps to prevent, default) usually leads to a fine or (in some cases) to imprisonment. Schedule 24 to the CA 1985 sets out in tabular form the offences arising under that Act, and the punishment. Schedule 10 to the IA 1986 does the same for offences under that Act.[61] There are references in the legislation to fines of 'the statutory maximum', and to fines not exceeding a certain level 'on the standard scale'. The statutory maximum means the prescribed sum within the meaning of the Magistrates' Courts

---

[56] Sections 166 and 183.
[57] The BNA 1985 is discussed further at **4.5** and **4.6**.
[58] LLP Act 2000, s 1(5).
[59] This is in addition to the power of the Secretary of State under LLP Act 2000, ss 15 and 17, discussed in **1.12–1.13**, to apply any law relating to companies to LLPs.
[60] The provisions of the Partnership Act 1890 which are incorporated, with modifications, as default provisions are ss 24(1), (2), (5), (6), (7), (8) and (9), 25, 28, 29(1) and 30. Although there is no express reference in the LLP Regulations 2001 to the 1890 Act, it is clear from LLP Act 2000, s 5(2) (as well as from the terms of the default rules themselves) that the default rules were made in exercise of the power to apply any law relating to partnerships.
[61] There are also offences under the LLP Act 2000 itself: see ss 2(3)–(4) and 9(4)–(6), and Sch, paras 4(8)–(9) and 7.

Act 1980. That sum is currently £5,000.[62] The standard scale is a scale of 5 levels, ranging from £200 (level 1) to £5,000 (level 5).[63]

GREAT BRITAIN

1.19 Apart from the provisions relating to taxation and LLPs, the LLP Act 2000 does not apply to Northern Ireland.[64] Taxation apart, therefore, the Act applies to Great Britain only (as opposed to the United Kingdom). Northern Ireland does, however, have its own LLP Act, passed in 2002,[65] and essentially re-enacting for Northern Ireland the provisions of the LLP Act 2000.

FINANCIAL SERVICES

1.20 An LLP is capable of being an 'authorised person' for the purposes of the Financial Services and Markets Act 2000 (FSMA), and is capable, therefore, of being permitted to carry on regulated activities.[66] For this permission to be granted, an application to the Financial Services Authority will be necessary. Given the organisational flexibility which LLPs have, the proposed organisational structure of the applicant LLP will need to be explained fully in the application.[67] Where an LLP carries on, or has previously carried on, a regulated activity without being an authorised person (ie in contravention of the general prohibition in FSMA 2000, s 19), the Financial Services Authority has the power to apply to the court for an administration order, or a winding up order, in relation to it.[68] Regulated activities include carrying on the business of establishing, operating or winding up a collective investment scheme in relation to property of any kind.[69] The possibility of an LLP itself amounting to a collective investment scheme under FSMA 2000, s 235 is discussed at **3.19–3.24**.

---

[62]   See the Magistrates Courts' Act 1980, s 32 and, generally, *Halsbury's Laws* (Butterworths, 4th edn), vol 11(2) paras 806–7

[63]   See the Criminal Justice Act 1982, s 37 and, generally, *Halsbury's Laws* (Butterworths, 4th edn), vol 11(2) para 808.

[64]   LLP Act 2000, s 19(4).

[65]   Limited Liability Partnerships Act (Northern Ireland) 2002. This Act was brought fully into operation on 13 September 2004 by SRNI 2004/306.

[66]   See FSMA 2000, ss 19, 31 and 40(1)(b). As to what constitute regulated activities, see FSMA 2000, s 22 and the Financial Services and Markets Act 2000 (Regulated Activities) Order 2001 S1 2001/544 and the Financial Services and Markets Act 2000 (Carrying on Regulated Activities by Way of Business) Order 2001 S1 2001/1177.

[67]   See the FSA's Authorisation Manual, chapter 3 para 3.23, where the authorisation of LLPs is discussed.

[68]   See FSMA 2000, ss 359 (administration order) and 367 (winding up order) as applied to LLPs by the LLP Regulations 2001 SI 2001/1090, reg 6. In relation to companies, s 359 has been substituted by the Enterprise Act 2002 with effect from 15 September 2003. The new administration regime has not been applied to LLPs (see **1.15** and, further, chapter 24). The effect of SI 2003/2093 Art 3(3)(b) is presumably to leave the previous s 359 in force for LLPs.

[69]   See the Financial Services and Markets Act 2000 (Regulated Activities) Order 2001 S1 2001/544 articles 4 and 51 and the Financial Services and Markets Act 2000 (Carrying on Regulated Activities by Way of Business) Order 2001, SI 2001/1177, Art 3.

GROUPS AND SUBSIDIARIES

1.21 As is mentioned in **2.2**, the members of an LLP do not need to be individuals. The members may all be, or include, companies or other LLPs. Equally, an LLP, as a separate entity able to own property and assets,[70] will be able to own shares in a company. It follows that LLPs may be 'parent' entities with wholly (or partly) owned subsidiaries, and also that (depending on the terms of the particular LLP agreement) they may be controlled by and be 'subsidiaries' of another LLP or company. The legislation recognises this, applying the provisions of Part VII of the CA 1985 regarding group accounts and related or subsidiary undertakings, and defining the circumstances in which a company is a subsidiary of an LLP and an LLP is a subsidiary (or a 'wholly-owned subsidiary') of a company or another LLP.[71]

---

[70] See further **3.1–3.5**.
[71] CA 1985, ss 736 and 736A.

Chapter 2

INCORPORATION

INTRODUCTION

2.1   In order for an LLP to be incorporated, there are three primary conditions which must be satisfied (set out as paragraphs (a), (b) and (c) in LLP Act 2000, s 2(1)) namely:

(a)   two or more persons associated for carrying on a lawful business with a view to profit subscribe their names to an 'incorporation document';

(b)   there is delivered to the Registrar the incorporation document or a copy of it authenticated in a manner approved by the Registrar; and

(c)   there is also delivered to the Registrar a statement, in a form approved by him, and made either by a solicitor engaged in the formation of the LLP or by one of the subscribers to the incorporation document, that the requirement imposed by paragraph (a) has been complied with.

It is convenient to deal with these three conditions in turn.

(a)   Two or more persons subscribe

'Persons'

2.2   The associated persons need not be individuals. The Interpretation Act 1978 provides that, in any Act, unless the contrary intention appears, 'person' includes a body of persons corporate or unincorporate.[1] The LLP Act 2000 expressly envisages the possibility of a subscribing person, or subsequent member, being a corporate body. This appears from the reference in s 4(1) to a subscribing person having been dissolved, and also from the references in s 18 to the address and name of a corporation which is a member of an LLP. The associated persons may, therefore, comprise or include, in addition to individuals, a company, another LLP, or some other form of corporate entity.

2.3   Whether or not 'person' in the LLP Act 2000 also includes an unincorporated body of persons is not so clear. In the authors' view, it is well arguable that an unincorporated body can constitute a 'person' for the purposes of the Act, and be a member of an LLP, and that there is no intention in the Act to the contrary. Such an argument is supported by the adoption (with modifications) for LLPs of CA 1985, s 734 (criminal proceedings against unincorporated bodies), which proceeds on the basis that a partnership or other unincorporated body can be

---

[1]   1978 Act, s 5, and Sch 1.

a member of an LLP.[2] It is well arguable, therefore, that a partnership, or a members' club which is an unincorporated association, or all the executors or trustees of an estate or trust,[3] or any other unincorporated body, can be a single member of an LLP. The Registrar, however, does not accept this and takes the view that a member of an LLP must either be an individual, or a body which the law recognises as having its own legal personality.[4] As a result, the Registrar will not accept registration of an unincorporated body as a member. If, therefore, a partnership or estate wishes to be a member of an LLP, it will be necessary for all the partners or executors, or for some of them on behalf of all, to be individual members of the LLP.[5]

2.4   In practice, most LLPs are likely to be made up of individuals. There is no requirement that the subscribers to the incorporation document, or persons becoming members subsequently, should be British nationals or resident in Great Britain. They may all (individuals or corporations) be foreigners resident offshore.[6] There is no upper limit on the permissible number of subscribers (or subsequent members); so that there can be as many subscribers as it is desired. There is no reason in principle why a company (or an LLP) in liquidation should not be a subscriber.[7] An undischarged bankrupt may not, however, be a subscriber without the leave of the court. It is an offence for a person who is an undischarged bankrupt (or in respect of whom a bankruptcy restriction order is in force) directly or indirectly to take part in or be concerned in the promotion or formation of an LLP (or subsequently act as a member) without such leave.[8]

(i)   'Associated'

2.5   Section 2(1)(a) of the LLP Act 2000 has echoes of both s 1 of the CA 1985 ('Any two or more persons associated for a lawful purpose may, by subscribing their names to a memorandum of association and otherwise complying with the requirements of this Act in respect of registration, form an incorporated company ...') and s 1(1) of the Partnership Act 1890 ('Partnership is the relation which subsists between persons carrying on a business in common with a view of profit'). Section 2(1)(a) effectively follows the format in the CA 1985, but injects the

---

[2] See the references in s 734 to CA 1985, ss 447, 450 and 451.

[3] It is to be noted in the context of executors and trustees that CA 1985, s360 (providing, inter alia, that no notice of any trust is to be receivable by the Registrar in the case of a company) is not applied to LLPs.

[4] This will permit a Scottish partnership (which has a legal personality distinct from the partners) to be a member (as LLP Act 2000 clearly envisages in the definitions of 'name' and 'address' in s 18), but not estates or trusts or English partnerships (as English partnership law presently stands). The express reference in the definitions of 'address' and 'name' in s 18 to a corporation or Scottish firm does lend support to the Registrar's view. But it is, perhaps, a slight basis on which to show a contrary intention from the general meaning in the Interpretation Act 1978. Section 18 defines 'address' and name' in relation to those members/persons being referred to, but it does not state that it is giving an exclusive definition of 'address' and 'name' for all members.

[5] As to fiduciaries as members of an LLP, see **8.25**.

[6] And the business of the LLP can be carried on outside Great Britain: see **2.12**.

[7] Although the compliance statement, discussed at **2.32–2.37**, would have to be very carefully considered.

[8] CDDA 1986, s 11 (as amended by the Enterprise Act 2002, s 257(3)). See further **32.32** as to disqualification.

Partnership Act requirement that there must be a business which is intended to be carried on with a view to[9] profit. The words 'in common', which appear in the phrase 'carrying on a business in common with a view of profit' in the Partnership Act 1890, are not carried over into the LLP Act 2000; but two or more persons have to be 'associated' for carrying on a lawful business before the LLP can be incorporated. 'Associated' can be taken to mean 'joined in a common purpose'.[10] The effect of the 'association' requirement is that the intended business, however wide,[11] must be an identifiable business for the carrying on of which all the subscribers to the incorporation document are intending that the LLP should be incorporated with them as members. It follows also from the requirement for a minimum of two persons to be associated for carrying on the business that at least two subscribers must be intended to contribute in at least some way to carrying on the business.[12] It would appear also to be the assumption of s 2(1)(a) that it must be the common intention of the subscribers that each of them (not simply a minimum of two out of a larger number of subscribers) will contribute in at least some way to the carrying on of the business.

(ii)   *'Business with a view to profit'*

2.6   The association of the subscribers must be for the purpose of carrying on a business with a view to profit. 'Business' includes every trade, profession or occupation.[13] It is undoubtedly a word of wide meaning in the context of s 2(1)(a).[14] 'Profit' is not defined, but means essentially excess of receipts over expenditure of the business.[15] Whether or not the intended activity constitutes a 'business' which is being carried on with a view to profit will turn ultimately, the authors suggest, on whether what is intended would ordinarily be seen and described as carrying on a business for profit.[16] In other words, the test is essentially objective; but if the intended acts are equivocal, it is suggested that the subjective purpose or object of the subscribers will become material in determining

---

[9]   There is no material difference between 'view of profit' and 'view to profit'. In *Blackpool Marton Rotary Club v Martin* [1988] STC 823, Hoffmann J (at 830j) treated the two expressions as interchangeable.

[10]   See *Oxford English Dictionary*.

[11]   The legislation envisages that an LLP may carry on business of two or more classes, which differ substantially from each other: see **18.14**(4).

[12]   It also follows, in the authors' view, that it must at least be doubtful whether 'off the shelf' LLPs can be created for sale to, and subsequent use by, entirely new members; and see also **2.32–2.37** as to the compliance statement.

[13]   LLP Act 2000, s 18. This is, in substance, the same meaning as 'business' has in the Partnership Act 1890, s 45.

[14]   There are many reported cases which consider the ambit of the word 'business' in different contexts: see, for instance, *Customs & Excise v Lord Fisher* [1981] 2 All ER 147 and *Institute of Chartered Accountants v Customs & Excise* [1999] 1 WLR 701 (HL), both VAT cases concerned with the issue whether a taxable supply was being made in the course of a business.

[15]   See, for instance, *Beauchamp v Woolworth Plc* [1990] 1 AC 478 at 489.

[16]   See *Armour v Liverpool Corporation* [1939] Ch 422 at 437, concerned with Companies Act 1929, s 357 (subsequently CA 1985, s 716, now repealed); and see also *In re Arthur Average Association for British, Foreign and Colonial Ships* [1875] LR 10 Ch App 542 (on Companies Act 1862, s 4) at 548 (col 2): is the association for a commercial undertaking?

the issue.[17] Investment can constitute carrying on a business,[18] but it may be difficult to see the mere holding of investments, or of the freehold reversion in tenanted land, without more, as constituting 'carrying on a business'. Actively speculating or trading, or exploiting a property, on the other hand, probably would do so.[19] It has been said (in the context of the statutory provision which became CA 1985, s 716) that for a business to be carried on, there must be a series or repetition of acts.[20]

2.7   The intended profit required by s 2(1)(a) must derive from the business for the carrying on of which the subscribers are associated, and must be a profit for the LLP. There is, however, no requirement that every member must be entitled to some share of the profit. There is no doubt, for instance, that there can be members of an LLP remunerated by fixed salary only.[21] But one issue which does arise is whether the profits of the business must be divisible amongst at least *some* of the members: is s 2(1)(a) satisfied if some or all of the profits of the business are to be distributed to a non-member?[22] The authors suggest that there is no requirement that the profits of the business must (all or in part) be divisible amongst some or all of the members.[23] What s 2(1)(a) is requiring is an intention that a profit will accrue to *the LLP* from the carrying on (by the LLP, acting through its members) of the business.

---

[17]   See *Iswera v Commissioners of Inland Revenue* [1965] 1 WLR 663 (PC), a tax case on profits from a 'trade'.

[18]   The view of the Inland Revenue (expressed in the context of 1890 Act and 1907 Act partnerships) is that investment carried on as a commercial venture comes within the definition of business: see the Law Commission Report on Partnership Law (Law Com No 283) of November 2003, para 4.34.

[19]   See, for instance, *Smith v Anderson* (1880) 15 Ch D 247 (CA) at 276, 279 and 283 (concerned with trustees), *Wigfield v Potter* (1882) 45 LT (NS) 612 at 615 and *Crowther v Thorley* [1884] 33 WR 330, all cases on the Companies Act 1862 s 4 (forerunner of CA 1985, s 716). See also *Simmons v IRC* [1980] 1 WLR 1196 (HL), a tax case on 'trade' for the purposes of Schedule D Case 1, at p 1199.

[20]   See *Smith v Anderson* above at 277/8, and *Crowther v Thorley* above at 332; and see also *Kirkwood v Gadd* [1910] AC 422 at p 431.

[21]   See further on employee members **8.26–8.32**.

[22]   Put another way, is s 2(1)(a) concerned solely with there being an intended profit for the LLP as an entity? This question is similar to the question which arose in the mid-19th century as to whether land allotment societies and mutual lending societies were required to be registered under s 2 of the Companies Act 1844 (which required the registration of any company, association or partnership 'established ... for any purpose of profit'): see *R v Whitmarsh* (1850) 15 QB 600 and *Bear v Bromley* (1852) 18 QB 101, which decided that one looked solely to see whether the company, association or partnership *as such* was established for such purpose. Subsequently, express reference to gain by the individual members of the company, association or partnership was inserted into the Companies Act 1862 s 4 (later CA 1985, s 716) in order to reverse the effect of these decisions: see *In re Padstow Total Loss and Collision Assurance Association* (1882) 20 Ch D 137 (a case on s 4 of the 1862 Act) at 149.

[23]   See in this connection IA 1986, s 110(4), which appears to contemplate the possibility of a person participating in the profits of an LLP although not a member, and LLP Act 2000, s 7(1)(d), contemplating the assignment by a member of his share in the LLP (discussed at **8.20**). This will also accord with what appears to be the partnership position (see *Lindley & Banks on Partnership* 18th edn, 2002, para 2-10) despite a possible indication to the contrary by Hoffmann J in *Blackpool Marton Rotary Club v Martin* [1988] STC 823 at 830. There is also, of course, the fundamental distinction between a partnership and an LLP, namely that with an LLP the corporate entity is separate from the members: the concept of profit accruing solely to the LLP is, therefore, easier to see.

2.8 A related issue which arises is whether, if the profits are to be shared amongst some only (or none) of the members, s 2(1)(a) will be satisfied if one or more members are not only not to receive a share of profits (as, for instance, a salaried member) but are not to receive any remuneration or financial benefit at all. The authors suggest that, in principle, and consistent with what has been said above as to the possibility of all the profits going to non-members, there is no objection to a member not receiving any remuneration or financial benefit from the carrying on of the business.

2.9 Another issue which arises is whether s 2(1)(a) (and the phrase 'with a view to profit') is satisfied if the intention is that the LLP – the separate entity – shows a profit, but this profit is in truth derived from the members of the LLP ie any profit shares which are divisible amongst members are in reality constituted by their own money.[24] It might be said that if (as suggested in **2.7**) s 2(1)(a) is concerned solely with there being an intended profit for *the LLP* as an entity, and there is no requirement that the profits must be divisible amongst at least some of the members, it would not matter that the money to come into the LLP as trading income was to come from the members. There is, in the view of the authors, no single answer to this question. The answer in any particular case will turn on the nature of the business venture. The essence of s 2(1)(a) is that the LLP must be a commercial venture: the subscribers are incorporating a commercial venture. The question will be: looking at the matter in an ordinary common sense way,[25] are the subscribers associated for carrying on a business with a view to profit? The fact that the trading income comes from the members will not automatically prevent s 2(1)(a) being satisfied;[26] but it may in such circumstances be difficult to see s 2(1)(a) being satisfied where it is the members' own money which is intended to go round, and there is no intended outside source of trading income for the LLP.

2.10 The requirements of s 2(1)(a) preclude a charitable body from being an LLP. A charity could, however, be a member of an LLP in the exercise of the charity's investment powers (assuming that they permit this), or if being associated with others for carrying on the business for profit is a proper part of fulfilling its charitable purposes.[27] Equally, a non-profit making body which does not have charitable status cannot be an LLP. Clubs and societies are unlikely, therefore, to be able to become LLPs; and an LLP is unlikely to be useable in the role occupied by, for instance, a property owners' service company.

---

[24] For instance, the members pay premiums into a mutual insurance association, or pay the LLP a fee for carrying out a business activity which the members desire, and then – as members – receive the net profits of the LLP from carrying out that activity.

[25] See the discussion in **2.6**.

[26] See, for instance, *In re Arthur Average Association for British, Foreign and Colonial Ships* (1875) LR 10 Ch App 542 (on Companies Act 1862 s 4) at 547–8. Compare *Bear v Bromley* above at 276: 'In fact, by profit [in the Companies Act 1844 s 2] is meant profit arising from others, not profits or advantages raised from, and accruing to, only the members of the company.'

[27] At least as charity law presently stands. A charity can engage in trading for profit in the course of fulfilling its raison d'être of carrying out its charitable purpose, and can have a subsidiary whose purpose is trading for profit, but it cannot be a body existing in order to trade for profit: see, for instance, *Halsbury's Laws* (Butterworths, 4th edn, 2001), vol 5(2), para 5.

(iii)   Legality of business

2.11 It is, strictly speaking, the *business* which must be lawful, not the means of carrying the business on. The latter may be subject to a separate regulatory regime. But a business which necessarily involves carrying out criminal acts or acts otherwise made illegal by statute will clearly not be a lawful business.[28] Similarly, a business will be unlawful which will necessarily involve, or whose principal purpose is, acting in breach of European legislation which has a direct effect in the United Kingdom.[29] A business which will necessarily involve, or whose principal purpose is, carrying on a trade involving illegal contracts or the committing of a tort against a third party will also be unlawful.[30] Equally, a business which could be carried on in a perfectly lawful manner, but which the subscribers in fact intend to carry on in an unlawful manner, is not a lawful business.[31] An example of a business to be carried on in an unlawful manner if it is to be carried on without the necessary licence or permit would be the business of bookmaking carried on by and for the account of an LLP without the LLP having a bookmaker's permit.[32] A business unacceptably offensive to public morals would also be unlawful.[33] Generally, it is probably correct to say that the business to be carried on would be unlawful if it were intended to be carried on in a manner which deceived the public as to the service or expertise on offer.[34] If an LLP did manage to be registered for the purpose of carrying on an unlawful business, that registration could

---

[28] See, for instance, *R v Registrar of Joint Stock Companies, ex parte More* [1931] 2 KB 197, refusing registration to a company formed to sell Irish Sweepstake tickets in England in breach of the Lotteries Act 1823.

[29] An example would be shipping waste across national frontiers without the proper authorisation in breach of the relevant EU Regulation.

[30] As to a trade involving illegal contracts, see *R v Registrar of Companies, ex parte Attorney-General* [1991] BCLC 476. An example of a business involving a tort against a third party would be passing off the LLP's goods for sale as those of another trader. For a discussion relevant for present purposes as to illegality and contracts, see *Chitty on Contracts* 29th edn, 2004, paras 16-007 and 16-014–16-074.

[31] See, for example, *Dungate v Lee* [1969] 1 Ch 545. (The issue was whether a partnership of two individuals running a betting office was unlawful. Only one of the partners had a bookmaker's permit under the Betting and Gaming Act 1960 (then the applicable Act). The answer turned on the construction of the Act, and on the intention as to their respective functions in the conduct of the business with which the two individuals entered into the partnership.) Where the intention is that the business should not be commenced until the required licence or permit has been obtained, the incorporation will not be for an unlawful business.

[32] See the Betting, Gaming and Lotteries Act 1963, s 2. The LLP legislation expressly foresees the possibility of an LLP being a bookmaker: see LLP Regulations 2001, Sch 5, para 8, inserting LLP references into the Betting and Gaming Duties Act 1981. Further examples would be carrying on a consumer credit business, which (subject to certain exemptions) requires a licence from the Director General of Fair Trading under the Consumer Credit Act 1974, or carrying on the business of deposit-taking which (again subject to certain exemptions) requires an authorisation from the Financial Services Authority under the Banking Act 1987.

[33] Such a business might well be unlawful on the ground discussed earlier that it involves contracts which are illegal, the illegality here being on the grounds of public policy. This was the position in *R v Registrar of Companies, ex parte A-G*, referred to in footnote 30 above. For a recent decision on whether or not a contract was so immoral as to be unenforceable see *Armhouse Lee Ltd v Chappell* (1996) *The Times*, August 7 (CA) (payment for advertisements for telephone sex lines enforced). The courts recognise that the notions of what is acceptable or unacceptable change with the times: see, for example Viscount Simonds in *Shaw v DPP* [1962] AC 220 at 268.

[34] As to restrictions on the use of certain words and expressions in the name of an LLP, see **2.20**.

subsequently be quashed by the court on an application by the Attorney-General on behalf of the Crown.[35]

2.12   There is no requirement that the business be carried on in Great Britain: it can be carried on abroad.[36] Complicated questions as to lawfulness may arise where the business is one which will necessarily involve, or the principle purpose of which is, acting in a foreign country in breach of that country's law.[37]

2.13   The definition of 'business' includes every profession. In the case of many professions it is unlawful, and a criminal offence, to practise or hold oneself out as qualified to practise as the specified professional without the necessary qualification (and current registration).[38] An intention on the part of the subscribers that the LLP should trade as, for example, 'solicitors' without all its members being qualified to act as solicitors[39] would constitute an unlawful business for the purposes of LLP Act 2000, s 2(1)(a). Any professionals considering incorporation as an LLP will clearly need to consider their own particular legislation (and professional rules). For solicitors, practising within a corporate body is envisaged by s 9 of the Administration of Justice Act 1985. The Solicitors' Incorporated Practice Rules 2001 enable solicitors to practise within LLPs (provided that the requirements of the Rules are met). For dentists, on the other hand, with certain limited exceptions, there is a prohibition on a body corporate carrying on the business of dentistry.[40]

(iv)   *Subscribing*

2.14   In the case of a subscriber who is an individual, the subscription does not need to be in his own hand. It can be done on his behalf by an agent duly

---

[35]   As in *R v Registrar of Companies, ex parte A-G*, referred to in footnotes 30 and 33 above where the registration of Lindi St Claire (Personal Services) Ltd was quashed. The application would be by way of judicial review to quash (ie declare completely invalid) the decision of the Registrar to register the LLP and issue a certificate of incorporation. In the event of such a quashing order being made, the position as to liabilities and assets of the now non-existent LLP will be as follows. As to liabilities incurred purportedly on behalf of the LLP, the individual acting will be personally liable under CA 1985, s 36C and/or for breach of warranty of authority. As to any assets, the LLP never having been incorporated, CA 1985, s 654 (bona vacantia on dissolution) will not apply and the assets will revert to their pre-incorporation ownership. See further, the discussion as to the conclusiveness of the certificate of incorporation at **2.39–2.41**. If an LLP, having been incorporated for the purposes of a lawful business, subsequently carries on an unlawful business, the Secretary of State can appoint inspectors under CA 1985, s 432(2) (see **20.2(2)**), or apply to the court for a winding-up order.

[36]   See, for instance, IA 1986, ss 95(6) and 98(4) referring to an LLP having no place of business in Great Britain.

[37]   See, for instance, the discussion in relation to contracts in *Chitty on Contracts* 29th edn, paras 16-031/2 and 30-171.

[38]   See, for instance, Solicitors Act 1974, ss 1, 20 and 21 and Dentists Act 1984, s 38.

[39]   In accordance with s 1 of the 1974 Act.

[40]   Dentists Act 1984, s 42.

authorised by him.[41] The name of the principal (ie the subscriber) should, however, be made clear.

(v)   Members reduced below two

2.15   The LLP Act 2000 requires that there be two or more subscribers for incorporation, and envisages that the corporate entity which is the LLP will continue to have a minimum of two members.[42] However, if and when subsequently there is only one member of the LLP left, the legislation does not require the LLP to cease business, and there is no automatic liquidation. Further members may be appointed to bring the number of members back to two or more. The legislation expressly envisages that the LLP can continue to carry on business although it only has one member.[43] If, however, it does carry on business with only one member for more than 6 months, that single member, if he knows that he is the only member, is liable, jointly and severally with the LLP, for payment of the LLP's debts contracted after the 6 months have passed.[44]

(b)   The incorporation document

2.16   The incorporation document of the LLP is the equivalent of the memorandum of association for a company.[45] The incorporation document must:[46]

(i)   be in a form approved by the Registrar (or as near to such a form as circumstances allow);

(ii)   state the name of the LLP;

(iii)   state whether the registered office of the LLP is to be situated in England and Wales,[47] in Wales or in Scotland;

(iv)   state the address of that registered office;

(v)   state the name and address of each of the persons who are to be members of the LLP on incorporation; and

(vi)   either specify which of those persons are to be designated members, or state that every person who from time to time is a member of the LLP is a designated member.

It is convenient to consider each of these requirements in turn. It is to be noted at the outset, however, that the incorporation document differs from the memorandum

---

[41]   See *Re Whitley Partners Ltd* (1886) 32 Ch D 337 as to subscribers signing the memorandum of association of a company.

[42]   In addition to s 2(1)(a), see the requirement for two designated members discussed at **2.29**.

[43]   CA 1985, s 24. There only being one member of the LLP is a ground on which the LLP may be wound up by the Court: see IA 1986, s 122(1)(c).

[44]   CA 1985, s 24.

[45]   Regulation 4(e) of the LLP Regulations 2001, applying provisions of the CA 1985 to LLPs, provides that references in the CA 1985 to the memorandum of association of a company shall include references to the incorporation document of an LLP. The CA 1985, as adopted for LLPs, includes such references in ss 42 and 711 (as to which see **2.31**). CA 1985, ss 1–6 are not adopted for LLPs.

[46]   LLP Act 2000, s 2(2).

[47]   See further **2.22–2.23**.

of association of a company in not being required to state the objects of the LLP, namely the business for which the members are associated.[48]

(i)   Approved form

2.17   The approved form is Form LLP 2 (Application for Incorporation of a Limited Liability Partnership). This sets out a format for the prescribed information to be given. In addition to the names and addresses of the persons who are to be the members of the LLP on incorporation ((v) above), Form LLP 2 also provides for the dates of birth of such persons to be given.

(ii)   Name of the LLP

2.18   The name must end with 'limited liability partnership' or 'llp' or 'LLP'.[49] If, however, the incorporation document states that the registered office is to be situated in Wales,[50] the name may end either with one of the above endings or with one of the specified Welsh equivalents.[51] Registration will not be permitted with a name which includes any of the above references to an LLP otherwise than at the end of the name;[52] nor with a name which is the same as the name of a company or other body appearing in the index of company and corporate names kept by the Registrar under CA 1985, s 714(1);[53] nor with a name the use of which by the LLP would in the opinion of the Secretary of State constitute a criminal offence;[54] nor with a name which in the opinion of the Secretary of State is offensive.[55]

2.19   In determining whether one name is the same as another (both for the purposes of initial incorporation[56] and on a change by the LLP of its name[57]) there is to be disregarded: (i) the definite article as the first word of the name; (ii) any of the following (or their Welsh equivalents, or abbreviations of them or Welsh equivalents of such abbreviations) at the end of the name – 'limited liability partnership', 'company', 'and company', 'company limited', 'and company limited', 'limited', 'unlimited', 'public limited company', 'investment company with variable capital' and 'open-ended investment company'; and (iii) type and

---

[48]   For companies, see CA 1985, s 2(1)(c). However, the SORP for accounting by LLPs (as to which, see **18.8**) provides for an annual Members' Report, which is to disclose, inter alia, the principal activities of the LLP and its subsidiary undertakings, indicating any significant changes during the year. This Report (together with the accounts and other financial statements) is to form part of the Annual Report which the SORP provides for: see further **18.14**(5).

[49]   LLP Act 2000, Sch (introduced by s 1(6) of the Act), para 2(1).

[50]   See **2.23**.

[51]   LLP Act 2000, Sch, para 2(2).

[52]   Ibid, Sch, para 3(1)(a).

[53]   Ibid, Sch, para 3(1)(b). The index includes limited partnerships registered under the 1907 Act, and now includes (new CA 1985, s 714(1)(da) inserted by LLP Act 2000, Sch, para 1) LLPs incorporated under the LLP Act 2000. For criteria for determining whether or not one name is the same as another, see **2.19**.

[54]   LLP Act 2000, Sch, para 3(1)(c).

[55]   Ibid, Sch, para 3(1)(d). As to restrictions on a person who was a member of a previous LLP at any time during the period of 12 months immediately prior to it going into insolvent liquidation being a member of a new LLP (or concerned in its formation or management) bearing the name of the previous LLP, see IA 1986, ss 216–217 discussed at **29.33–29.39**.

[56]   See **2.18**.

[57]   See **4.19** et seq.

case of letters, accents, spaces between letters and punctuation marks; and 'and' and '&' are to be taken as the same.[58] The effect of (ii) above is, inter alia, that for practical purposes the name of an LLP cannot be the same as the name of an existing company.

2.20 Except with the approval of the Secretary of State, registration will not be permitted with a name which in the opinion of the Secretary of State would be likely to give the impression that the LLP is connected in any way with the Government or with any local authority, or with a name which includes any words or expression for the time being specified in regulations made under CA 1985, s 29.[59] This section, inter alia, enables the Secretary of State to specify words or expressions for the registration of which as, or as part of, a company's corporate name his approval is required. Regulations have been made under it,[60] and the list of specified words and expressions includes words or expressions which, if misused, might give a false impression of professional association or recognised status.

2.21 If any person (ie individual or corporate body) carries on a business under a name or title which includes as the last words 'limited liability partnership' or their Welsh equivalent, or any contraction or imitation of such expression or its Welsh equivalent, then, unless that person is indeed an LLP (ie incorporated as such under the LLP Act 2000) or an 'oversea limited liability partnership',[61] he or it commits an offence, and is liable on summary conviction to a fine not exceeding level 3 on the standard scale.[62]

(iii) and (iv)   Situation and address of registered office

2.22 An LLP must at all times have a registered office, to which communications and notices may be sent.[63] The registered office must at all times be situated in England and Wales, or in Wales, or must at all times be situated in Scotland.[64] The effect of this requirement is that, on incorporation, the subscribers must choose forever thereafter whether the LLP's registered office is to be in England and Wales (or alternatively Wales), or in Scotland. The relevance of this choice is that it will determine where the LLP is to be registered (and whether by the Registrar of Companies in England and Wales or the Registrar of Companies in Scotland)[65] and

---

[58]   LLP Act 2000, Sch, para 8.
[59]   Ibid, Sch, para 3(2). 'Local authority' means any local authority within the meaning of the Local Government Act 1972 or the Local Government etc (Scotland) Act 1994, the Common Council of the City of London or the Council of the Isles of Scilly: ibid.
[60]   Ie the Company and Business Names Regulations 1981, SI 1981/1685, as amended from time to time, most recently by SI 2004/1771. The substance of these regulations is set out at *Halsbury's Laws* (Butterworths, 4th edn, 1996), para 168.
[61]   As defined in LLP Act 2000, s 14(3): see further chapter 17.
[62]   LLP Act 2000, Sch, para 7. A company cannot be registered with a name which includes at any place in the name the expression 'limited liability partnership' or its Welsh equivalent: CA 1985, s 26(1)(bbb), inserted by the LLP Regulations 2001
[63]   LLP Act 2000, Sch, para 9(1). A document may be served on an LLP by leaving it at, or sending it by post to, the LLP's registered office: CA 1985, s 725(1).
[64]   LLP Act 2000, Sch, para 9(1).
[65]   See ibid, s 3(1) with s 18 (meaning of 'the Registrar').

which is to be the legal system having jurisdiction over it. On incorporation, the situation of the registered office is that stated in the incorporation document.[66] The address of the registered office must be a full address, identifying a building and street. A PO Box number only will not be accepted by the Registrar.[67]

2.23 Where the incorporation document states that the registered office of an LLP is to be situated in Wales (as opposed to England and Wales), the LLP's name may end with 'partneriaeth atebolrwydd cyfyngedig' in place of 'limited liability partnership', or 'pac' or 'PAC' in place of 'llp' or 'LLP'.[68] Where the registered office is in fact situated in Wales, but the incorporation document does not state that it is to be situated in Wales (as opposed to in England and Wales), the LLP may at any time after incorporation deliver a notice to the Registrar stating that its registered office is to be situated in Wales.[69] Such a notice must be in a form approved by the Registrar and be signed by a designated member of the LLP or authenticated in a manner approved by the Registrar.[70] The approved form is Form LLP 287a (Notice that the Registered Office of a Limited Liability Partnership is Situated in Wales). The effect of such a notice is (presumably) to effect an alteration to the incorporation document, so that it now states that the registered office is situated in Wales with the result that the LLP can use the Welsh suffixes to its name mentioned above.[71]

(v) Names and addresses of members

2.24 The members of the LLP on incorporation are the two or more persons associated for carrying on a lawful business with a view to profit who have subscribed their names to the incorporation document (and who have not died or been dissolved between subscribing and incorporation).[72] The persons to be named in the incorporation document, therefore, are the persons who have subscribed their names to it. Form LLP 2 provides for each subscriber, beneath the details of his name, date of birth[73] and address, to sign a statement that he consents to act as a member of the LLP.

2.25 The 'name' of a member who is an individual is his forename and surname (or, in the case of a peer or other person usually known by a title, his title instead of

---

[66] LLP Act 2000, Sch, para 9(2). Changing the location of the registered office of an LLP after incorporation is considered at **3.15–3.18**.
[67] See the side note to Form LLP 2.
[68] LLP Act 2000, Sch, para 2(2).
[69] Ibid, Sch, para 9(3).
[70] Ibid, Sch, para 9(4).
[71] The Registrar publishes notice of the receipt by him of a Form LLP287a under CA 1985, s 711(1)(b) ('any document making or evidencing an alteration in a limited liability partnership's incorporation document').
[72] LLP Act 2000, s 4(1), discussed further in Chapter 8 below. As to the meaning of 'persons', see **2.2–2.3**.
[73] As mentioned at **2.17**, in addition to the name and address of a member, in the case of a member who is an individual Form LLP 2 provides for his date of birth to be given. Where a person becomes a member of an LLP after it has been incorporated, his date of birth is required to be given in the notice filed with Registrar: CA 1985, s 288(3).

or in addition to either or both his forename and surname); and of a corporation or a Scottish firm is its corporate or firm name.[74]

2.26 The 'address' of a member who is an individual is his usual residential address.[75] The incorporation document will be open to inspection by any member of the public under CA 1985, s.709(1) (which permits inspection of any records kept by the Registrar for the purposes of the LLP legislation),[76] and so any member of the public will be able to ascertain the usual residential address of any subscriber to the incorporation document. Where an individual who is subscribing considers that the availability for inspection by members of the public of particulars of his usual residential address is likely to create a serious risk that he or a person who lives with him will be subjected to violence or intimidation, he may apply to the Secretary of State for a 'confidentiality order' in his favour. The effect of such an order being made is that the right for the public to inspect records kept by the Registrar will not apply to so much of those records (contained in documents filed with the Registrar after the making of the order) as contain particulars of the usual residential address of the person for whose benefit the order is made.[77] The applicant for an order must supply a substitute address (a 'service address') to be used in documents filed with the Registrar. This must be an address where documents can be served on him.[78] If an individual who is subscribing to an incorporation document has the benefit of a confidentiality order, it is his service address which is to be stated in the incorporation document.[79] However, at the same time as the incorporation document is delivered to the Registrar, that individual's usual residential address must also be provided to the Registrar, but on a separate form approved by the Registrar.[80] If the incorporation document sent to the Registrar does not contain the service address of the individual having the benefit of the order, or it is not accompanied by the separate form containing that individual's usual residential address, the Secretary of State may (after giving the necessary prior notice) revoke the confidentiality order.[81] Confidentiality orders are more fully discussed at **8.9–8.13**.

2.27 The 'address' of a corporation (or Scottish firm) is its registered or principal office.[82] As is stated in **2.4**, a foreign corporation can be a subscriber, or later joining member, of an LLP. A company, or LLP, incorporated in Great Britain will

---

[74] LLP Act 2000, s 18. The same definition of 'name' is used in CA 1985, s 288 in the context of a person becoming a member after the LLP has been incorporated: see CA 1985, s 288, discussed at **8.6**. Clearly, an individual must subscribe, and have stated in the incorporation document, his true name, whether original or properly assumed. A name taken for a wrongful purpose will not be his true name: see generally on change of name *Halsbury's Laws* (Butterworths, 4th edn, 1994), vol 35, paras 1272–1279.

[75] LLP Act 2000, s 18. The same definition of address is used in CA 1985, s 288.

[76] As to inspection of records kept by the Registrar, see **1.11**.

[77] See generally CA 1985, ss 723B–723F.

[78] See generally the Limited Liability Partnerships (Particulars of Usual Residential Address) (Confidentiality Orders) Regulations 2002, SI 2002/915 (LLP Confidentiality Regulations 2002).

[79] LLP Act 2000, s 2(2A).

[80] Ibid, s 2(2B). The form which is used for this purpose is Form LLP 723(SR) introduced by the Limited Liability Partnerships (Forms) Regulations 2002 SI 2002/690.

[81] LLP Confidentiality Regulations 2002 reg. 11(1)(d).

[82] LLP Act 2000, s 18.

have a 'registered office'. The term 'principal office' will apply to corporate bodies not having a 'registered office' as well as to a Scottish firm.

(vi)   Specifying the designated members

2.28   The role of designated members is discussed in Chapter 10. In brief, they may be seen principally as the members of the LLP charged by the legislation with ensuring that the requirements of the legislation as to disclosure and notification to the Registrar are satisfied: LLP compliance officers.

2.29   So long as it has two or more members,[83] an LLP must always have at least two designated members.[84] As stated in **2.1**, there must be a minimum of two subscribers to the incorporation document. This document must adopt one of two courses for the purpose of identifying who the designated members are to be. It must either: (i) name those of the first members of the LLP who are to be the designated members,[85] in which case only the specified members become on incorporation the designated members;[86] or (ii) state that every person who from time to time is a member of the LLP is a designated member,[87] in which case every member (including everyone who subsequently becomes a member) is automatically a designated member.[88] Whichever course is adopted in the incorporation document, the document must provide for at least two designated members.[89] Form LLP 2 deals with all this quite simply, by requiring one of two boxes – 'Yes' or 'No' – to be ticked against the question 'Will all members from time to time be designated members?' Against the 'No' box, the form states: 'if no, at least two of the listed members must be designated members'. Where each subscriber's name and address is to be set out, there is a box for that subscriber to tick if he consents to act as a designated member. A duly completed incorporation document therefore, needs to have at least two of these individual boxes ticked by subscribers (whether or not the general 'Yes' box is ticked).

2.30   At any time after incorporation, an LLP can switch from one of the above options (some members only are designated members, or all are) to the other. Having originally chosen option (i), the LLP may at any time deliver to the Registrar a notice that every person who from time to time is a member of the LLP is a designated member.[90] Such a notice has the same effect as if this had been stated in the incorporation document, with the result that with effect from delivery of the notice every member of the LLP for the time being is automatically a designated member.[91] Likewise, having originally chosen option (ii), the LLP may at any time deliver to the Registrar a notice specifying named members as the

---

[83]   As to the possibility of an LLP having one member only, see **2.15**.

[84]   This follows from LLP Act 2000, ss 2(1)(a) and 8(2).

[85]   LLP Act 2000, s 2(2)(f).

[86]   Ibid, s 8(1)(a).

[87]   Ibid, s 2(2)(f).

[88]   Ibid, s 8(3).

[89]   Note that LLP Act 2000, s 2(2)(f) refers to designated members in the plural.

[90]   LLP Act 2000, s 8(4)(b).

[91]   Ibid, s 8(4), final part, with s 8(3). Presumably the intention is that the change has effect from delivery of the notice to the Registrar, and not that there should be a backdated effect.

designated members,[92] in which case thereafter[93] change will be by agreement amongst the members (and the notice requirements on any change will apply).[94] A notice to the Registrar switching from one option to the other must be in a form approved by the Registrar and be signed by a designated member or authenticated in a manner approved by the Registrar.[95] The approved form is Form LLP 8 (Notice of Designated Member(s) of a Limited Liability Partnership). On receipt of the notice, the Registrar is required to publish notice of it in the *London Gazette* under CA 1985, s 711(1)(b).[96]

Altering the incorporation document

2.31 There is no express provision in the legislation for alteration of the incorporation document. The legislation does, however, envisage that the incorporation document may be altered. CA 1985, s 42(1)(b) provides that, in certain circumstances, an LLP is not entitled to rely against persons other than members on any alteration of the LLP's incorporation document.[97] Section 711(1)(b) provides that, in certain circumstances, the Registrar is to publish in the *London Gazette* notice of the receipt by him of any document making or evidencing an alteration in an LLP's incorporation document. The question of what constitutes an alteration to the incorporation document is considered further at **3.13**.

(c)   Compliance statement

2.32   The third condition for an LLP to be incorporated is that there be delivered to the Registrar not only a duly completed incorporation document as referred to in LLP Act 2000, s 2(1)(b), but also a statement (in a form approved by the Registrar), made either by a solicitor engaged in the formation of the LLP or by one of the subscribers to the incorporation document, to the effect that the (two or more) subscribers to the incorporation document are associated for carrying on a lawful business with a view to profit, ie that the requirement for incorporation as an LLP imposed by LLP Act 2000, s 2(1)(a) has been complied with.[98]

2.33   The need for this compliance statement is particular to LLPs. Unlike a company, whose objects[99] are contained in its memorandum of association and are, therefore, scrutinised by the Registrar before registration, and published to the world, an LLP's incorporation document does not set out the business in which the LLP is to engage.[100] There is no equivalent to the objects clause in the memorandum of association of a company. The compliance statement, therefore, is the means of seeking to ensure that the proposed business is a lawful business, and

---

LLP Act 2000, s 8(4)(b).
Presumably, see footnote 91 above.
Section 8(4), final part, with s 8(1) and (2). See further **10.4**.
Section 8(5).
Ie as a document making or evidencing an alteration in the incorporation document. The Registrar considers that a Form LLP8 is a document falling within s 711(1)(b).
CA 1985, s 42 is discussed further at **3.10**.
LLP Act 2000, s 2(1)(c).
Which must also be for the carrying out of a 'lawful purpose': CA 1985, s 1(1).
[100] See **2.16**.

also that it is to be carried on with a view to profit. The approved form of the compliance statement is included in LLP Form 2 (Application for Incorporation of a Limited Liability Partnership). The statement is that 'the two or more persons named overleaf [ie the subscribing first members] are associated for carrying on a lawful business with a view to profit'.

2.34 The option of the compliance statement being made either by a subscriber (ie by one of the persons associated for carrying on the proposed business) or by the solicitor engaged in the formation of the LLP is perhaps reminiscent of the option given by the Civil Procedure Rules 1998 (CPR) for the statement of truth verifying a pleading to be made either by the party to the action or by his legal representative on his behalf.[101] It is to be noted, however, that whilst a CPR statement of truth is a statement of *belief* that the facts stated in the pleading are true,[102] the compliance statement under the LLP Act 2000 is a statement that the facts *are* true and that the business to be carried on is a lawful business, carried on with a view to profit. Whilst the LLP Act 2000 only provides for a sanction on the maker of the statement in the absence of belief by him as to its truth,[103] it is as well to bear in mind the absolute character of the compliance statement. Whether or not it is the solicitor who actually makes the statement, there is almost certainly going to be a duty on him to advise as to the accuracy of the statement. The compliance statement may well be made by the subscriber in reliance on that advice.

2.35 There is a substantial criminal sanction if a false compliance statement is made and the person who makes it either knows it to be false or does not believe it to be true. The maker of the false statement is guilty of an offence and liable (a) on summary conviction, to imprisonment for a period not exceeding 6 months or a fine not exceeding the statutory maximum, or to both; or (b) on conviction on indictment, to imprisonment for a period not exceeding 2 years or a fine, or to both.[104]

2.36 As stated in **2.32**, it is a pre-condition to incorporation of an LLP that the compliance statement be delivered to the Registrar. But it is also a separate pre-condition to incorporation that the requirement imposed by LLP Act 2000, s 2(1)(a) has been complied with.[105] The Registrar is not obliged to accept the compliance statement as true and accurate, and as sufficient evidence that the requirement for incorporation imposed by s 2(1)(a) has been complied with. The LLP Act 2000, s 3(2) makes it clear that he *may* do so; but the decision as to whether to be satisfied with the compliance statement, and that s 2(1)(a) has in fact been complied with, is his.[106] The Registrar can, therefore, reject the compliance

---

[101] CPR, r 22.1(6)
[102] CPR PD 22.2
[103] See **2.35**.
[104] LLP Act 2000, s 2(3) and (4).
[105] See the opening words of LLP Act 2000, s 2(1) and the reference in s 3(1) to para (a) of s 2(1).
[106] LLP Act 2000, s 3(2). In deciding whether or not to accept the compliance statement as sufficient evidence, the Registrar is fulfilling a quasi-judicial function, with a duty to determine whether the association of subscribers applying for registration is qualified to be registered: see *Bowman v Secular Society Ltd* [1917] AC 406 at 439 (in relation to registration of a company), adopted in *R v Registrar of Companies, ex parte A-G* [1991] BCLC 476.

statement, on the ground that he is not satisfied that it provides sufficient evidence of compliance with s 2(1)(a); and he can take into account information which comes to him otherwise than through the incorporation document, albeit the incorporation document is apparently verified by the compliance statement.

2.37 In the authors' view, it would be wise for the maker of the compliance statement to proceed on the assumption that if for any reason an event occurs between delivery of the incorporation document and issue of the certificate of incorporation which causes continuing compliance with the requirements of s 2(1)(a) to cease,[107] the maker of the statement is under an obligation to notify the Registrar of this fact. The existence of such a continuing obligation (and of an offence under s 2(3) if belief in the continuing accuracy of the statement is no longer held by the maker of it) is not clear; but at least until the position is established it would be wise to assume that such an obligation exists.[108]

CERTIFICATE AND REGISTRATION

2.38 LLP Act 2000, s 3(1) provides that, when the incorporation document and the compliance statement have been duly delivered to the Registrar, he is to retain the incorporation document (or an authenticated copy) delivered to him and, unless the requirement imposed by s 2(1)(a) has not been complied with (and, as discussed above, the Registrar is not bound to accept the accuracy of the compliance statement in this respect), he is to register the incorporation document (or copy) and give a certificate that the LLP is incorporated by the name specified in the incorporation document. This certificate is either to be signed by the Registrar or to be authenticated by his official seal.[109] When given, the certificate is conclusive evidence that the LLP is incorporated by the name specified in the incorporation document.[110] It is, therefore, the issue of the certificate which constitutes the LLP a body corporate, with its own legal personality separate from that of its members.[111] Thereafter the LLP can carry on business as a separate legal entity, with no restrictions as against the outside world on its capacity to do so.[112]

2.39 The certificate is stated in LLP Act 2000, s 3(4) to be conclusive evidence 'that the requirements of section 2 are complied with and that the limited liability partnership is incorporated by the name specified in the incorporation document'.

---

[107] For instance, the subscribers are reduced by death to one only, or the intended business becomes unlawful.
[108] Such an obligation would be analogous to the civil law obligation to correct a representation which, whilst true when made, has become untrue: see, for example, the discussion in *Chitty on Contracts* 29th edn, paras 6-016–6-018 and the criminal case of *Ray v Sempers* [1974] AC 370 (dishonestly obtaining by deception, where a continuing representation of an intention to pay for a restaurant meal changed from being honest at the beginning of the meal to being dishonest).
[109] LLP Act 2000, s 3(3).
[110] Ibid, s 3(4).
[111] Ibid, s 1(2). The fee payable to the Registrar for registration of the LLP is £95: see the Limited Liability Partnerships (Fees) (No 2) Regulations 2001, SI 2001/969.
[112] LLP Act 2000, s 1(3). As to the LLP's 'unlimited capacity', see further **3.4–3.5**.

This provision will prevent anyone (other than the Crown),[113] after issue of the certificate, challenging the validity of the incorporation and alleging that the LLP does not exist as such. In this respect, the effect is similar to that of CA 1985, s 13(7)(a) for companies.[114] The question which arises is whether LLP Act 2000, s 3(4) has any effect beyond this. The use of the present tense in the phrase 'are complied with' is in possible contrast to references earlier in s 3 to whether the requirements imposed by paras (a), (b) and/or (c) of s 2(1) 'have been' or 'has been' complied with.[115] It might be said, at first glance, that the use of the present tense in s 3(4) is intended to make the certificate conclusive evidence, on an ongoing basis, that the requirements of s 2 are complied with: namely, that there are at any time two or more members of the LLP who are associated for carrying on a lawful business with a view to profit. This, however, cannot have been intended; and would be inconsistent with the fact that the LLP continues to exist, and can continue to trade, if its membership is reduced to one person only,[116] and inconsistent also with the power for the Secretary of State to appoint inspectors to investigate the affairs of the LLP if he suspects that those affairs are being conducted for an unlawful purpose.[117]

2.40 Although the analogy between the requirement in LLP Act 2000, s 2(1)(a) that the subscribers be associated for a lawful purpose and the requirement in the CA 1985 that a company's objects stated in its memorandum of association be lawful is not exact, there seems no reason why the comments of the House of Lords in *Bowman v Secular Society Ltd*[118] as to the non-conclusiveness of a company's certificate of incorporation in relation to an issue as to the legality of its objects clause should not be equally applicable in relation to the question of the conclusiveness of an LLP's certificate of incorporation in relation to an issue as to the lawfulness of its business, or whether its business is to be carried on with a view to profit. In *Bowman*, the House of Lords made clear that, despite its stated conclusiveness,[119] the certificate does not prove that all the objects and powers in the memorandum are lawful.[120] Like the CA 1985 (and its statutory predecessor being considered in *Bowman*), the LLP Act 2000 is not expressed to bind the Crown. The authors suggest that, as in the case of a company which manages to be registered under CA 1985 and obtain a certificate of incorporation with objects specified in its memorandum which are unlawful, so in the case of an LLP it will

---

[113] See **2.40**.

[114] See, for instance, *Bowman v Secular Society Ltd* [1917] AC 406 at 421, 435 and 452 and *Cotman v Brougham* [1918] AC 514 at 523. For a still relevant statement of the importance of the conclusiveness of the certificate as to the validity of incorporation, see Lord Cairns in *Peel's Case* (1867) LR 2 Ch App 674 at 681–682. CA 1985, s 13(7)(a) provides: 'A certificate of incorporation given in respect of an association is conclusive evidence . . . that the requirements of this Act in respect of registration and of matters precedent and incidental to it have been complied with, and that the association is a company authorised to be registered, and is duly registered, under this Act'.

[115] See LLP Act 2000, s 3(1) and (2), and also s 2(1)(c).

[116] See **2.15**.

[117] CA 1985, s 432(2)(a). The grounds for DTI investigation are discussed in chapter 20.

[118] Above.

[119] As stated by s 1 of the Companies Act 1900, essentially the same as CA 1985, s 13(7)(a) quoted in footnote 114 above. CA 1985, s 1(1) provides that a company may be formed by any two or more persons associated for a lawful purpose subscribing their names to a memorandum of association.

[120] See [1917] AC 406 at 421, and at 439/40 and 452.

be open the Crown (acting through the Attorney-General) to apply to the court for judicial review of the Registrar's decision to give registration, and for an order quashing that registration,[121] where it transpires that the requirements of LLP Act 2000, s 2(1)(a) were not in fact complied with. It is also worth noting in the present context that one of the grounds on which the Secretary of State may appoint inspectors to investigate the affairs of an LLP is that he suspects that the LLP was formed for an unlawful purpose.[122]

2.41 The result of this discussion is that the conclusiveness of an LLP's certificate of incorporation referred to in LLP Act 2000, s 3(4) is not as far-reaching as might at first be thought. Probably, the use of the present tense in s 3(4) of the Act has no greater significance, as between the incorporated LLP and third parties, than to indicate that, for the purposes of valid and effective incorporation, the requirements of the Act in respect of registration and incorporation, and of all matters up to that moment, are to be assumed to have been complied with. This is an assumption which (subject to the right of the Crown referred to in **2.40**) the court must also make.[123] The position where the requirements of LLP Act 2000, s 2(1)(a) have been complied with on incorporation, but the LLP subsequently carries on business for an unlawful purpose, or otherwise than with a view to profit, is considered at **3.27-3.29**.

NOTICE OF ISSUE OF CERTIFICATE

2.42 In addition to the certificate being issued, the LLP will be allocated a registered number by the Registrar.[124] This, together with certain other information, must appear on its business letters and order forms.[125] The Registrar is also to publish in the *London Gazette* notice of the issue by him of the certificate of incorporation.[126]

INSPECTION

2.43 After the LLP has been incorporated, any person may inspect the incorporation document and the compliance statement, and also the certificate of incorporation, and take copies of them.[127] Any person can also require from the

---

[121] 'Revoke the incorporation' in the words of Lord Buckmaster in *Bowman* at 478. This is what was done in *R v Registrar of Companies, ex parte A-G* [1991] BCLC 476 referred to in **2.11**.

[122] CA 1985, s 432(2)(b). The grounds for DTI investigation are discussed in chapter 20.

[123] See the references to *Bowman v Secular Society Ltd* and *Cotman v Brougham* in footnote 114 above. But note also the reference by Lord Parker in *Bowman* at 439 to it being open to the court (in normal inter-partes litigation) to stay its hand until an opportunity has been given for taking the appropriate steps (ie the Attorney-General seeking judicial review) for the cancellation of the certificate of registration.

[124] CA 1985, s 705(1)–(3).

[125] Ibid, s 351(1). See further, **4.1–4.4**.

[126] Ibid, s 711(1)(a).

[127] Under the general right contained in CA 1985, s 709 to inspect any records kept by the Registrar.

Registrar a certificate of incorporation of an LLP signed by the Registrar or authenticated by his official seal.[128]

TRADING NOT COMMENCED

2.44 If the LLP does not start carrying on business within a year from its incorporation, it may be wound up by the court.[129] Winding up by the court on this and other grounds is discussed in Chapter 26.

---

[128] CA 1985, s 710.
[129] See IA 1986, s 122(1)(b).

Chapter 3

THE CORPORATE ENTITY

INTRODUCTION

3.1 Once incorporated (on the issue of the certificate of incorporation), the LLP, as a body corporate, is an entity with legal personality separate from that of its members,[1] and with its own rights and its own duties (whether statutory duties, or duties in tort or under the criminal law).[2] It will be the separate legal entity (as opposed to the individual members) which will carry on the business for which the first members have become associated.

3.2 It will be the LLP which will have rights of recovery from third parties on contractual claims or for wrongs done to it.[3] It will also be the LLP which (generally speaking) will own the property and assets of the business, and which will be the employer of the staff of the business (and which will be the recipient of restraint of trade covenants). It will have its own rights under the Human Rights Act 1998. As is mentioned in **2.15**, the LLP will continue to exist as a separate legal entity, even if the membership is reduced to one (or none), until it is wound-up and dissolved under the IA 1986.[4]

3.3 Like any corporate entity, the LLP can only act through others as its agents.[5] These others will clearly include (and in most cases will solely or principally comprise) its members. Section 6(1) of the LLP Act 2000 expressly provides that every member of an LLP is the agent of the LLP.[6] This sub-section serves a dual purpose in the LLP Act. First, it creates the framework within which the LLP may be bound to third parties by the acts of its members. Subject to the impact of s 6(2)

---

[1] LLP Act 2000, s 1(2): and see also, for instance, *Salomon v Salomon* [1897] AC 22 at 31.

[2] For example, under both the LLP Act 2000 and the CA 1985, an LLP has various obligations as to filing information with the Registrar, and itself commits an offence in the event of a variety such obligations not being met.

[3] See, as to companies, *Foss v Harbottle* (1843) 2 Hare 461, *Prudential Assurance Co Ltd v Newman Industries Ltd (No 2)* [1982] Ch 204 (CA) at 222–223, *Johnson v Gore Wood & Co* [2002] 2 AC 1 and *Giles v Rhind* [2003] Ch 618 (CA). An individual member may have a claim in respect of loss to him caused by the breach of a duty owed independently to him: *ibid*.

[4] Winding-up is considered in chapter 26.

[5] See, for example, *Meridian Global Funds Management Asia Ltd v Securities Commission* [1995] 2 AC 500 (PC).

[6] Broadly speaking, the position of the members will be similar to that of the directors of a company, for whose position the classic statement is that of Cairns LJ in *Ferguson v Wilson* (1866) 2 Ch App 77 at 89–90: 'What is the position of directors of a public company? They are merely agents of a company. The company itself cannot act in its own person, for it has no person; it can only act through directors, and the case is, as regards those directors, merely the ordinary case of principal and agent. Wherever an agent is liable those directors would be liable; where the liability would attach to the principal, and the principal only, the liability is the liability of the company'.

in relation to members, the acts of the LLP's members and employees will be attributed to it in accordance with the principles of agency (or the construction of the relevant statute, where a statutory duty is involved).[7] The degree to which an LLP is bound by the acts of its members, and of its non-member employees (and others), in dealings with third parties is considered in chapter 5. Secondly, s 6(1) establishes the internal relationship between the LLP and its members. It is from this relationship of principal and agent that the fiduciary obligations owed by members to the LLP arise. These obligations, and the other responsibilities and rights existing as between the members and the LLP, are considered in chapters 11 and 12.

'UNLIMITED CAPACITY'

3.4   Section 1(3) of the LLP Act 2000 provides that an LLP has 'unlimited capacity'. As against the outside world, therefore, an LLP has the same capacity and freedom to enter into any contract or other transaction as a private individual. Its capacity to enter into transactions is not limited in any way to transactions falling within the ambit of the business for the carrying on of which its first members subscribed their names to the incorporation document.[8] In this respect the position of an LLP is similar to that of a company since 1991,[9] namely the validity of an act done by it cannot be called into question on the ground of lack of capacity by reason of the precise or limited nature of the business for the carrying on of which it was formed. The doctrine of ultra vires, which used to be so important in relation to transactions entered into by companies, has no place in relation to LLPs.

3.5   In addition, therefore, to having the same capacity to enter into contracts as a private individual, the LLP will be able to own the assets of the business that it is carrying on, ranging from intellectual property rights to freehold or leasehold land; and not only will it be able to hold shares in a company, but it may be a member of another LLP, or be a partner in a partnership under the Partnership Act 1890 or the Limited Partnerships Act 1907, whatever business that other LLP, or those partnerships, may be carrying on.

---

[7]   See *Meridian Global Funds* above and *Attorney-General's Reference (No 2 of 1999)* [2000] 2 BCLC 257. If a member of an LLP acts illegally or dishonestly in relation to the LLP itself, knowledge of that illegality or dishonesty will not be attributed to the LLP: see *Belmont Finance Corporation Ltd v Williams Furniture Ltd* [1979] Ch 250 and *Attorney-General's Reference (No 2 of 1982)* [1984] 1 QB 624. This exception for attribution may be wider than cases of a member's illegality or dishonesty; and may cover other breaches of duty by the member to the LLP where justice and common sense must entail that it is impossible to infer the relevant knowledge on the part of the LLP: see *Arab Bank Plc v Zurich Insurance Co* [1999] 1 Lloyd's Rep 262 at 282/3.

[8]   As noted at **2.16**, the incorporation document does not contain any statement of the LLP's objects or business.

[9]   Ie the coming into force of the substituted CA 1985, s 35(1), introduced by the Companies Act 1989 (CA 1989).

BANKS AND LANDLORDS

3.6   It follows from the LLP being the entity which is carrying on the business that the primary banking relationship will (ordinarily) be between the LLP and the bank. Any property and other assets owned by the LLP can be used by it as security. There is no limitation on the LLP's capacity to borrow; and an LLP can give fixed and floating charges in the same way as a company.[10] To what extent *the bank* will see its relationship as being with the LLP to the exclusion of the individual members (and the requirement for guarantees from them) will no doubt depend on the particular circumstances.

3.7   The position will be similar in relation to leases. The LLP as a corporate entity will be able to enter into a lease (or take an assignment of a lease) as the tenant. But the extent to which a landlord will require individual members of the LLP to join in as sureties will no doubt depend on the landlord's perception of the LLP's financial stability, and on prevailing market conditions.

PIERCING THE CORPORATE VEIL

3.8   As is mentioned in **3.1**, once incorporated, the LLP, as a body corporate, will be a legally recognised entity, having an existence separate from its members. In this respect, its position will be similar to that of a limited company. In relation to companies, however, there are circumstances in which the court will disregard the company's separate existence ie where it will pierce the 'corporate veil'. Where the corporate veil is pierced, the company is treated as a mere vehicle for the person actually controlling it, and the company and that person are treated as one. The circumstances in which the corporate veil is pierced are not fully developed, but it has been said that the court will only do so where special circumstances exist which indicate that the company is a mere façade concealing the true facts.[11] A key factor will be the motive with which the corporate veil has been interposed in the first place ie why is the company there? Does it have any true independent rationale of its own, or is it a mere device that has been interposed in order to conceal liability on the part of others, or to evade some legal obligation?[12] In a well-known case in 1962,[13] the owner of some land who had contracted to sell it, in order to avoid having to complete the contract of sale, sold the land to a £100 company which was merely a vehicle for the purpose of him avoiding legal recognition as the owner. The court treated the company and the landowner as one: the company was said to be a mere device and sham, and its existence did not shield the landowner from an order to perform the contract.[14] In a more recent case, in 2001, the court held that the receipt by a company of moneys wrongfully taken from another company's bank account was the receipt personally of the

---

[10]   Charging the LLP's property is discussed in chapter 6.
[11]   See *Woolfson v Strathclyde Regional Council* 1978 SC (HL) 90 at 96.
[12]   See *Adams v Cape Industries Plc* in the Court of Appeal [1990] Ch 433 and *Trustor AB v Smallbone* [2001] 1 WLR 1177.
[13]   *Jones v Lipman* [1962] 1 WLR 832
[14]   An order for specific performance was made against both the landowner and the company.

wrongdoing director who had engineered the taking and whose vehicle the receiving company was.[15]

3.9　Given the requirement for the incorporation of an LLP that two or more persons must be associated for carrying on a business with a view to profit,[16] it is probable that an LLP will lend itself much less than a company to being used as a device to conceal the true facts. But, the authors suggest, if an LLP is used in circumstances where the use of a company would lead to its corporate veil being pierced, there is no reason in principle why the court should not similarly pierce the corporate veil of the LLP.

NOTIFICATION TO THE REGISTRAR

3.10　Reference has been made in **1.9–1.11** to the role of the Registrar in relation to LLPs, to the requirements for information relating to the LLP to be delivered to him, and to that information thereafter being available for inspection by any person.[17] Under CA 1985, s 711, the Registrar is required to publish in the London Gazette notice of the receipt by him of various documents relating to the LLP, including a winding-up order, an alteration in the incorporation document and a change in the situation of the registered office. In this context, CA 1985, s 42 provides, for the protection of persons dealing with LLP,[18] that an LLP is not entitled to rely against persons other than members of the LLP on:

(i)　　the making of a winding-up order in respect of the LLP or the appointment of a liquidator in a voluntary winding up of the LLP;

(ii)　　any alteration of the LLP's incorporation document;[19] or

(iii)　　(as regards service of any document on the LLP) any change in situation of the LLP's registered office,[20]

if the event has not been officially notified, by publication in the *London Gazette*,[21] at the material time and is not shown by the LLP to have been known at that time to the person concerned, or if the material time fell on or before the fifteenth day after[22] the date of publication in the Gazette (or, where the fifteenth day was a Saturday, Sunday or bank holiday, on or before the next day that was not) and it is shown that the person concerned was unavoidably prevented from knowing of the

---

[15]　*Trustor AB v Smallbone* above.

[16]　LLP Act 2000, s 2(1)(a).

[17]　Under CA 1985, s 709.

[18]　See *Official Custodian for Charities v Parway Estates Ltd* [1985] Ch 151 (CA), considering European Communities Act 1972, s 9(4), the predecessor of CA 1985, s 42.

[19]　Discussed at **2.31**.

[20]　Discussed at **3.15**.

[21]　'Officially notified' means (in the case of a voluntary liquidation) publication in the *London Gazette* of notice of the appointment of the liquidator and (in the other cases) publication in the *London Gazette* of notice of the receipt by the Registrar of the relevant document

[22]　In calculating 'the fifteenth day after', the date of the official notification is excluded: see *Dodds v Walker* [1981] 1 WLR 1027 (HL) (on s 29 of the Landlord and Tenant Act 1954) at 1029B–C.

event at that time.[23] The effect of s 42 is negative only. The provision that the LLP cannot rely on any of the specified events in the circumstances mentioned in s 42 does not have the result that, when notification in relation to that event *has been* published in the *Gazette*, knowledge or notice of the relevant event is thereby imputed to any third party.[24]

3.11 What does, and does not, constitute an alteration of the incorporation document is not clear; but it may be that for the purposes of CA 1985, s 42 an alteration of the incorporation document is constituted by any change from what is shown in the incorporation document. The argument against this is that the individual paragraphs of CA 1985, s 711(1) may be seen as intended to be mutually exclusive, so that an alteration of the incorporation document (paragraph (b)) is to be distinguished from, inter alia, a change among the members (paragraph (c)) and a change in the situation of the LLP's registered office (paragraph (n)). But it is by no means clear that the paragraphs of s 711(1) are mutually exclusive; and it is not easy to see why some changes only from what appears in the incorporation document should be categorised as alterations of the incorporation document.

THE REGISTERED OFFICE

3.12 As has been mentioned previously,[25] an LLP must at all times have a registered office, to which communications and notices may be sent;[26] and an irrevocable choice must be made at incorporation as to whether the registered office is to be situated in England and Wales (or in Wales), or in Scotland.[27] A document which is required to be served on an LLP may be served on it by leaving the document at, or sending it by post to, the registered office.[28] Where an LLP which is registered in Scotland carries on business in England and Wales, any court process in England and Wales may be served on that LLP by leaving the process at, or sending it by post to, the Scottish LLP's principal place of business in England and Wales, addressed to the manager or a designated member in England

---

[23] CA 1985, s 42(1) and (2)(b).

[24] See *Official Custodian for Charities v Parway Estates Ltd* [1985] Ch 151 (CA), concerned with the question whether a landlord who accepted rent after notification of the receipt by the Registrar of a winding-up order in respect of the tenant had been published in the *Gazette* had waived his right to forfeit by reason of that publication, although he was not actually aware of the liquidation.

[25] See **2.22**.

[26] LLP Act 2000, Sch, para 9(1).

[27] Ibid.

[28] CA 1985, s 725(1). A failure by a third party to comply with this provision in the service of court proceedings on an LLP, by serving such proceedings at an address other than the registered office, does not automatically render the proceedings a nullity, but is an irregularity which the court can deal with on its merits: see *Singh v Atombrook Ltd* [1989] 1 WLR 810 (on RSC Ord 2 r 1). For methods of service on a company see now CPR, r 6.2. Presumably this rule will be applied to LLPs. No clear meaning of 'senior position' in relation to an LLP is given for the purposes of CPR r 6.4 by the Practice Direction.

and Wales.[29] Where this latter course is followed, a copy of the document is to be sent by post to the LLP's registered office in Scotland.[30]

3.13 The following documents must be kept at the LLP's registered office, or (in the case of (i) and (ii) below) at such alternative place as is specified in the relevant section of CA 1985:

(i)	the LLP's accounting records;[31]
(ii)	any register of holders of debentures of the LLP;[32]
(iii)	a copy of every instrument creating a charge which requires to be registered;[33] and
(iv)	the register of charges, containing details of all charges specifically affecting the property of the LLP, and of all floating charges on the LLP's undertaking or any of its property.[34]

3.14 The address of the LLP's registered office must be mentioned on all its business letters and order forms;[35] and is also an item of information to be included in the annual return.[36]

3.15 An LLP may change its registered office at any time (within the English or Scottish jurisdiction originally chosen). This is done by delivering to the Registrar a notice in a form approved by him, and either signed by a designated member of the LLP or authenticated in a manner approved by the Registrar.[37] The approved form is Form LLP 287 (Change in situation or address of Registered Office of a Limited Liability Partnership). The change takes effect on the notice being registered by the Registrar; but until the end of the period of 14 days beginning with the date on which it is registered a third party may validly serve any document on the LLP at the previous registered office.[38] A PO Box number only will not be accepted by the Registrar as a registered office.[39] On receipt by him of the form, the Registrar is to publish notice of his receipt of it in the *London Gazette*.[40]

3.16 Section 42 of the CA 1985[41] provides that, as regards service of any document on an LLP, the LLP is not entitled to rely against persons other than its own members on any change in the situation of its registered office if either (i) at the time when the document is served notice of receipt by the Registrar of the form

---

[29]	CA 1985, s 725(2).
[30]	Ibid, s 725(3).
[31]	Ibid, s 222: see **18.2**. The alternative is 'such other place as the members think fit' .
[32]	Ibid, s 190: see **6.7**.
[33]	Ibid, s 406: see **6.10**.
[34]	Ibid, s 407: see **6.4**.
[35]	Ibid, s 351(1)(b): see **4.2**.
[36]	Ibid, s 364(a): see **4.26**.
[37]	LLP Act 2000, Sch, para 10.
[38]	CA 1985, s 287(1).
[39]	See the side note to Form LLP 287.
[40]	CA 1985, s 711(1)(n).
[41]	Discussed further at **3.10**.

has not been published in the *London Gazette*,[42] and it is not shown by the LLP that at that time the person serving the document knew of the change, or (ii) service of the document fell on or before the fifteenth day after publication in the *London Gazette* (or, where the fifteenth day was a non-business day, on or before the next day that was not), and it is shown that the person serving the document was unavoidably prevented from knowing of the change.[43]

3.17 With regard to the obligations to be met by the LLP itself in relation to its registered office,[44] it must start complying with these obligations in relation to its changed registered office from the moment that the Registrar registers the change.[45] Where an LLP unavoidably ceases to perform its obligation to keep any register or other document at its registered office in circumstances in which it was not practicable to give prior notice to the Registrar of a change of registered office, but (a) resumes performance of that obligation at other premises as soon as practicable, and (b) gives notice accordingly to the Registrar of a change in its registered office within 14 days of doing so, it is not to be treated as having failed to comply with that duty.[46] This would deal with a situation where, for instance, the registered office burns down. The statutory provision[47] also covers an LLP unavoidably ceasing to mention the address of its registered office in a document in circumstances in which it was not practicable to give prior notice to the Registrar of a change.

3.18 The legislation does not specify any particular internal procedure by which an LLP can decide to change its registered office. How a decision to change the LLP's registered office is to be made, therefore, is something to be covered, by a specific or general decision-making provision, in the LLP agreement. If a change of registered office is not covered by such a provision, the position will most probably be, by reason of the application of rule (6) of the default rules,[48] that it will require the consent of all the members (not simply a majority).

COLLECTIVE INVESTMENT SCHEMES

3.19 An LLP is capable of amounting to a collective investment scheme under s 235 of the Financial Services and Markets Act 2000 (FSMA 2000).[49] That is to

---

[42] See **3.10**. This publication is not the same as registration by the Registrar of the change of registered office.

[43] CA 1985, s 42(1)(d) with s 711(2).

[44] Referred to at **3.12** and **3.13**.

[45] See **3.15**. CA 1985, s 287(5) is not adopted for LLPs.

[46] CA 1985, s 287(2) as modified.

[47] Ibid. The provision is based on normal CA 1985, s 287(6), but adds in a reference to unavoidably ceasing to mention the address of the registered office. The reference in this context to 'resumes performance of that duty at other premises as soon as possible' presumably means giving another address on all its business letters, etc.

[48] Ie the rules provided by LLP Regulations 2001, regs 7 and 8 to form the LLP agreement in default of any terms otherwise: see **9.6–9.8**. Default rule (6) is considered at **14.6–14.7**.

[49] See the Financial Services and Markets Act 2000 (Collective Investment Schemes) Order 2001, SI 2001/1062 as amended by the Financial Services and Markets Act 2000 (Miscellaneous Provisions) Order 2001 SI 2001/3650. Paragraph 21(2) of the schedule to SI 2001/1062 expressly excludes

say, the association of the members of the LLP for carrying on a business with a view to profit is capable of amounting to a collective investment scheme. The issue will be whether that association constitutes arrangements with respect to property of any description (including money), the purpose or effect of which is to enable the members and/or other persons taking part in the arrangements ('the participants'), whether by becoming owners of the property or any part of it or otherwise, to participate in or receive profits or income arising from the acquisition, holding, management or disposal of the property or sums paid out of such profits or income.[50] If there are such arrangements and (i) the contributions of the participants, and the profits or income out of which payments are to be made to them, are pooled and/or the property is managed as a whole by or on behalf of the operator of the scheme,[51] and (ii) any of the persons who are to be the participants do not have day-to-day control over the management of the property (whether or not they have the right to be consulted or to give directions),[52] then the arrangements will amount to a collective investment scheme (unless they fall within the exemptions contained in an order made by the Treasury under FSMA 2000, s 235(5)).[53]

3.20 Where the association of the members of an LLP amounts to a collective investment scheme, it is probably going to be the case that the LLP will be the beneficial owner of the property in question (and of any contributions by the members) in exchange for rights of the members against the LLP under the LLP agreement.[54] In these circumstances, it will be the LLP itself which will constitute the collective investment scheme.[55]

3.21 The property in respect of which a collective investment scheme may be constituted is 'property of any description'. This includes moveable and immoveable, tangible and intangible, property. It includes, therefore, goodwill. Whenever an LLP is formed for the purpose of enabling the members to receive profits or income arising from the acquisition, holding, management or disposing of any such property, or the effect of the LLP agreement is to enable the members to receive such profits or income, the possibility arises of the LLP amounting to a collective investment scheme. This possibility arises even if the business of the LLP is a normal commercial or professional enterprise, not traditionally associated with investment activity, such as running a sweet shop or conducting a law practice. A key factor in arriving at an LLP being a collective investment scheme is likely to be an entitlement of members to receive profits or income from the exploitation of the property. If the LLP does amount to a collective investment scheme, there will be restrictions on communicating invitations or inducements to

---

LLPs from the general provision in para 21(1) that no body corporate other than an open-ended investment company amounts to a collective investment scheme.

[50]   See FSMA 2000, s 235(1).

[51]   Ibid, s 235(3). The ' operator of the scheme' is not defined for present purposes.

[52]   Ibid, s 235(2). As to day-to-day control, see further **3.22**.

[53]   The present exclusions are contained in SI 2001/1062 as amended by SI 2001/3650 referred to in footnote 49 above.

[54]   Ie the agreement provided for by LLP Act 2000, s 5 (discussed in chapter 9).

[55]   This would appear also to be the view of the FSA: see the FSA's Authorisation Manual, Appendix 2.4.

third parties to become members or other participants in the scheme.[56] There will also be issues as to who is the operator, and whether that person is operating the scheme by way of business. A person who operates a collective investment scheme by way of business must be an authorised person.[57]

3.22 If there is a possibility of an LLP amounting to a collective investment scheme, and this result is not desired, it can be avoided by all the members together having day-to-day control over the management of the property.[58] If any one or more of the members is not included in this day-to-day control, a collective investment scheme will not be avoided. FSMA 2000, s 235(2) makes it clear that a right to be consulted over the management, or to give directions as to the management of the property, will not be the same as having day-to-day control over the management.

> 'Just because one or more investors have a right to be consulted or can give directions, does not mean that they have control over the management of the property. In colloquial terms, what the subsection is directed towards is identifying who is or will be 'minding the shop' on a day-to-day basis. It may be that the person who is involved in a day-to-day basis is answerable to someone higher up the chain on whose behalf he is acting. But it is the former, not the latter, who has day-to-day control.'[59]

It is suggested that this day-to-day control will be achieved if the LLP agreement provides (and continues to provide[60]) for every member/participant to take part in the management of the property, and that any difference arising between members/participants as to such management may be decided by a majority of them.

3.23 The LLP agreement will also need to address, in the context of LLP Act 2000, s 7 (discussed at **8.17–8.24**), what is to happen in the event of the death or bankruptcy of a member/participant, or (if permitted by the LLP agreement) a member/participant voluntarily assigning his share in the LLP. LLP Act 2000, s 7(2) provides that a personal representative or trustee in bankruptcy or assignee of an LLP member may not interfere in the management or administration of any business or affairs of the LLP. In order to prevent the LLP from becoming a collective investment scheme, it will be necessary to ensure that day-to-day control by all members continues after a death, bankruptcy or assignment.

---

[56] FSMA 2000, ss 21 (with ss 25 and 30) and 238–240, and the Financial Services and Markets Act 2000 (Promotion of Collective Investment Schemes) (Exemptions) Order 2001, SI 2001/1060 made under FSMA 2000, s 238(6).

[57] See FSMA 2000, ss 19 and 22 and the Financial Services and Markets Act 2000 (Regulated Activities) Order 2001, SI 2001/544, Arts 4(1) and (2) and 51. Whether, and in what circumstances, a person operating an LLP/scheme is doing so by way of business is a matter of some uncertainty. An LLP will not amount to a collective investment scheme if it is operated otherwise than by way of business: see SI 2001/1062 Art 4.

[58] See FSMA 2000, s 235(2).

[59] Laddie J in *Russell-Cook Trust Co v Elliott* [2001] All ER (D) 197 (July) at para 20 (in the context of the statutory predecessor to FSMA 2000, s 235).

[60] Ie it is not impliedly varied by conduct.

3.24 A collective investment scheme which satisfies certain property and investment conditions also constitutes an open-ended investment company under FSMA 2000, s 236 (an 'oeic'). An LLP (a body corporate, as referred to in the property condition) which constitutes a collective investment scheme could, in principle, also constitute an oeic if the property and investment conditions are satisfied in relation to it.[61] There is, however, currently no provision in statute or statutory instrument under which LLPs may be authorised oeics. The Open-Ended Investment Companies Regulations 2001,[62] made under FSMA 2000, s 262 for the purpose of regulating oeics and permitting their incorporation upon authorisation by the FSA under those regulations, clearly do not contemplate the possibility of an LLP constituting an authorised oeic.

LLP CEASING TO SATISFY SECTION 2(1)(a)

3.25 The requirements of LLP Act 2000 s 2(1)(a) on incorporation are discussed in chapter 2. These requirements are that there must be two or more persons associated for carrying on a lawful business with a view to profit. If the Registrar is satisfied that these requirements have been complied with (and the formalities of LLP Act 2000, s 2 are also complied with), he will issue a certificate of incorporation under s 3. As is discussed in **2.38–2.40**, the certificate will be conclusive evidence of the existence of the LLP, and will prevent anyone other than the Crown challenging the validity of its incorporation. It may be, however, that after incorporation – and although s 2(1)(a) was complied with at the time of incorporation – the provisions of s 2(1)(a) cease to be met. It may be, for instance, that the LLP ceases to have two members, or the business being carried on by the LLP becomes unlawful, or the business is no longer being carried on with a view to profit. The question arises as to where this state of affairs leads. The application of s 2(1)(a) is limited to the initial incorporation of the LLP. The legislation does not impose an explicit ongoing requirement that s 2(1)(a) be complied with during the life of the LLP. For instance (and to answer the first possibility mentioned above), the legislation recognises that the LLP can function quite validly with one member only, albeit that the limited liability of that one member for the continuing business may be lost after six months.[63]

3.26 If the LLP carries on an unlawful business, there will be a number of possible or actual consequences. It will be a ground for the Secretary of State to appoint inspectors to investigate the affairs of the LLP that it appears to him that there are circumstances suggesting that those affairs are being conducted for a fraudulent or unlawful purpose.[64] The 'affairs' of an LLP clearly include the business it is carrying on. The Secretary of State can, in any event, and at any time, if he thinks there is good reason to do so, require an LLP to produce specified

---

[61]   The conditions are set out in FSMA 2000, s 236(2) and (3). The investment condition refers to 'shares in, or securities of' the body corporate. Whether or not there could be 'shares' in an LLP, there could be 'securities' of it.

[62]   SI 2001/1228.

[63]   See CA 1985, s 24, considered at **2.15**.

[64]   CA 1985, s 432(1)(a).

documents.[65] A report by inspectors, or information obtained under a requirement to produce documents, may lead to the Secretary of State applying to the court for the LLP to be wound up under IA 1986 s 124A (ie on the ground that winding up is expedient in the public interest). If the business is being carried on against the wishes of some of the members, those members will themselves be able to apply to the court for the LLP to be wound up on the 'just and equitable' ground.[66] Individual members who apply money or assets of the LLP for unlawful purposes will almost certainly be acting in breach of their fiduciary duty to the LLP.[67]

3.27 If the LLP ceases to carry on its business with a view to profit, a suspicion of this is not an express ground on which the Secretary of State may appoint inspectors to investigate the LLP's affairs; but such a suspicion could perhaps be made to fit one of the grounds for appointing inspectors set out in CA 1985, s 432(2).[68] As has been mentioned in **3.26**, the Secretary of State can, in any event, and at any time, if he thinks that there is good reason to do so, require an LLP to produce specified documents. Whether the Secretary of State would consider the fact that an LLP is no longer carrying on business with a view to profit to be a basis for presenting a winding up petition under IA 1986, s 124A is unclear; but the authors suggest that, given the policy behind the introduction of LLPs (as appearing from LLP Act 2000, s 2(1)(a)), he may well do so. If the new course of business being followed by the LLP is against the wishes of some of the members, those members will probably themselves be able to apply to the court for the LLP to be wound up on the 'just and equitable' ground, or alternatively for relief on the ground of 'unfair prejudice' under CA 1985, s 459 (if the right contained in that section has not been excluded by agreement under s 459(2)). If members' rights to apply to the court under s 459 have been excluded, it will still be open to the Secretary of State (if he has received a report from inspectors, or required documents to be provided under CA 1985 s 447) to make an application under CA 1985, s 460 on the ground of 'unfair prejudice' to the non-consenting members. There may, however, be more immediate and tangible dangers for an LLP and its members in the event of it ceasing to carry on business with a view to profit. If the LLP runs the danger of trading into insolvency, the members will need to bear in mind the provisions of IA 1986, s 214 (wrongful trading)[69] and also the CDDA 1986.[70] The continuing transparency for tax purposes of an LLP is dependent on its business being carried on with a view to profit.[71] Where the LLP ceases to carry on

---

[65]　CA 1985, s 447. The provisions of CA 1985, ss 431–452 (ie Part XIV) are discussed more fully in chapter 20.

[66]　Ie under IA 1986, s 122(1)(e), discussed in chapter 27.

[67]　See **11.6**(b). It must be unlikely that a duty to apply the money or assets of the LLP for lawful purposes only will be excluded by the LLP agreement: see **11.8**.

[68]　Eg possibly a suspicion that persons concerned with the management of the LLP's affairs have been guilty of misconduct towards the LLP or its members: CA 1985, s 432(2)(c).

[69]　Discussed at **29.3**.

[70]　Discussed in chapter 32.

[71]　See ICTA 1988, s 118ZA and TCGA 1992, s 59A.

business with a view to profit, an end to its tax transparency may have little impact in relation to income of the business, but it may have a substantial impact in relation to any unrealised capital gains.[72]

---

[72] Taxation of LLPs and members is considered in chapter 21.

Chapter 4

FORMALITIES AND REQUIREMENTS AFTER INCORPORATION

LLP IDENTIFICATION

Companies Act 1985 requirements

4.1　An LLP must have and keep its name painted or affixed in a conspicuous position and in easily legible letters on the outside of every office or place in which its business is carried on.[1] If an LLP does not do this, then it and every member of it who is in default is liable to a fine.[2]

4.2　All business letters of an LLP must mention in legible characters (i) its name,[3] (ii) its place of registration and its registration number,[4] and (iii) the address of the registered office.[5] In addition, if the LLP's name ends with the abbreviation 'llp' or 'LLP' there must be mentioned in legible characters on all its business letters the fact that it is a limited liability partnership.[6]

4.3　An LLP must also have its name mentioned in legible characters (i) on all its notices and other official publications, (ii) on all bills of exchange, promissory notes, endorsements, cheques and orders for money or goods purporting to be signed by or on its behalf, and (iii) on all its bills of parcels, invoices, receipts and letters of credit.[7] All order forms of an LLP must additionally mention in legible characters its place of registration and its registration number, the address of its registered office and, if its name ends with the abbreviation 'llp' or 'LLP', the fact that it is a limited liability partnership.[8]

4.4　If an LLP fails to comply with any of the requirements set out in **4.2** and **4.3**, it is liable to a fine;[9] and if a member of an LLP or a person on its behalf:

---

[1]　CA 1985, s 348(1).

[2]　Ibid, s 348(2).

[3]　Ibid, s 349(1)(a).

[4]　Ibid, s 351(1)(a). If the Registrar changes an LLP's registered number, the requirement that the number must be mentioned is, for a period of three years from the LLP being notified of the change of number, satisfied by use of either the old number or the new number: CA 1985, s 705(4).

[5]　CA 1985, s 351(1)(b).

[6]　Ibid, s 351(1)(c). There is an equivalent provision where the name ends with a Welsh abbreviation. As to names, see generally **2.18–2.21**.

[7]　CA 1985, s 349(1).

[8]　Ibid, s 351(1).

[9]　Ibid, ss 349(2) and 351(5)(a).

(i)   issues or authorises the issue of any business letter of the LLP in which the LLP's name, or place of registration and registration number, or address of its registered office or (if its name ends with the abbreviation 'llp' or 'LLP') the fact that it is a limited liability partnership is not mentioned as required above; or

(ii)   issues or authorises the issue of any notice or other official publication of the LLP, in which the LLP's name is not mentioned as required above; or

(iii)   signs or authorises to be signed on behalf of the LLP any bill of exchange, promissory note, endorsement, cheque or order for money or goods in which the LLP's name is not mentioned as required above; or

(iv)   issues or authorises the issue of any bill of parcels, invoice, receipt or letter of credit of the LLP in which its name is not so mentioned; or

(v)   issues or authorises the issue of any order form in which the LLP's place of registration or its registration number or the address of its registered office or if its name ends with the abbreviation 'llp' or 'LLP' the fact that it is a limited liability partnership is not mentioned,

he is liable to a fine.[10] If a member of the LLP or a person on its behalf signs or authorises to be signed on behalf of the LLP any bill of exchange, promissory note, endorsement, cheque or order for money or goods in which the LLP's name is not mentioned in legible characters, he is further personally liable to the holder of the bill of exchange, promissory note, cheque or order for money or goods for the amount of it (unless the amount is duly paid by the LLP).[11]

Business Names Act 1985

4.5   The Business Names Act 1985 (BNA 1985) is amended to apply in certain cases to LLPs.[12] The effect of the newly inserted s 1(1)(d), with s 1(2), is that the Act applies to any LLP which has a place of business in Great Britain and which carries on business[13] in Great Britain under a name which does not consist either solely of its corporate name or of its corporate name with an addition merely indicating that the business is carried on in succession to a former owner of the business. The BNA 1985 will not apply, therefore, to an LLP which is carrying on business under its corporate name (for instance, 'Smith & Jones LLP' carrying on its business under that name). Nor, it appears, will the Act apply to an LLP to which a partnership business, which has previously been carried on under the firm name of 'Smith & Jones', has been transferred, and which now carries on that business as, say, 'Kensington Surveyors LLP in succession to Smith & Jones'.

4.6   Where the BNA 1985 does apply to an LLP:

(1)   The LLP must not, without the written approval of the Secretary of State, carry on business in Great Britain under a name which would be likely to give the impression that the business is connected with the Government or

---

[10]   CA 1985, ss 349(3) and (4) and 351(5)(b).
[11]   Ibid, s 349(4).
[12]   By LLP Regulations 2001, reg 9 and Sch 5, paras 10–11.
[13]   'Business' includes a profession: BNA 1985, s 8(1).

with any local authority[14] or includes any word or expression for the time being specified for this purpose in regulations made under the BNA 1985[15] *save that* this restriction does not apply to the carrying on of a business by an LLP to which the business has been transferred and which carries on the business under the name which was its lawful business name[16] before that transfer during the period of 12 months beginning with the date of the transfer.[17]

(2)   Unless the LLP has more than 20 members and complies with sub-paragraph (3) below, it must state on all business letters, written orders for goods or services to be supplied to the business, invoices and receipts issued in the course of the business, and written demands for payment of debts arising in the course of the business, its corporate name and the name of each member (and an address in Great Britain at which service of any document relating in any way to the business will be effective).[18]

(3)   If the LLP has more than 20 members, sub-paragraph (2) above does not apply in relation to any document issued by it if it maintains at its principal place of business a list of the names of all the members and (a) none of the names of the members appears in the document otherwise than in the text or as a signatory, and (b) the document states in legible characters the address of the principal place of business of the LLP and that the list of the members' names is open to inspection at that place.[19]

(4)   In any premises where the business is carried on and to which the customers of the business or suppliers of any goods or services to the business have access, the LLP must display in a prominent position so that it may easily be read by such customers or suppliers a notice containing the name of each member and address[20] as mentioned in sub-paragraph (2) above.[21]

(5)   The LLP must secure that the names and address[22] required under sub-paragraph (2) above to be stated on its business letters, or which would have been so required had the LLP not come within sub-paragraph (3) above, are immediately given by written notice to any person with whom anything is

---

[14]   Ie any local authority within the meaning of the Local Government Act 1972, the Common Council of the City of London or the Council of the Isles of Scilly: BNA 1985, s 8(1).

[15]   The relevant regulations are the Company and Business Names Regulations 1981, SI 1981/1685 as amended from time to time, most recently by SI 2004/1771. These are the same regulations as are referred to in **2.20**; and their substance is set out at *Halsbury's Laws* (Butterworths, 4th edn, 1996), vol 7(1), para 168. See also the Company and Business Names (Chamber of Commerce, etc) Act 1999.

[16]   Ie a name under which the business was carried on without contravening s 2(1) of the BNA 1985 or s 2 of the Registration of Business Names Act 1916: BNA 1985, s 8(1).

[17]   BNA 1985, s 2(1) and (2). If the LLP contravenes this provision, it is guilty of an offence: BNA 1985, ss 2(4) and 7.

[18]   Ibid, s 4(1)(a)(iiia). Contravention without reasonable excuse is an offence: BNA 1985, s 4(6).

[19]   Ibid, s 4(3A). Where the LLP maintains a list of the members' names for this purpose, any person may inspect the list during office hours: BNA 1985, s 4(4A). Where a person is refused inspection, any member of the LLP who without reasonable excuse refuses the inspection, or permits it to be refused, is guilty of an offence: BNA 1985, s 4(7).

[20]   Or addresses, if different addresses are used for different members.

[21]   BNA 1985, s 4(1)(b). Contravention without reasonable excuse is an offence: BNA 1985, s 4(6).

[22]   See footnote 20 above.

done or discussed in the course of the business and who asks for such names and address.[23]

(6)   Any legal proceedings brought by the LLP to enforce a right arising out of a contract made in the course of a business in respect of which it was, at the time the contract was made, in breach of any of the requirements of sub-paragraphs (2), (4) and (5) above will be dismissed if the defendant to the proceedings shows (a) that he has a claim against the LLP arising out of that contract which he has been unable to pursue by reason of the LLP's breach of any of those requirements, or (b) that he has suffered some financial loss in connection with the contract by reason of the LLP's breach of such requirements, unless the court before which the proceedings are brought is satisfied that it is just and equitable to permit the proceedings to continue. This provision is without prejudice to the right of any person to enforce such rights as he may have against the LLP in any proceedings brought by that person.[24]

FORMALITIES FOR CONTRACTS, DEEDS AND OTHER DOCUMENTS

Generally

4.7   The formalities for making contracts and executing other documents are essentially the same for LLPs as for companies.[25] With some omissions and modifications CA 1985, ss 36–41 are adopted for LLPs.

4.8   A contract may be made by an LLP in writing under its common seal.[26] A contract may also be made on behalf of an LLP by any person acting with its express or implied authority.[27] Any formalities required by law in the case of a contract made by an individual also apply, unless a contrary intention appears,[28] to a contract made by or on behalf of an LLP.[29] There is no requirement that the LLP must contract in its registered name. If it does not contract in its registered name, whether or not it is the contracting party is to be gathered from the available evidence.[30]

---

[23]   BNA 1985, s 4(2). Contravention without reasonable excuse is an offence: BNA 1985, s 4(6).
[24]   Ibid, s 5.
[25]   Ie the position is essentially the same for GB LLPs as for companies incorporated in Great Britain. 'Limited liability partnerships' in CA 1985, s 36C means an LLP incorporated under the LLP Act 2000 (see LLP Act 2000, s 1(2)(b)). The modifications made by the Foreign Companies (Execution of Documents) Regulations 1994 (SI 1994/950, as amended by SI 1995/1729) to CA 1985, ss 36–36C in respect of companies incorporated outside Great Britain are not implemented for non-GB LLPs.
[26]   CA 1985, s 36
[27]   Ibid. The Corporate Bodies' Contracts Act 1960 does not apply to an LLP: see s 2 of the 1960 Act as amended by the LLP Regulations 2001, reg 9 and Sch 5, para 3.
[28]   Ie under some common law rule or statutory provision.
[29]   CA 1985, s 36.
[30]   See *OTV Birwelco Ltd v Technical and General Guarantee Co Ltd* [2002] 2 BCLC 723, considering the effect of CA 1985, ss 36 and 36A where a company contracted in its trading name.

4.9 An LLP does not need to have a common seal;[31] but if it does have one, the seal must have the LLP's name engraved on it in legible characters.[32] If the name is not so engraved, the LLP is liable to a fine;[33] and if a member of the LLP or a person on its behalf uses or authorises the use of any seal purporting to be a seal of the LLP on which the name is not properly engraved, he is liable to a fine.[34] Nevertheless, the use of a seal which does not have the LLP's name engraved on it for the purpose of the LLP entering into a document will not necessarily make the document void or unenforceable.[35]

4.10 A document is executed by an LLP either (a) by its common seal (if it has one) being affixed to the document, or (b) by the document being signed by two members of the LLP and expressed (in whatever form of words) to be executed by the LLP.[36] Strictly speaking, the position is (similarly to that for a company) that a document is executed by an LLP by the affixing of its common seal, but that a document signed by two members and expressed to be executed by the LLP has the same effect as if executed under the common seal. In favour of a purchaser in good faith for valuable consideration[37] (including a lessee, mortgagee or other person who for valuable consideration acquires an interest in property) a document is to be deemed to have been duly executed by an LLP if it purports to be signed by two members of the LLP.[38]

4.11 A document which is executed by an LLP (ie by its seal being affixed or by being signed by two members) and which makes it clear on its face that it is intended by the person or persons making it to be a deed has effect, upon delivery, as a deed.[39] Such a document is presumed, unless a contrary intention is proved, to be delivered upon its being so executed.[40] In favour of a purchaser in good faith for

---

[31] CA 1985, s 36A(3).

[32] Ibid, s 350(1).

[33] Ibid.

[34] CA 1985, s 350(2).

[35] See *OTV Birwelco Ltd v Technical and General Guarantee Co Ltd* above, where the seal had the contracting company's trading name engraved on it.

[36] CA 1985, s 36A(2) and (4). The Land Registry Rules 2003, SI 2003/1417, contain a form of execution to be used for land registration instruments executed by an LLP without using a common seal: see r 206(3) and Sch 9 form F. The Land Registry will accept execution by affixing of an LLP's seal where this is witnessed by two members (Practice Advice Leaflet 6, on Execution of Deeds).

[37] This can include a nominal sum: see *Midland Bank Trust Co Ltd v Green* [1981] AC 513.

[38] CA 1985, s 36A(6). If a document which is a disposition permitted by the Land Registry Rules 2003, SI 2003/1417 to be in electronic form has the electronic signatures of two members of the LLP, and is expressed to be executed by the LLP, CA 1985, s 36A(6) will have effect in relation to the document as if 'authenticated' were substituted for 'signed' in it: Land Registration Act 2002, s 91(9).

[39] CA 1985, s 36A(5); and see also Law of Property (Miscellaneous Provisions) Act 1989, s 1(2). The delivery (ie the party executing the document showing an intention to be bound by it) may be unconditional or in escrow. As a general rule, in order for the LLP to be able to sue or be sued on a deed made inter partes, the LLP needs to be described as a party to the deed, and the deed needs to be executed in its name: see *Bowstead & Reynolds on Agency*, 17th edn, 2001, Art 79.

[40] Ibid. The presumption of delivery in sub-s (5) is a difference in sub-s (5) from the Law of Property Act 1925, s 74(1), under which there is no deemed delivery on execution. It is, however, difficult to see how LPA 1925, s 74(1), with its references to a corporation's clerk, secretary or other

valuable consideration,[41] a document which purports to be signed by two members of the LLP, and which makes it clear on its face that it is intended by the person or persons making it to be a deed, is to be deemed to have been delivered upon its being executed.[42] Whether there is the same deemed delivery upon execution where the mode of execution is the affixing of the LLP's seal (without the document also being purportedly signed by two members) is unclear.[43]

4.12 A bill of exchange or promissory note is deemed to have been made, accepted or endorsed on behalf of an LLP if made, accepted or endorsed in the name of, or by or on behalf or on account of, the LLP by a person acting under its authority.[44]

4.13 An LLP may by writing under its common seal empower any person, either generally or in respect of any specified matters, as its attorney, to execute deeds on its behalf in any place elsewhere than in the United Kingdom; and a deed executed by such an attorney on behalf of the LLP has the same effect as if it were executed under the LLP's common seal.[45]

4.14 An LLP which has a common seal may also have an official seal for use in any territory, district or place elsewhere than in the United Kingdom. This is to be a facsimile of its common seal, with the addition on its face of the name of every territory, district or place where it is to be used.[46] The official seal, when duly affixed to the document, has the same effect as the LLP's common seal.[47] An LLP which has an official seal for use outside the United Kingdom may, by writing under its common seal, authorise any person appointed for the purpose in the foreign territory, district or place to affix the official seal to any deed or other document to which the LLP is party in that territory, district or place.[48] As between the LLP and a person dealing with such an agent, the agent's authority continues during the period (if any) mentioned in the instrument conferring the authority, or if no period is mentioned, then until notice of the revocation or determination of the agent's authority has been given to the person dealing with him.[49] The person affixing the official seal must certify in writing on the deed or other instrument to which the seal is affixed the date on which and the place at which it is affixed.[50]

---

permanent officer, and to its board of directors, council or other governing body, can be applied to LLPs.

[41] See **4.10**
[42] CA 1985, s 36A(6).
[43] The issue turns on what the first 'it' refers to in the phrase 'where it makes it clear on its face' in CA 1985, s 36A(6).
[44] Ibid, s 37. 'Authority' will include ostensible authority: see *Dey v Pullinger Engineering Co* [1921] 1 KB 77 and *Kreditbank Cassel GmbH v Schenkers* [1927] 1 KB 826.
[45] CA 1985, s 38.
[46] Ibid, s 39(1).
[47] Ibid, s 39(2).
[48] Ibid, s 39(3).
[49] Ibid, s 39(4).
[50] Ibid, s 39(5).

4.15 A document or proceeding requiring authentication by an LLP is sufficiently authenticated for the purposes of English law by the signature of a single member of the LLP.[51]

Pre-incorporation contracts

4.16 There are two provisions in the LLP legislation relating to contracts entered into before the LLP has been incorporated, namely CA 1985, s 36C and LLP Act 2000, s 5(2). The latter section relates to a pre-incorporation LLP agreement, and is considered in Chapter 9, dealing with LLP agreements.

4.17 Section 36C of the CA 1985 provides that a contract or a deed which purports to be made by or on behalf of an LLP at a time when the LLP has not been formed has effect, subject to any agreement to the contrary, as one made with the person purporting to act for the LLP or as agent for it, and he is personally liable on the contract or under the deed accordingly. In order for the person purporting to act for the LLP[52] or as its agent[53] in making the contract or deed ('contract') to avoid personal liability by relying on there being an 'agreement to the contrary', that agreement[54] must be a clear exclusion of such personal liability: there will be no inference drawn of such an agreement for the purposes of the section simply from the contract being signed 'on behalf of' or 'as agent for' the LLP.[55] Although s 36C(1) refers expressly only to *liability* under the contract for the person purporting to act, since the sub-section also refers to the contract as having effect as one made with that person (ie treats him as the contracting party), that person can also enforce the contract (subject, as with any contract, to the ordinary common law rules as to the enforceability of contracts).[56]

4.18 In order for the LLP, when it comes into existence, to have the benefit and be subject to the liabilities of the contract (and for the original person acting to be released from liability where such liability has not been excluded), there must be a new contract entered into by the LLP with the other party after incorporation.[57]

---

[51] CA 1985, s 41.

[52] Ie where the contract or deed purports to be made by the LLP.

[53] Ie where the contract or deed purports to be made on behalf of the LLP.

[54] Made between the person purporting to act for the LLP and the other party to the contract.

[55] *Phonogram Ltd v Lane* [1982] QB 938.

[56] *Braymist Ltd v Wise Finance Co Ltd* [2002] Ch 273 (CA), a company case. The text above reflects the views of the majority of the Court of Appeal (Latham and Judge LJJ). The view of Arden LJ (differing in this respect) was that the right of the person purporting to act for the company to enforce the contract does not follow automatically from s 36C(1) providing that the contract has effect as if made with that person, but that the intention of this provision is that whether that person can enforce the contract turns on the application of the common law rules to the facts of the particular case as to whether a person (and, in particular, an agent contracting as such) can enforce a contract personally: see esp paras 59 and 62-3.

[57] See, for example, *Halsbury's Laws* (Butterworths, 4th edn), vol 7(1), para 54 and vol 7(2), paras 1126 and 1127.

CHANGE OF NAME

4.19 An LLP may change its name at any time.[58] As with a change of registered office, the legislation does not specify any particular internal procedure by which an LLP can decide to change its name.[59] How a decision to change the LLP's name is to be made is, therefore, something to be covered, by a specific or a general decision-making provision, in the LLP agreement. If a change of name is not covered by such a provision, the position will probably be, by reason of the application of rule (6) of the default rules,[60] that it will require the consent of all the members (not simply a majority).

4.20 An LLP may also, in certain circumstances, be directed by the Secretary of State to change its name.

(1) Where the LLP has been registered with a name which is (a) the same as or, in the opinion of the Secretary of State, too like a name appearing at the time of registration in the index of company and corporate names,[61] or (b) the same as or, in the opinion of the Secretary of State, too like a name which should have appeared in the index at that time, the Secretary of State may within 12 months of the registration direct the LLP in writing to change its name within such period as he may specify.[62] In determining whether one name is the same as another (but not in determining whether one name is too like another name) there is to be disregarded the same matters as are mentioned in **2.19**.[63]

(2) If it appears to the Secretary of State (a) that misleading information has been given for the purpose of the registration of an LLP by a particular name, or (b) that undertakings or assurances have been given for that purpose and have not been fulfilled, he may, within 5 years of the date of its registration by that name, direct the LLP in writing to change its name within such period as he may specify.[64]

(3) If, in the Secretary of State's opinion, the name by which an LLP is registered gives so misleading an indication of the nature of its activities as to be likely to cause harm to the public, he may direct the LLP in writing to change its name within such period as he may specify.[65]

---

[58] LLP Act 2000, Sch, para 4(1).
[59] CA 1985, s 28, which governs a change of name by a company but which is *not* adopted for LLPs, provides for a company's change of name to be effected by special resolution.
[60] Ie the rules provided by LLP Regulations 2001, regs 7 and 8 to form the LLP agreement in default of any terms otherwise: see **9.6–9.8**. Default rule (6) is discussed at **14.5–14.6**.
[61] Kept by the Registrar under CA 1985, s 714(1).
[62] LLP Act 2000, Sch, para 4(2).
[63] Ibid, Sch, para 8.
[64] Ibid, Sch, para 4(3).
[65] Ibid, Sch, para 4(4).

4.21 Where the Secretary of State makes a direction under any of (1), (2) and (3) above specifying a period within which an LLP is to change its name, he may at any time before that period ends extend it by a further direction in writing.[66]

4.22 The LLP has what amounts to a right of appeal to the High Court against a direction by the Secretary of State to change its name under any of **4.20**(1), (2) and (3). The LLP may, within 3 weeks from the date of the Secretary of State's direction, apply to the High Court to set it aside, and the Court may set it aside or confirm it. If the direction is confirmed, the Court is to specify the period within which it must be complied with.[67]

4.23 If an LLP fails to comply with a direction to change its name, the LLP and any designated member in default commits an offence, and is liable on summary conviction to a fine not exceeding level 3 on the standard scale.[68]

4.24 Where an LLP does change its name (whether by its own decision, or by direction of the Secretary of State), it must deliver a notice of the change to the Registrar.[69] The notice must be in a form approved by the Registrar,[70] and must either be signed by a designated member of the LLP or be authenticated in a manner approved by the Registrar.[71] The approved form is Form LLP 3 (Notice of Change of Name of a Limited Liability Partnership). When the Registrar receives a notice, he is required to enter the new name in the index of corporate names kept by him under CA 1985, s 714, and to issue a certificate of the change of name,[72] unless the new name is one by which an LLP may not be registered.[73] The change of name has effect from the date on which the certificate is issued.[74] The requirement on the Registrar to issue a 'certificate of the change of name' differs from the equivalent requirement on him when a company changes its name, which is to 'issue a certificate of incorporation altered to meet the circumstances of the case'.[75] This wording for companies in the CA 1985 leads directly to the accompanying requirement on the Registrar (under CA 1985, s 711(1)(a)), when a company changes its name, to publish in the *London Gazette* notice of the issue of the new certificate,[76] and thus notice of the change of name. Section 711(1)(a) of the CA 1985 is adopted for LLPs; but it is not easy to read it as covering a 'certificate of the change of name' as specified in the LLP Act 2000. It is probably the case, however, that notice of the change of name of an LLP falls to be

---

[66] LLP Act 2000, Sch, para 4(7).
[67] Ibid, Sch, para 4(5) and (6). An LLP has a wider right of appeal in this respect than a company, which can apply to the court in respect of a direction under the CA 1985, equivalent of (3) above (CA 1985, s 32) but not in respect of the CA 1985, equivalents of (1) and (2) above (CA 1985, s 28).
[68] LLP Act 2000, Sch, para 4(8) and (9).
[69] Ibid, Sch, para 5(1).
[70] Ibid, Sch, para 5(2)(a).
[71] Ibid, Sch, para 5(2)(b).
[72] Ibid, Sch, para 5(3).
[73] Ie pursuant to LLP Act 2000, Sch, para 3, discussed at **2.20–2.21**.
[74] LLP Act 2000, Sch, para 5(4).
[75] CA 1985, s 28(6).
[76] Ibid, s 711(1)(a) refers to 'any certificate of incorporation of a company'.

published in the *London Gazette* by the Registrar under CA 1985, s 711(1)(b),[77] in that the change of name (or, more accurately, the notice given to the Registrar of the change of name) will constitute an alteration in the LLP's incorporation document.[78]

4.25 A change of name by an LLP does not affect any of its rights or duties or render defective any legal proceedings by it or against it; and any legal proceedings that might have been commenced by its former name, or continued against it by its former name, may be commenced or continued against it by its new name.[79]

ANNUAL RETURN

4.26 Every LLP must deliver to the Registrar each year an annual return which contains the following information:[80]

(1)   the address of the LLP's registered office;

(2)   the names, and usual residential addresses, of its members;[81]

(3)   if some only of the members are designated members,[82] which of them are those members; and

(4)   if any register of debenture holders (or a duplicate of any such register or a part of it) is not kept at the registered office, the address or place where it is kept.[83]

4.27 The return must be in a form approved by the Registrar, and be signed by a designated member of the LLP.[84] The approved form is Form LLP 363. It provides for the signing designated member to certify that the information given in the return is true to the best of his knowledge and belief.

4.28 The return is to be made up to a date not later than the 'return date' of the LLP,[85] and must be delivered to the Registrar within 28 days after that date.[86] The return date is the anniversary of the incorporation of the LLP or, if the last annual

---

[77]   Which, so far as presently material, refers to 'any document making or evidencing an alteration in an LLP's incorporation document'.

[78]   As to alterations to the incorporation document, see **2.31**.

[79]   LLP Act 2000, Sch, para 6.

[80]   CA 1985, s 364 with s 363(2)(b). If information regarding related undertakings of the LLP is excluded from the notes to the annual accounts under CA 1985, s 231(5) because of its excessive length, it must be annexed to the next annual return: CA 1985, s 231(6)(b).

[81]   Subject, in relation to usual residential address, to confidentiality orders: see **4.31**.

[82]   See **2.28–2.30**.

[83]   As to debentures, see footnote 28 to **6.7**.

[84]   CA 1985, s 363(2)(a) and (c). The fee payable on the filing of the annual return is £35: see the Limited Liability Partnerships (Fees) (No 2) Regulations 2001, SI 2001/969.

[85]   CA 1985, s 363(1).

[86]   Ibid, s 363(3). This period is indirectly specified, in that an offence is committed if the return is not delivered within 28 days: see **4.29**.

return delivered to the Registrar was made up to a different date,[87] the anniversary of that date.[88]

4.29 If the LLP fails to deliver an annual return within 28 days after the return date, the LLP is guilty of an offence and liable on summary conviction to a fine. The contravention continues until an annual return, satisfying the requirements set out in **4.26**, and made up to the return date, is delivered by the LLP to the Registrar.[89] In addition to the LLP, every designated member is similarly liable unless he shows that he took all reasonable steps to avoid the failure to deliver the return, or the continuance of the failure.[90]

4.30 In addition to this criminal sanction, if the LLP, having failed to deliver the annual return, fails to make good this failure within 14 days after service of a notice on it requiring it to do so, the court may, on an application made to it by any member or creditor of the LLP or by the Registrar, make an order directing the LLP or any designated member of it to make good the default within such time as the order specifies.[91] The court's order may also provide that all costs of and incidental to the application are to be borne by the LLP or by any of its members designated responsible for the default.[92]

4.31 The annual return delivered to the Registrar is open to inspection by any member of the public, and a copy may be obtained by any person.[93] If any individual who is a member of the LLP has the benefit of a confidentiality order made by the Secretary of State under CA 1985, s 723B,[94] as a result of which his usual residential address is exempted from disclosure in the documents filed by the LLP with the Registrar, the annual return is to contain, in place of that member's usual residential address, his 'service address' ie the address which he is required to supply for publicly available documents in place of his usual residential address.[95] Where a member of the LLP is the beneficiary of a confidentiality order, the form used for the annual return must be that version of Form LLP 363 prescribed by the Limited Liability Partnerships (Forms) Regulations 2002.[96]

---

[87]   For example, to an earlier date, as permitted under the requirement that the return be made up to a date 'not later than' the return date.

[88]   CA 1985, s 363(1).

[89]   Ibid, s 363(3).

[90]   Ibid, s 363(4).

[91]   Ibid, s 713(1) and (3).

[92]   Ibid, s 713(2).

[93]   Ibid, s 709.

[94]   Confidentiality orders are discussed at **8.9–8.13**.

[95]   CA 1985 s 723C(1)(b) as modified for LLPs by the Limited Liability Partnerships (No 2) Regulations 2002, SI 2002/913.

[96]   SI 2002/690, reg 4. This version contains a box to be ticked if the address being given for any member is a service address under a confidentiality order.

Chapter 5

THE LLP AND THE OUTSIDE WORLD

AGENCY

5.1   As has been mentioned in **3.3**, an LLP can only act through others as its agents. This is not the place to set out extensively the law as to an agent's authority.[1] It suffices here to say that an agent's authority may be actual or apparent (often termed 'ostensible').[2] Actual authority is the authority actually conferred by the principal (here, the LLP), either expressly or impliedly, on its agent. An agent will generally have implied authority from his principal to do whatever is ordinarily or necessarily incidental to carrying out the function for which he has express authority, and to do whatever is usually done by persons carrying out that function (for example, in acting as a solicitor).[3] Apparent, or ostensible, authority is 'the authority of an agent as it *appears* to others'.[4] It often coincides with actual authority, but can frequently be wider.[5] Apparent authority is, in brief, created by a representation made by the principal, by words or by conduct, and whether expressly or impliedly, that the agent has certain authority. The representation may be as to authority in relation to specific matters; or it may be of a far more general nature, to the world at large and not limited as to matters or transactions. For the principal to be bound by the act of the agent falling within the apparent authority, the third party must have acted in reliance on the representation.[6] The principal is estopped from denying that the agent had actual authority coinciding with the apparent authority which the principal has represented the agent as having.[7] The actual authority conferred on an agent will, therefore, be a matter of what has been agreed (expressly or impliedly) as to

---

[1]   For a fuller discussion, see *Bowstead & Reynolds on Agency*, 17th edn, 2001, or *Chitty on Contracts* 29th edn, 2004, vol II, paras 31-041–31-048.

[2]   See *Freeman & Lockyer v Buckhurst Park Properties (Mangal) Ltd* [1964] 2 QB 480 at 502–503.

[3]   See, generally for example, *Bowstead & Reynolds* above Articles 27 and 29.

[4]   *Hely-Hutchinson v Brayhead Ltd* [1968] 1 QB 549 at 583.

[5]   For an example of drawing a clear distinction between actual authority and apparent authority see *Waugh v H.B. Clifford & Sons* [1982] Ch 374 (CA), concerned with a solicitor's authority to compromise litigation, especially at 383E–G and 387D–388A. Other examples of apparent authority exceeding actual authority but nevertheless binding the principal are *Panorama Developments (Guildford) Ltd v Fidelis Furnishing Fabrics Ltd* [1971] 2 QB 711 (company secretary hiring cars) and *Gurtner v Beaton* [1993] 2 Lloyd's Rep 369 in particular at 378–380 (aviation manager of a company which owned aircraft, with his office at an airport, having apparent authority to use aircraft under his control for air taxi work notwithstanding that that work was not part of the company's business).

[6]   See *Freeman & Lockyer* above at 505–506, and for a fuller discussion *Bowstead & Reynolds* above Art 74 or *Chitty on Contracts* above para 31-056. The third party must, of course, believe that the agent has the relevant authority: see, for instance, *Criterion Properties Plc v Stratford Properties LLC* [2004] 1 WLR 1846 (HL) at para 31.

[7]   See, for instance, *Armagas Ltd v Mundogas SA (The Ocean Frost)* [1986] AC 717 at 777A–C.

authority between the principal and the agent; and an agent's apparent, or ostensible, authority, if wider than that agreed as his actual authority, will be a matter of what appearance has been given by the principal to the outside world.

5.2   LLP Act 2000, s 6(1) expressly provides that every member of an LLP is the agent of the LLP. The LLP Act 2000 makes no reference to the agency of non-member employees. It cannot have been the intention of the Act, however, that non-members should not be able to act as the agents of an LLP.

MEMBERS AND OTHER AGENTS ACTING WITHIN THEIR AUTHORITY

5.3   Whenever an issue arises as to whether an LLP is bound by the acts of a member or non-member employee (or other agent) in any dealing with a third party, the first question will be – what is the actual authority of the member or employee or other agent in question to act on behalf of the LLP? Where the agent of the LLP, whether member or non-member employee (or other agent), acts within his actual authority, the LLP Act 2000 leaves the general law of agency to apply; and there is no doubt that the LLP is bound. The LLP will, therefore, be liable under any contract made on its behalf by a member or employee (or other agent) acting within the scope of his actual authority, and will equally be able to enforce any such contract.[8] Similarly, the LLP will be liable for any wrong committed by a member or non-member employee (or other agent) acting within the scope of his actual authority.[9]

MEMBERS AND OTHER AGENTS ACTING OUTSIDE THEIR AUTHORITY

5.4   Where a non-member employee (or other non-member agent) of the LLP acts outside his actual authority, whether or not the LLP is bound by his acts as its agent will be determined by the general rules as to apparent authority outlined in **5.1**.[10] In the case of acts by a member, however, the position will not be so straightforward. The relationship between the provisions of the LLP Act 2000 regarding the agency of members and the general rules as to apparent authority is not wholly clear.[11] It will be convenient to consider the application of the general rules to non-member employees (and other agents) before considering the position of members and the effect of the LLP Act 2000 in relation to their agency.

---

[8]   See, for instance, *Bowstead & Reynolds* above, Art 73, or *Chitty on Contracts* above para 31-054.
[9]   See, for instance, *Bowstead & Reynolds* above, Art 92.
[10]   Considered further at **5.5–5.8.**
[11]   See further **5.9–5.16.**

Non-member employees (and other non-member agents)

5.5   The scope of the apparent authority of a non-member employee (and this term is used hereafter to include other non-member agents) of an LLP engaged in a business will depend greatly upon the nature and normal course of conducting such a business. Dealing first with the nature of the business, the position may perhaps be put as follows. There is a working presumption that a non-member employee, as the agent of 'a business' (which is how a third party would normally see an LLP), is not being held out as having authority to engage in a different business. But this is a working presumption only. In particular, it leaves open issues which may arise from the way in which the LLP describes or represents its business. The business as it appears to the outside world may include an activity which is not part of the actual business of the LLP as agreed and understood between the members. The result of this may be that an employee of the LLP has apparent authority to enter into a transaction relating to a particular activity which falls within the ambit of the business as it appears to the outside world, although he has no actual authority to do so.[12] It may be wise for the LLP in its representations to its customers and the public (eg in its letterheads and marketing literature) to make as clear as possible what its business is. Even if the business is clearly and accurately described to the outside world, issues could, of course, still arise as to what precisely that stated business covers.[13]

5.6   Turning to issues of apparent authority where an employee is acting broadly within the ambit of the LLP's actual business, it is clear from the decided cases that the extent of an agent's apparent authority owes much to the actual authority which a person in such a position as the agent holds usually has. When considering the scope of the apparent authority of an officer of a company (eg a managing director or company secretary), the issue is traditionally considered in terms of what actual authority an officer in such a position usually has.[14] This approach is not easily followed when one is considering the apparent authority of an employee of a professional firm. In these circumstances, the issue tends to be considered in terms of what is done in the ordinary course of that profession.[15] For the purpose of considering the apparent authority of an employee of an LLP, it is probably a fair working presumption that he has apparent authority to do (and only apparent authority to do) any act for carrying on in the usual way business of the kind

---

[12]   See, for example, *Gurtner v Beaton* [1993] 2 Lloyd's Rep 369 referred to in footnote 5 above.

[13]   See, for example, the comments as to changes in the ordinary course of solicitors' work of Staughton LJ in *United Bank of Kuwait v Hammoud* [1988] 1 WLR 1051 at 1063E–G.

[14]   See Diplock LJ in *Freeman & Lockyer v Buckhurst Park Properties (Mangal) Ltd* [1964] 2 QB 480 at 503–504 and *Bowstead & Reynolds*, above, para 8-018. But this approach is not to be slavishly and unrealistically followed in all situations: see the comments of Neill LJ in *Gurtner v Beaton* above at 379, col 2, to 380, col 1.

[15]   See *Union Bank of Kuwait v Hammoud* above (concerned with the issue, in two separate cases, of a solicitor's apparent authority to give an undertaking binding on his firm) especially at 1061F–H. The Court appears to have considered that there was no material distinction in the test for apparent authority between the first case, where the solicitor was a partner and the position was subject to s 5 of the Partnership Act 1890, and the second case, where the solicitor was not a partner.

carried on by the LLP.[16] But as with the working presumption mentioned in **5.5**, it must be appreciated that this is a working presumption only.

5.7   In deciding in any particular case whether or not an agent had apparent authority, the court may well be influenced by 'policy' considerations and err on the side of wide rather than narrow apparent authority.[17] In *Gurtner v Beaton*, Neill LJ said:[18]

> 'The development of the doctrine [of apparent authority] has been based in part upon the principle that where the Court has to decide which of two innocent parties is to suffer from the wrong-doing of a third party the Court will incline towards placing the burden upon the party who was responsible for putting the wrongdoer in the position in which he could commit the wrong.'

The scope of an agent's apparent authority is not uncontrollable by the principal, and can be made to coincide with the actual authority. There is no reason in principle why an LLP should not draw to the attention of third parties limits to the authority which an employee (or indeed a member) has, and which can therefore be attributed to him.[19]

5.8   It is worth bearing in mind in relation to apparent authority that there is, or may on particular facts be, a distinction to be drawn between, on the one hand, authority to enter into transactions and, on the other hand, authority to communicate on behalf of the principal (ie the LLP) in relation to transactions. The latter authority may be considerably wider than the former. This is illustrated by *First Energy v Hungarian International Bank*,[20] where the relevant manager of the bank did not have the authority (actual or apparent) to grant a loan facility, but he did have apparent (although not actual) authority to communicate that head office approved the facility. This accorded with the 'commercial realities of the situation'.[21]

Members

5.9   LLP Act 2000, s 6(1) states simply, and without more, that every member of an LLP is the agent of the LLP.[22] Section 6(2) provides that an LLP is not bound by anything done by a member in dealing with a third party if (a) the member in

---

[16]   Ie a working presumption in the same terms as are used in s 5 of the Partnership Act 1890.

[17]   See, for example, the approach of Brightman LJ in *Waugh v HB Clifford & Sons* [1982] Ch 374 at 388D–H as to the scope of the apparent authority of solicitors to bind their clients to a compromise. The narration by Brightman LJ in the same case at 383G–387C of the history of the courts' decisions as to the authority of solicitors to compromise on their clients' behalf illustrates how policy can change.

[18]   [1993] 2 Lloyd's Rep 369 at 379, col 2.

[19]   See, for instance, Brightman J in *Overbrooke Estates Ltd v Glencombe Properties Ltd* [1974] 1 WLR 1335 at 1341C–D.

[20]   [1993] 2 Lloyd's Rep 194 (CA).

[21]   Per Evans LJ at 206, col 1. There can also be apparent authority to receive communications: see *El Ajou v Dollar Holdings Plc* [1994] 2 All ER 685 at 703c–e (Hoffmann LJ).

[22]   As is mentioned in **3.3**, s 6(1) serves a dual purpose in the LLP Act, namely to establish the relationship between the LLP and its members, and to create the framework within which the LLP may be bound to third parties by the acts of its members.

fact has no authority to act for the LLP by doing that thing *and* (b) the third party either knows this, or does not know or believe the person with whom he is dealing to be a member of the LLP.[23] Section 6(1) does not provide for any limitation on the scope of the authority which a member may have, or be taken by third parties to have, either as to business engaged in or as to acts done in the course of that business.[24] However, since s 6(2) expressly envisages that there may be limits on a member's actual authority, it is clear that s 6(1) is not intending to provide that every member has, by force of statute, unlimited actual authority to act on behalf of, and to bind, the LLP; and it is not the position, therefore, that a member of an LLP has, for instance, actual authority by statute to commit the LLP in respect of any business or activity (however divorced that business or activity may be from the business in which the LLP is actually engaged), or has actual authority to act in the conduct of the LLP's business in any manner (however unusual acting in that manner would be). As between the member and the LLP, s 6(1) establishes the agency status of a member. The sub-section is not concerned with determining the scope of his actual authority as agent. The members are free to agree amongst themselves what actual authority individual members will have. A partnership under the Partnership Act 1890 frequently puts limits on the authority of partners to act on behalf of the firm in certain respects.[25] It will be open to the members of an LLP, and probably as equally desirable as at present with traditional partnerships, to provide in the LLP agreement[26] for limits on the authority of members to act on behalf of the LLP. These limits will still, however, leave open issues of apparent authority and the intended effect of the LLP Act 2000 in circumstances where a member is acting outside the scope of his actual authority.

5.10 The principal issue of construction of s 6(1), read together with s 6(2) and its opening word 'But', is whether the sub-section is creating in relation to each member the effect of unlimited apparent authority subject only to the LLP not being bound in the circumstances set out in s 6(2), or whether there is to be implied into the statement in s 6(1) that every member is the agent of the LLP a statement that the LLP's commitment for a member's acts is subject to the normal rules as to a principal's commitment for his agent's acts save to the extent that those rules are varied by what is provided in s 6(2) as to the LLP not being bound in the circumstances there set out. On the first approach, s 6(1) will effectively read for present purposes: every member of an LLP is the agent of the LLP and every act of his binds the LLP save only in the circumstances specified in s 6(2). On the second approach, s 6(1) will effectively read for present purposes: every member of an

---

[23] Section 6(2) is similar to the second part of s 5 of the Partnership Act 1890: 'unless the partner so acting has in fact no authority to act for the firm in the particular matter, and the person with whom he is dealing either knows that he has no authority, or does not know or believe him to be a partner'. LLP Act 2000, s 6(2)(b) excludes the LLP being bound 'if...the [third party] knows that [the member] has no authority'. This reference to 'no authority' must be to 'authority to act for the limited liability partnership by doing that thing' as referred to in s 6(2)(a).

[24] Compare s 5 of the Partnership Act 1890: 'Every partner is an agent of the firm and his other partners for the purpose of the business of the partnership and the acts of every partner who does any act for carrying on in the usual way business of the kind carried on by the firm of which he is a member bind the firm and his partners, unless [as in footnote 23 above]'.

[25] For instance, lending firm money or releasing debts due over a certain amount.

[26] Ie in the agreement provided for by LLP Act 2000, s 5, discussed in chapter 9.

LLP is the agent of the LLP and his acts bind the LLP where that is the effect of the general principles of agency law save where s 6(2) cuts down the liability of the LLP further than the general principles of agency law would provide. The significance of this issue will turn on the meaning which is to be given to the word 'knows' in s 6(2)(b). This is considered at **5.12–5.13**. It is suggested that the more natural reading, and more likely intended effect, of sub-ss (1) and (2) together, linked as they are by the word 'But' at the beginning of sub-s (2), is that sub-s (1) is creating a universal liability on the LLP for the acts of its members, subject only to the exonerating circumstances set out in sub-s (2) ie the first approach referred to above. This conclusion as to the intended effect of sub-s (2) is by no means clear, however.[27]

5.11   It has been seen from **5.9** that the concept of 'knowing' arises in two contexts in sub-s 6(2)(b): first, in the context of whether the third party knows that the member with whom he is dealing has the relevant authority to act on behalf of the LLP and, secondly, in the context of whether the third party knows (or believes) that the person with whom he is dealing is a member of the LLP at all. Issues could arise in either of these two contexts as to what constitutes 'knowledge' by the third party.

Third party 'knowing' that no authority

5.12   Assuming that the third party knows that he is dealing with a member of an LLP, for the LLP to be within s 6(2), and so escape being bound, the third party must 'know' that the member does not have the relevant authority. If the approach to s 6(1) preferred in **5.10** is accepted, the more restricted the concept of 'knowledge' used in the first part of sub-s (2)(b), the greater the potential for the LLP to be liable under the Act for the acts of its members, even where such members are acting outside the scope of their apparent authority under the general law of agency.[28] An example might be where the member is acting outside the scope of his actual authority and the scope of the authority that he would normally be expected to have,[29] but the third party is unaware of that fact and simply knows or believes himself to be dealing with a member of the LLP.

5.13   It is most probably correct to say that knowledge here will include, in any event, the first three of the five categories of knowledge accepted by Peter Gibson J in *Baden v Société Generale*,[30] namely: (i) actual knowledge; (ii) wilfully shutting one's eyes to the obvious; and (iii) wilfully and recklessly failing to make such enquiries as an honest and reasonable man would make. These three

---

[27]   On the second approach, it is difficult to see what function s 6(2) has. The conclusion reached in the text is consistent with the approach of the Government Minister (Lord McIntosh of Haringey) in relation to these provisions in the House of Lords at Committee stage and at Report stage on the bill; but the Minister's statements are not clear on this point: see *Hansard HL* 24 January 2000 columns 1376–1379 and 6 March 2000 columns 868–869.

[28]   If s 6(1) is subject to the limits on apparent authority inherent in the general law of agency, it does not matter how narrow an interpretation is given to the concept of knowledge in s 6(2).

[29]   Ie he has neither actual nor apparent authority under the general law of agency.

[30]   [1993] 1 WLR 509 at 575–576.

categories have been said to constitute actual knowledge or its equivalent.[31] Put in the terms of an alternative categorisation, knowledge here will probably include 'blind-eye knowledge' ie knowledge which exists when a person deliberately refrains from inquiring further lest his firmly grounded suspicion of wrongdoing be confirmed.[32] Where a third party has this level of knowledge as to the member's lack of authority, therefore, it is most probably the case that the LLP will not be bound under the Act by the member's actions.[33] The remaining two *Baden* categories of knowledge are: (iv) knowledge of circumstances which would indicate the facts to an honest and reasonable man; and (v) knowledge of circumstances which would put an honest and reasonable man on inquiry. These two categories have been said to constitute – broadly speaking, and not as a rigid rule – constructive knowledge.[34] Whether such constructive knowledge by the third party of lack of authority on the part of the member – or some other category of knowledge, however described, which is short of actual knowledge or its equivalent – would be considered as knowledge for the purposes of s 6(2)(b), and as a result the LLP not be bound, is unclear.[35] The authors suggest that if the Act had intended to incorporate shades of knowledge going beyond actual knowledge (eg lack of knowledge through carelessness or negligence), it could easily have done so expressly.[36] For these reasons, it is suggested that 'knows' in the first part of s 6(2)(b) is – in broad terms – restricted to actual knowledge in the sense of the first three *Baden* categories.

5.14 If the conclusion reached in **5.13** is correct, the liability of an LLP for the acts of its members may be significantly wider than for the acts of its non-member employees (which is understandable as a matter of policy) and potentially wider than that of a company for the acts of its directors (which is perhaps less easy to justify). To revert to the example given in **5.12**, the LLP would be liable for the acts of its member, although it would probably not be so liable under the general law of agency. The LLP Act 2000 has here widened the circumstances in which an LLP may be liable for the acts of a member beyond those in which a principal

---

[31] See, for instance, *BCCI v Akindele* [2001] Ch 437 at 454E–F (CA).

[32] See, for instance, *Manifest Shipping Co Ltd v Uni-Polaris Co Ltd* [2003] 1 AC 469 at paras 112–116 and *White v White* [2001] 1 WLR 481 (HL). In *White*, it was said that even on a strict and narrow interpretation of what constituted knowledge for the purposes of the EC directive there being construed, blind-eye knowledge was included: see paras 14–16.

[33] Since this degree of knowledge would almost certainly negate any apparent authority which would otherwise exist, there would not be liability under the general law of agency either.

[34] See, for instance, *BCCI v Akindele* above at 454E–H (CA). And see Millett LJ in *Agip (Africa) Ltd v Jackson* [1990] Ch 265 at 293 warning against over refinement or a too ready assumption that categories (iv) and (v) are necessarily cases of constructive knowledge only.

[35] At least in the context of normal commercial transactions, and 'knowing receipt' cases, the court is generally setting its face against *Baden* categories (iv) and (v) constituting knowledge: see, for instance, *Cowan de Groot Properties Ltd v Eagle Trust plc* [1992] 4 All ER 700 at 759g–760c and the discussion in *BCCI v Akindele* above. The House of Lords has rejected a 'conscionability' approach to knowledge in the context of apparent authority: see *Criterion Properties Plc v Stratford Properties LLC* [2004] 1WLR 1846.

[36] Section 6(2)(a) could, for instance, have said 'knows or ought to know'. Equally, it could have said 'knows or believes', as the second part of s 6(2)(b) does say.

would be liable under the general law of agency, or an 1890 Act partnership would be liable for the acts of a partner.[37]

No 'knowledge or belief' by third party as to membership

5.15　LLP Act 2000 s 6(2) only applies in circumstances where the member is acting beyond his actual authority, if the third party does not know or believe that the person with whom he is dealing is a member of the LLP. If the approach to s 6(1) preferred in **5.10** is accepted, the more restricted the concept of 'knowledge' used in the second part of sub-s (2)(b), the greater the potential for the LLP not to be liable under the Act for the acts of its members. In the context of a third party's knowledge and belief of the status of a member, and unlike the circumstances being covered by the first part of s 6(2)(b), a more restricted concept of 'knowledge' is to the advantage of the LLP. It would seem to be broadly correct to say that, for the third party to be able to hold the LLP bound (and for the LLP not to be absolved) under s 6, the third party must have placed some reliance on the person he was dealing with being a member of the LLP. Proceeding on this basis, and bearing in mind that s 6(2)(b) is referring to the third party knowing or *believing*, it is suggested that knowledge in the present context is likely to be interpreted as actual knowledge, and belief as actual belief. In other words, and put broadly, for the purposes of s 6(2), in order for the LLP to be capable of being bound, the third party must have an actual knowledge or belief that the person he is dealing with is a member of the LLP. In policy terms, it may be said that it is the actual knowledge or belief that he is dealing with a member which justifies the additional protection conferred on the third party by the restricted meaning of 'knowledge' in the first part of sub-s (2)(b).

5.16　Circumstances may arise, however, where a member of an LLP is dealing with a third party who does not know that the person with whom he is dealing is a *member*, but he does know that this person is acting on behalf of the LLP (albeit he has no knowledge that the person is acting outside his authority). An example would be a client dealing with a member of an LLP of solicitors: the client knows that he is dealing with a solicitor of the LLP, but believes that the solicitor is not a member, but an associate. It would be a strange, and surely unintended, result of s 6(2)(b) if in these circumstances, and if the member is acting within the apparent authority of a non-member employee, the LLP were not bound by the actions of the member. If the member had in fact been the non-member employee he was believed to be, the LLP would be bound in accordance with the normal principles of apparent authority. The answer, it is suggested, is that, whilst (as suggested in **5.10**) s 6(1) is creating a universal liability on the LLP for the acts of its members (subject only to the exonerating circumstances set out in sub-s (2)), this universal liability is supplementing, rather than replacing, any liability to be attributed to the LLP under the general law of agency or otherwise. Sub-sections (1) and (2) of s 6 are effectively stating for present purposes as follows: without prejudice to any liability under the general law of agency or otherwise, the LLP is liable under this Act for the acts of its members, but in the circumstances specified in sub-s (2)(a)

---

[37]　See (as to the general law) *Criterion Properties Plc v Stratford Properties LLC* above at para 31 and (as to partnerships) the first part of s 5 of the 1890 Act set out in footnote 24 above.

and (b) it is not liable *under this Act*. The possibility of liability outside the subsections is left open.

5.17 If the member has committed a wrongful act or omission for which he is personally liable, the LLP will, in any event, be liable under LLP Act 2000, s 6(4).[38]

CESSATION OF MEMBERSHIP

5.18 Where a person ceases to be a member, he will (subject to any agreement to the contrary) cease to be the agent of the LLP and will, therefore, cease to have actual authority to bind the LLP. The effective date of a person ceasing to be a member is the date when he ceases to be a member in accordance with the terms of the LLP agreement[39] rather than the date of notification to the Registrar of his ceasing to be a member.[40] The former member will continue, however, to be regarded in relation to anyone dealing with the LLP as still being a member[41] unless either (a) the person dealing with the LLP has notice that the (now former) member has ceased to be a member, or (b) notice that the (now former) member has ceased to be a member has been delivered to the Registrar.[42] 'Notice' in (a) presumably means actual or constructive notice as generally understood. A person can have notice of a matter yet not know it.[43] The notice referred to in (b) is that which s 9(1)(a) provides must be delivered to the Registrar within fourteen days of a person ceasing to be a member.[44]

VICARIOUS LIABILITY FOR TORTS AND OTHER WRONGS

5.19 In addition to being liable for breaches of its own duties, the LLP will be vicariously liable to third parties for the torts or other wrongs of its members and employees acting in the course of the business of the LLP.[45]

Acts of members

5.20 LLP Act 2000, s 6(4) expressly provides for the LLP to be vicariously liable for the torts or other wrongs of its members. Section 6(4) states that where a member is liable to any person (other than another member of the LLP) as a result of a wrongful act or omission of his in the course of the business of the LLP or with its authority, the LLP is liable to the same extent as the member. The words 'wrongful act or omission' include not only a common law wrong (such as negligence or deceit), but also an equitable wrong (such as dishonest participation

---

[38]   Considered at **5.20**.
[39]   Or LLP Act 2000, s 4(3), discussed in **16.6–16.9**.
[40]   See **8.33–8.35**.
[41]   So that the provisions of LLP Act 2000, s 6(2), discussed above, will continue to be applicable.
[42]   LLP Act 2000, s 6(3).
[43]   See, for example, *Eagle Trust Plc v SBC Securities Ltd* [1992] 4 All ER 488 at 497j–498d.
[44]   See further at **8.34**.
[45]   See, generally, on vicarious liability *Clerk & Lindsell on Torts* 18th edn, 2003, chapter 5

in a breach of trust) and probably any act leading to fault-based liability.[46] The wrongful act or omission must have been done 'in the course of the business' of the LLP (or with its authority). The broad issue will be whether the wrongful conduct was so closely connected with acts which the member could properly do in the course of the business that, for the purpose of liability of the LLP to third parties, that conduct may fairly and properly be regarded as having been done by the member in the course of the LLP's business.[47] The decision as to whether or not an act is within the course of a particular business will be a decision made by the court, taking into account the policy behind the principle of vicarious liability, on the basis of the primary facts.[48] Reference is made in **15.29** to professional positions which can only be occupied by individuals. Such positions include actuaries of occupational pension schemes and insolvency practitioners. Individuals acting in these positions will, in any event (and subject to the effect of any exoneration clause), have personal liability for their own negligence or other wrongdoing when so acting. Issues may arise in some circumstances as to whether, although acting in an individual capacity, a person acting in such a position who is a member of an LLP is also to be regarded as acting in the course of the business of the LLP. All will depend upon the particular facts. The reality is likely to be, in many cases, that the individual has been chosen to hold the position because of his membership of a particular LLP. In such cases, anyway, it is suggested that – depending upon the detailed facts – the court may well conclude that the negligent or other wrongful conduct may fairly and properly be regarded as done by the individual while acting in the course of the LLP's business. Similar issues may arise in relation to individual members of an LLP who act as trustees or company directors. These also are personal positions; but in many cases it may be unrealistic to see them as not undertaken in the course of the business of the LLP.[49]

5.21 By the words '(other than another member of the limited liability partnership)', s 6(4) excludes from the vicarious liability of the LLP the wrongful act of a member done in the course of the business of the LLP, or with its authority, where the personal liability of the wrongdoing member is to another member.[50] An issue which may arise in this context is whether the reference in the

---

[46] See *Dubai Aluminium Co Ltd v Salaam* [2003] 2 AC 366 at paras 10 and 103, considering the same words in the Partnership Act 1890, s 10. These words embrace every kind of wrong capable of causing damage to non-members: ibid para 108.

[47] See *Dubai Aluminium Co Ltd v Salaam* above, a partnership case under the Partnership Act 1890, s 10. The relevant words in s 10 of the 1890 Act are 'in the ordinary course of the business of the firm'. The equivalent words in LLP Act 2000, s 6(4) are 'in the course of the business' of the LLP ie they omit 'ordinary'. This, if anything, widens the scope for an LLP being vicariously liable for the wrongs of its members.

[48] Compare the approach of Lord Nicholls in *Dubai Aluminium Co Ltd v Salaam* above at para 24 ('The conclusion is a conclusion of law, based on primary facts, rather than a simple question of fact') and that of Lord Millett at para 112 ('It is not, of course, a question of primary fact, but a factual conclusion based on an assessment of the primary facts').

[49] See, for instance, as to trusteeships, *Walker v Stones* [2001] 1 QB 902 (CA) at 950F. The statutory presumption arising under the Partnership Act 1890 referred to in that case that individual trusteeships which a partner undertakes are not undertaken in the ordinary course of business of a firm (see 949E–951A) is not carried into the LLP Act 2000.

[50] It seems probable that s 6(4) is intended positively to exclude such liability; but this must always be without prejudice to any direct cause of action which the wronged member may have against the LLP.

words quoted above to 'another member' is to another member in any circumstances or capacity, or is only to another member qua member. It may be, for instance, that a member of an LLP, assuming a personal responsibility, carries out work for another member in the same manner as he would for a normal customer. If the work is carried out negligently, the other member in such circumstances may be said not to suffer loss qua member, but as a customer. It is not clear whether the intention of s 6(4) is to exclude vicarious liability on the part of the LLP in such circumstances. The issue may, however, prove to be of little practical importance. In the example above, it is probable that the personal responsibility of the member carrying out the work was not assumed by him to the exclusion of the LLP's responsibility.[51] Whatever the precise ambit of the exclusion from vicarious liability to one member for the acts of another, the LLP can be vicariously liable to a member in respect of the tort or other wrong of a non-member employee committed in the course of his employment: this is not excluded by LLP Act 2000, s 6(4).

Acts of non-member employees

5.22 As in the context of agency, the LLP Act 2000 makes no reference to non-member employees; but the LLP will be liable for the torts and other wrongs of its employees committed in the course of their employment on the normal principles of vicarious liability.[52] The broad issue will be whether the wrongful conduct was so closely connected with the nature of his employment and the class of activities which the employee was employed to carry out that, for the purpose of liability of the LLP to third parties, that conduct may fairly and properly be regarded as having been done by the employee in the course of his employment.[53]

---

[51] And if it was, it may not be unreasonable that there should be no liability on the part of the LLP.

[52] On vicarious liability generally, see footnote 45 above.

[53] See *Lister v Hesley Hall Ltd* [2002] 1 AC 215. The fact that the wrongdoing was intentional or dishonest, or done for the benefit of the employee alone, or contrary to express instructions to him, is not of itself a defence for the employer.

Chapter 6

PROPERTY AND CHARGES

INTRODUCTION

6.1   As has been mentioned earlier,[1] an LLP is able to own property and assets; and it has the same capacity and freedom to enter into transactions in relation to its property and assets as a private individual. In addition, there is no limitation on its capacity to borrow.[2]

6.2   An LLP is, therefore, able to charge its property as security for borrowing. It will be able to issue debentures, and give fixed or floating charges.[3] This will include an ability to issue 'perpetual debentures' (ie debentures which are irredeemable, or which are redeemable only on the happening of a certain event or on the expiration of a fixed period)[4] and to re-issue debentures previously redeemed (unless it has contracted or shown an intention that there will be no re-issue).[5] Like a company, an LLP is obliged to maintain a register of charges.[6] In addition, broadly speaking, any charge must be registered with the Registrar.[7]

6.3   Holders of the LLP's debentures will be entitled to receive copies of its accounts (together with a copy of the auditors' report) within one month of the accounts being signed; and will be entitled to receive, also, on request, a copy of the LLP's last annual accounts (and auditors' report).[8]

REGISTER OF CHARGES

6.4   Every LLP must keep at its registered office:[9] (i) a register of charges;[10] and

---

[1]   See **3.5**.
[2]   Although, of course, the LLP agreement may restrict the level of borrowings as a matter of internal management.
[3]   There is no reason in principle why an LLP cannot give a floating charge, and the legislation assumes that it can: both CA 1985, ss 196 (dealing with payment of debts out of assets subject to a floating charge) and 396 and IA 1986, s 245 (dealing with the avoidance of certain floating charges) are adopted for LLPs. CA 1985, Part XVIII, concerned with floating charges in Scotland, is also adopted. See further as to floating charges **29.27**.
[4]   CA 1985, s 193.
[5]   Ibid, s 194. As to the duty of the LLP to issue certificates of debentures allotted or transferred, see CA 1985, s 185.
[6]   See **6.4–6.7**.
[7]   See **6.8–6.15**.
[8]   CA 1985, ss 238 and 239, discussed further at **18.24**.
[9]   Subject to what is said in **6.6**(2).
[10] CA 1985, s 407(1).

also (ii) a copy of every charge requiring registration under CA 1985, s 395–405.[11] There must be entered in the register of charges all charges affecting property of the LLP and all floating charges on the LLP's undertaking or any of its property.[12] The entry must in each case give a short description of the property charged, the amount of the charge and, except in the case of securities to bearer, the names of the persons entitled to it.[13] The obligation on the LLP is to keep a register of charges, whether or not any charge has in fact been granted. The right of inspection referred to in **6.5** is, inter alia, a right to see whether there are any charges. The register may, therefore, on inspection have no entries in it at all. If a member of the LLP knowingly and wilfully authorises or permits the omission of an entry required to be made in the register, he is liable to a fine.[14] But a mere failure to enter a charge on the register will not invalidate the charge.[15]

6.5   The register of charges kept by the LLP, and copies of charges requiring registration under the CA 1985, are to be open for inspection during business hours[16] by any creditor or member of the LLP without fee.[17] The register (but not the copies) is also required to be open to inspection by any other person on payment of such fee, not exceeding 5 pence, as the LLP may prescribe.[18] If inspection of the copies or of the register is refused, every member of the LLP who is in default is liable to a fine;[19] and the court may make an order compelling an immediate inspection of the copies or the register.[20]

6.6   The register may be kept either by making entries in bound books or by recording the charges and their details in any other manner.[21] Where the entries are made otherwise than in bound books, the LLP must take adequate precautions for guarding against falsification, and for facilitating the discovery of any falsification;[22] and if there is default in taking these precautions, the LLP and every member of it who is in default is liable to a fine and, for continued contravention, to a daily default fine.[23] The power to keep the register otherwise than in bound books includes the power to keep the register otherwise than in a legible form (eg on a computer), so long as the entries are capable of being reproduced in a legible form.[24] If the register is kept on computer, the following conditions apply.

---

[11]   CA 1985, s 406(1). In the case of a series of uniform debentures, a copy of one debenture of the series is sufficient: s 406(2). For charges requiring registration, see **6.10**.
[12]   Ibid.
[13]   CA 1985, s 407(2). As to entering on the register a transfer of a debenture, see CA 1985, s 183; and as to the effect of a certification by the LLP of an instrument of transfer of a debenture, see s 184.
[14]   Ibid, s 407(3).
[15]   *Wright v Horton* (1887) 12 App Cas 371.
[16]   Subject to such reasonable restrictions as the LLP may impose, but so that inspection is available for not les than 2 hours in each day.
[17]   CA 1985, s 408(1).
[18]   Ibid, s 408(2).
[19]   Ibid, s 408(3). As to the meaning of 'in default', see CA 1985, s 730(5) and **10.9**.
[20]   Ibid, s 408(4).
[21]   Ibid, s 722(1).
[22]   Ibid, s 722(2).
[23]   Ibid, s 722(3). As to the meaning of 'in default', see footnote 19 above.
[24]   Ibid, s 723(1). The section is headed 'Use of computers for company records'.

(1) The duty on the LLP of allowing inspection of the register[25] is converted into a duty to allow inspection of a reproduction of the register in a legible form (ie a computer printout).[26]

(2) The duty to allow inspection continues to be a duty to allow inspection at the LLP's registered office; but the LLP will not be required to keep the register at the registered office.[27]

6.7 Although an LLP is obliged to keep a register of charges, and the prescribed particulars of most charges are required to be registered with the Registrar, there is no statutory obligation to keep a separate register of *holders* of charges (although in practice a charge or other debenture[28] actually issued may well contain a condition that such a register will be kept by the LLP). Where, however, a register of debenture holders *is* kept, certain statutory obligations are imposed. The register is to be kept either at the LLP's registered office or at the place where the work of making it up is done.[29] The register is to be open to inspection by the registered holder of any debenture without fee, and by any other person on payment of the prescribed fee for copies.[30] The person inspecting may require a copy of the register or any part of it, on payment of the prescribed fee.[31] The register is to be available for inspection for a minimum of 2 hours on each business day.[32] If inspection is refused, or a copy is refused, the LLP and every member of it who is in default is liable to a fine;[33] and the court may order an immediate inspection of the register or direct that the copies required be sent to the person requiring them.[34] Without prejudice to any lesser applicable limitation period, liability incurred by an LLP from the making or deletion of an entry in its register of debenture holders, or from a failure to make or delete any entry, is not enforceable more than 20 years

[25] Ie under CA 1985, s 408, discussed in **6.5**.

[26] Ibid, s 723(3).

[27] The Companies (Registers and other Records) Regulations 1985, SI 1985/724, para 2, made under CA 1985, s 723(4). These Regulations are applied to LLPs by LLP Regulations 2001, reg 10. Further reference should be made to the 1985 Regulations if the register is to be kept on computer or in other non-legible form.

[28] The term 'debenture' in the CA 1985 includes debenture stock, bonds, and any other securities of an LLP, whether constituting a charge on its assets or not. The term does, therefore, include a mortgage over a single property to a single mortgagee: CA 1985, s 744.

[29] CA 1985, s 190. If the register is not kept at the LLP's registered office, notice of where it is kept (and any change) must be given to the Registrar: ibid. And see CA 1985, s 364(c) as to the annual return (discussed in **4.26**).

[30] CA 1985, s 191(1). As to the prescribed fee, see the Companies (Inspection and Copying of Registers, Indices and Documents) Regulations 1991, SI 1991/1998, made under CA 1985, s 723A. These Regulations are applied to LLPs by LLP Regulations 2001, reg 10, but their only application to LLPs is to the register of debenture holders.

[31] CA 1985, s 191(2). As to the prescribed fee, see SI 1991/1998 above. The person inspecting the register is to be permitted to copy any information which is available for inspection by taking notes or himself writing out the information (reg 3(2)). The LLP is not obliged to present the register for inspection in a manner which shows debenture holders by location or nationality or whether they are individuals or corporations (reg 4(2)(b)); nor is it obliged to provide copies by reference to such categories (reg 4(3)(b)).

[32] SI 1991/1998.

[33] CA 1985, s 191(4). As to the meaning of 'in default', see footnote 19 above.

[34] Ibid, s 191(5).

after the date on which the entry was made or deleted, or the failure to make or delete the entry first occurred.[35]

REGISTRATION OF CHARGES

6.8   The LLP legislation adopts for LLPs the provisions of the CA 1985 as to the registration in a public register maintained by the Registrar[36] of the prescribed particulars of certain charges[37] created by the LLP, together with the instrument creating or evidencing them. If the prescribed particulars, together with the instrument (if any)[38] creating or evidencing the charge, are not delivered to or received by the Registrar for registration within 21 days after the date of the creation of the charge, then so far as any security on the LLP's property or undertaking is conferred by the charge, the charge is void as against the liquidator or administrator, and any creditor, of the LLP.[39] It is, however, only the security which is void. The contract or obligation for repayment of the money secured by the charge remains valid; and when a charge becomes void for non-registration, the money secured by it becomes immediately payable.[40]

6.9   The purpose of the register is so that those dealing with an LLP, or considering doing so, are able, by searching the register, to find out whether the LLP has incumbered its property.[41] The register is open to inspection by any person.[42] The requirement for registration applies to both legal and equitable charges. It does, however, only apply in respect of charges which the LLP has itself created,[43] so that it does not apply in respect of a charge or lien arising solely by operation of law, such as an unpaid vendor's lien.[44] The requirement applies whether the charge is created in writing or otherwise (for instance, by deposit).

6.10   The charges the prescribed particulars of which must be registered are as follows:[45]

---

[35]   CA 1985, s 391(7).

[36]   Under ibid, s 401

[37]   The statutory provisions on registration refer to 'charges' of the LLP. This includes mortgages: CA 1985, s 396(4).

[38]   So that registration is required even if there is no instrument (and see footnote 44).

[39]   CA 1985, s 395(1). And see *Smith v Bridgend County BC* [2002] 1 AC 336 as to an unregistered charge being void against the administrator. As to the prescribed particulars, see **6.13** and Form LLP 395. For each registration of a charge, there is a fee of £20: see the Limited Liability Partnerships (Fees) (No 2) Regulations 2001, SI 2001/969.

[40]   CA 1985, s 395(2).

[41]   See *Re Jackson and Bassford Ltd* [1906] 2 Ch 467 at 476.

[42]   CA 1985, s 401(3).

[43]   See the reference in CA 1985, s 395(1) to 'a charge created by an LLP'.

[44]   See *London and Cheshire Insurance Co Ltd v Laplagrene Property Co Ltd* [1971] Ch 499. Compare *Re Wallis & Simmonds (Builders) Ltd* [1974] 1 WLR 391 (equitable charge arising by deposit of title deeds does require registration).

[45]   CA 1985, s 396(1). The prescribed particulars are set out in **6.13**

(i)   a charge for the purpose of securing any issue of debentures;[46]
(ii)   a charge created or evidenced by an instrument which, if executed by an individual, would require registration as a bill of sale;[47]
(iii)   a charge on land (wherever situated) or any interest in it, but not including a charge for any rent or other periodical sum issuing out of the land;[48]
(iv)   a charge on book debts of the LLP;[49]
(v)   a floating charge on the LLP's undertaking or property;[50]
(vi)   a charge on a ship or aircraft, or any share in a ship; and
(vii)   a charge on goodwill or any intellectual property (ie any patent, trade mark, registered design, copyright or design right, or any licence under or in respect of any such right).[51]

6.11 It is the LLP's duty to send to the Registrar the particulars of every charge created by it which requires registration.[52] But a charge may also be registered by any person interested in it.[53] If the LLP fails to register the charge, and the charge has not been registered by some person interested in it, both the LLP and every member of it who is in default are liable to a fine and, for continued contravention, to a daily default fine.[54]

6.12 Where the LLP acquires property which is already subject to a charge of a kind which would have been required to be registered if it had been created by the LLP after the acquisition of the property, the LLP must register the charge (and also deliver to the Registrar a certified copy of the instrument by which it was

---

[46]   As to meaning of 'debenture', see footnote 28 above. An 'issue of debentures' is not defined in the legislation. *Gore-Browne on Companies* para. 18.9.1 suggests that probably what is intended to be covered by (i) is not the issue of any debenture, but rather the issue of a series of debentures.

[47]   A mortgage or charge on personal chattels as defined by the Bills of Sale Acts will require registration under this head.

[48]   As to 'any interest' in land, CA 1985, s 396(3) provides that the holding of debentures entitling the holder to a charge on land is not for the purposes of head (iii) deemed to be an interest in land. A charge on unregistered land will also need to be registered under the Land Charges Act 1972. The exemption from registration under s 3(7)–(8) of that Act for floating charges over land applies only to such charges created by companies, and so will not apply to floating charges created by LLPs. A charge over registered land will require to be registered at the Land Registry under the Land Registration Act 2002.

[49]   The expression 'book debts' is not defined in the legislation. 'Book debts of the LLP' can perhaps be defined as 'debts arising in the busines of the LLP which in the ordinary course of one conducting a busines of that nature are entered in well-kept books relating to it (whether in fact the debts are entered in the books of the LLP or not)': see *Paul & Frank Ltd v Discount Bank (Overseas) Ltd* [1967] Ch 348 at 360–1. A charge on future book debts is covered by head (iv): see *Independent Automatic Sales Ltd v Knowles & Foster* [1962] 1 WLR 974. A charge over book debts (present and future) can be either a fixed charge or a floating charge. As to which it is in any case, see *Re Spectrum Plus Ltd* [2004] 3 WLR 503 (CA) (leave given to appeal to the House of Lords).

[50]   As to a floating charge over land, see footnote 48 above.

[51]   See CA 1985, s 396(3A).

[52]   Ibid, s 399(1).

[53]   Ibid: Where the charge is registered by such a person, he is entitled to recover from the LLP the fees paid to the Registrar on the registration: CA 1985, s 399(2).

[54]   Ibid, s 399(3). As to the meaning of 'in default', see footnote 19 above.

created or is evidenced) within 21 days after completion of the acquisition.[55] If default is made in registering a charge after the acquisition of a property subject to it, both the LLP and every member of it who is in default are liable to a fine and, for continued contravention, to a daily default fine.[56]

6.13   The particulars which must be registered are as follows.[57]

(a)   In the case of any charge other than a charge to the benefit of which the holders of a series of debentures are entitled:
    (i)   if it is a charge created by the LLP, the date of its creation, and if it is a charge which was existing on property when the property was acquired by the LLP, the date of the acquisition of the property;
    (ii) the amount secured by the charge;
    (iii) short particulars of the property charged; and
    (iv) the person entitled to the charge.
(b)   In the case of a charge to the benefit of which the holders of a series of debentures are entitled:
    (i)   the total amount secured by the whole series;
    (ii) the dates of the determinations of the LLP authorising the issue of the series and the date of the covering deed (if any) by which the security is created or defined;
    (iii) a general description of the property charged; and
    (iv) the names of the trustees (if any) for the debenture holders.

6.14   When a charge has been registered, the Registrar will give a certificate of the registration, either signed by him, or authenticated by his official seal, stating the amount secured by the charge.[58] The certificate is conclusive evidence that the requirements for registration of the charge have been satisfied.[59] The LLP is required to cause a copy of the certificate of registration to be endorsed on every debenture or certificate of debenture stock which is issued by it, and the payment of which is secured by the charge.[60] If a person knowingly and wilfully authorises or permits the delivery of a debenture or certificate of debenture stock which is required to have endorsed on it a copy of a certificate of registration, without the copy being so endorsed on it, he is liable (without prejudice to any other liability) to a fine.[61]

6.15   Where the debt secured by the charge is paid off, or the property charged is released from the security (or has ceased to form part of the LLP's property or undertaking), on receipt by the Registrar of a statutory declaration in the prescribed

---

[55]   CA 1985, s 400(1) and (2). If the property is situated, and the charge was created, outside Great Britain, the 21 days is extended to allow a period for posting: CA 1985, s 400(3).
[56]   CA 1985, s 400(4). As to the meaning of 'in default', see footnote 19 above.
[57]   Ibid, s 401.
[58]   Ibid, s 401(2).
[59]   Ibid, s 401(2)(b).
[60]   Ibid, s 402(1). This does not apply to any debenture or certificate of debenture stock issued by the LLP before the charge was created: s 402(2). For the meaning of 'debenture' see footnote 28.
[61]   CA 1985, s 402(3).

form verifying this,[62] under CA 1985, s 403 he may enter a memorandum to this effect on the register.[63] Where the memorandum is of satisfaction of the whole debt, the LLP can require a copy of the memorandum from the Registrar.[64]

POWER OF COURT TO EXTEND TIME AND RECTIFY

6.16   There is power for the court under CA 1985, s 404, on the application of the LLP or of a person interested, and on such terms and conditions as the court thinks just and expedient, to order that the time for registration of a charge shall be extended or that an omission or misstatement in the register of 'any particular with respect to' a charge (or an omission or misstatement in 'a memorandum of satisfaction') be rectified.[65] The reference to 'any particular with respect to' a charge is a reference to the particulars which the Registrar is required to enter on the register under CA 1985, s 401(1), and the reference to 'a memorandum of satisfaction' is a reference to the memorandum of satisfaction which the Registrar may enter on the register under CA 1985, s 403. The power of rectification given to the court does not extend to mistakes otherwise than in such particulars or memorandum.[66] In any event, before making an order under CA 1985, s 404, the court will need to be satisfied that the omission to register a charge within the required time, or the omission or misstatement in the register or memorandum of satisfaction, was accidental, or due to inadvertence or to some other sufficient cause, or is not of a nature to prejudice the position of creditors of the LLP, or that on other grounds it is just and equitable to grant relief.[67] There is no wider or other inherent general jurisdiction, beyond that given by CA 1985, s 404, for the court to order rectification of the register.[68]

---

[62]   Or a statement by a designated member (or administrator or administrative receiver) in an electronic communication satisfying s 403(1A).

[63]   CA 1985, s 403(1).

[64]   Ibid, s 403(2).

[65]   Ibid, s 404.

[66]   See *igroup Ltd v Ocwen* [2004] 1WLR 451, where the court was asked (unsuccessfully) to rectify prescribed forms which had been filed relating to deeds of discharge and to new charges, in order to delete unnecessary information which had been attached to the forms.

[67]   Ibid.

[68]   *Exeter Trust Ltd v Screenways Ltd* [1991] BCLC 888.

Chapter 7

CONVERSION FROM A PARTNERSHIP

INTRODUCTION

7.1 Many LLPs will be formed for the purpose of incorporating existing partnerships. The issues facing a firm contemplating conversion will be similar to those arising on any business transfer. Much will depend, of course, upon the circumstances of the particular partnership; and many of the issues will raise tax questions. The purpose of this chapter is to identify the kind of issues that may arise.

THE DECISION TO CONVERT

7.2 The decision to transfer the business and assets of the partnership to an LLP, and (at the same time or subsequently) to dissolve and wind up the partnership, will fall to be made by the partners. Unless the partnership agreement provides for the relevant decisions as to transfer and dissolution to be made by majority resolution, unanimity amongst the partners is likely to be required. There may, however, be an existing power for the majority to amend the agreement; and this power *may* be wide enough to introduce a power for the majority to decide on a transfer and dissolution.[1] Where unanimity is required, and one or more partners refuse to agree to the necessary transfer and dissolution, it is difficult to see how such a refusal can of itself be characterised as 'bad faith' (possibly giving rise to a liability to expulsion), however desirable the majority of partners may consider conversion to be. Like any other action on the part of a partner, however, a refusal may be capable of being so characterised if actual bad faith can be positively shown as the motive for the refusal.

7.3 A stalemate amongst the partners as to whether or not to convert into an LLP may give rise to a situation where it is just and equitable for the partnership to be dissolved by the court under s 35(f) of the Partnership Act 1890, so that those partners wishing to incorporate as an LLP may do so. It may also be possible for a majority of partners who wish to transfer the business and assets of the partnership to an LLP to obtain a '*Syers v Syers* order' that they may buy out the interest in the partnership of the opposing minority, so that they are in a position to transfer all interest in the business and assets of the partnership to the LLP.[2]

---

[1] A variation has to be distinguished from a substitution of a new contract: see, generally, *Halsbury's Laws* (Butterworths, 4th edn, 1988), vol 9(1), para 1024.

[2] In relation to *Syers v Syers* orders, see *Lindley & Banks on Partnership* 18th edn, 2002, paras 23-187–23-190 and *Mullins v Laughton* [2003] Ch 250, paras 107–111.

7.4 Where a partnership deed is being drafted to provide for the partnership to be able to convert into an LLP at some time in the future on the vote of a specified majority, it may be wise to provide for the senior partner, or some other member of the firm, to have a power of attorney to execute any necessary documents on behalf of all partners. Provision should also be made in the deed as to whether dissenters are to be obliged to join the LLP on conversion or whether they are to be permitted (or required) to retire at (or prior to) conversion.[3] If the deed makes no provision for the retirement of dissenters, and they do not join the LLP, they will continue to be partners for the purposes of the dissolution and winding up of the partnership. This can cause difficulties. For instance, the dissenters are likely to be entitled to insist on being paid out their share of the partnership assets at market value rather than simply the balances on their current and capital accounts. Where the book value of the assets of the partnership represents an undervalue (because, for instance, certain assets are shown at cost) the difference may be significant.

STAMP DUTY AND STAMP DUTY LAND TAX

7.5 Consideration needs to be given to securing the exemption from stamp duty, and from stamp duty land tax, on transfers of property from the partners to the LLP contained in LLP Act 2000, s 12 (stamp duty) and Finance Act 2003, s 65 (stamp duty land tax). The conditions for this exemption relate to the persons who are the partners in the existing partnership, and are to be the first members of the LLP, and to the shares of the existing partners in the property, and their shares in the property of the LLP. These conditions are discussed at **21.73–21.76**.

TRANSFER OF THE PARTNERSHIP BUSINESS AND ASSETS

7.6 In most cases, the partners will wish to transfer the whole of the business and assets of the partnership to the LLP as a going concern. Indeed, partial incorporation may give rise to a number of significant tax issues.[4] Where liabilities are 'transferred', the LLP will, in practice, discharge the partnership's liabilities whether or not they have been formally novated to the LLP. The consideration for the transfer by the partners of their shares in the partnership assets will be the shares or interests in the LLP which they take on the transfer. Thought will obviously need to be given to whether particular assets or liabilities ought to remain in the partnership, and whether the transfers which are to be made will require compliance with any formalities. Issues arising in relation to particular categories of assets and liabilities are discussed in the following paragraphs.

CUSTOMER/CLIENT CONTRACTS

7.7 Some professional service firms which are planning well ahead for conversion into an LLP provide in the terms of engagement agreed between the

---

[3] Perhaps immediately before incorporation of the LLP: see **21.73–21.76**.
[4] See **21.57–21.58**.

firm and the client that the client will accept the professional service being provided by the LLP in place of the partnership when conversion takes place. In the absence of such a provision in the terms of engagement, the burden of a client contract (ie the obligation to provide the services) cannot be assigned (or, more accurately novated) to the LLP without the agreement of the client.[5] However, in the absence of contractual prohibitions, the benefit of a retainer, or at least the 'fruits' of the retainer, can be assigned to the LLP or to a trust declared for the benefit of the LLP.[6] Professional service firms will, on any given day, have a large number of part-performed client retainers. Serious consideration will need to be given to whether the consent of each client is to be obtained to a formal novation. Firms will have to balance the practical difficulty and potential embarrassment of seeking to persuade a client of the sense of novating a part-performed retainer against the fact that the partners will continue to have unlimited liability in respect of retainers which are completed as run-off matters in the partnership. In most cases, part-performed retainers are likely to be completed by the partnership; and, as new matters arise, retainers will be created between the LLP and the clients.

7.8   If retainers are to be completed by the partnership (whether still continuing for run-off purposes or in dissolution), a decision will need to be made as to whether fees generated by work done after incorporation are to accrue to the benefit of the LLP or are to be left in the partnership. A decision will also have to be made as to whether the benefit of work in progress and receivables as at the date of incorporation is to be assigned to the LLP. There may be reason to retain part in the partnership in order to fund any liabilities from which it is desired to insulate the LLP. In making any of the decisions mentioned in this paragraph, consideration will need to be given to the tax consequences of partial incorporation of the business.[7]

EMPLOYEES

7.9   The Transfer of Undertakings (Protection of Employees) Regulations 1981[8] will apply on a conversion. The contracts of the employees of the partnership will, therefore, not be terminated by the transfer of the business (and the dissolution of the partnership) but will be treated as having been made with the LLP (subject to the right of any employee to object to becoming employed by the LLP).[9] For firms where staff are employed by a service company, no change is necessary unless it is desired to move the employees to the LLP.

---

[5]   See *Chitty on Contracts* 29th edn, 2004, paras 19-085–19-088.

[6]   *Don King Productions Inc v Warren* [2000] Ch 291 at 318–320 (Lightman J at first instance).

[7]   See **21.29** and **21.57–21.58**.

[8]   SI 1981/1794

[9]   Regulation 5. See generally *Harvey on Industrial Relations and Employment Law*, Division F. If an employee does object to becoming employed by the LLP, his objection will operate so as to terminate his employment with the partnership, but he will not be treated as having been dismissed by the partnership: reg 5(4A) and (4B).

LEASES

7.10 In many cases, leases of premises used by the firm will have been taken in the names of up to four of the partners, who will hold the premises on trust for all the partners. The consent of the landlord may well be required to the assignment of a lease to the LLP; and a personal guarantee from the members may be required by the landlord as a condition of giving consent. Whether such a demand is reasonable will depend upon the financial position of the LLP.[10] Consideration will also need to be given to whether (and if so, what) provision ought to be made for contingent liabilities accruing under leases which are assigned.

BANKING

7.11 New banking facilities will need to be negotiated. As with leases, a key issue will be whether banks insist on personal guarantees from members in respect of borrowings. It is of the essence of an LLP that, where money is lent to the entity, the lender will (generally speaking) have no recourse against the individual members unless personal liability is expressly placed on the members. In addition (or as alternatives) to guarantees, banks may require covenants from members as to the level of members' capital to be maintained,[11] or to the effect that LLP indebtedness to members is subordinated to indebtedness to the bank. As is mentioned at **6.2**, an LLP is able to give floating, as well as fixed, charges over its assets; and banks may require one or other of such forms of charge. The transfer of an existing partnership overdraft to the LLP may well require continuing personal liability.

INVESTMENTS

7.12 Many firms will have acquired assets (such as shares taken in lieu of fees or interests in offshore trust companies) which are held on trust for the partners. Consideration will need to be given to whether such assets are to be transferred to the LLP or whether fresh declarations of trust should be executed. Particular thought will need to be given to how equity between partner years is to be maintained, and how effect is to be given to any policy that the firm may have in this regard.

PROFESSIONAL INDEMNITY INSURANCE

7.13 Professional indemnity cover will be required both for the LLP and, on a run-off basis, for the partnership. LLPs are unlikely to wish to reduce the level of cover from that previously taken by the partnership merely because of the limitation on liability resulting from incorporation, at least until there is some

---

[10] See, for instance, *Woodfall, Landlord and Tenant*, vol 1, para 11.143.
[11] Capital, and the unrestricted ability under the legislation to reduce it, is discussed at **13.1–13.7**.

judicial clarification as to the circumstances in which an individual member who is responsible for a wrong committed by the LLP (eg negligence) may himself be personally liable, in addition to the LLP.[12] In this latter respect, care will be needed to ensure that the individual members, as well the LLP itself, are covered by the insurance. In some professions, despite incorporation as an LLP, the responsibility for the work is by statute that of the individual professional.[13] A decision will need to be made as to whether the LLP should give the partners in the superseded partnership an indemnity against professional negligence claims made against them in that capacity. If the LLP gives the previous partners a general indemnity against professional negligence claims it will become exposed to claims that overtop the partnership's run-off indemnity insurance limit. It may be thought preferable to keep the LLP insulated from any 'mega' claim which is made against the previous partners.

INDEMNITIES

7.14   It will usually be appropriate for the LLP to give the partners an indemnity against liabilities taken over by the LLP.[14]

ANNUITIES

7.15   Annuities are likely to provide one of the greatest difficulties on incorporation.[15] Careful consideration will need to be given to the terms of any annuities and to the effect of incorporation in relation to them. For example, some annuity provisions stipulate that incorporation is to act as a capitalisation trigger in favour of the annuitants. A decision will need to be made as to whether the liability to pay annuities is to be transferred to the LLP and, if not, how the annuity payments are to be funded. A transfer of the liability would require a formal novation (ie agreement with all those who are beneficiaries or potential beneficiaries of the annuity provisions). If liability to pay the annuities is novated to the LLP, or the LLP assumes the responsibility for discharging the annuities (for instance, by agreeing in the business transfer agreement to indemnify the partners against the liability to pay the annuities), the quantum of the total annuity liability will need to be capitalised and provided for on the LLP's balance sheet in respect of this liability. This is discussed further in **7.16**. This consequence can be avoided by all the members, including all future members (who will need to execute deeds of adherence), but not the LLP, entering into an agreement under which they agree to discharge the annuity liability pro rata to their profit shares in the LLP.

---

[12]   This issue is discussed in chapter 15.
[13]   Examples are actuaries of occupational pension schemes and insolvency practitioners, discussed further at **15.29**.
[14]   Although see **7.13** in relation to professional negligence claims.
[15]   Although transfers to the LLP will not generally speaking be a chargeable transfer for capital gains tax purposes: see **21.61** et seq.

'TRUE AND FAIR' ACCOUNTS

7.16 The LLP will need to prepare an annual balance sheet and profit and loss account, giving a 'true and fair view' of the position in accordance with CA 1985, s 226. This will involve (as a general rule) complying with the applicable accounting standards issued by the Accounting Standards Board, and with the Statement of Recommended Practice (SORP) for LLPs.[16] It is generally considered advisable for partnerships which are contemplating converting into an LLP to go through the exercise, well before actual conversion, of producing a balance sheet and profit and loss account in the formats required for LLPs by the CA 1985, and in accordance with the applicable accounting standards and the LLP SORP. This will give an early indication of how individual items will now fall to be treated for accounting purposes. Particular accounting issues may arise in relation to annuities. Where a partnership has obligations to pay annuities to past members or employees, and the liability is to be transferred to the LLP (or assumed by the LLP), this liability will need to be recognised in the LLP's balance sheet.[17] In relation to annuities payable to former partners (as for annuities subsequently payable to former members of the LLP), the LLP SORP requires the accounts to show (recalculated annually) the present value of the best estimate of the expected liability for future payments to the former partners (or members).[18]

PARTNERSHIPS OF ACCOUNTANTS

7.17 An existing partnership of accountants which, as a firm, has been appointed as a company auditor[19] will need to consider how that appointment is going to be transferred to the LLP. The LLP, provided that it is eligible for appointment as a company auditor, will be capable of holding the appointment in the same way as the partnership.[20] CA 1989, s 26(5) provides that where a partnership ceases (ie either on a technical or a full dissolution), and its appointment as company auditor does not devolve automatically under s 26(3), then that appointment may – with the consent of the company – be treated as transferred ('extending') to a person eligible for the appointment who succeeds to the business of the former partnership or who succeeds to such part of that business as the company agrees is to be treated as comprising the appointment. 'Person' here will include an LLP. Section 26(5) provides a route, therefore, to the partnership's appointment as auditor of a company being transferred to the LLP. But s 26(5) only applies if s 26(3) does not apply. On a partnership ceasing, s 26(3), with s 26(4), causes the partnership's appointment as a company auditor to devolve automatically on a successor partnership where the whole, or substantially the whole, of the business of the ceasing partnership passes to that successor partnership, provided that the successor partnership is itself eligible for appointment as an auditor and that it

---

[16] Accounts, and audit requirements, are considered in chapter 18.
[17] See LLP SORP, para 58.
[18] LLP SORP, paras 44 and 48.
[19] As permitted by CA 1989, Part II.
[20] See CA 1989, s 25 and the definition of 'firm' in s 53 (a body corporate or a partnership).

comprises substantially the same members as the ceasing partnership.[21] If the business of the ceasing partnership does not pass to a successor partnership, but rather passes to an individual or a body corporate who or which (as well as being eligible for appointment) previously carried on the partnership practice as a partner in the ceasing partnership, then s 26(3), with s 26(4), causes the ceasing partnership's appointment to devolve automatically on that successor individual or body corporate. If there is any automatic transfer of the ceasing partnership's appointment under s 26(3) as set out above, s 26(5) will not be available. The authors suggest that a scheme under which, say, a partner retires immediately prior to the firm transferring its business to the LLP would bring s 26(3) into operation, and would as a result not bring s 26(5) into operation: although the retirement would cause the partnership to 'cease', the appointment as auditor would – albeit for a brief moment only between the retirement and transfer – have been automatically transferred (to the continuing firm) under s 26(3).[22] The easiest way to bring s 26(5) into operation will be for the partnership to go into full dissolution, and for its business to be transferred from the partnership in dissolution to the LLP. In these circumstances, the partnership will have 'ceased', but there will be no automatic transfer of the appointment as auditor under s 26(3). As to the requirement under s 26(5) for 'the consent of the company', it is suggested that the company can act by its directors for these purposes (in the same way as under CA 1985, s 388(1)[23] the directors can fill a casual vacancy in the office of auditor). If a full dissolution of the partnership on transfer of its business to the LLP is not convenient, the easiest alternative will probably be for the partnership to resign as company auditor immediately prior to dissolution,[24] and for the LLP to be appointed in its place under CA 1985, s 388.[25]

7.18   Under some UK, and overseas, legislation there are restrictions on a body corporate being appointed as auditor.[26] Accountancy partnerships which carry out audits will need to consider whether they have any clients which cannot be audited by a body corporate.

FSMA 2000 AUTHORISED PERSONS

7.19   A partnership may, as a firm, be an 'authorised person' for the purposes of the Financial Services and Markets Act 2000 (FSMA 2000).[27] Where an authorised

---

[21]   This covers the normal coming and going of partners in a firm of auditors.

[22]   It might be possible to devise a scheme making use of s 26(3), under which the LLP became a member of the partnership and then 'succeeded' to the appointment under ss (3)(b), or a scheme under which, on the retirement of a partner (and, therefore, the partnership 'ceasing'), the business of the partnership (or the audit business) falls to be automatically transferred to the LLP.

[23]   Applying here to companies.

[24]   The notice of resignation will need to be accompanied by a statement under CA 1985, s 394.

[25]   Applying here to companies. As with any resignation of a company auditor, this will have to be in accordance with CA 1985, s 392.

[26]   See, for instance, (in the UK) the Trade Union and Labour Relations (Consolidation) Act 1992, s 34, which provides that a body corporate may not act as auditor of a trade union, and (overseas) the Irish Companies Act 1990, s 187, which provides that a body corporate is not qualified for appointment as auditor of a company or as public auditor of a society or a friendly society.

[27]   See FSMA 2000, ss 32 and 40.

firm is dissolved, the authorisation continues in relation to a successor firm (ie comprising substantially the same members and taking on substantially the whole of the previous firm's business).[28] But where an *LLP* succeeds to the firm's business (whether the firm is dissolved or not), there is no continuation of the authorisation, and the LLP (which can in principle be an authorised person) will need to make its own application for authorisation under FSMA 2000, Part IV.[29]

---

[28]   FSMA 2000, s 32
[29]   And see the *FSA Handbook* chapter 3, paras 3.23.4–3.23.5

Chapter 8

MEMBERSHIP: GENERAL MATTERS

INTRODUCTION

8.1 Whilst, as has been seen earlier,[1] an LLP has an existence separate and distinct from that of its members, it is nevertheless of the essence of an LLP that it has members.[2] An individual member is part of a triangle, made up of (i) himself, (ii) the other members, and (iii) the LLP. He has a legal relationship with each of the other two, each relationship being a bundle of rights and obligations. These legal relationships are considered in the following chapters. The purpose of this chapter is to consider a number of general matters relating to membership.

FIRST MEMBERS

8.2 An LLP does not exist as an entity, and there are no members of it, until it has been incorporated.[3] On incorporation, those persons[4] who subscribed their names to the incorporation document become the LLP's first members, save for any individuals who have died between subscribing and incorporation, and save also for any bodies of persons which have been dissolved between subscribing and incorporation.[5] It is to be noted, in relation to bodies of persons, that it is only dissolution which causes a subscribing body not to become a member. A company (or another LLP) which subscribes to an incorporation document and then goes into voluntary or compulsory winding up, but which has not been dissolved before the certificate of incorporation is issued, will, therefore, still become a member of the LLP on the issue of the certificate.[6]

8.3 The legislation gives no express guidance as to what happens if the death before incorporation of an individual who has subscribed his name to the incorporation document (or the dissolution of a body of persons which is a subscriber) reduces the number of future first members to one only (or none). An LLP can exist, and continue to trade with limited liability (for a 6-month period), with one member only.[7] In practice, a sole surviving subscriber, or the personal

---

[1] Chapter 3.
[2] One of the grounds on which an LLP may be wound up by the court is that the number of members is reduced below two: IA 1986, s 122(1)(c).
[3] Ie the certificate of incorporation has been issued under LLP Act 2000, s 3.
[4] As to the meaning of 'persons', see **2.2–2.3**.
[5] LLP Act 2000, s 4(1).
[6] But if the company or the other LLP is one of only two subscribers to the incorporation document, an issue may arise as to whether the compliance statement under LLP Act 2000, s 2(1)(c) remains true: see further the discussion in **8.3**.
[7] See **2.15**.

representatives of a deceased sole surviving subscriber, will probably wish to inform the Registrar of the position, and to withdraw the incorporation document and what is, in effect, the application for incorporation.[8] The Registrar would accede to this because the compliance statement delivered to him under LLP Act 2000, s 2(1)(c) would no longer be accurate.[9] In the absence of the Registrar becoming aware of the altered position after receiving the compliance statement, he will, obviously, simply issue the certificate of incorporation. There may well, however (and as discussed at **2.37**), in any event be an obligation on the maker of the compliance statement, between delivery of that statement and issue of the certificate of incorporation, to inform the Registrar of any event of which he has become aware which has caused continuing compliance with the requirements of s 2(1)(a) to cease.

8.4   If an individual who subscribed his name to the incorporation document dies (or, in the case of a body of persons which subscribed, has been dissolved) before incorporation, but the Registrar has not, for whatever reason, been notified of this fact before issuing the certificate of incorporation, LLP Act 2000, s 9 is likely to be interpreted as requiring that (within 14 days after the certificate of incorporation) notice of that death or dissolution, is to be notified to the Registrar as discussed in **8.34**.

NEW MEMBERS

8.5   After the LLP has been incorporated with its first members, the membership may, of course, change. Section 4(2) of the LLP Act 2000 provides that any other person may become a member by and in accordance with an agreement with the existing members.[10] In other words, and as with a traditional partnership, becoming a member of an LLP is a matter of contract. The LLP agreement will, therefore, need to make provision as to new members joining. In the absence of any such provision, default rule (5) will apply.[11] This provides that no person may be introduced as a member without the consent of all existing members.

8.6   As has been discussed in **2.24–2.27**, the names and addresses of the first members of the LLP must be stated in the incorporation document.[12] Where, after incorporation, a person becomes a member of the LLP, notice of his joining must be given to the Registrar within 14 days of his becoming a member.[13] The giving of this notice is the responsibility of the LLP; but if it is not given, both it and

---

[8]   Given that at best the LLP could only trade with one member for 6 months before that member became personally liable for the LLP's debts (see CA 1985, s 24 discussed at **2.15**), there would in most cases be little incentive for a sole surviving subscriber to proceed to incorporation.

[9]   See **2.36**.

[10]   As to the meaning of any 'person' who may become a member, see **2.2–2.4**.

[11]   The default rules are discussed at **9.6–9.8**.

[12]   LLP Act 2000, s 2(2)(e).

[13]   Ibid, s 9(1)(a). The approved form of notice to the Registrar referred to below requires the date of joining of the new member to be specified.

every designated member is guilty of an offence.[14] The notice is to be in a form approved by the Registrar, and must be signed by a designated member or authenticated in a manner approved by the Registrar.[15] The notice must give the member's name and usual residential address[16] (or, in the case of a corporation or Scottish firm, its registered or principal office), and also (in the case of an individual) his date of birth.[17] The form to be used when a person becomes a member is Form LLP 288a (Appointment of a Member to a Limited Liability Partnership). This provides that the designated member signing on behalf of the LLP cannot be the new member himself. Form LLP 288a does, however, require a 'consent signature' by the new member,[18] following on from the requirement of LLP Act 2000, s 9(3) that notice of a person becoming a member of an LLP must contain a statement by him that he consents to becoming a member. If notice of the new member is not given to the Registrar, that member (or any other member, or a creditor, or the Registrar himself) may operate the procedure of CA 1985, s 713[19] to enforce the giving of the notice.

CHANGES IN A MEMBER'S NAME OR ADDRESS

8.7   Where there is any change in the name, or the address, of a member, notice of the change must be given to the Registrar (in a form approved by the Registrar) within 28 days.[20] This applies in relation both to a first member and to any subsequent member. As with notice to the Registrar of a person becoming a member of an LLP, the responsibility for giving notice of a change in a member's name or address lies with the LLP (but, as with a new member joining, if the notice is not given, both it and every designated member is guilty of an offence).[21] The notice must be signed by a designated member or authenticated in a manner approved by the Registrar.[22] The approved form of notice is Form LLP 288c (Change of Particulars of a Member of a Limited Liability Partnership). This provides that the designated member signing on behalf of the LLP cannot be the member whose change of particulars are being given in the form. It also provides for the member whose particulars have changed himself additionally to sign the form (ie a renewed 'consent signature'). As with the requirement that notice of a new member be given to the Registrar, if notice of a change in a member's name or address is not given to the Registrar, the member concerned (or any other member,

---

[14]   LLP Act 2000, s 9(4)–(6). It is a defence for a designated member to prove that he took all reasonable steps for securing that the notice was given: see further, **10.23–10.24**.
[15]   LLP Act 2000, s 9(3)
[16]   Subject to the existence of a confidentiality order: see **8.9–8.13**
[17]   CA 1985, s 288. As to the meaning of 'name', see **2.25**.
[18]   'I consent to act as a member of the above named limited liability partnership'.
[19]   Ie notice to the LLP requiring the default to be made good within 14 days, and if it is not, an application to the court. And see also **12.3**.
[20]   LLP Act 2000, s 9(1)(b). As with the approved form of notice to the Registrar of a new member, the approved form of notice of a change in particulars of a member requires the date of the change to be specified.
[21]   See footnote 14 above.
[22]   LLP Act 2000, s 9(3)(b).

or a creditor, or the Registrar himself) may operate the procedure of CA 1985, s 713[23] to enforce the giving of the notice.

NOTICE IN THE *LONDON GAZETTE*

8.8 On receipt by him of any notification of a 'change among the members' of the LLP the Registrar is required under CA 1985, s 711(1)(c) to publish a notice in the *London Gazette* that he has received such notification. The effect of this provision is that, when any changes in the composition of the membership of the LLP, or in the name or address of a member, have been notified to the Registrar as required by LLP Act 2000, s 9(1),[24] details of the actual change are not published in the *Gazette*; but what is published is notice that a change has been notified to the Registrar. An interested party can then inspect the relevant form sent to the Registrar under the right of inspection given by CA 1985, s 709 in order to see the details.

CONFIDENTIALITY ORDERS

8.9 Under CA 1985, s 709(1) any records kept by the Registrar in relation to the LLP may be inspected (and copies taken) by any member of the public. Such records will include the incorporation document,[25] the annual return[26] and Forms LLP 288a and 288c referred to in **8.6** and **8.7**. Each of these documents will contain the usual residential address of a member. Where an individual who is a member of an LLP, or is proposing to become a member, considers that the availability for inspection by members of the public of particulars of his usual residential address creates, or is likely to create, a serious risk that he or a person who lives with him will be subjected to violence or intimidation, he may apply to the Secretary of State for a 'confidentiality order' in his favour. If the Secretary of State is satisfied that such a serious risk exists, he is obliged to make an order.[27] The effect of a confidentiality order in relation to an individual is that CA 1985, s 709(1) does not apply to documents containing particulars of that individual's usual residential address which are delivered to the Registrar after the order has been made.[28] A confidentiality order does not, therefore, delete from public inspection details which are contained in documents filed with the Registrar before the order was made.

8.10 Although subsequently filed details of a member's residential address are hidden from public inspection, the beneficiary of a confidentiality order is obliged,

---

[23] Ie notice to the LLP requiring the default to be made good within 14 days, and if it is not, an application to the court. And see also **12.3**.
[24] Ie notice on Form LLP 288a of a member's joining (see **8.6**) or notice on Form 288b of a member leaving (see **8.34**) or notice on Form LLP 288c of a change of a member's name or address (see **8.7**).
[25] Discussed at **2.16–2.31**.
[26] Discussed at **4.26–4.31**.
[27] CA 1985, s 723B(1)–(3).
[28] Ibid, s 723C(1)(a); and see also the definition of 'confidential records' in CA 1985, s 723D(3).

on his application for the order, to provide a substitute address at which documents may be served on him (a 'service address').[29] A service address cannot be a PO or DX Box Number, and must be at a place where documents can be served by being physically delivered, and where that delivery is capable of being recorded by means of the server obtaining an acknowledgement of delivery.[30] The service address must be within a state which is a member of the European Community or be in Iceland, Norway or Liechtenstein.[31] A service address can be changed from time to time. If it is changed, the member must notify the LLP of the changed address,[32] and within 28 days of the LLP being so notified notice of the change must be given to the Registrar in the same way (and with the same sanctions for non-compliance) as on a change in the usual residential address of a member without a confidentiality order.[33] The position in relation to the beneficiary of a confidentiality order who subscribes to an incorporation document for a new LLP is discussed at **2.26**. When the beneficiary of an order becomes a new member of an already existing LLP, it is his service address (and not his usual residential address) which is given for him in the notice to the Registrar required under LLP Act 2000, s 9(1)(a).[34] When an individual who is an existing member of an LLP obtains a confidentiality order, notice of his service address must be given to the Registrar within 28 days of the order being made.[35] It is his service address (and not his usual residential address) which is given for a member who is the beneficiary of a confidentiality order in the LLP's annual return.[36]

8.11 Although the member's usual residential address is thus sheltered from inspection by the public under CA 1985, s 709, he is still required to provide that address to the Registrar. For an individual becoming a new member of the LLP, this is required by CA 1985, s 288A(b), and is done on Form LLP 723(SR) ('Notification of Details of Usual Residential Address Following Grant of Confidentiality Order'). [37] It appears also to be intended that where it is an existing member of an LLP who obtains an order, notification of his usual residential

---

[29] CA 1985, ss 723B(5) and 723C(7) together the Limited Liability Partnerships (Particulars of Usual Residential Address) (Confidentiality Orders) Regulations 2002, SI 2002/915 (LLP Confidentiality Regulations 2002), regs 2(2)(b) and 9. Where the applicant for the order is already the member of an LLP, he must also notify the LLP of the service address: ibid, reg 6.

[30] LLP Confidentiality Regulations 2002, reg 9(2).

[31] Ibid, reg 9(3).

[32] Ibid, reg 7.

[33] LLP Act 2000, s 9(3B)(b) (inserted into the LLP Act 2000 by the LLP Confidentiality Regulations 2002). Change in a member's usual residential address is discussed in **8.7**. An additional sanction is the possible revocation of the confidentiality order (subject to the notice requirements for doing so referred to in **8.12**): see LLP Confidentiality Regulations 2002, reg 11(1)(c).

[34] Ie in Form LLP 288a referred to in **8.6**: see CA 1985, s 288A(a). The new member must notify the LLP of his service address: LLP Confidentiality Regulations 2002, reg 8. Form LLP 288a has a box to be ticked if the address shown on it is a service address under a confidentiality order.

[35] LLP Act 2002, s 9(3A) (inserted into the LLP Act 2000 by LLP Confidentiality Regulations 2002). The obligation is on the LLP to ensure that the notice is given. There appears to be no sanction on the LLP if this obligation is not met; but if the notice is not given within the 28 day period the Secretary of State may revoke the confidentiality order (subject to the notice requirements for doing so referred to in **8.12**): LLP Confidentiality Regulations 2002, reg 11(1)(b).

[36] CA 1985, s 723C(1)(b) as modified for LLPs by the LLP (No 2) Regulations 2002, SI 2002/913. The annual return is discussed at **4. 26–4.31**.

[37] See the Limited Liability Partnerships (Forms) Regulations 2002, SI 2002/690.

address should be given to the Registrar on Form LLP 723 (SR), although this is not expressly provided for. Notice of any change in the usual residential address of a member with a confidentiality order must be given to the Registrar within 28 days of the change,[38] and is done (it appears) on Form LLP 723 (change).[39] The forms which are sent to the Registrar notifying him of the usual residential address of an individual who has the benefit of a confidentiality order are sent to the Secured Register Unit, and are kept at offices of the DTI separate from Companies House. The 'confidential records' in relation to such an individual (ie the documents filed with the Registrar after the making of the confidentiality order and recording that individual's usual residential address[40]) may be inspected by a number of 'competent authorities'.[41] The manner of such inspection is to be determined by the Registrar.[42] There are 39 'competent authorities' listed in the regulations, and they include the Secretary of State, an inspector appointed under Part XIV of the CA 1985,[43] the Commissioners of HM Customs and Excise, the Commissioners of Inland Revenue, a police force and an overseas regulatory authority within the meaning of CA 1989, s 81. Although there is a broad prohibition on disclosure of the usual residential address of the beneficiary of an order,[44] a competent authority may disclose such information for the purpose of facilitating the carrying out of a 'public function' i.e. broadly, any function conferred by UK or Community legislation, or any similar function conferred by non-UK law, or any function relating to the investigation of any criminal offence.[45]

8.12   A confidentiality order remains in force for 5 years, but the beneficiary of it can apply for a further order.[46] There is no limit on the number of possible renewals. There are detailed provisions as to the making of the application for a confidentiality order.[47] In particular, the Secretary of State may require an application to be supported by a statement by the LLP that the LLP wishes a confidentiality order to be made in respect of the applicant together with a statement of reasons for that wish; and the Secretary of State may also refer to a police force (or to any other person whom he considers may be able to assist) any question relating to an assessment of the nature and extent of any risk of violence or intimidation considered by the applicant as likely, or any question as to the nature and extent of any risk of violence or intimidation likely to be created as a result of the individual's involvement in the activities of the particular LLP or category of LLPs, or as a result of his involvement in a particular sector of commerce or particular type of business activity.[48] If an application for a

---

[38]   LLP Act 2000, s 9(3B)(a).
[39]   See the Limited Liability Partnerships (Forms) Regulations 2002, SI 2002/690. In addition to sanctions in LLP Act 2000, s 9 for non-compliance, a sanction for non-compliance is possible revocation of the order (subject to the notice requirements for doing so): see ibid, reg 11(1)(c).
[40]   This is presumably the intended meaning of 'confidential records' in the LLP Confidentiality Regulations, following that in CA 1985, s 723D(3).
[41]   LLP Confidentiality Regulations 2002, reg 13 and Sch 1.
[42]   Ibid.
[43]   The appointment of inspectors is discussed in **20.1–20.7**.
[44]   LLP Confidentiality Regulations 2002, reg 14.
[45]   Ibid.
[46]   LLP Confidentiality Regulations 2002, reg 10.
[47]   See LLP Confidentiality Regulations 2002, regs 2–5.
[48]   Ibid.

confidentiality order is refused, there is a right of appeal to the High Court (but only with the leave of that court) on the grounds that the refusal was unlawful or irrational or unreasonable or was made on the basis of procedural impropriety or otherwise contravened the rules of natural justice.[49] A confidentiality order can be revoked by the Secretary of State at any time on a number of specified grounds, which are essentially (i) if it transpires that the beneficiary of the order has provided the Secretary of State with false, misleading or inaccurate information[50] or (ii) there is a failure to comply with requirements as to filing details of the beneficiary's service address and usual residential address with the Registrar.[51] Before a confidentiality order is revoked, however, notice must be given to the beneficiary of the order stating the grounds on which it is proposed to revoke the order, and giving the beneficiary a period of 21 days in which to make representations as to why the order should not be revoked.[52] Where an individual is the beneficiary of both a confidentiality order under the LLP Confidentiality Regulations and an order under the equivalent Companies Confidentiality Regulations,[53] and the latter order is revoked under those regulations, any confidentiality order made under the LLP Confidentiality Regulations is automatically also revoked.[54] If a confidentiality order is revoked (or expires and is not renewed) the erstwhile beneficiary of it must notify the LLP.[55]

8.13 The benefit of a confidentiality order extends to particulars contained in the register of disqualification orders made under the CDDA 1986 and maintained by the Secretary of State under CDDA 1986, s 18 (and open to inspection). Where the beneficiary of a confidentiality order is the subject of a disqualification order to the effect that he shall not be a member of an LLP and, as is required,[56] particulars of the order are furnished to the Secretary of State for inclusion in the register, the form on which the particulars are so furnished provides for the beneficiary's service address to be shown rather than his usual residential address.[57]

LIMITED LIABILITY

8.14 As discussed in **3.1**, generally speaking it will be the corporate entity, distinct from the individual members, which carries on the business, and which (to the exclusion of the individual members) bears the duties and liabilities. There is no minimum financial contribution which a member must make to the funds of the

---

[49] See LLP Confidentiality Regulations 2002, regs 2–5.
[50] It is an offence, in an application, knowingly or recklessly to make a false statement in a material particular. Liability is to imprisonment or a fine or both: LLP Confidentiality Regulations 2002, reg. 17.
[51] LLP Confidentiality Regulations 2002, reg. 11.
[52] Ibid.
[53] The Companies (Particulars of Usual Residential Address) (Confidentiality Orders) Regulations 2002, SI 2002/912.
[54] LLP Confidentially Regulations 2002, reg 11(2). There is also automatic revocation the other way if an LLP confidentiality order is revoked: see Companies Confidentiality Regulations 2002, reg 11(2).
[55] LLP Confidentiality Regulations 2002, reg 12.
[56] By the Companies (Disqualification Orders) Regulations 2001, SI 2001/967.
[57] See the Companies (Disqualification Orders) (Amendment No 2) Regulations 2002, SI 2002/1834.

LLP, either as a going concern or in a liquidation. Any contribution is determined by agreement. The funding of an LLP as a going concern is discussed in chapter 13. The liability of an individual member to the outside world for the debts and liabilities of the LLP in the event of winding up is (subject to what is said in **8.15**) limited to the sum (if any) which he has agreed with the other members or with the LLP that he will be liable to contribute, in the circumstances which have arisen, towards what is sufficient for the payment of the LLP's debts and liabilities.[58] This sum may be nominal only (as is commonly the case for members of a company limited by guarantee). It will be specified in the LLP agreement.[59] This limited obligation on a winding-up is, however, without prejudice to any other outstanding contractual obligation on the member to pay sums to the LLP which continues to be enforceable after the commencement of the winding up (for instance, an obligation to contribute capital under the LLP agreement).

8.15　In the event of the LLP being wound up, it and its members will be subject to the regime of the IA 1986 in relation to the winding up of companies.[60] This regime includes the possibility of a member being required under s 212 (misfeasance), s 213 (fraudulent trading) or s 214 (wrongful trading),[61] if any of these sections are applicable to him, to make such a contribution to the assets of the LLP in the winding up as the court thinks fit. The regime also includes a provision[62] under which a member can be required to put back into the LLP any sums[63] which he withdrew from it during the 2 years prior to the winding up if, in brief, at the time of the withdrawal: (i) he knew (or had reasonable grounds for believing) that the LLP was unable to pay its debts or would be unable to pay its debts by reason of his and any other contemplated withdrawals; and (ii) he knew or ought to have concluded that there was no reasonable prospect that the LLP would avoid going into insolvent liquidation.[64]

8.16　It is relevant to mention here also that members of an LLP will be subject to the CDDA 1986 in the same way as company directors. Under this Act, a person may in certain circumstances be disqualified from being a member of, or taking part in the formation or management of, an LLP (or from being a director of, or taking part in the formation or management of, a company).[65]

---

[58]　LLP Act 2000, s 1(4) with IA 1986, s 74. See further, **26.17**.
[59]　The LLP agreement is discussed in chapter 9.
[60]　The IA 1986 being applied (with modifications) to LLPs on the basis that 'company' includes LLP and 'director' or 'officer' includes member.
[61]　These sections are considered in Chapter 29.
[62]　IA 1986, s 214A – Adjustment of withdrawals.
[63]　Ie a share of profits, salary, repayment of a loan (or interest on it) or otherwise: s 214A(2)(a).
[64]　Section 214A is considered in more detail at **29.6–29.10**.
[65]　The CDDA 1986 is considered in chapter 32. Also under the CDDA 1986 (s 15) a member who is an undischarged bankrupt will be (jointly and severally with the LLP) personally liable for the debts of the LLP incurred while he is a member unless he has the leave of the court to be a member.

A MEMBER'S SHARE AND INTERESTS

8.17   The legislation proceeds on the basis that a member of an LLP has a 'share', and 'interests', in the LLP;[66] and it contemplates that the share, or an interest, of a member is (potentially[67]) transferable. There is, however, no definition of a 'share' or 'interest'; nor is there any explicit guidance given as to what a share or interest comprises. Broadly speaking, a member of an LLP will have financial rights and obligations (for instance, a right to share in the profits, and an obligation to contribute capital), and governance rights and obligations (for instance, the right to vote on various LLP business and administrative affairs, and the obligation to comply with certain contractual and statutory duties). Put another way, a member will have an economic interest and a management interest in the LLP. The nature and extent of these rights and interests for any one member may well vary, depending upon the point in time at which, and the context in which, they are being considered. The authors suggest, however, that the 'share' of a member is the totality of the contractual or statutory rights and obligations of that member which attach to his membership; and that an 'interest' of a member is one or more of the components of his share.

8.18   There is no reason why individual members, or groups of members, should not have shares and interests in the LLP, whether economic interests or management interests, which differ from those of other members or groups of members (but subject always to the irreducible statutory obligations and rights which all members have[68]). In this respect, therefore, there can be different classes of members (and different classes of 'shares').

8.19   A consideration of the nature and extent of the share or interests of a member in an LLP is likely to be relevant in the following contexts:

(1)   *while the LLP is a going concern*, in the context of (i) an assignment (or other alienation) by a member of the whole or any part of his share or interests (considered in **8.20**), (ii) an application by a member for a 'buy-out' order under CA 1985, ss 459–461[69] (considered in chapter 27), and (iii) an outgoing member's financial entitlement (considered in chapter 16); and

---

[66]   See the references to a member's 'share' in LLP Act 2000, s 7(1)(d) and CA 1985, ss 432(2)(a) and (4) and 461 (all concerned with the assignment or transfer or purchase of a member's share); and the references to a member's 'interest' or 'interests' in CA 1985, s 736A(7) (referring to a member's interest held by way of security), CA 1985, Sch 4 (balance sheet formats requiring 'Members' other interests' to be shown), IA 1986, s 107 (distribution in a voluntary winding up of the LLP's property), IA 1986, s 111(2) (purchase of a member's interest by the liquidator) and LLP Regulations 2001, reg 7(5) (default rule as to assigning an interest in an LLP). One may note also the references in IA 1986, ss 88 and 127 to a transfer of a member's interest in the property of an LLP, and that LLP Act 2000, s 12(3)(a) is worded as if members have a direct interest in property transferred to the LLP.

[67]   See further **8.20**.

[68]   See generally chapters 11 and 12, and also **8.28–8.29**.

[69]   CA 1985, s 461(2)(d) enables the court to order that the shares of any members in the LLP shall be purchased by other members or by the LLP itself.

(2)   *when the LLP has gone into liquidation*, in the context of (i) the possible
        purchase of a member's interest under IA 1986, s 110 (considered in chapter
        29), and (ii) the distribution of the LLP's surplus assets on dissolution
        (considered in chapter 30).

ALIENATION OF A SHARE OR INTEREST

8.20   As mentioned in **8.17**, the legislation contemplates that the share, or an
interest, of a member in the LLP is potentially transferable. LLP Act 2001, s 7
expressly contemplates (and effectively declares) that a member may assign the
whole or any part of his share in the LLP (absolutely or by way of charge or
security).[70] Section 7 also contemplates that a member's share may be transferred
to non-members by operation of law, specifically to his trustee in bankruptcy or his
personal representatives.[71] Where there is such a voluntary assignment or transfer
by operation of law, s 7(2) provides that the assignee or transferee may not
interfere in the management or administration of any business or affairs of the LLP
(but that this does not affect any right to receive an amount from the LLP).[72]
Effectively, therefore, and subject always to the provisions of the LLP agreement,[73]
the economic interest of a member in the LLP can be assigned or transferred, but
the assignment or transfer will not carry the member's management interest; nor,
perhaps more fundamentally, does it give the assignee a right to be registered as a
member.[74] The management and administration of the LLP's business and affairs
may be carried on (provided that they are carried on bona fide in the interests of the
LLP) without any acknowledgment of, or reference to, the assignee or transferee.[75]

8.21   Although LLP Act 2000, s 7(2) provides that an assignee or transferee of a
member's share (and also a retired member) 'may not interfere' in the management
or administration of the LLP's business and affairs, this is, the authors suggest,
subject to any contrary agreement. The effect of s 7(2) is that, however wide the
assignment or transfer, it cannot of itself carry a right for an assignee or transferee

---

[70]   Note IA 1986, s 127, which provides that in a winding up by the court any transfer by a member of
       the LLP of his interest in the property of the LLP made after the commencement of the winding-up
       is, unless the court orders otherwise, void. The LLP's property is, of course, owned by the LLP and
       not by the members. Query whether s 127 is to be interpreted as rendering an assignment of a
       member's share in the LLP after the commencement of compulsory winding-up void. In relation to
       a voluntary winding-up, see IA 1986, s 88. See further, **26.29**.
[71]   See LLP Act 2000, s 7(1)(a) and (b) and (2)(a) and (b). A share will vest in a member's trustee in
       bankruptcy under IA 1986, s 306. As to a member who becomes bankrupt, see further, **16.11**
       referring to CDDA 1986, ss 11 and 15. The share, or an interest, of a member in the LLP is not
       capable of being the subject matter of a charging order under the Charging Orders Act 1979, as it
       does not fall within the categories of property set out in s 2 of that Act.
[72]   Section 7(2) and (3). 'An amount from' the LLP would clearly cover, for instance, a distribution of
       a profit share.
[73]   See **8.25**.
[74]   Compare the assignee of a share in a company (subject to the provisions of the articles of
       association).
[75]   This may include, for instance, alteration to the remuneration of members and the sums received by
       the assignee or transferee: see *In re Garwood's Trusts* [1903] 1 Ch 236 (a case on the Partnership
       Act 1890, s 31).

to interfere; but this does not preclude the members from agreeing to the assignee or transferee or retiree (or any other third party) taking part in the conduct of the LLP's affairs. Such an agreement may be made generally and in advance of an assignment, or on an ad hoc basis following an assignment.

8.22 In the case of a voluntary assignment, and assuming that the assignor does not cease under the terms of the LLP agreement to be a member on making the assignment (and subject in any event to the effect of any provisions in the LLP agreement), s 7(2) does not prohibit the assignor/member from validly agreeing with the assignee that he (the assignor) will act in relation to governance issues in accordance with the assignee's instructions.[76] If there is such an agreement, however, the assignor will nevertheless continue as a member. He will, therefore, continue to be subject to the statutory duties imposed on members,[77] the non-statutory duties discussed in chapter 11, and the obligations to comply with the standards of probity and competence imposed by the CDDA 1986.[78] It will also be the case that, whilst the assignee will not become a member by reason of the assignment, an agreement with the assignor for the latter to act in accordance with the assignee's instructions could in certain circumstances render the assignee a 'shadow member' and, as a result, subject to liabilities in a winding-up.[79]

8.23 The discussion in **8.20–8.22** needs to be seen in the context of default rule (5) of the LLP agreement[80] which provides that no person may voluntarily assign an interest in an LLP without the consent of all existing members. Like all the default rules, this provision may be altered by agreement. Given, however, the existence of the default rule and the fact that, if there is a provision in the LLP agreement permitting the assignment, that provision will have been expressly considered, the chances of controversy within the LLP in relation to assignments of members' shares or interests will be lessened. The consequence of the restriction in default rule (5) being on any 'person' is that (as a default rule) not only is a member precluded from voluntarily assigning an interest in the LLP without the agreement of all current members, but any assignee from him (whether by way of voluntary assignment or operation of law) is equally precluded. The trustee in bankruptcy of a member, and the personal representative of a deceased member, may both be affected by this.

8.24 If there is provision in the LLP agreement permitting the assignment of a member's share, the agreement is likely also to address the rights which an assignee may have to receive information as to transactions of the LLP and to inspect the LLP's books of account. In the absence of such a provision, it will be a matter of interpretation of the assignor's contractual rights under the LLP agreement, and of the nature and ambit of the assignment, as to what contractual rights the assignee will take the benefit of. This interpretation will need to be

---

[76] CA 1985, s 736A(7) appears to envisage this. And see *Russell v Northern Bank Development Corpt* [1992] 1 WLR 588(HL), considering a shareholders' agreement.

[77] See **11.16–11.17**.

[78] See **14.10** and chapter 32.

[79] See **8.37**.

[80] The default rules generally are considered at **9.6–9. 8**

made against the background that the assignor will be remaining the member. An assignment will not, it is suggested, automatically carry the benefit of the member's statutory right under CA 1985, s 222(1) to inspect the LLP's accounting records.

FIDUCIARIES AS MEMBERS

8.25 Persons who are executors, trustees or other fiduciaries may be members of an LLP.[81] Section 360 of CA 1985, which provides for companies that no notice of any trust, express, implied or constructive, is to be entered on any register, is not applied in any way to LLPs. If trustees or other fiduciaries are members of an LLP, therefore, there is no reason why the LLP agreement should not expressly recognise and address this to any extent that is desirable. The other members (like any persons dealing with trustees) will be potentially subject to equitable remedies at the instance of beneficiaries of the trust for wrongful receipt of trust monies or dishonest assistance in a breach of trust.[82] If the LLP agreement provides for members to contribute funding,[83] or to make contributions towards payment of the LLP's debts and liabilities in a winding-up,[84] it will be a matter of construction of the agreement as to whether, if the trust estate is not sufficient to cover the contribution, the liability of the trustee members for that contribution will be limited to the amount of the trust estate. The trustees will, on the face of it, be personally liable up to the contractual amount.[85]

EMPLOYMENT

8.26 Section 4(4) of the LLP Act 2000 provides that a member of an LLP is not to be regarded for any purpose as employed by the LLP unless, if he and the other members were partners in a partnership, he would be regarded for that purpose as employed by the partnership. The essential purpose of this provision is to prevent the general position being that a member of an LLP is an employee of the corporate body (with all the implications and results of employment status). The general position, therefore, will be that a member is self-employed.[86] The provision clearly does envisage, however, that a member can be an employee of the LLP.[87] As has been mentioned previously, there is no requirement that in order to be a

---

[81] See the discussion at **2.3** to the effect that only a 'person' who or which the law recognises as having its own legal personality will be accepted by the Registrar as a single member of an LLP.

[82] As discussed in *Royal Brunei Airlines v Tan* [1995] 2 AC 378 and *Twinsectra Ltd v Yardley* [2002] 2 AC 164.

[83] On funding, see **13.1–13.7**.

[84] See **8.14**.

[85] See, for instance, *Muir v City of Glasgow Bank* (1879) 4 App Cas 337, where individuals took a transfer of shares 'as trustee disponees'.

[86] And see ICTA 1988, s 118ZA (inserted by LLP Act 2000, s 10) discussed at **21.6–21.18**.

[87] This possibility appears also to be envisaged by the IA 1986, s 214A, referring in sub-s (2)(a) to 'salary'. The fact that the Inland Revenue see all members as liable to Class 2 National Insurance Contributions (see **21.59**) does not, it is submitted, stop a member being an employee if that is his contractual status.

member of an LLP a person must be entitled to a share of the LLP's profits.[88] There can, therefore, be 'salaried' or 'fixed share' members, namely persons who are to the outside world full members, but who do not in fact share in the profits, and who may be employees.

8.27   The wording of s 4(4) – 'unless, if he and the other members were partners in a partnership, he would be regarded for that purpose as employed by the partnership' - is not particularly happy, however, in that a person cannot in fact be both a partner for the purposes of the Partnership Act 1890 and an employee of the partnership.[89] But the general intention of the subsection seems reasonably clear: if the LLP was a partnership, and a person was held out as a partner for the purposes of s 14 of the 1890 Act but was actually an employee of the partnership rather than a partner,[90] the same criteria which determined his status as between employee and partner will apply to determine whether or not he is an employee of the LLP. These criteria are of the most general kind.[91] Important amongst them, but not exclusively determinative, are whether the 'partner' in question is entitled to share in the profits[92] and whether he is obliged to contribute to the losses.[93] The concept of a contribution to the losses of an LLP is not entirely the same as that of a contribution to the losses of a partnership.[94] It is of the essence of an LLP that (save insofar as the LLP agreement provides otherwise) there is no unlimited liability for losses on the part of any members, and that a member (of any description) is only liable to contribute to the assets of the LLP (whether in the event of losses or otherwise) to the extent that he has agreed to do so.[95] The analogy assumed by s 4(4), therefore, between 'salaried partners' and 'salaried members' for determining their respective employment status is not exact. The point may, however, be more theoretical than practical. Ultimately, and as with partnerships, the answer will turn on the particular facts of the particular case.[96]

8.28   There is, however, an important difference between the position of employee partners in an 1890 Act partnership and employee members of an LLP. The former, although appearing as partners to the outside world, are not in fact members of the partnership; and their rights to information, and to participate in the decision-making of the firm, may be severely limited. The latter, although employees, and not profit-sharers, are members of the LLP for the purposes of the LLP legislation. Essentially, therefore, and subject always to any particular provisions in the LLP agreement, the relationship between employee members (as members) and the LLP, and between employee members and the other members, will be the same as the relationship enjoyed by 'full' (ie non-employee) members

---

[88]   See **2.7**.
[89]   See, for example, *Stekel v Ellice* [1973] 1 WLR 191 at 198F and 199H–200A.
[90]   Ie the position of many 'salaried partners'.
[91]   See, for example, Megarry J in *Stekel v Ellice* above at 199G–H: whether or not a 'salaried partner' is a partner in the true sense depends on the substance of the relationship.
[92]   See Partnership Act 1890, s 2(3).
[93]   See, for example, *Briggs v Oates* [1990] ICR 473 at 475C–D.
[94]   See **13.13–13.14**
[95]   Contribution in the event of a winding up is discussed at **26.17** et seq.
[96]   For a general discussion of the factors relevant to identifying whether a contract of employment exists, see, for instance, *Chitty on Contracts* 29th edn, 2004, paras 39-010–39-028.

with the LLP and with the other members. In particular, employee members (as 'members' for the purposes of the legislation) will be subject to the statutory duties and prohibitions set out in **11.17**, and will be liable to penalties if 'in default' and found guilty of an offence in relation to the failure by the LLP to observe its duties set out in **11.18**. Employee members will also have the statutory rights to information, and to enforcing the filing of accounts and other documents with the Registrar, as are set out in **12.2** and **12.3** (save to the extent that such rights can be and are written out in the LLP agreement). Similarly, employee members will (in the absence of agreement to the contrary) have the contractual rights contained in default rules (7) and (8) considered in **12.5** and **12.6**. Certain duties and responsibilities are laid by the CA 1985 on the members as a whole.[97] This will include employee members.

8.29   There may be a desire on the part of the 'full' members to exclude employee members (or, indeed, some other class of members) from being party to carrying out the duties and responsibilities laid on the members as a whole, and from having some vote in relation to them. The question of delegation of such duties to particular members only is considered at **14.13–14.15**. Whilst the authors consider that such duties can in principle be delegated,[98] given the potential liabilities which all members have if the LLP goes into insolvent liquidation referred to in **8.15**,[99] it must be doubtful whether, save in unusual circumstances, it would be fair or proper to exclude employee members (or any other class of members) from taking part in the approval of the annual accounts. There may also be a desire on the part of the 'full' members to exclude employee (or other) members from exercising some or all of the statutory rights given to all members (for instance, to inspect the LLP's accounting records).[100] The issue is the extent to which members intended to be excluded can validly waive these rights. This in turn involves an issue as to the intention and policy of the statutory provisions.[101] The authors suggest that it must be doubtful whether these statutory rights given to members can be validly and effectively waived. The practical answer may be that, in the light of the provisions of the IA 1986 and the CDDA 1986, a well-advised employee (or other) member will be unlikely to agree to be excluded from taking part in approving the accounts or to having his statutory rights excluded.[102]

8.30   In addition to the above, employee members will, of course, have the employer/employee relationship with the LLP arising under their contracts of employment. This will have significance in the event of the LLP going into

---

[97]   See **11.16**.
[98]   Save (as discussed in **14.15**) in relation to their residual responsibility to appoint auditors.
[99]   And note the reference to 'salary' in IA 1986, s 214A(2)(a).
[100]   See **12.2–12.4**.
[101]   See *Equitable Life Assurance Society of the United States v Reed* [1914] AC 587 and *Kammins Ballrooms Co Ltd v Zenith Investments (Torquay) Ltd* [1971] AC 850 at 860 and 877, and generally as to waiver of statutory rights *Halsbury's Laws of England* (Butterworths, 4th edn, 1995), vol 44(1), para 1364.
[102]   As a possible alternative, an employee might require an indemnity; but it must be doubtful whether this would provide satisfactory protection.

insolvent liquidation. In such an event, an employee member will presumably be able to prove in the winding up for any unpaid salary.[103]

8.31 One practical result of employee members being members of the LLP for the purposes of the legislation is that their rights and obligations, as members, will need to be provided for in any LLP agreement, whether to be found in one document or otherwise, governing the mutual rights and duties of the members, and the mutual rights and duties of the LLP and its members, under LLP Act 2000, s 5.[104] It may be, however, that structures will be devised under which the employee members do not see some of the terms of the agreement relating solely to the profit-sharing members: for instance, the 'equity' members of the LLP may be party to one agreement, containing their rights and obligations, and the salaried members may be party to a separate agreement setting out their (probably limited) rights and obligations qua members. Alternatively, the rights and obligations of the employee members could be contained in their respective contracts of employment.

8.32 Default rule (4) provides that no member shall be entitled to remuneration for acting in the business or management of the LLP. This is an adoption of s 24(6) of the Partnership Act 1890 (with the addition of the words 'or management').[105] In the partnership context, it applies only to partners properly so called and not to salaried/employee partners. If there are to be employee members of the LLP, default rule (4) will need to be varied.[106]

LEAVING MEMBERS

8.33 An individual ceases to be a member on his death; and a corporation ceases to be a member on its dissolution.[107] Subject to this, and to the statutory right next mentioned, the duration of a person's membership, and the events upon which he ceases to be a member (either at his choice or at the choice of the other members), will be governed by agreement between the members ie will be governed by the terms of the LLP agreement.[108] The Act does provide, however, that where a person wishes to cease to be a member but there is no governing agreement between the members as to cessation of membership, either generally or covering the particular case, the person wishing to leave may do so by giving 'reasonable notice' to the other members.[109] This right of a member to leave (and what will constitute 'reasonable notice') is considered further in chapter 16.

---

[103] See further, **28.3**.
[104] The LLP agreement is considered in Chapter 9.
[105] Section 24(6) states: 'No partner shall be entitled to remuneration for acting in the partnership business'. Default rule (4) is considered further at **14.2–14.3**.
[106] If an LLP agreement provides for salaried/employee members, it will most probably vary rule (4) by necessary implication anyway.
[107] LLP Act 2000, s 4(3). A corporate member which is in liquidation will, therefore, remain a member until it is dissolved, subject to the LLP agreement providing otherwise.
[108] LLP Act 2000, s 4(3).
[109] Ibid.

8.34   As with a person becoming a member, where a person ceases to be member of the LLP (for whatever reason), notice of his leaving must be given to the Registrar within 14 days of his ceasing to be a member.[110] The giving of the notice is the responsibility of the LLP; but if the notice is not given, both the LLP and every designated member is guilty of an offence.[111] The notice is to be in a form approved by the Registrar, must be signed by a designated member or authenticated in a manner approved by the Registrar.[112] The form to be used is Form LLP 288b (Terminating the Membership of a Member of a Limited Liability Partnership). This provides that the designated member signing on behalf of the LLP cannot be the leaving member himself. The notice is not required to be signed by the leaving member or his representative.

8.35   As is stated in **8.33**, the cessation of membership is governed by the LLP agreement or (in the absence of agreement) by LLP Act 2000, s 4(3). It is not the giving of the notice to the Registrar which effects the cessation of a person's membership (any more than it is the giving of the relevant notice to the Registrar, discussed in **8.6**, which causes a person to become a member), but the working of the contractual or statutory termination provisions.[113] Two results flow from this. First, a false notice will have no effect on actual membership, although it may have effect on the apparent authority of the member in question to bind the LLP.[114] Secondly, after he has ceased to be a member under the contractual or statutory termination provisions, the ceasing member will not be able to operate the procedure of CA 1985, s 713 (referred to in **8.6** and **8.7**) to enforce the giving to the Registrar of notice of his departure.

8.36   A person who has ceased to be a member, like the assignee or transferee of a member's share, may not interfere in the management or administration of any business or affairs of the LLP.[115] This inability to interfere does not affect a leaving member's right to receive his entitlement on leaving the LLP.[116] As in the case of an assignee or transferee, it is probably the case that there is no prohibition on the members agreeing, if they and the leaving member so wish, that a member who has left can interfere.[117]

SHADOW MEMBERS

8.37   The LLP legislation refers in a number of contexts to 'shadow members', following the concept of 'shadow directors' in company law. A 'shadow member' is a person who is not actually a member of the LLP, but in accordance with whose

---

[110]   LLP Act 2000, s 9(1)(a). The approved form of notice requires the date of the member leaving to be specified.

[111]   Ibid, s 9(4)–(6). See footnote 14 above, and further, **10.23–10.24**.

[112]   Ibid, s 9(3).

[113]   See, for the analogous position in relation to companies, *POW Services Ltd v Clare* [1995] 2 BCLC 435 at 440/1.

[114]   See further the discussion in chapter 5.

[115]   LLP Act 2000, s 7

[116]   Ibid, s 7(3)

[117]   See **8.21–8.22**

directions or instructions the members of the LLP are accustomed to act, save that a person is not to be deemed to be a shadow member by reason only of the fact that the members act on advice given by him in a professional capacity. This definition appears in CA 1985, s 741, CDDA 1986, s 22(5) and IA 1986, s 251. Certain provisions of the latter two Acts, relating to disqualification and liability in a liquidation, apply to shadow members as they apply to actual members.[118] Although the definition is contained in the CA 1985, there appear to be no other provisions in that Act as it is modified for LLPs which refer to, or apply in relation to, shadow members.

---

[118] See **29.3–29.5**, **29.33–29.39** and **32.1–32.15**.

Chapter 9

THE LLP AGREEMENT

LLP ACT 2000, SECTION 5(1)

9.1   Section 5(1) of the LLP Act 2000 provides that, except as far as otherwise provided by the Act itself or any other enactment, the mutual rights and duties of the members of an LLP, and the mutual rights and duties of an LLP and its members, shall be governed (a) by agreement between the members, or between the LLP and its members, or (b) in the absence of agreement as to any matter, by any provision made in relation to that matter by regulations made under s 15(c) of the Act, ie by regulations establishing terms to have effect in default of agreement.

9.2   The agreement envisaged by s 5(1) (what we will call 'the LLP agreement') is, in broad terms, the equivalent of the articles of association for a company. It is, however, like a traditional partnership agreement (and unlike articles of association), a private agreement which is not required to be disclosed to the outside world. Indeed, there may be no written agreement at all.[1] And further like a traditional partnership agreement, the LLP agreement can be tailor-made to the requirements of the members in relation to such matters as decision-making and management, the provision of capital, profit-sharing (and what to do if losses are made), retirement and other relevant matters – subject only to what is excepted from free agreement and dictated by statute.[2]

9.3   There is, however, a fundamental difference between an LLP agreement and a traditional partnership agreement, reflecting the fundamental difference between an LLP and a partnership. A traditional partnership agreement is concerned solely with the legal relations (ie the mutual rights and duties) between the individual partners. The LLP agreement (as reflected in s 5(1)) covers not only the relationship between the individual members, but also the relationship between the members and the LLP. It will be essential when drafting an LLP agreement to bear in mind that it will be the LLP which will carry on the business, and own the assets of the business;[3] and to bear in mind also that there will be rights and duties to be considered between the members inter se, and between the members and the corporate entity.

9.4   Section 5(1) states that the LLP agreement (or the provisions having effect in default) will govern the mutual rights and duties mentioned 'except as far as otherwise provided by this Act or any other enactment'. This exception really covers three categories of statutory provision:

---

[1]   See **9.5**.
[2]   As to which, see **9.4**.
[3]   See, generally, chapter 3 discussing the corporate entity.

(i) the duties and responsibilities placed on designated members, both by the LLP Act 2000 itself and by the CA 1985 and the IA 1986 as adopted for LLPs;[4]

(ii) the duties and responsibilities placed on all members, and the rights given to all members, by the CA 1985 and the IA 1986;[5] and

(iii) substantive provisions contained in the LLP Act 2000 itself (for instance, in s 6 as to a member's agency for the LLP and in s 8 as to identifying designated members), and in legislation amended by the LLP Regulations 2001 to apply to LLPs, such as the Sex Discrimination Act 1975 and the Race Relations Act 1976.[6]

9.5   The LLP agreement is a contract, and will be subject to normal contract law in relation both to its existence and to its construction. There is no legal requirement for the agreement to be in writing. All or part of its terms may, therefore, be agreed orally. Consistently with this, there is no statutory right for members to be supplied with a copy of the agreement,[7] or requirement that a copy of the agreement be kept anywhere. In accordance with the normal principles of contract law, terms may be agreed by conduct.[8] There may equally be implied terms,[9] and estoppels may arise. Also, and in accordance with the normal principles of contract law,[10] the terms of the LLP agreement may be expressly or impliedly varied. Where there is a power to vary the agreement conferred on a majority, the power cannot be exercised so as to take away rights already accrued to a non-consenting minority.[11]

THE POSITION IN DEFAULT

9.6   Section 15(c) of the LLP Act 2000, which is referred to in s 5(1) of the Act as the basis for provisions governing the mutual rights and duties of the members and the LLP in the absence of actual agreement as to any matter, provides that regulations may be made applying or incorporating, with such modifications as appear appropriate, any law relating to partnerships. Pursuant to s 15(c), the LLP Regulations 2001[12] contain default provisions whose purpose is expressed to be to determine the mutual rights and duties of the members, and the mutual rights and duties of the LLP and the members, subject to the provisions of the general law and

---

[4]   The duties and responsibilities of designated members are considered in chapter 10.

[5]   As to the duties and responsibilities, see chapter 11: as to the rights, see chapter 12.

[6]   See LLP Regulations 2001, reg 9 and Sch 5. With effect from 1 October 2004, provisions of the Disability Discrimination Act 1995 apply in relation to partners in a traditional partnership and in relation to members of an LLP: see ss 6A–6C of the 1995 Act.

[7]   Unlike the members of a company being entitled to a copy of the memorandum and articles of association under CA 1985, s 19.

[8]   See, for instance, *Chitty on Contracts*, 29th edn, 2004, paras 2-004 and 2-028, and *Ho Tung v Man On Insurance Co Ltd* [1902] AC 232, where particular articles of association of a company were held to have been adopted by a long course of dealing.

[9]   As the LLP Regulations 2001, reg 2 (defining 'limited liability partnership agreement') and reg 8 explicitly recognise.

[10]   Not under s 19 of the Partnership Act 1890: see LLP Act 2000, s 1(5) discussed at **1.17**.

[11]   See *James v Buena Ventura Nitrate Grounds Syndicate* [1896] 1 Ch 456 at 466.

[12]   SI 2001/1090.

to the terms of any actual LLP agreement. The default provisions are, however, very far from being a complete default LLP agreement, and should not be seen as the LLP equivalent of Table A articles of association for a company.

9.7 If no clear LLP agreement is made, and a dispute arises between the members as to any matter which is not covered by the default rules, there may be considerable uncertainty as to the basis for resolving the dispute. The court (or arbitrator) will be casting around to find some agreement by conduct or otherwise between the members which provides an answer. As mentioned in Chapter 1,[13] one cannot simply look to partnership law to provide an answer. The LLP Act 2000 expressly provides that partnership law is not a long-stop.[14] It will undoubtedly be the wise course for there to be a full written LLP agreement, save in the most unusual circumstances.

9.8 The default provisions contained in the LLP Regulations 2001 (what we will refer to as the 'default rules') cover eleven matters.[15] The rules apply, with modifications, some (but not all) of the provisions contained in ss 24–30 of the Partnership Act 1890. The matters covered by the default rules, in outline, are as follows (references to section numbers are to the section in the Partnership Act 1890 being applied):

(1)   sharing in capital and profits (s 24(1));[16]
(2)   indemnity to members (s 24(2));[17]
(3)   right to take part in management (s 24(5));[18]
(4)   no entitlement to remuneration (s 24(6));[19]
(5)   introduction of a new member and voluntary assignment of a member's interest (s 24(7));[20]
(6)   ordinary matters connected with the business to be decided by majority (s 24(8));[21]
(7)   books and records to be available for inspection by any member (s 24(9));[22]
(8)   each member to render true accounts and full information to any member (s 28);[23]

---

[13] See **1.17**.
[14] LLP Act 2000, s 1(5), which provides that 'Accordingly, except as far as otherwise provided by this Act or any other enactment, the law relating to partnerships does not apply to a limited liability partnership'. 'Accordingly' follows from the earlier provisions establishing the body corporate separate from its members. The words 'does not apply to' an LLP are presumably intended to cover the relations between members, and between members and the LLP.
[15] Ten matters are covered by reg 7, and one (expulsion) by reg 8. The default rules contained in reg 7 are displaced by express or implied agreement: the expulsion rule in reg 8 is displaced only by express agreement between the members.
[16] See further, chapter 13.
[17] See further, **12.5**.
[18] See further, **14.2**.
[19] See further, **14.2**.
[20] See further, **8.5** and **8.20**.
[21] See further, **14.6–14.8**.
[22] See further, **12.5**.
[23] See further, **11.30** and **12.6**.

(9)   obligation to account to the LLP for any profits made from a competing business without consent (s 30);[24]

(10)   obligation to account to the LLP for any private benefit derived without consent from use of LLP property (s 29(1));[25] and

(11)   no majority power to expel without express agreement as to such power (s 25).[26]

In addition to these default rules (applying existing partnership law provisions) LLP Act 2000, s 4(3) creates a default rule that a member of an LLP may cease to be a member by giving reasonable notice to the other members.[27]

POINTS FOR THE LLP AGREEMENT

9.9   Partnership agreements provide a useful starting point for LLP agreements, in particular in relation to management and decision-making, retirement (voluntary and compulsory), and the consequences of retirement (eg financial entitlement of the leaver) and restrictive covenants. But the fundamental difference between the two types of agreement mentioned in **9.3** needs to be fully appreciated. The following points are put forward by way of assistance in considering terms which are or may be required for an LLP agreement but which do not, or do not naturally, fall within a traditional partnership agreement. They are not put forward as an exhaustive list of such points.

Accounting obligations

(1)   There are statutory obligations as to the keeping of accounting records, and as to the preparation, auditing and approval (and filing) of annual accounts which comply with the requirements of the CA 1985.[28] The duty of preparing the accounts and approving them is laid on the members.[29] The primary duty of appointing the auditors is laid on the designated members.[30] There is also an obligation for the LLP to preserve accounting records for three years.[31] Consideration needs to be given to provisions being put into the agreement to ensure that the statutory obligations as to accounts and the appointment of auditors are met.

---

[24]   See further, **11.7**.
[25]   See further, **11.7**.
[26]   See further, **16.13**.
[27]   On cessation of membership generally, see **8.33–8.36**.
[28]   See generally, chapter 18.
[29]   See **11.16**. As to the possibility of this duty being delegated, see **14.13–14.15**. The duty of signing the accounts and filing them is laid on the designated members: see **10.10–10.11**.
[30]   See **10.13–10.21** and **19.2–19.8**.
[31]   See **18.3**. Every member has an obligation in this respect. There is also an obligation on members to keep records relating to the LLP's tax position: see **11.18**(iv).

Designated members

(2)   The agreement should deal with the appointment of designated members and the carrying out of their responsibilities.[32] The incorporation document will specify whether all the members are automatically to be designated members, or whether the designated members are to be some named members only.[33] It would be sensible for the LLP agreement also to set out what is agreed in this respect. If the designated members are to be some named members only, consideration needs to be given to a procedure for determining who they will be (and how and when they will cease to be designated members); and to ensuring that there is always a minimum number of two named members. As to the carrying out of the designated members' responsibilities (which the LLP agreement may cast wider than the responsibilities imposed on the designated members by the legislation), consideration should be given to establishing a decision-making procedure for the designated members,[34] and for the signing and filing with the Registrar of the various documents which are to be signed by a designated member and filed.[35]

(3)   The possibility of a designated member's liability to the LLP for a failure to carry out his functions as a designated member being excluded, and the possibility of a designated member having an indemnity from the LLP, are discussed at **10.35–10.36**. Whether or not there is to be such an exclusion and/or indemnity, and if so the extent of it,[36] should be considered.

Funding

(4)   The agreement should deal with capital funding for the LLP, including any provisions for increasing or reducing capital contributions.[37] Is capital contributed by members, or loans made by members to the LLP, to carry interest? Any specific procedure and authority for the LLP to enter into fixed or floating charges over its assets should be covered.[38]

Profits and losses

(5)   The agreement will clearly deal with the members' respective shares in profits made by the LLP. It should also cover the division of those profits amongst the members in accordance with their respective shares (eg crediting shares to individual members' current accounts), and any drawing on account of profits.[39] In the light of the tax transparency of LLPs (and individual members being taxed under the self-assessment rules as if they are partners in a partnership),[40] it may be

---

[32]   See chapter 10.
[33]   See **2.29**.
[34]   See **10.38**. There will be decision-making in relation to the appointment and remuneration, and possibly the removal, of the auditors; and also if the LLP goes into a members' voluntary winding up.
[35]   For instance, the annual return to be filed under CA 1985, s 363 and notices of change of designated members under LLP Act 2000, s 9.
[36]   It may, for instance, be limited so as not to cover fraud or wilful default.
[37]   See **13.1–13.7**.
[38]   Charges are considered in chapter 6
[39]   See **13.8–13.12**.
[40]   See chapter 10.

convenient to provide for the amount of an individual member's tax liability on his share of the profits to be retained by the LLP, and to be paid to the tax authorities on his behalf when due. Provision should also be made for the eventuality of the LLP making a trading loss (eg by providing that a specified membership vote may decide that further contributions of capital are to be made by members to meet any resulting deficiency).[41]

New members

(6)   The circumstances in which a person may become a member should be set out, if the default position (requiring the consent of all existing members to a new member joining) is not desired. It may also be wise to set out a procedure for the requisite notice of a new member joining being given to the Registrar under LLP Act 2000, s 9.[42]

Property

(7)   The LLP is capable of owning property, and may be intended to own the assets of the business. The agreement (or the transfer of assets agreement, in the case of an existing partnership converting into an LLP) will need to make clear which assets are to be vested in and owned by the LLP, and which assets (if any) are to be retained in the ownership of some or all of the individual members and simply made available for use by the LLP.[43]

Exclusion of liability to the LLP, and indemnity

(8)   The members will individually owe a duty of care to the LLP.[44] The possibility of a member's liability under that duty of care being excluded, and the possibility of a member having the benefit of an indemnity from the LLP for personal liability to a third party, are discussed at **12.7–12.9**. Whether or not there is to be such an exclusion and/or indemnity, and if so the extent of it,[45] should be considered. Is the LLP going to fund separate indemnity insurance for individual members?

(9)   Are any exclusions and indemnities offered to current members in relation to breaches of duty of care to be offered also to outgoing members? Are the exclusions and indemnities for outgoing members to be the same as those for current members?

Declaring an interest

(10)   Reference is made in **11.6** to the obligation of a member not to put himself in a position where his duty to the LLP and his own interests may be in conflict

---

[41]   See **13.13–13.14**.

[42]   On new members, see **8.5–8.6**

[43]   If there are to be such assets made available for use by the LLP, the agreement may need to specify, in principle if not in detail, the terms of such availability.

[44]   See **11.12–11.13**.

[45]   It may, for instance, be limited so as not to cover fraud or wilful default. It may also have a financial cap.

(and not to make a profit for himself out of a transaction in which the LLP is involved), and to the resulting duty of disclosure which in practice a member has. It is for consideration whether the LLP agreement should provide that a member may, to some extent or in relation to some transactions (and probably subject to relevant disclosure), profit from a transaction in which he is interested.[46] Equally, it is for consideration whether the agreement should provide a procedure for disclosure,[47] and for subsequent limits on the ability of the interested member to vote where there is a conflict or potential conflict between his declared interest and the interest of the LLP.[48]

Authority

(11)   The LLP agreement will no doubt set out the nature of the business which the LLP is to carry on. The agreement may also be an appropriate place to set out how that business is to be described to the outside world.[49] What limits are to be placed on the authority of individual members to bind the LLP? Are certain members to have specific authorities?[50] In this regard, it may be convenient to set out who are the members who have authority to execute (or authorise the execution of) documents on behalf of the LLP.[51] If the LLP has a seal,[52] the agreement should specify the authority to affix it to any document.[53] Where a traditional partnership is converted into an LLP, it may also be wise to have a provision reminding members that they are carrying on business on behalf of the LLP, and prohibiting them from holding themselves out as being in partnership with their co-members or as having authority to act as agent for any fellow member.

Assignment by a member of his share

(12)   Default rule (5) provides that a member (or any other person) may not voluntarily assign an interest in the LLP without the consent of all the existing members. This rule differs from the default position under the Partnership Act 1890, which permits an assignment by a partner of his share in the partnership (although the effect of such an assignment is limited).[54] The nature of a member's share and interests in the LLP, and the alienation of such a share or interest, are discussed at **8.17–8.24**. It is for consideration whether the default restriction on assignment is to be loosened; and if it is to be loosened, what rights (if any) are to be accorded to an assignee.

---

[46]   See, for instance, in a company context, regs 85–86 in CA 1985, Table A.
[47]   For instance, disclosure to the management committee will suffice as disclosure to the whole membership. Strict adherence to the provision would be required for the disclosure to satisfy it: see *Gwembe Valley Development Co Ltd v Koshy* [2004] 1 BCLC 131.
[48]   See, for instance, in a company context regs 94–96 in CA 1985, Table A.
[49]   See **5.5–5.7**.
[50]   See chapter 5.
[51]   As to execution of documents generally, see **4.7–4.15**.
[52]   See **4.7–4.10**.
[53]   See, for instance, in a company context, reg 101 in CA 1985, Table A.
[54]   Partnership Act 1890, s 31. It is, however, common for partnership deeds to prohibit or restrict assignments.

Duty of good faith?

(13)   The duty of good faith existing between the members of a traditional partnership, and the fact that that duty will not automatically exist (at least, to its full extent) as between the members of an LLP, is discussed at **11.24–11.26**. It is for consideration whether the agreement should provide that the members should act towards each other with that same good faith which is required of traditional partners to each other.

Unfair prejudice

(14)   The legislation adopts for LLPs CA 1985, ss 459–461 (protection of members against unfair prejudice).[55] Section 459(1A) provides that the members may (by unanimous agreement) in writing exclude the right of a member to apply to the court under s 459(1).[56] Consideration should be given as to whether or not to exclude this right. If a full written LLP agreement is adopted, exclusion of this right is likely to be sensible, and the authors' experience is that in professional service LLPs it is routinely excluded.[57]

Employee members

(15)   If there are to be employee members (or 'salaried members'),[58] care will need to be taken that the statutory duties and responsibilities, and rights, which they share with 'full' members are recognised.[59] Default rule (4) will need to be varied.[60] Are the employee members to be liable to contribute in the event of a winding up?[61] A possible point for consideration is whether employee members should be given some indemnity against having to put back into the LLP under IA 1986, s 214A the whole or part of their salary taken over the 2 years prior to an insolvent liquidation.[62] Any such indemnity would have to be given by other members, as opposed to by the LLP itself.

Meetings

(16)   There are no provisions in the legislation, or in the default rules, as to the holding or conduct of meetings of the members of an LLP. Accordingly, the LLP agreement needs to contain provisions as to the convening and conduct of meetings of the membership, including such matters as quorum and proxies. There is a default provision as to voting majorities needed,[63] namely any difference arising as to ordinary matters connected with the business of the LLP may be decided by a

---

55   See chapter 27.
56   See **27.6**.
57   See **27.12**.
58   See **8.26–8.31**.
59   See **8.28–8.29**.
60   See **8.32**.
61   See **9.9**(24).
62   See **8.15** and **8.29**.
63   Default rule (6).

majority of the members.[64] Any non-ordinary matters will (unless the LLP agreement provides otherwise) require unanimity.

Management and decision making

(17)   The default position is that every member may take part in the management of the LLP (and that, as mentioned above, any difference arising as to ordinary matters connected with the business of the LLP may be decided by a majority of the members).[65] Any tailor-made management and decision-making structure which varies this position will need to be considered in the light of the statutory duties and rights which all members have,[66] and the general responsibilities (and potential liabilities in the event of insolvent liquidation) laid on all members by the legislation.[67] It may be convenient to make express provision for ensuring that certain statutory duties placed on *the LLP* are complied with, for instance that the LLP's name and other prescribed particulars appear in all business letters as required by CA 1985, ss 349 and 351,[68] and that the annual return is filed.[69] Other statutory duties placed on the LLP are set out at **11.18**.

Change of name or registered office or business of the LLP

(18)   There are a number of matters which may require change during the course of the LLP's life, but which will not be 'ordinary matters' to be decided by a majority of the members under the default rule. Two of these are a change in the registered office of the LLP and a change in change the name of the LLP.[70] Another such matter is a change in the nature of the business carried on by the LLP. It is for consideration whether some level of majority vote should be sufficient to change the name, or the registered office, or the business carried on by the LLP.

Power of expulsion

(19)   There is no default power of expulsion (or forced retirement) of a member.[71] Default rule (11) (following Partnership Act 1890, s 25) provides that 'no majority … can expel any member' without an express power to that effect agreed to by the members. If such a power is desired, therefore, it needs to be expressly included in the agreement.[72] The authors consider that there is no objection in principle to a power of expulsion being conferred on specified members (constituting a minority of members) if that is what is desired and agreed.

---

[64]   Management and decision making is discussed in chapter 14.
[65]   Default rule (3).
[66]   See **11.16–11.17** (duties) and **12.2–12.4** (rights).
[67]   See further, chapter 14.
[68]   See **4.1–4.4**.
[69]   See **4.26**.
[70]   See **3.17** (change of registered office) and **4.19** (change of name).
[71]   See **16.13**.
[72]   The effect of default rule (11) is that a power of expulsion cannot be implied into an LLP agreement.

Leaving members

(20)   The circumstances in which a person is to cease to be a member should be set out if the uncertainties of a member leaving on 'reasonable notice' (as permitted in default by LLP Act 2000, s 4(3)) are to be avoided.[73] Equally, the financial consequences of a person ceasing to be a member should be set out if considerable uncertainty as to the position is to be avoided.[74] As with a new member joining, it may be wise to set out a procedure for the requisite notice of a member leaving being given to the Registrar under LLP Act 2000, s 9.

Restrictive covenants

(21)   As with a traditional partnership agreement, consideration should be given to the need for any restrictive covenants on a leaving member, and any `garden leave' provisions. It will be the LLP which will be the beneficiary of any restrictive covenants. Some traditional partnership deeds restrict the right of a partner serving out a retirement notice, or on 'garden leave', to have access to the office and to participate in decision-making. As with salaried members, care will need to be taken that the statutory duties and responsibilities, and rights, of members in this position are recognised.

Liquidation, administration and arrangements with creditors

(22)   The legislation gives to the LLP specific powers in relation to going into administration or liquidation, and as to making arrangements with its creditors; but none of the statutory provisions conferring these powers establishes how the LLP is to make the relevant decision. Under the IA 1986 the LLP may (i) make a proposal for a voluntary arrangement;[75] (ii) apply to the court for an administration order;[76] (iii) determine to go into voluntary liquidation[77] (and, if it does go into liquidation, determine that it is to appoint a liquidator);[78] (iv) confer authority on a liquidator in a members' voluntary winding up to receive, as consideration for the transfer of the business or property of the LLP to another company or LLP, interests in the transferee company or LLP;[79] and (v) determine that it present a petition to be wound up by the court.[80] Under CA 1985, s 425 the LLP may effect a scheme of compromise or arrangement with its creditors, or between the LLP and its members.[81] Consideration should be given to whether decisions on such matters are to be unanimous or not, and if not, what the required majorities are to be.

---

[73]   On cessation of membership generally, see **8.33–8.36** and chapter 16.
[74]   Cessation of membership and its consequences are considered in chapter 16.
[75]   IA 1986, s 1(1): see **23.4**.
[76]   Ibid, s 9(1): see **24.3**.
[77]   Ibid, s 84(1): see **26.1**. A provision for going into voluntary liquidation may be used to create, in effect, a fixed term LLP.
[78]   IA 1986, ss 91 and 92: see **26.4** (and see also s 100(2) and **26.7**).
[79]   Ibid, s 110: see **31.6**. An arrangement under s 110 may be seen as the equivalent of dissolution and merger provisions in a traditional partnership agreement.
[80]   IA 1986, s 122(1)(a): see **26.10**.
[81]   See **31.2–31.3**.

(23)   Consideration should be given also to including a provision as to the division or destination of surplus assets in a liquidation.[82]

Liability to contribute in a winding-up

(24)   The legislation provides that the liability of the members to contribute to the assets of the LLP in the event of it being wound up is limited to what (if anything) they have agreed to contribute in these circumstances.[83] The agreement needs to state what the members do agree to contribute. This may be a nominal sum only. Although members are free to agree that they will not contribute anything, if they are, without doubt, to be 'contributories', provision should be made for payment of at least a nominal sum.[84]

Default rules

(25)   The default rules should be considered in order to see in what respects they are not wanted, and need to be varied.

Variation of agreement

(26)   As is mentioned in **1.13**, regulations made under ss 14-17 of the LLP Act 2000 are a fundamental part of the LLP legislation. These regulations (and, indeed, primary statutory provisions) may be altered by statutory instrument made by the Secretary of State and approved by Parliament. In the light of this power of the Secretary of State, and of the fact that LLP law is in its early stages of development (and that, in any event, new issues may arise for the members), consideration should be given to a provision enabling variations to be made to the agreement, at least in some respects, by some form of majority vote of the members or other mechanism.

EXECUTE BEFORE INCORPORATION?

9.10   In many cases where an LLP is being incorporated, it is likely that, by the time the incorporation document is subscribed to, the subscribers will already have agreed the terms of the LLP agreement, and that the actual incorporation will itself be part of the terms agreed, or alternatively will be seen as merely the final formality to be completed. In these circumstances, the 'partners' may wish to sign up to the terms before the incorporation is actually completed. Section 5(2) of the LLP Act 2000 is clearly directed to enabling this. The subsection provides that an agreement before the incorporation of an LLP between the persons who subscribe their names to the incorporation document may impose obligations on the LLP (to take effect at any time after its incorporation).

---

[82]   See **28.2**.
[83]   IA 1986, s 74. This is subject to any contributions which may be required under IA 1986, ss 212–214A: see **8.14**.
[84]   'Contributories' have certain rights under the IA 1986: see, for instance, ss 124(1), 133(2), 136, 139 and 147; and see further **26.17–26.22**.

9.11 It will be noted that s 5(2) refers only to obligations: it does not say that after incorporation the LLP will also have the benefit of the agreement, and will be able itself to enforce obligations stated (expressly or impliedly) in the agreement to be owed by members to it. It is a general principle of contract law that a person cannot acquire rights arising under a contract to which he is not a party.[85] By referring only to obligations on the LLP (and not to obligations owed to the LLP by the contracting persons), s 5(2) is, on the face of it at least, providing for a partial LLP agreement only to be made prior to incorporation. The obligations owed to the LLP contained in the agreement could include such matters as the provision of capital by members, the obligations contained in default rules (9) and (10) as to accounting for profits made from a competing business or for any personal benefit derived from using LLP property, or a leaver's restrictive covenant. The Contracts (Rights of Third Parties) Act 1999 will not, it appears, be available to make obligations owed to the LLP enforceable by it. Section 6(2A) of that Act[86] provides that s 1 of it confers no rights on a third party (ie the LLP here) in the case of any limited liability partnership agreement (or incorporation document).[87] It might be thought that, by reason of the `pure benefit and burden principle',[88] the individual subscribers cannot take the benefit of the agreement without also assuming the burden of obligations owed by them under it to the LLP. Whether or not this is correct (and this 'pure principle' has been heavily doubted by the House of Lords[89]), the problem for the LLP would remain that it is not a party to the agreement.

9.12 Although the absence of a reference in s 5(2) to obligations owed to an LLP should be borne in mind, it may be that this absence will not in practice cause problems. An LLP agreement entered into before incorporation may provide for the subscribers to procure that the LLP becomes an additional party on incorporation. Alternatively, the subscribers may agree that certain rights of theirs under the agreement will be assigned to the LLP on incorporation. Another possible course is for the subscribers to enter into an agreement which schedules the LLP agreement in draft, and which contains an agreement amongst the subscribers to enter into that draft agreement, and to cause the LLP to enter into it, after incorporation. In any event, the members may be able themselves to enforce obligations of co-members owed to the LLP by way of an order for specific

---

[85] See, for example, *Chitty on Contracts* 28th edn, 2004, para 18-021.

[86] Inserted by LLP Regulations 2001, reg 9 and Sch 5, para 20. This insertion equates for the purposes of the 1999 Act an LLP incorporation document and an LLP agreement to a company's articles of association, which (under s 6(1) of the 1999 Act) cannot confer rights on a third party.

[87] Ie agreement between the members of an LLP or between the LLP and the members which determines the mutual rights and duties of the members, and their rights and duties in relation to the LLP (LLP Regulations 2001, reg 2). It might be argued that s 6(2A) of the 1999 Act does not apply to a pre-incorporation agreement made under LLP Act 2000, s 5(2) – so that rights can be conferred by such an agreement on the LLP when incorporated (see s 1(3) of the 1999 Act) – because such an agreement is not an LLP agreement, being made not between `members' but between persons who subscribe their names to the incorporation document. However, when the third party/LLP came to enforce an obligation owed to it in the agreement, the agreement would be an LLP agreement.

[88] As recognised by Megarry J in *Tito v Waddell (No 2)* [1977] Ch 106 at 301 et seq.

[89] *Rhone v Stephens* [1994] 2 AC 310 at 322.

performance[90] or damages,[91] or by way of an injunction.[92] However, if the LLP agreement is to be entered into before the LLP is incorporated, it would be wise for the LLP itself, in all cases, to become a party to the agreement immediately on incorporation.

9.13   Although s 5(2) is an adjunct to s 5(1), it does not, at least expressly, contain any limitation on the nature of the agreement between subscribers to which it is referring, nor on the identity of the persons to whom the LLP may be obligated by the agreement. Any such agreement, and the imposing by it of obligations on the LLP, will be subject to the fiduciary and other duties and responsibilities owed by the members to the LLP,[93] including a duty not to impose an obligation on the LLP for an unlawful or improper purpose. One obligation which may be imposed by a s 5(2) agreement is an obligation for the LLP to pay for or reimburse its (proper) costs of incorporation. If these costs have been paid by, or are outstanding to, a person who is not a party to the agreement, there is nothing in s 5(2) to preclude an obligation being placed on the LLP to pay or reimburse that third party.

9.14   A point of uncertainty which may be felt in relation to s 5(2) is the impact on it of CA 1985, s 36C.[94] The position is that there is probably no impact.[95] An agreement between the subscribers which imposes (the word used in subsection 5(2)) an obligation on the LLP is not a contract which purports to be made by or on behalf of the LLP.[96]

RECTIFICATION

9.15   The articles of association of a company, having statutory operation under CA 1985, s 14, cannot be rectified by the court under its equitable jurisdiction to rectify documents which do not give effect to the actual intention of the parties.[97] An issue may arise as whether there is jurisdiction enabling the court to order rectification of an LLP agreement. In the authors' view, there is. A fundamental reason for there being no jurisdiction in relation to the articles of association of a company is that the articles are a publicly available document, and (whether specifically drafted and filed with the Registrar, or constituted by a complete adoption of Table A) are required to be registered in order for the company to be incorporated.[98] An LLP agreement, on the other hand,[99] is a private agreement, which is not required to be disclosed to the outside world; and it is difficult to equate LLP Act 2000, s 5(1) with CA 1985, s 14. There appears to be no reason in principle why an LLP agreement should not be subject to rectification in the same

---

[90]   See, for example, the discussion in *Chitty on Contracts* above, paras 27-048–27-051.

[91]   As to the provision of capital: see, generally on damages, *Chitty on Contracts* above, para 18-046.

[92]   See *Chitty on Contracts* above, para 18-065.

[93]   See chapter 11.

[94]   Considered at **4.17**

[95]   But see footnote 96 below.

[96]   It would, however, be wise to ensure that the wording of a s 5(2) agreement cannot be construed as bringing the agreement within this description.

[97]   See *Scott v Frank F Scott (London) Ltd* [1940] Ch 794 and *Bratton Seymour Service Ltd v Oxborough* [1992] BCLC 693

[98]   See *Scott v Frank F Scott* above at 802 and *Bratton Seymour* above at 696f-h.

[99]   If indeed there is one beyond the default rules.

way as any other commercial agreement (including a traditional partnership agreement). That said, the difficulties facing a claim for rectification of a multi-lateral agreement (at least a claim not founded on an error in the execution of the document caused by clerical mistake) are obvious.

RESCISSION FOR MISREPRESENTATION

9.16 It is stated in **11.10** that, by reason of the fiduciary relationship between a member and the LLP, if a person who becomes a member of an already-established LLP fails to make disclosure in any material respect, *the LLP* will probably be able to rescind the LLP agreement. It is probably not the case, however, that the other members will have a similar right (there being no general fiduciary relationship between members). It may well be in practice, however, that (depending on the facts) the other members will have a common law right of rescission for misrepresentation.[100] Where, in relation to an incoming member, the failure to make full disclosure is the other way, ie is on the part of the existing members, the incoming member may well (depending on the facts) equally have a common law right to rescind the LLP agreement as between him and the other members. It is, it appears, rescission of the LLP agreement as between the incoming member and the other members (as opposed to rescission of the agreement as between the incomer and the LLP) that will cause the incoming member to cease to be (or, more accurately, to be treated as never having been) a member.[101] Where there is rescission of the LLP agreement for misrepresentation as between one (or more than one) incoming member and the other members, the likely position is that the LLP agreement will not be rescinded as between the other (remaining) members, and that the mutual rights and obligations under the agreement as between those members will remain in place.[102] The common law right to rescind for misrepresentation will be applicable where a member has been induced to become a member by a material misrepresentation by the existing members or where, conversely, the existing members have been induced by a material misrepresentation by a prospective member to take him as a member. A rescission of the LLP agreement will not, of course, dissolve the LLP.

9.17 The common law right to rescind for misrepresentation is subject to a number of qualifications. In particular, it is subject to restitutio in integrum being possible, to the representee not having affirmed the agreement after discovering the misrepresentation, and (in the case of non-fraudulent misrepresentation) to the discretion which the court has under s 2(2) of the Misrepresentation Act 1967 to award damages in lieu of rescission.[103] A further important qualification is that the right to rescind may be barred by the intervention of the rights of third parties. In

---

[100] As to the distinction between a pure non-disclosure and a misrepresentation, see *Chitty on Contracts* 29th edn, 2004, para 6-013.

[101] See LLP Act 2000, s 4, which provides for membership to be a matter of agreement between members.

[102] See *Hurst v Bryk* [2002] 1 AC 185 at 195G–196A (considering repudiation).

[103] As to rescission for misrepresentation generally, see *Chitty on Contracts* 29th edn, paras 6-100–6-130.

relation to an LLP agreement, these third parties may include persons who have become members since the member who made or received the misrepresentation joined, and creditors of the LLP. As to creditors, it is likely that rescission will be barred if the LLP goes into insolvent liquidation, at least if the member who made or received the misrepresentation has contributed capital, or has agreed to contribute in a winding-up.[104] Equally, it is likely that there can no longer be rescission if the LLP, although not yet being wound up, is in fact insolvent.[105]

REMEDIES FOR BREACH

9.18 The LLP agreement is a contract; and, the authors suggest, there is no reason in principle why the usual remedies for breach of contract, including in particular damages and discharge by reason of breach, should not be available to a wronged party. A member may have a claim for breach of the agreement against either the LLP (assuming that it is a party to the agreement in the relevant respect) or against one or more of the other members. The LLP agreement may itself provide remedies (for instance, expulsion) in the case of some breaches; but its remedies may well not cover all breaches, or provide for compensation where financial loss has been caused. As to discharge by breach (or termination by reason of the acceptance of a repudiation of the agreement),[106] the authors suggest that in principle an LLP agreement can be terminated by an acceptance of a repudiation of that agreement. Its effect, however, may be unclear. In any event, such an acceptance will not, of course, dissolve the LLP. Where (as is likely to be the case in an LLP with more than two members) a repudiation gives rise to two camps amongst the members of the LLP, namely the alleged repudiators and the acceptors of the alleged repudiation, the acceptance of the repudiation will probably not operate to discharge the parties in the same camp (whether the camp of the guilty or of the innocent) from their obligations under the LLP agreement to each other.[107] It is relevant to mention in this context that it is now generally considered to be the position that a traditional partnership agreement cannot be automatically terminated (and the partnership dissolved) by the acceptance by one partner or group of partners of a repudiation of the agreement by one or more of the other partners; and that, if termination of the agreement, and dissolution of the partnership, are to be the result of a serious breach of the agreement, then (failing any relevant provision in the agreement itself) an order of the court is required

---

[104] See, for instance, *Tennent v City of Glasgow Bank* (1879) 4 App Cas 615 and *In re Scottish Petroleum Co.* (1883) 23 Ch D 413 (company cases).

[105] See *Tennent v City of Glasgow Bank* above at 622. See also, generally, *West Mercia Safetywear Ltd v Dodd* [1988] BCLC 250 and *Official Receiver v Stern (No 3)* [2002] 1 BCLC 119 as to the interests of creditors becoming paramount when a company is insolvent or of doubtful solvency. The position will be similar for LLPs.

[106] See, generally, on discharge of a contract by breach, *Chitty on Contracts* 29th edn, 2004, chapter 24. Whilst an acceptance of a repudiation leads to the agreement being terminated, this is not the same as a rescission of the agreement (for instance, on the ground of misrepresentation: see **9.16**), where the status quo ante is restored. On a termination resulting from an accepted repudiation the agreement is not rescinded ab initio: what is ended is the primary contractual obligations of the parties which remain unperformed: see *Chitty on Contracts*, para 24-047.

[107] See *Hurst v Bryk* [2002] 1 AC 185 at 195G–196A.

under the Partnership Act 1890, s 35.[108] The reason for this is that partnership is considered to be more than a simple contract. It is a continuing personal as well as commercial relationship; and by entering into that relationship the parties are taken to have submitted themselves to the jurisdiction of the court of equity, and to have renounced their right by unilateral action to bring about the automatic dissolution of their relationship by acceptance of a repudiatory breach of the partnership contract.[109] As has been mentioned in **1.17**, there is no general default application of partnership law to LLPs. The authors suggest that the reasoning which applies to preclude a traditional partnership agreement (and resultant partnership relationship) from being terminated by an accepted repudiation of that agreement does not apply in relation to an LLP agreement.

GOVERNED BY FOREIGN LAW?

9.19   The members of an LLP which, in the day to day conduct of its affairs, is to have only a tenuous link with Great Britain may wish to have the LLP agreement governed by some law other than English law.[110] In the authors' view, this could, at most, only be achieved to a limited extent. The Rome Convention,[111] which provides that as a general rule a contract is to be governed by the law chosen by the parties, does not apply to 'questions governed by the law of companies and other bodies corporate or unincorporate such as the creation, by registration or otherwise, legal capacity, internal organisation or winding up of companies and other bodies corporate or unincorporate and the personal liability of officers and members as such for the obligations of the company or body'.[112] It is clear that an LLP is an 'other body corporate'. The LLP agreement default rules (introduced by legislation), and any provisions agreed by the parties in the place of the default rules, are probably part of 'the law of companies and other bodies corporate'. In any event, 'internal organisation' will include such matters as the appointment of new members, voting rights of members and the division and allocation of profits. It will include also the fiduciary obligations owed by a member to the LLP.[113] It is difficult to see any matters of significance for an LLP agreement which fall outside this exception from the general rule in the convention. The result of (in broad terms) the Rome Convention not covering an LLP agreement is that the proper law of the agreement (ie the law governing the interpretation and validity, mode of performance and consequence of breaches) will fall to be determined by common law rules. These rules provide for the proper law of a contract to be the law chosen (expressly or impliedly) by the parties for this purpose, or in the absence of any such discernible choice, for the proper law to be that system of law with which,

---

[108]   *Hurst v Bryk* above at 193-196 (Lord Millett) and *Mullins v Laughton* [2003] Ch 250 at paras 86-93
[109]   See *Hurst v Bryk* above at 194D–196B–D.
[110]   'Foreign connections' generally are discussed in chapter 17.
[111]   Given the force of law in the United Kingdom (with limited exceptions) by the Contracts (Applicable Law) Act 1990.
[112]   Article 1.2(e). For a fuller discussion of this exception from the general rule, see *Dicey & Morris on The Conflict of Laws* 13th edn, 2000, para 30-025.
[113]   *Base Metal Trading Ltd v Shamurin* [2004] EWCA (Civ) 1316 at paras 56 and 65.

viewed objectively, the contract has the closest and most real connection.[114] This right of choice, however, is subject to certain rather ill-defined limitations, in particular that the choice must be 'bona fide and legal', and that the application of the foreign law will not be contrary to public policy.[115]

9.20 An LLP is a creature of United Kingdom legislation; and certain obligations on the part of the membership, and (probably) certain rights of members, are under that legislation fundamental conditions of the LLP's existence.[116] It seems clear that an English court would not recognise the provisions of an LLP agreement which purported to render nugatory any of these statutory obligations or rights.[117] It is probably correct to say that any provision which would be null and void on the basis that the proper law of the agreement is English law would be held to be null and void even though purporting to be governed by a foreign law.[118] But, subject to these limitations, consideration could be given, if this is desired, to certain specific issues of membership covered by the LLP agreement being governed by a foreign law, with the agreement generally being governed otherwise by English law.[119] The issue of jurisdiction over LLPs is considered at **17.2–17.3**.

---

[114] See, for instance, *Amin Rasheed Shipping Corpt v Kuwait Insurance Co* [1984] AC 50 at 60/1, and generally *Dicey & Morris* above paras 32-003–32-007.

[115] *Vita Food Products Inc v Unus Shipping Co Ltd* [1939] AC 277 (PC) at 290.

[116] For instance, obligations to have a minimum two designated members, and to prepare and file with the Registrar each year annual accounts; and the right of every member to inspect the accounting records of the LLP (on which, see **12.2**).

[117] See, for instance, *Walker v London Tramways Co* [1879] 12 Ch D 705, holding that a company's articles cannot deprive the company of the statutory right to alter the articles under what is now CA 1985, s 9.

[118] See, for instance, *The Hollandia* [1983] AC 565 at 576C–E. And in relation to any wish to exclude fiduciary obligations owed by a member to the LLP, see *Base Metal Trading Ltd v Shamurin* above (a company case), at pars 69–75.

[119] See *Dicey & Morris* above paras 32-046–32-049.

Chapter 10

DESIGNATED MEMBERS

INTRODUCTION

10.1 Unless the membership of an LLP falls to being one person only, at all times at least two of its members must be 'designated members'.[1] The two options which an LLP has for identifying who the designated members are to be have been discussed earlier.[2] As has also been discussed earlier,[3] a company or corporation, as well as an individual, can be a member of an LLP; and there is no requirement that a member of an LLP must be resident in Great Britain. All the members can, therefore, be foreign individuals, or foreign corporations, or some combination of these. There is no distinction in this respect between ordinary members and designated members.[4]

10.2 Whilst the LLP Act 2000 establishes (in s 8) the office or role of designated member, and requires there to be two such members, it does not attempt any overall description or definition of the functions and responsibilities of a designated member. These functions and responsibilities are to be found principally in a combination of the LLP Act 2000 itself, the CA 1985 and the IA 1986. It is difficult to detect a clear distinguishing thread running through all of the the designated members' functions and responsibilities, but they are concerned principally with requirements of the legislation as to disclosure and notification to the Registrar. The designated members may also come to be seen in other, general, legislation as convenient and identifiable representatives of the LLP for the purpose of fulfilling particular roles or functions.[5]

10.3 The scheme of this chapter is, first, to discuss the appointment and retirement of members as designated members; secondly, to set out the duties,

---

[1] This follows from LLP Act 2000, ss 2(1)(a) and 8(2).

[2] At **2.29**. The two options are, in brief, (i) specify named members or (ii) state that every member is automatically a designated member.

[3] At **2.2**.

[4] When the Bill was going through Parliament, the Government recognised this. On Second Reading in the House of Commons, Dr Kim Howells, Parliamentary Under-Secretary for Trade and Industry, said that the Government did not believe that they needed to prevent an offshore member being a designated member: if there was a breach of obligation by the designated members, the LLP itself could be pursued: *Hansard*, HC, 23 May 2000, col 915.

[5] There are two examples of this. The Criminal Justice Act 1967, s 9 is amended by the LLP Regulations 2001 to provide that any written statement made under that section may be served on an LLP by being delivered or sent to any designated member of the LLP; and a designated member of an LLP is specified as the person to whom an initial request for consultation is to be addressed by an enforcer in relation to enforcement proceedings against the LLP under Part 8 of the Enterprise Act 2002 (relating to the enforcement of certain consumer legislation): see the Enterprise Act 2002 (Part 8 Request for Consultation) Order 2003, SI 2003/1375, para 6(c).

powers and responsibilities of the designated members; and, thirdly, to consider the relationship between the designated members and the LLP, and to address some additional matters concerning designated members.

APPOINTMENT AND RETIREMENT OF DESIGNATED MEMBERS

Option (i): specifying named members

10.4   Where the option is chosen (either on incorporation or by a later change) of specifying named members to be the designated members (as opposed to stating that every member is automatically a designated member),[6] the members may at any time after incorporation agree amongst themselves changes in the identity of the designated members, and that a member not currently a designated member should become one or that a member who is currently a designated member should cease to be one.[7] There may, for instance, be provision in the LLP agreement as to the members of the LLP who are for the time being to be the designated members. If at any time, as the result of agreement amongst the members, or deaths or retirements, there is only one designated member, then every member of the LLP automatically becomes a designated member.[8]

10.5   Notice of any change in the designated members (ie of any person becoming or ceasing to be a designated member) must be given to the Registrar within 14 days of the change.[9] The obligation of ensuring that such notice is given is an obligation of the LLP.[10] The notice must be in a form approved by the Registrar and signed by a designated member (or authenticated in a manner approved by the Registrar).[11] Where it is notice of a person becoming a designated member, it must contain a statement signed by that person (or authenticated in a manner approved by the Registrar) that he consents to becoming a designated member.[12] The approved form of notice is Form LLP 288c (Change of Particulars of a Member of a Limited Liability Partnership). Although notice of a change in the designated members is required to be given to the Registrar, the change takes effect by reason of the agreement between the members, and is not dependent on notice being given within the 14-day period.[13] However, there are criminal sanctions if notice of a change in the designated members is not given to the Registrar within 14 days of the change.[14] In addition to individual notices of change as to the designated

---

[6]   See the discussion as to these options in **2.29** and **2.30**. There can be a switch between these options at any time after incorporation: ibid.

[7]   LLP Act 2000, s 8(1).

[8]   Ibid, s 8(2): '...if there would otherwise be no designated members, or only one, every member is a designated member'.

[9]   Ibid, s 9(1)(a). The particulars to be contained in the notice are the same as for a person becoming an ordinary member: CA 1985, s 288, discussed at **8.6**.

[10]   Ibid, s 9(1). But there are possible penalties on the designated members for breach: see further, **10.24**.

[11]   Ibid, s 9(3).

[12]   Ibid.

[13]   See ibid, s 8(1): 'in accordance with an agreement'.

[14]   See **10.24**.

members, the annual return which the LLP is obliged to deliver to the Registrar must state which of the members are designated members.[15]

Option (ii): all members automatically designated members

10.6 Where the option is chosen of all members automatically being designated members, the relevant notification to the Registrar is that of a person becoming or ceasing to be a member: no separate notice is required as to changes in *designated* members.[16]

Ceasing to be a member

10.7 Whichever option as to nominating designated members is chosen, when a person ceases to be a member of the LLP for any reason, he also automatically ceases to be a designated member.[17]

DUTIES, POWERS AND RESPONSIBILITIES OF THE DESIGNATED MEMBERS

10.8 The duties, powers and responsibilities of the designated members fall under a number of topics; and it will be convenient to consider them in this way. They can, however, be seen as broadly divided into two categories: first, those duties and powers which are given directly to the designated members by the legislation; and secondly, those responsibilities for compliance with the legislation which the designated members carry, in that it is such members who are or may be guilty of an offence if a requirement of the legislation is not complied with.

10.9 Under a number of statutory provisions, designated members who are 'in default' are guilty of an offence.[18] A designated member will be 'in default' if he has knowingly and wilfully authorised or permitted the default or contravention mentioned in the relevant statutory provision.[19] 'Knowingly' means with knowledge of the facts which constitute the default or contravention: it does not require knowledge that there is a breach or contravention of the relevant statutory requirement.[20] 'Wilfully' means that the act is done deliberately and intentionally, not by accident or inadvertence.[21]

---

[15] CA 1985, s 363. The annual return is discussed at **4.26–4.31**.

[16] LLP Act 2000, s 9(1) and (2), discussed further in **8.6** and **8.34**.

[17] Ibid, s 8(6).

[18] See **10.19, 10.20, 10.21, 10.28** and **10.31**.

[19] CA 1985, s 730(5). Note that the reference to the CA 1985 includes a reference to the LLP Act 2000: LLP Regulations 2001, reg 4(1)(b).

[20] See *Burton v Bevan* [1908] 2 Ch 240 at 247. Knowledge will almost certainly include 'blind-eye knowledge' ie knowledge which exists when a person deliberately refrains from inquiring further lest his firmly grounded suspicions of wrongdoing be confirmed: see, for instance, *Manifest Shipping Co Ltd v Uni-Polaris Co Ltd* [2003] 1 AC 469 at paras 112–116 and *White v White* [2001] 1 WLR 481 (HL) at paras 14–16.

[21] See *R v Senior* [1899] 1 QB 283 at 290–291, and also *De Maroussem v Commissioner of Income Tax* (2004) *The Times*, September 13 (PC), considering 'wilful neglect'.

Annual accounts and audit

Signing and filing the accounts

10.10   As discussed more fully in Chapter 18, annual accounts (ie a balance sheet and profit and loss account) for every LLP must, together with the auditors' report, be filed with the Registrar (subject to certain exemptions). The duty of preparing the accounts in compliance with the requirements of the CA 1985 lies with the members as a whole.[22] And it is to the members as a whole that the auditors make their report on the accounts.[23] The accounts are, however, to be signed by a designated member (on behalf of all the members);[24] and the copy of the balance sheet which is delivered to the Registrar is to be signed by a designated member.[25]

10.11   The duty of filing the annual accounts (together with a copy of the auditors' report) with the Registrar within the required period [26] is a duty laid directly on the designated members.[27] If the accounts and auditors' report are not filed with the Registrar within the required period every person who, immediately before the end of the relevant period, was a designated member is guilty of an offence.[28] It is a defence for a designated member charged with this offence to prove that he took all reasonable steps for securing that the accounts and auditors' report would be delivered to the Registrar within the required period.[29] It is not a defence, however, to show that the accounts and report were not in fact prepared as required by the Act.[30] As to the ability of any member or creditor of the LLP, or the Registrar, to apply to the court for an order against the designated members requiring them to file the accounts and auditors' report, see **18.20**.

10.12   Other functions of the designated members in relation to accounts include (a) claiming for the LLP a 3-month extension of the period allowed for filing the LLP's accounts where the LLP carries on business, or has interests, outside the United Kingdom, the Channel Islands and the Isle of Man,[31] and (b) the duty,

---

[22]   CA 1985, s 226.

[23]   Ibid, s 235(1).

[24]   Ibid, s 233(1). The signature is on the balance sheet. Every copy of the balance sheet which is circulated, published or issued is to state the name of the designated member who signed: CA 1985, s 233(2) and (3).

[25]   Ibid, s 233(4).

[26]   As to which, see **18.19**.

[27]   CA 1985, s 242(1).

[28]   Ibid, s 242(2). The liability is to a fine and, for continued contravention, to a daily default fine. Someone becoming a designated member after an accounting year has ended but before the accounts and auditors' report for that year are delivered to the Registrar is therefore assuming responsibility for those accounts being delivered. In addition to the designated members being guilty of an offence, the LLP itself is liable to a civil penalty under CA 1985, s 242A: see further, **18.21**.

[29]   CA 1985, s 242(4).

[30]   Ibid, s 242(5).

[31]   Ibid, s 244(3). See further, **18.19**. Section 244(3) may be repealed with effect from 1 January 2005 as respects LLPs' financial years which begin on or after 1 January 2005 by Regulations made in late 2004 after this book goes to print: see draft Companies Act 1985 (International Accounting Standards and Other Accounting Amendments) Regulations 2004 laid before Parliament in October 2004. The authors understand that it is intended that the amendments to be made to the CA 1985 by

where the LLP has as a subsidiary undertaking a body corporate incorporated outside Great Britain which does not have an established place of business in Great Britain, and whose activities are so different from those of the LLP that it is not included in consolidated accounts, and its individual accounts are appended to the LLP's accounts, to annex a copy of those accounts translated into English if they are not in English.[32]

Appointment, removal and remuneration of auditors

10.13   Control of the appointment (and removal) of the auditors, and their remuneration, is primarily in the hands of the designated members.

10.14   Where the LLP has a duty to appoint auditors (which it will have unless it is exempted from audit requirements as a small or dormant LLP[33]), it is the designated members who are to carry out this duty and appoint auditors within the specified time limits for each financial year.[34] If the designated members fail to make the appointment for any financial year, the membership as a whole may do so in a meeting convened for that purpose.[35]

10.15   Where a casual vacancy occurs in the office of auditor, the designated members may make an appointment filling it.[36]

10.16   The remuneration of the auditors is to be fixed by the designated members unless the membership as a whole determines some other manner of fixing the auditors' remuneration.[37]

10.17   Provided that the requisite procedure is gone through, the designated members can at any time remove the auditors from office (without prejudice to any claim which the auditors may have against the LLP as a result of such removal).[38]

10.18   If the auditors resign of their own accord by depositing notice in writing to that effect at the registered office of the LLP,[39] and they accompany the notice

---

these Regulations should apply to LLPs at the same time as to companies, but with modifications to be introduced by a further statutory instrument.

[32]   CA 1985, s 243(4). Section 243 may be repealed or modified with effect from 1 January 2005 as respects LLPs' financial years which begin on or after 1 January 2005 by Regulations made in late 2004 after this book goes to print: see the draft Regulations referred to in footnote 31 above.

[33]   CA 1985, s 384(1), discussed in **18.38–18.41**.

[34]   Ibid, ss 385(2) and 388A(3) (where an LLP ceases to be exempt from the obligation to appoint auditors).

[35]   Ibid, ss 385(4) and 388A(5). If in respect of any financial year auditors are not appointed within the specified time limits: (i) the Secretary of State may appoint auditors to fill the vacancy; (ii) the LLP must within a week of the end of the relevant period notify the Secretary of State that his power has become exercisable; and (iii) if the LLP fails to give this notice, both it and every designated member in default is guilty of an offence and liable to a fine and, for continued contravention, to a daily default fine: CA 1985, s 387 (discussed at **19.4**).

[36]   CA 1985, s 388(1).

[37]   Ibid, s 390A(1).

[38]   Ibid, ss 391 and 391A. Notice must be given to the Registrar: see further, **10.20**. As to the requisite procedure, see **19.14** and **19.15**.

[39]   Ibid, s 392(1).

by a signed requisition calling on the designated members to convene a meeting of
the whole membership of the LLP for the purpose of considering a statement by
them of the circumstances of their resignation,[40] the designated members must
within 21 days from the deposit of the requisition convene a meeting of all the
members for a day not more than 28 days after the date on which the notice
convening the meeting is given; and if this is not done every designated member
who has failed to take reasonable steps to secure that a meeting was convened in
accordance with these requirements is guilty of an offence and liable to a fine.[41]

10.19   Where the designated members propose to remove, or not to re-appoint,
the auditors, the LLP is obliged to send to each member a copy of any
representations which the auditors may make and request to be notified to the
members.[42] If a copy of any such representation is not sent out as so required, any
designated member in default (and the LLP itself) commits an offence.[43]

10.20   Where the designated members have made a determination to remove the
auditors, they must, within 14 days of that decision, give notice of it to the
Registrar.[44] If such notice is not given, every designated member who is in default
is guilty of an offence.[45]

10.21   Where the auditors resign of their own accord (by depositing a notice in
writing to that effect at the registered office of the LLP, accompanied by a
statement under CA 1985, s 394), the LLP must send a copy of the auditors' notice
of resignation to the Registrar within 14 days of the auditors depositing it with the
LLP.[46] If a copy of the notice is not sent to the Registrar as required, every
designated member who is in default (and the LLP itself) is guilty of an offence.[47]

Annual return

10.22   As discussed at **4.26–4.31**, the LLP must file an annual return each year
with the Registrar. The annual return must be signed by a designated member.[48] If
there is a failure to file the annual return, in addition to the LLP itself every

---

[40]   CA 1985, s 392A(2).
[41]   Ibid, s 392A(5). If an auditor ceasing to hold office deposits a statement under CA 1985,
s 394, the obligation to circulate the statement (or the right to apply to the court) is that of the LLP,
and penalty for default is on the LLP and on every member in default: see further, **19.19**.
[42]   Ibid, s 391A(4).
[43]   Ibid, s 391A(5). The liability is, on summary conviction, to a fine.
[44]   Ibid, s 391(2).
[45]   Ibid. The liability is to a fine and, for continued contravention, to a daily default fine. It is not clear
whether the LLP itself is also guilty of an offence if the notice is not given to the Registrar: contrast
the obligation put on the designated members (only) in the first para of s 391(2) and the reference to
the LLP failing to give the notice referred to in the second para of the subsection.
[46]   Ibid, s 392(3).
[47]   Ibid. The liability is to a fine and, for continued contravention, a daily default fine.
[48]   Ibid, s 363(2)(c).

designated member is guilty of an offence unless he shows that he took all reasonable steps to avoid the failure to deliver the return.[49]

Notices to the Registrar

10.23   The LLP Act 2000 provides for various notices to be given by the LLP to the Registrar. They are all to be signed by a designated member (or authenticated in a manner approved by the Registrar):

(a)   a notice of any change in the membership of the LLP, or change in the identity of the designated members, or change in the name or address of any member, as required by LLP Act 2000, s 9(1);[50]

(b)   a notice by the LLP exercising its right to change from specifying named members as designated members to all members automatically being designated members, or vice versa;[51] and

(c)   notices by the LLP exercising its right (or acting on a direction of the Secretary of State) to change its name,[52] or (where its registered office is in fact situated in Wales) to state that its registered office[53] is to be situated in Wales (as opposed to in England and Wales).[54]

10.24   Responsibility for compliance by the LLP with its duty to give notice of any change mentioned in **10.23** is carried by the designated members. If the LLP fails to give notice within the specified periods,[55] every designated member (and the LLP itself) commits an offence: but it is a defence for a designated member to prove that he took all reasonable steps for securing that the necessary notice was given.[56]

Other duties, powers and responsibilities

Statement of release of charge

10.25   Where property of an LLP is released from a charge on payment of the debt, instead of notice being given to the Registrar by a statutory declaration under CA 1985, s 403,[57] notice may be given to the Registrar by a statement by a

---

[49]   CA 1985, s 363(4). The liability is to a fine. Responsibility for any failure by the LLP to file annual returns is a matter to be taken into account on an application for disqualification under the CDDA 1986: see CDDA 1986, s 9 and Sch 1, para 4(f).

[50]   LLP Act 2000, s 9(3)(b). The obligation of the LLP is expressed as one to ensure that the relevant notice is given to the Registrar. As to such changes, see **8.6**, **8.7** and **8.34**.

[51]   Ibid, s 8(5)(b).

[52]   Under ibid, Sch, paras 4 and 5, discussed at **4.19–4.25**.

[53]   Under ibid, Sch, para 10, discussed at **3.12–3.18**.

[54]   Under ibid, Sch, para 9, discussed in **2.23**.

[55]   Ie 14 days for change in members or designated members, and 28 days for change in the name or address of a member.

[56]   LLP Act 2000, s 9(4) and (5). There is liability to a fine on summary conviction not exceeding level 5 on the standard scale: s 9(6). As to 'the standard scale', see **1.18**.

[57]   See **6.15**.

designated member in electronic form verifying the payment and release and giving certain other information as to the charge and the chargee.[58]

Application to strike off the register

10.26   If the LLP has not traded or otherwise carried on business for the previous three months (and certain other conditions are satisfied), any two or more of the designated members can apply to the Registrar for the LLP's name to be struck off the register (resulting in the dissolution of the LLP and its property vesting in the Crown as *bona vacantia*).[59]

Voluntary arrangement

10.27   Where an LLP makes a proposal for a voluntary arrangement under Part I of the IA 1986,[60] and the nominee is not the liquidator or administrator of the LLP, it is the designated members of the LLP who are to submit to the nominee a document setting out the terms of the proposed voluntary arrangement and a statement of the LLP's affairs.[61] It is also the designated members who may apply to the court for the nominee to be replaced by another insolvency practitioner if the nominee fails to submit his report to the court within the prescribed period.[62]

Winding up

10.28   If the LLP determines to go into a voluntary winding up, a copy of the determination must be sent to the Registrar within 15 days of it being made. If this is not done, every designated member who is in default (and the LLP itself) is guilty of an offence.[63]

10.29   A statutory declaration of solvency made for the purposes of the LLP going into a members' voluntary winding up is to be made by the designated members (or, if there are more than two, the majority of them) at a meeting of the designated members.[64]

10.30   If the LLP goes into a creditors' voluntary winding up, it is the designated members who are to make the statement as to its affairs (verified by affidavit by

---

[58]   CA 1985, s 403(1A). A designated member making a statement which he knows to be false or does not believe to be true is liable to imprisonment or a fine, or both: s 403(2A).

[59]   Ibid, s 652A. Where designated members make such an application, they are under a duty to ensure that a copy of the application is given to all the members of the LLP, and also all employees and creditors; CA 1985, s 652C. Striking an LLP off the register is more fully discussed in chapter 20.

[60]   And the proposal is not made by the administrator or liquidator.

[61]   IA 1986, s 2(3).

[62]   Ibid, s 2(4).

[63]   Ibid, s 84(4). The liability is to a fine.

[64]   Ibid, s 89(1). A designated member making a declaration without having reasonable grounds for the opinion that the LLP will be able to pay its debts in full, with interest at the official rate, within the period specified is liable to imprisonment or a fine, or both: s 89(4).

some or all of them); and one of the designated members is to attend the meeting of creditors and preside at it.[65]

Change of name

10.31 The LLP must change its name (by sending a notice of change to the Registrar) if directed by the Secretary of State to do so on one of the grounds set out in LLP Act 2000, Schedule, paras 4(2)–(4).[66] If the LLP fails to comply with a direction of the Secretary of State, any designated member in default (and the LLP itself) commits an offence.[67]

Enforcement of duty to file with the Registrar

10.32 Reference has been made elsewhere to the right of any member or creditor of the LLP, or the Registrar, to serve a notice on the designated members requiring them to make good a default by them in complying with their obligation to deliver to the Registrar a copy of the LLP's annual accounts and auditors' report.[68] Section 713 of the CA 1985 provides that where *the LLP* is in default in complying with any requirement of the LLP Act 2000 or the CA 1985 as to delivering a document to the Registrar[69] or giving notice to him of any matter,[70] any member or creditor of the LLP, or the Registrar, may serve a notice on the LLP requiring the default to be made good.[71] If, after receiving such a notice, the LLP fails to make good the default within 14 days of the notice being served on it, an application can be made to the court (by any member or creditor, or the Registrar) for an order directing the LLP and any designated member of it to make good the default within such time as the order specifies.[72] The order may provide that all the costs of and incidental to the application are to be borne by the LLP or by any designated member responsible for the default.[73] Such an order could clearly, therefore, in at least some circumstances, be directed against designated members. Finally, any order made by the court under this provision is without prejudice to the possible imposition of penalties on the LLP or on designated members provided for in respect of any default.[74]

10.33 It is worth noting that, although under CA 1985, s 713 an order can be directed against the designated members (as opposed to members who are not designated members), the requirements as to delivering a document to the Registrar

---

[65] IA 1986, s 99(1) and (2). In the event of default, see IA 1986, s 166(5).
[66] Discussed in **4.20**.
[67] LLP Act 2000, Sch, para 4(8). The liability on summary conviction is to a fine not exceeding level 3 on the standard scale: Sch, para 4(9). As to the standard scale, see **1.18**.
[68] See **18.20**.
[69] See **10.21**, **10.22**, **10.23**, **10.28** and **10.33**.
[70] See **10.23**.
[71] Although not explicitly stated in the section, it is reasonably to be assumed that any of the possible applicants to the court under the section can also serve a notice under it.
[72] CA 1985, s 713(1). Whilst having the right to serve a notice and apply to the court under this section, the Registrar is probably not under any obligation to do so: see *Re Normandie House (Kensington) Ltd* (1967) 111 SJ 131 (the Companies Act 1948 did not impose a positive legal obligation on the Registrar to take any action against a defaulting company).
[73] CA 1985, s 713(2).
[74] Ibid, s 713(3).

or giving notice to him which can be enforced under the section are not confined to those requirements laid directly on the designated members or for which they carry responsibility. One such requirement is that contained in CA 1985, s 400 to deliver to the Registrar a copy of a charge over property which has been acquired by the LLP already charged.[75]

DESIGNATED MEMBERS AND THE LLP

10.34   The designated members of an LLP are members of the LLP, with all the normal duties and responsibilities (statutory and otherwise) of a member towards the LLP.[76] By reason of them being designated members, they have additional duties and responsibilities, and powers. All these functions must be carried out consistently with the core fiduciary obligation owed by every member to the LLP of single-minded loyalty, and in the promotion of the best interests of the LLP. Equally, the authors suggest, the designated members will (unless excluded by agreement) owe a duty to the LLP to use reasonable care and skill, and diligence, in carrying out their functions as designated members.

10.35   The possibility of the LLP agreement containing an exclusion of liability of a member to the LLP for a breach of his duty of care is discussed in **12.7–12.9** (where it is concluded that there can be such an exclusion). There is no reason in principle why liability on the part of a designated member to the LLP for breach of his duty of care in carrying out his functions as a designated member should not also be covered by an exclusion clause.

10.36   A provision in the LLP agreement excluding liability on the part of a designated member to the LLP will not, however, serve to exclude a designated member from criminal sanctions which may be imposed on him where a responsibility has not been met. As has been seen from the foregoing paragraphs, there are a considerable number of absolute obligations (either laid upon the designated members directly or upon the LLP) in respect of which the designated members are potentially liable to criminal sanctions (mostly fines) if the obligations are not met. The extent to which the LLP agreement may validly and effectively provide for a designated member to be indemnified against a fine imposed on him is not clear. As a matter of general law, there is scope for a valid and effective indemnity against a criminal sanction where the offence is one of strict liability and the breach was wholly innocent.[77] It may be, therefore, that the LLP agreement can provide for a designated member to be indemnified against a fine which has not resulted in any way from his own wilful default or negligence. In practice, however, it is unlikely that a fine would be imposed in such circumstances, given the requirement in many cases that the designated member must be 'in default' before he commits an offence, and given also the availability in other cases of a defence of having taken all reasonable steps. The LLP probably

---

[75]   See **6.12**. The obligation is on the LLP.
[76]   See, generally, chapter 11.
[77]   See *Chitty on Contracts* 29th edn, 2004, para 16-168.

can, in any event, agree to indemnify a designated member against his costs of successfully defending himself when charged with an offence.[78]

10.37 The practical impact of the approach of the legislation to responsibility is that (as obviously intended) the designated members have a definite incentive to ensure that the various obligations are fulfilled. Where the business of the LLP is sizeable, and there is a large number of members, it must be for consideration whether it would not be sensible (and fair to the designated members if not all the members are automatically designated members) for the LLP agreement to contain, or to provide for the creation of, procedures aimed at ensuring that the obligations as to notification and disclosure to the Registrar are fulfilled. Consideration might also be given to the inclusion in the LLP agreement of powers for the delegation of the responsibilities for particular duties to particular designated members.

10.38 A number of the duties and powers of the designated members require decisions to be made by them as a body.[79] There is no reason in principle why the LLP agreement should not provide for decision-making by the designated members to be by majority vote, with a necessary quorum and chairman's casting vote and such like. In default of such a provision in the LLP agreement, decision-making by the delegated members is likely to have to be unanimous.

COMPANY DIRECTORS DISQUALIFICATION ACT 1986

10.39 The application of the CDDA 1986 to LLPs is discussed in chapter 32. It is, however, worth noting the provisions of s 3 of that Act here. Section 3 provides that the court may make a disqualification order against a person where it appears to the court that that person has been persistently in default in relation to provisions of the legislation[80] requiring any return, account or other document to be filed with, delivered or sent, or notice of any matter to be given, to the Registrar. This will cover defaults in delivering the LLP's annual accounts and the annual return to the Registrar,[81] and in giving notice to the Registrar of removal of the auditors or notice of their resignation.[82] It will also cover default in giving notice to the Registrar of changes in members or designated members, or their addresses, as required by the LLP Act 2000, s 9.[83]

---

[78] See CA 1985, s 310(2)(b)(i) (applying only to companies), which permits this indemnity for company officers.

[79] See, for example, **10.13–10.17** (relating to the auditors) and **10.27** (replacement of nominee). This is not true of all designated members' powers: see **10.25** and **10.26**.

[80] The reference in CDDA 1986, s 3(1) to 'the companies legislation' includes references to the LLP Act 2000: LLP Regulations 2001, reg 4(2)(b).

[81] See **10.11** and **10.22**.

[82] See **10.20** and **10.21**.

[83] See **10.24**.

Chapter 11

THE DUTIES AND RESPONSIBILITIES OF MEMBERS

INTRODUCTION

11.1 This chapter is concerned with the duties owed by members to the LLP and to other members, including what may be called the public duties and responsibilities of members.

11.2 Most LLPs will have a written LLP agreement (or the default rules will apply so far as not varied or excluded),[1] and this will be an important source of duties and responsibilities of members. But it will not be the only source. A member will be in a fiduciary relationship with the LLP. This relationship arises out of a member's position as an agent of the LLP, and his consequential power to affect the legal relations of the LLP with third parties.[2] The fiduciary obligations which will usually arise out of this relationship are discussed in the following paragraphs; but it should be borne in mind that the precise nature and scope of a member's obligations will depend on the particular circumstances of the relationship between the member and the LLP.[3] The discussion at **11.6–11.9** is based on the assumption that each of the members of the LLP will be actively working in the business of the LLP. In addition to obligations arising out of the position of members as agents of the LLP, and as part of the price for the members being able to carry on their business with limited liability through the LLP, the CA 1985 places on the members in any event a number of duties and responsibilities relating to the LLP.

11.3 It will be seen, therefore, that the duties and responsibilities of a member are to be found in a combination of what is contained in the LLP agreement (or the default rules), what is inherent in the relationship of principal and agent existing between the LLP and its members, and in the duties and responsibilities placed on members by the CA 1985. Although it is convenient for discussion purposes to make a division between the duties owed by a member to the LLP and the duties owed by him to his co-members, there may well be particular circumstances where a duty is owed by the member both to the LLP and to his co-members.

---

[1]   The LLP agreement generally is discussed in chapter 9

[2]   An agent has long been recognised as owing fiduciary obligations to his principal: see generally *Bowstead & Reynolds on Agency* 17th edn, 2001, paras 1-001, 1-014 and 6-032–6-038. And see Lord Browne-Wilkinson in *White v Jones* [1995] 2 AC 207 at 271E–G referring to an agent coming under fiduciary duties by reason of assuming responsibility for the affairs of the principal.

[3]   See *NZ Netherlands Society 'Oranje' Inc v Kuys* [1973] 1 WLR 1126 (PC). As to the LLP agreement possibly excluding these obligations, see **11.8**.

A MEMBER'S NON-STATUTORY DUTIES TO THE LLP

11.4   A member's non-statutory duties to the LLP arise essentially out of his role and activities in carrying on the business of the LLP, ie out of his role as a worker in the business and agent for the LLP. This role may, very broadly, be equated to that of a director of a company, who is an agent for his company and owes it various fiduciary and other duties.[4]

Duty to account

11.5   An agent is under a general duty to pass over to his principal (or pay as the principal directs) any money which he receives on behalf of the principal, and to render any appropriate account to the principal.[5] The member of an LLP will clearly be under a duty to pay over to the LLP at some point any money (or perhaps net money after expenses) which he receives on behalf of the LLP (for instance, where he receives payment from a customer of the LLP for work done). Whether the duty is, in a particular case, a fiduciary duty (with the member being a trustee of any money which he receives on behalf of the LLP) will depend on what trust obligations, or (to the contrary) independent rights, he has over the money.[6]

Fiduciary obligations

11.6   As mentioned in **11.2**, the member will be in a fiduciary relationship with the LLP, and owe fiduciary obligations to it. The core obligation of a fiduciary is that of single-minded loyalty to his principal.[7] The member of an LLP must act in the LLP's interest in preference to his own. This core obligation will be represented by several separate duties or restrictions, which as a general rule will include the following (but these are not offered as an exhaustive list).[8]

(a)   The member must at all times act in good faith towards the LLP in the relationship between the LLP and him.[9] This essentially means that when acting on the LLP's behalf he must act honestly and in what he believes to

---

[4]   See **3.3** and footnote 6 at p 34.

[5]   See *Bowstead & Reynolds* above paras 6-097 and 6-098.

[6]   See *Paragon Finance v D B Thakerar & Co* [1999] 1 All ER 400 (CA) at 415–6 and *Coulthard v Disco Mix Club Ltd* [2000] 1 WLR 707.

[7]   See generally the judgment of Millett LJ in *Bristol and West Building Society v Mothew* [1998] Ch 1 at 16–22 and the approval of his dictum as to fiduciary obligations by the Privy Council in *Arklow Investments Ltd v Maclean* [2000] 1 WLR 594. The Privy Council said (at 598G–H) that the concept of loyalty 'encaptures a situation where one person is in a relationship with another which gives rise to a legitimate expectation, which equity will recognise, that the fiduciary will not utilise his or her position in such a way which is adverse to the interests of the principal'. See also *University of Nottingham v Fishel* [2000] ICR 1462 at 1490C–D: the obligation of loyalty is a duty to act in the interests of another.

[8]   See **11.2** and footnote 3 at p 133. Equity is flexible in adjusting obligations to make them fit what it sees as the requirements of the particular situation: see, for instance, *Medforth v Blake* [2000] Ch 86 (CA) at 102D. And see also Lord Upjohn in *Boardman v Phipps* [1967] 2 AC 46 at 123: 'Rules of equity have to be applied to such a great diversity of circumstances that they can be stated only in the most general terms and applied with particular attention to the exact circumstances of each case.' And see **11.8** as to the ability to vary these duties or restrictions by agreement.

[9]   See, for example, *Bowstead & Reynolds* above, para 6-063.

be the best interests of the LLP, and not for some ulterior purpose or separate interest (for instance, his own).[10] This duty includes doing one's best to promote the business of the LLP,[11] and making full and fair disclosure to the LLP of all material facts.

(b) The member must not misapply money or property of the LLP. He has the duties of a trustee in relation to the LLP's money and property: his power to deal with the LLP's money and property must be exercised for the purposes, and in the interests, of the LLP.[12] As part of this duty, the member must not apply LLP money for an illegal purpose[13] or for a purpose which is unlawful for the particular LLP (as, for instance, being in breach of trust obligations which it owes to others in relation to the moneys).[14]

(c) The member must not put himself in a position where his duty to the LLP and his own interests are in conflict, or may be in conflict (in the sense that there is a real sensible possibility of such a conflict).[15] The classic example (but certainly not the only example) of a breach of this duty would be where a member has a personal financial interest in a contract of sale to, or purchase from, the LLP ('self-dealing'). The member can, generally speaking, avoid being in breach of this duty if he makes a full and frank disclosure of his interest to the LLP, and the LLP – fully informed of the real state of things by him – gives its consent to the position.[16] This duty leads in practice to a duty to disclose to the LLP any interest which a member has in a contract or proposed contract between the LLP and a third party.[17] In the absence of any provision in the LLP agreement governing declarations of a member's interests, the disclosure will need to be made to a general meeting of the members. Provided that a member has made such

---

[10] As to these being the key elements in good faith, see *Medforth v Blake* above at 103B–E.

[11] See, for instance, *Scottish Co-operative Wholesale Society Ltd v Meyer* [1959] AC 324 at 366/7 and *Guinness Plc v Saunders* [1990] 2 AC 663 at 691A–B.

[12] See *Re Lands Allottment Co* [1894] 1 Ch 616 (CA) at 631 and 638, and *JJ Harrison (Properties) Ltd v Harrison* [2002] 1 BCLC 162 (CA) on company directors. The liability for wrongful application or dissipation (and obligation to replace the moneys) will be the same as that of a trustee.

[13] See Lord Parker of Waddington in *Bowman v Secular Society Ltd* [1917] AC 406 at 439, referring to directors who apply company funds for an illegal object being guilty of misfeasance and liable to replace the money. And see also *Re Loquitur Ltd* [2003] 2 BCLC 442 at paras 133–7 (concerned with company directors paying an unlawful dividend).

[14] See *Bishopsgate Investment Management Ltd v Maxwell (No 2)* [1994] 1 All ER 261 (CA) esp 265j.

[15] See *Parker v McKenna* (1874) 10 Ch App 96 at 118 and *Boardman v Phipps* above at 123D–124D; and also *Regal (Hastings) Ltd v Gulliver* in 1942 reported [1967] 2 AC 134 at 137F–138G. A recent example of a breach of this duty is *Longstaff v Birtles* [2002] 1 WLR 470 (CA) (see esp para 35).

[16] See *Dunne v English* (1874) 18 Eq 524, *Boulting v Association of Cinematograph, Television and Allied Technicians* [1963] 2 QB 606 (CA) at 636 and *NZ Netherlands Society 'Oranje' v Kuys* above at 1131H–1132A. As to the degree of acquiescence required to amount to consent precluding action being taken against the self-dealing member, see *Knight v Frost* [1999] 1 BCLC 364 at 374.

[17] CA 1985, s 317 expressly places on company directors a duty to disclose an interest in a contract to a meeting of directors, in that a failure to disclose leads to the criminal sanction of a fine. Section 317 is not adopted for LLPs; but this does not mean that the fiduciary duty to avoid a conflict of interest (leading to a civil claim and remedy if breached) does not exist for members of an LLP. A civil claim against a director arises not from s 317 but from breach of fiduciary duty: see *Cowan de Groot Properties Ltd v Eagle Trust Plc* [1992] 4 All ER 700 at 762.

disclosure, and if the terms of the LLP agreement do not preclude him from doing so,[18] it is suggested that the member will be able to exercise any voting rights which he has in relation to the transaction, at least if such voting is at a general meeting of the members.[19]

(d)   The duty of disclosure may well also include a duty on a member to disclose any material breach by him of his fiduciary duties to the LLP (and a duty to disclose any material breach by another member, of which he is aware, of that other member's fiduciary's duties to the LLP).[20]

(e)   The member must, in addition, disclose to the LLP all information which he obtains which is of legitimate interest to the LLP in the conduct of its business.[21] It does not matter that the LLP will not be able to turn the information to account for itself.[22]

(f)   The member must not (without the fully informed consent of the LLP) compete in business with the LLP. This is an application of the wider duty to act in the manner best calculated to promote the interests of the LLP.[23] This duty will include a prohibition on soliciting the clients or customers of the LLP for a competitor business which the member will be starting or joining after he has ceased to be a member.[24]

(g)   The member must not misuse his position as a member of the LLP for his own advantage – by, for example, using the property of the LLP, or any opportunity or knowledge which he obtains as a member, for his own private benefit without the LLP being fully aware of the circumstances, and consenting.[25] This is an application of that aspect of duty (c) that a fiduciary

---

[18]   In a company context, for instance, see reg 94 in CA 1985, Table A.

[19]   See *North-West Transportation Co v Beatty* (1887) 12 App Cas 589 and *Burland v Earle* [1902] AC 83 at 94 ('Unless otherwise provided by the regulations of the company, a shareholder is not debarred from voting or using his voting power to carry a resolution by the circumstance of his having a particular interest in the subject-matter of the vote': Lord Davey). The member will, however, have to exercise his voting rights in good faith in accordance with duty (a) above and as discussed in **11.24–11.25**.

[20]   See *Item Software (UK) Ltd v Fassihi* [2004] EWCA Civ 1244 and *British Midland Tool Ltd v Midland International Tooling Ltd* [2003] 2 BCLC 523.

[21]   See, for example, *Industrial Development Consultants Ltd v Cooley* [1972] 1 WLR 443 at 453A–B, and also *University of Nottingham v Fishel* [2000] ICR 1462 (an employee case). The duty includes disclosing not only positive news (eg a business opportunity), but also negative news (eg that a determined effort is being made by a competitor to take the LLP's customers or employees): see *British Midland Tool Ltd v Midland International Tooling Ltd* above esp at para 90.

[22]   *Industrial Developments Ltd v Cooley* above at 449A–C

[23]   See, for example, *Regal (Hastings) Ltd v Gulliver* above at 138F–G and *Industrial Developments v Cooley* above at 452E–F. This is similar to the implied duty of good faith owed by an employee, and applied in *Hivac Ltd v Park Royal Scientific Instruments Ltd* [1946] Ch 169 and *Sanders v Perry* [1967] 1 WLR 753. The proposition as to not competing in duty (f) is a sound working rule, but like all these duties falls to be applied to the specific facts of the case in issue. For an illustration of this, see *In Plus Group Ltd v Pyke* [2002] 2 BCLC 201 (CA), where the competing director had been effectively excluded from the claimant company.

[24]   Ibid. For an example of this principle applied to a director, see *Balston Ltd v Headline Filters Ltd (No 2)* [1990] FSR 385 and also *British Midland Tool Ltd v Midland International Tooling Ltd* above, esp at para 89. For a recent consideration of these principles in a partnership context, see *Kao Lee & Yip v Koo* [2003] WTLR 1283 (HK).

[25]   See *Don King Productions Inc v Warren* [2000] Ch 291 (CA) (a partnership case) at 340H–341F. An example of misuse of position is *Industrial Development Consultants Ltd v Cooley* above, where the managing director of a company received valuable information as to possible contracts,

must not obtain a secret profit for himself out of his fiduciary position, however honourably or legitimately he may consider he is acting.[26] The position in partnership law may not be quite so severe, in that it appears that a partner may be able to use information which he has obtained as a partner if it cannot reasonably be considered to be of any commercial interest to the partnership as it is outside the scope of the partnership business.[27] It would be unwise, however, for a member of an LLP to proceed otherwise than on the strict basis set out above.

11.7 The authors suggest that the fiduciary obligations set out above will exist unless they are expressly (and properly[28]) excluded by the LLP agreement or it is clear from a consideration of all the circumstances that particular duties are inapplicable.[29] Not all of these duties, however, are reflected in the default rules. The duty at **11.6**(f) above is reflected in default rule (9).[30] This provides as follows:

'If a member, without the consent of the limited liability partnership, carries on any business of the same nature as and competing with the limited liability partnership, he must account for and pay over to the limited liability partnership all profits made by him in that business.'

And the duty at **11.6**(g) is reflected in default rule (10), which provides as follows:

'Every member must account to the limited liability partnership for any benefit derived by him without the consent of the limited liability partnership from any transaction concerning the limited liability partnership, or from any use by him of the property of the limited liability partnership, name or business connection.'

Both these rules are taken from the Partnership Act 1890: rule (9) is s 30 of the 1890 Act, modified; and rule (10) is s 29(1) of the 1890 Act, modified. There is no reflection in the default rules of the duties owed to the LLP at **11.6**(a)–(e). This does not mean, however, in the authors' view, that these fiduciary duties are not owed by the members to the LLP. These duties would normally flow from a principal/agent relationship, and be owed by the agent to his principal. The default rules are not, in the authors' view, intended to exclude these duties from the

---

and dishonestly obtained release from his position with the company in order to obtain the contracts for himself. He was held liable to account to the company for his profits from the contract. For more recent examples, see *CMS Dolphin Ltd v Simonet* [2001] 2 BCLC 704 (Lawrence Collins J, whose judgment, at paras 98–105, also discusses the position where the director exploits the opportunity through a new corporate vehicle or partnership) and *Bhullar v Bhullar* [2003] 2 BCLC 241 (CA). Another example would be accepting a bribe, namely an incentive to act in breach of the duty of single-minded loyalty to the LLP: see *A-G for Hong Kong v Reid* [1994] 1 AC 324.

[26] See, for instance, *Regal (Hastings) Ltd v Gulliver* above at 144G–145A and 153B–F, and *Gwembe Valley Development Co Ltd v Koshy* [2003] EWCA Civ 1478, [2004] 1 BCLC 131, at paras 44–5 and 144–5.

[27] See *Aas v Benham* [1891] 2 Ch 245, approved by Lord Hodson (in a partnership context) in *Boardman v Phipps* above at 107E–110E.

[28] See the discussion in **11.8**.

[29] See NZ *Netherlands Society 'Oranje' Inc v Kuys* above.

[30] Ie para (9) of reg 7 of the LLP Regulations 2001.

principal/agent relationship expressly stated to exist between an LLP and every member of it.[31]

11.8 It is perhaps unlikely, at least in the case of a professional services LLP, that there would be any wish by the members to exclude to any significant extent the obligations set out in **11.6**, or that mentioned in **11.5**. But if there were such a wish, careful thought would need to be given to any such exclusion and the propriety of it. Generally speaking, it is the case that a fiduciary relationship, and obligations arising out of it, are dependent on the terms of any contract existing between the principal and the fiduciary, and must accommodate themselves to the terms of that contract.[32] Equally, the members acting together (unanimously, in the absence of any clear provision to the contrary in the LLP agreement, and honestly) can authorise or ratify a breach of any of these obligations.[33] But against this must be set the considerations that the members will probably be under a de facto continuing obligation[34] to carry on the LLP's business with a view to profit, and that they must not act so as to put in jeopardy the solvency of the LLP or cause loss to its creditors.[35] In the result, the scope for the members to allow circumvention of the obligations set out in **11.5–11.6**, if otherwise desired, should not be seen as unlimited.

11.9 The remedies of a wronged principal for the breach of a fiduciary obligation which results in the fiduciary obtaining a benefit, or the principal suffering loss, are principally restitution ie payment over to the principal of the wrongfully obtained benefit[36] or equitable compensation.[37] These are the principal remedies which the LLP would have against a member who has in breach of his fiduciary obligation to

---

[31]   See LLP Act 2000, s 6(1). And see the reference in LLP Regulations 2001, reg 7 to 'the provisions of the general law'.

[32]   See *Kelly v Cooper* [1993] AC 205 (PC), especially at 213H–214B and 215A–D, and *Henderson v Merrett Syndicates Ltd* [1995] 2 AC 145 at 206B–D.

[33]   See, for instance, *Multinational Gas and Petrochemical Co v Multinational Gas and Petrochemical Services Ltd* [1983] Ch 258 (CA), considering the right of shareholders of a company to ratify the acts of directors and *Bowthorpe Holdings Ltd v Hills* [2003] 1 BCLC 226 at paras 48–50. Where the LLP agreement permits the authorising or ratifying of a breach by majority vote of the members (as opposed to unanimity) it is likely that any breach of duty involving dishonesty on the relevant individual member's part cannot be authorised or ratified by a majority only ie the majority cannot force an actual fraud on the minority: see *Mason v Harris* (1879) 11 Ch D 97. Equally, a majority could not authorise or ratify what would amount to a 'fraud on the minority' as discussed at **12.11**.

[34]   See **3.25–3.27**.

[35]   Where an LLP is insolvent, or of doubtful solvency, the interests of the creditors will become paramount: see *West Mercia Safetywear Ltd v Dodd* [1988] BCLC 250 (CA) and *Official Receiver v Stern (No 3)* [2002] 1 BCLC 119 (CA) esp at paras 32 and 51.

[36]   'Equity … insists that it is unconscionable for a fiduciary to obtain and retain a benefit in breach of duty': Lord Templeman in *A-G for Hong Kong v Reid* above at 331B–C. And see the references to *Don King Productions Inc v Warren* and to *Regal (Hastings) Ltd v Gulliver* in footnotes 25 and 26 above. There may also be a right for the wronged principal to trace into property representing the principal's moneys or assets wrongfully obtained: see, for instance, *Clark v Cutland* [2004] 1 WLR 783.

[37]   Ie compensation to make good the loss in fact suffered by the principal and which, using hindsight and common sense, can be seen to have been caused by the breach: see *Target Holdings Ltd v Redferns* [1996] AC 421 and *Swindle v Harrison* [1997] 4 All ER 705 (CA) esp at 731h–735d.

the LLP obtained a benefit for himself or caused a loss to the LLP.[38] Where the member has a personal (but not fully disclosed) interest in a transaction with the LLP in breach of duty (c) at **11.6**, the transaction may in addition be voidable at the option of the LLP, provided that the transaction is avoided within a reasonable time of the non-disclosure being discovered and that equity can do what is practically just to restore the position to what it was before the transaction took place.[39]

11.10 It is probably (although not certainly) the position that a prospective member is under a duty – prior to becoming a member, but in the light of the fiduciary relationship which he and the LLP are intending to enter into – to make full disclosure to the LLP (ie in practice, to the other members on behalf of the LLP) of matters which are clearly material to his proposed status as a member and agent of the LLP.[40] Assuming that this is the position, if the member has failed to make such disclosure, the LLP will probably have the right to rescind the LLP agreement between it and that member, provided that such right is exercised within a reasonable time of the non-disclosure being discovered and that the position existing before the individual became a member can be practically restored.[41] A rescission of the agreement by the LLP, however, is unlikely of itself to rescind the LLP agreement as between the non-disclosing member and *the other members*; and the effect of a rescission by the LLP alone is likely to be unclear. As is discussed in **9.16**, the right of the other members to rescind the LLP agreement as between themselves and the non-disclosing member (if it exists) will probably be a common law right to rescind for misrepresentation. Where, in relation to an incoming member, the failure to make full disclosure is on the part of the LLP (acting by its existing members) and/or the existing members, the incoming member will probably have similar rights of rescission of the LLP agreement as the LLP and/or the other members would have where it is the incomer who fails to disclose. A rescission of the LLP agreement will not, of course, in any circumstances, dissolve the LLP. Whether or not, upon a rescission, the incoming member ceases to be a member will, it appears, depend upon whether or not the LLP agreement is rescinded as between him and the other members.[42]

---

[38] If the LLP goes into liquidation, there could also be a claim against the delinquent member under IA 1986, s 212.

[39] See, for instance, *Armstrong v Jackson* [1917] 2 KB 822; *Hely-Hutchinson v Brayhead Ltd* [1968] 1 QB 549 (CA) at 585C–E, 589F–590C and 594F-G; *Bristol and West Building Society v Mothew* [1998] Ch 1 at 18C–E; and *Guinness Plc v Saunders* [1990] 2 AC 663 at 697G–698B. For a fuller discussion of remedies in relation to benefits acquired in breach of fiduciary duties, see Goff & Jones, *The Law of Restitution* 6th edn, 2002, chapter 33. As to the application of the Limitation Act 1980 in relation to claims for breach of fiduciary duty against a member, see *Gwembe Valley Development Co Ltd v Koshy* [2003] EWCA Civ 1478.

[40] See *Bell v Lever Bros Ltd* [1932] AC 161 at 227 (Lord Atkin referring to certain fiduciary relationships) and *United Dominions Corporation Ltd v Brian Proprietary Ltd* (1985) 157 CLR 1 (concerned with obligations between parties prospectively in a fiduciary relationship), also discussed at **11.22**. Compare the duty of disclosure between prospective partners contained in clause 10 of the draft Partnerships Bill 2003 presented to Parliament by the Law Commission in November 2003 (Law Com No 283).

[41] See, for instance, *Hely-Hutchinson v Brayhead Ltd* and *Guinness Plc v Saunders* referred to in footnote 39 above, concerned with non-disclosure of an interest by an existing fiduciary.

[42] See LLP Act 2000, s 4, which provides for membership to be a matter of agreement between members.

Other (non-statutory) duties and responsibilities of a member

11.11   Although a member is in a fiduciary relationship with the LLP, this does not mean that all the duties which he owes to the LLP are fiduciary duties.[43] In addition to the fiduciary duties discussed in **11.6**, a member will (again, subject to the terms of the LLP agreement) owe certain other duties to the LLP, arising in equity or in tort or out of the express or implied terms of the LLP agreement.

Duty of care

11.12   The principal duty will be a duty of care, arising in equity or in tort, owed by a member to the LLP in carrying out his functions on behalf of the LLP.[44] There will probably also be an implied term (if there is not an express term) in the LLP agreement to the same effect. The extent of the duty (and whether or not there has been a breach of it by the member) will in all circumstances be affected by the terms of the LLP agreement and the particular circumstances. It is not easy to state what, in general terms, will be the standard of care owed by a member to the LLP, nor to state the degree of negligence which will lead to liability on the member's part to the LLP. The standard of care owed at common law by a director to a company is now said to be that stated in s 214(4) of the 1A 1986, namely that a director must display the conduct of 'a reasonably diligent person having both – (a) the general knowledge, skill and experience that may reasonably be expected of a person carrying out the same functions as are carried out by the director in relation to the company, and (b) the general knowledge, skill and experience that that director has'.[45] With the substitution of 'member' and 'limited liability partnership' for 'director' and 'company', s 214 is adopted for LLPs. This is an objective standard of reasonable care. The common law duty of care owed by an agent to his principal[46] can be stated in the following terms: 'Every agent acting for reward is bound to exercise such skill, care and diligence in the performance of his undertaking as is usual or necessary in or for the ordinary or proper conduct of the profession or business in which he is employed, or is reasonably necessary of the proper performance of the duties undertaken by him'.[47] This again is an objective standard of reasonable care.

11.13   In the context of partnerships, and in particular professional partnerships, there is still uncertainty as to what level of failure of care in the conduct of the partnership business will lead (in addition to partnership liability to a third party) to

---

[43]   For a discussion of the ambit of fiduciary duties, and the distinction between these duties and other duties which may be owed by a person in a fiduciary position, see the judgment of Millett LJ in *Bristol and West Building Society v Mothew* above at 16–17.

[44]   Whether the duty in any situation is seen as arising in equity out of the member's fiduciary relationship with the LLP or in tort (as to which, see generally Lord Browne-Wilkinson in *Henderson v Merrett Syndicates Ltd* [1995] 2 AC 145 at 205F–H, and in *White v Jones* [1995] 2 AC 207 at 271C–272B), the measure of compensation or damages (as also the limitation period) will be the same in equity as in tort: see as to damages Millett LJ in *Mothew* above at 17H and as to limitation *Companhia de Seguros v Heath (REBX) Ltd* [2000] 1 WLR 112.

[45]   Following *Norman v Theodore Goddard* [1991] BCLC 1028 and *Re D'Jan of London Ltd* [1994] 1 BCLC 561.

[46]   A member of the LLP is an agent of the LLP: see LLP Act 2000, s 6(1).

[47]   *Bowstead & Reynolds on Agency* 17th edn, 2001, Art 42.

the negligent partner being personally accountable and liable for resulting loss to his co-partners. It has historically been the position that the standard of care owed by a partner to his co-partners is the standard of care which he adopts in his own affairs, and that a partner can only be liable to his co-partners for 'culpable' or 'gross' negligence (in addition to fraud or wilful default).[48] Whether this historical approach is still the law is uncertain. Even if it is, there is no necessity for it to continue in the context of LLPs.[49] The authors suggest that the courts are likely to move to viewing the duty of care owed by a member to the LLP as a duty to observe an objective standard of reasonable care in all the circumstances.

Act within authority

11.14   There has been discussion in **5.9–5.16** of the possibility of the LLP being bound by the actions of a member which, although done by the member outside his actual authority on behalf of the LLP, were within his apparent authority. The member will be under a duty to the LLP to act within the scope of his actual authority, and not to exceed that authority.[50]

Liability of the member

11.15   Subject to the LLP agreement providing otherwise (and to any ratification of the member's actions by the LLP), in the case of a breach by a member of either of the duties set out in **11.12–11.14**, the member will be liable to compensate or indemnify the LLP for loss caused to it as a result of the breach. The possibility of excluding the liability of a member to the LLP, and the possibility also of the LLP giving an indemnity to a member against personal liability to a third party, are discussed at **12.7–12.9**.

STATUTORY DUTIES AND RESPONSIBILITIES

Duties and responsibilities on members as a whole

11.16   The members of the LLP as a whole are given certain duties and responsibilities by the CA 1985 in relation to the LLP's accounts. These include the following:[51]

(i)   It is the duty of the members to prepare for each financial year of the LLP a balance sheet and a profit and loss account which comply with the provisions of the CA 1985 and give a true and fair view of the LLP's

---

[48]   See, for instance, *Thomas v Atherton* (1878) 10 Ch D 185 at 199. This used also to be the position for company directors: see *Gore-Browne on Companies*, para 27-19.

[49]   As mentioned in **1.17**, there is no automatic or default application to LLPs of the law relating to partnerships.

[50]   See generally, *Bowstead & Reynolds* above paras 6-002–6-004.

[51]   The extent to which these duties and responsibilities may be delegated by the members as a whole is considered at **14.13–14.15**.

financial position.[52] This includes the exercise of judgements and discretions provided for in the statutory provisions: for instance, whether there are special reasons for departing from the accounting principles set out in CA 1985, Sch 4,[53] and whether the LLP is carrying on business of two or more classes which differ substantially from each other, so that the amount of turnover attributable to each class should be stated separately.[54] Consistently with this duty, the report on the accounts by the auditors is made to the members.[55]

(ii)   The accounts, prior to filing with the Registrar, are to be approved by the members.[56] If annual accounts are approved which do not comply with the requirements of the CA 1985, every member of the LLP who is a party to their approval and who knows that they do not comply or is reckless as to whether they comply is guilty of an offence.[57]

(iii)   It is for the members to determine whether a financial year of the LLP ends with the last day of the relevant accounting reference period, or with a day not more than 7 days before or after the end of that period.[58]

(iv)   It is for the members to decide where the LLP's accounting records are to be kept.[59]

(v)   If the designated members fail to appoint auditors for any financial year within the periods specified in the CA 1985, the members as a whole may make the appointment in a meeting convened for that purpose.[60]

Duties (with penalties for non-observance) on individual members

11.17   There are a number of statutory duties or prohibitions laid on individual members, with penalties for non-observance. These include the following:

(i)   Every member is obliged to give to the LLP's auditors such information and explanations as the auditors require from him as being necessary for the performance of their duties as auditors.[61]

(ii)   A member must not on behalf of the LLP issue or authorise the issue of or sign documents of various descriptions in which some or all of the LLP's name, place of registration, registration number, address of its registered office and fact that it is a limited liability partnership, are not mentioned as

---

[52]   CA 1985, s 226. Accounting requirements are considered in detail in chapter 18. Where the LLP is a parent, there is, generally speaking, a similar duty on the members to prepare group accounts: CA 1985, ss 227–8.

[53]   See CA 1985, Sch 4, para 15.

[54]   Ibid, Sch 4, para. 55. In additional to paras 15 and 55 of Sch. 4, see for example, paras 27(1) and (5), 31(3), 48(3) and 56(5) of Sch 4, and paras 27(1), 31(3) and 49 of Sch 8.

[55]   Ibid, s 235(1).

[56]   Ibid, s 233(1).

[57]   Ibid, s 233(5). The liability is to a fine.

[58]   Ibid, s 223(2) and (3).

[59]   Ibid, s 222(1), which provides that the accounting records are to be kept at the registered office or at such other place as the members think fit.

[60]   Ibid, s 385(4) and s 388A(5); and see further **14.15**. The appointment of auditors is discussed in chapter 19.

[61]   Ibid, s 389A: see further, **19.9** as to giving misleading, false or deceptive information or explanations, and the penalties.

required by the CA 1985, nor sign or authorise to be signed on behalf of the LLP any bill of exchange, promissory note, endorsement, cheque or order for money or goods in which the LLP's name is not mentioned in legible characters.[62] In addition to liability to a fine, if a member does sign or authorise to be signed on behalf of the LLP any bill of exchange, promissory note, endorsement, cheque or order for money or goods in which the LLP's name is not mentioned in legible characters, he is personally liable to the holder for the amount of it (unless the amount is duly paid by the LLP).[63]

(iii)   A member must not use or authorise the use of a seal purporting to be the seal of the LLP on which the name of the LLP is not engraved in legible characters. If he does so, he is liable to a fine.[64]

(iv)   If a member knowingly and wilfully authorises or permits the omission of an entry which should be made on the LLP's charges register, he is liable to a fine.[65]

(v)   A member must not destroy mutilate or falsify (or be privy to the destruction, mutilation or falsification of) a document (ie any recorded information[66]) affecting or relating to the LLP's property or affairs, nor make (or be privy to the making of) a false entry in such a document.[67] A member who does any of these things is guilty of an offence (and liable to imprisonment or a fine, or both), unless he proves that he had no intention to conceal the state of affairs of the LLP or to defeat the law.[68]

(vi)   If the BNA 1985 applies to the LLP,[69] and the LLP maintains a list of its members' names at its principal place of business, and any third party seeks to exercise his right to inspect the list during office hours, a member must not without reasonable excuse refuse to allow the inspection. Any member of the LLP who is party to refusing the inspection is guilty of an offence, and liable to a fine.[70]

(vii)   If the Secretary of State makes an application to the court under CA 1985, s 245B for a declaration that the annual accounts of the LLP do not comply with the requirements of the CA 1985, and for an order requiring the members to prepare revised accounts, and the court finds on the application that the accounts did not comply with the requirements of the CA 1985, the court may order that the costs of the application and of preparing the revised accounts are to be borne by such of the members as were party to the approval of the defective accounts. For this purpose, every member at the time the accounts were approved is to be taken to have been a party to their

---

[62]   CA 1985, ss 349 and 351. The various descriptions of documents are considered in **4.2** and **4.3**. There is liability to a fine for transgression.

[63]   CA 1985, s 349(4).

[64]   CA 1985, s 350(2). The LLP's seal is discussed at **4.9–4.10**

[65]   CA 1985, s 407(3). As to the meaning of 'knowingly and wilfully', see **10.9**.

[66]   CA 1985, s 450(5).

[67]   CA 1985, s 450(1).

[68]   CA 1985, s 450(1) and (3). It is also an offence (with similar liability) for a member fraudulently to part with, alter or make an omission in any document (or to be privy to any such action): CA 1985, s 450(2). And see IA 1986, ss 206 and 209 as to a member destroying or falsifying the LLP's books when the LLP is being wound up, or during the 12 months immediately preceding the commencement of the winding up.

[69]   As to which, see **4.5** and **4.6**.

[70]   BNA 1985, ss 4(7) and 7.

approval unless he shows that he took all reasonable steps to prevent their being approved.[71]

(viii) If the LLP's affairs are investigated by DTI inspectors, every member (and past member) must, if required by the inspectors to do so, give to the inspectors all assistance in their investigation which he is reasonably able to give, including producing all documents relating to the LLP which he has in his custody or power.[72] Failure to comply can lead to the inspectors referring the matter to the court, which may punish the member (or past member) as if guilty of contempt of court.[73]

(ix) If the LLP is required to produce documents to a DTI appointee under CA 1985, s 447, every member (and past member) must, if required by the DTI appointee to do so, provide an explanation of any of the documents.[74] The penalty for failure to comply is a fine.[75]

(x) If the LLP goes into administration or liquidation, every member (and past member) must give to the administrator or liquidator such information concerning the LLP and its business and affairs as the administrator or liquidator may reasonably require. If a member (or past member) fails without reasonable excuse to do so, he is liable to a fine and, for continued contravention, to a daily default fine.[76]

11.18 In the case of a number of statutory duties which are placed on the *LLP* (expressly or impliedly), the penalty for non-compliance is laid on every member 'who is in default' (or an equivalent) or, in one case,[77] fails to take all reasonable steps to secure compliance by the LLP. A member is 'in default' if he knowingly and wilfully authorises or permits the default or contravention.[78] Where a member is in default in respect of the failure by the LLP to observe its duty, that member is guilty of an offence and liable to a fine (and in three cases to imprisonment or a fine, or both[79]). In addition to any member in default, in most cases[80] the LLP itself is also guilty of an offence. The statutory duties on the LLP (expressly or impliedly) being referred to include the following:

[71] CA 1985, s 245B(4). In making a costs order, the court is to have regard to whether the members party to the approval of the defective accounts knew or ought to have known that the accounts did not comply with the Act's requirements. The costs order may differ as between members: CA 1985, s 245B(5).
[72] CA 1985, s 434: see further, **20.4**.
[73] CA 1985, s 436
[74] CA 1985, s 447(5): see further, **20.7**.
[75] CA 1985, s 447(6).
[76] IA 1986, s 235. There are also specific obligations (with sanctions for non-compliance without reasonable excuse) on members (and past members) to provide statements as to the affairs of the LLP to an administrator where an administration order has been made (IA 1986, s 22) and to the official receiver where a winding-up order has been made by the court (IA 1986, s 131). See also, in relation to an LLP being wound up either by the court or voluntarily, IA 1986, s 208 as to a member (or past member) withholding papers or information or property from the liquidator and IA 1986, s 210 as to a member (or past member) making any material omission in any statement relating to the LLP's affairs.
[77] Sub-paragraph (iv) below.
[78] See CA 1985, s 730(5). The meaning of 'in default' is discussed further at **10.9**.
[79] Sub-paragraphs (i), (ii) and (iii) below.
[80] But not under sub-paragraphs (i), (ii), (iii) and (xiv) below.

(i) to keep accounting records, under CA 1985, s 221;[81]

(ii) to keep the accounting records at its registered office (or such other place as the members think fit), under CA 1985, s 222;[82]

(iii) to keep its accounting records at all times open to inspection by the members, under CA 1985, s 222;[83]

(iv) to preserve its accounting records for 3 years from the date on which they are made, under CA 1985, s 222;[84] in addition to this obligation on the LLP under CA 1985, the Taxes Management Act 1970, s 12B places an obligation on the members to keep records of all items relating to the tax position in relation to the LLP's business until the end of the fifth anniversary of the 31 January next following the end of the tax year in which the relevant accounting period ended;[85]

(v) not to circulate, publish or issue a copy of the balance sheet without it having been signed on behalf of all the members by a designated member as required by CA 1985, s 233;[86]

(vi) not to circulate, publish or issue a copy of the auditors' report, or send it to the Registrar, without the name of the auditors being stated, or (where it is sent to the Registrar) being signed by the auditors as required by CA 1985, s 236;[87]

(vii) not to file with the Registrar a copy of the balance sheet which has not been signed by a designated member as required by CA 1985, s 233;[88]

(viii) to send a copy of the annual accounts and auditors' report to every member, and to every debenture holder, within the specified period, under CA 1985, s 238;[89]

(ix) to supply on demand to any member a copy of the last annual accounts and auditors' report, under CA 1985, s 239;[90]

(x) not to publish any of its statutory accounts without such accounts being accompanied by the relevant auditors' report as required by CA 1985, s 240;[91]

(xi) to take adequate precautions to guard against any register or accounting records being falsified and any falsification not being discovered;[92]

---

[81] CA 1985, s 221(5) and (6). It is a defence for the member to show that he acted honestly and that in the circumstances in which the LLP's business was carried on the default was excusable. As to the meaning of 'accounting records', in *DTC (CNC) Ltd v Gary Sargeant & Co* [1996] 1 WLR 797 (accountants asserting a lien for unpaid fees over accounting records of a company) these were said ordinarily to include sales invoices, purchase invoices, cheque books, paying-in books and bank statements.

[82] CA 1985, s 222(4). There is a similar defence for the member as stated in footnote 81.

[83] Ibid.

[84] CA 1985, s 222(6). Every member must take all reasonable steps for securing that this duty on the LLP is complied with. A failure to do this, or intentionally causing the LLP to default on its obligation of preserving the records, is an offence with liability to imprisonment or a fine or both.

[85] See further, **21.10–2.11**.

[86] CA 1985, s 233(6).

[87] Ibid, s 236(4).

[88] Ibid.

[89] Ibid, s 238(5).

[90] Ibid, s 239(3).

[91] Ibid, s 240(6).

[92] Ibid, s 722(3). The duty exists where the register or accounting records are not kept in bound books.

(xii)   to circulate to every member and debenture holder any statement by auditors under CA 1985, s 394 of the circumstances of their ceasing to be auditors which the auditors consider should be brought to the attention of members or creditors;[93]

(xiii)   to register with the Registrar the prescribed particulars of any charge created by the LLP under CA 1985, s 399,[94] or of any charge over property acquired by the LLP already subject to a charge under CA 1985, s 400;[95]

(xiv)   to allow inspection of copies of the charges given by the LLP requiring registration with the Registrar, and of the LLP's charges register, under CA 1985, s 408;[96]

(xv)   to notify the transferee of a debenture of the LLP of any refusal to register the transfer under CA 1985, s 183;[97]

(xvi)   to complete certificates of debentures under CA 1985, s 185;[98]

(xvii)   to allow inspection of the register of debenture holders, and to supply a copy of the register to any registered debenture holder requiring a copy, under CA 1985, s 191;[99]

(xviii)   to keep the LLP's name in a conspicuous position and in easily legible letters on the outside of every office or place where its business is carried on, under CA 1985, s 348;[100]

(xix)   to file with the Registrar an office copy of any court order sanctioning an arrangement under CA 1985, s 425;[101]

(xx)   to give notice in the London Gazette under IA 1986, s 85 within 14 days of a determination by the LLP that it should be wound up voluntarily;[102] and

(xxi)   if an administration order is in force in relation to the LLP, or the LLP is being wound up (whether by the court or voluntarily), not to issue any invoice, order or business letter on behalf of the LLP and carrying the LLP's name which does not also contain a statement that the LLP's affairs are being managed by the administrator, or a statement that the LLP is being wound up, as required by IA 1986, 12 (administration) or IA 1986, s 188 (winding-up).[103]

---

[93] CA 1985, s 394A(4).

[94] Ibid, s 399(3). There is no offence if the charge is registered by the chargee or some other person.

[95] CA 1985, s 400(4).

[96] Ibid, s 408(3).

[97] Ibid, s 183(6).

[98] Ibid, s 185(5)–(7). LLP Regulations 2001, Sch 2, Pt 1 expressly modify CA 1985, Sch 24 to exclude references to CA 1985, ss 183(6) and 185(5). This is clearly an error, given that these sections themselves are earlier included by Sch 2, Pt 1.

[99] CA 1985, s 191(4)

[100] Ibid, s 348(2)

[101] Ibid, s 425(4). And see also CA 1985, ss 426 and 427.

[102] IA 1986, s 85(2)

[103] In the case of an administration, a member who without reasonable excuse authorises or permits a default is liable to a fine: IA 1986, s 12(2). In the case of a winding-up, a member who knowingly and wilfully authorises or permits a default is liable to a fine: IA 1986, s 188(2). There is a similar requirement as to a statement on invoices, orders or business letters where a receiver or manager of the LLP's property has been appointed: IA 1986, s 39.

Company Directors Disqualification Act 1986

11.19   The CDDA 1986, which applies to members of LLPs, is discussed in chapter 32. It is worth noting here, however, that amongst the matters to which the court is to have regard on an application for a disqualification order against a member on the ground that his conduct as a member makes him unfit to be concerned in the management of an LLP[104] is the extent of that member's responsibility for any failure by the members or the LLP to comply with, inter alia, the provisions of the CA 1985 as to preparing accounts,[105] approving the accounts,[106] keeping accounting records[107] and registering charges.[108] The matters to which the court is directed have regard to under the CDDA 1986 are considered at **32.13–32.15**.

A MEMBER'S DUTIES TO HIS CO-MEMBERS

11.20   The issue of what duties are owed by members of an LLP to each other is, very broadly, similar to the issue of what duties are owed by shareholders in a company to each other. The relationship between one member and another (as opposed to the relationship between a member and the LLP) will be concerned principally with their roles as co-owners of the LLP (as opposed to their roles as co-managers of its business).[109]

Fiduciary duties?

11.21   When the LLP is incorporated and carrying on business, the members will be acting as agents of the LLP and not on behalf of themselves as members.[110] Proceeding on the basis that a fiduciary is 'someone who has undertaken to act for or on behalf of another in a particular matter in circumstances which give rise to a relationship of trust and confidence',[111] the members will, generally speaking,[112] not owe fiduciary duties to each other but, rather, to the LLP.

---

[104]   See CDDA 1986, ss 6 and 9 and Sch 1, paras 4 and 5.
[105]   See **11.16**(i).
[106]   See **11.16**(ii).
[107]   See **11.18**(i)–(iii).
[108]   See **11.18**(xi).
[109]   For a discussion of the distinction between the role of a director of a company voting as such and the role of a shareholder voting as such, see *Northern Counties Securities Ltd v Jackson & Steeple Ltd* [1974] 1 WLR 1133 at 1144 E–H.
[110]   This is a key distinction between an LLP and an 1890 Act partnership. See **1.3**.
[111]   Per Millett LJ in *Bristol and West Building Society v Mothew* [1998] Ch 1 at 18A, approved by the Privy Council in *Arklow Investments Ltd v Maclean* [2000] 1 WLR 594.
[112]   But not inevitably: see, for instance, Millett LJ in *Stein v Blake* [1998] 1 All ER 724 at 727d, referring to the position of two 50 per cent shareholders in a company: 'I have no doubt that circumstances may exist in which [a fiduciary duty owed by one to the other personally] may exist'. And see also *Peskin v Anderson* [2001] 1 BCLC 372 (CA), discussing company directors owing fiduciary duties to shareholders in special circumstances. The problem for the wronged member may be to establish loss to him personally from the breach, rather than loss to the LLP or loss which is merely a reflection of loss for which the LLP may recover: see *Johnson v Gore-Wood* [2002] 2 AC 1 (HL) and *Giles v Rhind* [2003] Ch 618 (CA), both company cases.

11.22   But the position may not be the same as between prospective members prior to the LLP being incorporated, especially if the LLP agreement has been entered into prior to incorporation under LLP Act 2000, s 5(2)[113] and steps are being taken towards carrying out the intended business of the LLP. If this is the case, the prospective members may well already be persons who are in fact associated for carrying on a business with a view to profit[114] (as they will be under LLP Act, s 2(1) when they subscribe to the incorporation document[115]). In these circumstances, and pending the incorporation of the LLP, they may owe fiduciary duties to each other in the taking of the preliminary steps towards the business intended to be carried on by the LLP (if and when incorporated).[116] Whether fiduciary duties do exist in any particular case between persons whose connection is that they are prospective LLP members will depend on the circumstances of that case;[117] but it is suggested that in principle they can.[118] If fiduciary duties do arise in any particular case, and there is a breach by a prospective LLP member, the possible remedies will be as discussed in **11.8**. Where there is an issue as to the destination of property which has been purchased by a prospective member of the future LLP under a pre-acquisition agreement that the property would be injected into the LLP when incorporated, the issue may more properly fall to be analysed in terms of constructive trusts and proprietary estoppel.[119]

11.23   There may also, depending on the particular circumstances, be a duty owed by all the prospective LLP members to each other, or by some prospective LLP members to others, to make full disclosure of any matters relevant to their association for carrying on a business with a view to profit.[120]

---

[113]   Section 5(2) is discussed at **9.10–9.14**.

[114]   In that the underlying venture has been embarked upon: see *Khan v Miah* [2000] 1 WLR 2123 (HL), a partnership case.

[115]   See 2.5–2.10.

[116]   See *United Dominions Corporation Ltd v Brian Proprietary Ltd* (1985) 157 CLR 1 (concerned with the relationship between three prospective joint-venturers who had not yet entered into the formal joint venture agreement) especially at 10–12 (Mason, Brennan and Deane JJ) and 16 (Dawson J) and *Fawcett v Whitehouse* (1829) 1 Russ & M 132 (intending partner obtaining secret benefit from negotiations conducted by him on behalf of intended partnership).

[117]   As to the moulding of fiduciary duties to the particular circumstances, see *NZ Netherlands Society 'Oranje' Inc v Kuys* [1973] 1 WLR 1126 (PC).

[118]   Where, for example, negotiations are already being conducted by one of the intending members on behalf of the 'business' which it is intended, or intended possibly, to incorporate into an LLP. And see *United Dominions Corporation* above at 12–13 (Mason, Brennan and Deane JJ).

[119]   See *Banner Homes Group Plc v Luff Developments Ltd* [2000] Ch 372 (CA).

[120]   See, for instance, in relation to the second possibility, *Directors of Central Railway Co of Venezuela v Kisch* (1867) LR 2 HL 99 (concerned with a dishonest prospectus inviting the public to subscribe): 'In my opinion, the public, who are invited by a prospectus to join in any new adventure, ought to have the same opportunity of judging of everything which has a material bearing on its true character, as the promoters themselves possess. It cannot be too frequently or too strongly impressed upon those who, having projected any undertaking, are desirous of obtaining the co-operation of persons who have no other information on the subject than that which they choose to convey, that the utmost candour and honesty ought to characterise their published statement' (Lord Chelmsford LC at 113). Compare the duty of disclosure between prospective partners contained in clause 10 of the draft Partnerships Bill 2003 presented to Parliament by the Law Commission in November 2003 (Law Com No 283).

Duty of good faith?

11.24 It is an axiom of the law of traditional partnerships that partners owe to each other a duty of the utmost good faith. The basis of this duty is the fact that each partner is the agent for all the others in carrying on the partnership business.[121] The duty extends to the conduct of the purely internal affairs of the partnership, and can perhaps be described as a duty of fair and conscionable dealing between partners in relation to the partnership and all its affairs.[122] As has been discussed earlier, the member of an LLP is not the agent for his co-members, but is the LLP's agent (and as such owes a duty of good faith to the LLP as part of his wider fiduciary obligations).[123] There is no general application of partnership law to LLPs;[124] and the default rules for LLP agreements do not expressly contain (as many partnership deeds do) a requirement of good faith as between members.[125] It is not the position, therefore, that there is an automatic, or default, duty of good faith on the individual members of an LLP ('limited liability partners') to their co-members in the same manner as there is on individual partners in a traditional partnership. It may be, however, that in some circumstances (for instance, in an LLP of professionals) there will be implied into the LLP agreement a term, similar to the standardised default term of mutual trust and confidence implied into contracts of employment,[126] to the effect that a member will not without reasonable and proper cause engage in conduct likely to undermine the trust and confidence between members which is required if the relationship between members is to continue in the manner which the LLP agreement implicitly envisages.

11.25 A duty on each member towards the other members to act honestly and fairly in the relevant interest and for the relevant purpose, and not for some separate interest or ulterior purpose,[127] will, the authors suggest, in any event generally be implied into the LLP agreement so as to apply to the making of decisions which require a majority vote of members, and which are to be binding on the minority. As with the default rules for LLP agreements, the articles of association of a company do not usually contain any express requirement for good faith between shareholders. Nevertheless, the principles of good faith are generally implied into the articles so as to apply to the making of decisions by a majority

---

[121] See the discussion in *Blackett-Ord on Partnership* 2nd edn, 2002, para 10.1

[122] For an example of the application of the duty of good faith between partners, see *Mullins v Laughton* [2003] Ch 250 ('Bullying, seeking to trap and intentionally taking by surprise with a view to shock, in hope of obtaining an advantage for the co-partners and a disadvantage for the partner concerned, must, in my view, amount to a breach of good faith': Neuberger J at para 100). And see also *R v Dept of Health, ex parte Source Informatics Ltd* [2001] QB 424 (CA) at para 31, where 'good faith' in the context of use of confidential information was characterised in terms of conscience.

[123] See **3.3** and **11.6**(a)

[124] See **1.17**

[125] The default rules are considered at **9.6–9.8**.

[126] See *Mahmud v BCCI* [1998] AC 20. Such an implied term must always yield to the express provisions of the relevant contract: see *Reda v Flag Ltd* [2002] IRLR 747 (PC), at para 45.

[127] Ie the key elements in the duty of good faith: see *Medforth v Blake* referred to in footnotes 8 and 10 above, and *Redwood Master Fund Ltd v TD Bank Europe Ltd* referred to in footnote 133 below.

vote of shareholders and which are binding on the minority.[128] This implication is
based on the general principle 'applicable to all authorities conferred on majorities
of classes enabling them to bind minorities, namely that the power must be
exercised for the purpose of benefiting the class as a whole, and not merely
individual members only',[129] and is usually expressed in a company context in
terms that the right of a shareholder to vote must be exercised 'bona fide for the
benefit of the company as a whole'.[130] The authors suggest that, generally
speaking, and by way of implication into the provisions of the LLP agreement, this
principle will be equally applicable to decision-making by the members of an LLP,
and that when considering matters which require a majority vote the members must
(like a company's shareholders) act in what, in their honest opinion, is for the
benefit of the LLP as a whole. An application of this principle has to take into
account, however, the fact that the right to vote of an individual shareholder (of a
company) or individual member (of an LLP) is a right of property which that
shareholder or member may exercise in his own separate interests, and that these
interests will sometimes be, to a greater or lesser extent, in conflict with the
interests of other shareholders or members.[131] In the light of this, the principle that
a member must exercise his voting power 'bona fide in the interests of the LLP as a
whole' is best seen as a negative requirement, namely that a member must not
exercise his voting power (i) in a manner which is dishonest or unfairly
discriminatory against another member or (ii) otherwise than truly for the purpose
for which it was conferred.[132] Put another way, the majority must not use their
position in order to discriminate dishonestly or unfairly against a minority or to
secure for themselves some special collateral advantage.[133] In relation to some
matters where there is provision in the LLP agreement for decisions by majority
vote, the application of the principle of acting bona fide in the interests of the LLP
as a whole will perhaps be seen most easily in terms of taking an individual
hypothetical member and considering whether what is proposed is for that
hypothetical person's benefit.[134] Such matters may include, for instance, the
expulsion of a member[135] or varying the LLP agreement.[136] In relation to other
matters where there is provision for decisions by majority vote, the application of
the principle will perhaps be seen most easily in terms of the negative requirement

---

[128] See, for instance, *Allen v Gold Reefs of West Africa Ltd* [1900] 1 Ch 656 (CA) at 671.
[129] Viscount Haldane in *British America Nickel Corp Ltd v MJ O'Brien Ltd* [1927] AC 369 at 371. The implication, if made, will be on the basis that the principle is required for business efficacy purposes, or was intended to apply as a matter of obvious inference, or was necessary to give effect to the reasonable expectations of the parties.
[130] See *Allen v Gold Reefs of West Africa Ltd* above and *Greenhalgh v Arderne Cinemas Ltd* [1951] Ch 286 (CA).
[131] See, for instance, *Re Astec (BSR) plc* [1998] 2 BCLC 556 at 584 (Jonathan Parker J).
[132] This was clearly the preferred approach of Evershed MR in *Greenhalgh v Ardern Cinemas Ltd* above at 291 (second full paragraph).
[133] See the valuable discussion of this topic by Rimer J in *Redwood Master Fund Ltd v T D Bank Europe Ltd* [2002] EWHC 2703 (Ch), [2002] All ER (D) 141 (Dec) concerned with the variation of a syndicated loan facility by a majority of all the lenders, the variation being binding on the different classes of lenders with potentially differing interests.
[134] See *Greenhalgh v Arderne Cinemas Ltd* above at 291.
[135] See further **16.13** and **16.14**.
[136] See *Allen v Gold Reefs of West Africa Ltd* above and *Sidebottom v Kershaw, Leese & Co Ltd* [1920] 1 Ch 154, both cases concerned with the variation of articles of association.

set out above. Such matters may include, for instance, the distribution of profits amongst the members or an increase in capital contributions.

11.26   When considering whether or not an impugned majority decision has been taken in good faith in accordance with the principles set out in **11.25**, the court will not take as its yardstick what decision it, the court, would have taken; but, rather, will consider whether the decision which the majority has taken can be said to be one which no reasonable man could consider to have been taken in good faith for the benefit of the LLP as a whole.[137] If the court concludes that this is the position, it will declare the decision to be invalid.[138]

11.27   A breach by a majority of members of the principles set out in **11.25** and **11.26** will usually constitute oppressive, or 'unfairly prejudicially', conduct on the part of that majority. In a company context, such a breach will often lead to a petition to the court under CA 1985, s 459, if there is no other satisfactory exit route for the oppressed minority.[139] Section 459 (in a modified form) applies to LLPs, but its application can be excluded by the LLP agreement; and it is likely that many LLP agreements will exclude it.[140] In these circumstances, over time the above principles may take on more importance in the context of LLPs than they currently have in the context of companies.

11.28   As part of his 'share' in the LLP, a member will have certain rights and interests, whether under the LLP agreement or arising as a matter of law, which belong to and/or are exercisable by him alone.[141] Examples are the right to retire as a member[142] and a member's interest in the capital of the LLP. An exercise of such rights, or a dealing with such an interest, or an assignment of a member's share in the LLP,[143] will not be subject to any duty of good faith or requirement to act for the benefit of the LLP as a whole: the subject-matter being dealt with is the right or property of the member personally, existing solely for his own benefit and with which he may deal as he wishes (subject to contractual provisions).[144] This is

---

[137] See *Shuttleworth v Cox Brothers & Co (Maidenhead) Ltd* [1927] 2 KB 9 (CA) at 18, 23 and 27 (concerned with the variation of articles of association). 'Proof of matters of this sort [eg the majority being motivated by malicious discrimination] may of course be difficult, and in many cases the complainants may have no independent evidence enabling them to level attacks on the exercise of the power on grounds such as these. They may, and usually will, be able to do no more than point to the manner of the exercise of the power and invite the inference that it is so manifestly disadvantageous, discriminatory or oppressive towards them that the only conclusion that can be drawn is that it must have been motivated by dishonest considerations inconsistent with a proper exercise of the power for the purpose for which it was intended. If the facts are strong enough, the court may well be prepared to draw such a conclusion' (Rimer J in *Redwood Master Fund* above at para 105).
[138] See also the discussion at **12.11** as to the right for a minority to take a 'derivative action' in the event of a 'fraud on the minority'.
[139] So that there are few recent cases considering the principles discussed in **11.24** and **11.25**.
[140] See **9.9**(14).
[141] See **8.17–8.19**.
[142] Either under the LLP agreement or under LLP Act 2000, s 4(3).
[143] See **8.20**.
[144] See, for instance, *Russell v Russell* (1880) 14 Ch D 471 at 480–1 (a power for one partner to determine the partnership could be exercised capriciously); and *CMS Dolphin Ltd v Simonet* [2001] 2 BCLC 704 at paras 87 and 95 (a director's power to resign from office is not a fiduciary power: it

subject to the caveat, however, that if a member exercises an individual right which he has in the interests or pursuit of fraud, the exercise is likely to be void.[145]

11.29 In partnership law, the general duty of good faith between partners imposes a duty on one partner who is purchasing the share of another partner, or who is selling his own partnership share to another partner, and who knows (and is aware that he knows) more about the state of the partnership's assets and finances than the other, not to conceal what he alone knows, but to put the other in possession of all the material facts. If he does not do this, the purchase or sale will be voidable at the instance of the other (less informed) partner.[146] In the absence of any term in the LLP agreement imposing duties of good faith between members, the partnership position set out above will probably not obtain as between LLP members (although the general law as to misrepresentation will, of course, be applicable).

Duty to render 'true accounts' etc

11.30 Default rule (8) provides as follows:

> 'Each member shall render true accounts and full information of all things affecting the limited liability partnership to any member or his legal representatives.'

This rule is an adoption of s 28 of the Partnership Act 1890, essentially substituting 'member' for 'partner'. It would perhaps have been more logical for the rule to have been framed in terms of rendering accounts and information to the LLP. It may be that the practical effect will be much the same. The rule does, however, give *any* member the right to require information 'affecting' the LLP from any other member. This rule is considered further (as creating a member's right) in chapter 12.

---

can be exercised however damaging this may be to the interests of the company). And see *Cassels v Stewart* (1881) 6 App Cas 64, a partnership case concerning the disposal by a partner of his share in the partnership: the general 'good faith' duties of traditional partners do not apply in relation to a partner's purely personal right or interest, because in exercising the right or dealing with the interest he is not acting as the agent of his co-partners. Similarly, a shareholder does not owe any duties of good faith to the company when dealing with his shares.

145   On the basis that 'fraud unravels all'. See, for instance, *Walters v Bingham* [1988] 1 FTLR 260 at 267/8, where it was held (obiter) that a notice of dissolution of a partnership served by a partner with a view to impeding an investigation of his own fraudulent actions was void and of no effect.

146   See *Law v Law* [1905] 1 Ch 140, and also *Bell v Lever Brothers Ltd* [1932] AC 161 at 227.

Chapter 12

THE RIGHTS OF MEMBERS

INTRODUCTION

12.1   An individual member's rights, as against both the LLP and other members, are likely to be considerably more dependent on the express terms of the LLP agreement than are his duties and responsibilities. Many of the latter (as has appeared from chapter 11) will probably arise in any event from the agent/principal relationship existing between the member and the LLP, or as a matter of implied terms in the LLP agreement. There are, however, a number of rights given by the CA 1985 to every member. We will consider these statutory rights first, and then consider rights arising under the default rules or otherwise.

STATUTORY RIGHTS OF EVERY MEMBER

12.2   The statutory rights given to every member by the legislation are principally rights to information relating to the LLP's accounts, its accounting records and its financial position. The general obligations of preparing and filing annual accounts (and of keeping accounting records) are considered in Chapter 18. The rights to information which the legislation gives to every member include the following:

(i)   the right at all times to inspect the accounting records of the LLP (ie the accounting records which the LLP is required to keep under CA 1985, s 221);[1]

(ii)   the right to receive a copy of the LLP's accounts, together with a copy of the auditors' report on those accounts, within one month of their being approved and signed on behalf of the membership, and in any event not later than 10 months after the end of the relevant accounting period;[2]

(iii)   the right to be furnished, on demand and without charge, with a copy of the LLP's last annual accounts and the auditors' report on those accounts;[3]

(iv)   where the designated members are proposing to remove the auditors, or not to re-appoint them (in favour of other auditors), the right to receive a copy of

---

[1]   CA 1985, s 222(1). As to where these records are to be kept, see **11.18**(ii). And see footnote 81 to **11.18**(i) referring to *DTC (CNC) Ltd v Gary Sergeant & Co* [1996] 1 WLR 797.

[2]   Ibid, s 238(1). Where advantage is taken of an exemption from the audit requirements of the CA 1985 under s 249A (discussed in **18.38**), there is no right to a copy of an auditors' report: CA 1985, s 249E(1)(a).

[3]   Ibid, s 239. See footnote 2 above where advantage is taken of an exemption from the audit requirements of the CA 1985.

any representations from the auditors which they may wish to make to the members (via the LLP) as to their removal or non-reappointment;[4]

(v)   where the auditors resign of their own volition, the right to receive and consider at a meeting of members any statement from the resigning auditors explaining the circumstances of their resignation and which they consider should be brought to the attention of a meeting of the members;[5]

(vi)   where the auditors are in fact removed, or not re-appointed, or do not seek re-appointment, or cease to be the LLP's auditors for any other reason, the right to receive a copy of any statement from those auditors of the circumstances of their ceasing to hold office which they consider should be brought to the attention of the members;[6]

(vii) the right to inspect the LLP's charges register, and (if it keeps one) its register of holders of charges, without fee.[7]

12.3   Every member also has statutory rights to enforce the filing of documents with the Registrar.

(a)   If the designated members fail to file with the Registrar a copy of the LLP's annual accounts within the permitted period,[8] any member may serve a notice on the designated members requiring the accounts to be filed, and may follow this up with an application to the court if the accounts are not filed within 14 days.[9]

(b)   If there is a failure on the part of *the LLP* to meet a statutory obligation on it to deliver any document or give any notice to the Registrar (for example, to give notice to the Registrar of a person becoming or ceasing to be a member of the LLP as required by LLP Act 2000, s 9[10]), any member may serve a notice on the LLP requiring the document to be delivered or notice to be given, and may follow this up with an application to the court if the statutory obligation is not complied with within 14 days.[11]

12.4   There is also a right for not less than one-fifth in number[12] of the members of an LLP to apply to the Secretary of State for the appointment by him of

---

[4]   CA 1985, s 391A. This is subject to the right of the LLP under CA 1985, s 391A(6) to apply to the court on the ground that the auditors are abusing their right to make representations: see further as to such an application, **19.14**.

[5]   Ibid, s 392A.

[6]   Ibid, s 394. This right (which the holders of the LLP's debentures also have) is also subject to the right of the LLP under CA 1985, s 394(3)(b) to apply to the court on the ground that the auditors are using the statement to secure needless publicity for defamatory matter: see further as to such an application, **19.19**.

[7]   Ibid, ss 408 (register of charges) and 191 (register of holders). As to these registers, see **6.4–6.7**.

[8]   See generally on filing the accounts with the Registrar, **18.18–18.21**. The duty to file the accounts is a duty of the designated members: CA 1985, s 242(1).

[9]   Ibid, s 242(3).

[10]   The failure constitutes an offence by the LLP, and also by the designated members: s 9(4) and (5).

[11]   CA 1985, s 713.

[12]   As appearing from notifications given to the Registrar.

inspectors to investigate the affairs of the LLP and report to him.[13] This is considered at **20.2–20.6**.

NON-STATUTORY RIGHTS

Default rules

12.5   The default rules contain what may be seen as two clear rights of individual members against the LLP.

(1)   Rule (2) gives members the right to an indemnity from the LLP. The rule provides:

'The limited liability partnership must indemnify each member in respect of payments made and personal liabilities incurred by him –

(a)   in the ordinary and proper conduct of the business of the limited liability partnership; or

(b)   in or about anything necessarily done for the preservation of the business or property of the limited liability partnership.'

This is an adoption of s 24(2) of the Partnership Act 1890, and is in accordance with the general principles of agency.[14] Paragraph (a) refers to "the ordinary and proper conduct of the business" of the LLP. The indemnity will not cover liabilities incurred by the member as a result of acts in breach of duty owed by him to the LLP[15] (including his duty of care to the LLP, and his duty to act within his authority[16]), and as a general rule will not cover, therefore, personal liability which a member may incur in negligence to a customer or client.[17] Nor will it cover acts known by the member to be unlawful.[18]

(2)   Rule (7) gives every member the right to inspect the books and records of the LLP. The rule provides:

'The books and records of the limited liability partnership are to be made available for inspection at the registered office of the limited liability partnership or at such other place as the members think fit and every member

---

[13]   CA 1985, s 431(2).
[14]   See *Bowstead & Reynolds on Agency*, 17th edn, 2001, Art 64 and *Chitty on Contracts* 29th edn, 2004, para 31-156.
[15]   Compare *Bowstead & Reynolds* above, Art 65 and *Chitty on Contracts* above, para 31-157.
[16]   See **11.11–11.14**.
[17]   But this is not an invariable rule: a member's breach of a personal duty of care owed by him to a customer or client will not *necessarily* be a breach of his duty of care to the LLP: see footnote 23 below. The possibility of a member owing a personal duty of care to a customer or client is discussed in chapter 15.
[18]   See footnote 15 above.

of the limited liability partnership may when he thinks fit have access to and inspect and copy any of them.'

This is an adoption (with additions) of s 24(9) of the Partnership Act 1890.[19] This right to inspect the 'books and records' of the LLP is a wider right than that given by CA 1985, s 222(1) to inspect the 'accounting records'.[20] Default rule (7) may come under close consideration where an LLP agreement is being drafted for both 'full' and 'salaried' (ie employee) members.[21] There may be a desire to restrict what books and records of the LLP employee members may inspect and take copies of; and there may be a desire, therefore, to restrict the scope or application of this default provision. It will be necessary, however, to bear in mind the statutory rights to information (and statements from the auditors) which are in any event given to all members, and which are set out in **12.2**.

12.6   The default rules also contain, in rule (8), the right for one member to obtain information directly from another member. Rule (8) provides:

> 'Each member shall render true accounts and full information of all things affecting the limited liability partnership to any member or his legal representatives.'

This is an adoption of s 28 of the Partnership Act 1890, essentially substituting 'member' for 'partner'. One member can, therefore, require such full information from another member. 'Affecting' is a word of wide ambit. This rule, like default rule (7) mentioned in **12.5**(2) above, may come under close consideration where an LLP agreement is being drafted with employee members. These default rules can, of course, be varied by the LLP agreement. It is worth mentioning here, however, that one of the grounds on which the Secretary of State may, on his own initiative, appoint inspectors to investigate the affairs of the LLP is that it appears to him that there are circumstances suggesting that the LLP's members have not been given all the information with respect to its affairs which they might reasonably expect.[22]

Possibility of excluding a member's liability to the LLP for negligence

12.7   Reference is made in **11.12–11.13** to the duty of care which the member will owe to the LLP. The existence of this duty could have great significance if (to take the most obvious, but not the only, example) the LLP was liable to a third party under a claim for negligence in excess of its insurance cover. In such a situation, the LLP (or its liquidator) might consider it necessary to seek to recover the excess of the liability over the insurance cover from the member whose negligence (in possible breach of his own duty of care owed to the LLP[23]) caused the liability to

---

[19]   The words in the rule 'at the registered office . . . or at such other place as the members think fit' are a reflection of CA 1985, s 222(1).

[20]   See **12.2**(ii).

[21]   Employee members are considered at **8.26–8.32**.

[22]   CA 1985, s 432(2)(d), discussed further at **20.2**(2).

[23]   It is important to appreciate, however, that the duty of care owed by the individual member to the LLP is not *necessarily* co-extensive with the duty of care owed by the LLP (acting by the member in question) to the client: see in this respect *Ross Harper & Murphy v Banks* 2000 SLT 699 (a Scottish case on the duty of care by a partner to his co-partners) at 705 (Lord Hamilton). When *Ross-Harper & Murphy* was before the Inner House, the pursuer partnership withdrew their claim:

be incurred.[24] The question therefore arises as to whether the member and the LLP can agree in the LLP agreement or separately for an exclusion of liability on the part of the member to the LLP for loss caused to the LLP as a result of that member's negligence in carrying out his functions as a member. There is no reason in principle why there cannot be such an exclusion clause. In this respect, the position of a member of an LLP differs from that of a director of a company, who is precluded by CA 1985, s 310 from having such an exclusion clause.[25] Section 310 of CA 1985 is not adopted for LLPs. (It is worth noting in this context that equally CA 1985, s 727, which contains a power for the court to grant relief to a director in respect of any negligence or breach of duty if he acted honestly and reasonably and ought fairly to be excused, is also not adopted for members of the LLP.[26]) Such an exclusion clause will not, it is suggested, be subject to the Unfair Contract Terms Act 1977,[27] and so will not need to satisfy the requirement of reasonableness. That Act (so far as presently material) does not extend to any contract so far as it relates to the constitution of any body corporate or to the rights or obligations of the corporators or members of any body corporate.[28] This is clearly wide enough, it is suggested, to cover the tortious or contractual duty of care owed by a member to the LLP (or, should the issue arise, to other members).[29]

12.8 Where the LLP is liable to a third party in negligence, the member whose negligence caused the liability to be incurred may himself, in addition to the LLP, be independently liable to the third party (if he assumed a personal responsibility), and thus a joint tortfeasor with the LLP.[30] In these circumstances, it would be open to the LLP to seek a contribution from the member in question (whether or not the member was pursued directly by the third party) under the Civil Liability (Contribution) Act 1978. This right to contribution can be regulated or excluded by agreement between the members and the LLP.[31] The LLP agreement can therefore contain a provision excluding (or limiting) the LLP's right to seek contribution under the 1978 Act from a negligent member who is also himself personally liable to the third party.

---

see the Law Commission Report of November 2003 (Law Com No 283), para 11.8. See further the discussion at **11.13**.
[24] For the position if the member was a joint tortfeasor, see **12.8**.
[25] A company can, however, purchase insurance against such liability for a director. Equally, it is suggested (see **12.9**), an LLP can purchase insurance for a member.
[26] But it is adopted for auditors of an LLP, as for auditors of a company: see **19.22**.
[27] Section 2(2) of which (subject to exclusions from the Act) provides that in the case of loss or damage other than death or personal injury liability for negligence cannot be excluded or restricted except in so far as the exclusion satisfies the requirement of reasonableness.
[28] Section 1(3) of UCTA 1977 and Sch 1, para 1(d)(ii). The Unfair Terms in Consumer Contracts Regulations 1999 (discussed in **15.25**) will also, it is suggested, not be applicable to the agreement between the LLP and the members: see *Chitty on Contracts* above, para 15-028. It is difficult to see an LLP agreement as a 'consumer contract'.
[29] Insofar as the duty of care may arise in equity, UCTA 1977 will in any event have no application, as it does not apply to exclusions or restrictions of liability for breach of a duty of care arising in equity.
[30] For the position of the individual member, see chapter 15. The liability of the LLP for the member's negligence may also arise under LLP Act 2000, s 6(4) discussed in **5.20–5.21**.
[31] Section 7(3) of the 1978 Act.

12.9   The possibility of an individual member being himself liable to the third party leads to a consideration of two matters: insurance for individual members, and an indemnity for members from the LLP. As to insurance, clearly individual members can have their own indemnity insurance;[32] and there is no reason why the LLP agreement cannot provide for the premiums for this to be paid by the LLP. As to an indemnity, it might be thought that an exclusion of a negligent member's liability to the LLP as discussed in **12.7** and an exclusion of the LLP's right to seek contribution under the 1978 Act as discussed in **12.8** will be the equivalent to an indemnity. This would, however, be wrong. A third party may choose to sue only the individual member who has assumed personal responsibility, and not the LLP as well; or may choose to sue both the LLP and the individual member, but to enforce recovery of damages against the individual member only. In the first case, the individual member would be exposed to the third party's claim, whilst the LLP would not be exposed and would have no contribution claim to make.[33] In the second case, the LLP would have no financial loss to make a claim in respect of. Full protection for the individual member, therefore, would include an indemnity from the LLP.

Claims by a member against the LLP

12.10   There is no reason in principle why the LLP (which, as previously mentioned, can only act by its members or other agents or employees[34]) cannot be liable for breach of contract or in tort (or for other wrongdoing) to an individual member. There could, therefore, be circumstances in which the LLP is liable to one member as a result of the negligent or other wrongful acts of some or all of the other members (which are attributable to the LLP).[35]

Derivative action by minority

12.11   Reference has been made in Chapter 11 to the fiduciary and other obligations owed by members to the LLP. In the event of a breach of these duties, it is the LLP (and not individual members) which will have the claim, and bring any action, against the wrongdoing member or members in respect of the breach. Company law has well-developed principles to meet the situation where the wrongdoing members are the majority, benefiting themselves at the expense of the company (or otherwise causing the company to engage in illegal activity) and using their majority voting power to prevent the company taking any action. In such situations the minority are enabled to bring, in their own names but for the benefit of the company, the action against the wrongdoing majority which the company ought to (and would) bring but for the majority's abuse of their power by blocking the company bringing such an action. The minority is enabled to bring a

---

[32]   In *Merrett v Babb* [2001] QB 1174, the Court of Appeal clearly signalled that individual professionals will be expected to have personal insurance: see May LJ at para 46. And see also Lord Griffiths in *Smith v Bush* [1990] 1 AC 831 at 858H referring to all prudent professional men carrying insurance.

[33]   Although a claim for contribution under the 1978 Act by the member *against* the LLP might be considered.

[34]   See **3.3**.

[35]   As to the issue of vicarious liability of the LLP for the wrongful act of one member to another member, see **5.20–5.21** considering LLP Act 2000, s 6(4).

'derivative action'.[36] It is suggested that the courts will apply similar principles in the event of a 'fraud on the minority' of an LLP. The classic case is where the majority seek directly or indirectly to appropriate to themselves property or opportunities belonging to the company. The court will[37] permit the minority to bring an action for the benefit of the company for recovery of the property, or for other appropriate relief.[38] There seems no reason why the court should not equally permit a minority of LLP members to bring an action in the same situation, or in other situations where it would permit minority shareholders in a company to bring an action for the benefit of the company.[39] It is also worth noting here the power of the Secretary of State to take civil proceedings in the name and on behalf of an LLP under CA 1985, s 438.

---

[36] See *Wallersteiner v Moir (No 2)* [1975] QB 373 at 390–391 and *Prudential Assurance Co Ltd v Newman Industries Ltd (No 2)* [1982] Ch 204 at 210–211.

[37] As a general rule: reference should be made to more detailed works on this topic in relation to both substance and procedure.

[38] See, for example, *Daniels v Daniels* [1978] Ch 406 where directors, who were also the majority shareholders, were allegedly acting in breach of duty. 'The principle . . . is that a minority shareholder who has no other remedy may sue where directors use their powers, intentionally or unintentionally, fraudulently or negligently, in a manner which benefits themselves at the expense of the company' (Templeman J at 414D–E). See, generally, on 'fraud on the minority', *Gore-Browne on Companies* Ch 28.

[39] CPR, r 19.9 (setting out the procedure for 'Derivative Claims') applies not only in relation to *a company*, but also where any 'other incorporated body' (which will include an LLP) is alleged to be entitled to claim a remedy and a claim is made by one or more members of the body for it to be given that remedy.

Chapter 13

FUNDING AND PROFITS AND LOSSES

FUNDING

13.1 Like any business, the LLP will need working capital. As in the case of a limited company (or a traditional partnership), this can be provided by way of either 'equity' or 'debt', that is to say, by way of members' 'capital' or by way of loan to the LLP. Funds can, of course, also be borrowed by the LLP from the bank or another third party.

13.2 The legislation clearly recognises the concept of members' capital,[1] and also clearly recognises the distinction between this and sums advanced to the LLP by members by way of loan.[2] A loan will (expressly or impliedly) carry terms as to repayment, and will constitute a debt of the LLP to the member (or third party) making it. The essence of a loan is the lending of a sum of money for a period with an obligation for repayment at some time and under some circumstances.[3] Capital, on the other hand, is money invested in the business and exposed to the risk of loss: it will not constitute a debt of the LLP to the member contributing it.[4] Whether funds provided by members are provided as capital or by way of loan will be a matter of the intention of the members. In the absence of the funds being clearly designated as capital, they will be assumed to constitute a loan, and to be a debt owing from the LLP to the members providing the funds.[5] There is no reason why loans cannot be made, or capital designated, in a foreign currency.[6]

13.3 There are two practical distinctions for a member between contributing capital and making a loan. The first relates to the member leaving. The second

---

[1] See Balance Sheet Formats 1 and 2 in CA 1985, Sch 4 and Sch 8; and also default rule (1) considered in **13.5**. See also the reference to the amount contributed by a member as capital in ICTA 1988, s 118ZC, inserted by LLP Act 2000, s 10(1).

[2] See the Balance Sheet Formats referred to in footnote 1 and **18.14**(1)–(2). The balance sheet is required to show separately 'Loans and other debts due to members' and 'Members' capital'.

[3] See, for instance, In re *Southern Brazilian Rio Grande do Sul Ry Co Ltd* [1905] 2 Ch 78 at 83 and *Champagne Perrier SA v HH Finch Ltd* [1982] 3 All ER 713 at 717 d–e.

[4] See *Lee v Neuchatel Asphalte Co* (1889) 41 Ch D 1 at 23 and *Verner v General and Commercial Investment Trust* [1894] 2 Ch 239 at 264. If there is a surplus in a winding up, then (and not before) the LLP will be a debtor to the members for their capital: ibid. The SORP for LLPs (see **18.8**) defines Members' capital as amounts subscribed or otherwise contributed by members for longer-term retention in the business (para 13).

[5] See, for instance, *Seldon v Davidson* [1968] 1 WLR 1083 (CA): the payment of money *prima facie* imports an obligation to repay it. The repayment of loans to the LLP made by members may be subordinated to debts owing by the LLP to outside parties, and may, for instance, be made contingent on the solvency of the LLP or repayable out of a particular fund only.

[6] As to capital, see for instance *In re Scandinavian Bank Group Plc* [1988] Ch 87 (under CA 1985, s 2(5)(a) a company's share capital can be expressed in a non-UK currency).

relates to a liquidation. In relation to the member leaving, it is the authors' view that a leaving member will not be entitled to a return of his capital in the absence of a positive agreement to that effect,[7] whereas (and as stated in **13.2**) a loan will necessarily carry terms (express or implied) as to repayment.[8] In relation to a liquidation, whilst a member should be able to prove in a liquidation, alongside other unsecured creditors, for a loan made by him to the LLP (subject to the specific terms of the loan), he will not be able to prove for his capital in a liquidation (which, as stated in **13.2**, will not constitute a debt of the LLP).[9]

13.4 As in a traditional partnership context, capital (cash or its equivalent contributed by members) is wholly distinct from the assets (owned by the LLP).[10]

13.5 Default rule (1)[11] provides as follows:

> 'All the members of a limited liability partnership are entitled to share equally in the capital and profits of the limited liability partnership.'

This is an adoption (with modifications) of s 24(1) of the Partnership Act 1890. Its relevance in the context of discussing capital is that the default position will be that all capital contributed (in whatever shares) will be owned equally by the members. If this is not what is desired, the LLP agreement should contain provisions as to entitlement to capital.[12] It is worth noting here that (disregarding profits for the moment) default rule (1) is concerned solely with the entitlement to what is designated as capital in the accounts of the LLP. Specifically, it is not making provision as to the sharing between members of a surplus of assets over liabilities in a winding-up. It is also worth noting that there is no default provision for contributions of capital to carry interest; and they will only do so if the LLP agreement provides for interest on capital.

13.6 Whilst an LLP's working capital can be provided, wholly or in part, by contributions of 'capital' by the members, there is no requirement in the legislation that members do contribute capital. If, however, amounts of capital have been contributed, there is no objection in principle (subject to compliance with the relevant provisions of the LLP agreement) to these amounts at any time being wholly or in part reduced, that is to say being repaid to the members or being converted into loans to the LLP (ie being converted into debt owing by the LLP to the members).[13] Although there is no statutory restriction on such conversion of

---

[7]   See further, chapter 16.
[8]   See further, **16.23**.
[9]   See further, **28.3–28.5**. The SORP for LLPs (see **18.8**) para 34 requires the notes to an LLP's accounts to explain where 'Loans and other debts due to members' shown in the balance sheet would rank in relation to other creditors who are unsecured in the event of a winding up.
[10] In the partnership context, see *Popat v Shonchhatra* [1997] 1 WLR 1367 at 1371F–H.
[11] As to the default rules generally, see **9.6–9.8**.
[12] In reality, the slightest indication of an implied agreement between the members that their share in capital should correspond with their contributions to it will suffice to displace the default rule that they are entitled to share equally: see *Popat v Shonchhatra* above at 1373B–C.
[13] The rule in *Trevor v Whitworth* (1887) 12 App Cas 409 for companies does not apply to LLPs. Note also that CA 1985, s 461(2)(d) enables the court to order that the share of a member (which

capital into debt, caution will need to be exercised before this is done. The members will need to consider the solvency of the LLP. If the LLP is at the time insolvent, or of doubtful solvency, the interests of the creditors will be paramount,[14] and will need to be fully taken into account in any decision to convert capital into debt.[15]

13.7 In like manner as funds originally provided by way of capital can be converted into debt owing by the LLP, funds originally provided by members by way of loan can be redesignated as capital contributed by them. As is discussed at **18.14**(5), the SORP for LLPs[16] provides that the Members' Report forming part of the annual accounts should disclose the policy of the LLP regarding the subscription, and repayment, of members' capital, and any transfers from capital to debt which have taken place.

PROFITS AND LOSSES

Profits

13.8 Profits (or losses) are an accounting measure of the LLP's performance over a given period.[17] At least one given period for an LLP, by reason of the accounting requirements of the CA 1985, is one year.[18] The LLP agreement will make provision (either expressly or by default[19]) as to the members' respective shares in profits made by the LLP. When the profits for any year (or other chosen period) have been established, it will be a matter of interpretation of the LLP agreement as to when (and if) those profits are to be divided amongst the individual members in accordance with the profit-sharing provisions (or, for instance, are to be placed in reserves). The agreement may provide for the profits, when ascertained, automatically to be divided amongst the members. Alternatively, the agreement may provide that a decision (by the membership, or some part of it) as to division is first required before members are to be entitled to call for payment by the LLP to them of their respective shares.[20]

13.9 As indicated above, the LLP agreement may provide for the automatic division of profits when the profits of the LLP for the relevant period have been established. But it is probably the position that default rule (1) set out in **13.5** – as a default rule in all circumstances – does not so provide, and is solely making

---

will include capital contributions made by him: see **8.17**) shall be purchased by the LLP, without the need (required by s 461(2)(d) for companies) that the court also authorise a reduction of capital.
[14] See *West Mercia Safetywear Ltd v Dodd* [1988] BCLC 250 (director's misfeasance case) and *Official Receiver v Stern (No 2)* [2002] 1 BCLC 119 (director's disqualification case).
[15] The repayment of a loan to a member within a period of 2 years prior to winding-up may be subject to 'claw-back' under IA 1986, s 214A: see **29.6–29.10**.
[16] See further, **18.8**.
[17] See, for example, *Reed v Young* [1986] 1 WLR 649 at 654D.
[18] As to the accounting requirements, see chapter 18.
[19] See default rule (1) set out in **13.5**.
[20] Analogous to the decision of a company to declare a dividend.

provision as to shares of profit if and when there is a decision to divide them.[21] As has been mentioned at **9.5**, the terms of an LLP agreement may be agreed by conduct; and, where the default rules are being relied upon to constitute the agreement, it may be that the members will in fact proceed on the basis of automatic division, and so create an agreement to that effect. It may also be that the slightest indication that profits are to be automatically divided will be held by a court sufficient to justify finding an implied agreement to that effect.

13.10   If the LLP agreement does provide for the automatic division of profits, the profits allocated to individual members in accordance with the agreed profit shares will be credited directly to the individual accounts with the LLP of the members and, subject again to the provisions of the LLP agreement,[22] thereupon become debts due from the LLP to the members. Where the LLP agreement provides for a separate decision to be made as to division, profits which have been ascertained but which have not been the subject of such a decision will be shown in the LLP's balance sheet under 'Other reserves' (within 'Members' other interests'), and until allocated to the individual members will not constitute debts for which the members may sue or prove in a liquidation.

13.11   Members of professional and trading LLPs will usually expect to be entitled to drawings on account of profits during a financial year, with a balancing payment or repayment when the accounts for that year have been prepared and approved and the profits divided. This again is a matter for decision by the members. In the absence of agreement as to this, there is no default right to drawings on account of profit during the year.[23] If there is provision for members to draw on account of profits not yet divided, such drawings will constitute loans by the LLP to the members receiving the drawings, and will therefore appear on the balance sheet of the LLP as indebtedness of members to the LLP. In these circumstances, over a period of a year (or more, namely until the accounts for the relevant financial year have been approved) considerable indebtedness on the part of the members to the LLP may build up. Some LLPs may wish to provide for quarterly (or other periodic) divisions of profit during a year in order to lessen this build up of members' indebtedness. Such periodic divisions will need to be based on properly prepared and approved periodic accounts ie on accounts which will be consistent with the year-end accounts.[24]

---

[21]   The legal opinion of Robin Potts QC annexed to Appendix 1 to the SORP for LLPs also takes the view that default rule (1) is solely concerned with shares of profit and not division.

[22]   There may, for instance, be an agreement for members not to withdraw all profits allocated to them, and to redesignate part of such profits as capital.

[23]   The SORP for LLPs para 39 requires the 'Members' Report' to disclose the overall policy followed by the LLP in relation to members' drawings, including an indication of the policy applicable where the cash requirements of the business compete with the need to allow cash drawings by members.

[24]   A withdrawal of a share of allocated profits will be potentially subject to 'claw-back' under IA 1986, s 214A in the event of the LLP going into liquidation: see the reference to 'a share of profits' in sub-s (2)(a). Such periodic accounts will not need to be audited.

13.12   'Profits' in default rule (1) will include capital profits, that is to say any profits on the realisation of assets of the LLP.[25] As with income profits discussed above, the point at which an entitlement for an individual member to receive a share of any capital profits crystallises will be a matter for agreement.[26] If an LLP agreement makes no clear distinction between shares of revenue profits and shares of capital profits, the latter will be shared in the same proportions as the former.[27]

Losses

13.13   An LLP may be a going concern but nevertheless making trading losses. Losses are conceptually quite distinct from the debts and liabilities of the firm, and from the assets which are available to meet them.[28] If an LLP makes a trading loss in a particular period, some financial provision will need to be made to cover that loss, both in actual cash terms and in terms of appropriating the loss in the accounts. Consideration will need to be given to this in drafting the LLP agreement. The essential question when drafting the LLP agreement will be: in the event of a trading loss, is there to be a substantive provision as to division of loss (up to a limited amount) amongst the members by debiting their current accounts, or members being obliged to contribute – either by way of capital contribution or loan – to cover the loss.[29] An alternative approach would be to provide for any losses to be debited to a separate 'Other reserves' account,[30] coupled with a provision enabling a decision to be made requiring members to contribute more capital or money on loan to the LLP. An LLP agreement should not provide that losses are to be divided between members and automatically allocated to them individually in their respective profit shares: such a provision would make members, indirectly, personally liable for the LLP's debts and would risk undermining the primary purpose of the members being in the LLP, namely limited liability.[31]

13.14   What is the position in default of agreement as to covering trading losses? The liability of the members for the debts and liabilities of the LLP is limited, in the sense that in a winding up their liability to contribute for the benefit of creditors of the LLP is limited to what they have agreed to contribute.[32] Consistently with this, default rule (1) does not adopt the second part of s 24(1) of the Partnership Act 1890, which provides '...and must contribute equally towards the losses...

---

[25]   See *Popat v Shonchhatra* above at 1373D and 1374B–1375A.
[26]   And see the discussion as to entitlement to a share of any increased (but not realised) value on cessation of membership in chapter 16.
[27]   See *Robinson v Ashton* (1875) 20 Eq 25.
[28]   See *Reed v Young* above at 654A.
[29]   For an LLP of professionals, circumstances might arise, for instance, where a negligence liability exceeds professional indemnity insurance cover, but the creditor will accept payment of the excess over a period of years.
[30]   See footnote 33 below and the text to it.
[31]   In the event of any overdrawing on a member's current account, that member will, in most cases anyway, either expressly or by necessary implication come under an obligation – enforceable by the LLP or a liquidator – to repay to the LLP the amount of such overdrawing.
[32]   Subject to ss 212–214A of the IA 1986. See **8.14–8.16**.

sustained by the firm'.[33] It is not the default position for LLPs, therefore, that trading losses are to be shared amongst, or made good by, members in equal (or in any other) shares. If the LLP is trading at a loss, the members will, however, need to have in mind the provisions of ss 212–214A of the IA 1986;[34] and ultimately the LLP may be put into liquidation. As a matter of accounting, where there is no provision in the LLP agreement for a trading loss to be allocated to individual members, it will be debited to 'other reserves' (within 'Members' other interests') on the balance sheet.[35] If there *is* provision in the LLP agreement that losses (either generally or of any specific nature or up to any specific amount) are to be borne by the individual members, but there is no provision as to the shares between the members in which the losses are to be borne, the inference will be, it is suggested (and in the absence of anything to the contrary), that they are to be borne in the same shares as profits are divisible.[36]

[33] Section 24(1) of the 1890 Act is a default rule of internal management as to the allocation between partners of losses arising out of debts and liabilities for which, as against third parties, the partners are jointly (or jointly and severally) liable.
[34] For instance, fraudulent trading or wrongful trading: see chapter 29.
[35] See the SORP for LLPs para 32. 'Other reserves' may, as a result, be a negative figure.
[36] See *Re Albion Life Assurance Society* (1880) 16 Ch D 83.

Chapter 14

MANAGEMENT AND DECISION MAKING

INTRODUCTION

14.1 Like a traditional partnership, the members of an LLP can adopt whatever management and decision-making structure they wish with whatever voting structure they wish.[1] It needs to be remembered, however, that there are certain duties and responsibilities placed by statute on the members as a whole;[2] and the impact should not be overlooked of ss 214 (wrongful trading) and 214A (adjustment of withdrawals) of the IA 1986, and of the CDDA 1986.[3]

MANAGEMENT

14.2 Default rules (3) and (4)[4] provide as follows:

'Every member may take part in the management of the limited liability partnership.

No member shall be entitled to remuneration for acting in the business or management of the limited liability partnership.'

14.3 These rules are an adoption of s 24(5) and (6) of the Partnership Act 1890. The LLP agreement can depart from these rules and create any management structure (and remuneration for management) that is desired. 'Remuneration', the essence of which is that it is consideration for work done or to be done, can take many forms, and is not limited to a conventional direct payment.[5]

14.4 If there is to be a management committee (to which management of the LLP is to be delegated), its composition and functions, and the ambit of its delegated authority (or the method for establishing that authority) need to be set out clearly in the LLP agreement. There should also be provision as to how matters are to be decided by the committee (for instance, by majority vote), and as to the quorum for a meeting of it. If the committee is to have power to delegate any of its powers to

---

[1] The legislation envisages that an LLP may be a subsidiary, of a company or of another LLP, in that the 'parent' holds under the LLP agreement a majority (or, through itself and/or other subsidiaries, all) of the voting rights in the LLP: CA 1985, ss 736 and 736A. In other words, the legislation appears to be envisaging that voting rights and control can be distributed amongst the members by the LLP agreement in any manner which is desired.

[2] See **11.16**.

[3] See **14.10–14.12**.

[4] As to the default rules generally, see **9.6–9.8**.

[5] See *Currencies Direct Ltd v Ellis* [2002] 2 BCLC 482.

any other committee or sub-committee, that power needs to be contained in the LLP agreement.

14.5 One of the decisions which will need to be taken at the time of incorporation, even if an LLP agreement is not yet in place, is whether all members are automatically to be designated members or whether the designated members will be some specified members only.[6] When drafting the LLP agreement, it will probably be convenient to consider this issue at the same time as the management structure and any express management and administrative powers and duties to be set out in the LLP agreement.

DECISION MAKING

14.6 Default rule (6) provides as follows:

> 'Any difference arising as to ordinary matters connected with the business of the limited liability partnership may be decided by a majority of the members, but no change may be made in the nature of the business of the limited liability partnership without the consent of all the members.'

14.7 This is an adoption of s 24(8) of the Partnership Act 1890. It will be a matter of fact, to be considered in the context of the LLP itself and current commercial practice, what matters fall within 'ordinary matters'. But the matters which may be decided by a majority of the members must be matters 'connected with the business' of the LLP. Profit sharing, or other matters solely regulating affairs between members, will not be such matters. It is suggested that, generally speaking, changing the registered office, or changing the name of the LLP, although connected with the business of the LLP, will not be 'ordinary matters'.[7]

14.8 Mention has been made earlier of the need, when drafting an LLP agreement, for careful consideration to be given to the position of 'salaried members'.[8] Default rule (6), and also default rules (3) and (4) mentioned above, as they stand, embrace all members.

DEATH OF A MEMBER OR ASSIGNMENT OF HIS SHARE

14.9 LLP Act 2000, s 7(2) provides that neither the personal representatives of a deceased member, nor the trustee in bankruptcy of a member, nor the assignee of a member's share in the LLP may 'interfere in the management or administration of any business or affairs' of the LLP. Section 7(2) is considered further at **8.20–8.22**.

---

[6]   See **2.28–2.30**. The duties and responsibilities of the designated members are considered in chapter 10.

[7]   See **3.15** and **4.19**.

[8]   See **8.26–8.32**.

THE 1986 LEGISLATION

14.10   An LLP of any appreciable size is likely to have a management committee or its equivalent. It may be that a loose analogy will be seen between the members of an LLP and its management committee on the one hand, and the shareholders of a company and its board of directors on the other hand. However, members of an LLP should guard against adopting this analogy too closely. All members are effectively equated to directors by the application of the CA 1985;[9] and, as has been mentioned elsewhere,[10] members are potentially subject to the personal liability provisions of the IA 1986,[11] and to disqualification under the CDDA 1986.[12] The emphasis of modern company legislation is to impose standards of conduct and carrying of responsibility on individual directors which are calculated to protect the public and in particular creditors dealing with the directors' company. It follows from the application of the two 1986 Acts to LLPs and their members that, in principle, these same standards of conduct and carrying of responsibility must be accepted by LLP members. 'Those who trade under the regime of limited liability and who avail themselves of the privileges of that regime must accept the standards of probity and competence to which the law requires company directors to conform'.[13] 'LLP members' may be substituted for 'company directors' in this statement. The fact that a company, unlike an LLP, has third-party shareholders as well as creditors does not, in the authors' view, lessen the application of this judicial statement to LLPs.

14.11   Both s 214 (wrongful trading) and s 214A (adjustment of withdrawals) of the IA 1986 can lead to a member being required to make a contribution to the assets of the LLP (over and above what he may have agreed in the LLP agreement to contribute) if the LLP goes into insolvent liquidation. Such a contribution can be required from a member if he knew or ought to have concluded that there was no reasonable prospect that the LLP would avoid going into insolvent liquidation.[14] For these purposes, the facts which a member ought to know or ascertain and the conclusions which he ought to reach, and (in the case of wrongful trading) the steps which he ought to take, are those which would be known or ascertained or reached or taken by a reasonably diligent person having both (a) the general knowledge, skill and experience that may reasonably be expected of a person carrying out the same functions as are carried out by that member in relation to the LLP,[15] and (b) the general knowledge, skill and experience that that member has.[16] This, then, is the duty of care and standard of conduct in the management of the LLP's finances and affairs which every member owes to the LLP, in that if he fails

---

[9]   Thus leading to the statutory duties set out in chapter 11.
[10]   See **8.15–8.16**.
[11]   Sections 212–213A.
[12]   The relevant provisions of these Acts are considered in chapters 29 and 32.
[13]   Neill LJ in *Re Grayan Building Services Ltd* (a director's disqualification case) [1995] Ch 241 at 258. And see Henry LJ in the same case quoted in footnote 17 to **1.8**.
[14]   IA 1986, ss 214(2)(b) and 214A(5).
[15]   Including (in the context of liability to contribute under IA 1986, s 214 where there has been wrongful trading) any functions which he does not in fact carry out but which have been entrusted to him: IA 1986, s 214(5).
[16]   IA 1986, ss 214(4) and 214A(6). See further **29.3–29.5**.

to meet it (and the LLP goes into liquidation unable to meet its debts and liabilities) he may be called upon to contribute to the shortfall.

14.12 It is usual in traditional partnerships of any appreciable size for the partners to receive periodic management reports showing income and expenditure for a preceding period. In the light of ss 214 and 214A of the IA 1986, and the CDDA 1986, consideration needs to be given to the members receiving regular financial projections ie reports as to income and expenditure over *future* periods. This will enable (or at least help) members to conclude (or otherwise) on a periodic basis that there is every reasonable prospect of the LLP not going into insolvent liquidation, and will assist them to fulfil their collegiate responsibility for the conduct of the LLP's affairs.[17]

DELEGATION OF DUTIES LAID ON MEMBERS AS A WHOLE

14.13 Certain duties and responsibilities are laid on the members of the LLP as a whole by the CA 1985. These are referred to at **11.16**. They include, in particular, preparing the annual accounts in compliance with the provisions of the CA 1985 (ie so that the accounts give a 'true and fair view' of the LLP's financial position), and approving those accounts. An issue which arises in the present context is the extent to which the LLP agreement may provide that such duties and responsibilities are to be delegated by the members as a whole to a smaller body of members. The authors suggest that there is no objection in principle to such a provision. Whether or not such a provision will be wise, however, or may lead to potential liabilities for individual members who make the delegation, will depend upon the particular circumstances of the LLP. In many cases where the LLP agreement provides, expressly or impliedly, that the preparation and/or approval of the accounts is a matter for the membership as a whole, the reality is likely to be that some of the members will rely on other members (and the auditors) with a greater grasp of the relevant information, and a greater relevant expertise, for the purpose of deciding the details of preparation of the accounts, and whether or not to approve the accounts when completed. Provided that those members who are so relying on others do so reasonably in all the circumstances (judged by an objective standard of reasonable care),[18] they will not be liable to the LLP (acting, for instance, by a liquidator) for breach of a duty of care, nor be liable to disqualification under the CDDA 1986, if the accounts turn out to be materially wrong.[19]

14.14 The view may be taken by the members that the circumstances of the LLP are such that the members as a whole can reasonably delegate to (and rely on) a particular committee of members to act on behalf of all the members in preparing

---

[17] See the discussion as to collegiate responsibility in **32.19–32.21**.

[18] As to the general duty of care of a member to the LLP, see **11.12**.

[19] See, for instance, *Davey v Cory* [1901] AC 477 and *Re D'Jan of London Ltd* [1994] 1 BCLC 561 (cases of negligence alleged against directors) and *Re Cladrose Ltd* [1990] BCLC 204 (disqualification case); and see the reference in para 5 of Sch 1 Part 1 to the CDDA 1986 to the extent of the member's responsibility for any failure to comply with CA 1985, ss 226/7 or 233.

and/or approving the annual accounts, or in deciding the details of the financial year of the LLP and where the LLP's accounting records are to be kept.[20] The risk will be that, in permitting the LLP agreement to provide that such matters shall be done by a committee, the members will be institutionalising their own view as to the reasonableness of reliance by the general body of members. Before permitting such provision in relation to the approval of the annual accounts, the members will need to be satisfied that they are not, in doing so, being reckless as to whether or not those accounts comply with the requirements of the CA 1985.[21]

14.15   In addition to the duties and responsibilities on the members as a whole referred to in **14.14**, the members as a whole have a responsibility (or a power) to appoint the auditors of the LLP for a financial year if the designated members fail to do so.[22] This power is exercisable by the members 'in a meeting convened for the purpose'. The authors suggest that the effect of these words is that it is indeed only the members as a whole, in a meeting, who can exercise this power; and that there is no scope for a delegation of it to a committee.

---

[20]   See **11.16**(i)–(iv).
[21]   See CA 1985, s 233(5).
[22]   See **11.16**(v) referring to CA 1985, ss 385(4) and 388A(5).

Chapter 15

THE MEMBER AND THE OUTSIDE WORLD

INTRODUCTION

15.1 In the case of a traditional partnership, where there is no legal entity separate from the individual partners contractually connected to each other, each partner is, on the principles of agency, liable for the contracts entered into, and the wrongs committed by, any other partner acting in the course of the partnership's business.[1] The cardinal feature of the LLP Act 2000 is that it creates a legal entity – the LLP – separate from the members. As previously discussed,[2] the LLP is now the principal, and the members are agents for it rather than agents for their co-members. The result is that, in accordance with the principles of agency (and LLP Act 2000, s 6), it is now the LLP which is liable for the contracts entered into, and the wrongs committed by, any member acting within the scope of his actual or ostensible authority on behalf of the LLP.[3] The existence of the LLP serves, therefore (in broad terms), to shelter the individual member from personal liability for the acts of another member (or an employee) carried out in the course of the business. This is one of the fundamental benefits to the individual member of incorporation as an LLP.

15.2 The position of the LLP as against the outside world has been considered in Chapter 5. The position which remains to be considered is that of the individual member as against third parties (eg suppliers or customers) with whom he is the individual dealing on behalf of the LLP.

CONTRACTS

15.3 As a general rule, where a member, as the agent of the LLP, makes a contract solely on behalf of the LLP, the member will not himself be liable under the contract to, nor himself be able to enforce the contract against, the other contracting party. But it must be clear from the contract that the member is contracting solely on behalf of the LLP; and it is important that any liability on the part of the member himself be expressly or impliedly negatived.[4] It is perfectly possible for the contract to be so written that the member *is* himself liable and able to enforce the contract, either alone or concurrently with the LLP. The true position

---

[1]   Generally speaking: see Partnership Act 1890, ss 5, 9 and 10.
[2]   See **3.3** and chapter 5.
[3]   See chapter 5.
[4]   A statement that the member is signing 'for' or 'on behalf of' the LLP should normally suffice: see *Bowstead & Reynolds* on Agency 17th edn, 2001, Art 101(c), and *The Swan* [1968] 1 Lloyd's Rep 5 at 13 (Brandon J).

is to be gathered from the parties' intention as determined by an objective construction of the contract in its surrounding circumstances in accordance with normal principles of construction of contracts.[5]

DEEDS

15.4 It has been mentioned previously that, as a general rule, in order for an LLP to be able to sue or be sued on a deed made inter partes, the LLP needs to be described as a party to the deed, and the deed needs to be executed in its name.[6] Conversely, if a member is described as a party to the deed and executes it in his own name, even if he is described in the deed as acting on behalf of the LLP he will be personally liable (and entitled to sue) on it.[7]

TORTS

15.5 An agent acting on behalf of his principal can incur personal liability in tort, as well as impose attributed liability on his principal.[8] The LLP Act 2000 expressly envisages the possibility of a member being personally liable to a third party as a result of a wrongful act or omission of his done in the course of the business of the LLP or with its authority.[9]

Negligence in the performance of services causing economic loss

15.6 The particular situation which we will consider here is where the member, in carrying out his work on behalf of the LLP, is negligent and, as a result, the client or customer[10] suffers economic loss. As in any situation of negligence, the key question when considering whether the individual member is personally liable to the customer (in addition to the LLP being liable) is whether the member personally owed a duty of care to the customer. In the case of a traditional partnership, there is seldom any need to consider whether there is a distinction for the partner dealing with a customer's matter between a direct duty of care owed by him, and the duty of care owed by the principals as a whole (ie the firm) of whom he is one. It is to be remembered, however, that an employee dealing with a customer's matter can certainly owe a duty of care to the customer, and be liable for a breach of that duty, even if in practice he is often not made a defendant to a claim.[11] The answer to the question whether the negligent individual LLP member

---

[5] See, generally, *Bowstead & Reynolds* above, Articles 99–101 or *Chitty on Contracts* 29th edn, 2004, paras 31-082–31-084. As to the principles of construction of contracts, see *Investors Compensation Scheme Ltd v West Bromwich Building Society* [1998] 1 WLR 896 (HL) at 912F–913F (Lord Hoffmann).

[6] At **4.11**.

[7] See *Bowstead and Reynolds* above, Art 104.

[8] See *Bowstead & Reynolds* above, Art 115 and *Williams v Natural Life Health Foods Ltd* [1998] 1 WLR 830 at 835 B–C.

[9] LLP Act 2000, s 6(4), discussed at **5.20–5.21**.

[10] We will use the term 'customer' hereafter to cover both client and customer.

[11] See, for instance, *Fairline Shipping Corporation v Adamson* [1975] QB 180 at 191A–B (Kerr J) and *Punjab National Bank v de Boinville* [1992] 1 WLR 1138 at 1154B–E (Staughton LJ). In the

(or employee) personally owes a duty of care to the customer will turn on the fundamental question – what was the relationship between the member (or employee) and the customer? The fact that the contract for the services to be supplied to the customer was solely between the customer and the LLP will not necessarily preclude a duty of care on the member personally arising outside the contract.[12] Whether there is in any case a duty of care owed by one person to another will depend upon the relationship between them: is the relationship such a special relationship as to give rise to a duty of care on the part of one to the other?[13]

15.7 Whether there is in tort a special relationship between A and B, leading to the existence of a duty of care on the part of A to B, is determined essentially by reference to one of two approaches:

(a) the 'threefold' test of foreseeability of damage, proximity (or neighbourhood) and whether it is fair just and reasonable that the law should impose a duty of care in the particular situation;[14] or

(b) the 'assumption of responsibility' test (originating with *Hedley Byrne & Co Ltd v Heller & Partners Ltd*[15]), namely whether in the particular circumstances there has been, objectively viewed,[16] an acceptance or assumption by A of responsibility towards B for carrying out a task: where there has been such an acceptance or assumption of responsibility by A, there is attached by the law to it a duty owed by A to B to carry out the task with reasonable care; and if there has been reliance (in most cases[17]) by B on that assumption of responsibility, and that reliance was reasonable,[18] there will be legal liability on the part of A to B for loss suffered by B as a result of the task not having been carried out with reasonable care.[19]

---

latter case, the employees (insurance brokers) were defendants, and were held liable as being in breach of their own duty of care. This was also the case with the employee surveyor in *Harris v Wyre Forest District Council* [1990] 1 AC 831.

[12] See, for instance, *Fairline Shipping Corporation* above at 190C–191B and *White v Jones* [1995] 2 AC 207 at 274C–E and 275A (Lord Browne-Wilkinson).

[13] See, for instance, Lord Goff in *Henderson v Merrett Syndicates Ltd* [1995] 2 AC 145 at 180C and Lord Browne-Wilkinson in *White v Jones* above at 271F–H, 272B–D and 274E–H.

[14] See, for instance, *Caparo Industries Plc v Dickman* [1990] 2 AC 605 at 617G–618C (Lord Bridge) and 632C–633D and 635B–636B (Lord Oliver) and *Gran Gelato Ltd v Richcliff (Group) Ltd* [1992] Ch 560 at 569D–E (Nicholls V-C).

[15] [1964] AC 465.

[16] Lord Goff in *Henderson* at 181B.

[17] The exception is the disappointed will beneficiary or similar who probably does not know of, and is not relying on, the solicitor drafting the document: *White v Jones* above at 268C–D (Lord Goff), 276F (Lord Browne-Wilkinson) and 294A–B (Lord Nolan). And see subsequently *Carr-Glynn v Frearsons* [1999] Ch 326 (CA) and *Gorham v British Telecommunications Plc* [2000] 1 WLR 2129 (CA).

[18] See *Williams v Natural Life Health Foods Ltd* [1998] 1 WLR 830 at 836F-837B; and see the discussion of reliance in *Hagen v ICI Chemicals and Polymers Ltd* [2002] IRLR 31 at paras 105–127 (Elias J).

[19] See, generally, Lord Goff in *Henderson* above at 180–181 and 193C, Lord Browne-Wilkinson in *White v Jones* above at 272–274 and Lord Steyn in *Williams* above at 834D–H. The assumption of responsibility is for the task, not an assumption of legal liability: see Lord Browne-Wilkinson in

15.8 There has been much judicial debate in recent years as to which of these approaches or methodologies is to be used in different circumstances to determine whether a duty of care has arisen. In the context of determining whether, in circumstances where a customer has retained an LLP to provide services and economic loss has resulted from the work being carried out negligently, an individual member of the LLP carrying out the work owed a personal duty of care to the customer, the assumption of responsibility approach appears to be that which the courts are most likely to adopt.[20] We will consider the question whether an individual member owes a personal duty of care (and is personally liable for his own negligence) in the terms of this approach.

Assumption of personal responsibility, and reliance on it

15.9 Whether the member is to be seen as assuming a personal responsibility (or, to put it another way, as being willing to be personally answerable[21]) to the customer for carrying out the work will depend upon whether such an assumption (or willingness) appears from an objective view of all the circumstances of the particular case.[22] 'The touchstone of liability is not the state of mind of the defendant. An objective test means that the primary focus must be on things said or done by the defendant or on his behalf in dealings with the plaintiff. Obviously, the impact of what a defendant says or does must be judged in the light of the relevant contextual scene.'[23] Taking this 'objective view' as to whether there has been an assumption of responsibility gives the court scope to arrive at what it sees as the generally acceptable and just result in the particular case. In *Phelps v Hillingdon LBC*,[24] Lord Slynn, after referring to the test of assumption of responsibility being an objective one, said: 'The phrase [assumption of responsibility] means simply that the law recognises that there is a duty of care. It is not so much that responsibility is assumed as that it is recognised or imposed by the law.'[25] In *Merrett v Babb*,[26] May LJ discussed the two approaches ('strands of consideration') referred to in **15.7** for determining whether or not there was a duty of care in cases where economic loss has been caused. After quoting Lord Slynn's words set out above, May LJ said that the two approaches in reality merge, and went on: 'In my view, it is very often a helpful guide in particular cases to ask whether the defendant is to be taken to have assumed responsibility to the claimant to guard against the loss for which damages are claimed. But I also think that it is reaching for the moon – and not required by authority – to expect to accommodate every circumstance which may arise within a single short abstract formulation. The

---

White v Jones at 273G–274B and Morritt LJ in *Peach Publishing Ltd v Slater & Co* [1998] PNLR 364 at 372E.

[20] See *Williams* above, especially at 834F–G. For a general discussion of the different approaches, see *Clerk & Lindsell on Torts* 18th edn, 2003, paras 7-84–7-96.

[21] See Lord Steyn in *Williams* above at 838A–B. Lord Steyn also speaks of an 'assumption of risk': 838B.

[22] See footnote 16 above

[23] Lord Steyn in *Williams* above at 835F–H.

[24] [2001] 2 AC 619, concerning, inter alia, alleged negligence on the part of a local authority educational psychologist. *Williams* appears not to have been cited or referred to in *Phelps*.

[25] At 654D–F. See previous similar remarks in *Smith v Bush* [1990] 1 AC 831 at 862E–F (Lord Griffiths) and *Caparo v Dickman* above, at 628F–H (Lord Roskill).

[26] [2001] QB 1174 (CA), considered further at **15.12**.

question in each case is whether the law recognises that there is a duty of care.'[27] Although the assumption of responsibility test is said to obviate the need to embark upon an enquiry as to whether it is 'fair, just and reasonable' to impose liability,[28] at some stage in the court's reasoning the issue is going to be addressed as to whether responsibility to the claimant *should* be imposed on the individual member by a deemed assumption of responsibility.[29]

15.10   The above having been said, any general consideration of the issue of personal liability for negligence of an individual member of an LLP must embrace a consideration of the important House of Lords decision in *Williams v Natural Life Health Foods Ltd*.[30] The principles stated in *Williams* are fundamental to an assessment of whether in any particular case there will be personal liability for negligence on the part of an individual member of the LLP. The leading judgment in *Williams* was given by Lord Steyn, with whom the other Law Lords agreed. *Natural Life Health Foods Ltd* had been incorporated by a Mr Mistlin, on the strength of his expertise in the retail health food trade, in order to franchise the concept of retail health food shops. The plaintiffs approached the company with a view to obtaining a franchise for such a shop. On the basis of a brochure and financial projections supplied to them by the company, they entered into a franchise agreement with the company and took a lease of a shop (from an unrelated third party). In the event, the turnover of the shop was substantially less than the projections which had been supplied by the company, and the plaintiffs' business ceased trading after 18 months. They sued the company (which was soon wound up) and Mr Mistlin. The company was held to have given negligent advice. The issue in the House of Lords was whether, in addition to the company, Mr Mistlin was personally liable to the plaintiffs for the loss resulting from that negligent advice. In considering this issue, Lord Steyn made it clear that, whilst the particular facts of *Williams* were concerned with the question of liability to a third party on the part of a director of a company, the applicable principles were not confined to companies and directors but applied equally to any issue as to the personal liability in tort to a third party of an agent who is acting on behalf of a principal with a separate legal identity.[31] In the case of a director of a company (and the position will be similar in the case of a member of an LLP), the inquiry must be 'whether the director, or anybody on his behalf, conveyed directly or indirectly to the [customer] that the director assumed personal responsibility

[27]   Paragraph 41. For a later review of the two approaches or methodologies, see *Customs & Excise Commissioners v Barclays Bank* [2004] 2 All ER 789 esp at 32–51 (Colman J).

[28]   See Lord Goff in *Henderson* above at 181D–E: '...once the case is identified as falling within the *Hedley Byrne* principle, there should be no need to embark upon any further enquiry whether it is "fair, just and reasonable" to impose liability for economic loss'

[29]   See, for instance, Lord Browne-Wilkinson in *White v Jones* above at 275D–276B referring to 'fair just and reasonable' in the context of an assumption of responsibility, and see also Lord Oliver in *Caparo v Dickman* above at 637F–H: the phrase 'voluntary assumption of responsibility' is a convenient phrase 'but it is clear that it was not intended to be a test for the existence of the duty for, on analysis, it means no more than that the act of the defendant in making the statement or tendering the advice was voluntary and that the law attributes to it an assumption of responsibility if the statement or advice is inaccurate and is acted upon. It tells us nothing about the circumstances from which such attribution arises.'

[30]   [1998] 1 WLR 830.

[31]   At 835A–B.

towards the [customer]'.[32] If this is conveyed to the customer (and there is negligence) the next question will be whether the customer was in fact relying on *the director's* assumption of personal responsibility.[33] This reliance will be essential if the customer is to have a cause of action against the individual director Additionally, this reliance on the individual director's assumption of responsibility (objectively viewed) must be reasonable.[34] One can substitute 'LLP member' for 'director' in the foregoing sentences.

15.11   Applying these principles to Mr Mistlin's position, the House of Lords held (reversing the trial judge and a majority Court of Appeal) that on the facts there was no assumption of personal responsibility by Mr Mistlin, although he was the owner and controller of the company, and the company's brochure made clear that its expertise to provide advice was derived from him; and although also he had played a prominent part in the production of the projections supplied to the plaintiffs. Clearly central to this conclusion was the fact that there were no personal dealings between Mr Mistlin and the plaintiffs, who had dealt solely with an employee.[35]

> 'There were no exchanges or conduct crossing the line which could have conveyed to the plaintiffs that Mr Mistlin was willing to assume personal responsibility to them . . . I am also satisfied that there was not even evidence that the plaintiffs believed that Mr Mistlin was undertaking personal responsibility to them. Certainly, there was nothing in the circumstances to show that the plaintiffs could reasonably have looked to Mr Mistlin for indemnification of any loss.'[36]

Also material was the fact that documents sent to the plaintiffs were on company notepaper.[37]

15.12   The subsequent case of *Merrett v Babb* in the Court of Appeal[38] has been seen as difficult to reconcile with the approach of the House of Lords in *Williams*, where consideration of the facts focussed largely on the degree of direct contact between the plaintiffs and Mr Mistlin. In *Merrett v Babb* a firm of surveyors was engaged by a building society to produce a valuation of a modest house, which valuation, in the usual way, was to be passed on to the prospective mortgagors (and purchasers) of the property. The valuation report was duly passed on to them, and it proved to be negligently inaccurate. The action was a claim by the mortgagors against the individual surveyor who had carried out the valuation, Mr Babb. A professionally qualified surveyor and valuer, he was a salaried employee of the firm. The mortgagors had no contact with him, and did not know who he was. (The copy of the valuation report which was supplied to them omitted both his name and the name of the firm.) They were not themselves the clients of the firm.

---

[32]   At 835H.

[33]   Ie a reliance regardless of the corporate character of the company.

[34]   See 836F–G and 837B.

[35]   See 838C–D.

[36]   Lord Steyn at 838C–D.

[37]   See 833A–B. And see the reference at 835H–836B to *Fairline Shipping v Adamson* above.

[38]   [2001] QB 1174. Leave to appeal to the House of Lords was refused by the Lords: [2001] 1 WLR 1859.

Nevertheless, Mr Babb was held to be personally liable to them for the negligent valuation. He knew that the valuation would be relied on by the mortgagors, and he signed the report as a valuer in his personal capacity.[39] On these facts, he was held by a majority of the Court of Appeal to have assumed responsibility to the mortgagors for the valuation. It is important to appreciate that the facts were very similar to two previous cases decided by the House of Lords, in which valuers engaged by mortgagees of modest houses were held liable in negligence to the mortgagors;[40] and it is clear that particular policy considerations are in play in relation to responsibility for such valuations.[41] *Merrett v Babb*, it is suggested, is best seen as an illustration of the importance of the 'objectivity' of the court's approach to determining whether or not there has been an assumption of personal responsibility, and as a case involving particular policy considerations.[42]

15.13   The first issue in any particular case relating to an LLP, therefore, will be whether there has been an assumption of personal responsibility by the individual member, namely whether (to adapt Lord Steyn's words quoted in **15.10**) the member, or anybody on his behalf, has conveyed directly or indirectly to the customer that the member has assumed personal responsibility for the work in hand towards the customer. If this has been conveyed to the customer, the second issue will be whether it has, in fact, been relied on by the customer, and relied on reasonably. Inevitably, in any dispute the court will be looking at the situation with hindsight, when loss has been suffered by the customer and the court is considering whether a remedy against the individual member for that loss ought to be available.[43] The criteria by which the reasonableness of reliance is to be assessed are not wholly clear from *Williams*. But given the clear connection between reliance on a person carrying out a task and indemnification by that person if the task is carried out negligently, it appears that an element at least (or way of looking at the matter) in determining whether it is reasonable for a customer to rely on an assumption of personal responsibility by an individual member of an LLP will be whether it is reasonable for the customer to rely on indemnification by that member personally in the event of negligence in the carrying out of the work on behalf of the LLP.[44] And it may be also that a factor for the court in forming an

---

[39]   See the judgments at paras 5, 10, 44 and 61-3.

[40]   *Smith v Bush* and *Harris v Wyre Forest DC* reported together at [1990] 1 AC 831.

[41]   See May LJ at paras 13, 23 and 30 and Wilson J at para 58 in *Merrett v Babb*. In *Williams* (at 837D), Lord Steyn described *Smith v Bush* and *Harris v Wyre Forest DC* as having been decided on special facts.

[42]   It is to be remembered also that in *White v Jones* [1995] 2 AC 207 (the disappointed will beneficiary case), the testator's solicitor was held to have assumed a responsibility to the beneficiary, although the latter had had no contact with the solicitor: see 268D and 270B.

[43]   Although couched in terms of the 'threefold' test, rather than the presently applicable 'assumption of responsibility' test, see Lord Oliver in *Murphy v Brentwood District Council* [1991] AC 398 at 486A–B: 'The essential question which has to be asked in every case, given that damage which is the essential ingredient of the action has occurred, is whether the relationship between the plaintiff and the defendant is such – or, to use the favoured expression, whether it is of sufficient "proximity" – that it imposes upon the latter a duty to take care to avoid or prevent that loss which has in fact been sustained'. And see Lord Goff in *Henderson* above at 186H: 'an assumption of responsibility coupled with reliance by the plaintiff which, in all the circumstances, makes it appropriate that a remedy in law should be available for such negligence'.

[44]   See Lord Steyn at 836G–837B.

objective view as to whether there has, in any event, been the initial *assumption of responsibility* will be whether the individual LLP member has shown a willingness to be personally answerable out of his own pocket.[45]

15.14   There is clearly scope for policy considerations to play a part both in the objective view which is taken of all the particular circumstances when reaching a decision as to whether there has been an assumption of personal responsibility, and in determining whether reliance by the customer on that assumption of responsibility (if existing in fact) was reasonable.[46] The starting point, however, may be the one which appears to have been adopted by the New Zealand Court of Appeal in *Trevor Ivory Ltd v Anderson*[47] (referred to by Lord Steyn in *Williams*), namely that where individuals have formed a limited liability entity, separate and distinct from its members, in accordance with legislative policy, the limitation of liability should not be undermined by an unreasonable finding of an assumption of personal responsibility on the part of a member. There is a balance to be found between giving proper recognition to the separate legal personality of the LLP and allowing an adequate remedy for the wrong done.

Professional advisers

15.15   The issues discussed above will be essentially the same whether the LLP is a firm of professionals (eg accountants or solicitors) or non-professionals, and the crucial core question will still be – has there been an assumption of personal responsibility? But when considering the position of an individual member of an LLP of professionals, it is perhaps worth considering also the possibility of a fiduciary relationship being said to have arisen between a member personally and the client. A fiduciary relationship arises where one person has undertaken to act for or on behalf of another either generally or in a particular matter in circumstances which give rise to a relationship of trust and confidence.[48] Most relationships between professional adviser and client are seen as fiduciary relationships.[49] The effect of there being a fiduciary relationship is that a duty of

---

[45]   See Lord Steyn at 836H quoting La Forest J in the Canadian Supreme Court case of *Edgeworth Construction v Kuehne Nagel International* [1993] 3 SCR 206 at 212. And see also Lord Reid in *Hedley Byrne* [1964] AC 465 at 486.

[46]   And see in this context Lord Steyn's reference in *Williams* at 837D–E to 'practical justice'. For a wider discussion as to the judicial approach to policy and discretion, see *Clerk & Lindsell on Torts* above, paras 7-13–7-20.

[47]   [1992] 2 NZLR 517. The company was a one-man company which, through Mr Ivory, the major shareholder and managing director, carried on the business of an agricultural supplier and adviser. Acting by Mr Ivory, it gave negligent advice as to the use and application of a herbicide for the plaintiffs' raspberry plantation, as a result of which negligent advice the raspberry plants had to be dug up. The Court of Appeal (reversing the trial judge) held that there had been no assumption of responsibility by Mr Ivory. There was merely 'routine' involvement by him for and through the company, and no singular feature which would satisfy the belief that he was accepting a personal commitment as opposed to the known company obligation (McGechan J at 532).

[48]   See Millett LJ in *Bristol and West Building Society v Mothew* [1998] Ch 1 at 18A–B, approved by the Privy Council in *Arklow Investments Ltd v Maclean* [2000] 1 WLR 594.

[49]   See Lord Upjohn in *Brown v IRC* [1965] AC 244 at 265F–G: 'a professional adviser, whether he be solicitor, factor, stockbroker or surveyor is of course in a fiduciary relationship to his client'. The relationship between solicitor and client has long been recognised as a fiduciary relationship: see, in addition, for instance, *McMaster v Byrne* [1952] 1 All ER 1362 (PC).

care is imposed on the fiduciary in the carrying out of the matters in respect of which he has undertaken to act. The basis of this imposition is an assumption or acceptance of responsibility by him for those matters.[50] In other words, its basis is exactly the same as the basis for the imposition of the common law duty of care arising under the *Hedley Byrne* principle discussed in the foregoing paragraphs.[51]

15.16   Where the LLP is a firm of professionals, with an individual member advising the client on its behalf, there will be a fiduciary relationship between the LLP and the client. Whether there is, in addition, a fiduciary relationship between the individual member and the client will turn on whether (to use the language of fiduciary relationships[52]) the *individual member* has undertaken to act for or on behalf of the client in the relevant matter in circumstances which give rise to a relationship of trust and confidence between him personally and the client. Strictly speaking, this should be seen as just another way of posing the crucial core question in the context of an LLP of professional advisers. To say that there is a fiduciary relationship between the member personally and the client is merely to attach the label 'fiduciary' to a relationship where an assumption of personal responsibility is seen – on an objective view – to have been accepted by the individual professional.[53] Nevertheless, given the personal trust and confidence between client and individual adviser which in many situations is seen as the essence of a professional relationship, and given also the entrenched learning that the relationship between client and professional adviser is a 'fiduciary relationship',[54] it may be that the courts will have a predisposition, at least in some professional contexts, to see trust and confidence having been reposed by the client in (and accepted by) the individual member personally, leading to there being a

---

[50]   See Lord Browne-Wilkinson in *White v Jones* above at 271G–H.

[51]   See Lord Browne-Wilkinson in *Henderson* above at 205E–H ('The liability of a fiduciary for the negligent transaction of his duties is not a separate head of liability but the paradigm of the general duty to act with care imposed by law on those who take it upon themselves to act for or advise others') and in *White v Jones* above at 271D–H and 274F–H. In *Medforth v Blake* [2000] Ch 86 (CA), concerned with the scope of the duties of a receiver (including the duty of care), the court declined to distinguish between the answer at common law and in equity: see 102D–E. Although the duty arises out of the fiduciary relationship, the duty of care is not itself a fiduciary duty; and equitable compensation for breach of the duty is given on the same principles as common law damages: see Millett LJ in *Bristol and West Building Society v Mothew* above at 17C–H. 'There is no reason in principle why the common law rules of causation, remoteness of damage and measure of damages should not be applied by analogy in such a case': *ibid.*

[52]   See footnote 48 above.

[53]   'Although the historical development of the rules of law and equity have, in the past, caused different labels to be stuck on different manifestations of the duty, in truth the duty of care imposed on bailees, carriers, trustees, directors, agents and others is the same duty: it arises from the circumstances in which the defendants were acting, not from their status or description. It is the fact that they have all assumed responsibility for the property or affairs of others which renders them liable for the careless performance of what they have undertaken to do, not the description of the tradeor position which they hold': Lord Browne-Wilkinson in *Henderson* above at 205F–H.

[54]   See footnote 49 above. In defence of the individual member, it will be said that there is indeed such a relationship, but the 'professional adviser' is the LLP.

duty of care on that member personally (whether put in common law terms, or in terms of equity[55]) in addition to the duty of care on the LLP.

15.17   Even if an individual assumption of responsibility is found, however, there will still remain the issues of reliance on that individual assumption and, if there was reliance, whether it was reasonable.[56]

Excluding liability in the retainer letter

15.18   The obvious practical conclusion from the above discussion (at least for an LLP of professionals) is that, from the individual member's point of view, consideration needs to be given to the terms of a retainer letter, written when the LLP is first instructed, making clear that the client or customer is dealing solely with the LLP,[57] and that there is no acceptance or assumption of responsibility by any member personally (as opposed to the LLP) for carrying out the relevant work. The question arises, however, as to the impact on such a letter of the Unfair Contract Terms Act 1977, and also of the Unfair Terms in Consumer Contracts Regulations 1999.[58] It is convenient to consider the 1977 Act first.

The Unfair Contract Terms Act 1977

15.19   This Act (UCTA 1977) provides that a person cannot by reference to any contract term or to a notice given to persons generally or to particular persons exclude or restrict his liability for a breach by him of any common law duty to take reasonable care or exercise reasonable skill (ie exclude or restrict his liability for common law 'negligence') except in so far as the term or notice satisfies the requirement of 'reasonableness' set out in the Act. This exception is itself subject to the saving that where the loss or damage is death or personal injury there can be no exclusion or restriction of liability at all.[59] It is also provided that where a contract term or notice purports to exclude or restrict liability for such negligence, a person's agreement to or awareness of it is not of itself to be taken as indicating his voluntary acceptance of any risk.[60] It is relevant to note that UCTA 1977 has no application to exclusions or restrictions of liability for breach of a duty of care arising in equity.[61] If, therefore, a member's individual duty of care were to exist in equity (ie be imposed by equity as a result of a fiduciary relationship), but not at common law, the retainer letter could exclude or restrict liability for breach of that

---

[55]   As to the possible relevance of a distinction between the existence of a common law duty of care and a duty in equity, see **15.18** discussing UCTA 1977.

[56]   For further consideration of the position in relation to LLPs of professionals, see *Whittaker* 'Professional LLPs: Liability in Negligence after *Merrett v Babb*' [2002] JBL November Issue, 601.

[57]   See **15.3**.

[58]   SI 1999/2083.

[59]   UCTA 1977, s 2(1) and (2) with s 1(1)(b). The Act also applies in relation to contractual obligations to take reasonable care in the performance of the contract. The present discussion is concerned solely with the duty of care in tort, and assumes that there is no direct contractual obligation to take reasonable care owed by the individual member to the client.

[60]   UCTA 1977, s 2(3).

[61]   See the discussion in **15.15** and **15.16**.

duty of care without interference from UCTA 1977.[62] It must be very doubtful, however, whether the courts would allow any distinction between common law and equity in this context to permit professionals (at least in the general run of work) to escape a restriction on clauses excluding liability for negligence which applies to non-professionals.[63] This discussion of UCTA 1977, and the retainer letter, proceeds on the basis that if a duty of care on an individual member is to be found, it will be held to exist at common law.

15.20   The question is whether a statement in the retainer letter[64] to the effect that no individual member of the LLP accepts or assumes responsibility for carrying out the relevant work constitutes an exclusion or restriction by the relevant individual member or members[65] of their liability (and, if it does, whether it satisfies the reasonableness test). It might be argued that UCTA 1977 cannot apply, on the basis of the following reasoning: what the Act prevents or impedes is the exclusion of liability for negligence; negligence is defined in the Act[66] as the breach of a duty of care; this duty arises from an assumption of responsibility; what the retainer letter is doing (if anything) is excluding such an assumption of responsibility; therefore, there being no duty arising between the individual member and the client, there is in fact no exclusion of liability for breach of that duty because there is simply no duty. The courts have, however, emphasised that the substance of a contractual term or notice must be looked at in order to see whether it is an exclusion or restriction for the purposes of the Act.[67] Specifically, the above line of reasoning has been rejected by the House of Lords in *Smith v Bush*.[68] The House of Lords pointed, inter alia, to s 13(1) of the Act, which provides (so far as presently relevant) that to the extent that s 2 prevents the exclusion or restriction of any liability, it also prevents excluding or restricting liability by reference to terms and notices which exclude or restrict the relevant obligation or duty.

15.21   It appears, therefore, that in order to determine whether an individual member is excluding his duty of care for the purposes of UCTA 1977 (with the result that the 'reasonableness' of the exclusion needs to be established), the essential question is whether, regardless of the retainer letter, he is – objectively viewed, and taking into consideration the matters referred to in **15.9–15.14** – assuming a personal responsibility to the client, ie would the individual member be

---

[62]   But not (where the disclaimer is a term of the contract between the LLP and the client) without interference from the Unfair Terms in Consumer Contracts Regulations 1999. These Regulations do not distinguish between liabilities arising at common law or in equity.

[63]   See the discussion in **15.15** and **15.16**.

[64]   Which, it is being assumed, will be a letter from the LLP.

[65]   Ie any member or members who actually do work for the client.

[66]   Section 1(1)(b).

[67]   See *Phillips Products Ltd v Hyland* [1987] 1 WLR 659 at 666B (Slade LJ) and *Johnstone v Bloomsbury Health Authority* [1992] QB 333 at 346C–E (Stuart-Smith LJ).

[68]   [1990] 1 AC 831 (concerned with the liability of building society surveyors to purchasers borrowing on mortgage): see Lord Templeman at 848C–849C, Lord Griffiths at 856E–857H and Lord Jauncey at 872H–874A. The above line of reasoning was accepted by the Court of Appeal in *Harris v Wyre Forest DC* [1988] QB 835, one of the two cases heard in the House of Lords (where the Court of Appeal was reversed) and reported under the title of *Smith v Bush* above.

assuming that responsibility but for what is said in the retainer letter.[69] The practical result may perhaps be put as follows. The retainer letter will not of itself determine whether there is or is not a duty of care owed by any individual member or members of the LLP to the client, that is to say whether there is or is not (objectively viewed) any individual assumption of personal responsibility to the client. But the letter may conveniently provide evidence militating against a finding of an individual assumption of responsibility.

15.22   If the retainer *does* amount to an exclusion or restriction of liability for negligence, the application of UCTA 1977 means that there can be no exclusion or restriction by a member of liability for death or injury resulting from negligence.[70] In relation to other loss or damage (eg economic loss from negligent advice) there can be exclusion or restriction of liability if such exclusion or restriction is 'reasonable' in accordance with UCTA 1977, s 11. It is relevant at this stage to consider the legal status of the statement in the letter which negatives the existence of any individual member's duty of care. Assuming that the retainer letter is a contract between the LLP and the client, and that the statement as to no personal responsibility on the part of a member has contractual effect, the requirement of reasonableness is that the term should have been a fair and reasonable one to be included having regard to the circumstances which were, or ought reasonably to have been, known to or in the contemplation of the parties (ie the LLP and the client) when the contract was made.[71] If, however, the statement made to the client is merely a notice, not having contractual effect, the reasonableness test is whether it is fair and reasonable to allow reliance on the notice, having regard to all the circumstances obtaining when the liability arose or (but for the notice) would have arisen.[72]

15.23   This is not the place to discuss extensively the test of reasonableness and its application.[73] At whichever time the test falls to be applied, however, it is a broad general test.[74] The onus will be on the member to show that the exclusion or restriction of liability was reasonable.[75] In the same way as there is room for policy considerations to play a part when considering the question whether in a particular case a member has assumed a personal responsibility,[76] so here also there is clear scope for a degree of policy consideration: is it reasonable to allow individual professionals as members of an LLP to exclude or restrict personal liability? The following statement by Lord Griffiths in *Smith v Bush*[77] is to be noted:

---

[69]   This is the 'but for' test stated by Lord Griffiths in *Smith v Bush* above at 857D.

[70]   This will clearly be relevant to LLPs which are building contractors.

[71]   Ie broadly speaking, at the beginning of the retainer and before the work is carried out: UCTA 1977, s 11(1).

[72]   UCTA 1977, s 11(3).

[73]   For a fuller discussion, see, for example, *Chitty on Contracts* 29th edn, 2004, paras 14-084–14-102.

[74]   '...the court must entertain a whole range of considerations, put them in the scales on one side or the other, and decide at the end of the day on which side the balance comes down': Lord Bridge in *George Mitchell (Chesterhall) Ltd v Finney Lock Seeds Ltd* [1983] 2 AC 803 at 815–816. And see also the factors enumerated by Lord Griffiths in *Smith v Bush* [1990] 1 AC 831 at 858–859.

[75]   UCTA 1977, s 11(5).

[76]   See **15.14**.

[77]   [1990] 1 AC 831 at 859D–E.

'I would not, however, wish it to be thought that I would consider it unreasonable for professional men in all circumstances to seek to exclude or limit their liability for negligence. Sometimes breathtaking sums of money may turn on professional advice against which it would be impossible for the adviser to obtain adequate insurance cover and which would ruin him if he were to be held personally liable. In these circumstances it may indeed be reasonable to give the advice upon a basis of no liability or possibly of liability limited to the extent of the adviser's insurance cover.'

15.24   This statement was, of course, made before LLPs were in view. Nevertheless, it is a judicial recognition that there are circumstances where an individual professional man can reasonably exclude or restrict his personal liability. In the case of an individual member of an LLP being considered here, unless the LLP seeks to exclude or restrict its own liability there will be, in any event (and subject to issues of solvency), the LLP for the client to look to. It may be that in the light of this, and provided that the LLP has what is a reasonable level of insurance cover in the circumstances, the court will look favourably on an exclusion of personal liability on the part of the individual member. Alternatively, it may be that a restriction of personal liability up to a certain insurable limit for the individual member will be reasonable.[78]

The Unfair Terms in Consumer Contracts Regulations 1999

15.25   In addition to UCTA 1977, it will be necessary to consider the possible impact of the Unfair Terms in Consumer Contracts Regulations 1999[79] on any exclusion or restriction of a member's personal liability. These regulations are concerned, inter alia, with 'unfair terms' in contracts made between a seller or supplier (whether corporate or a natural person), who is acting for purposes relating to his trade, business or profession, and a natural person (the 'consumer'). These regulations have no application, therefore, where the client of the LLP is a corporate body. An unfair term is not binding on the consumer.[80] The test for whether or not a term is 'unfair' is more complex than the reasonableness test under UCTA 1977,[81] but for the purposes of considering terms restricting or excluding liability is not likely to lead to differing results. The relevant contract for present purposes is the contract between the LLP (the seller or supplier) and the client (the consumer) constituted by the retainer letter,[82] and the relevant term is that there is no personal responsibility on the part of a member.

15.26   Two particular points on these regulations should be noticed in the present context. First, a term which has not been individually negotiated[83] may specifically

---

[78]   See UCTA 1977, s 11(4), and the cases referred to in *Chitty on Contracts* above, para 14-087.

[79]   SI 1999/2083.

[80]   Regulation 8(1).

[81]   Regulation 6(1) provides that: 'the unfairness of a contractual term shall be assessed, taking into account the nature of the goods or services for which the contract was concluded and by referring, at the time of conclusion of the contract, to all the circumstances attending the conclusion of the contract and to all the other terms of the contract or of another contract on which it is dependent'.

[82]   See footnote 59.

[83]   Which it will not have been where it has been drafted in advance and the consumer has not been able to influence it: reg 5(2).

be regarded as unfair.[84] Secondly, Sch 2 to the Regulations contains an indicative and non-exhaustive list of the terms which may be regarded as unfair. Paragraph (b) of these terms is relevant, being a term which has the object or effect of 'inappropriately excluding or limiting the legal rights of the consumer vis-à-vis the seller or supplier or another party in the event of total or partial non-performance or inadequate performance by the seller or supplier of any of the contractual obligations.' The client of the LLP will be the consumer, and the LLP itself will be the seller or supplier: 'another party' will include the individual member of the LLP. If there is a breach by the LLP of its contractual duty of care[85] which causes loss to the client, this will be through the negligence of the individual member acting on behalf of the LLP. This, of course, will not be a breach of a contractual duty owed by the individual member to the client, but (assuming for present purposes that there has been an assumption of personal responsibility by the member) it will be a breach of his personal duty of care to the client (whether arising at common law or in equity).[86] There is no requirement in paragraph (b) that the legal rights of the consumer against another party must be for breach of the *seller or supplier's* contractual obligation, only that they arise 'in the event of' a breach of the seller's contractual obligation. In any event paragraph (b) is only indicative.[87] The conclusion from this discussion is that where the client or customer of the LLP is a private individual, and there is to be an exclusion of liability for negligence for individual members of the LLP, the 1999 Regulations need to be borne in mind as well as UCTA 1977.

Other torts causing economic loss

15.27   The reasoning in *Williams* is not expressly confined to the tort of negligence, and to determining whether an agent has assumed a personal responsibility for work being carried out with due care.[88] It has subsequently been decided by the House of Lords, however, that this reasoning does not apply to liability for fraudulent acts done by an agent. In *Standard Chartered Bank v Pakistan National Shipping Corp (No 2)* the Court of Appeal had applied the reasoning in *Williams* to a claim brought against a director personally for a fraudulent misrepresentation made by him on behalf of his company. The false statement was attributed to the company: the issue was whether the director was personally liable as well. The Court of Appeal decided that he was not, because he never led the plaintiff bank to believe that he was assuming personal responsibility for the representation, and the bank believed that it was dealing with the company.[89] The House of Lords reversed this, on the basis that a person cannot escape liability for his fraud by saying that he made it clear he was not personally liable.[90]

---

[84]   Regulation 5(1).

[85]   Ie 'non-performance or inadequate performance' of its contractual obligation.

[86]   The 1999 Regulations have no distinction between rights arising at common law or in equity.

[87]   Regulation 5(5).

[88]   Lord Steyn at [1998] 1 WLR 830 at 835B–C refers simply to 'personal liability in tort'.

[89]   [2000] 1 Lloyd's Rep 218.

[90]   [2003] 1 AC 959.

Joint liability with the LLP

15.28   A member of an LLP can in certain circumstances be liable to a third party as a joint tortfeasor with the LLP for the LLP's tort. These circumstances will, in broad terms, be where the tortious act is to be seen as a joint act done by the member and the LLP in pursuance of a common purpose between them. This may, in particular, be the case where the member has ordered or procured the tortious act to be committed. The degree of participation in the act which is required from the member in order to make him liable as a joint tortfeasor with the LLP has been said (in the context of directors of companies) to be 'elusive', and to involve – at least in some cases – broad considerations of policy.[91] Generally speaking, a member will not be treated as jointly liable with the LLP for the latter's tort if he does no more than carry out the proper functions allotted to him in accordance with the LLP agreement for the purposes of the LLP's management or business.[92] The mere fact that a person is a member of an LLP will not of itself render him liable for torts committed by the LLP during his membership.[93]

Individual status of certain professionals

15.29   Legislation provides that some professional positions can only be occupied by an individual (and not, therefore, by a partnership or a corporate body such as an LLP). Examples are the actuary of an occupational pension scheme,[94] a cathedral architect,[95] an insolvency practitioner[96] or a receiver of the property of an LLP.[97] In cases where such an individual is a member of an LLP, he will clearly assume a personal responsibility to the client; and will (subject to any exoneration clause) be personally liable in the event of his services being provided negligently. Similarly, an individual who is a member of an LLP and undertakes a trusteeship or directorship will be personally liable for his own wrongdoing in such positions. Whether or not the LLP will in addition be liable under LLP Act 2000, s 6(4) for the individual's negligence or other wrongdoing is discussed at **5.20**.

LIABILITY IN AN INSOLVENT LIQUIDATION

15.30   As has been mentioned at **8.15–8.16** and **14.10–14.12**, the members of an LLP may, in certain circumstances, find themselves exposed to personal liability to general creditors of the LLP in the event of the LLP going into insolvent liquidation.

---

[91]   See *C Evans Ltd v Spritebrand Ltd* [1985] 1 WLR 317 (CA) at 330–1.
[92]   See, generally, *MCA Records Inc v Charly Records Ltd* [2003] 1 BCLC 93 (CA).
[93]   See, for instance, *C Evans v Spritebrand Ltd* above at 323H.
[94]   See Pensions Act 1995, s 47.
[95]   See Cathedrals Measure 1999, ss 9(1)(f) and 35(1).
[96]   See IA 1986, s 390.
[97]   See ibid, s 30.

Chapter 16

CESSATION OF MEMBERSHIP AND ITS CONSEQUENCES

INTRODUCTION

16.1 The cessation of a person's membership of an LLP, and the requirement to give notice of it to the Registrar, has been mentioned in outline at **8.33–8.36**. The purpose of this chapter is to consider the routes to cessation of a person's membership in more detail, and then to consider the consequences of a cessation of membership.

CESSATION OF MEMBERSHIP

Cessation by agreement or by 'reasonable notice'

16.2 Section 4(3) of the LLP Act 2000 provides that, in addition to ceasing to be a member by death or dissolution, a person may cease to be a member of an LLP in accordance with an agreement with the other members or, in the absence of agreement with the other members as to cessation of membership, by giving reasonable notice to the other members. Section 4(3), therefore, does two things: it entitles a member to retire in accordance with an agreement with the other members, and it provides a default right of retirement.[1] This default right is for a member to retire, not for the other members to expel.[2]

16.3 Partnership law provides no equivalent default right to retire: a partner has no right to retire in the absence of an express or implied agreement with his partners.[3] The explanation for this is that a partnership is the relationship which exists between all the partners together: there is no relationship between one partner and a separate entity. What partnership law does give, in a partnership at will, is the right for any member to dissolve the partnership (ie to bring the relationship to an end) and, *prima facie* at least, to have the assets sold and the business wound up. An LLP, however, continues to exist as the same corporate entity, notwithstanding that members have left or new members have joined. Given this, and the separate relationship between each member and the corporate entity, it

---

[1] We will use the expressions 'retire' and 'retirement' to mean 'cease to be a member' and 'cessation of membership'.

[2] Expulsion is discussed in **16.13–16.14**.

[3] *Lindley & Banks on Partnership* 18th edn, 2002, paras 24–90 to 24–94; Blackett-Ord, *Partnership* 2nd edn, 2002, paras 13.34–13.38.

is, the authors suggest, appropriate that a person has a right to cease to be a member in the absence of an agreement with the other members as to leaving.[4]

By agreement

16.4   An agreement amongst the members as to retirement may form part of a general LLP agreement. Alternatively, such an agreement can be made on an ad hoc basis as and when a member wishes to retire. As with a traditional partnership, if the members make an agreement which operates to restrict, or impose conditions on, the right to retire (for example, by fixing the necessary notice period, or by limiting the number of members who may leave during a particular period), a member will have to comply with the terms of that agreement in order to cease to be a member.

16.5   What is not entirely clear is whether the members of an LLP are entitled to contract out of the s 4(3) default right altogether. Can the members agree that there will be no right of retirement at all, or no right of retirement during a specified period? If such a provision is agreed, the result will be that a member will only cease to be a member by death (in the case of an individual member), by dissolution (in the case of a corporate member), pursuant to an express power of expulsion, or the dissolution of the LLP following winding up.[5] Whilst an agreement containing an exclusion of the right to retire is likely to be rare, there may in particular circumstances be good commercial justification for it, especially in smaller LLPs. The issue on s 4(3) is whether the words 'in the absence of agreement with the other members as to cessation of membership' mean 'in the absence of an agreement between the members allowing individual members to cease to be members' or mean 'in the absence of any agreement at all relating to cessation'. In other words, is an agreement that there shall be no right to retire an agreement 'as to cessation'? The drafting of s 4(3) is unhappy; but it is suggested that an agreement that there shall be no right to retire is an agreement 'as to cessation'. In principle, members should be entitled to make an agreement that they shall not be entitled to retire, and in the authors' view they can do so.[6]

On reasonable notice

16.6   If there is no relevant agreement as to retirement (permitting it or excluding it), what period of notice will be regarded as reasonable? Clearly, this will vary from LLP to LLP in the light of all the relevant circumstances, and may even vary

---

4   Cf the position of a member of a company limited by guarantee. In the absence of a provision in the Articles of Association permitting him to do so, he cannot cease to be a member. And contrast also the position of a member of company limited by shares who can only cease to be a member by transfer of his shares: the articles of association of many private companies impose restrictions on the ability of members to transfer their shares, and members wishing to dispose of their shares may be forced to rely upon the unfair prejudice provisions of CA 1985, s 459.

5   Or by an order for the purchase of his share in the LLP pursuant to CA 1985, s 459. See chapter 27.

6   Very careful thought will need to be given before such a term is agreed. If relations between the members break down and the majority are not prepared to agree to allow a dissatisfied member to leave, such a member may be forced to petition for relief under CA 1985, s 459 (if not also excluded by agreement under s 459(1A)), or for the winding up of the LLP on the just and equitable ground pursuant to IA 1986, s 122(1)(e): see chapter 27.

between different members of the same LLP. A longer period may be more reasonable for a long established member who has significant contact with clients than for a junior member who has little client involvement. Although a fixed default notice period in s 4(3) would have been somewhat arbitrary, the certainty of a fixed period (which could, of course, have been varied by agreement) might have been preferable to the uncertainty to which the reasonable notice requirement may well give rise.

16.7 It is possible to identify some factors that are likely to be relevant in determining the reasonable period; but, until some judicial guidance is given, it is difficult to predict with any degree of confidence the approach that is likely to be taken by the courts. It is suggested that some or all of the following factors are likely to be relevant.

(i)   The nature of the LLP's business, and the role of the outgoing member in the business. Does the outgoing member have a significant involvement or contact with clients/customers? To what extent (as a matter of commercial reality) is the 'goodwill' of the business vested in the members generally or in the outgoing member? Is the member likely to take clients/customers with him? Does the LLP agreement impose restrictive covenants on outgoing members; and if it does not, is this significant?[7]

(ii) The length of time that the outgoing member has been a member.

(iii) The need for the LLP to replace the outgoing member, the ease with which this can be done and the length of time the replacement process is likely to take.

(iv) The notice periods imposed by other LLPs, firms or companies in the same business. This is likely to be of limited relevance, but it may provide some general guidance. For example, notice periods for professionals (both for partners and employees) tend to be longer than those for manual workers.

(v)   The absence of an agreement as to the notice period. The court may infer from the fact that the members have not agreed a notice period that they did not intend a long period. This may be particularly so if the LLP has no written agreement at all: a court may infer from the relative informality adopted by the members that they did not intend lengthy restrictions on leaving.

(vi) The solvency of the LLP. A member may wish to cease to be a member as a consequence of concluding that the LLP is insolvent and will not avoid going into insolvent liquidation. If a member takes such a view, and is unable to persuade his fellow members to implement appropriate steps, he will expose himself to liability pursuant to s 214 of the IA 1986 unless he ceases to be a member.[8] In such circumstances, a court is likely to consider that a very short period of notice is reasonable.

---

[7]   Given that a restrictive covenant (if there is one) will in practice be in a written LLP agreement, and that a written LLP agreement is likely to provide for a fixed notice period for retirement, a consideration of the impact of restrictive covenants which are in place is in practice unlikely to arise.

[8]   See chapter 29. As an alternative to giving 'reasonable notice', the member may be able to present a winding-up petition as a contributory.

(vii) The default provisions in partnership and employment law. A partner in a partnership at will can serve a notice dissolving the partnership without notice. The statutory minimum notice to be given by an employee is one week.[9] This is likely to be of limited relevance but, again, tends to point towards shorter rather than longer notice periods.

16.8 It is suggested that, in general, courts are likely to favour shorter rather than longer notice periods in the absence of persuasive reasons to the contrary. Notice periods for partners in professional service firms tend to vary between about 3 months and 1 year. It is unusual to find shorter, but not that uncommon to find longer, periods. For example, some firms provide that at least 1 year's notice must be given to expire at the end of the firm's accounting period. The notice period in these cases can, therefore, be up to 2 years. It is suggested that the courts will tend to favour notice periods at the bottom end of this range for professionals ie between 3 and 6 months. For non-professional service LLPs, it is suggested that the courts will tend to favour an even shorter period ie perhaps about one month. It is to be stressed, however, that each case will turn on its own facts, and that no reliable view can be expressed until a body of case law has developed.

16.9 The discussion in **16.6–16.8** has been in relation to 'full' members of the LLP, that is to say members who are not also employees of the LLP. The existence of employee members has been discussed in chapter 8.[10] An employee member is likely to have a fixed notice period in relation to his employment. If he does not, there is a body of case law as to what will constitute the proper notice period.[11] The termination of his employment, and the termination of his membership of the LLP, may (depending on the terms of any agreement) be two quite separate matters; and there is no necessity for the two to coincide. Nevertheless, if the court is faced with an issue as to what is 'reasonable notice' for an employee member to cease to be a member, it is likely to find as a general rule, the authors suggest, that the period is the same as the notice period for terminating his contract of employment.

Death/dissolution

16.10 The intention (or at least the assumption) behind the legislation appears to be that a member ceases to be a member on death (in the case of an individual member) or dissolution (in the case of a corporate member). LLP Act 2000, s 4(3) provides that 'A person may cease to be a member... (as well as by death or dissolution) in accordance with an agreement with the other members...'. In the case of the dissolution of a corporate member, there can be no doubt that the dissolution causes a cessation of membership (although theoretically the membership, viewed as a bundle of rights and obligations, could vest in the Crown as *bona vacantia*[12]). In the case of death, however, s 4(3) is to be contrasted with LLP Act 2000, s 7. Section 7(1) provides that s 7 applies where a member of an

---

[9] See Employment Protection (Consolidation) Act 1978, s 49(2).
[10] See **8.26–8.32**
[11] See, for example, *Chitty on Contracts* 29th edn, 2004, para 39-155.
[12] Under CA 1985, s 654. This would be subject to the effect in such circumstances of the LLP Act 2000, s 7(2), discussed at **8.20–8.23**.

LLP has either ceased to be a member or: (a) has died; (b) has become bankrupt or been wound up; (c) has granted a trust deed for the benefit of his creditors; or (d) has assigned the whole or part of his share in the LLP (absolutely or by way of charge or security). This appears to assume that death does not automatically cause cessation: if death causes a cessation, s 7(1)(a) would be unnecessary. Section 7(2) provides that 'in such an event' the former member or (a) his personal representative; (b) his trustee in bankruptcy or liquidation; (c) his trustee under the deed for the benefit of his creditors; or (d) his assignee may not interfere in the management or administration of any business or affairs of the LLP. The authors suggest that the reference to death in s 7 should either be regarded as a drafting error or, alternatively, as part of an intention to recite, for the avoidance of doubt, that personal representatives are not entitled to interfere in the management etc of the LLP. This latter view of the provision gains support from the fact that there is a reference in s 7(2) to a former member: a former member is clearly not entitled to interfere in the management of the LLP; and so (the authors consider) the reference in paragraph (a) of each of s 7(1) and s 7(2) to death or personal representatives must have been included for the avoidance of doubt. Construing ss 4(3) and 7 together, the better view is that death does cause an automatic cessation of membership for the member and his estate.

Bankruptcy/liquidation of a member

16.11 The bankruptcy of an individual member does not cause a cessation of his membership unless the LLP agreement provides for this, either automatically or at the election of the other members.[13] If the bankrupt does not cease to be a member, his share or interest in the LLP will vest in his trustee in bankruptcy on appointment.[14] But the trustee has no right to become a member, and may not interfere in the management or administration of any business or affairs of the LLP.[15] If the bankrupt member ceases to be a member, either because he is expelled or pursuant to an agreement with the other members, the financial entitlement of the trustee will depend upon the terms of the LLP agreement. The position if there is no agreement as to an outgoing member's share is discussed in **16.28–16.41**.[16]

16.12 The liquidation of a corporate member likewise does not result automatically in cessation of membership although, again, cessation can be agreed

---

[13] It is, however, a criminal offence for a person who is an undischarged bankrupt to act as a member of an LLP except with the leave of the Court: CDDA 1986, s 11. See also CDDA 1986, s 15.

[14] IA 1986, s 306.

[15] LLP Act 2000, s 7(2)(b), discussed further at **8.20–8.24**.

[16] *Quaere* whether, despite CDDA 1986, s 11, a bankrupt can voluntarily cease to be a member without the consent of his trustee after commencement of the bankruptcy if, by doing so, his share or interest would vest in the other members without financial compensation in full. *Quaere* also the effect of IA 1986, ss 339 and 340 (transactions at an undervalue and preference) in relation to pre-bankruptcy agreements. *Quaere* also the application of the rules relating to forfeiture in the event that a member leaving because of his bankruptcy is not entitled to compensation for his share: see *Krasner v Dennison* [2001] Ch 76 (CA) and *Rowe v Saunders* [2002] BPIR 847.

by the members. A liquidator may not interfere in the management or administration of any business or affairs of the LLP.[17]

Expulsion/compulsory retirement

16.13   In the absence of agreement between the members as to expulsion or
compulsory retirement, a member cannot be expelled or required to retire. This is
the effect of default rule (11)[18] (adopting s 25 of the Partnership Act 1890) which
provides as follows:

> 'No majority of the members can expel any member unless a power to do so has been
> conferred by express agreement between the members.'

16.14   In partnership law, a power to expel must be exercised in good faith and
not for an ulterior motive.[19] Company law applies a similar principle to the
exercise of powers conferred on majority shareholders that enable them to bind
minorities. It is most likely, therefore, that the exercise of a power of expulsion or
compulsory retirement of a member will be subject to a requirement of good faith,
ie that the power be exercised bona fide for the benefit of the LLP as a whole.[20]

CONSEQUENCES OF CESSATION OF MEMBERSHIP

Notification to the Registrar and cessation of agency

16.15   As has been discussed previously, where a person ceases to be a member
(i) the LLP must ensure that notice of this is delivered to the Registrar within 14
days, and (ii) that person will (subject to any agreement to the contrary) cease to be
the agent of the LLP and to have authority to bind the LLP.[21]

Rights and obligations of the outgoing member

16.16   Cessation of membership will result in the member ceasing to be subject
to most of the obligations incidental to his membership, for instance, the obligation
not to compete in business with the LLP[22] and the statutory obligation to take all
reasonable steps for securing that the LLP's accounting records are preserved.[23]
The legislation does not, however, even in the default rules, make any express
provision for the financial consequences of cessation of membership.[24]

---

[17]   LLP Act 2000, s 7(2)(b).
[18]   LLP Regulations 2001, reg 8.
[19]   *Blisset v Daniel* (1853) 10 Hare 493; *Lindley & Banks on Partnership* above, paras 10.120–10.121.
        And see in an employment context *Reda v Flag Ltd* [2002] IRLR 747 (PC), concerned with an
        employer company's contractual right to dismiss an employee without cause, at para 43.
[20]   See further the discussion as to good faith at **11.24–11.26**.
[21]   At **8.34** (notification to the Registrar) and **5.18** (cessation of agency).
[22]   See **11.6**(f), subject to any restrictive covenant binding to him.
[23]   See **11.18**(iv).
[24]   An attempt was made by Lord Goodhart during the third reading of the Bill in the House of Lords
        to introduce a default provision entitling an outgoing member to receive from the LLP an amount
        equal to the value of his share in the capital and profits of the LLP, but the proposed amendment
        was defeated; see *Hansard* HL, vol 611, no 71, 6 April 2000, cols 1420–1427.

Accordingly, in default of agreement between the members, an outgoing member has no express statutory right to receive any payment for the value of his 'share' in the LLP,[25] either from the continuing members or from the LLP itself. As will appear from what is said in the following paragraphs, it is important that members agree (preferably in a written LLP agreement) not only how, and in what circumstances, persons will cease to be members, but also the financial consequences of cessation of membership.

16.17 Most modern partnership agreements provide for the outgoing partner's share to vest in the continuing partners and for the outgoing partner to be entitled to be paid (in addition to his share of accrued profits) a sum representing his capital and/or his share of the firm's assets. Partners are free to decide the basis upon which the amount of the outgoing partner's entitlement is to be calculated. In professional practices, the entitlement of an outgoing partner is often limited to repayment of capital and does not include a share of the excess of the true value of the assets over their balance sheet value (ie unrealised capital profits).[26] LLP agreements, especially for professionals, are likely to adopt a similar approach. In all cases where a member leaves an LLP, however, it will be sensible for him to have in mind the provisions of s 214A of the IA 1986 (adjustment of withdrawals).[27] A member who believes that he is leaving a sinking ship will need to consider, at least, whether he wishes to take some or all of his luggage with him as he seeks to float away.

Potential financial interests

16.18 Before analysing what the position may be in the absence of any agreement as to the financial entitlement of an outgoing member, it is convenient to consider what in fact an outgoing member's financial interests potentially are. It is suggested that they are the following:

(a) a share of profits for a previously finished financial year;
(b) a share of profits for the current year in respect of the period to cessation of membership;
(c) sums contributed by him (or credited to him) as capital;
(d) sums advanced by him to the LLP by way of loan;
(e) a share of the excess of the true value of the assets over their balance sheet value (ie unrealised capital profits); and
(f) a share of any reserve (for instance, a tax reserve or a revaluation reserve).

(a) Share of profits for a previously finished year

16.19 An outgoing member's entitlement to share in the profits of the business made by the LLP prior to his cessation of membership will depend on the

---

[25] As to the legislation recognising that a member has a 'share' and 'interests' in the LLP, see **8.17**.
[26] Issues can arise on the construction of financial provisions in a partnership agreement as to whether the outgoing partner is entitled to a share of goodwill or of unrealised capital profits: see, for instance, *Re White (Dennis) Deceased* [2001] Ch 393 (CA).
[27] See **8.15**.

agreement between the members as to sharing, and division, of profits.[28] The default rule (having effect in the absence of any agreement as to profit sharing) is that all the members share equally in the profits.[29] If an outgoing member leaves at the financial year-end, or after a financial year-end but before the profits for that financial year have been determined, it must be very unlikely that any agreement will provide that he is not entitled to a share of profits for that year on their division. This may, however, be subject to a provision as to retention of profits to a capital account or a reserve account. Given the statutory requirement for annual accounts (which must show, inter alia, the profit or loss for the year in question),[30] and the fact that the outgoing member will have been a member of the LLP during the whole of financial year/accounting period in question, the position under the default rule, it is suggested, will be that the outgoing member is entitled to his share of the profits for the previous financial year when those profits have been determined (and divided) in the same way as a continuing member.[31]

16.20   If profits for a previous year have been determined, and the entitlement of each member to his share in them has crystallised, and there is no agreement as to retention of them,[32] the outgoing member will be entitled to take such of his share as he has not yet drawn.[33]

(b)   *Share of profits for current year*

16.21   If a member leaves during a financial year, the position may be less clear. Again, it must be very unlikely that any agreement will provide that he is not entitled to any share of profits for the financial year during which he leaves. But there may be a question of construction of the agreement as to whether he has a right to a time-apportioned share of the profits for the whole financial year during which he leaves (in which case the ascertainment of his entitlement will have to await the end of the financial year and the drawing up of the accounts), or a right to call for special accounts to be drawn for the period of the financial year up to the date of his ceasing to be a member. As mentioned in **16.19**, the default rule is that all members are entitled to share equally in the profits. 'Members' in the rule, it is suggested, means members for the time being, ie at the time in respect of which one is applying the rule. It follows from this, it is suggested, that the position under the default rule (if applicable) is that special accounts should be drawn up to the date of the outgoing member's cessation of membership for the purpose of calculating his share of profits during the time of his membership. Consistently with this, it is suggested that (unless there is some clear agreement to the contrary) an outgoing member has no right to share in profits made after he has ceased to be a member. There would seem to be no justification for construing 'members' in the default rule as including 'former members'.

---

[28]   See **13.8–13.10**.

[29]   Default rule (1): see **13.5**.

[30]   CA 1985, s 226. Annual accounts are discussed in chapter 18.

[31]   See **13.8-13.10**, and also *Re White (Dennis) Deceased* [2001] Ch 393 at 404–405 (Chadwick LJ, paras 28–30) and 417 (Peter Gibson LJ, para 74), albeit construing a particular agreement.

[32]   Ie the undrawn profits are in a member's 'current' or 'drawings' account.

[33]   See **13.8–13.10**.

(c) Capital

16.22   As has been mentioned in **13.2**, the legislation clearly recognises the concept of members' capital. Where there is an LLP agreement, it is likely to provide a right to repayment of a member's capital on his ceasing to be a member. What is the position in default of agreement? Default rule (1) does not, in the authors' view, contain any provision as to distribution or payment out of capital. All it does is to specify the share of each member; it includes no provision as to how and when that entitlement can be realised. The court may well strive to find an agreement that a leaving member is entitled to repayment of his capital; the slightest indication may be sufficient to justify the finding of an implied agreement.[34] But if no agreement to this effect can be found, whether an outgoing member will be entitled to be paid out his capital will turn on the effect of his cessation of membership on his 'share' in the LLP. This is discussed in **16.28– 16.32**.

(d) Loans

16.23   Sums advanced by way of loan will be repayable according to the terms on which they were loaned.[35]

(e) Unrealised capital profits

16.24   For an outgoing member of a partnership, it is sometimes an issue of construction of the partnership agreement as to whether he is entitled to a share of the excess of the true value of the partnership assets over their balance sheet value.[36] The assets of a partnership are owned by the partners; and in the absence of any agreement to the contrary they are owned in equal shares by all the partners.[37] With an LLP, however, generally speaking the assets of the business will be owned by the corporate entity. When considering the position of a leaving member, therefore, one will be looking to see whether there is any agreed provision which entitles the outgoing member to a share of the surplus value of the LLP's assets. Such a provision will need to do two things: first, appropriate to the outgoing member a share of the surplus value and, secondly, give him an entitlement to take it on leaving. Default rule (1) does neither of these things. The rule follows s 24(1) of the Partnership Act 1890 as to entitlement to share equally in the 'capital and profits' of the LLP. It is clearly established that in s 24 'capital' does not include the assets of the partnership, but is confined to the capital properly so called.[38] There seems no reason why default rule (1) should be interpreted

---

[34]   To adopt the words of Nourse LJ in *Popat v Shonchhatra* [1997] WLR 1367 at 1373B (in the context of displacing the default rule of s 24(1) of the Partnership Act 1890 that all partners are entitled to share equally in the capital).

[35]   Where money is loaned to the LLP without any stipulation as to the time of repayment, it will generally be repayable at once or, in practice, on demand: see, for instance, *Chitty on Contracts* 29th edn, 2004, para 28-036.

[36]   See, for example, *Re White (Dennis) Deceased* [2001] Ch 393.

[37]   This is a rule of general partnership law outside s 24(1) of the Partnership Act 1890. See *Popat v Shonchhatra* above at 1372F–G (Nourse LJ). The law relating to partnerships does not apply to LLPs except so far as expressly applied by statute: see **1.17**.

[38]   See *Popat v Shonchhatra* above at 1372H–1373C.

differently, treating 'capital' (ie members' capital) as including the assets of the LLP. Even if 'capital' could be so treated, there remains the point mentioned in **16.22** that the rule does not contain any provision as to distribution or payment out. Whether, therefore, an outgoing member will be entitled to a share of the surplus value of the assets of the LLP, and if so at what value, if there is no LLP agreement governing the position, will turn on whether any share in such surplus value is appropriated to his 'share' in the LLP, and the effect of his cessation of membership on that 'share'.[39]

(f)   Reserve

16.25   Although the payment of income tax on an individual partner's share of profits is that partner's personal responsibility, some partnership agreements provide for part of a partner's share of profits to be credited to a 'tax reserve' to be available when the tax falls due. The position as to tax on the share of profits of an individual member of an LLP will be the same as for a partner in a traditional partnership.[40] It may be, therefore, that some LLP agreements will have similar 'tax reserve' provisions. If there is a tax reserve, it is difficult to imagine that there will not be, as a matter of express or implied agreement, an entitlement for the outgoing member to be paid the amount reserved in respect of his liability, either immediately or as and when the tax becomes due.

16.26   In relation to any other reserve (for instance, a revaluation reserve), in the absence of any agreement as to entitlement, an outgoing member's entitlement will turn on what that reserve represents and the principles applicable to the underlying item represented.

LLP in liquidation

16.27   IA 1986, s 127 provides that, in a winding up by the court, any disposition of the LLP's property which is made after the commencement of the winding-up is, unless the court otherwise orders, void. The commencement of the winding-up is the time of the presentation of the winding-up petition or if, before the presentation of the petition, the LLP has determined to go into voluntary winding-up, the time of such determination.[41] Payment by the LLP of any sums in satisfaction of the interests set out in **16.18** will involve a disposition of the LLP's property. The commencement of a compulsory winding-up of the LLP will, therefore, have a material effect on the entitlement of an outgoing member to realise his financial entitlement. The remainder of this chapter proceeds on the basis that there is no winding up of the LLP.

NO AGREEMENT AS TO ENTITLEMENT ON CESSATION

16.28   As has appeared from **16.19–16.21**, and **16.23**, an outgoing member is likely to have little or no difficulty in establishing in principle his entitlement to his

---

[39]   See further, **16.28–16.32**.
[40]   See generally on taxation, chapter 21.
[41]   IA 1986, s 129.

share of any profits of the business made prior to the date of his leaving, and to the repayment of loans made by him to the LLP. But difficult questions arise as to an outgoing member's entitlement to repayment of his capital, and to a share of the surplus value of assets, where the LLP agreement does not deal with the issue of such entitlement. As has been discussed previously, the legislation does envisage that a member has a 'share', and 'interest', in the LLP.[42] This fact of itself, however, does not take matters very far. There remains to be decided how the composition of a share is determined, and whether the legislation gives it any particular rights and entrenched existence in relation to a member leaving.

16.29   Two questions arise. First, in the absence of any agreement dealing with entitlement on cessation, is a leaving member entitled to receive (from the LLP or from his fellow members) a payment representing the value of his 'share' in the LLP, or that part of his share which is not covered by any agreement; and, secondly, if not, what is the effect of cessation of his membership on a member's 'share'?

Does a leaving member have a right to payment for the value of his 'share'?

16.30   A member's share is the bundle of contractual or statutory rights and obligations incidental to his membership of the LLP. Does the legislation contain any deemed contractual provision (or other inherent provision) as to what a 'share' comprises. Does the legislation contain any deemed contractual right (or other inherent right) for a leaving member to be entitled to a payment representing his 'share'? As to the first of these questions, the nature and extent of a member's rights and obligations will probably vary, depending upon the point in time at which, and the context in which, they are being considered. There is no definition, or comprehensive statement, in the legislation of what a member's 'share' comprises.

16.31   As to the second of the above questions, s 4(3) of the LLP Act 2000 is the only serious candidate for containing an entitlement for an outgoing member to receive some 'share' on leaving. This subsection gives a member the right to retire in accordance with any agreement or, in the absence of any agreement as to cessation of membership, the right to retire on giving reasonable notice.[43] In partnership law, a partner cannot retire from the partnership unless there is some agreement between the partners to that effect:[44] if there is such an agreement, but no agreement as to the financial consequences, it appears to be implied from the agreement for retirement that the outgoing partner's share or interest in the partnership assets vests in the continuing partners in exchange for the outgoing partner becoming entitled to a sum equal to the value of his share of the partnership assets.[45] Can it be said that s 4(3) is properly viewed as a deemed term of the agreement between members, or between members and the LLP, which applies in

[42]   See **8.17**.
[43]   See **16.2–16.9**.
[44]   See footnote 3 above. If the partnership is a partnership at will, he can, of course, dissolve it.
[45]   See *Sobell v Boston* [1975] 1 WLR 1987.

default of any other agreement; and that there is to be implied into this deemed agreement a term (similar to that which appears to be implied in partnership law) that the member leaving under it is entitled to a sum equal to the value of his 'share'? In the authors' view, there are strong arguments against this. First, the wording of s 4(3) does not lend itself easily to being viewed as containing deemed contractual terms. The right to give reasonable notice applies 'in the absence of agreement with the other members'. This suggests that the right is more a free standing statutory right. If it was intended to be a default term in an LLP agreement, one would have expected to find it in reg 7 of the LLP Regulations 2001.[46] Secondly, the reasonable notice right in s 4(3), and whatever flows from it, does not apply to a person ceasing to be a member by reason of death. It is unlikely that the legislation was intended to give rise to different financial consequences for a person ceasing to be a member upon reasonable notice and a member ceasing to be a member on death. Thirdly, if there is agreement amongst the members as to the ability of members to leave, but no agreement as to financial entitlement on leaving, it is difficult to see any scope for s 4(3) applying; and it is unlikely that the legislation contains a deemed term as to financial entitlement where there is no agreement as to the ability of a member to leave, but does not contain the term where there is agreement as to leaving. Finally, if the subsection does provide a right to payment, it is difficult to say whether the obligation to make the payment falls on the continuing members or on the LLP.[47]

16.32   The view of the authors is that, on a proper construction of the LLP legislation, if a member exercises his right to cease to be a member, whether under the LLP agreement or under s 4(3), without reaching an agreement as to the financial consequences with the continuing members, he has no automatic right to payment for the value of his 'share'; and, specifically, he has no automatic right to payment of his capital or a share in the surplus value of the LLP's assets. The position will be the same for the estate of a member who ceases to be a member by reason of death.

Does the 'share' of a leaving member survive cessation?

16.33   If an outgoing member has no automatic right to payment of the value of his 'share' on his ceasing to be a member, what is the effect of cessation on his 'share'? There are two possibilities: either the outgoing member continues to be entitled to a 'share' in the LLP, notwithstanding that he has ceased to be a member, or the outgoing member's 'share' is determined on cessation.

16.34   In addressing this question, it is necessary to examine what is meant by a 'share' or 'interest' in an LLP in more detail. As stated previously, the legislation does not contain a definition of a 'share' or 'interest', but does contemplate that a

---

[46]   And compare the introductory wording of reg 7 with s 4(3).

[47]   There is also the problem of seeking to imply into the Act, where there is possible ambiguity, what would in effect be a statutory substantive right for a leaving member (or his estate) to be paid out in circumstances where the Government refused to accept an amendment which would have provided such a right in default of agreement. See footnote 24 above.

'share' or 'interest' is (potentially) capable of transfer.[48] Consequently, whatever 'share' or 'interest' may mean in any particular context, it would appear that ownership of a 'share' or 'interest' can become vested in someone other than the member himself.[49] It does not follow from this, however, that a 'share' or 'interest' can survive the cessation of membership and be vested in a non-member. Assuming, as we are, no relevant terms in the LLP agreement, a 'share' in an LLP is, it is suggested, no more than the bundle of the rights and obligations incidental to membership, and an 'interest' is one or more of such rights. If this is correct (and on the assumption mentioned above) the existence of a 'share' or 'interest' in an LLP is dependent on the continuation of the relationship between the member and the LLP (ie the membership) from which the rights and obligations originated.

Comparison with companies and partnerships

16.35   The position of a member of a company limited by guarantee (without a share capital) is not, in this regard (that is to say, in relation to the existence of his 'share' being dependent on the continuation of his membership), dissimilar to that of a member of an LLP. Pursuant to Art 4 of Table C, [50] a member may at any time withdraw from the company by giving at least 7 days' clear notice to the company, and membership is not transferable and ceases on death. Although the company does not have a share capital, a member of such a company owns a 'share' of the company in the sense that he has a right, as a member, to share in any distribution of profit (in proportion to the amount of his guarantee) made by the company, or to share in the company's surplus assets on a winding up.[51] If, however, the member ceases to be a member by giving notice, his right to participate in any distributions must come to an end, and the subsequent profits or surplus are distributable amongst the current members at the relevant time.

16.36   In the case of a company limited by shares, a share is the expression of the proprietary relationship between the shareholder and the company (ie a share gives the shareholder proportionate ownership of the company) and comprises a bundle of rights and duties.[52] In *Borland's Trustee v Steel*[53] Farwell J defined a 'share' as:

> 'the interest of a shareholder in the company measured by a sum of money, for the purpose of liability in the first place, and of interest in the second, but also consisting of mutual covenants entered into by all the shareholders inter se in accordance with [s 14 of the CA 1985]. The contract contained in the articles of association is one of the original incidents of the share. A share is not a sum of money . . . but is an interest

---

[48]   LLP Act 2000, s 7(1), discussed at **8.20**. See also, for example, CA 1985, ss 432(4) and 461(2)(d) and IA 1986, s 127. (Default rule (5) provides that no person can voluntarily assign an 'interest' in an LLP without the consent of all existing members.)

[49]   As well as being capable of voluntary assignment, the share or interest may also vest in non-members by operation of law, for example, in a trustee in bankruptcy of a member pursuant to IA 1986, s 306: see LLP Act 2000, s 7(1)(b).

[50]   SI 1985/805.

[51]   See *Palmer's Company Law* paras 2.008–2.013.

[52]   *Palmer's Company Law* paras 6.001 and 6.002. See generally *Gower and Davies' Principles of Modern Company Law* 7th edn, 2003, pp 615–618.

[53]   [1901] 1 Ch 279, at 288.

measured by a sum of money and made up of various rights contained in the contract, including the right to a sum of money of a more or a less amount.'

16.37   Although a share in a company limited by shares is clearly a form of property (namely, a chose in action), the bundle of rights and obligations that comprise the share are nevertheless merely incidents of the shareholder's membership of the company. The difference between a company limited by shares, on the one hand, and a company limited by guarantee, or an LLP or a partnership, on the other, is that (subject to restrictions in the company's articles) a member of a company limited by shares is entitled to transfer his shares to another person, and that person is entitled to become registered as a member.[54] Nevertheless, the 'share' is still a bundle of rights incidental to membership. The transferee becomes a member on registration; the transferor does not cease to be a member until the transferee has become registered.[55]

16.38   In partnership law, a partner is free (subject to any contrary agreement) to assign his share in the partnership absolutely or by way of charge.[56] However, the effect of such an assignment is extremely limited. An assignee does not, as a result of the assignment, become a partner or acquire the right to become a partner: the assigning partner continues to be a partner until his death, expulsion or retirement. An assignee is not entitled to interfere in the management or administration of the partnership business or affairs, or to require accounts of any transaction or to inspect the books. An assignee's right is limited, by statute, to an entitlement to receive the share of profits to which the assigning partner would have been entitled and, on a dissolution, to the share of assets to which the assigning partner is entitled as between himself and the other partners.[57] If, therefore, a partner ceases to be a partner (and the continuing partners carry on the business) in circumstances in which the outgoing partner is not entitled to compensation, the rights of an assignee, being incidental to the partner's membership of the firm, will come to an end.

LLPs

16.39   Is there anything in the LLP legislation which, expressly or by implication, contemplates that a member's share or interest will continue even if his membership has ceased? It is our view that there is not. Indeed, as has been seen, default rule (1) provides that the members are to share equally in the capital and profits of the LLP. Assuming that 'members' in the rule means 'members for the time being',[58] the rule would seem to be inconsistent with any suggestion that an outgoing member has any interest in the capital or profits of the LLP on an ongoing basis or in the assets on a winding up.

---

[54]   *Palmer's Company Law* above, para 6.602.
[55]   Ibid, para 7.017.
[56]   Partnership Act 1890, s 31(1).
[57]   Ibid, s 31.
[58]   See **16.21**.

If ceased member does have continuing 'share' or 'interest'

16.40   If we are wrong in the view expressed in **16.39**, and an outgoing member (who ceases to be a member pursuant to s 4(3)) does (in the absence of any agreement with the continuing members) continue to have a share or interest in the LLP, how does the former member realise his share? If, notwithstanding his cessation, the former member continues to be entitled to receive a profit share without any obligation to provide services, this is likely to be some incentive for the continuing members to agree terms in respect of the former member's share. If, however, agreement cannot be reached, the question arises as to how the former member can extract the value of his share from the LLP. There would seem to be two possibilities: first, a petition to wind up the LLP on the just and equitable ground pursuant to s 122 (1)(e) of the IA 1986 and, secondly, a petition for unfair prejudice pursuant to s 459 of the CA 1985. The objective of a petition pursuant to s 122(1)(e) would be to have the LLP wound up and for the former member to receive payment for the value of his share. The objective of a petition pursuant to s 459 would be an order that the continuing members purchase the interest of the former member at a value to be agreed or determined by the court. There are, however, serious issues as to the locus standi of a former member to present a petition pursuant to either section; and, indeed, serious issues as to whether relief can be granted under these provisions in the absence of unfairly prejudicial conduct on the part of the respondents to the petition. A refusal to buy the outgoing member's share may not be regarded as such conduct. Petitions pursuant to ss 459 and 122(1)(e) are discussed in chapter 27. If a past member has no right to present a petition for winding up on the just and equitable ground or for unfair prejudice, he will have no cause of action to extract the value of his share from the LLP, and he will be forced to wait for the LLP to be wound up at the instance of the other members or a creditor.

Conclusion

16.41   It is our view that if a member leaves without any agreement as to the financial consequences, his capital will accrue to the other members; and that the surplus value of the assets will remain with the LLP until appropriated to members.

16.42   While these issues as to financial entitlement on leaving remain unresolved, a member who is contemplating retirement, in circumstances where there is no agreement providing for the financial consequences of retirement, will obviously be wise to seek to agree terms with the other members before giving his notice. If satisfactory terms cannot be agreed, his only remedy may be (while still a member) to present a petition to the court under s 459 of the CA 1985 (unfair prejudice) or s 122(1)(e) of the IA 1986 (just and equitable winding up).[59]

---

[59]   See chapter 29.

Chapter 17

FOREIGN CONNECTIONS AND OVERSEA LLPs

FOREIGN CONNECTIONS OF GREAT BRITAIN LLPs

17.1 An LLP incorporated under the LLP Act 2000 will, of course, be incorporated in Great Britain. It will have a registered office in Great Britain where documents (including court proceedings) may be served on it.[1] It will also at all times be subject to the statutory filing requirements.[2] Nevertheless, in the conduct of its day-to-day business the LLP's connection with Great Britain may be tenuous. There is no restriction in the legislation on foreign membership, so that all the members of an LLP (including the designated members) may be resident or incorporated outside Great Britain.[3] Equally, there is no restriction on an LLP carrying on all its business outside Great Britain: it need not have any place of business in Great Britain.[4] It has unlimited capacity to own property and other assets abroad.[5] It may borrow funds, and designate the capital contributed by its members, in a foreign currency;[6] and there is no restriction as to the currency in which its accounts may be prepared.[7] The extent to which an LLP agreement may be governed by a foreign law is considered at **9.19–9.20**.

JURISDICTION OVER GREAT BRITAIN LLPs

17.2 The jurisdiction of the High Court is founded upon service of process: the High Court has jurisdiction over a defendant if he or it is properly served with process (whether in England or abroad).[8] At common law, the English Court has jurisdiction over persons present in England at the time of service and, in certain other specific cases, the English court permits service outside the jurisdiction.[9] The common law position has been modified substantially by the EC Council Regulation on jurisdiction and the recognition and enforcement of judgments in civil and commercial matters ('the Regulation'),[10] the Brussels and Lugano Conventions ('the Conventions') and the Civil Jurisdiction and Judgments Act

---

[1] See **3.12**.
[2] An LLP which carries on business, or has interests outside the United Kingdom, the Channel Islands and the Isle of Man may claim a 3-month extension of the period for filing its accounts and auditors' report: see CA 1985, 244(3), discussed at **18.19**.
[3] See **2.4** and **10.1**.
[4] See **2.12**.
[5] As to an LLP's unlimited capacity, see **3.4–3.5**.
[6] See **13.2.**
[7] So that they may, for instance, be prepared in Euros.
[8] Dicey & Morris, *The Conflict of Laws* 13th edn, 2000, paras 11R-001 et seq.
[9] *Dicey & Morris* above, para 11-004; and CPR, r 6.20.
[10] Council Regulation (EC) No 44/2001.

1982.[11] Pursuant to the Regulation and the Conventions, save for various matters in respect of which another state has exclusive jurisdiction, the English Court has jurisdiction in respect of a claim (within the scope of the Regulation or the Conventions) against an LLP domiciled in England.[12] As a body corporate, an LLP is domiciled where it has its (a) statutory seat or (b) central administration or (c) its principal place of business.[13] The 'statutory seat' of an LLP will be the place of its registered office.[14]

17.3 Article 22.2 of the Regulation provides that the courts of the Member State in which a company, legal person or association of natural or legal persons has its seat has *exclusive jurisdiction* over proceedings 'which have as their object the validity of the constitution, the nullity or the dissolution of' the entity, or 'the validity of the decisions of their organs'.[15] In determining the seat of the entity for these purposes, the court applies its rules of private international law.[16] Article 22(2) clearly applies to LLPs.[17] The relevant UK rules for determining the seat of an entity are contained in para 10 of Sch 1 to the Civil Jurisdiction and Judgments Order 2001.[18] This provides that an entity has its seat in the UK if (and only if) it was incorporated or formed under the law of a part of the UK, or its central management and control is exercised in the UK.[19] By analogy with company law, it appears that Art 22.2 applies to any dispute as to the extent of an individual member's liability, qua member, for the debts or engagements of the LLP or to a dispute as to the extent of a member's duties to the LLP.[20]

17.4 The Regulation does not apply to proceedings relating to the winding-up of insolvent companies or legal persons (which clearly includes LLPs), judicial arrangements, compositions or analogous proceedings.[21] The EC Council Regulation on insolvency, which confers jurisdiction in relation to insolvency proceedings, is discussed at **22.3**.

---

[11] The Regulation has substantially (but not completely) superseded the Brussels and Lugano Conventions: see generally chapter 11 of the Third Supplement to *Dicey & Morris* above.

[12] Regulation Art 2, and *Dicey & Morris* above, 3rd supplement, paras S11R-232–S11-237.

[13] Regulation Art 60.1, and *Dicey & Morris* above, 3rd supplement, paras 11R-059–11-060.

[14] Regulation Art 60.2.

[15] See on these words *Dicey & Morris* above, 3rd supplement, paras S11R-343–S11-348.

[16] Regulation Art 22.2.

[17] See, for instance, in relation to partnerships, *Phillips v Symes* [2002] 1 WLR 853 at paras 42/3.

[18] SI 2001/3929.

[19] Para 10(2). The entity has its seat in another Regulation State if it was incorporated or formed under the law of that state; and it is not to be regarded as having its seat in a Regulation State other than the UK if it has its seat in the UK, or if it is shown that the courts of that other state would not regard it for the purposes of Art 22.2 as having its seat there: para 10(3) and (4).

[20] *Dicey & Morris* above, para 30-024 and 3rd supplement para 30-024, citing *Konamaneni v Rolls-Royce Industrial Power (India) Ltd* [2002] 1 WLR 1269.

[21] Regulation Art 1.2(b).

OVERSEA LLPs

Requirements for carrying on business in Great Britain

17.5 For the purposes of the LLP Act 2000 and the LLP Regulations 2001 a 'limited liability partnership' is an entity incorporated as such in Great Britain under the LLP Act 2000.[22] A number of other jurisdictions also enable 'limited liability partnerships' to be established.[23] The LLP Act 2000 recognises this, and provides that regulations may apply existing company, insolvency and partnership law not only to domestic LLPs incorporated under the Act,[24] but also to bodies incorporated or otherwise established outside Great Britain and having such connection with Great Britain and such other features as the regulations may prescribe (defined as 'oversea limited liability partnerships').[25] The only regulations relating to oversea LLPs which have so far been made (namely, the LLP Regulations 2001 applying CA 1985, s 693 with modifications) relate to bodies incorporated or otherwise established outside Great Britain whose names under their law of incorporation or establishment include the words 'limited liability partnership'.[26] Every such oversea LLP is required:

(a)   in every prospectus inviting subscriptions for its debentures in Great Britain, to state the country in which it is incorporated or established;[27]

(b)   to conspicuously exhibit on every place where it carries on business in Great Britain its name and the country in which it is incorporated or established; and

(c)   to cause its name and the country in which it is incorporated or established to be stated in legible characters in all bill heads, letter paper, and in all notices and other official publications and communications of it.

This is the only provision of UK legislation or domestic law which has so far been applied to oversea LLPs carrying on business in Great Britain. In relation to *companies* incorporated outside Great Britain ('oversea companies') and which have established a branch or other place of business in Great Britain, CA 1985, Part XXIII[28] creates a regime for the filing with the Registrar of detailed information, including (i) a list of the company's directors and of the names and

---

[22]   See LLP Act 2000, ss 1(2) and 14(3)

[23]   Ie in particular, states of the United States of America and provinces of Canada: see **17.7–17.10**. Singapore also appears set to introduce LLPs, based on the US Revised Uniform Partnership Act model: see the Ministry of Finance Press Statement of 5 April 2004.

[24]   As is done by the LLP Regulations 2001 and the LLP Regulations 2002.

[25]   See LLP Act 2000, ss 14, 15 and 18.

[26]   See CA 1985, s 693(2) as modified. It may be argued that an LLP formed outside Great Britain which is not an entity separate from its members, but is an 'aggregate' partnership, is not a 'body' for the purposes of s 693. The authors suggest that 'body' in s 693 is likely to be interpreted as including a body of persons forming together a partnership, whether or not the resultant partnership is a separate entity. As to the relevance of the distinction, see **17.17** et seq.

[27]   CA 1985, s 693(1) provides essentially as (a), (b) and (c) in the text, but does not include the words 'or established' in the phrase 'country in which it is incorporated or established'. It seems reasonably clear from s 693(2), however, that what is intended by s 693(1) is that the country of incorporation or establishment (whichever is appropriate) should be stated or exhibited in the circumstances specified in (a), (b) and (c).

[28]   Sections 690A–703R.

addresses of the persons resident in Great Britain authorised to accept on the company's behalf service of any proceedings or notice required to be served on it; (ii) annual accounts; and (iii) details of charges over property. No such details are currently required to be filed with the Registrar by oversea *LLPs* carrying on business in Great Britain.

17.6 The explanation for the current paucity of Companies Act provisions being made applicable to oversea LLPs carrying on business in Great Britain, and for the very general definition of 'oversea LLP' used for the purposes of CA 1985, s 693,[29] no doubt lies in the nature of North American limited liability partnerships. An increasing number of oversea LLPs of professionals are carrying on business in Great Britain, and it is worthwhile considering what their nature is, and how they may be treated by the English courts.

US LLPs (and LLCs)

17.7 In the US, LLPs are the creatures of individual state laws. Since 1999, all the states have had statutes providing for the creation of LLPs.[30] Whilst there are common core features uniting all US LLPs, there are also some distinctions between them (for instance, as to the need for annual registration, and as to limitation of liability). The key point for the English lawyer to appreciate is that it is a core feature of US LLPs that, unlike GB LLPs, they are not corporate entities (in the language of the CA 1985, they are not 'incorporated'), but are general partnerships which have elected, under and in accordance with their chosen state law, to have the status of 'limited liability partnership'. Having said this, it is also to be appreciated that a majority of states (but not all states) have adopted (with individual variations) the Revised Uniform Partnership Act 1994 ('RUPA'), which provides that a partnership is an entity distinct from its partners.[31] Where RUPA has been adopted, therefore, a general partnership (and, as a result, an LLP which it becomes),[32] although not a corporate entity, will generally[33] have a legal personality separate from that of the individual partners. Where RUPA has not been adopted, the general partnership will be an 'aggregate' partnership, like an English partnership under the Partnership Act 1890. The mechanics of a general partnership electing to have LLP status differ from state to state; but, generally speaking, the election involves the existing partnership filing an application with a designated public official setting out certain basic information, such as the

---

[29] A body incorporated or otherwise established outside Great Britain whose name under its law of incorporation or establishment includes the words 'limited liability partnership'.

[30] The first LLP statute was enacted in Texas in 1991, in the aftermath of the savings and loan crisis of the 1980s, which resulted in many substantial claims against accounting and law firms.

[31] RUPA, s 201(a). States which have adopted the RUPA entity model include California, Delaware and Florida. States which have not adopted this model include Illinois, New York and Pennsylvania.

[32] RUPA, s 201(b), which provides that an LLP continues to be the same entity that existed before the filing of a statement of qualification as provided for in s 1001.

[33] But not invariably. The Delaware RUPA, for instance, provides that a partnership (and so an LLP which it becomes) is a separate legal entity from its partners unless otherwise provided in a statement of partnership existence and in a partnership agreement: s 15-201(a). Although, under RUPA, a partnership has its own legal personality, the partners in a general partnership (but not an LLP) remain jointly and severally liable for all of its obligations: RUPA, s 306(a).

partnership's name (which must end with 'LLP' or variant) and principal office, and the number of partners and nature of the partnership's business. Upon this filing (and payment of a fee), the partnership becomes a 'limited liability partnership'. Most states require the application to be renewed annually if the status of LLP is to be retained; and some states restrict LLP status to partnerships of professionals only.[34] No state requires the filing of accounts.

17.8   As is most likely the case for members of a GB LLP, limitation of liability for individual partners is the driving force behind US LLPs. The degree of protection from vicarious liability differs from state to state; but it appears to be the position that all US states will hold a partner in an LLP personally liable in respect of claims arising from his own misconduct or negligence, or for the misconduct or negligence of those under his direct supervision or control.[35] In this respect, and owing to the separate corporate status of a GB LLP, the position of a US partner differs from the position of a member of a GB LLP.[36] This uniform personal liability apart, there are differences between individual state laws as to the extent of the departure which LLP status affords from the position of every partner having joint and several liability for the debts and obligations of the partnership. The broad difference is that some states ('partial shield states') only protect an individual partner from vicarious liability for the negligence or misconduct of others in the partnership (so long as that partner was not personally involved) and not from the LLP's general commercial liabilities, whilst other states ('full shield states') provide substantial protection to an individual partner from *all* partnership liabilities (excluding those arising from his own misconduct as mentioned above), whether arising in contract or tort or otherwise, and so will substantially protect him from personal liability for the partnership's general business and commercial debts and liabilities (such as leases or guarantees).[37] Most states also require an LLP to carry a minimum amount of insurance.

17.9   As has been seen from what is said in **17.7** and **17.8**, apart from the fact that they share the use of 'LLP' in their names, US LLPs and GB LLPs are only distantly related. The US entity to which a GB LLP can much more closely be equated is the 'limited liability company', which is again a creature of statute in individual states. There are considerable similarities between an LLC and a GB LLP. Both are separate legal entities distinct from their members, with unlimited capacity (subject to restrictions in some US states on the business activities in which an LLC may engage), with pass-through tax treatment and (broadly speaking) with no personal liability for their members for the contractual and

---

[34]   Examples of such states are California and New York. Delaware has no such restriction. Some other states, on the other hand, prohibit certain professionals from practising as an LLP.

[35]   The liability of an individual partner for his own negligence or misconduct is either expressed in statutes or arises as a matter of common law.

[36]   How wide this difference will turn out to be in practice will depend much on the approach of the English courts to applying the principle of "the assumption of personal responsibility" to members of GB LLPs: see the discussion at **15.5–15.14**.

[37]   Examples of states providing such substantial protection are Delaware and New York.

tortious liabilities of the entity.[38] An LLC is incorporated by the filing of 'articles of organisation' similar to the incorporation document for a GB LLP, and the relationship of the members to each other and to the LLC is governed by a private 'operating agreement' similar to an LLP agreement for GB LLPs (with the US statutes, like the LLP Act 2000, providing default rules as to such matters as management and sharing of profits if not covered by the operating agreement actually made).[39]

Canadian LLPs

17.10   A number (although not all) of the provinces of Canada, led by Ontario in 1998, have introduced the ability for partnerships of specified professionals to become LLPs.[40] Canadian LLPs are essentially the same as US LLPs (ie general partnerships which have elected under their chosen provincial law to register as 'limited liability partnerships'), and are not separate corporate entities as in Great Britain. Equally, Canadian LLPs (and general partnerships) do not follow the US RUPA model of being entities distinct from their members; but are 'aggregates' in the same way as English general partnerships. In broad terms, protection from personal liability does not extend to a partner's liability for his own negligence or misconduct[41] or (with some variations between provinces) for the negligence or misconduct of those under his direct supervision or control, or for negligence or misconduct which he knew of and failed to take reasonable steps to prevent. Broadly speaking, a partner remains personally liable to a third party for all such negligence or misconduct. Beyond this, the Canadian statutes mostly follow the more narrow approach outlined in **17.8** (ie 'the partial shield states'), and only protect an individual partner from personal liability for the negligence and/or (in some cases only) wider misconduct of others in the partnership in which he has no involvement, and not from personal liability for the ordinary debts of the partnership incurred in the course of its business.[42]

Jersey LLPs

17.11   Jersey introduced limited liability partnerships in 1997. Under the Limited Liability Partnerships (Jersey) Law 1997, a Jersey LLP is a legal person (although not a corporate body) distinct from the partners of whom it is composed.[43] Any contract which binds the LLP is made only with this separate legal person. A partner is personally liable for any loss caused by him (for instance, arising out of

---

[38]   The legislation in some US states expressly provides that the case-law which states the conditions and circumstances under which the corporate veil of a corporation may be pierced shall also apply to LLCs. For a discussion of the English law position as to personal liability, see chapter 15.

[39]   For a fuller discussion of US LLPs and LLCs, see *Limited Liability Companies and Limited Liability Partnerships* by Thomas A Humphreys (Law Journal Press, 2004).

[40]   Other provinces which have introduced LLPs include Alberta, Manitoba, New Brunswick, Nova Scotia and Saskatchewan.

[41]   See, for instance, s 10(3) of the Ontario Partnership Act 1990.

[42]   Exceptions are New Brunswick and Saskatchewan ('full shield provinces'), which provide that a partner is personally liable only for negligence or other wrongful acts for which he would be personally liable if he was not a member of the partnership, and for any partnership obligation for which he would be liable if the partnership were a corporation of which he was a director.

[43]   Article 2(4).

his own negligence or misconduct); but beyond this, he is not personally liable for any debt or loss of the partnership (including any debt or loss caused by the act of any partner) save where, in certain circumstances, he withdraws capital or profits at a time when the LLP is (or becomes within 6 months from the withdrawal) unable to pay its debts. Although the LLP is obliged to keep full accounting records going back ten years, it is not obliged to have its accounts audited or filed with the Registrar.

JURISDICTION OF ENGLISH COURT OVER OVERSEA LLPs

The juridical party

17.12   As is mentioned in **17.2**, the jurisdiction of the English court depends upon service. The English court will have jurisdiction in respect of a claim against an oversea LLP if proceedings can be validly served on the LLP in accordance with English procedural law. Given that those countries which have LLPs are not parties to the Regulation, or to the Conventions, discussed at **17.2–17.3**, the significance of the Regulation and the Conventions will be limited.[44] As has been seen at **17.7–17.11**, LLPs in other jurisdictions are not bodies corporate. At present, all oversea LLPs are general partnerships. Some of them are, under their domestic legislation, separate entities distinct from their members; and others of them retain the 'aggregate' approach of English general partnerships. Under English procedural law, and whether or not it has separate legal personality, if a partnership is carrying on business in England, it can be sued in the name of the individual partners or in the firm name.[45] If the oversea partnership is *not* carrying on business in England, the position is probably as follows: if it does not have separate legal personality, it must be sued in the names of the individual partners; and if it does have separate legal personality, it can nevertheless still be sued in the name of the individual partners,[46] and can as an alternative be sued in the name of the entity.[47] The same principles will apply where the oversea partnership is itself suing. Whether or not the oversea partnership will be regarded by English law as having separate legal personality (and, therefore, capable of being a party to English proceedings) will be determined by reference to the law of the place of its formation.[48] In this respect, English law's approach to recognition is the same as its approach to the question whether or not a foreign corporation exists, namely that

---

[44]   Some of the provisions of the Regulation apply regardless of the domicile: see, for example, Art 22.1 which gives exclusive jurisdiction in proceedings which have as their object rights *in rem* in immoveable property or tenancies of immoveable property to the courts of the state in which the property is situated; Art 23 in relation to jurisdiction agreements; and Arts 27–30 in relation to proceedings pending in more than one state.

[45]   See CPR, Sch 1 RSC Ord 81.1; and see *Worcester City and County Banking Co v Firbank, Pauling & Co* [1894] 1 QB 784. As to when business is being carried on in England, see *Grant v Anderson & Co* [1892] 1QB 108 and *Dicey & Morris* above, paras 11-100 et seq.

[46]   See *Oxnard Financing SA v Rahn* [1998] 1 WLR 1465.

[47]   Ibid.

[48]   See *Associated Shipping Services v Department of Private Affairs of H H Sheikh Zayed Bin Sultan Al-Nahayan* (1990) *Financial Times*, July 31, CA (concerning the private office of the Ruler of Abu Dhabi), *Bumper Development Corporation v Commissioner of Police of the Metropolis* [1991] 1 WLR 1362 (recognising a temple in India as a juridical entity), *The 'Gilbert Rowe'* [1997] 2 Lloyd's Rep 218 (on appeal [1998] CLC 1574) (concerning a Dutch commercial partnership) and *Oxnard Financing SA v Rahn* above (concerning a Swiss banking partnership).

its existence (or dissolution) will be determined by reference to the law of the place where it was formed (subject to any issues of English public policy).[49]

Service within the jurisdiction

17.13   Where partners (in a domestic partnership or an oversea partnership) are sued in the name of their partnership (whether it is a separate entity or not), postal or DX service within the jurisdiction will generally be effected by serving solicitors authorised to accept service on behalf of the partnership.[50] Where there is no solicitor authorised to accept service, service will be at an address for service within the jurisdiction provided by the partnership or (if there is no solicitor authorised and no address for service within the jurisdiction given) at the principal or last known place of business of the partnership within the jurisdiction.[51] Where service on a partnership is to be by way of personal service,[52] the partnership will be served by leaving the claim form with (a) a partner, or (b) a person who, at the time of service, has the control or management of the partnership business at its principal place of business at the usual (or last known) residence of that person, or at the principal (or last known) place of business of the partnership, within the jurisdiction.[53] Where partners are sued individually, only those partners in England at the time of service may be served as of right. A consideration of the method of service on an oversea partnership should include consideration of the implications of CPR Sch 1, r 81.5 as to enforcement of any judgment against the partnership.

Service out of the jurisdiction

17.14   If the claimant wishes to serve the oversea LLP or individual partners out of the jurisdiction (and assuming that the claim does not fall under the Civil Jurisdiction and Judgments Act 1982 or the Regulation),[54] he must obtain permission to do so. CPR r 6.20 provides for categories of claim where the court may grant permission. The categories most likely to apply to claims against oversea LLPs or their members are:

(i)   a claim made in respect of a contract made within the jurisdiction or by or through an agent trading or residing within the jurisdiction or made subject to an English law governing clause or jurisdictional clause;[55]

(ii)   a claim made in respect of a breach of contract committed within the jurisdiction;[56]

---

49   See *Dicey & Morris* above, Rule 153, and paras 30-010/011; and the cases referred to in footnote 48 above.
50   See CPR, r 6.4(1).
51   See CPR, r 6.5(6). This would appear to be the intention of CPR r 6.5.
52   Personal service can always be used as a method of service (see CPR r 6.2(1)(a)); and is required for certain documents eg injunctions.
53   See CPR, r 6.4(5) and 6PD.4.
54   See the text of **17.12** to footnote 44 above.
55   CPR, r 6.20(5).
56   CPR, r 6.20(6).

(iii)   a claim made in tort where the damage was sustained within the jurisdiction or resulted from an act committed within the jurisdiction;[57]

(iv)   a claim made to enforce any judgment or arbitral award;[58] and

(v)   a claim relating wholly to property located within the jurisdiction.[59]

An application for permission to serve out of the jurisdiction must be accompanied by evidence stating the grounds on which the application is made, that the claimant believes his claim has a reasonable prospect of success and the defendant's address, or if not known, the place or country in which the defendant is, or is likely to be found.[60] The application is made under CPR Part 23.[61] Once permission to serve out of the jurisdiction has been granted, the claim form may be served by any method permitted by the law of the country in which it is to be served or in accordance with CPR r 6.25 or 6.26A.

RECOGNITION OF LIMITED LIABILITY OF OVERSEA LLP MEMBERS

17.15   There are an increasing number of foreign professional firms carrying on business in England, particularly firms of US lawyers. Subject to any relevant regulatory restrictions, a foreign firm carrying on business in England can choose to do so by setting up a branch of its existing partnership, or it can form an English general partnership or an English LLP. An important issue for oversea LLPs carrying on business in England (and an important factor in any decision as to how the English part of the business should be structured) is whether the English court will recognise the limitation on personal liability of the partners of an oversea LLP which the LLP's domestic law confers on those partners. The following possible scenario illustrates the issues which may arise in relation to an oversea LLP carrying on business in England.

> Smith LLP is a law firm formed in Yellow State. Yellow State is a common law jurisdiction. By statute, Yellow State permits general partnerships to become LLPs by the partners completing and filing a form. A, B, C, D and E are the partners. A, B and C work in Yellow State, and D and E work in England. Yellow State law provides the partners with a shield: they are not jointly and severally liable for the negligence or misconduct of the other partners.[62] Each partner is, however, by express statutory provision, liable for his own negligence or misconduct. D is retained by a client to give English law advice to an English company, Z Ltd, in England. D carries out the retainer in a manner which the client alleges was negligent.

This situation gives rise to a number of issues raising possible conflict of laws problems. What is the status of Smith LLP, and what law governs this issue? Who

[57]   CPR, r 6.20(8).
[58]   CPR, r 6.20(9).
[59]   CPR, r 6.20(10).
[60]   CPR, r 6.21.
[61]   See the notes to CPR, r 6.21 in the White Book for further detail.
[62]   See **17.8**

are the parties to the client retainer, and what is the law governing this issue? Has the contract of retainer been breached, and what law governs this issue? Was D's negligence a breach of a tortious duty owed by (a) him and/or (b) Smith LLP and/or (c) his partners; and what is the proper law of any tort claim?

17.16   A convenient starting point for considering such issues is the following statement by Staughton LJ in *Macmillan Inc v Bishopsgate Investment Trust Plc (No 3)*:[63]

> 'In any case which involves a foreign element it may prove necessary to decide what system of law is to be applied, either to the case as a whole or to a particular issue or issues. [Counsel] for Macmillan Inc has referred to that as the proper law; but I would reserve that expression for other purposes, such as the proper law of a contract, or of an obligation. Conflict lawyers speak of the lex causae when referring to the system of law to be applied. For those who spurn Latin in favour of English, one could call it the law applicable to the suit (or issue) or, simply, the applicable law. In finding the *lex causae* there are three stages. First, it is necessary to characterise the issue that is before the court. Is it for example about the formal validity of a marriage? Or intestate succession to moveable property? Or interpretation of a contract? The second stage is to select the rule of conflict of laws which lays down a connecting factor for the issue in question. Thus the formal validity of a marriage is to be determined, for the most part, by the law of the place where it is celebrated; intestate succession to moveables, by the law of the place where the deceased was domiciled when he died; and the interpretation of a contract, by what is described as its proper law. Thirdly, it is necessary to identify the system of law which is tied by the connecting factor found in stage two to the issue characterised in stage one.'

17.17   As stated above, LLPs in other jurisdictions (at least at present) are not bodies corporate, but are general partnerships. Some of these partnerships, nevertheless, have separate legal personality, whilst others are 'aggregates' in the same way as English partnerships.[64] It is convenient to consider the issue of whether English law will recognise limitations on personal liability by reference, first, to oversea LLPs which have separate legal personality and, secondly, by reference to oversea LLPs which are 'aggregates'.

Oversea LLP has separate legal personality

17.18   Although LLPs in other jurisdictions are not bodies corporate, a starting point is to consider how English law approaches issues involving foreign corporations. As has been seen above,[65] whether or not a corporation is recognised by English law as existing depends upon the law under which it was formed. If the existence of the corporation is recognised, ancillary 'status' issues such as those concerning the constitution of the corporation, who are the corporation's officials authorised to act on its behalf, or the extent of a member's personal liability (qua member) for the debts and liabilities of the corporation, are also governed by the

---

[63]   [1996] 1 WLR 387 at 391G-392B. And see also *Raiffeisen Zentralbank Osterreich AG v Five Star Trading LLC* [2001] QB 825, at paras 26–29 (Mance LJ).

[64]   See **17.7** and **17.10**.

[65]   See **17.12**.

law of the place of incorporation.[66] As has also been seen above,[67] English law's approach in relation to the existence of foreign entities which do *not* constitute corporations is the same as its approach in relation to the existence of corporations. There seems to be no reason in principle why English law should not take the same approach to ancillary 'status' issues in relation to non-corporation foreign entities as it does in relation to corporations. Recent decisions of the English courts support this.[68]

17.19   In *Johnson Matthey & Wallace Ltd v Ahmed Alloush* in 1984,[69] the Court of Appeal was concerned with the question whether or not individual partners in a Jordanian 'ordinary limited company' were personally liable upon promissory notes which had been issued by this entity. The entity had separate legal personality, but in other respects was akin to an English partnership. The court, whilst holding that the individual partners were personally liable on a proper interpretation of the relevant Jordanian statute, clearly proceeded on the basis that it would have been open to Jordanian law, as the governing law of the entity, to limit the liability of its members as a matter of substantive law; and that if it had done so, English law would have given recognition to this. The relevant statutory provision was s 19 of the Jordanian Companies Law (No 12 of 1964), which provided that 'every partner shall be liable jointly with the other partners, as well as severally, for all the debts and liabilities of the company which were incurred while he was a partner.... provided always that no execution order shall be issued against any partner in respect of his several liability for the company's debts or liabilities unless the company has been dissolved, or unless a creditor has obtained judgment and the company does not have sufficient funds to meet the judgment debt...'. Giving the leading judgment, Sir John Donaldson MR cited the following passage from *Dicey & Morris on the Conflict of Laws*, 10th edn:

> 'If the *lex causae* regards the defendant as under no liability whatever unless other persons are sued first, the rule is substantive and must be applied in English proceedings. If on the other hand the *lex causae* regards the defendant as liable, but makes his liability conditional on other persons being sued first, then the rule is procedural and is ignored in English proceedings...'

He then went on:

> '...As it seems to me, it is open to the proper law of a company to limit the liability of its members and officers by adopting either a substantive law route or a procedural law route. The choice is that of the relevant legislature. If it chooses to adopt the

---

[66]   See *Dicey & Morris* above, para 30-24, citing, inter alia, *Risdon Iron and Locomotive Works v Furness* [1906] 1 KB 49 (concerned with an issue as to whether shareholders in an English company, and as such having limited liability for the company's debts, could nevertheless be held liable for such debts under a California statute to this effect. 'The authority to do these things is given to a limited company, and it can only do them subject to the limited liability of its shareholders, which is a fundamental condition of its existence': Collins MR at 56).

[67]   See **17.12**.

[68]   Ancillary 'status' issues may, however, in some circumstances, fall to be seen more accurately as matters of contract, to be governed by the proper law of the membership contract (itself likely to be the same as the law of the place of formation).

[69]   24 May 1984 (CAT 234), reported in summary form only at (1985) 135 NLJ 1012.

substantive law route, that law will have extra-territorial effect, at any rate so far as England is concerned. If, on the other hand, it chooses to adopt the procedural law route, it will only have intra-territorial effect. The Jordanian legislature has chosen to adopt the procedural route and I see no reason why the ordinary consequences, as foreshadowed in the paragraph which I have read from Dicey, should not follow.'

17.20　　The approach of the court in *The 'Gilbert Rowe'* in 1996[70] was consistent with the approach of the Court of Appeal in *Johnson Matthey*. The *'Gilbert Rowe'* was concerned with the personal position of partners in a Dutch commercial partnership (a VOF) which was alleged to have acted in breach of a contract of towage. A VOF was described in the judgment as a hybrid. 'It is not like an English partnership. (a) It is not simply a name representing the sum of individual partners and is therefore not simply akin to an English law partnership. (b) But it is not as such a complete or independent legal person like a corporation. (c) However, it represents the separate persona of its partners 'taken together' and jointly or 'the partners as a whole'. (d) As such it has a separate legal existence or recognition, viz. it is a *'persona standi in judicio'*, for the purposes of suit.'[71] The court clearly proceeded on the basis that issues as to the personal exposure to liability of the individual partners for breach of contract by the VOF was governed by Dutch law.[72] The approach of the Court of Appeal in *Oxnard Financing SA v Rahn* in 1998 [73] was also consistent with this approach. The issue in *Oxnard* was the procedural issue as to whether a Swiss banking partnership could be sued in the names of the four individual partners. Nevertheless, it seems clear that the court proceeded on the basis that, on the substance of liability, English law would give effect to the rule of substantive Swiss law as to the limits on the individual liability of the partners personally.[74]

17.21　　Reverting to the scenario set out in **17.15**, it is suggested that as a general rule the position will be as follows. If the law of Yellow State provides that Smith LLP is an entity distinct from its partners (ie the LLP is by the law of the place of its formation a separate legal entity) English law will recognise the existence of this separate entity. Provided that D has made it clear that he is acting solely on behalf of the LLP, English law will recognise the entity as the party contracting with Z Ltd to provide the legal services.[75] The governing law of the contract between the LLP and Z Ltd will probably be English law (as was the governing law of the contract in *The 'Gilbert Rowe'*). In these circumstances, whether or not there has been a breach of the contract will be determined by English law. Save

---

[70]　*Rowan Companies Inc v Lambert Eggink Offshore Transport Consultants VOF* [1997] 2 Lloyd's Rep 218 (Clarke J). The case went to the Court of Appeal (reported at [1998] CLC 1574), but the basis on which the judge proceeded was not questioned.

[71]　Page 222, col 1. The judge went on to say that a VOF did not have a legal personality as such, but that it appeared to have something very like it in that it could enter into a contract in its own name and could sue and be sued in its own name: p 223, col 2.

[72]　See p 224, col 1.

[73]　[1998] 1 WLR 1465.

[74]　See in particular 1470C–D and 1475G–H.

[75]　This may also be the case where by its domestic law the LLP does not have legal personality as such, but can nevertheless by the law of its formation enter into contracts in its own name: see footnote 71 above.

insofar as the contract may itself stipulate where any liability lies,[76] English law will treat as a matter of 'status' of the entity any issue as to personal liability of individual members of the LLP, qua members, for a breach of the contract by the LLP (ie a breach of the express or implied term to use all proper skill and care). If and to the extent that the governing law of the LLP provides, as an attribute of the LLP, that the members are not personally liable, qua members, for a breach of contract, English law will give effect to such a provision.

17.22   The tort analysis will be similar. A claim by Z Ltd against the LLP in tort will, prima facie, be governed by English law as the place where the advice was given: that is to say, English law will be the law governing the question whether an actionable tort has occurred (namely, whether there has been a breach of a duty of care recognised in English law).[77] If a tort has been committed by the LLP, English law will treat as a matter of 'status' of the entity any issue as to personal liability of individual members, qua members, for the tort. The matter being one of 'status' of the LLP, a consideration of the possible impact of the Unfair Contract Terms Act 1977 (UCTA 1977) will not be relevant. The provision of law in Yellow State that a member of an LLP shall not be jointly and severally liable for the negligence or misconduct of the other members (creating the 'status' of non-liability of members) is to be contrasted, however, with a term of the contract between Smith LLP and Z Ltd which itself contains a limitation on the liability for negligence of the LLP as an entity, or of its members. The provisions of UCTA 1977 will be relevant to such a contractual term.[78]

17.23   In addition to determining whether or not the LLP has committed a tort, English law (assuming it is the applicable law) will also determine whether D, the individual partner carrying out the work, has personally committed a tort ie whether D has assumed a personal responsibility for the work and has breached a personal duty of care.[79] This latter issue may become important. It has been said as a general statement in **17.8** that it appears to be the position that all US States will hold a partner in an LLP personally liable in respect of claims arising from his own misconduct or negligence. As stated in **17.10**, the position is similar in those Canadian provinces with LLPs. It may be, however, that an analysis as to how the law of Yellow State arrives at this result will be necessary in order to determine how and if D is personally liable in the English court. There may, for instance, be an issue as to whether the Yellow State statute is providing that the negligent partner has personal liability to a third party for any negligent act done by him as a partner (in which case there would be no protection for D personally in our scenario) or it is providing, rather, that D is not protected if there is a breach by him of an independent duty of care owed by him (but if there is no such breach by him, then he is not personally liable).[80] If D is to be personally liable for his own

---

[76]   See further, **17.23**.

[77]   See the Private International Law (Miscellaneous Provisions) Act 1995, ss 9(4) and 11(1).

[78]   Assuming that the contract is governed by English law (or if UCTA 1977 is, in any event, properly regarded as a mandatory rule: see *Dicey & Morris* Rules 175 and 181).

[79]   See chapter 15.

[80]   See, for instance, the New Brunswick and Saskatchewan provisions referred to in footnote 42 above. The Delaware RUPA (s 15-306) provides simply 'An obligation of a partnership incurred while the partnership is a limited liability partnership, whether arising in contract, tort or otherwise,

negligence, it may be necessary, therefore, to find an assumption of personal responsibility by him.[81]

17.24   Although the members of an oversea LLP can be assumed to wish to have the benefit of limitations on personal liability which the domestic law of the LLP provides, the possibility should not be excluded of facts arising from which it can be inferred that the partners have authorised the LLP to trade in England, or to contract with a particular third party, on the basis of unlimited personal liability as in a traditional partnership.[82]

Oversea LLP does not have separate legal personality

17.25   An analysis of the personal position of members of an oversea LLP where the LLP is not, under the law of its formation, a distinct entity is less straightforward.[83] Where the LLP is not an entity, it will, generally speaking, be an 'aggregate' partnership, namely (and like an 1890 Act partnership in England) a relationship subsisting between the partners, based on agreement between them, and under which they are all agents for each other. The core issue is whether English law will, in such a case, recognise and give effect to limitations on personal liability contained in legislation of the jurisdiction of the place of formation.

17.26   The first question is: how will English law characterise this issue? As appears from **17.18–17.23**, in relation to corporate bodies, and also (generally speaking) bodies having separate legal personality which are not corporations, English law characterises the issue of personal liability of a member as an issue of, or at least ancillary to, 'status': the limitation on liability being an attribute of the entity itself. Where, however, the oversea LLP does not have separate legal personality, it is by no means obvious that the same characterisation can or should be applied. Where a claimant asserts that he has suffered a contractual or tortious wrong and seeks to sue an entity, and/or its individual members, in England, English conflict of laws rules are applied to determine the law applicable to the wrong, namely the law governing the issue whether or not there has been a breach of contract or a tortious wrong committed.[84] The purpose in this context of the application of foreign law to 'status' issues is to determine whether or not the 'entity' being sued is indeed a separate entity and, if it is, whether the members of it, qua members, in addition to the entity itself, are liable in respect of the wrong. If

---

is solely the obligation of the partnership. A partner is not personally liable, directly or indirectly, by way of indemnification, contribution, assessment or otherwise, for such an obligation solely by reason of being or so acting as a partner' without any carving out of a partner's liability for his own negligence or wrongful conduct.

[81]   The question whether there has been an assumption of personal responsibility by D will also be relevant to an issue of vicarious liability of the LLP for his negligence: see *Dicey & Morris* above, para 35-038.

[82]   See, for instance, *Risdon Iron and Locomotive Works v Furness* [1906] 1 KB 49.

[83]   See *Lindley & Banks on Partnership* 18th edn, 2002, paras 28-12–28-13; Blackett-Ord *Partnership* 2nd edn, 2002, para 1.13; *Higgins & Fletcher*, Law of Partnership in Australia and New Zealand 8th edn, 2000, p 275; *Fletcher* Interstate Trade: The Last Hurdle for Limited Partnerships (1993) 11 C & S LJ 433.

[84]   See **17.21–17.22**.

the law applicable to the wrong is determined to be English law (and the entity is indeed a separate entity), the issue of the liability of the individual members, qua members, will only arise if they are not, in any event, personally liable for the wrong; that is to say, the issue will only arise if the members are not regarded as themselves parties to the contract (the contract being formed between the claimant and the entity) and/or as having assumed a personal responsibility. Where it is determined that there is no separate entity, the relationship between the partners or members is just that: a relationship. Even if the law governing that inter-member relationship is properly regarded as a foreign law,[85] it does not follow that limitations on the personal liability of the members under that foreign law should be recognised as having application to the (quite separate) relationship, and issues arising, between the members and a third party.

17.27   Turning to the scenario set out in **17.15**, where Smith LLP does not have separate legal personality, English law will probably regard the partners in it as mutual agents; and the issue of personal liability of the partners as one of agency. For the purpose of determining what law governs contractual relations in an agency context, English law distinguishes between, on the one hand, the relationship between principal and agent ie in a partnership context, the relationship between all the partners ('the internal relationship') and, on the other hand, the relationship between principal (ie the partners together) and third party who the agent (ie one or more of the partners) deals with on the principal's behalf ('the external relationship'). The rights and liabilities arising out of the internal relationship are, put broadly, governed by the law chosen for the purpose by the principal and agent,[86] whilst the rights and liabilities arising out of the external relationship are, again put broadly, governed by the law applicable to the contract made between the agent and the third party or applicable to the tort alleged to have been committed.[87] Even if the foreign law that purports to limit the liability of the partners does so in a way which is intended to apply to both the internal and the external relationships, and in a way which is intended to have extra territorial effect, English law will not consider itself obliged to give extra territorial effect (ie effect in England) to legislation of a foreign jurisdiction governing issues of liability arising under a contract or tort, if the law of that foreign jurisdiction would not otherwise be the law applicable to the wrong.[88] In other words, if the law applicable to the wrong is English law, English law determines, in a contractual context, who are the parties

---

[85]   The applicable law of the relationship between the partners may properly be regarded as an ordinary contractual applicable law issue, although it must of course be borne in mind that the relationship (at least according to English law) is not simply a contractual one. See, for instance, Lord Millett in *Hurst v Bryk* [2002] 1 AC 185 (concerned with an English 1890 Act partnership) at 194C–D: '…while partnership is a consensual arrangement based on agreement, it is more than a simple contract …; it is a continuing personal as well as commercial relationship'. In the authors' view, it certainly cannot be assumed that the proper law of the relationship between the partners can be determined merely by a 'place of formation' approach. In the absence of a choice of law, the place of formation (even if one can be identified) may well not be determinative. As mentioned in **17.28** and footnote 89 below, the Rome Convention will not apply to determine the law governing the contract of partnership.

[86]   See *Dicey & Morris* above, Rule 197, and further below.

[87]   See *Dicey &* Morris above, Rule 198, and further below.

[88]   As to extra-territoriality of UK legislation, see *Halsburys Laws* (Butterworths, 4th edn, 1995) vol 44(1), paras 1317 et seq.

to the contract and who is liable for breach and, in a tortious context, who owed a duty of care and who was negligent. An attempt by a foreign law to limit the liability of partners (where that law is not the law applicable to the wrong ie to the external relationship) is, in the authors' view, of no effect in England. As stated in **17.26**, the purpose of the application of the 'status' approach in entity cases is to determine whether anyone, in addition to the entity itself, is liable, *qua member*, for a contractual or tortious wrong in circumstances in which (by application of the law applicable to the wrong) the entity is liable but those other persons do not have separate liability. Even where there is a separate entity, a law in the place of formation that excludes liability on the part of the members of an entity cannot 'override' the liability of those members in contract or tort according to the application of the law applicable to the wrong.

17.28   As discussed in **17.21**, whether or not Smith LLP is a separate entity or an 'aggregate' will be determined by reference to the law of Yellow State. Proceeding on the basis that this exercise shows Smith LLP to be an 'aggregate', the relationship between the partners (ie between principals and agent) will almost certainly be governed by Yellow State law. One arrives at this by two possible routes. Assuming that the relationship between the partners of the LLP is properly seen as contractual, the governing law will be that determined in accordance with common law rules to be the proper law of the contract ie the law chosen (expressly or impliedly) by the partners for this purpose, or in the absence of any such discernible choice, that system of law with which, viewed objectively, the partnership contract has the closest and most real connection.[89] If the relationship between the partners is not to be seen as contractual, it is likely to be seen as more accurately a creature of a statute of Yellow State. If this is the case, generally speaking[90] it is difficult not to see the English court concluding that the relationship between the partners is governed by Yellow State law. An issue, if it arises, which will be governed by Yellow State law, as the law governing the relationship between the partners, will be an issue as to the actual authority to act on behalf of the other partners which an individual partner has.[91]

17.29   In the scenario which is being considered (set out in **17.15**), the governing law of the contract under which D, on behalf of Smith LLP, is giving advice will probably be English law. Proceeding on this basis, it appears to be correct to say that it will, therefore, be English law which governs the external relationship (ie the rights and liabilities) between the individual members of Smith LLP on the one hand and Z Ltd on the other hand, including specifically whether or not the acts of D will bind his partners as his principals.[92] An issue which will, if it arises, be governed by English law on this basis will be an issue as to what apparent authority to act on behalf of the other partners D had.[93] There is no reason in

---

[89]   See, for instance, *Amin Rasheed Corpt v Kuwait Insurance* [1984] AC 50 at 60/1, and generally *Dicey & Morris* above, paras 32-003–32-007. The Rome Convention will not apply to determine the law governing the contract of partnership as the partnership will be a 'body unincorporate' within Art 1.2(e) of the Convention (on which, see *Dicey & Morris* above, paras 30-025/6).

[90]   But possibly not in all circumstances: see **17.32**.

[91]   See *Dicey & Morris*, above, paras 33-402 and 33-422–33-426.

[92]   See *Dicey & Morris*, above, Rule 198 and paras 33-417–33-430.

[93]   See *Dicey & Morris*, above, para 33-422.

principle why the position should be different in the context of an alleged tort; and, assuming that a claim in tort by Z Ltd will be governed by English law,[94] it appears to be correct to say in this context also that it will be English law which governs the relationship between the members of Smith LLP and Z Ltd.

17.30   It is clearly a line of argument for Z Ltd to say that D was acting as the agent for all the partners of Smith LLP, that their liability to Z Ltd as D's principals is governed by English law, that it (Z Ltd) is not a party to the contract or relationship between the partners (in respect of which a foreign law purports to limit the partners' liability to third parties), that that limitation is not a matter of English law, and that, as a result, all the partners of the partnership which is Smith LLP are liable, as D's principals, to it. In answer to this, the partners may contend that, on a true interpretation of the contract or relationship between the partners under Yellow State law, D did not have authority to act on behalf of Smith LLP otherwise than on the basis of limited liability of the partners, and that this limit on D's authority is a matter governed by Yellow State law.[95] In reply to this defence, Z Ltd may argue that nevertheless D had apparent authority in England to act without limitation of liability of the partners (and that Z Ltd relied on this).[96] This last argument raises the issue (if it has not appeared previously) of what someone dealing in England with 'Smith LLP' can or should reasonably be taken to have expected: in the context of an apparent authority argument, could there be a representation, reasonably relied upon, that D was acting on behalf of the other partners of Smith LLP without limitation on liability? It is to be remembered that an oversea LLP carrying on business in Great Britain must, under CA 1985, s 693, conspicuously exhibit at its office in England, and state on its communications, its name and where it is established.[97] The purpose of this requirement is presumably to alert persons in Great Britain dealing with an oversea LLP that that is what they are dealing with, and that there are likely to be limitations on liability. The authors suggest that, whilst the mere existence of the requirements of CA 1985, s 693 will not preclude an argument by a third party of apparent authority, the fact (if it be established) that the LLP complied with these requirements may make it more difficult. It might be possible to take the argument for the LLP one step further and say that, if the third party is clearly aware that he is (at his own choice, presumably) dealing with an oversea LLP, whether a separate entity or an 'aggregate', established (in our scenario) in Yellow State, then he should be estopped from denying the limited liability to him of the partners. The existence of such an estoppel would be governed by English law.[98] Whether there is, in any particular case, such an estoppel will, of course, ultimately depend on the particular facts and (as with all estoppels) issues of conscionability.

17.31   Prior to undertaking the work for Z Ltd, Smith LLP may have contracted expressly with Z Ltd that the personal liability of the partners was limited in accordance with the law of Yellow State. Whilst there is nothing in principle to

---

[94]   See **17.22**.
[95]   See **17.28**.
[96]   On apparent authority generally, see **5.1**.
[97]   See **17.5** (and footnote 26).
[98]   See **17.27** and **17.29**

prevent Smith LLP stipulating this, such a term will (if the contract is governed by English law and, possibly, even if it is not)[99] be subject to the provisions of UCTA 1977.[100] The limitation on liability, in accordance with the law of Yellow State, would have to be 'reasonable' in accordance with s 11 of UCTA 1977 for the partners of Smith LLP to be able to rely on it to limit (in fact, exclude) their liability.

17.32 Despite the considerations which have been canvassed in **17.26–17.31**, it may be thought that, in at least some circumstances, there is a short route to the conclusion that all the members of an 'aggregate' oversea LLP have unlimited liability for the acts in Great Britain of any one partner. In a wholly English context, two or more persons who are carrying on a business in common with a view of profit are in the relation of partnership governed by the Partnership Act 1890, whether or not they are aware of the fact. It may be said that persons who are carrying on business in England in common with a view of profit fall within the grasp of the 1890 Act, and fall, therefore, to be treated in England as in a partnership governed by the 1890 Act. The result of this, *inter alia*, would be unlimited personal liability on the part of the partners to third parties dealing with one of their number in the course of the firm's business. There are, however, a number of difficulties with this conclusion. As has been mentioned in **17.27**, for the purpose of determining what law governs contractual relations in an agency context, English conflict of laws rules distinguish between the principal/agent relationship and the principal/third party relationship (with the former being governed by the law chosen for the purpose by the principal and agent); and, as discussed in **17.28**, this distinction between the two sets of relationships is equally likely to be drawn where the principal/agent relationship is seen as governed by statute rather than contract. The Partnership Act 1890 governs both sets of relationships. To apply this Act to the principal/agent relationship existing between the partners of an oversea LLP would be to act contrary to the well-established conflict of laws rule;[101] and it is difficult to see a logical basis upon which only those provisions in the Act concerned with the principal/third party relationship should be said to be applicable. To apply the Partnership Act 1890 to the relationship between the partners would also be to give the Act an extra-territorial application which, the authors suggest, it was not intended to have.[102] The provisions of the Act are as capable of applying to a partnership which has a separate identity as to an 'aggregate' partnership.[103] If the Act were to be applicable to an oversea 'aggregate' partnership, it is difficult to see why it should not equally be applicable to an oversea 'separate entity' partnership. To apply it to an oversea separate entity, however, would also be to act contrary to what appear to be sound and well-established conflict of laws principles.[104] In the scenario set out in **17.15**, a majority of the partners of Smith LLP are in Yellow State; and, for

---

[99] See *Dicey & Morris* above, Rule 181.

[100] Discussed in the context of personal liability of a member of a GB LLP at **15.19–15.24**.

[101] See **17.27–17.28**, and *Dicey & Morris* above, Rule 197.

[102] See, for instance, generally on extra-territorial application of UK legislation, *Halsbury's Laws* (Butterworths, 4th edn, 1995) vol 44(1), para 1319 and *Clark (Inspector of Taxes) v Oceanic Contractors Ltd* [1983] 2 AC 130 at 152C–D.

[103] See, for instance, s 4(2) of the Act, referring to Scottish partnerships.

[104] See **17.18–17.22**.

the reasons set out above, the authors suggest that the relationship between them will be governed by Yellow State law, and will not be subject to the Partnership Act 1890. Accordingly, it is suggested that in this scenario the Partnership Act 1890 has no role to play, and that issues of liability to Z Ltd will be governed by the English common law (and conflicts) rules of agency as discussed in **17.29–17.30**. English law might view the position differently, however,[105] if a preponderance of the partners was carrying on business in England and/or a preponderance of the oversea LLP's business was in England.[106]

---

[105] Perhaps applying a 'central management and control' test. English common law conflict of laws rules do not recognise a wholly unrestricted right of parties to choose the proper law of their contract. The choice must be 'bona fide and legal' and not contrary to public policy: see *Vita Foods Inc v Unus Shipping Co Ltd* [1939] AC 277(PC) at 290.

[106] In relation to the internal relationship between partners, the conclusion might be that the Partnership Act applies to the extent that its 'default' provisions are not varied by the oversea LLP agreement or law of the place of formation.

Chapter 18

INDIVIDUAL ACCOUNTS AND AUDIT

INTRODUCTION

18.1 Subject to modifications, additions and deletions made by the LLP Regulations 2001, Part VII of the CA 1985 (ie ss 221 to 262A) dealing with accounts and audit apply to LLPs.[1] This chapter is concerned with the accounting and auditing requirements which must be met for the individual accounts of LLPs. It does not consider the detailed requirements in relation to group accounts.[2] The appointment and position of auditors is discussed separately in Chapter 19.

ACCOUNTING RECORDS

18.2 An LLP must keep accounting records which are sufficient to show and explain its transactions and which are such as to: (a) disclose with reasonable accuracy, at any time, the financial position of the LLP at that time; and (b) enable the members to ensure that the balance sheet and profit and loss account which they are obliged[3] to prepare for each financial year comply with the requirements of the Act.[4] The accounting records must contain in particular: (i) entries from day to day of all sums of money received and expended by the LLP, and the matters in respect of which the receipt and expenditure takes place; and (ii) a record of the assets and liabilities of the LLP.[5] If the LLP's business involves dealing in goods, the accounting records must also contain: (iii) statements of stock held by it at the end of each of its financial years; (iv) all statements of stocktakings from which any such statement of stock has been or is to be prepared; and (v) except in the case of goods sold by way of ordinary retail trade, statements of goods sold and purchased, showing the goods and the buyers and sellers in sufficient detail to enable all these to be identified.[6]

18.3 The accounting records are to be kept at the LLP's registered office, or at such other place as the members think fit; and are at all times to be open to

---

[1] LLP Regulations 2001, reg 3(1). Inter alia, references to a company in the CA 1985 are to include references to an LLP, and references to a director or to an officer of the company are to include references to a member of the LLP: reg 3(2).

[2] There is a fuller discussion of accounting and auditing for LLPs in Boadle and Lang, *Accounts and Audit of Limited Liability Partnerships* (Tolley, 2002).

[3] Under CA 1985, s 226. The obligation to deliver the accounts to the Registrar is an obligation of the designated members: see further, **18.18–18.21**.

[4] CA 1985, s 221(1).

[5] Ibid, s 221(2).

[6] Ibid, s 221(3).

inspection by any member.[7] All accounting records which the Act requires an LLP to keep (ie as set out in **18.2**) must be preserved for a period of three years from the date on which they were made.[8] If any accounting records are kept outside Great Britain, accounts and returns with respect to the business dealt with in those accounting records must be sent to, and kept at a place in Great Britain, and must also be open at all times to inspection by any member.[9] These accounts and returns sent to Great Britain must be such as to: (a) disclose with reasonable accuracy the financial position of the business in question at intervals of not more than six months; and (b) enable the members to ensure that the LLP's balance sheet and profit and loss account comply with the requirements of the Act.[10]

ANNUAL ACCOUNTS

18.4   As mentioned in **18.2**, the members of an LLP are obliged to prepare for each financial year of the LLP: (a) a balance sheet as at the last day of that year; and (b) a profit and loss account.[11] As discussed in **18.6–18.9**, the obligation is to prepare a balance sheet and account which gives a 'true and fair view' of the position. When the annual accounts have been prepared and approved, subject to certain exemptions for small or dormant LLPs discussed later, a copy of those accounts (together with a copy of the auditors' report on them) must be delivered to the Registrar.[12] Thereafter, the accounts will be in the public domain and open to inspection by anybody under CA 1985, s 709. In other words, they can be obtained by anybody doing an 'LLP search'.

FINANCIAL YEAR

18.5   The 'financial year' of an LLP is determined as follows.

(1)   The first financial year of an LLP begins on the date of its incorporation;[13] and ends (unless the LLP alters this date under the procedure mentioned in (2)–(4) below) on the last day of the month in which the first anniversary of its incorporation falls (which is the LLP's first 'accounting reference date'[14]) or such other date, not more than 7 days before or after the first accounting reference date, as the members may determine.[15]

(2)   However, the first financial year can be shortened to less than a year, or extended to more than a year, by altering the first accounting reference date. The first financial year must end on a date more than 6 months from (and

---

[7]   CA 1985, s 222(1).
[8]   Ibid, s 222(5) (subject to any rules made under s 411 of the IA 1986). There are also obligations under TMA 1970 to keep tax records: see **21.10–21.11**.
[9]   CA 1985, s 222(2).
[10]   Ibid, s 222(3).
[11]   Ibid, s 226(1).
[12]   See further, **18.18**.
[13]   CA 1985, ss 223(2) and 224(4).
[14]   Ibid, s 224(3A).
[15]   Ibid, s 223 with s 224(3A) and (4).

beginning with) the date of incorporation,[16] and must not last for a period of more than 18 months from (and beginning with) the date of incorporation.[17]

(3)   To take an example, if an LLP is incorporated on 15 March 2005, its first financial year begins on 15 March 2005 and ends on 31 March 2006 (or, if the members so decide, another date which is within 7 days either side of 31 March 2006). This first financial year can, however, be shortened or extended so as to end, for example, on 30 September 2005 or 31 August 2006.

(4)   The procedure for the first financial year being shortened or extended as mentioned above is that the LLP gives notice to the Registrar in the prescribed form specifying a new accounting reference date.[18] This notice does not have to be given by any particular time (so that, in the example given in (3) above, it can be given before or after 31 March 2006) save that it must be given before the expiration of 10 months from the first anniversary of the incorporation of the LLP.[19] To follow the example given in (3) above, notice altering the first financial year must be given by the LLP at the latest by 15 January 2007 (with, if notice is given on the last available date, the accounts and auditors' report for the altered first financial year).

(5)   Subsequent financial years begin with the day immediately following the end of the previous financial year and end with the next anniversary of the end of the previous financial year (which is the LLP's accounting reference date for subsequent financial years) or such other date, not more than 7 days before or after the accounting reference date, as the members may determine.[20] In other words, financial years are successive periods of 12 months, ending on the LLP's accounting reference date with a 7-day leeway at the discretion of the members.

(6)   Like the first financial year, any subsequent financial year can be shortened or extended by notice given to the Registrar, either during or after the end of the financial year in question, specifying a new accounting reference date.[21] There appears to be no limit as to how short a particular financial year (or, more accurately, accounting reference period) can be made; but (unless an administration order is in force under Part II of the IA 1986) it cannot be extended so as to exceed 18 months.[22] To be effective to specify a new accounting reference date, a notice to the Registrar must be given before the expiration of the period allowed for delivering to the Registrar the accounts and auditors' report for the financial year as it exists before any notice has

---

[16]   CA 1985, s 224(4) with s 225(1) and (3)(a).
[17]   Ibid, s 224(4) with s 225(1) and (3)(b).
[18]   Ibid, s 225(1) and (3). The prescribed form is Form LLP 225: 'Change of accounting reference date of a Limited Liability Partnership'.
[19]   Ie the period within which, under CA 1985, s 244, the LLP's accounts and auditors' report for its first financial year must be delivered to the Registrar: see CA 1985, s 225(5).
[20]   CA 1985, ss 223(3) and 224(5).
[21]   Ibid, s 225(1) and (3). The prescribed form is again Form LLP 225.
[22]   Ibid, s 225(6). The words in CA 1985, s 225(4) and (6) 'an administration order is in force' have been changed for companies to 'the company is in administration' by the Enterprise Act 2002, s 248(3) and Sch 17, brought into force in September 2003 by SI 2003/2093. But this is subject to the former administration provisions in the IA 1986 continuing to apply to LLPs: see SI 2003/2093, Art 3(3)(b). In view of this, the authors consider that CA 1985, s 225(4) and (6) remain unaltered for LLPs. See further, **24.1**.

been given,[23] and provided also that if a financial year has previously been extended by giving notice to the Registrar specifying a new accounting reference date, a notice altering the accounting reference date again to extend a subsequent financial year cannot be given less than 5 years after the end of the financial year which was previously extended (save that the Secretary of State can waive this restriction in any particular case and save also that this restriction does not apply where an administration order is in force under Part II of the IA 1986).[24]

ACCOUNTING PRINCIPLES: 'TRUE AND FAIR VIEW'

CA 1985 provisions

18.6   The balance sheet of the LLP must give a true and fair view of the state of affairs of the LLP as at the end of the financial year; and the profit and loss account must give a true and fair view of its profit and loss for the financial year.[25] The balance sheet and the profit and loss account together are referred to in the CA 1985 as the LLP's 'individual accounts'.[26] Subject to certain limited exemptions for small and medium-sized LLPs (discussed in **18.26–18.37**), and to the overriding obligation to present a true and fair view of the position, the LLP's individual accounts must comply with the provisions of Sch 4 to the CA 1985 as to the form and content of the balance sheet and the form and content of the profit and loss account, and as to additional information to be provided by way of notes to the accounts.[27] The overriding obligation to present a true and fair view can be seen from the provisions in the CA 1985 that:

(i)   where compliance with the provisions of Sch 4, and the other provisions of the CA 1985 as to matters to be included in the accounts or in notes to the accounts, would not be sufficient to give a true and fair view, the necessary additional information must be given in the accounts or in a note to them;[28] and

(ii)   if in special circumstances compliance with any of the statutory provisions is inconsistent with the requirement to give a true and fair view, the members are to depart from the statutory provision in question to the extent necessary to give a true and fair view (with particulars of any such departure, and the reasons for it and its effect, being given in a note to the accounts).[29]

18.7   Schedule 4 to the CA 1985 contains considerable detail as to the information which   is   to   be   included   in   the   accounts.   Paragraphs   9–14   of   Sch   4

---

[23]   Ie before the expiration of 10 months from the end of the financial year as specified in CA 1985, s 244(1): see CA 1985, s 225(5).

[24]   CA 1985, s 225(4). See footnote 22 above.

[25]   Ibid, s 226(2).

[26]   Ibid, s 226(1).

[27]   Ibid, s 226(3).

[28]   Ibid, s 226(4).

[29]   Ibid, s 226(5).

set out the essential accounting principles to be followed in preparing the annual accounts.

(1)   The LLP is to be presumed to be carrying on business as a going concern.
(2)   Accounting policies are to applied consistently from one financial year to the next.
(3)   The amount of any item is to be determined on a prudent basis, and in particular:
    (a)   only profits realised at the balance sheet date are to be included in the profit and loss accounts; and
    (b)   all liabilities and losses which have arisen or are likely to arise in respect of the financial year to which the accounts relate or a previous financial year are to be taken into account, including those which only become apparent between the balance sheet date and the date on which it is signed on behalf of the members of the LLP as required by CA 1985, s 233.
(4)   All income and charges relating to the financial year to which the accounts relate are to be taken into account, without regard to the date of receipt or payment, ie income should be included on the basis of when it was earned, rather than when actually received. Similarly with costs, which should be included on the basis of when they were incurred rather than actually paid (the 'accruals' basis).
(5)   In determining the aggregate amount of any item the amount of each individual asset or liability that falls to be taken into account is to be determined separately.

Paragraph 15 of Sch 4 provides that these principles can be departed from in respect of any particular year if the members consider that there are special reasons for doing so, and that not to do so would result in the accounts not giving a true and fair view. If the principles are departed from, particulars of the departure, and the reasons for it and its effect, must be given in a note to the accounts.[30] Such departures are likely to be rare.

ACCOUNTING STANDARDS AND SORP

18.8   The notes to an LLP's accounts must, in any event, state the accounting policies which have been adopted,[31] and must also state whether the accounts have been prepared in accordance with the applicable accounting standards; and where there has been any material departure from those standards, the accounts must give particulars of the departure and the reasons for it.[32] The 'applicable accounting standards' are the statements of standard accounting practice which have been issued by the Accounting Standards Board (the ASB) and which are relevant to the LLP's circumstances and to its accounts.[33] The ASB is the body which is

---

[30]   CA 1985, Sch 4, Part II, para 15.
[31]   Ibid, Sch 4, para 36.
[32]   Ibid, Sch 4, para 36A.
[33]   Ibid, s 256

prescribed under CA 1985, s 256 for the purpose of issuing such statements.[34] As a general rule (but not a rigid rule), the obligation for an LLP to present a true and fair view in its accounts will involve the accounts following any applicable accounting standard.[35] In addition to itself issuing general purpose standards, the ASB authorises particular other bodies to issue more detailed guidance for accounting in particular industries or sectors. This more detailed guidance is issued in the form of Statements of Recommended Practice (SORPs).[36] A SORP for accounting by LLPs has been issued (in May 2002) by the Consultative Committee of Accountancy Bodies (the CCAB), which is recognised by the ASB for this purpose.[37] Accordingly, and as a general rule, in order to present a true and fair view, the annual balance sheet and profit and loss account of an LLP will need to follow the requirements of the SORP for LLPs, together with the body of general accounting standards which are relevant to the LLP's circumstances and accounts.[38] This body of general accounting standards is known as the UK Generally Accepted Accounting Practice (UK GAAP).[39] Where more than one accounting policy would meet the requirements of UK GAAP, the LLP should adopt that policy which is most appropriate to its circumstances. This work is not the place to set out an extensive account of what the SORP for LLPs provides. References are made elsewhere in the text to particular points.

18.9 For financial years starting on or after 1 January 2005, listed companies which are governed by the law of an EU member state must prepare their consolidated accounts in conformity with international accounting standards (IAS) ie on the basis of accounting standards issued by the International Accounting Standards Board which are adopted by the European Commission.[40] EU member states may also permit or require listed companies to prepare their individual accounts in accordance with adopted IAS, and – relevant for present purposes - may permit or require other companies to prepare their consolidated and/or individual accounts in accordance with IAS.[41] For these purposes, 'companies'

---

[34]   By the Accounting Standards (Prescribed Body) Regulations 1990, SI 1990/1667, applied to LLPs by the LLP Regulations 2001, para 10 and Sch 6 Part I.

[35]   See *Lloyd Cheyham & Co Ltd v Littlejohn & Co* [1987] BCLC 303 at 313: the standards will be very strong evidence of what is the proper standard which should be adopted.

[36]   SORPs are recommendations for specialised industries or sectors. They are not issued by the ASB, but they supplement accounting standards which have been issued by the ASB, and other legal and regulatory requirements.

[37]   The SORP states that the CCAB will keep it under review for changes in accounting practice and new developments. It also states that it is to be used in conjunction with the LLP Regulations 2001 (applying the CA 1985 with modifications) and accounting standards rather than on a stand-alone basis. In the event of conflict, the LLP Regulations 2001 and accounting standards take precedence over it.

[38]   The *Introduction to Accounting Standards* published by the ASB states as follows (para 16): 'Accounting standards are authoritative statements of how particular types of transaction and other events should be reflected in financial statements and accordingly compliance with accounting standards will normally be necessary for financial statements to give a true and fair view.'

[39]   UK GAAP incorporates the Statements of Standard Accounting Practice (SSAPs, issued by the Accounting Standards Committee, predecessor to the ASB), the Financial Reporting Standards and the Urgent Issues Task Force (UITF) Abstracts that are currently in existence.

[40]   Council Regulation (EC) No 1606/2002 of the European Parliament and of the Council on the application of international accounting standards.

[41]   Ibid, Art 5.

includes LLPs. The UK Government has decided in principle that (subject to the requirement existing in any event in relation to the consolidated accounts of listed companies) British companies are to have the option, in relation to consolidated and/or individual accounts, either to switch to preparing their accounts in accordance with adopted IAS, or to continue to prepare their accounts in accordance with the provisions of the CA 1985 and UK GAAP. To this end amendments will be made to the CA 1985.[42] The Government intends that the option to switch to adopted IAS should extend to LLPs.[43] Accordingly, it will in time be open to LLPs to prepare their accounts in accordance with IAS, in preference to domestic accounting standards. Any differences between these two sets of standards should, however, diminish in that the ASB aims in the longer term to bring UK standards into line with the standards set by the IASB.[44]

FORMATS

18.10   The balance sheet to be prepared for each financial year must follow one of the two balance sheet formats set out in section B of Part I of Sch 4 to the CA 1985, in the sense of showing the items listed in the chosen format in the order and under the headings and sub-headings contained in it; and the profit and loss account must similarly follow either Format 1 or Format 2 profit and loss account set out in section B.[45] Having chosen to adopt one of the two permissible formats in each regard, that format should continue to be used for subsequent financial years unless there are, in the opinion of the members, special reasons to change.[46] And if there is a change in the format adopted, particulars of it are to be disclosed, and the reasons for it explained, in a note to the balance sheet or profit and loss account in which the changed format is first adopted.[47]

18.11   The permissible formats are not, however, complete straightjackets. Indeed, attention has been drawn in **18.6** to the overriding objective of the accounts of an LLP being to give a true and fair view of its state and of its profit and loss. Schedule 4 expressly provides that an item required by the formats to be shown may be shown in greater detail than the relevant format requires, and that items representing or covering the amount of any asset or liability, or income or expenditure, not otherwise covered by any item listed in the relevant format, may

---

[42] See the DTI Consultation Paper '*Modernisation of Accounting Directives/IAS Infrastructure*' (March 2004), paras 1.4–1.5 and 3.3–3.4. The Government has, in October 2004, laid before Parliament a draft statutory instrument (Companies Act 1985 (International Accounting Standards and Other Accounting Amendments) Regulations 2004) introducing the option for all companies of preparing their individual accounts in accordance with IVAs. These regulations are intended to come into force on 1 January 2005, and to have effect as respects companies' financial years which begin on or after 1 January 2005.

[43] Ibid, para 1.16. The authors understand that it is intended that the amendments to be made to the CA 1985 by the Regulations referred to in footnote 42 above should apply to LLPs at the same time as to companies, but with modifications to be introduced by a further statutory instrument.

[44] Ibid, para 3.18.

[45] CA 1985, Sch 4, para 1.

[46] Ibid, Sch 4, para 2(1).

[47] Ibid, Sch 4, para 2(2).

be included.[48] Scope is also expressly given for adapting the arrangement and headings of a format where the special nature of the LLP's business so requires;[49] and for combining what would otherwise be separate items.[50]

18.12   The amounts set out in the annual accounts may also be shown in the same accounts translated into euros provided that they have been translated at the relevant exchange rate prevailing on the balance sheet date and the rate is disclosed in the notes to the accounts.[51]

INFORMATION COMING INTO THE PUBLIC DOMAIN

18.13   Both formats of balance sheet contained in Sch 4 lead to the same information being shown.[52] This is not the case with both formats of profit and loss account; but it is the position that under both of these there will be shown, inter alia, turnover and profit or loss for the financial year before members' remuneration and profit shares.[53] For those considering whether or not to incorporate their business as an LLP, a consideration of what information must be contained in the accounts, and what information will therefore come into the public domain,[54] will be material.

18.14   In addition to turnover, and gross and net profit and loss, and related matters, the CA 1985 (as adopted for LLPs) provides, inter alia, for the information referred to in (1)–(4) below to be included.

The balance sheet

(1)   Under the heading 'Loans and other debts due to members', the following amounts are to be shown separately:[55]

    (a)   the aggregate amount of money advanced to the LLP by the members by way of loan;

    (b)   the aggregate amount of money owed (ie allocated) to members by the LLP in respect of profits;[56]

    (c)   any other amounts due to members.

---

[48]   CA 1985, Sch 4, para 3(1) and (2): save that the following are not to be treated as assets in any balance sheet – (a) preliminary expenses; (b) expenses of and commission on any issue of debentures; and (c) costs of research.

[49]   CA 1985, Sch 4, para 3(3).

[50]   Ibid, Sch 4, para 3(4).

[51]   Ibid, s 242B. This section refers to ECUs. A reference to ECUs is to be read as a reference to euros at the rate of one euro to one ECU: see Council Regulation (EC) 1103/97.

[52]   Including the division under 'Creditors' of moneys due within one year and moneys due after one year: although Format 2 on the face of it differs from Format 1 in combining these two, note (13) to Format 2 requires these two categories to be shown separately.

[53]   Ie items 1 and 20 (Format 1) or 22 (Format 2).

[54]   Subject to certain exemptions for small or medium-sized LLPs.

[55]   CA 1985, Sch 4, note (12) on the balance sheet formats.

[56]   Profits not yet allocated to members are shown as part of 'Other reserves': see **18.14**(2).

And in a note to the balance sheet (if not in the balance sheet itself) under the same heading, the following further information[57] is to be given:

(i)   the aggregate amount of loans and other debts due to the members as at the date of the beginning of the financial year,

(ii) the aggregate amounts contributed by members during the financial year,

(iii) the aggregate amounts transferred to or from the profit and loss account during that year,

(iv) the aggregate amounts withdrawn by members or applied on behalf of members during that year,

(v)   the aggregate amount of loans and other debts due to members as at the balance sheet date, and

(vi) the aggregate amount of loans and other debts due to members that fall due after one year.

The SORP for LLPs provides that the notes to the accounts should explain where amounts in 'Loans and other debts due to members' would rank in relation to other creditors who are unsecured in the event of a winding up, and should include details of any protection afforded to creditors in such an event which is legally enforceable and cannot be revoked at will by the members. Where there is no such protection in respect of loans and other debts due to members, this fact should be disclosed.[58]

(2)   There is also to be set out in the balance sheet, under the heading 'Members' other interests', the following items: members' capital,[59] revaluation reserve and other reserves. This last item will include profits (and also a loss) for the year not allocated to members.[60]

Profit and loss account

(3)   In addition to the profit or loss for the year before members' remuneration and profit shares, in a note to the profit and loss account (if not in the account itself), under the heading 'Particulars of members', the following information is to be given:[61]

(a)   Particulars of the average number of members of the LLP in the financial year. (This number is determined by dividing the 'relevant annual number' by the number of months in the financial year. For these purposes, the 'relevant annual number' is determined by ascertaining for each month in the financial year the number of members of the LLP for all or part of that month, and adding together all the monthly numbers.)

(b)   Where the profit for the financial year before members' remuneration and profit shares exceeds £200,000, the amount of profit (including

---

[57] CA 1985, Sch 4, Part III, paras 35 and 37A.
[58] SORP para 34
[59] As to which, see **13.1–13.7**
[60] See the SORP paras 18 and 32, and **13.10** and **13.13**.
[61] CA 1985, Sch 4, Part III, paras 35 and 56A. Providing the information specified in paras 52–57 is subject to CA 1985, s 230 where the LLP is a 'parent company'.

remuneration) which is attributable to the member with the largest entitlement to profit (including remuneration).

For the purposes of (b) above, 'remuneration' includes any emoluments, or sums[62] under long-term incentive schemes, which are paid by the LLP (or by any subsidiary of it or any other person) to members for their services as members (or which are receivable by members for their services from the LLP or any subsidiary or other person), and includes contributions paid by the LLP (or subsidiary or other person) into a money purchase benefit pension scheme in respect of members' services.

(4)   If in the course of any financial year the LLP carries on business of two or more classes which, in the opinion of the members, differ substantially from each other, the profit and loss account must show the amount of turnover attributable to each class separately.[63] Similarly, turnover attributable to the supply of substantially different geographical markets must be shown separately.[64] In analysing for these purposes whether the LLP is carrying on separate classes of business, or supplying different markets, the members are to have regard to the manner in which the LLP's activities are organised.[65] Where, however, the members consider that the disclosure of separate turnover figures for different classes of business or markets would be seriously prejudicial to the interests of the LLP, the information need not be given in the accounts, but the fact that it has not been disclosed must be stated.[66]

The members' report

(5)   The SORP for LLPs provides for the annual accounts (more precisely, 'the Annual Report and Financial Statements') to include a 'report to the members' (the Members' Report). This should disclose the following information:[67]

(i)   the principal activities of the LLP and its subsidiary undertakings, indicating any significant changes during the year;

(ii)   an indication of the existence of any branches[68] outside the UK;

(iii) the identity of anyone who was a designated member during the year; and

(iv)   the overall policy followed in relation to members' drawings, including an indication of the policy applicable where the cash requirements of the business compete with the need to allow cash drawings by members. There should also be disclosed any transfers of members' interests from capital to debt during the period of the accounts and up to the date that the accounts are approved, and the

---

62   Or net value of assets.
63   CA 1985, Sch 4, para 55(1). See footnote 61 above
64   Ibid, Sch 4, para 55(2). In both cases, immaterial amounts attributable to one class, or market, may be included in the amount stated in respect of another: para 55(4). See footnote 61 above.
65   CA 1985, Sch 4, para 55(3). See footnote 61 above.
66   Ibid, Sch 4, para 55(5). See footnote 61 above.
67   SORP paras 22 and 39.
68   As defined in CA 1985, s 698(2).

policy under which members' capital is subscribed to, and repaid by, the LLP.

GROUP ACCOUNTS

18.15   Subject to certain exemptions (for instance, where the LLP is itself a wholly-owned subsidiary of a parent undertaking established under the law of an EU member state, and certain conditions are met),[69] if at the end of a financial year an LLP is a 'parent company',[70] the members are obliged to prepare, in addition to individual accounts for the year, group accounts for the LLP and its subsidiaries. These accounts are to comprise (a) a consolidated balance sheet dealing with the state of affairs of the parent LLP and its subsidiary undertakings, and (b) a consolidated profit and loss account dealing with the profit and loss of the parent LLP and its subsidiary undertakings. These consolidated accounts must give a true and fair view of the state of affairs as at the end of the financial year, and the profit or loss for the financial year, of the undertakings included in the consolidation as a whole, so far as concerns members of the LLP. Subject to the overriding obligation to present a true and fair view of the position, the group accounts must comply with the provisions of Sch 4A to the CA 1985 as to the form and content of the consolidated balance sheet and the consolidated profit and loss account, and as to additional information to be provided by way of notes to the accounts.[71]

AUDITING

18.16   The annual accounts of an LLP are to be submitted to its auditors, who are to make a report on them to the members.[72] The auditors' report is to state whether in the auditors' opinion the accounts have been properly prepared in accordance with the Act, and in particular whether a true and fair view is given: (a) in the case of the balance sheet, of the state of affairs of the LLP as at the end of the financial year; and (b) in the case of the profit and loss account, of the profit and loss of the LLP for the financial year.[73] In preparing their report, the auditors are to carry out such investigations as will enable them to form an opinion as to: (i) whether proper accounting records have been kept by the LLP, and proper returns adequate for the audit have been received from branches not visited by them; and (ii) whether the LLP's accounts are in agreement with the accounting records and returns.[74] If the auditors consider that proper accounting records have not been kept, or that proper returns adequate for their audit have not been received from branches not visited by them, or if the LLP's accounts are not in agreement with the accounting records and returns, the auditors are to state that fact in their report.[75] The auditors are also

---

[69]   CA 1985, s 228
[70]   See ibid, s 258(1).
[71]   Ibid, s 227. There are similar provisions in sub-ss (5) and (6) of s 227 to sub-ss (4) and (5) of s 226 set out at **18.6**(i) and (ii).
[72]   CA 1985, s 235(1).
[73]   Ibid, s 235(2).
[74]   Ibid, s 237(1).
[75]   Ibid, s 237(2).

to state, if it be the case, that they have failed to obtain all the information and explanations which, to the best of their knowledge and belief, are necessary for the purpose of their audit.[76] The auditors' report is to state the names of the auditors and to be signed by them;[77] and every copy which is circulated, published or issued is to state the names of the auditors.[78] There is to be stated in a note to the accounts the amount of the auditors' remuneration.[79]

APPROVING THE ACCOUNTS

18.17   The LLP's annual accounts are to be approved by the members and signed on behalf of all the members by a designated member.[80] The signature is to be on the balance sheet;[81] and every copy of the balance sheet which is circulated, published or issued is to state the name of the person who signed it on behalf of the members.[82] If annual accounts are approved which do not comply with the requirements of the CA 1985, every member who is a party to their approval, and who knows that they do not comply or is reckless as to whether they comply, is guilty of an offence and liable to a fine. For this purpose, every member at the time the accounts are approved is to be taken to be a party to their approval unless he shows that he took all reasonable steps to prevent their being approved.[83]

FILING WITH THE REGISTRAR

18.18   A copy of the annual accounts in respect of each financial year, together with a copy of the auditors' report on those accounts, must be delivered to the Registrar.[84] The copy of the balance sheet that is delivered to the Registrar must be

---

[76]   CA 1985, s 237(3).

[77]   Ibid, s 236(1). Amendments to CA 1985, s 236(1) having effect from 1 January 2005 may also require the auditors' report to be dated: see the draft Regulations referred to in footnotes 42 and 43 above.

[78]   CA 1985, s 236(2). If a copy of the report is circulated, published or issued without the auditors' names being stated, the LLP and every member of it who is in default is guilty of an offence and liable to a fine: CA 1985, s 236(4).

[79]   CA 1985, s 390A(3)–(5). This remuneration need not be stated in the accounts of an LLP qualifying as a small LLP: see **18.27**(5).

[80]   CA 1985, s 233(1).

[81]   Ibid, s 233(2).

[82]   Ibid, s 233(3). If a copy of the balance sheet is circulated, published or issued without the balance sheet having been so signed, or without the required statement of the signatory's name being included, the LLP itself and every member of it who is in default is guilty of an offence and liable to a fine: CA 1985, s 233(6). As to the meaning of 'in default', see **10.9**.

[83]   CA 1985, s 233(5).

[84]   Ibid, s 242(1). The duty of delivering the accounts is on the designated members of the LLP: see further, **18.20**. There is an exemption for small LLPs from delivering the auditors' report: see **18.27**(4) and **18.33**.

signed on behalf of the members by a designated member;[85] and the copy of the auditors' report must state the name of the auditors and be signed by them.[86]

18.19   The period allowed for delivering the accounts and auditors' report to the Registrar is 10 months after the end of the relevant financial year[87] save that: (a) if the relevant financial year is the LLP's first accounting reference period and is a period of more than 12 months, the period allowed is whichever is the longer of 10 months from the first anniversary of the incorporation of the LLP or 3 months from the end of the accounting period;[88] (b) if the LLP carries on business, or has interests outside the United Kingdom, the Channel Islands and the Isle of Man, the designated members may, in respect of any financial year, give to the Registrar before the end of the 10-month period (or, in the case of the LLP's first financial year, before the end of the period specified in (a) above) a notice in the prescribed form stating that the LLP so carries on business or has such interests and claiming a 3-month extension of the period for delivering the accounts and report, and on such notice being given the period is extended accordingly;[89] (c) if the LLP shortens its financial year (ie by notice under CA 1985, s 225),[90] the period for delivering the accounts and report is whichever is the longer of the period applicable under what has been said above or 3 months from the date of the notice of the shortening;[91] and (d) the Secretary of State may in any case by notice in writing to the LLP extend the period by such further period as he specifies if for any special reason he thinks fit to do so on an application made to him before the expiry of the period otherwise allowed.[92]

18.20   If a copy of the accounts and auditors' report is not delivered to the Registrar within the relevant period, every person who was a designated member of the LLP before the end of the accounting period in question is guilty of an offence and liable to a fine (and for continued contravention, to a daily fine).[93] Further, if the designated members fail to make good the default within 14 days after the service of a notice on them by any member or creditor or the Registrar[94] requiring compliance, the court may on the application of any member or creditor, or of the Registrar, make an order directing the designated members (or any of them) to make good the default within such time as it may specify.[95] It is a defence

---

[85]   CA 1985, s 233(4). For the sanction for contravention, see footnote 82 above.
[86]   Ibid, s 236(3). If the copy balance sheet delivered to the Registrar is not properly signed or the copy auditors' report does not comply with s 236(3), the LLP itself and every member who is in default is guilty of an offence and liable to a fine: CA 1985, ss 233(6)(b) and 236(4)(b).
[87]   CA 1985, s 244(1), with s 244(6).
[88]   Ibid, s 244(2).
[89]   Ibid, s 244(3). The prescribed form is Form LLP 244. This provision may be repealed with effect from 1 January 2005 as respects LLPs' financial years which begin on or after 1 January 2005 by Regulations made in late 2004 after this book goes to print: see the draft Regulations referred to in footnotes 42 and 43 above.
[90]   See **18.5**(4) and **18.5**(6).
[91]   CA 1985, s 244(4).
[92]   Ibid, s 244(5).
[93]   Ibid, s 242(2).
[94]   Ibid, s 242(3) appears to assume that any of these may serve a notice.
[95]   Ibid, s 242(3). The court's order may provide that all costs of and incidental to the application are to be borne by the designated members: ibid.

for a designated member charged with an offence as above to prove that he took all reasonable steps for securing that the accounts and report would be delivered within time;[96] but it is not a defence, either to being charged with an offence or to an application made to the court for a directing order, for a designated member to prove that the accounts and report were not in fact prepared as required by the Act.[97]

18.21   In addition to liability of the designated members as set out in **18.20** for failure to deliver the annual accounts and auditors' report within the permitted time, if the accounts and report are not delivered within such time the LLP itself is automatically liable to a civil penalty (recoverable by the Registrar and to be paid by him into the Consolidated Fund), the amount of which is to be determined by reference to the length of the period between the end of the period allowed for delivering the accounts and report and the day on which they are delivered as follows:[98]

Length of period	Penalty
Not more than 3 months	£100
More than 3 months but not more than 6 months	£250
More than 6 months but not more than 12 months	£500
More than 12 months	£1,000

Similarly to the position for designated members, it is not a defence for the LLP to prove that the accounts and report in question were not in fact prepared as required by the CA 1985.[99]

REVISING THE ACCOUNTS

18.22   If it appears to the members of the LLP that any annual accounts did not comply with the requirements of the CA 1985 (ie the accounts do not give a true and fair view of the state of affairs of the LLP at the end of its financial year, or of its profit and loss for the financial year), the members may prepare revised accounts.[100] Where copies of the previous (non-complying) accounts have already been delivered to the Registrar, the revisions are to be confined to the correction of those respects in which the previous accounts did not comply, and the making of

---

[96]   CA 1985, s 242(4).

[97]   Ibid, s 242(5).

[98]   Ibid, s 242A(3). The Registrar has a limited discretion as to whether or not to pursue recovery of the penalty: see *R (POW Trust) v Chief Executive and Registrar of Companies* [2003] 2 BCLC 295 at para 14.

[99]   CA 1985, s 242A(4).

[100]   Ibid, s 245(1).

any necessary consequential alterations.[101] If the accounts which have been delivered to the Registrar do comply with the statutory requirements (ie they do give a true and fair view), there is no right for the members, nevertheless, to prepare revised accounts in order to take out extraneous or superfluous material subsequently discovered to be embarrassing in some way; and the court does not have any inherent jurisdiction to permit the filing of revised accounts beyond what is permitted by CA 1985, s 245(1).[102]

18.23 There is also power for the Secretary of State, where it appears to him that there is, or may be, a question whether the accounts (or revised accounts) delivered to the Registrar comply with the requirements of the CA 1985, by notice to the members of the LLP to ask for an explanation of the accounts.[103] The Secretary of State's sanction, if no satisfactory explanation is given, is to apply to the court.[104] The application will be for a declaration that the accounts in question do not comply with the requirements of the CA 1985, and for an order requiring the members of the LLP to prepare revised accounts.[105] The court can also give consequential directions (including directions as to auditing and bringing the making of the order to the notice of people likely to be relying on the previous, non-complying accounts);[106] and can order all or any of the costs of the application, and of the reasonable expenses incurred by the LLP in connection with or as a consequence of the preparation of the revised accounts, to be paid by all or some of the persons who were the members at the time the defective accounts were approved.[107]

CIRCULATION AND PUBLICATION OF ACCOUNTS

18.24 A copy of the LLP's accounts (together with a copy of the auditors' report on those accounts[108]) is to be sent to every member of the LLP, and also to every holder of any debentures issued by the LLP, within one month of the accounts being signed in accordance with CA 1985, s 233(1), and in any event not later than 10 months after the end of the relevant accounting reference period.[109] In addition

---

[101] CA 1985, s 245(2). The auditors are to report on the revised accounts. The Companies (Revision of Defective Accounts and Report) Regulations 1990, SI 1990/2570 made under CA 1985, s 245(3)–(5), are applied to LLPs with such modifications as the context requires for the purpose of giving effect to the provisions of CA 1985 which are applied by the LLP Regulations 2001: see the LLP Regulations 2001, reg 10(1)(a) and Sch 6, Part I.

[102] *In re a Company (No 007466 of 2003)* [2004] 1 WLR 1357.

[103] CA 1985, s 245A.

[104] Ibid, s 245A(3).

[105] Ibid, s 245B(1). The application can also be made by the Financial Reporting Review Panel Limited: The Companies (Defective Accounts) (Authorised Person) Order 1991, SI 1991/13, is applied to LLPs: see LLP Regulations 2001, reg 10 and footnote 101 above.

[106] CA 1985, s 245B(3).

[107] Ibid, s 245B(4) and (5). Notice of the result of the application to the court is to be given to the Registrar: s 245B(6).

[108] See **18.16**.

[109] CA 1985, s 238(1). This can be done (by agreement) by electronic communication: s 238(4A) and (4B). Copies need not be sent to a person of whose address the LLP is unaware, nor to more than one of the joint holders of debentures, unless (it appears) there are debenture holders who are

to the above entitlement to receive copies of the accounts, a member of the LLP and any holder of debentures issued by the LLP is entitled to be furnished, on demand and without charge, with a copy (ie single copy) of the LLP's last annual accounts and auditors' report on those accounts.[110] If a demand made in exercise of this entitlement is not complied with within 7 days, the LLP and every member who is in default is guilty of an offence and liable to a fine (and, for continued contravention, to a daily default fine).[111]

18.25 If an LLP publishes[112] any of its statutory accounts,[113] they must be accompanied by the relevant auditors' report.[114] An LLP which publishes non-statutory accounts for any financial year otherwise than as part of its statutory accounts, must[115] publish with them a statement indicating: (a) that they are not the statutory accounts; (b) whether statutory accounts dealing with the financial year in question have been delivered to the Registrar; (c) whether there is an auditors' report on the statutory accounts for the year; and (d) whether any auditors' report so made was qualified or contained a statement that proper accounting records had not been kept etc[116] or a statement that the auditors had failed to obtain all necessary information and explanations etc.[117] The LLP must not publish with the non-statutory accounts any auditors' report on the statutory accounts. [118]

EXEMPTIONS FOR SMALL- AND MEDIUM-SIZED LLPS

18.26 There are modifications to the requirements as to accounts that an LLP must prepare and/or deliver to the Registrar for a financial year if in relation to that year the LLP qualifies as a small- or a medium-sized LLP.[119]

---

entitled to receive notices of general meetings of the membership (in which case, copies of the accounts must be sent to all debenture holders so entitled): CA 1985, s 238(2). If default is made in the sending out of copies of the accounts (and auditors' report), the LLP and every member of it who is in default is guilty of an offence and liable to a fine: CA 1985, s 238(5).

[110] CA 1985, s 239(1) and (2). The obligation can be met (by agreement) by sending the copies by electronic communication: s 239(2A).

[111] CA 1985, s 239(3).

[112] 'Publishing' a document means here publishing, issuing or circulating or otherwise making available for public inspection in a manner calculated to invite members of the public generally, or any class of members of the public, to read it: CA 1985, s 240(4).

[113] Ie its accounts for a financial year required to be delivered to the Registrar under CA 1985, s 242 (discussed in **18.18**): s 240(5).

[114] CA 1985, s 240(1). The sanction for breach is liability to a fine for the LLP and for any member who is in default: CA 1985, s 240(6).

[115] CA 1985, s 240(3). The sanction for breach is the same as for publishing statutory accounts without the relevant auditors' report: CA 1985, s 240(6).

[116] Ie a statement under CA 1985, s 237(2) referred to in **18.16**.

[117] Ie a statement under CA 1985, s 237(3) referred to in **18.16**.

[118] Ie auditors' report under CA 1985, s 235: see CA 1985, s 240(3). The sanction for breach is the same as for publishing statutory accounts without the relevant auditors' report: CA 1985, s 240(6).

[119] These modifications do not apply if the LLP (where otherwise qualifying as a small or as a medium-sized LLP) is, or was at any time during the financial year in question, a person (other than a banking limited liability partnership) who has permission under Part 4 of the FSMA 2000 to carry

Small LLP

18.27   In respect of any financial year in which an LLP qualifies as a small LLP the following will apply.

(1)   The LLP is absolved from the obligation of preparing a balance sheet and profit and loss account complying with CA 1985, Sch 4; and instead its obligation to prepare accounts will be satisfied if it prepares a simplified form of balance sheet adopting one of the two formats set out in CA 1985, Sch 8, and a profit and loss account adopting either Format 1 or Format 2 set out in Sch 8.[120]

(2)   A copy of the profit and loss account need not be delivered to the Registrar.[121]

(3)   The balance sheet to be *delivered to the Registrar* need only be in abbreviated form which adopts one of the two formats set out in CA 1985, Sch 8A ('abbreviated accounts').[122]

(4)   If the LLP does avail itself of the above entitlement to deliver abbreviated accounts only to the Registrar, subject to certain conditions[123] it need not deliver a copy of the auditors' report on its accounts.[124]

(5)   Neither the abbreviated accounts, nor any fuller accounts which the LLP chooses to file with the Registrar under CA 1985, s 242, need state the amount of the auditors' remuneration.[125]

(6)   In place of complying with all the applicable accounting standards issued by the ASB,[126] the LLP's accounts may follow the accounting standard for small entities issued by the ASB, namely the Financial Reporting Standard for Smaller Entities (the FRSSE), which covers LLPs. The basic measurement requirements in the FRSSE are the same as those in other accounting standards (although with some modifications), but many of the disclosure and presentation requirements of other standards are not included.

Qualifying as a small LLP

18.28   An LLP qualifies as a small LLP in relation to a financial year if: (i) in the case of its first financial year, it satisfies two or more of the following conditions in that year; and (ii) in the case of any subsequent financial year ending on or after 30 January 2004 (save where the financial year is made to end on or after that date by

---

on one or more regulated activities: CA 1985, s 247A(1)(a). A banking LLP is defined in CA 1985, s 262.

[120]   CA 1985, s 246(1) and (2). The accounts may adopt the Sch 8 provisions in some respects only, complying with the corresponding provisions of Sch 4 when not following Sch 8. Sch 8 is discussed further in **18.30** and **18.31**.

[121]   CA 1985, s 246(5)(a).

[122]   Ibid, s 246(5)(c). The term 'abbreviated accounts' comes from CA 1985, s 247B(1)(a): see further, **18.32**.

[123]   Discussed in **18.33**.

[124]   CA 1985, s 247B. The abbreviated accounts do need to be accompanied by a special report of the auditors certifying that the LLP is entitled to deliver abbreviated accounts and that the filed accounts are properly prepared as abbreviated accounts: see further, **18.33**.

[125]   CA 1985, s 246(6)(d).

[126]   See **18.8**.

an alteration of the accounting reference date under CA 1985, s 225[127]), it satisfies two or more of the following conditions in that year and in the preceding year (the figures in brackets are the previous figures which continue to apply for financial years ending before 30 January 2004):[128]

(1)		Turnover			Not more than £5.6m (£2.8m)

(2)		Balance sheet total		Not more than £2.8m (£1.4m)

(3)		Number of employees	Not more than 50

For the purposes of these conditions:

(a)	if an LLP's financial year is not in fact a year, the maximum figure for turnover (£2.8 million) is to be proportionately adjusted;[129]
(b)	turnover means the amounts derived from the provision of goods and services falling within the LLP's ordinary activities, after deduction of trade discounts, value added tax and any other taxes based on the amounts so derived;[130]
(c)	the balance sheet total means the aggregate of the amounts shown in the balance sheet (following Format 1 or Format 2 in Sch 4) under the headings 'fixed assets', 'current assets', and 'prepayments and accrued income';[131] and
(d)	the number of employees means the average number of persons employed by the LLP in the year determined on a monthly basis, ie by dividing the relevant annual number of employees by the number of months in the financial year, where the relevant annual number of employees is determined by ascertaining for each month in the financial year the number of persons employed under contracts of service by the LLP in that month (whether throughout the month or not).[132]

18.29		If an LLP qualifies in relation to a financial year as a small LLP under (i) referred to in **18.28** (ie it satisfies two or more of the conditions in its first financial year) or under (ii) referred to in **18.28** (ie it satisfies two or more of the conditions in two consecutive financial years, being the year in question and the preceding year), then it will be treated as also qualifying as a small LLP in relation to the next financial year (ie year 2 under (i) above or year 3 under (ii) above – 'the deemed qualifying year') and may, for the purposes of its next financial year after the deemed qualifying year (the 'next following year') (ie year 3 under (i) above or year 4 under (ii) above) and of needing a preceding year in which it met the

---

[127]	See **18.5**(6)
[128]	CA 1985, s 247(1)(a) and (b) and (3). The figures set out in the text for financial years ending on or after 30 January 2004 are the figures substituted for the previous figures by way of amendment made to CA 1985, s 247(3) by the Companies Act 1985 (Accounts of Small and Medium-Sized Enterprises and Audit Exemption) (Amendment) Regulations 2004, SI 2004/16. As to the assumption that these figures are intended to apply to LLPs, see **1.14**. If this assumption is correct, the transitional provisions contained in reg 7 of the 2004 regulations referred to above (including application of the new figures to a determination of whether a company is to be treated as having qualified as a small company in any previous financial year) can also be assumed to apply to LLPs.
[129]	CA 1985, s 247(4).
[130]	Ibid, s 262(1).
[131]	Ibid, s 247(5).
[132]	Ibid, s 247(6), with Sch 4, para 56(2) and (3). See footnote 61 above.

qualifying conditions in order to qualify as a small LLP under (ii) above for the next following year, treat the deemed qualifying year as a year in which it met the qualifying conditions.[133] The result is that if an LLP qualifies as a small LLP in relation to its first financial year, it is automatically treated as so qualifying in relation to its second financial year; and if it meets two or more of the conditions for two consecutive years, it is automatically treated as qualifying as a small LLP for the third year, and continues to qualify for the fourth year provided that in *that* year it actually does meet two or more of the qualifying conditions.

Schedule 8

18.30 What is said in **18.10** and **18.11** with regard to the formats set out in Sch 4 is equally applicable to the Sch 8 formats.[134] The accounting principles set out in **18.7** are equally to be followed for accounts prepared under Sch 8.[135] Again, there is no difference in the information being shown under the two formats of balance sheet.[136] The Sch 8 balance sheet requires the same itemised amounts as set out under **18.14**(1)(a)–(c) to be shown[137] under the heading of 'Loans and other debts due to members'; and requires the same information as is set out under **18.14**(1)(i)–(vi) to be given, either in the balance sheet or in a note to it.[138] It also requires the same information as is set out in **18.14**(2) to be given.

18.31 Formats 1 and 2 of a profit and loss account contained in Sch 8 are identical to Formats 1 and 2 contained in Sch 4. There is no requirement in a Sch 8 profit and loss account to give the information as to 'Particulars of members' (including, where the profit for the financial year exceeds £200,000, the amount of profit attributable to the member with the largest entitlement) set out under **18.14**(3).[139] There is also no requirement to break down the turnover as set out in **18.14**(4), the corresponding obligation being that if the LLP has supplied geographical markets outside the UK during the financial year in question the profit and loss account is to state the percentage of turnover that, in the opinion of the members, is attributable to those markets.[140]

Abbreviated accounts

18.32 The two formats of balance sheet set out in CA 1985, Sch 8A provide for simplified statements of assets and creditors. They require 'Loans and other debts due to members' to be included but not the detailed breakdown set out in **18.14**(1). They require also, under the heading 'Members' other interests', the items set out in **18.14**(2) to be included.

---

[133] CA 1985, s 247(2). The terms 'deemed qualifying year' and 'next following year' are the authors', in order to help the explanation.

[134] CA 1985, Sch 8, paras 1–5 mirror CA 1985, Sch 4, paras 1–5.

[135] Ibid, Sch 8, paras 9–15 mirror CA 1985, Sch 4, paras 9–15.

[136] Including the division under 'Creditors' of moneys due within one year and money due after one year.

[137] CA 1985, Sch 8, note (9) on the balance sheet formats.

[138] Ibid, Sch 8, Part III, paras 35 and 37A.

[139] Ibid, Sch 4, Part III, para 56A is not mirrored in CA 1985, Sch 8.

[140] Ibid, Sch 8, para 49.

No filing of auditors' report

18.33   If the LLP files abbreviated accounts only with the Registrar, the conditions upon which it need not deliver a copy of the full auditors' report on its accounts are as follows.

(1)   The abbreviated accounts when delivered are accompanied by a copy of a special report of the auditors stating that in their opinion (a) the LLP is entitled to deliver abbreviated accounts (ie the LLP qualifies as a small LLP) and (b) the abbreviated accounts have been prepared in compliance with CA 1985, Sch 8A.[141]

(2)   If the auditors' report (ie the report not being delivered) is qualified, the special report sets out the auditors' report in full together with any further material necessary to understand the qualification.[142]

(3)   If the auditors' report contains a statement that proper accounting records have not been kept, or that proper returns adequate for their audit have not been received from branches not visited by the auditors, or that the LLP's individual accounts are not in agreement with the accounting records and returns,[143] or a statement that the auditors have failed to obtain all the information and explanations which, to the best of their knowledge and belief, are necessary for the purposes of their audit,[144] the special report sets out the relevant statement in full.[145] Like a full auditors' report,[146] the special report (and the copy delivered to the Registrar) must state the name of the auditors and be signed by them;[147] and there are similar sanctions on the LLP and members if a copy of the special report is circulated, published or issued without stating the auditors' names (or without being signed by them, in the case of the copy delivered to the Registrar).[148]

Medium-sized LLP

18.34   There are no exemptions for a medium-sized LLP from the requirements of the CA 1985 for filing with the Registrar copies of its balance sheet and profit and loss account, together with a copy of its auditors' report. It remains obliged to comply with all the requirements of CA 1985, Sch 4 (ie inter alia, what is set out in **18.6–18.13**) save that, in respect of any financial year in which it qualifies as a medium-sized LLP, an LLP is entitled to the following alleviations from the requirements of Sch 4.

(1)   The accounts do not need to state whether they have been prepared in accordance with the applicable accounting standards, nor state particulars of

---

[141]   CA 1985, s 247B(2).
[142]   Ibid, s 247B(3)(a).
[143]   Ie a statement under CA 1985, s 237(2) referred to in **18.16**.
[144]   Ie a statement under CA 1985, s 237(3) referred to in **18.16**.
[145]   CA 1985, s 247B(3)(b).
[146]   See **18.16**, referring to CA 1985, s 236.
[147]   CA 1985, s 247B(4).
[148]   Ibid, s 247B(4) with CA 1985, s 236(4) referred to in footnote 78 above.

any material departure from those standards and reasons for such departure.[149]

(2) The profit and loss account delivered to the Registrar may combine turnover, cost of sales, gross profit or loss and other operating income distribution costs (otherwise required to be shown separately in the profit and loss account) as one item under the heading 'gross profit or loss'.[150]

(3) There is no obligation to state in the accounts particulars of turnover referable to different classes of business carried on by the LLP.[151]

18.35   Where the accounts of a medium-sized LLP delivered to the Registrar take advantage of the exemptions in **18.34**(2) and (3), the accounts so delivered must contain a statement in a prominent position on the balance sheet above the signature of a designated member as required by CA 1985, s 233[152] that the accounts have been prepared in accordance with the special provisions of the CA 1985 relating to medium-sized LLPs.[153]

Qualifying as a medium-sized LLP

18.36   An LLP qualifies as a medium-sized LLP in relation to a financial year if (a) in the case of its first financial year, it satisfies two or more of the following conditions in that year, and (b) in the case of any subsequent financial year ending on or after 30 January 2004 (save where the financial year is made to end on or after that date by an alteration of the accounting reference date under CA 1985, s 225[154]), it satisfies two or more of the following conditions in that year and in the preceding year (the figures in brackets are the previous figures which continue to apply for financial years ending before 30 January 2004):[155]

(1)   Turnover   Not more than £22.8m (£11.2m)

(2)   Balance sheet total   Not more than £11.4m (£5.6m)

(3)   Number of employees   Not more than 250

For the purposes of these conditions, (a), (b), (c) and (d) in **18.28** apply equally as they apply in relation to determining whether an LLP satisfies the small LLP conditions.[156]

---

[149]   CA 1985, s 246A(2).
[150]   Ibid, s 246A(3)(a). The above text is in relation to Format 1 of the profit and loss accounts. The permitted combination under the single heading is different for Format 2.
[151]   CA 1985, s 246A(3)(b): see **18.14**(4).
[152]   See **18.17**.
[153]   CA 1985, s 246A(4).
[154]   See **18.5**(6).
[155]   CA 1985, s 247(1)(a) and (b) and (3). The figures set out in the text for financial years ending on or after 30 January 2004 are the figures substituted for the previous figures by way of amendment to CA 1985, s 247(3) by the Companies Act 1985 (Accounts of Small and Medium-Sized Enterprises and Audit Exemption) (Amendment) Regulations 2004, SI 2004/16. See further footnote 128 above.
[156]   CA 1985, s 247(6), with Sch 4, para 56(2) and (3).

18.37   What is said in **18.29** (as to qualifying as a small LLP in subsequent financial years) is also equally applicable in relation to qualification as a medium-sized LLP in subsequent financial years.[157]

TOTAL EXEMPTIONS FROM AUDIT REQUIREMENTS

18.38   In certain circumstances, an LLP is exempted from the requirement of the CA 1985 that its accounts be audited[158] (and is exempt also from the obligation to appoint auditors[159]). An LLP is exempt from audit requirements in respect of a financial year ending on or after 31 March 2004 where for that financial year it meets the following 'total exemption' conditions (the figures in brackets are the previous figures which continue to apply for financial years ending before 31 March 2004):[160]

(a)   it qualifies as a small LLP in relation to that year;[161]

(b)   its turnover for that year[162] is not more than £5.6m (£1 m); and

(c)   its balance sheet total[163] for that year is not more than £2.8m (£1.4 m); and[164]

(d)   its balance sheet contains a statement by the members[165] to the effect that (i) for the year in question the LLP was entitled to the exemption, and (ii) the members acknowledge their responsibilities for ensuring that the LLP keeps accounting records which comply with CA 1985, s 221[166] and acknowledge their responsibilities also for preparing accounts which give a true and fair view of the state of affairs of the LLP as at the end of the financial year and of its profit and loss for the financial year in accordance with the requirements

---

[157]   CA 1985, s 247(2).

[158]   Ibid, s 249A.

[159]   Ibid, s 388A(1).

[160]   Ibid, s 249A(3). The figures set out in the text for financial years ending on or after 31 March 2004 are the figures substituted for the previous figures by way of amendment to CA 1985, s 249A(3) by the Companies Act 1985 (Accounts of Small and Medium-Sized Enterprises and Audit Exemption) (Amendment) Regulations 2004, SI 2004/16. See further footnote 128 above. This exemption cannot apply to an LLP in respect of a financial year if at any time within that year it was a person (other than a limited liability partnership) who had permission under Part 4 of the FSMA 2000 to carry on a regulated activity, it was an appointed representative within the meaning of FSMA 2000, s 39, it was a special register body as defined in s 117(1) of the Trade Union and Labour Relations (Consolidation) Act 1992 or an employers' association as defined in s 122 of that Act, or it was a parent LLP or a subsidiary undertaking (subject to certain ameliorating qualifications in relation to parents and subsidiaries): CA 1985, s 249B(1).

[161]   See **18.28** and **18.29**.

[162]   For a period which is an LLP's financial year but not in fact a year the maximum figure for turnover is to be proportionately adjusted: CA 1985, s 249A(6). Turnover has the same meaning as for qualification as a small or medium-sized LLP, set out in **18.28**(b).

[163]   As described in CA 1985, s 247(5): see **18.28**(c).

[164]   CA 1985, s 249B(4).

[165]   Above the required signature of a designated member on behalf of all the members: CA 1985, s 249B(5) with s 233(1).

[166]   See **18.2**.

of CA 1985, s 226[167] and which otherwise comply with the requirements of the CA 1985 relating to accounts so far as applicable to the LLP.

18.39   Where an LLP is exempt under the above conditions, and the members have taken advantage of that exemption, the provisions of the CA 1985 which give every member of the LLP, and also the holders of any debentures issued by the LLP, the right to be sent a copy of the LLP's accounts within one month of them being signed, and to demand a copy of the last annual accounts,[168] are to be read as not including a right to an auditors' report.[169] In addition, no copy of an auditors' report need be delivered to the Registrar.[170]

18.40   An LLP is also exempt from audit requirements (including the obligation to appoint auditors) if it has been dormant from the time of its incorporation, or if it has been dormant since the end of the previous financial year and it is entitled in respect of that previous year to prepare its accounts as a small LLP.[171] The exemption is also conditional upon the balance sheet containing a statement as set out in **18.38**(d).[172] An LLP is 'dormant' during a period in which no significant accounting transaction occurs.[173]

18.41   Where a dormant LLP is exempt from audit requirements, the position in relation to the entitlement of members and debenture holders to copies of the accounts is the same as set out in **18.39**.[174] In addition, no copy of an auditors' report need be delivered to the Registrar.[175]

---

[167]   See **18.6**.
[168]   Under CA 1985, ss 238 and 239, discussed in **18.24**.
[169]   CA 1985, s 249E(1)(a).
[170]   Ibid, s 249E(1)(b).
[171]   Ibid, ss 249AA(1) and 388A(1). There is no exemption if the LLP was at any time during the financial year in question a person (other than a banking limited liability partnership) who has permission under Part 4 of the FSMA 2000 to carry on one or more regulated activities: CA 1985, s 249AA(3).
[172]   CA 1985, s 249B(4).
[173]   Ie a transaction which is required to be entered in the LLP's accounting records under CA 1985, s 221(1). The payment of certain fees and penalties are not 'significant accounting transactions': CA 1985, s 249AA(5).
[174]   CA 1985, s 249E(1)(a).
[175]   Ibid, s 249E(1)(b).

Chapter 19

AUDITORS

INTRODUCTION

19.1 Every LLP, save for those small or dormant LLPs which qualify for exemption from audit requirements,[1] must each year appoint auditors,[2] to whom the annual accounts for that year must be submitted, and who are to make a report on those accounts to the members.[3]

APPOINTMENT

19.2 The auditors for the first financial year of the LLP in respect of which auditors are appointed are to be appointed before the end of that year.[4] The appointment is to be made by the designated members.[5] The 'first financial year in respect of which auditors are appointed' will be the first financial year[6] of the LLP unless the LLP is exempt from audit requirements for that year.[7]

19.3 For subsequent financial years in respect of which auditors are required, the designated members are to appoint the auditors within 2 months following the approval[8] of the LLP's accounts for the preceding financial year.[9] The auditors for the previous year can, of course, be re-appointed.

19.4 If the designated members fail to appoint auditors for any financial year in respect of which auditors are required by the appointed time,[10] the members of the LLP as a whole may appoint the auditors in a meeting convened for that purpose.[11] And if in any financial year in respect of which auditors are required no auditors have been appointed (either by the designated members or by all the members in a meeting) by the appointed time, the LLP must, within one week of the end of that period, give notice to the Secretary of State that no auditors have been appointed (and that the Secretary of State's next-mentioned power to do so has become

---

[1]   Ie under CA 1985, s 249A or s 249AA: see **18.38–18.41**. As to small or dormant LLPs which, having been exempt, then cease to qualify for exemption, see **19.6**.
[2]   CA 1985, s 384(1), with s 388A(1).
[3]   Ibid, s 235, discussed in **18.16**.
[4]   Ibid, s 385(2)
[5]   Ibid.
[6]   As to the determination of an LLP's first financial year, see **18.5**.
[7]   Ie as a qualifying small LLP or a dormant LLP: see **19.1**.
[8]   Ie approval by the members: CA 1985, s 233(1), discussed in **18.17**.
[9]   CA 1985, s 385(2).
[10]   Ie as stated in **19.2** and **19.3**.
[11]   CA 1985, s 385(4).

exercisable).[12] The Secretary of State may then appoint auditors.[13] If the LLP fails to give such a notice to the Secretary of State, it and every designated member of it who is in default[14] is guilty of an offence and liable to a fine and, for continued contravention, to a daily default fine.[15]

19.5 If a casual vacancy occurs in the office of auditors (by, for instance, the removal or resignation of the auditors) the designated members may fill it.[16]

19.6 Reference is made in **19.1** to those small or dormant LLPs which qualify for exemption from audit requirements. If an LLP which has been so exempt ceases to be exempt auditors for it are to be appointed as in the normal situation, ie by the designated members[17] or, if they do not do so, by all the members in a meeting convened for that purpose.[18]

19.7 The auditors (whenever appointed, and whether by the designated members, by all the members in a meeting or by the Secretary of State) hold office until not later than the expiration of 2 months following the approval[19] of the LLP's accounts for the financial year in respect of which they were appointed[20] (ie until the expiration of the period during which auditors are to be appointed for the next financial year).[21]

19.8 Only persons who satisfy the eligibility criteria contained in Part II of the CA 1989 for being appointed as company auditors may be appointed auditors of an LLP.[22] This means, in brief, that they must be members of a recognised supervisory body and be eligible to be appointed auditors under the rules of the body.[23] They must also be independent of the LLP.[24] Part II of the CA 1989, concerned with eligibility for appointment as company auditors, applies in respect of auditors of LLPs in the same way as it applies to companies registered under the CA 1985.[25]

ACCESS TO LLP

19.9 The auditors have a right of access at all times to the LLP's books, accounts and vouchers, and are entitled to require from its members such information and

---

[12]   CA 1985, s 387(2).
[13]   Ibid, s 387(1).
[14]   Ie it appears, in default of giving notice to the Secretary of State.
[15]   CA 1985, s 387(2).
[16]   Ibid, s 388(1).
[17]   Ibid, s 388A(3).
[18]   Ibid, s 388A(5).
[19]   See footnote 8 above.
[20]   CA 1985, ss 385(3) and 388A(3). Auditors for the next financial year must be appointed before the expiration of this 2-month period: see **19.3**.
[21]   See **19.3**.
[22]   CA 1985, s 384(4).
[23]   CA 1989, ss 25(1) and 30 et seq.
[24]   Ibid, s 27.
[25]   CA 1985, s 384(5).

explanations as they think necessary for the performance of their duties as auditors.[26] A member of the LLP commits an offence if he knowingly or recklessly makes to the auditors a statement (whether written or oral) which conveys or purports to convey any information or explanations which the auditors require, or are entitled to require as auditors, and which is misleading, false or deceptive in a material particular.[27] A member guilty of this offence is liable to imprisonment or a fine, or both.[28]

19.10   The auditors are entitled to receive all notices of, and other communications relating to, any meeting which a member of the LLP is entitled to receive and where any part of the business of the meeting concerns them as auditors,[29] and are entitled to attend any meeting of the LLP where any part of the business of the meeting concerns them as auditors.[30]

REMUNERATION

19.11   The remuneration[31] of auditors appointed by the designated members or by the members in meeting is to be fixed by the designated members or in such manner as all the members may determine.[32] The remuneration of auditors appointed by the Secretary of State[33] is to be fixed by the Secretary of State.[34]

19.12   The amount of the auditors' remuneration for carrying out their role as auditors is to be stated in a note to the LLP's annual accounts.[35] There is also to be stated in notes to the annual accounts (save, broadly, in the annual accounts of a 'small LLP' which is entitled not to deliver to the Registrar a copy of its profit and loss account, and need only deliver ' abbreviated accounts')[36] the aggregate of any remuneration paid by the LLP during the year to its auditors for non-audit work.[37]

---

[26]   CA 1985, s 389A(1).

[27]   Ibid, s 389A(2).

[28]   Ibid.

[29]   Ibid, s 390(1)(a).

[30]   Ibid, s 390(1)(b). If the auditors are themselves a corporate body or partnership, the attendance is by an individual authorised in writing by that body or partnership: CA 1985, s 390(3).

[31]   Including expenses and the nature and value of any benefits in kind: CA 1985, s 390A(4) and (5).

[32]   CA 1985, s 390A(1). This sub-section refers to the remuneration of auditors 'appointed by the LLP', in contrast to the remuneration of auditors appointed by the Secretary of State (referred to in s 390A(2)), and is therefore referring to appointment of auditors under CA 1985, ss 385(2) and (4) and 388A(3), discussed at **19.2–19.6**

[33]   Ie under CA 1985, s 387 if the LLP fails to appoint auditors within the required period: see **19.4**.

[34]   CA 1985, s 390A(2).

[35]   Ibid, s 390A(3).

[36]   As to qualification as a 'small LLP', see **18.28–18.29**. As to the entitlement mentioned, see **18.27**.

[37]   Companies Act 1985 (Disclosure of Remuneration for Non-audit Work) Regulations 1991, SI 1991/2128, made under CA 1985, s 390B. These regulations are adopted for LLPs by the LLP Regulations 2001. The text above is a simplified summary only of them.

TERMINATION OF APPOINTMENT

19.13   The auditors may at any time before their term of office expires have their appointment as auditors terminated and be removed from office by the designated members, notwithstanding anything in any agreement with them.[38] These last words are without prejudice, however, to any right of the auditors to compensation or damages payable in respect of the termination of their appointment, or the termination of any appointment terminating with that as auditors.[39]

19.14   Before the designated members can remove the auditors in mid-term, there is a procedure which must be gone through. The designated members must first give 7 days' written notice to the auditors of the proposal to remove them.[40] The auditors may then make representations in writing to the LLP on the proposal (not exceeding a reasonable length), and request that the members be notified of these representations.[41] If the auditors take this course, the LLP must send a copy of the representations to every member of the LLP within 21 days of the representations being received.[42] There is, however, a caveat to this. Copies of the representations need not be sent out to the members if, on an application to the court by either LLP or any other person claiming to be aggrieved, the court is satisfied that the right of the auditors to make representations is being abused in order to secure needless publicity for defamatory matter. If the court is so satisfied, it may order the LLP's costs on the application to be paid in whole or in part by the auditors, notwithstanding that they are not party to the application.[43] Whilst the legislation provides that such an application can be made to the court by the LLP (or any other person claiming to be aggrieved), it should nevertheless be borne in mind that an allegation that the auditors are abusing their position by seeking to secure needless publicity for defamatory matter is an allegation of acting in bad faith, and as such is a very serious allegation.[44]

19.15   Where, after the procedure described in **19.14** has been gone through, the designated members have determined to remove the auditors, the LLP must within 14 days give notice of that decision in the prescribed form to the Registrar.[45] If the LLP fails to give this notice to the Registrar, both the LLP and every designated member who is in default is guilty of an offence and liable to a fine and, for continued contravention, to a daily default fine.[46] Having been removed, the

---

[38]   CA 1985, s 391(1). The words 'with him' at the end of s 391(1) will cover the position whether the relevant agreement is seen as made between the LLP and the auditors or the designated members and the auditors.

[39]   CA 1985, s 391(3).

[40]   Ibid, s 391A(1)(a). The statutory provision merely says 'give notice' to the auditors. The notice must, presumably, be of the designated members' proposal as to the auditors.

[41]   CA 1985, s 391A(3).

[42]   Ibid, s 391A(4).

[43]   Ibid, s 391A(6). The sub-section only refers to the costs of the LLP. Query whether the court could order the costs of an aggrieved other person to be paid by the auditors.

[44]   See further, **19.20**.

[45]   CA 1985, s 391(2). The form is Form LLP 391.

[46]   Ibid.

auditors will be required to deposit at the LLP's registered office a s 394 statement as discussed in **19.19**.

19.16 Notwithstanding their removal mid-term, auditors who have been removed are entitled, in relation to any meeting of the LLP at which their term of office would otherwise have expired, or at which it is proposed to fill the vacancy caused by their removal, to receive all notices of, and other communications relating to that meeting which a member of the LLP is entitled to receive, to attend that meeting and to be heard at it on any part of the business which concerns them as former auditors.[47]

19.17 The same procedure as is set out in **19.14** must be gone through where the designated members propose simply not to re-appoint the existing auditors for the following financial year,[48] ie the designated members must give notice to the auditors of the designated members' proposal not to re-appoint them, and the auditors may make representations in writing to the LLP on the proposal. If, after this procedure, the auditors are not re-appointed, they will be required to deposit at the LLP's registered office a s 394 statement as discussed in **19.19**.

19.18 The auditors may themselves resign as auditors at any time by depositing a notice in writing to that effect at the LLP's registered office.[49] To be effective, however, the notice must be accompanied by the statement which is required by CA 1985, s 394.[50]

SECTION 394 STATEMENT

19.19 Whenever auditors cease for any reason to hold office (ie whether as a result of removal, resignation or simply not being re-appointed, and whether by their own choice or that of the LLP), they are required by CA 1985, s 394 to deposit at the LLP's registered office a statement of any circumstances connected with their ceasing to hold office which they consider should be brought to the attention of the members or the creditors of the LLP or, if they consider that there are no such circumstances, a statement that there are none.[51] The statement is to be deposited within a period of 14 days beginning with the date on which the auditors cease to hold office (save where the auditors resign, when the statement is to accompany the notice of resignation, and save also where the auditors do not seek re-appointment, when the statement is to be deposited not less than 14 days before the end of the time allowed for next appointing auditors).[52] If the statement is indeed of circumstances which the auditors consider should be brought to the

---

[47] CA 1985, s 391(4) with s 390(1).
[48] Ibid, s 391A(1)(b).
[49] Ibid, ss 392(1) and 394(2). The auditors may, when depositing their notice of resignation, require the designated members to call a meeting of the membership of the LLP to consider an explanation by the auditors of the circumstances connected with their resignation: CA 1985, s 392A.
[50] Ibid.
[51] CA 1985, s 394(1).
[52] Ibid, s 394(2).

attention of the members or the creditors of the LLP, the LLP must within 14 days of the statement being deposited with it send a copy of it to every member and to every holder of the LLP's debentures,[53] unless the LLP applies to the court for an order that the statement need not be sent out on the ground that the auditors are using the statement in order to secure needless publicity for defamatory matter.[54] If the LLP wishes to make such an application to the court, it must do so within the 14-day period (or the statement must be sent out). The 14-day period is mandatory and cannot be extended by the court.[55] If the LLP does make this application to the court, it must notify the auditors of the application. Unless the auditors receive notice of such an application before the end of the period of 21 days beginning with the day on which they deposited the statement, they are within a further 7 days to send a copy of the statement to the Registrar.[56] If, however, the LLP does make an application to the court:

(i)   if the court is satisfied that the auditors are using the statement to secure needless publicity for defamatory matter, the court is to direct that copies of the statement need not be sent out, and it may also order that the LLP's costs on the application be paid in whole or in part by the auditors, notwithstanding that they are not party to the application; and the LLP must with 14 days send to every member and to every holder of the LLP's debentures a statement setting out the effect of the order;[57]

(ii) if the court is *not* satisfied that the auditors are using the statement to secure needless publicity for defamatory matter, the LLP must within 14 days of the court's decision send copies of the auditors' statement to the members and debenture holders and notify the auditors of the court's decision; and the auditors must within 7 days of receiving such notice send a copy of the statement to the Registrar.[58]

19.20   An allegation that auditors are using a statement under CA 1985, s 394 to secure needless publicity for defamatory matter is a very serious allegation, 'tantamount to an allegation of dishonesty', against professional accountants.[59] If the LLP makes an application to the court on this ground but fails to establish that the auditors are misusing the statement as alleged, or if the LLP commences but then discontinues such an application, it can expect to be ordered to pay the auditors' costs of the application on an indemnity basis.[60]

---

[53]   Ie to the persons to whom copies of the LLP's annual accounts are to be sent under CA 1985, s 238(1): see **18.24**.

[54]   CA 1985, s 394(3).

[55]   *P & P Design Plc v Pricewaterhouse Coopers* [2002] 2 BCLC 648.

[56]   CA 1985, s 394(5). The combined effect of the making of an application by the LLP to the court and CA 1985, s 394(3) and (5) will be to suspend the obligation of the LLP to send the statement out to members and debenture holders, and to suspend also the obligation of the auditors to send a copy to the Registrar.

[57]   CA 1985, s 394(6).

[58]   Ibid, s 394(7).

[59]   *Per* Lightman J in *Jarvis Plc v Pricewaterhouse Coopers* [2000] 2 BCLC 368 at para 16(2).

[60]   See the judgment of Lightman J referred to in footnote 59 above. 'Proceedings which seek to silence, and which pending judgment do silence, auditors reporting matters which may require

19.21   If auditors fail to comply in any respect with s 394, they are guilty of an offence and liable to a fine (subject to the defence that they took all reasonable steps and exercised all due diligence to avoid committing the offence).[61] If the LLP makes any default in complying with s 394, both it and every member who is in default is guilty of an offence and liable to a fine and, for continued contravention, to a daily default fine.[62]

SECTION 727 RELIEF

19.22   Section 727 of the CA 1985 as adopted for LLPs[63] gives power to the court, similar to that given by the Trustee Act 1925, s 61 in relation to trustees, to grant relief from liability to auditors in certain circumstances. The section provides that if in any proceedings for negligence, default, breach of duty or breach of trust against auditors it appears to the court that they are or may be liable in respect of the negligence, default, breach of duty or breach of trust, but that they have acted honestly and reasonably, and that, having regard to all the circumstances of the case (including those connected with their appointment), they ought fairly to be excused for the negligence, default, breach of duty or breach of trust, the court may relieve them, either wholly or in part, from their liability on such terms as it thinks fit. If the auditors think that a claim will or might be made against them, they can make a pre-emptive application to the court for relief under the section.[64]

---

urgent communication to interested persons are high risk and are not to be undertaken lightly': ibid, para 17.
[61]   CA 1985, s 394A(1) and(2).
[62]   Ibid, s 394A(4).
[63]   As adopted, CA 1985, s 727 applies only to auditors: it does not apply to members of the LLP. On the liability of a member, see **11.11–11.13**.
[64]   CA 1985, s 727(2).

Chapter 20

INVESTIGATIONS AND STRIKING OFF

DTI POWER TO INVESTIGATE OR REQUIRE INFORMATION

Introduction

20.1 The powers given by the CA 1985 to the Secretary of State to appoint inspectors to investigate the affairs of companies, or to require the production of documents, are adopted (with modifications) for LLPs. In specified circumstances, therefore, inspectors can be appointed to investigate the affairs of an LLP, and to report on them to the Secretary of State. Alternatively, the Secretary of State can require the LLP to produce documents to his appointee. For the purposes of the power to investigate, the 'affairs of an LLP' will comprise all its business affairs, including its assets and transactions and its profits and losses.[1] The Secretary of State has similar powers in relation to LLPs as he has in relation to companies to apply to the court for a winding-up order, or for other orders, as a result of what he learns from an inspector's report, or from documents produced to his appointee.

Investigation by inspectors

20.2 There are two sets of circumstances in which the Secretary of State may, at his discretion, appoint inspectors.

(1)   Application by the LLP or members of it

He may do so on the application of the LLP itself, or on the application of not less than one-fifth in number of those persons who appear from notifications which have been given to the Registrar to be the current members of the LLP.[2] The application must be supported by such evidence as the Secretary of State may require for the purpose of showing that those seeking the investigation have good reason.[3] The Secretary of State may also, before appointing inspectors, require the applicants to give security[4] for payment of the costs of the investigation.[5]

---

[1]   See *R v Board of Trade, ex parte St Martin Preserving Co Ltd* [1965] 1 QB 603 at 613 and 618 (on Companies Act 1948, s 165, predecessor to CA 1985, s 432).

[2]   CA 1985, s 431(2). The notifications will be essentially notices of persons becoming or ceasing to be members given under LLP Act 2000, s 9(1).

[3]   CA 1985, s 431(3).

[4]   Currently, not exceeding £5,000.

[5]   CA 1985, s 431(4).

(2)   On the Secretary of State's own initiative

The Secretary of State may also appoint inspectors[6] if it appears to him that there are circumstances suggesting:

(a)   that the affairs of the LLP are being or have been conducted with intent to defraud its creditors or the creditors of any other person, or otherwise for a fraudulent or unlawful purpose, or in a manner which is unfairly prejudicial to some part of its members;[7] or

(b)   that any actual or proposed act or omission of the LLP (including an act or omission on its behalf) is or would be unfairly prejudicial to some part of its members, or that the LLP was formed for any fraudulent or unlawful purpose; or

(c)   that persons concerned with the LLP's formation or the management of its affairs have in connection with such formation or management been guilty of fraud, misfeasance or other misconduct towards the LLP or towards its members; or

(d)   that the LLP's members have not been given all the information with respect to its affairs which they might reasonably expect.

If he does decide to appoint inspectors on one or more of these grounds, the Secretary of State's decision cannot be challenged, and he cannot be compelled to give his reasons, unless some case can be shown for lack of good faith on his part.[8]

20.3   In contrast to the discretion which the Secretary of State has in the circumstances set out in **20.2**, if the court declares that the affairs of an LLP ought to be investigated, then the Secretary of State *must* appoint inspectors to investigate those affairs, and to report to him in such manner as he directs;[9] and he is to supply a copy of the inspectors' report to the court.[10]

20.4   If an LLP's affairs are investigated (on any of the grounds mentioned in **20.2** and **20.3**), it will be the duty of the past and present members of the LLP, and also of past and present 'agents' of it such as solicitors and bankers and auditors, to attend before the inspectors, and to give all assistance to the inspectors that they reasonably can give, including producing all documents which they have relating to the LLP, if required by the inspectors to do so.[11] If any person fails or refuses to comply with any such requirements of the inspectors, the inspectors may refer the

---

6   Under CA 1985, s 432(2).

7   'Members' here (and in (b)) includes any person who is not a member but to whom a member's share in the LLP has been transferred or transmitted by operation of law: CA 1985, s 432(4). As to transfer of a member's share, see **8.20–8.24**.

8   *Norwest Holst Ltd v Secretary of State* [1978] Ch 201.

9   CA 1985, s 432(1).

10   Ibid, s 437(2).

11   Ibid, s 434. This is subject to a right to refuse to disclose on grounds of legal professional privilege, save that a lawyer can be required to disclose the name and address of his client: s 452(1). There are additional restrictions if the LLP is carrying on a banking business: s 452(1A). For a discussion of the demands that can reasonably be placed on persons by the inspectors, see *Re an Inquiry into Mirror Group Newspapers Plc* [1999] 1 BCLC 690 at 708–713.

matter to the court, which may punish the offender as if he had been guilty of contempt of court.[12]

20.5 An investigation under CA 1985, Part XIV, and any questioning by the inspectors, is carried out in private.[13]

20.6 In all cases of an investigation and report, the Secretary of State may, if he thinks fit, supply a copy of the report to the LLP.[14] He may also, if requested to do so (and on payment of a fee), supply a copy to any member of the LLP, to anyone whose conduct is referred to in the report, to the LLP's auditors or to the applicants for the investigation.[15] He may also publish the report.[16] Where, however, the Secretary of State appoints inspectors on his own initiative (ie on one of the grounds set out in **20.2**(2)), he can exclude this ability to supply copies and publish the report by making it a term of the appointment of the inspectors that their report is not for publication.[17] This will not, however, preclude the Secretary of State from being able himself to disclose, or to authorise or require the inspectors to disclose, any information obtained by the inspectors to certain government or regulatory bodies, or for certain essentially regulatory purposes.[18] Such information may also be disclosed by the inspectors to a person appointed to carry out various investigations under the FSMA 2000, or authorised to require production of documents under CA 1985, s 447 (discussed in **20.7**).[19]

Production of documents

20.7 As an alternative to the inevitably rather high-profile route of investigating an LLP's affairs by appointing inspectors, the Secretary of State may follow the lower-key and more discreet route, if at any time he thinks that there is good reason to do so, of requiring an LLP (or any person who appears to be in possession of the documents) to produce any documents which he may specify to a DTI appointee.[20] When such documents are produced, any present or past member, or employee, of the LLP can be required to provide an explanation of them;[21] and there are criminal sanctions for knowingly or recklessly giving a false explanation.[22] If documents are not produced, the person who was required to produce them can be required to

---

[12] CA 1985, s 436.

[13] See *Re an Inquiry into Mirror Group Newspapers Plc* above at 704–705.

[14] CA 1985, s 437(3).

[15] Ibid.

[16] Ibid.

[17] Ibid, s 432(2A).

[18] Ibid, s 451A(1) and (2). The government and regulatory bodies, and the regulatory purposes, are set out in CA 1985, s 449.

[19] CA 1985, s 451A(3).

[20] Ibid, s 447. This is subject to the right not to produce documents covered by legal professional privilege: s 452(2). 'Documents' includes information recorded in any form: s 447(9).

[21] CA 1985, s 447(5)(a). The explanation required can be wide-ranging: see *A-G's Reference (No 2 of 1998)* [2000] QB 412.

[22] CA 1985, s 451. It can also be an offence for a member of an LLP to destroy or falsify documents relating to an LLP's property or affairs: see CA 1985, s 450 and **11.17**(v).

state, to the best of his knowledge and belief, where they are.[23] No document or information obtained by the Secretary of State or his appointee under this route can, without the previous consent in writing of the LLP, be published or disclosed except to a 'competent authority',[24] unless the publication or disclosure is required for one or more of various regulatory purposes or for the purposes of various proceedings.[25] These proceedings include disqualification proceedings as mentioned in **20.8** and any disciplinary proceedings relating to the exercise by a solicitor, auditor, accountant, valuer or actuary of his professional duties.[26]

Applications to court by the Secretary of State

20.8 An inspectors' report into the affairs of an LLP, or information obtained by the Secretary of State by the alternative route outlined in **20.7**, may be the basis of: (a) disqualification proceedings taken by the Secretary of State against a person who is or has been a member of the LLP, under the CDDA 1986 as applied to LLPs;[27] and (b) an application by the Secretary of State to the court for the winding up of the LLP if it appears to him from the report or information that it is expedient in the public interest that the LLP should be wound up.[28] Alternatively, if it appears to the Secretary of State that the affairs of the LLP are being or have been conducted in a manner which is unfairly prejudicial to the interests of its members generally or some part of its members, or that any actual or proposed act or omission of the LLP (including any act or omission on its behalf) is or would be so prejudicial, he may apply to the Court for an order under CA 1985, s 461.[29] If it appears to the Secretary of State from an inspectors' report, or from information obtained by him outlined in **20.7**, that any civil proceedings ought in the public interest to be brought by the LLP (or by any other body corporate), he may himself bring such proceedings in the name and on behalf of the LLP (or other body corporate).[30] But he must indemnify the LLP (or other body corporate) against the costs or expenses of such proceedings.[31]

---

[23] CA 1985, s 447(5)(b). If the LLP fails to comply with requirements as to documents placed on it by the DTI appointee, see also CA 1985, s 733 as to the possibility of an individual member being guilty of an offence together with the LLP itself.

[24] Ie various government or regulatory bodies listed in CA 1985, s 449(3).

[25] CA 1985, s 449. The purposes are listed in s 449(1). Additional purposes (relating to criminal investigations and criminal proceedings) are contained in the Anti-terrorism, Crime and Security Act 2001, s 17: see Sch 4, para 24 applying s 17 to CA 1985, s 449(1).

[26] CA 1985, s 449(1)(l).

[27] Ibid, ss 441 and 449(1)(ba) and CDDA 1986, s 8. See further **32.29**. Information or documents obtained by the Secretary of state under s 447 are admissible in evidence in the disqualification proceedings; see *Re Rex Williams Leisure Plc* [1994] Ch 1.

[28] IA 1986, s 124A.

[29] CA 1985, s 460. CA 1985, Part XVII is discussed more fully in chapter 27.

[30] CA 1985, s 438(1). The DTI has been advised that the Secretary of State cannot under this section take over existing litigation: see *Re London United Investments Plc* [1992] 1 BCLC 91 at 108.

[31] CA 1985, s 438(2).

STRIKING THE LLP's NAME OFF THE REGISTER

Introduction

20.9 An LLP which (at any time in its life) is not carrying on business or in operation may be struck off the register by the Registrar.[32] The result of a striking off is that the LLP is dissolved. An LLP may be struck off the register by the Registrar either on his own initiative,[33] or on an application made to him, in circumstances which permit it, by two or more designated members.[34] The result of the LLP being dissolved will be that (subject to the possibility of the dissolution being unscrambled by the Court as mentioned below, and subject also to the possibility of an agreement amongst members in the circumstances as to the division amongst them of assets[35]) all property and rights whatsoever vested in or held on trust for the LLP immediately before the dissolution (but not property held on trust for others) will pass as *bona vacantia* to the Crown,[36] save to the extent that the Crown disclaims any such property.[37]

Registrar's initiative

20.10 The procedure under which the Registrar can strike an LLP off the register on his own initiative is as follows.[38]

(1) If the Registrar has reasonable cause to believe that an LLP is not carrying on business or in operation, he may send it a letter inquiring whether it is carrying on business or in operation.

(2) If within one month of sending the letter he does not receive any reply, he is to send to the LLP by post within the next 14 days a registered letter referring to the first letter, and stating that no answer to it has been received, and that if an answer is not received to the second letter within one month from its date, a notice will be published in the *London Gazette* with a view to striking the LLP's name off the register.

(3) If the Registrar either receives an answer to the effect that the LLP is not carrying on business or in operation, or does not within one month after sending the second letter receive any answer, he may then publish in the *London Gazette*, and send to the LLP by post, a notice that at the expiration of 3 months from the date of that notice, unless cause is shown to the contrary, the name of the LLP will be struck off the register and it will be dissolved.

---

[32] As has been mentioned previously (at **2.44**) if an LLP does not start carrying on business within a year from its incorporation, it may be wound up by the court: IA 1986, s 122(1)(b). It may also be wound up if it suspends its business for a whole year.

[33] Under CA 1985, s 652: see further, **20.10**.

[34] Under CA 1985, s 652A(1): see further, **20.11**.

[35] See *Neville v Wilson* [1997] Ch 144.

[36] CA 1985, s 654. Under CA 1985, s 656.

[37] Under CA 1985, s 656. The effect of a disclaimer by the Crown will be to determine, as from the date of the disclaimer, all interest (and liabilities) of the LLP in or in respect of the property disclaimed; but will not otherwise affect the rights and liabilities of third parties: CA 1985, s 657.

[38] CA 1985, s 652(1), (2), (3) and (5).

(4)   Where an LLP is being wound up, if the Registrar has reasonable cause to believe either that no liquidator is acting, or that the affairs of the LLP are fully wound up, and the returns required to be made by the liquidator have not been made for a period of 6 consecutive months, the Registrar is to publish in the *London Gazette* and send to the LLP or the liquidator (if any) a similar notice to that mentioned in (3) above.

(5)   At the expiration of the time mentioned in the notice the Registrar may, unless the LLP has shown cause to the contrary, strike its name off the register. And if he does this, notice of the striking off is to be published in the *London Gazette*; and on that publication the LLP is dissolved.

Application by designated members

20.11   There are a number of restrictions on an application being made by designated members for an LLP to be struck off the register.[39] The first is that the LLP must not have been trading or otherwise carrying on business during the 3 months prior to the application.[40] In addition, the application cannot be made if at any time during the 3 months prior to the application the LLP has:[41]

(i)   changed its name; or

(ii)   made a disposal for value of property or rights which, immediately before ceasing to trade or otherwise carry on business, it held for the purpose of disposal for gain in the normal course of trading or otherwise carrying on business; or

(iii)   engaged in any other activity, except one which is necessary or expedient for the purpose of the designated members making the application, or for the purpose of concluding the affairs of the LLP, or for the purpose of complying with any statutory requirements, or specified by the Secretary of State by order for these purposes.

The application also cannot be made at a time when any of the following is the case:[42]

(a)   an application has been made to the court under CA 1985, s 425 on behalf of the LLP for the sanctioning of a compromise or arrangement and the matter has not been finally concluded;[43]

---

[39]   The application is made on Form LLP 652a.

[40]   CA 1985, s 652B(1)(b). Merely making a payment in respect of a liability incurred in the course of trading or otherwise carrying on business prior to the 3 months will not itself constitute trading or carrying on business during the 3 months: CA 1985, s 652B(2).

[41]   CA 1985, s 652B(1).

[42]   Ibid, s 652B(3). See further s 652B(4) and (5). Any designated member who makes an application where there are circumstances prohibiting the application is guilty of an offence (and liable to a fine), although it will be a defence for him to prove that he did not know, and could not reasonably have known, of the existence of the relevant circumstances: CA 1985, s 652E(1) and (3). It is also an offence knowingly or recklessly to give information to the Registrar which is false or misleading in a material particular: CA 1985, s 652F.

[43]   As to what constitutes final conclusion of such an application, see s 652B(4).

(b)   a voluntary arrangement in relation to the LLP has been proposed under Part I of the IA 1986 and the matter has not been finally concluded;[44]

(c)   an administration order in relation to the LLP is in force under Part II of the IA 1986 or a petition for such an order has been presented and not finally dealt with or withdrawn;[45]

(d)   the LLP is being wound up under Part IV of the IA 1986, whether voluntarily or by the court, or a petition under that Part for the winding up of the LLP by the court has been presented and not finally dealt with or withdrawn; or

(e)   there is a receiver or manager of the LLP's property.

Broadly speaking, if any of the above circumstances which prohibit an application being made by designated members for the LLP to be struck off come into existence after the application has been made and before it is dealt with or withdrawn,[46] there is an obligation on every designated member of the LLP to secure that the application is withdrawn forthwith.[47]

20.12   The designated members making the application are required to ensure that a copy of it is given, within 7 days of it being made (unless the application is withdrawn within those 7 days), to every person who was on the day of the application a member of the LLP. A copy is also to be given to every person who was on that day an employee or creditor of the LLP, or a manager or trustee of any pension fund established for the benefit of the employees of the LLP.[48]

20.13   In addition to the obligation on all the designated members mentioned at the end of **20.11**, if at any time after the application has been made (and not formally dealt with or withdrawn) any person becomes a member of the LLP, or becomes an employee or creditor of the LLP,[49] there is an obligation on all the

---

[44]   As to what constitutes final conclusion of such an application, see s 652B(5).

[45]   CA 1985, ss 652B(3)(c) and 652C(4)(d) are amended by the Enterprise Act 2002, s 248(3) and Sch 17, brought into force in September 2003 by SI 2003/2093. But this is subject to the former administration provisions in the IA 1986 continuing to apply to LLPs: see SI 2003/2093 reg 3(3)(b). In view of this, the authors consider that CA 1985, ss 652B(3)(c) and 652C(4)(d) remain unaltered for LLPs.

[46]   And also if LLP had determined during this period to go into voluntary winding up.

[47]   CA 1985, s 652C(4)–(7). As to s 652C(4)(d), see footnote 45 above. Failure by a designated member to comply with this obligation will constitute an offence; but it will be a defence for him to prove either that at the time of the failure he was not aware of the application having been made or that he took all reasonable steps to carry out the obligation: CA 1985, s 652E(1) and (5). The application is withdrawn on Form LLP 652c.

[48]   CA 1985, ss 652B(6)–(8) and 652D. A failure to ensure that a copy of the application is given as required above will constitute an offence; although it will be a defence for the designated member to prove that he took all reasonable steps to perform the duty: CA 1985, s 652E(1), (2) and (4). If the designated members fail to supply a copy of the application with the intention of concealing it, they are liable to imprisonment: see subsection (2).

[49]   Or a manager or trustee of any pension fund established for the benefit of the employees of the LLP.

designated members at that time to ensure that a copy of the application is given to the new member or employee or creditor within 7 days.[50]

20.14   Where the Registrar strikes an LLP off the register pursuant to an application by designated members, he must publish notice of it in the *London Gazette*; and on publication of that notice, the LLP is dissolved.[51]

After striking off

20.15   Although if an LLP is struck off the register it is dissolved, this is not an end to all matters relating to the LLP.

(1)   The liability (if any) of every member of the LLP continues and may be enforced as if the LLP had not been dissolved.[52]

(2)   The court continues to have power to wind up the LLP.[53]

(3)   The court may, on the application of any person appearing to it to be interested, make an order on such terms as the court thinks fit (for instance, relating to property which has vested in the Crown as bona vacantia under CA 1985, s 654) declaring the dissolution to have been void.[54] Such an application may, for instance, be made by a liquidator wishing to distribute an asset overlooked in the winding-up, or by a creditor making a claim which he has not previously made.

(4)   Where the Registrar has struck an LLP off the register on his own initiative (ie under CA 1985, s 652), if the court is satisfied on an application made by the LLP,[55] or by any member or creditor of the LLP who feels aggrieved that it has been struck off, and made before the expiration of 20 years from publication of the notice of striking off, that the LLP was at the time of the striking off carrying on business or in operation, or otherwise that it is just that the LLP be restored to the register, the court may order the LLP's name to be restored.[56]

(5)   Where the Registrar has struck an LLP off the register following an application by designated members, on an application made by any persons to whom a copy of the application to the Registrar should have been given as mentioned in **20.12** and **20.13**, and made before the expiration of 20 years

---

[50]   Or to a manager or trustee as above: CA 1985, s 652C(1)–(3). The position on a failure to carry out this obligation is the same as set out under footnote 48 above.

[51]   CA 1985, s 652A(4) and (5).

[52]   Ibid, ss 652(6)(a) and 652A(6).

[53]   Ibid, ss 652(6)(b) and 652A(7). As to the desirability of the dissolution being declared void before a winding-up order is made, see *In re Thompson & Riches Ltd* [1981] 1 WLR 682.

[54]   CA 1985, s 651. Generally speaking, the application must be made within 2 years from the date of dissolution: s 651(4)–(7). The power of the court under s 651 is not confined to cases where the LLP is dissolved as a result of being struck off the register: the primary use of s 651 in relation to companies is by liquidators, after the completion of a winding up, seeking to recover assets which have been overlooked.

[55]   Although, *ex hypothesi*, it does not exist. In relation to companies, it is the practice of the court not to permit such applications to be made by the company alone, but to require a contributory or creditor to join in: see *Re Portrafram Ltd* [1986] BCLC 533 at 534. This practice is likely to be followed for LLPs. There may, in any event, be an issue as to whether 'the LLP' has given authority for the application to be made.

[56]   CA 1985, s 653(1) and (2). The application needs to be served on the Treasury Solicitor.

from publication of the notice of striking off, the court may order the LLP's name to be restored to the register if satisfied that any duty to give to the applicant a copy of the original application was not performed, or that the original application was made in circumstances where such an application was prohibited (as set out in **20.11**) or that it is for some other reason just to restore the LLP's name to the register. [57]

(6)   The court may also order the LLP's name to be restored to the register on an application by the Secretary of State made before the expiration of 20 years from publication of the notice of the striking off if the court is satisfied that it is in the public interest to do so.[58]

(7)   Where the court orders an LLP's name to be restored to the register under (4), (5) or (6) above, on an office copy of the court's order being delivered to the Registrar, the LLP is deemed to have continued in existence as if its name had not been struck off.[59] In the order restoring the name, the court may also give such directions and make such provisions as seem just for placing the LLP and all other persons in the same position (as nearly as maybe) as if the LLP's name had not been struck off.[60] The court is thus enabled to add where necessary to the order for restoration special directions designed to achieve an 'as-you-were position' between the LLP and third parties.[61] Such directions and provisions will be relevant, inter alia, to property which has vested in the Crown as bona vacantia.

(8)   Where an order is made by the court either declaring the dissolution to have been void (ie under (3) above), or restoring an LLP's name to the register, the order does not affect any disposition already made by the Crown of property which vested in it as bona vacantia; but the Crown is to pay to the LLP an amount equal to the amount of any consideration received by it for the property or the value of any such consideration at the time of the disposal, or if no consideration was received an amount equal to the value of the property disposed of as at the date of the disposal.[62]

---

[57]   CA 1985, s 653(2B) and (2C).
[58]   Ibid, s 653(2D).
[59]   Ibid, s 653(3).
[60]   Ibid.
[61]   See *Tymans Ltd v Craven* [1952] 2 QB 100 (CA) at 110/111 and 126. As to the giving of a limitation direction in favour of the LLP, see *Regent Leisuretime Ltd v Natwest Finance Ltd* [2003] BCC 587 (CA) esp at paras 89–91.
[62]   CA 1985, s 655(2).

Chapter 21

TAXATION OF A LIMITED LIABILITY PARTNERSHIP AND ITS MEMBERS

INTRODUCTION

21.1   The explanatory notes to the first draft of the Limited Liability Partnerships Bill issued in September 1998 very helpfully stated that 'the treatment of an LLP as a partnership, and the members as partners, will apply for all tax purposes....'. Whilst, it is believed, there had been only limited consultation between the DTI and the Inland Revenue at that stage, this statement clearly set out the Government's intention with regard to the taxation of an LLP. It seems fair to say that this statement continues to reflect the Government's intention.

21.2   Discussions between interested professional bodies and the DTI, the Inland Revenue and Customs & Excise have been continuing to take place since September 1998. This has been achieved through the helpful co-operation of all parties towards achieving a coherent system of taxation for LLPs. The discussions have covered a large number of issues. The preferred approach of the Government bodies to these issues has been to deal with them by the publication of practice notes.

21.3   The main publications used for this purpose are the *Inland Revenue Tax Bulletin*[1] and the *Customs & Excise Business Brief*[2] covering LLPs. Equally important is the new Statement of Recommended Practice (SORP) for LLPs issued in May 2002 by the Consultative Committee of Accountancy Bodies.[3] The author of this chapter and his colleagues have been closely involved in these discussions, and this chapter therefore includes sections which are based upon the discussions with the Government and professional bodies.

COMPUTATION OF TAXABLE PROFITS

21.4   The profits of an LLP will be taxed in accordance with the taxation rules which apply to the members of the LLP. In the case of individual members, the

---

[1]   The *Tax Bulletin* issue 50 sets out the Inland Revenue's interpretation on various practical issues relating to the taxation of an LLP and was released in December 2000. This chapter contains extracts from the *Tax Bulletin* which are © Crown copyright and reproduced with the kind permission of the Controller of Her Majesty's Stationery Office. Each issue of the *Tax Bulletin* contains certain qualifications which should be referred to before reliance is placed on an interpretation of it.

[2]   *Customs & Excise Business Brief* No 3/2001 issued in February 2001.

[3]   See further **18.8**.

profits will be calculated in accordance with the income tax rules.[4] Those members liable to corporation tax will have their share of profits calculated in accordance with corporation tax rules.[5] It should be noted that, whilst in the majority of cases similar rules apply to both income tax and corporation tax, this is not the case in relation to all expenditure.

Capital allowances

21.5   Where an LLP succeeds to a business previously carried on by a partnership, this will not give rise to a balancing event for the purposes of the capital allowance provisions.[6] Members of the LLP will therefore be able to continue to claim capital allowances in the normal way.

Income tax

21.6   Section 10 of the LLP Act 2000, inserting ICTA 1988, s 118ZA, is the main provision in the LLP Act 2000 covering the annual taxation of an LLP, and runs to no more than seven lines. It operates by stating that a trade, profession or business carried on by an LLP shall be treated as though carried on in partnership by its members. The effect of this section is to ensure that members of an LLP are taxed under the self-assessment rules as though they were partners in a partnership.

21.7   In addition, the Inland Revenue have confirmed that they will not treat the incorporation of the whole of an existing partnership business into an LLP as a cessation under the income tax rules and will therefore, in effect, ignore the incorporation into an LLP for income tax purposes.[7] This will therefore mean that partners in a partnership incorporating into an LLP will be unaffected by the incorporation for income tax purposes. The Inland Revenue have also confirmed that the partnership/LLP tax return, and partner's/member's tax returns, can be prepared on the basis of there being no change in the self-employed business activity carried on.[8] This means that only one return will be required from a partnership which fully incorporates into an LLP part way through an accounting period. It should perhaps be noted, however, that in these circumstances a partnership converting to an LLP may need to prepare separate accounts up to incorporation, and after incorporation, in order to establish the financial position to which the previous partnership agreement (and law), and the new LLP agreement (and law), respectively apply. Income tax self-assessment rules make each individual partner liable for the tax due on that partner's profit share in a personal capacity, and the income tax liability would not be a partnership or LLP liability.

21.8   The basis of taxation for an LLP will therefore follow the same rules as apply to partnerships and partners. Thus, an LLP will be required to submit an annual tax return to the Inland Revenue which sets out the tax figures relevant to

---

[4]   Ie in accordance with ICTA 1988, s 111.
[5]   Ibid, s 114.
[6]   *Tax Bulletin* issue 50.
[7]   Ibid.
[8]   Ibid.

that fiscal year.[9] An LLP member will be taxed upon the profits arising for the accounting period ending during the relevant tax year. For example, if an LLP has an accounting reference date of 30 April, the annual accounts to 30 April 2004 fall in the tax year 2004/05 (period 6 April 2004 to 5 April 2005), and will therefore form the basis of the LLP's 2004/05 tax return.

21.9 A partnership tax return requires details of the profit and loss account and, normally, the balance sheet to be set out using the Inland Revenue's standard accounts information format. The same will apply to an LLP, except that the balance sheet information will become mandatory as the balance sheet will form part of the accounts which will need to be filed annually with Companies House[10]. For partnerships and LLPs with a turnover in excess of £15 million, the standard accounts information does not have to be completed in full, but separate taxation computations and a set of the firm's accounts must accompany the tax return. The LLP tax return should be signed by a nominated member, normally the senior or managing member, on behalf of all the members.[11]

21.10 An LLP will be required to maintain records of all items relating to the firm's taxation position. These records need to be maintained for 5 years and 10 months following the end of the tax year in which the accounting period ended.[12]

21.11 Failure to maintain such records can result in penalties being applied of up to £3,000 for each default and, in the case of an LLP or partnership, these penalties can be multiplied by the number of members/partners during the relevant LLP tax return basis period.[13]

21.12 It should be noted that, like a partnership, the tax liability arising on an LLP's income is the liability of the individual members and not of the LLP. This is the case even if the profits are not allocated to members in the LLP's accounts. Accordingly, the 'appropriation' of profits which are unallocated in the accounts will need to be agreed before the firm's and members' tax returns are submitted to the Inland Revenue. In the absence of agreement the Revenue will seek to tax the unallocated profits on the basis of the firm's profit sharing contained within the Members Agreement.

21.13 The LLP tax return needs to be filed on or before 31 January following the end of the tax year in question.[14] For example, an LLP with a year end date of 30 April will need to file its April 2004 accounts as part of its 2004/05 tax return on or before 31 January 2006. In this case, the relevant tax records need to be kept until 31 January 2011.

---

[9] TMA 1970, s 12AA.
[10] The statutory requirements as to accounts are considered in chapter 18.
[11] TMA 1970, s 12AA(3).
[12] Ibid, s 12B.
[13] Ibid, s 12B(5).
[14] Ibid, s 12AA(4).

21.14   Penalties also apply where the LLP tax return is submitted after the 31 January filing deadline. In this case an automatic penalty of £100 per member will be levied and this is doubled if the return is still outstanding 6 months later.[15] The LLP's tax return sets out the allocation of the firm's income, allowances and reliefs arising within the LLP between the members of the LLP. This declaration also includes a statement of each member's full name, unique taxpayer reference and address.

21.15   Whilst the accounting period is the basis period for which the LLP's income is generally taxed, this is not the case in respect of income of the LLP received net of income tax such as dividends and taxed interest income.[16] In these cases, the income is taxed on the basis of what is actually received during the relevant tax year in question. Again, any additional liability to tax in respect of taxed income is personal to the members and dependant on each member's share of the income concerned.

21.16   An LLP is required to submit annual accounts to Companies House, and these accounts have to be prepared using generally accepted accounting practice and applying the LLP SORP. Likewise, partnerships have been required to prepare their accounts, for tax purposes, using generally accepted accounting practice since 24 July 2002.[17] Thus, the basis for the profits chargeable to taxation for an LLP should be broadly similar to that for a partnership. There will, however, be some differences as a result of the application of the LLP SORP.

21.17   On the change to a 'true and fair' basis of accounting[18] for tax purposes for a partnership, there was often an additional charge, known as the 'catching up charge', which reflected the increase in taxable profits arising from this adjustment.[19] This 'catching up charge' for a partnership is statutorily spread over 10 tax years from 1999/2000 to 2008/09.[20] The charge can be brought forward, by an election on behalf of all of the partners.[21] This charge is allocated each year in accordance with the profit sharing arrangements for the 12 months to the anniversary date of the charge.[22] In addition, the charge is subject to capping rules; although any balance not previously charged to tax will be taxed in the final year, ie 2008/09.[23]

21.18   The Inland Revenue have indicated (see **21.7**) that, where applicable, partnerships with a 'catching up charge' which incorporate the whole of their business into an LLP, will continue to be able to spread the balance of this charge

---

[15]   TMA 1970, s 93A.
[16]   ICTA 1988, s 111(8) only relates to untaxed income, therefore leaving taxed income to be assessed without reference to the partnership.
[17]   FA 1998, s 42 as amended by FA 2002, s 103(5).
[18]   Which is part of generally accepted accounting practices
[19]   FA 1998, Sch 6, s 3.
[20]   Ibid, Sch 6, s 4.
[21]   Ibid, Sch 6, ss 5 and 6(3)(b).
[22]   Ibid, Sch 6, s 6(4).
[23]   Ibid, Sch 6, s 4(5).

in the normal way over the 10-year period.[24] Complications may arise where only part of the business of the partnership is so incorporated, as the Revenue has indicated that they will treat such situations as a demerger of the previous business. In such cases, the 'catching up charge' will either follow one of the successor businesses where one successor business is recognisably 'the business' carried on by the partnership or, possibly, the cessation rules will apply to the whole charge. Where the cessation rules are deemed to apply, the balance of the 'catching up charge' will continue to be spread over the balance of the remaining 10-year period but be allocated in accordance with the profit sharing arrangements for the 12 months up to cessation and will not be subject to the capping rules.[25]

Corporation tax

21.19   Companies are also able to be members of an LLP. Such companies are not subject to the complex self-assessment income tax rules but are subject to the separate corporation tax rules. Accordingly, a corporate member's share of profits needs to be calculated in accordance with the corporation tax regime, and will be taxed according to the accounting period of the company concerned.[26] Thus a company will be taxed on the profits arising from the LLP during that actual accounting period. It is therefore preferable for corporate members to ensure that their accounting reference date is identical to that of the LLP in order to avoid complex apportionment being necessary.

21.20   A company will need to comply with the corporation tax self-assessment regime. Details of these rules are outside the scope of this book.

ASSOCIATES AND CONNECTED PERSONS

21.21   The Taxes Acts have a number of provisions which are used to determined the 'control' of a company and whether it is 'close' for tax purposes – which can affect the rate of tax, amongst other issues. For these purposes it is necessary to review ownership; and this is achieved by looking at the owners, their associates and persons with whom they are connected. Partners in a partnership are defined as falling within the definition of 'associates and connected persons',[27] and members of an LLP also fall within this definition.[28] This will be beneficial where members also own a company (for example, to carry out certain kinds of regulated business), because it will help them to qualify for tax relief on interest on loans to buy shares in the company.

---

[24]   *Tax Bulletin* issue 50.
[25]   FA 1998, Sch 6, s 6(4).
[26]   ICTA 1988, s 114.
[27]   Ibid, s 839 and TCGA 1992, s 286.
[28]   Ibid, s 118ZA

Individual members' taxation

21.22	As stated above, details of a member's income from an LLP will be reported to the Inland Revenue via the LLP's annual tax return.[29] The individual detail for each member shown on the LLP's tax return will also need to be shown on the relevant pages of the individual member's tax return. The individual member's tax return will also need to show details of the individual's other income and outgoings for the relevant tax year.

21.23	An individual member of an LLP is subject to the same filing date requirements and record keeping requirements as the LLP. In this case, the penalties are £100 for a late filed tax return, increasing to £200 if more than 6 months late,[30] and up to £3,000 in respect of a record-keeping failure.[31] These penalties apply, and are charged to each individual, and are not therefore multiplied by the number of members in an LLP.[32]

21.24	As a result, the individual member will need to report details of his income from the LLP on the basis of his share of the taxable profits arising in the accounting period ending in the relevant tax year. Thus, for an LLP with a year end of 30 April, the individual partner will be required to declare in his 2004/05 tax return details of his share of the taxable profits of the LLP arising in the accounting period ended 30 April 2004. The member will also have to declare details of his other income arising in the tax year 6 April 2004 to 5 April 2005 (including details of LLP income received net of income tax).

21.25	Complications arise in the year of commencement, and in the year of cessation, of self-employment, whether the individual is a member of an LLP or a partner in a partnership. These complications are discussed at **21.2–21.33**.

Commencement rules

21.26	In the year of commencement of self-employment, for example as a new member of an LLP, the income tax rules apply so that the individual is taxed on his or her share of the taxable profits arising in the business during the relevant tax year.[33] Thus, for a new member admitted to an LLP on, say, 1 May 2003, his taxable profits for the tax year 2003/04 will be his share of the taxable profits of the LLP for the period 1 May 2003 to 5 April 2004. In the second year of the individual's self-employment as a member of the LLP, the normal basis of assessment will apply[34] so that he will be taxed on his share of the full year's profits of the LLP for the year ended 30 April 2004.

21.27	As a result of these opening year rules, there is a period which falls to be assessed to taxation twice in the first couple of years of the member's self-

---

[29]	For salaried members who are treated as employees, see **21.46**.
[30]	TMA 1970, s 93.
[31]	Ibid, s 12B(5).
[32]	See **21.11** in relation to a default by an LLP
[33]	ICTA 1988, s 61.
[34]	Ibid, s 60.

employment. This period which is doubly assessed for income tax is known as the 'overlap' period and, in the example above, relates to the taxable profits of the member for the period 1 May 2003 to 5 April 2004. The underlying principle of self-assessment is that during an individual's self-employment he will be taxed on the whole of his self-employment income, not a penny more or a penny less. As a result, the taxable profits for the 'overlap' period are calculated and a record is maintained so that relief is given for this 'overlap' period either as a result of certain changes of accounting reference date of the business (see **21.30–21.32**) or upon the cessation of the individual member's self-employment (see **21.33**).

21.28   In the case of LLPs, the Inland Revenue have confirmed that the incorporation of the whole of the business of a partnership into an LLP will not be a trigger event for overlap relief for the individual members/partners.[35] This therefore means that the overlap relief on an individual becoming a partner in a partnership incorporated as an LLP will be carried through to his participation as a member of the LLP, such that relief will only be given on a change to a later accounting reference date in the tax year, or on retirement from the LLP.

21.29   Complications may arise where only part of the business of a partnership is incorporated into an LLP, as the Revenue have indicated that they will treat such situations as a demerger.[36] Where one of the successor businesses is sufficiently large in relation to the rest as to be recognisably 'the business' as previously carried on, then this may be treated as a continuation of the old business.[37] In this case, the other successor business will be treated as a new business such that the commencement rules will apply to members/partners. Perhaps more worryingly, if neither of the successor businesses is sufficiently large in relation to the rest, then the old business will be deemed to have ceased, and two or more new businesses will be deemed to have commenced. In this case, both the cessation and commencement rules will apply to each member/partner, although accrued overlap reliefs will be available for offset against taxable profits.

Change of accounting reference date

21.30   Where an LLP changes its accounting reference date to one later in the tax year, an appropriate proportion, calculated on a time basis, of the overlap relief is released in order to be offset against the profits assessable in that tax year.[38] It will be appreciated that the accounting period, or period ending in the relevant tax year, will exceed 12 months in length and that this is the reason why part of the overlap relief is released. Thus, in the case of an LLP whose accounting reference date has been 30 April, and which then switches in the tax year 2004/05 to a 31 October accounting reference date, the assessable profits for 2004/05 will be the 12 months to 30 April 2004 plus 6 months to 31 October 2004. Against these profits there will be a release of the overlap relief representing the period 1 May to 31 October, out

---

[35]   *Tax Bulletin* issue 50.
[36]   Ibid.
[37]   *Statement of Practice* 9/86.
[38]   ICTA 1988, s 62.

of the total period 1 May to 5 April, ie amounting to 183 days out of a total of 340 days.

21.31 Where the accounting reference date is moved to a date earlier in the tax year, there will be a corresponding increase in the member's overlap relief available for carry forward as a result of a period falling into the basis period for two tax years. For example, where a firm moves from a 30 September 2004 reference date to 30 April 2004, the assessment periods become:

> 2003/04 – year ended 30 September 2003
>
> 2004/05 – year ended 30 April 2004.
>
> Thus the additional overlap period is 1 May 2003 to 30 September 2003.

21.32 There are specific rules to ensure that businesses cannot frequently change accounting reference date without having good commercial reasons for the change.[39]

Cessation

21.33 When a member leaves an LLP he will be deemed to have ceased his self-employment in respect of that LLP's business. As a result, the cessation rules[40] will apply to the individual concerned, with the release of his overlap relief being crystallised. In the year of cessation, the member is taxed on his share of the LLP's profits for the period since the end of the basis period for the previous tax year to the end of his membership of the LLP. In the case of a member who retires from an LLP on, say, 31 July 2005, and whose previous tax year's basis period is the accounts to 30 April 2004, the basis period to the year of cessation is the 12 months to 30 April 2005 plus the three months to 31 July 2005. Against this can be offset the whole of his accrued overlap relief in respect of that business. In terms of assessable periods, the individual will have been taxed on a 15-month period from 1 May to 31 July, and will have received overlap relief for 1 May through to 5 April, thus resulting in the assessable period, in terms of time only, being the period arising during the relevant tax year. However, as overlap relief is not index linked, it is likely that the overlap relief in terms of actual taxable profits will be significantly different from the equivalent profits accrued during the period of offset. This deficit, or potential excess, reflects the cashflow benefit or disbenefit of having an accounting reference date early in the tax year.

Loss relief

21.34 The members of an LLP will be entitled to relief in respect of losses incurred in the business of the LLP, either through the income tax or the corporation tax rules. In the case of an LLP carrying on a profession (as distinct from a trade, a distinction which has generated some confusing case-law), this relief is unrestricted and equal to the loss.[41] Relief can be given against total

---

[39] ICTA 1988, s 62A.

[40] Ibid, s 37.

[41] *Tax Bulletin* issue 50.

taxable income of the current or previous tax years, and failing this by carry forward against subsequent shares of profit from the LLP. The loss for the year will need to be 'appropriated' for tax purposes when submitting the LLP and members' personal tax returns, accordingly the accounting treatment may differ from the tax treatment.

21.35   However, the amount available for relief against total income ('sideways' relief) for a member of an LLP *which carries on a trade* is restricted to the amount of the member's contribution to the business.[42] The amount of the member's contribution is further defined as the greater of the amount subscribed by the member and the amount of the member's liability on a winding up. The amount 'subscribed' is a reference to capital contributed and not to income retained within the LLP.[43]

21.36   The undrawn profits of a member of a trading LLP cannot normally be added to that member's subscribed capital in order to calculate the limit of his entitlement to current and subsequent year loss relief. This is because, subject to any agreement between the members, a member's undrawn profits will normally be regarded as a debt of the LLP. Accordingly, the member ranks, for that sum, alongside the other creditors in the event of liquidation. If, however, the terms of the agreement between the members specifically provide that the undrawn profit stands as part of a member's capital contribution, and that agreement is unconditional, then that amount can be taken into account in calculating the limit.

Example

The following useful example of how the relief provisions discussed in **21.35** and **21.36** will apply was included in the December 2000 *Tax Bulletin*.

Mr A becomes a member of a trading LLP on 6 April 2003. He introduces capital of £10,000 into the partnership. The LLP carries on a trade. During the year ended 5 April 2006 he makes a further capital contribution of £6,000.

His share of the LLP's trading loss is as follows and he claims for those losses against his other income.

Year ended 5 April 2005:   £6,000

Year ended 5 April 2006:   £3,000

Mr A is entitled to loss relief as follows:

---

[42]   ICTA 1988, s 118ZC–118ZD and the *Tax Bulletin* issue 50.
[43]   ICTA 1988, s 118ZC(3)

2003/04:   £6,000 (unrelieved capital contribution £4,000)

2004/05:   £4,000^a (unrelieved loss £2,000)

2005/06:   £5,000^b (unrelieved capital contribution £1,000)

ᵃ   Loss relief is restricted to the unrelieved capital contribution brought forward of £4,000. The balance of the loss of £2,000 (£6,000 – £4,000) is carried forward.
ᵇ   Loss relief of £5,000 available, ie loss of the year of £3,000 plus unrelieved loss brought forward of £2,000. Unrelieved capital contribution carried forward is £1,000 (ie total contributions of £16,000 less total loss relief given of £15,000).

21.37   Where a member of a trading LLP makes a capital contribution in order to meet a liability of the LLP for negligence for which the member is personally responsible (and he is obliged by the other members to make that contribution), then that amount will be taken into account in determining the amount of the member's capital contribution to the LLP. Provided that the conditions for relief are otherwise met, that member will be entitled to loss relief up to a maximum of the amount of the additional contribution.[44]

21.38   When these special rules apply to limit 'sideways' loss relief for a trading LLP member, any unrelieved losses can still be carried forward for relief against future profit shares.

Salaried members

21.39   Paragraphs **8.26** and **8.27** discuss the criteria by which a member of an LLP will be treated as an employee of the LLP. In these circumstances, the salaried member will be treated for taxation purposes in the same way as an employee of the LLP. The salaried member's income will need to be paid via the LLP's payroll and subject to the Pay As You Earn (PAYE) taxation system in the normal way for an ordinary employee.

21.40   It is understood that the Revenue has issued some rulings under Code of Practice 10 to the effect that certain salaried members are to be taxed as self-employed under Schedule D for taxation purposes. Such rulings are dependent upon the particular circumstances of each set of facts, and are also capable of being withdrawn at any time. It is the view of the author of this chapter that if it is intended that salaried members are to be taxed as self-employed their arrangements should be capable of meeting the normal criteria of self-employment. Typically this would include the requirement for the members in question to provide capital to the LLP and participate in the variable profits of the business (and possibly losses to some degree[45]).

Partnership annuity payments

21.41   Before the introduction of the LLP Act 2000, partnerships regularly paid annuities to former partners and/or their surviving spouses. These annuities

---

[44]   *Tax Bulletin* issue 50
[45]   See the discussion at **13.13**.

invariably recognised the ongoing benefit for the remaining partners of the former partner's work for the firm. These annuities specifically qualify for tax relief as charges on each individual partner's personal income from the business.[46] As can be seen from what is said at **7.15**, partnership annuities can give rise to considerable difficulties upon the incorporation of a partnership into an LLP. The result may be that, upon incorporation, the annuities are carried through from the former partnership into the LLP, or they are specifically left behind as obligations of the former partners.

21.42   In the former case (annuities carried through), the Revenue has confirmed that income tax relief for those partners who become members of the LLP will continue as though the annuities were paid via the continuing partnership route.[47] Newly admitted members of the LLP who assume a proportion of the liability, either by joining in the liability or out of whose profit share the annuities are paid, will also qualify.

21.43   Where the liability to pay an annuity is not transferred to the LLP, and the members of the old partnership continue to pay the annuity personally, those members will continue to obtain higher rate income tax relief. This relief will cease on the earlier of the paying member ceasing to be a member of the LLP or when the business originally carried on by the partnership ceases.[48]

21.44   It will also be possible to pay similar annuities to former members of an LLP and obtain tax relief under these provisions, even if the annuity liability is stated to be that of the LLP.

Partnership annuity transfers

21.45   The Revenue has confirmed that the transfer to an LLP of a partner's annuity rights and/or the transfer to an LLP of annuity obligations owed to former members of the partnership will not be regarded as chargeable disposals, provided that the rights and obligations remain substantially the same as those existing in relation to the old partnership. Where an annuitant agrees to substitution of the LLP, and the terms otherwise remain substantially the same, the annuitant will not be treated as making a chargeable disposal for capital gains tax purposes.[49]

Pension relief

21.46   As the members of an LLP are to be treated in the same way as partners in a partnership, the existing pension relief rules will apply to members of an LLP in an identical manner as they apply to partners in a partnership. This means that individuals with pension contracts under the old retirement annuity schemes (ie

---

[46]   ICTA 1988, s 660A(9)(a).
[47]   *Tax Bulletin* issue 50.
[48]   Ibid.
[49]   Ibid.

policies taken out before 1 July 1988), will continue to receive income tax relief in respect of premiums paid within the limits applicable to those policies.[50]

21.47   Similarly, those members contributing to personal pension policies will also continue to receive relief for their premiums paid, subject to meeting the appropriate percentage of 'net relevant earnings' rules.[51] However, it should be noted that personal pension policies will be affected by the new stakeholder pension rules which came into effect from 6 April 2001. These rules will restrict the ability to carry forward unused relief from past years and limit the ability to carry back premiums in certain circumstances.[52]

21.48   The table below shows the available percentage of 'net relevant earnings' which may be paid into pension schemes either under a retirement annuity policy or under a personal pension/stakeholder scheme policy. It should be noted that there is a cap on the amount that may be contributed to a personal pension/ stakeholder policy, which is determined in the annual Budget. For the year 2004/05 the personal pension relief cap amounted to £102,000.[53]

Retirement Annuity Policies		*Personal Pension and Stakeholder Policies*	
Age at start of tax year	Maximum %	Age at start of tax year	Maximum %
50 or less	17.5	35 or less	17.5
51–55	20	36–45	20
56–60	22.5	46–50	25
61 or over	27.5	51–55	30
		56–60	35
		61 or over	40

21.49   At the time of writing, the Chancellor of the Exchequer has confirmed that pension simplification will go ahead with effect from 6 April 2006, when the current pension regimes will come to an end and be replaced by a single universal regime. There will be two key controls in the new regime, namely:

An annual allowance

A lifetime allowance

21.50   Individuals will be able to invest each year the lower of £215,000 or their net relevant earnings into a tax privileged pension arrangement. This annual allowance will increase by steps between the fiscal years 2007/08 and 2010/2011 to £255,000.

---

[50]   ICTA 1988, s 626.
[51]   Ibid, s 640.
[52]   FA 2000, Sch 13, paras 17–19.
[53]   ICTA 1988, s 640A.

21.51   The lifetime allowance for the first year, 2006/07, will be £1.5m. This, in turn, will increase over the next four years as follows:

2007/08   £1.6m

2008/09   £1.65m

2009/10   £1.75m

2010/11   £1.8m

21.52   If pension benefits exceed the lifetime allowance, there will be a 'recovery charge' in respect of the excess value equivalent to 25 per cent of the fund (and further tax up to a total of 55 per cent if taken as a lump sum). Individuals will be able to protect their existing schemes provided that they register their intent to do so within three years of the change.

Loan interest relief

21.53   Historically, partnerships have been funded mainly either by partners' personal capital contributions or by retained profits. Partners have been able to obtain income tax relief in respect of the interest incurred on a loan taken out to introduce monies into a partnership as long as the monies are used for one of the following purposes:

(a)   purchasing a share in a partnership; or
(b)   contributing money to a partnership by way of capital or premium where the money is used wholly for the purposes of the partnership business; or
(c)   paying off another loan where relief would have been available under the above criteria.

21.54   Where these criteria are met, and the individual partner has not recovered any capital from the partnership, he has been able to offset the loan interest paid against his assessable profits, and thus obtain income tax relief.[54] This loan interest relief will continue to be available to members of an LLP in the same manner as it is available to partners in a partnership.[55]

21.55   The Finance Act 2001 introduced anti-avoidance provisions in respect of interest on a loan to purchase an interest in an investment LLP (see **21.93–21.94**).

21.56   Nevertheless, as an LLP will have a personality separate from its members under the LLP Act 2000,[56] it may be preferable for such entities to seek a degree of corporate funding through the business, thus removing the personal liability of the members in the event of a default. However, it is expected that banks will, in a number of circumstances, look for personal guarantees from the members of an LLP for such borrowing, which may negate some of the benefits of this level of borrowing.

---

[54]   ICTA 1988, s 362.
[55]   See ibid, s 362(2)(a), amended by LLP Act 2000, s 10(2)
[56]   See the discussion in chapter 3.

PARTIAL INCORPORATION TO AN LLP

21.57 It is quite possible that a number of partnerships wishing to obtain LLP status will not be able to achieve full incorporation of their business into an LLP. This may result from an inability to novate existing contracts,[57] the difficulties associated with the transfer of liability for annuity payments,[58] or other specific circumstances. On this basis, it may well be that many partnerships will only be able to partially incorporate their business into an LLP. This partial incorporation will raise a number of significant issues, such as the effect on overlap relief, and the catching up charge referred to above.

21.58 In the case of incorporation into a limited company, the Revenue has, in practice, normally been prepared to accept the incorporation of a partnership as fully achieved as long as the performance and conduct of all contracts, and the economic benefit or otherwise of the partnership business, has been transferred by the partners to the new corporate entity. It appears that a similar pragmatic and commercial approach has been adopted by the Revenue in respect of incorporation of a partnership into an LLP. In these circumstances it is also recommended that the clients of the partnership are notified of the transfer of the business to the LLP, in order to be able to demonstrate to the Revenue the intended transfer of the business, although the clients may refuse to accept that this restricts their legal rights in any way.

NATIONAL INSURANCE CONTRIBUTIONS

21.59 Following lobbying, the LLP Act 2000 includes a specific provision which states that members of an LLP will be liable to Class 4 National Insurance contributions and not the alternative employee contribution system.[59] The provision is silent in respect of the other classes of National Insurance contributions, but the Revenue have confirmed that members of an LLP will also be liable to Class 2 National Insurance contributions and/or, where applicable, Class 3 National Insurance contributions.[60]

CAPITAL GAINS TAX (CGT)

21.60 As the members of an LLP will be treated similarly to the partners in a partnership, the existing rules in relation to partners' CGT will apply to the members of an LLP. These rules (as applied to LLPs) provide that the individual assets of an LLP are treated for tax purposes as though owned by the members in proportion, rather than separately by the LLP itself.[61] This can present many

---

[57] See the discussion at **7.5–7.6**.

[58] See **7.14–7.15**.

[59] LLP Act 2000, s 13, inserting a new sub-s (3A) into s 15 of the Social Security Contributions and Benefits Act 1992.

[60] *Tax Bulletin* issue 50.

[61] TCGA 1992, s 59A.

complexities, particularly in areas where members join and leave an LLP, or where there is a change in the profit and asset sharing ratios within the LLP.

21.61   Historically, partnerships have been subject to an Inland Revenue Statement of Practice D12 ('SPD12'), which enables firms to deal with these issues, in circumstances where there is not a revaluation of assets, as though transactions between partners take place at historic cost. As a result there is no CGT charge arising on the acquisition or disposal of interests in the partnership. SPD12 has been updated to provide a similar position for members of an LLP.[62]

21.62   Where there *is* a revaluation of partnership assets, and subsequent changes in the asset sharing ratios, then each such change results in a disposal and acquisition for CGT purposes. Each individual member will be required to do a CGT computation in respect of his proportionate change arising at the date of the event giving rise to the change in asset sharing ratios. This can require quite complex CGT records and computations to be maintained, and may result in partners suffering an unexpected charge to CGT. It is therefore likely that most LLPs will wish to apply the practice as set out in the revised SPD12. There may be some complications for LLPs, in that their accounts will need to be prepared using generally accepted accounting practices and comply with the LLP SORP. This may have an impact on the values attributable to assets held within the LLP's balance sheet.

21.63   The transfer of a business from a partnership to an LLP will have no effect for CGT purposes, as the assets before transfer will be deemed to be owned by the partners individually and, following incorporation, the assets will still be deemed to be owned by the members individually, thus resulting in no disposal arising for CGT purposes. Obviously, if there were to be a change in ownership ratios at the time of incorporation then a chargeable gain could arise, subject to the application of the revised SPD12. However, as noted at **21.73–21.80**, this is unlikely to be desirable in any event.

21.64   As a result of there being no disposal by the partners on incorporation into an LLP, the transfer of the business and assets will have no effect upon the availability of any existing indexation allowance and the accrual period for CGT taper relief purposes.[63] Equally, the incorporation will not be a disposal whereby former partners will be able to take advantage of the retirement relief provisions which were phased out by 5 April 2003.[64]

21.65   As an LLP will be required to produce its accounts under generally accepted accounting practice and using the LLP SORP, a merger is likely to have to be treated as an acquisition in the LLP's accounts. This will result in the balance sheet having to reflect the value of the assets acquired at their market value and will, in most cases, result in goodwill being reflected on the LLP's balance sheet. In accordance with generally accepted accounting practice, the goodwill will

---

[62]   Statement of Practice D 12 revised October 2002
[63]   *Tax Bulletin* issue 50.
[64]   TCGA 1992, ss 163–164 and Sch 6.

normally be written down through the LLP's profit and loss account over a period of years.

21.66   The valuation of goodwill arising in such cases would result in the members of the LLP not being able to take advantage of the practice set out in SP D12 in relation to goodwill.

CGT rollover relief

21.67   Where an individual sells a privately owned 'qualifying' asset (for example, farmland which he has used for his own farming business) resulting in a capital gain arising and, within a period of one year before or three years after the disposal, acquires an interest in another 'qualifying' asset held in an LLP, rollover relief can be claimed to defer the capital gains tax until the LLP asset is sold. Assets which 'qualify' include land, buildings or goodwill used in a trade or profession. The same relief can also apply in the reverse situation where there is a sale by an LLP of a 'qualifying' asset and a subsequent acquisition by a member of the LLP of another 'qualifying' asset. This relief works at the individual member level and therefore the proceeds reinvested would be restricted in each case to either the member's share of the LLP asset disposed or the member's share of the asset acquired.

LIQUIDATIONS/WINDING UP

21.68   The Income Tax and CGT transparency of an LLP applies only while the LLP is carrying on activities with a view to profit. Accordingly, where an LLP ceases to carry on a trade or profession, it will no longer have equal treatment with that of a partnership, and for the purposes of Income Tax and CGT will instead be regarded as body corporate and no longer transparent.[65]

21.69   For income purposes the loss of tax transparency will result in the profits of the LLP being taxed as though the LLP were a company with corporation tax being levied at the corporate level. The members will either be taxed on distributions as employment income or as income or capital distributions depending upon the nature of the payment being made by the liquidator.

21.70   The members will be liable to taxation in respect of the gain or losses that will arise on the disposal of their capital interest in the LLP. The costs of the members' capital interest in the LLP will be deemed to be the allowable acquisition costs of each partner's interest in the LLP, determined by reference to the capital contributions made as if the LLP had never been transparent.[66] It will therefore be necessary for members to maintain accurate records of their capital contributions made to an LLP and not just their share of the interest of each individual asset owned by the LLP.

---

[65]   ICTA 1988, s 118ZA(4), inserted by LLP Act 2000, s 10(1) and TCGA 1992, s 59A(2), inserted by LLP Act 200, s 10(3).

[66]   *Tax Bulletin* issue 50.

21.71 The Revenue have also stated that where members of an LLP are able to wind up the LLP's affairs in an orderly way, without the formal appointment of a liquidator, in the course of a cessation of commercial activity, then transparency for CGT purposes will be preserved subject to:

(a) the LLP not being wound up for reasons connected in whole or in part with the avoidance of tax; and

(b) that following the cessation of the LLP's business the period of winding up is not unduly protracted taking account of the LLP's assets and liabilities.[67]

21.72 Once a liquidator has been appointed, however, transparency will be lost and potential double charges to capital gains tax – at the LLP level and individual member level – may arise. Also, any previously 'rolled over' or 'held over' capital gains will crystallise, and CGT which has been deferred will become payable, without any additional taper relief for the period since the date of disposal which gave rise to the rollover claim.

STAMP DUTY

21.73 The LLP Act 2000 includes a specific stamp duty exemption on the incorporation of a partnership business into an LLP.[68] This exemption applies to instruments by which property is conveyed or transferred by a partner to an LLP within the period of one year, beginning with the date of incorporation of the LLP.[69] It should be noted that the exemption only applies to the transfer of assets to an LLP within one year of the date of the incorporation of the LLP as, in the corporate world, it is common practice for a company to be incorporated well before transfer of a business to the limited company. Care will therefore need to be taken to ensure that an LLP is not incorporated so early that it is not possible to transfer all of the assets of a partnership to the LLP within the one year timescale.

21.74 The stamp duty exemption contained in the LLP Act 2000 is subject to two conditions.

(1) The first condition[70] is that the partners in the partnership immediately before the incorporation of the LLP are the same as the persons who are to be members of the LLP.[71] There has been much debate about this condition, as it is likely that firms will wish to incorporate their partnership business into an LLP at its normal year end, which is also the time at which partners are admitted and retire. The Revenue has stated that, provided all the other

---

[67] *Tax Bulletin* issue 50.
[68] LLP Act 2000, s 12.
[69] Ibid, s 12(1).
[70] Ibid, s 12(2)(a).
[71] It is assumed here that the property being conveyed or transferred to the LLP has been acquired by the partnership before incorporation of the LLP. In relation to property which is acquired by the partnership after the LLP has been incorporated, the first condition is that the partners in the partnership immediately after the acquisition of the property are the same as the persons who are or are to be members of the LLP: see LLP Act 2000, s 12(5)(a).

conditions for the exemption are met, they will accept that the stamp duty charge can be averted by arranging matters so that the change of partners takes place the instant before or after the incorporation of the LLP.[72] However, to confirm the position, the Stamp Office has said that it will need to see all associated documents affecting the change in membership of the old partnership, and of membership of the LLP, prior to and/or after incorporation. This position could cause problems if certain partners do not agree to become LLP members, as one dissenting partner could result in the loss of this stamp duty relief. The Stamp Office has confirmed that the exemption will apply in cases where the LLP incorporation document (being the registration form submitted to Companies House)[73] includes, say, only two members but further members are added prior to the business transfer such that at the time of the business transfer the members of the LLP are identical to the partners in the partnership. The death of a partner should not trigger a problem as the deceased partner no longer exists (unless the Partnership Agreement provides for a partner's executors to take his place as partner). The first condition also extends the exemption where the property conveyed or transferred was previously held by a nominee or bare trustee for one or more of the partners in the partnership.[74]

(2)   The second condition[75] requires that for the exemption to be applied, the individual partners' respective ownership proportions of property conveyed or transferred into an LLP must either be unchanged between the moment immediately before incorporation of the LLP[76] and the moment immediately after transfer, or that the proportions must not have changed during this period for tax avoidance reasons. Strictly speaking (as the property transferred to the LLP will become owned by the corporate entity), the partners' respective interests in the LLP will replace their interests in the old partnership assets. However, the Revenue have stated that they will not take this point.[77]

STAMP DUTY LAND TAX

21.75   Stamp duty land tax (SDLT) introduced by the Finance Act 2003, came into general effect from 1 December 2003. A similar exemption applies on the conversion of a partnership to an LLP as applies to stamp duty.[78]

21.76   If the partners (on behalf of the partnership) are assigning a leasehold interest, and that leasehold interest is a market rent lease with no inherent value, then that will be an assignment for no chargeable consideration which is not notifiable and can be self-certified. For assignments of leases which do have value,

---

[72]   *Tax Bulletin* issue 50.
[73]   See **2.16** et seq.
[74]   LLP Act 2000, s 12(2)(b).
[75]   Ibid, s 12(3).
[76]   Or acquisition of the property where it was acquired after incorporation of the LLP.
[77]   *Tax Bulletin* issue 50.
[78]   FA 2003, s 65

or for transfers of freeholds, these will be notifiable transactions. Provided the conditions of the relief are met, no SDLT will be due. The first condition of the relief is that the 'effective date' of the transaction is not more than one year after the date of incorporation of the limited liability partnership.[79] Often, the date of the business transfer agreement will be an 'effective date' (even if the assignment/ transfer completes later) as, from the date of the business transfer agreement, the LLP (and not the partnership acting via the partners) will normally become entitled to occupy the premises (or receive rents) and so substantial performance will have occurred.[80] The first land transaction return will be due within 30 days of this date, claiming the conversion relief. The later completion of the assignment or transfer (say, once the landlord's consent has been received) will be another notifiable event.[81] it is not clear whether that later completion will be another 'effective date' for the purposes of the conversion relief – so that the completion (as well as substantial performance) of the land transaction must be within one year of the date of incorporation of the LLP in order to get the relief from SDLT. The legislation seems to suggest that there can only be one effective date[82] – and if substantial performance precedes completion, substantial performance will be the effective date. This would lead to the conclusion that as long as substantial performance occurs within one year of the incorporation of the LLP, the conversion relief should be available even if the land transaction actually completes outside the one-year period. However, the Inland Revenue has indicated that this is not the way it intends the relief to work. It considers that for the conversion relief to be available, both substantial performance and completion must occur within one year of incorporation of the LLP. The legislation currently does not appear to support the Inland Revenue's stance on this. For now, it would be prudent to ensure that completion of all land transactions on conversions to LLP occur within the year after incorporation of the LLP, if an argument with the Inland Revenue is to be avoided.

21.77 The application of SDLT to transactions involving partnerships and LLPs was deferred until Royal Assent to the Finance Act 2004. From that date SDLT applies to the acquisition of interests in land by partnerships and LLPs, and also to transfers of interests between the partners/members.

21.78 Under SDLT, the duty on new lease rents will probably mean much higher charges than under the old stamp duty regime. SDLT, at a rate of 1 per cent, is due on the net present value of the property for the life of the lease. However, net present value is calculated by discounting future rents by only 3.5 per cent per annum. The increase can be seen from the example below:

---

[79]   FA 2003, s 65(1).
[80]   Ibid, s 44(4).
[81]   Ibid, s 44(8).
[82]   Ibid, s 44(4).

Example

Assume a 10-year lease at a rent of £100,000 per annum. Under the old system, stamp duty of £2,000 would be payable. However the increased liability under stamp duty land tax will be £6,816.

21.79 The new rules (as set out in Part 3, Sch 15 to the FA 2003 as substituted by the Finance Act 2004) will mean that (subject to the exemption for conversion from a partnership to an LLP):

– SDLT will be charged on a proportion of the market value of any land transferred into an LLP by an existing member, or by anyone in exchange for an interest in the LLP. The proportion will be calculated to be equal to the proportion of the market value of the property acquired by the other members plus the members retained portion of any consideration paid for the land.

– SDLT will be charged where an existing member transfers all or part of his interest in the LLP to another member, or to someone who becomes a member for money or money's worth, or where an existing member reduces his interest, and takes out money or money's worth. SDLT will be due on the additional proportion acquired by the member plus the members retained proportion of any consideration paid for the land. The position, however, can be more complex where the land was acquired by the LLP or the member increases his profit share after 19 October 2003.

– SDLT will be charged on the proportion of the market value of land transferred out of an LLP to a member or former member. SDLT will only be due on the proportion of the market value that has not already been subject to tax.

Example

Three members, A, B and C, are in an LLP as solicitors sharing profits equally, and own an office worth £2m. A retires and extracts capital of £100,000. As a result B and C increase their interest by 16.7 per cent each. They must each pay SDLT on a value of £333,333 (16.7 per cent x £2m). It appears that if A had retired without extracting any capital, no SDLT will be due. However, consideration is probably given as A may be giving up liabilities

21.80 The rules are far reaching and will apply not only where LLPs own land, but also, for example, where a member retires, extracts capital and is also released from the LLP's lease. No SDLT is due where the consideration (in this case the proportion of the market value of the interest acquired) is less than £150,000 (for non residential properties); and it is therefore hoped that this will exempt the majority of transactions.

21.81 Nevertheless, these new rules are complex, and potentially onerous, and will need to be considered on any changes of interests between members, even though on the face of it the transaction may not seem to involve an acquisition of property. The new rules are likely to require modification as they contain various anomalies, for example, SDLT applies where there are changes in income sharing ratios even though capital sharing ratios remain the same.

DOUBLE TAXATION RELIEF

21.82   One of the guiding principles behind double taxation treaties is that they are enacted to ensure that relief is obtained for the taxation suffered in one country against the taxation charge arising on the same profits in another country. Most double taxation agreements have historically been worded so that relief for corporate taxes suffered in one country is obtained against corporate taxes suffered in the other country. Likewise, income tax relief is given for income taxes suffered in the source country. The difficulty with LLPs is that whilst they may be taxed under income tax rules in the UK, they may well be subject to corporate taxes in the foreign country. The Inland Revenue has stated that they will allow tax credit relief to be obtained in respect of the proportionate share of the foreign tax paid on the profits of the overseas branch of a UK LLP where that branch is taxed by the overseas tax authority as a body corporate,[83] thus avoiding the distinction between corporate and income taxes. The same treatment does not necessarily apply in reverse (eg relief only being granted for income tax against income tax or corporate tax against corporate tax), and great care will need to be taken when considering the overseas taxation of an LLP.

21.83   A similar position arises in respect of dividends received from an overseas source. In the normal course of events, the individuals will be able to claim relief for the withholding tax suffered. However, this does not apply to the underlying taxes suffered on the profits out of which the dividend has been paid.[84]

21.84   The taxation of UK registered LLPs will vary from country to country depending upon how the UK LLP is regarded by the relevant tax authority. Due to the fact that the UK LLP is a body corporate,[85] it is likely that a number of countries will consider the UK LLP as opaque for tax purposes. In these cases the LLP will be taxed as a corporate entity in the foreign jurisdiction, and payments to members will fall within that country's regime for taxing employed individuals. The tax status for domestic purposes of a UK LLP remains unclear in a number of countries, including in particular France[86] and Germany. The position is clear, however, in Belgium, Denmark and the United States of America. Belgium accepts a UK LLP as 'transparent' for its tax purposes, with the result that a UK LLP will be taxed there as if a partnership. The position is the same in Denmark. In the USA, a UK LLP can elect, using Form 8832, to be treated as a partnership.

---

[83]   *Tax Bulletin* issue 50.
[84]   Ibid.
[85]   LLP Act 2000, s 1(2)
[86]   Although it is generally considered that under the terms of the proposed new Double Taxation Treaty between the UK and France (awaiting ratification at the time of this text going to print), a UK LLP will be taxed in France in the same way as a UK partnership operating in France.

21.85   In the exceptional circumstances where an LLP has ceased to be treated as transparent (see **21.69**), then the LLP will itself be able to claim relief for the foreign taxes and, if appropriate, the underlying taxes suffered in respect of the dividend received.[87]

UK BRANCHES OF OVERSEAS LLPs

21.86   A clear distinction needs to be made between a UK LLP and the UK branch of an oversea LLP. The Inland Revenue has published its views on how some such oversea LLPs should be regarded for taxation purposes.[88] Some overseas LLPs will be taxed as though liable to corporation tax in the UK,[89] whereas others will be regarded as a partnership, resulting in the members being separately liable to income tax on their share of the branch profits under the existing legislation for partnerships rather than under the LLP Act 2000. The LLP tax rules do not apply to the UK branch of an oversea LLP, or to an oversea LLP operating solely within the UK.

INHERITANCE TAX (IHT)

21.87   The LLP Act 2000 has a very short section covering inheritance tax.[90] In effect, the section states that members of an LLP will be treated in the same way as partners in a partnership and an LLP will be treated in the same way as a partnership, for all IHT purposes. This has the effect of ensuring that the specific reliefs for business property[91] and agricultural property[92] will apply as if members of an LLP were the partners in a partnership. Equally, where a partnership incorporates as an LLP, these reliefs will continue as though there had been no change in ownership, and therefore the qualifying periods of ownership will not be regarded as interrupted.[93]

21.88   The other IHT reliefs and exemptions available to partners in a partnership will be available to members of an LLP including, importantly, the exemption for transfers not intended to confer any gratuitous benefit.[94]

---

[87]   *Tax Bulletin* issue 50.
[88]   Ibid.
[89]   *Tax Bulletin* issue 50 states that this will be the case where the oversea LLP is regarded as a 'body corporate' for the purposes of the UK Taxes Acts. The Inland Revenue's 'entity classification' of various oversea LLPs is also set out in *Tax Bulletin* issue 50. The nature of oversea LLPs is discussed in chapter 17.
[90]   LLP Act 2000, s 11, inserting IHTA 1984, s 267A.
[91]   IHTA 1984, s 103.
[92]   Ibid, s 115.
[93]   *Tax Bulletin* issue 50.
[94]   IHTA 1984, s 10.

VALUE ADDED TAX (VAT)

21.89   Customs & Excise have stated that they will view an LLP as a body corporate for the purposes of the VAT legislation. This provides a potential advantage over the existing rules applicable to a partnership. The advantage is that an LLP, being a body corporate, will be able to be a member of a group registration for VAT purposes.[95] A decision as to whether a group registration is appropriate is a complex one, and needs to be considered in relation to the various other members of the VAT group as well as the LLP.

21.90   Customs & Excise have also indicated that they consider the transfer of the whole of the business of a partnership to an LLP to be a 'transfer of a going concern', such that VAT will not be chargeable on the transfer.[96] They have also indicated that it will be possible to carry over the existing VAT registration number to the LLP in similar circumstances.[97]

21.91   Where it is only possible to achieve a partial incorporation, each individual case will need to be reviewed on its own merits to see whether the 'transfer as a going concern' rules can apply, and the VAT number can be transferred.

COSTS OF CONVERSION

21.92   The process of conversion of an existing partnership business into an LLP will inevitably result in a number of costs arising. For example, the process of conversion will involve legal, taxation and accounting advice on both the decision to incorporate and drawing up the appropriate members' agreement and transfer agreement, and (where the partnership is of professionals) in relation to regulatory compliance. The question therefore arises as to whether these costs will be allowable for taxation purposes.

21.93   A decision of the Special Commissioners in respect of the conversion of the Halifax Building Society from a mutual body to a PLC found, as a fact, that on balance the conversion was made in order to transfer the business from a restrictive regulatory regime to a more favourable regulatory regime which would enable it to continue trading profitably. As a result, the expenses associated with the conversion process were an allowable expense for taxation purposes. Accordingly, based on the facts of each particular case, it may be possible to obtain a degree of tax relief for at least part of the expenses of conversion. However, it is likely that the Revenue will resist such claims either on the grounds that the expenditure is 'capital', or that it fails to meet the 'wholly and exclusively' test for the purpose of earning the profits of the trade or profession.

---

[95]   *Customs & Excise Business Brief* no 3/2001, issued in February 2001.
[96]   Ibid.
[97]   Ibid.

ANTI-AVOIDANCE LEGISLATION

21.94 The Finance Act 2001 introduced anti-avoidance provisions to prevent tax loss through LLPs which are used for investment and property investment.[98] The three major concerns covered by the anti-avoidance legislation are to ensure that:

(i) exempt bodies are taxed on any income from property they receive in their capacity as members of an LLP;

(ii) the same consequences follow for shareholders in a company that disincorporates to form an LLP, as currently follow when a company disincorporates to form a partnership; and

(iii) loans used to provide money to purchase an interest (or a 'share') in an investment LLP will not qualify for tax relief.

21.95 The definitions of 'investment LLP' and 'property investment LLP' are as follows:

(a) an 'investment LLP' means a limited liability partnership whose business consists wholly or mainly in the making of investments and the principal part of whose income is derived therefrom; and

(b) a 'property investment LLP' means a limited liability partnership whose business consists wholly or mainly in the making of investments in land and the principal part of whose income is derived therefrom.[99]

21.96 It is understood that the specific intention of these proposals was to ensure that LLPs are not used to create a UK tax-transparent corporate property investment vehicle with tradeable interests. This was understood to be Government policy. However the Government has recently announced proposals to consider the establishment of Property Investment Funds which are expected to be similar to the US Real Estate Investment Trusts. Nevertheless, the UK LLP is proving to be an attractive vehicle to invest in property due to its flexible structure. The anti-avoidance provisions, whilst effective in the areas of concern for the Revenue, do not have a material adverse effect if the structure does not rely heavily on the members borrowing to invest into the LLP. As a result, such property investment LLPs will arrange borrowings at the LLP level with the expectation that the members will provide their capital from personal resources, rather than non tax efficient borrowings.

21.97 The Finance Act 2001 also introduced sundry measures to prevent various tax favoured entities obtaining a benefit from the availability of LLPs. These rules ensure that:

– pension funds are denied exemption from tax on income derived in their capacity as members of property investment LLPs;[100]

---

[98] FA 2001, s 76
[99] ICTA 1988, s 842B.
[100] Ibid, s 659E

– income received by pension funds as a member of a property investment LLP is taxable at the rate applicable to trusts;[101]

– where s 271 of the TCGA 1992 provides certain miscellaneous capital gains tax exemptions some of which relate to pension funds or schemes, these are disapplied in respect of gains on assets held by pension funds or schemes as members of property investment LLPs;[102]

– insurance companies are taxable on income and gains received as members of a property investment LLP;[103]

– a policyholder's share of income and gains is charged to corporation tax if it relates to an insurance company's membership of a property investment LLP, and is referable to pension business. For these purposes, income from a property investment LLP is treated as derived from a separate property business, and is chargeable to tax at a corporation tax rate equal to the basic rate of income tax. The income is not treated as 'relevant profits' in the tax computations of insurance companies, but is included in the calculation of pension business profit;[104] and

– the corporation tax exemption for friendly societies on profits from life or endowment business[105] or the other business of a registered friendly society or an incorporated friendly society[106] is not given on income and gains received as a member of a property investment LLP.

21.98 It is interesting to note that whilst these specifically targeted provisions prevent other tax favoured entities from benefiting from the LLP structure, they do not apply to charities,[107] which will be taxed on their LLP income and gains in the normal way.

---

[101] ICTA 1988, s 686(6A)
[102] TCGA 1992, s 271(12)
[103] ICTA 1988, s 438B and s 438C
[104] Ibid, s 438B
[105] Ibid, s 460(cb)
[106] Ibid, s 461(3A) and s 461B(2A)
[107] As to a charity being a member of an LLP, see **2.10**.

Chapter 22

INSOLVENCY AND WINDING UP OF LLPs – A GENERAL INTRODUCTION

INTRODUCTION

22.1   The scheme of the LLP legislation is to apply to LLPs the statutory provisions relating to the insolvency and winding up of companies (including the CDDA 1986) with modifications.[1] Unless otherwise stated, references to the IA 1986, the CA 1985 and the CDDA 1986 are to those Acts as modified by the LLP Regulations 2001 to apply to LLPs. This reflects the stated intention of the Government that LLPs are, in most respects, to be treated as corporate entities. In fact, relevant corporate insolvency law has been applied virtually wholesale with little modification, and puts LLPs more or less on the same footing as companies. The IA 1986 applies to both solvent and insolvent LLPs. Consequently, members of an LLP will not share the flexibility enjoyed by partners to dissolve and wind up a solvent partnership informally and without the need for the involvement and expense of an insolvency practitioner.[2] It is not the purpose of this work to provide a detailed exposition of the law of corporate insolvency. What follows is an outline of the relevant provisions as they apply to LLPs.[3]

22.2   Since the enactment of the LLP Act 2000, the IA 1986 has been substantially amended by the Insolvency Act 2000 and the Enterprise Act 2002. Save in relation to the new administration procedure,[4] the statutory instruments that bring the relevant parts of that legislation into force for companies do not refer to LLPs. The authors understand from the DTI that the government intends to bring statutory instruments into force specifically applying the new legislation to LLPs with modifications (in the same form as the LLP Regulations 2001). In the meantime, it is not entirely clear whether the new provisions apply automatically to LLPs. The view of the authors, as discussed at **1.14–1.15**, is that amendments to the primary legislation[5] do apply automatically to LLPs unless the contrary is provided (expressly or by necessary implication) in the amending legislation. Save

---

[1]   LLP Act 2000, s 14 and LLP Regulations 2001, reg 4(2) and Part II of Sch 2 (applying, with modifications, the CDDA 1986), reg 5 (applying, with modifications, Parts I to IV, VI and VII of the First Group of Parts and the Third Group of Parts of the IA 1986 (as amended)), and reg 10 and Sch 6 (applying subordinate legislation).

[2]   Since 1986 an insolvent partnership can be wound up as an 'unregistered company' pursuant to Part V of the IA 1986 applied, initially, by the Insolvent Partnerships Order 1986, SI 1986/2142, and now by the Insolvent Partnerships Order 1994, SI 1994/2421, as amended by the Insolvent Partnerships (Amendment) Order 2001, SI 2001/767.

[3]   For a detailed exposition see, for instance, Totty and Moss, *Insolvency* and *Palmer's Company Law* Parts 14 and 15.

[4]   Introduced by the Enterprise Act 2002.

[5]   Applied to LLPs by the LLP Regulations 2001.

for the statutory instrument bringing ss 248 and 249 of the Enterprise Act 2002 into force, which specifically states that the new administration procedure does not apply to LLPs, the new primary and secondary legislation is silent as to its application to LLPs.[6] Until a specific statutory instrument is brought into force or there is a decided case, the application of the new provisions to LLPs should be treated as uncertain. The text in Chapters 23–32 assumes that the authors' view is correct. For an outline of the law as it was before the coming into force of the Insolvency Act 2000 and the Enterprise Act 2002, see the first edition of this book.

22.3   On 31 May 2002 the EC Council Regulation No 1346/2000 on insolvency proceedings came into force. It has direct effect in the UK. The Regulation applies to natural and legal persons,[7] which clearly includes LLPs, and affects winding up by or subject to the supervision of the court, creditors' voluntary winding up (with confirmation by the court), administration and voluntary arrangements under insolvency legislation.[8] The courts of the Member State within the territory of which the centre of an LLP's main interests is situated have jurisdiction to open insolvency proceedings.[9] The place of the registered office is presumed to be the centre of the LLP's main interests in the absence of proof to the contrary.[10] Where the LLP's main interests are situated within the territory of a Member State, the courts of another Member State have jurisdiction to open insolvency proceedings only if the LLP has an establishment within the territory of that other State, but the effect of such proceedings is restricted to the assets situated in that territory.[11] Where insolvency proceedings have been opened under Art 3(1), any proceedings opened subsequently under para 2 of Art 3 are secondary proceedings and must be winding-up proceedings.[12] An LLP which has its centre of main interests outside the UK and does not have an establishment within the UK is not, therefore, liable to be wound up by the court in England and Wales.[13] The Regulation does not apply to voluntary winding up except for creditors' voluntary liquidation where the court has made an order of confirmation that the Regulation applies.[14]

---

[6]   The Enterprise Act 2002 (Commencement No 4 and Transitional Provisions and Savings) Order 2003, SI 2003/2093.

[7]   Recital (9).

[8]   Arts 1, 2(a) and (c) and Annexes A and B.

[9]   Art 3(1). 'Centre of main interests' is the place where the LLP conducts the administration of its interests on a regular basis: Recital (13). Any judgment opening insolvency proceedings handed down by a court of a Member State which has jurisdiction pursuant to Art 3 is to be recognised in the other Member States: Art 16(1). See also Art 25.

[10]   Article 3(1).

[11]   Article 3(2). Establishment means any place of operations where the LLP carries out a non-transitory economic activity with human means and goods: Art 2(h).

[12]   Art 3(3).

[13]   IA 1986, s 117 has been amended so that it is subject to Art 3 of the Regulation: s 117(7).

[14]   Insolvency Rules 1986, r 7.62 inserted by Insolvency (Amendment) Rules 2002, SI 2002/1307, Art 9.

Chapter 23

VOLUNTARY ARRANGEMENTS

WHAT IS A VOLUNTARY ARRANGEMENT?

23.1 A voluntary arrangement is a composition in satisfaction of an LLP's debts, or a scheme of arrangement of an LLP's affairs, made between the LLP and its creditors. The purpose of a voluntary arrangement is, usually, to enable an LLP to trade out of its financial difficulties or to effect a more advantageous realisation of its assets than could be achieved in a liquidation. An LLP (like a company or other legal person) is free to enter into contractually binding arrangements with its creditors, but such arrangements can be defeated by a dissentient creditor. Part I of the IA 1986 contains provisions relating to voluntary arrangements. The principal advantage of compliance with the procedures set out in the IA 1986 is that dissenting creditors are bound to the terms of the arrangements so long as the terms are supported by at least three-quarters in value of the LLP's creditors.

THE PROPOSAL

23.2 The voluntary arrangement procedure is initiated by the LLP making a proposal to its creditors for a composition in satisfaction of its debts or a scheme of arrangement of its affairs.[1] Where the LLP is subject to an administration order or is being wound up, a proposal can be made by the administrator or liquidator (respectively); but in such a case it must also be made to the LLP.[2]

23.3 In relation to companies, it is the directors who make the proposal pursuant to IA 1986, s 1(1). The proposal is made to both the company and its creditors and, to take effect, the proposal must be approved at meetings of the members and the creditors. The requisite majority for members is (subject to any express provision to the contrary in the articles) more than one-half in value of the members present in person or by proxy and voting on the resolution.[3] A company can, therefore, subject to approval by its creditors, enter into a voluntary arrangement so long as it is approved by its directors and one-half in value of the members.

23.4 Section 1(1) of the IA 1986 (as modified for LLPs) provides for the LLP itself to make the proposal. The modified section does not, however, specify how the LLP is to decide whether to make a proposal, or how it is to decide on the

---

[1]   IA 1986, s 1(1). It is an offence for a member of an LLP to make a false representation or to do or omit to do anything fraudulently for the purpose of obtaining the approval of a voluntary arrangement: IA 1986 s 6A (inserted by IA 2000, s 2, Sch 2, Part I, paras 1 and 8).
[2]   IA 1986, s 1(3).
[3]   Insolvency Rules 1986 (IR 1986), r 1.20(1).

terms. It seems very unlikely that the making of a proposal would be regarded as an ordinary matter connected with the business of the LLP so as to be capable of being decided by a simple majority of members.[4] In the absence of a general majority voting provision in the LLP agreement, therefore, it would seem that a proposal can only be made if it is supported by all the members. Clearly, an LLP agreement ought to make provision for the way in which such a determination is to be made and, if it is to be made by resolution of the members, the requisite majority.

23.5 The proposal must provide for a nominee (a qualified insolvency practitioner) to act in relation to the voluntary arrangement, either as trustee or otherwise for the purpose of supervising its implementation.[5] Notice of the proposal is given to the nominee and, within 7 days, the LLP must deliver to the nominee a statement of the LLP's affairs.[6] Within 28 days after being given notice, the nominee submits a report to the court stating whether in his opinion the proposed voluntary arrangement has a reasonable prospect of being approved and implemented, whether a meeting of the LLP's creditors should be summoned to consider the proposal and, if so, when and where he proposes the meeting should be held.[7] If it appears to the nominee that he cannot properly prepare his report on the basis of the information in the proposal, he can seek additional information, including access to the LLP's accounts and records.[8] Ordinarily, the nominee will have been instructed by the LLP to prepare the proposal. He will, therefore, have obtained adequate information for the purpose of preparing the proposal and will have indicated in advance whether the proposal should be submitted to the creditors.

23.6 A proposal can also be made by an administrator or liquidator of an LLP, and can provide either for the administrator/liquidator or a third party to act as the nominee. Where the proposal is made by an administrator or liquidator, it must also be made to the LLP.[9] In such a case, a separate set of modifications apply to IA 1986, ss 2 and 3 for LLPs. Section 2(2) is modified to provide that where the nominee is not the liquidator or administrator, the nominee submits a report to the court stating whether meetings of the members of the LLP and its creditors should be summoned to consider the proposal; and s 3 is modified to provide for the nominee to summon meetings of the members of the LLP and creditors. Where the nominee is the liquidator/administrator, there is no requirement for a report, and the nominee simply fixes a venue and gives notice of meetings of creditors and the members of the LLP.[10]

---

4   LLP Regulations 2001, reg 7(6): default rule (6).

5   IA 1986, s 1(2).

6   Ibid, s 2(3); IR 1986, rr 1.4 and 1.5. Given that s 2(3) provides for the designated members to submit the proposal and the statement of affairs to the nominee, references in IR 1986, rr 1.4 and 1.5 to directors are probably properly read as references to designated members rather than members.

7   IA 1986, s 2(2); IR 1986, r1.7.

8   IR 1986, r 1.6.

9   IA 1986, s 1(3); IR 1986, rr.1.10, 1.12.

10   Ibid, s 3(2).

MORATORIUM

23.7 One of the principal drawbacks of the corporate voluntary arrangement legislation has been the absence of provisions imposing a moratorium on actions by creditors during the period in which the proposal was being considered. This was to be contrasted with the personal insolvency regime which imposes a moratorium from the moment an application for an interim order is made.[11] This lacuna has, for eligible LLPs, now been remedied by the amendments to the IA 1986 made by the Insolvency Act 2000 with effect from 1 January 2003.[12] The provisions relating to moratoria are set out in Schedule A1 to the IA 1986.[13]

23.8 An LLP is eligible for a moratorium if it meets the requirements of para 3 of Sch 1A to the IA 1986. The qualifying conditions are that it satisfies (on the date on which the documents referred to in para 7(1) of Sch A1 are filed with the court or in the financial year of the LLP which ended last before that date) two or more of the requirements for being a small LLP set out in s 247(3) of the CA 1985, namely, a turnover of not more than £5.6 million, a balance sheet total of not more than £2.8 million and not more than 50 employees.[14] A number of exclusions from eligibility are set out in para 4 and paras 4A–4K of Sch A1, including if the LLP is in administration or being wound up.

23.9 Where an LLP[15] wishes to obtain a moratorium, it submits to the proposed nominee a document setting out the terms of the proposed voluntary arrangement, a statement of affairs and such other information requested by the nominee to enable him to comply with sub-para (2) of IA 1986, Sch A1 para 6.[16] This provides that the nominee then submits a statement to the LLP indicating whether, in his opinion, the proposed voluntary arrangement has a reasonable prospect of being approved and implemented, whether the LLP is likely to have sufficient funds available to it during the proposed moratorium to enable it to carry on its business and whether meetings of the members of the LLP and its creditors should be summoned to consider the proposed voluntary arrangement.[17] The moratorium is obtained by the LLP filing a number of documents with the court:[18]

(a)   a document setting out the terms of the proposed voluntary arrangement;

---

[11]   IA 1986, ss 253 et seq.
[12]   Insolvency Act 2000 (Commencement No 3 and Transitional Provisions) Order 2002, SI 2002/2711.
[13]   IR 1986 rr 1.35-1.54 apply where there is a moratorium.
[14]   IA 1986, Sch A1 paras 2 and 3. Para 3(4) provides that an LLP is not eligible if it is a holding LLP of a group of LLPs which does not qualify as a small or medium-sized group. As to the turnover and other figures, see **18.28**.
[15]   The reference in IA 1986, Sch A1 para 6(1) as it applies to companies is to the directors but it is assumed that it should, consistently with the modifications to s 1, be read as a reference to the LLP rather than the members of the LLP.
[16]   IA 1986, Sch A1 para 6(1)
[17]   Ibid, Sch A1 para 6(2). It is assumed that para 6(2)(c) should be read (to apply to LLPs) as requiring meetings of both the members and the creditors; cf the alternate IA 1986 ss 2 and 3.
[18]   IA 1986, Sch A1 para 7(1).

(b)   a statement of affairs;

(c)   a statement that the LLP is eligible for a moratorium;

(d)   a statement from the nominee that he consents to act; and

(e)   a statement from the nominee that the proposed voluntary arrangement has a reasonable prospect of being approved and implemented, that the LLP is likely to have sufficient funds available to it during the proposed moratorium to enable it to carry on its business and meetings of the members of the LLP and that its creditors should be summoned to consider the proposed voluntary arrangement.

The moratorium comes into force when the documents are filed with the court.[19] The moratorium ends at the end of the day on which the meetings of creditors and members (which are summoned under para 29(1) of Sch A1) are first held (or, if they are held on different days, on the later of those days) unless the moratorium is extended under para 32 of Sch A1.[20]

23.10   If either of the meetings has not been held within 28 days of the moratorium coming into force, the moratorium ends at the end of the day on which those meetings were to be held (or, if the meetings were to be held on different days, the later of those days), unless the moratorium is extended under para 32.[21] If the nominee fails to summon either meeting within 28 days, the moratorium ends at the end of the last day of the 28-day period.[22] If the moratorium is extended (or further extended) under para 32, it ends at the end of the day to which it is extended (or further extended).[23] A moratorium can also come to an end if the nominee withdraws his consent to act (para 26(3)), an order is made by the court under paras 26(3), 27(3) or 40 or a decision to end the moratorium is made by one of the meetings summoned under para 29. If the moratorium has not previously come to an end in accordance with sub-paras (2)–(6) of para 26, it ends at the end of the day on which a decision under para 31 to approve a voluntary arrangement takes effect under para 36.[24] When a moratorium comes into force, the LLP notifies the nominee[25] and the nominee advertises the moratorium and notifies the registrar of companies and any petitioning creditor of whose claim he is aware.[26] When a moratorium comes to an end, the nominee advertises that fact and notifies the court, the Registrar of Companies, the LLP and any creditor of the LLP of whose claim he is aware.[27]

23.11   During a moratorium:[28]

(a)   no petition may be presented for the winding up of the LLP;

---

19   IA 1986, Sch A1 para 8(1).
20   Ibid, Sch A1 para 8(2).
21   Ibid, Sch A1 para 8(3).
22   Ibid, Sch A1 para 8(4).
23   Ibid, Sch A1 para 8(5).
24   Ibid, Sch A1 para 8(7).
25   Ibid, Sch A1 para 8(9).
26   Ibid, Sch A1 para 8(10).
27   Ibid, Sch A1 para 8(11).
28   Ibid, Sch A1 paras 8(12).

(b)   no meeting of the LLP may be called except with the consent of the nominee or the leave of the court and subject (where the court gives leave) to such terms as the court may impose;

(c)   no resolution may be passed or order made for the winding up of the LLP;

(d)   no petition may be presented for an administration order in relation to the LLP;

(e)   no administrative receiver of the LLP may be appointed;

(f)   no landlord or other person to whom rent is payable may exercise any right of forfeiture by peaceable re-entry in relation to premises let to the LLP in respect of a failure by the LLP to comply with any term or condition of its tenancy of such premises, except with the leave of the court and subject to such terms as the court may impose;

(g)   no other steps may be taken to enforce any security over the LLP's property, or to repossess goods in the LLP's possession under any hire-purchase agreement, except with the leave of the court and subject to such terms as the court may impose; and

(h)   no other proceedings and no execution or other legal process may be commenced or continued, and no distress may be levied, against the company or its property except with the leave of the court and subject to such terms as the court may impose.

23.12   Where a petition (other than an excepted petition[29]) for the winding up of the company has been presented before the beginning of the moratorium, IA 1986, s 127 does not apply in relation to any disposition of property, transfer of any interest in the LLP or alteration in status of the members made during the moratorium.[30]

23.13   In addition, the rights of a holder of an uncrystallised floating charge over the property of an LLP are put on hold while a moratorium is in force. A charge holder is not entitled to give notice causing either the crystallisation of the charge or a restriction on the disposal of any property of the LLP, and any event that would otherwise cause crystallisation or such a restriction does not have that effect. The charge holder is entitled to give notice as soon as practicable after the moratorium has come to an end.[31] Security granted by an LLP at a time when a moratorium is in force may only be enforced if, at that time, there were reasonable grounds for believing that it would benefit the LLP.[32]

23.14   Paragraphs 24–28 of Sch A1 contain provisions relating to the nominee. Paragraph 24 imposes a duty on the nominee to monitor the LLP's affairs for the purpose of forming an opinion as to whether the proposed voluntary arrangement (without or without modifications) has a reasonable prospect of being approved and implemented, and as to whether the LLP is likely to have sufficient funds

---

[29]   Primarily public interest winding-up petitions under IA 1986, s 124A: IA 1986, Sch A1 para 12(5).

[30]   Or at a time mentioned in para 37(5)(a): IA 1986, Sch A1 para 12(2).

[31]   IA 1986, Sch A1 para 13.

[32]   Ibid, Sch A1 para 14. Paragraphs 15–23 contain various provisions relating to the conduct of the LLP's affairs during a moratorium, such as an obligation to state on invoices, orders and letters that a moratorium is in force: para 16(1).

available to it during the remainder of the moratorium to enable it to carry on its business. Paragraph 25 deals with the withdrawal by a nominee of his consent to act. Paragraph 26 deals with challenges to the actions of the nominee. Paragraph 28 provides for the replacement of the nominee.

THE MEETING(S)

23.15   The IA 1986 now contains parallel sets of provisions the application of which depends upon whether a moratorium is in place or not. Sections 3–7 apply where there is no moratorium and paras 29 to 39 of Sch A1 apply where there is. The provisions are broadly similar. The text below follows ss 3–7 with the references to Sch A1 footnoted.

23.16   Once a report has been filed in court by the nominee, he summons the meeting(s) (of creditors and/or members) at the time and place proposed in his report.[33] The procedure does not require any judicial input from the court, and the filing of the nominee's report is merely an administrative exercise. Notice of the creditors' meeting is served on all the creditors of the LLP.[34] Notice is also given to all the members of the LLP, although the chairman has the power to exclude any member from attendance (either completely or for any part).[35] The purpose of the meeting is for the creditors to decide whether to approve the proposed arrangements. The nominee acts as the chairman of the creditors' meeting.[36] The creditors may approve the arrangements with or without modifications,[37] although no proposal or modification can be approved which would affect the rights of a secured creditor to enforce its security except with the consent of the creditor concerned.[38] Further, the meeting cannot approve any proposal or modification under which any preferential debt is paid otherwise than in priority to any non-preferential debts, or under which a preferential creditor is paid a smaller proportion of his debt than that paid to another preferential creditor except with the concurrence of the creditor concerned.[39]

23.17   In the case of a proposal made by the LLP, if modifications are proposed at the meeting of creditors, the chairman shall, before the conclusion of the meeting, ascertain from the LLP whether or not it accepts the proposed modifications, and if at the conclusion the LLP has failed to respond it shall be presumed not to have agreed to it.[40] This provision (which only applies to LLPs) is required because the modified legislation does not provide for a meeting of the members of the LLP to approve the proposal where the LLP itself made the

---

[33]   IA 1986, s 3(1); IR 1986, rr 1.9, 1.11 and 1.13. (IA 1986, Sch A1 para 29(1) if there is a moratorium.)

[34]   IA 1986, s 3(3); IR 1986, rr 1.9(2)(a), 1.11(a). (IA 1986, Sch A1 para 29(2) if there is a moratorium.)

[35]   IR 1986, r 1.16.

[36]   Ibid, r 1.14.

[37]   IA 1986, s 4(1). (IA 1986, Sch A1 para 31(1) if there is a moratorium.)

[38]   Ibid, s 4(3). (IA 1986, Sch A1 para 31(4) if there is a moratorium.)

[39]   Ibid, s 4(4). (IA 1986, Sch A1 para 31(5) if there is a moratorium.)

[40]   Ibid, s 4(5A). There is no equivalent in Sch A1.

proposal. The reference to the conclusion of the meeting will presumably be construed as being the conclusion of the meeting following any adjournments. This again raises the question of the basis on which an LLP is to take the necessary decisions. Unless all the members of the LLP, or one or more members with authority to bind the LLP, are present at the meeting, adjournments to enable a meeting of the LLP to be held would appear inevitable.

23.18 Every creditor who is given notice of the meeting is entitled to vote.[41] Votes are calculated according to the amount of the creditor's debt as at the date of the meeting (or, where the LLP is being wound up or in administration, the date of it going into liquidation or administration).[42] A creditor may vote in respect of a debt for an unliquidated amount, or any debt whose value is not ascertained, but (for the purposes of voting) his debt is valued at £1 unless the chairman agrees to put a higher value on it.[43] The chairman has the power to admit or reject a creditor's claim for the purpose of entitlement to vote.[44] There are provisions for an appeal against a chairman's decision.[45]

23.19 A resolution to approve a proposal or modification requires a majority in excess of three-quarters in value of the creditors present in person or by proxy.[46] Any other resolution put to a meeting requires a majority in excess of one-half.[47] The meeting can be adjourned.[48] The chairman reports the result of the meeting to the court.[49]

23.20 In the case of a proposal made by the LLP, once approved by the meeting of creditors, the voluntary arrangement binds every person who, in accordance with the rules, had notice of, and was entitled to vote at, that meeting (whether or not he was present or represented at the meeting) as if he were a party to the voluntary arrangement.[50]

23.21 In the case of a proposal made by a liquidator or administrator (and subject to the operation of IA 1986, s 4A), the approval of both the meeting of creditors and the meeting of members is required.[51] With effect from 1 January 2003, if the proposal is approved by the creditors' meeting it takes effect subject to the right of a member to apply to the court.[52] The court may order the decision of

---

[41] IR 1986, r 1.17(1).
[42] Ibid, r 1.17(2).
[43] Ibid, r 1.17(3).
[44] Ibid, r 1.17A(2).
[45] Ibid, r 1.17A(3)–(7).
[46] Ibid, r 1.19(1). A vote in respect of any claim or part of a claim shall be left out of account: (a) where written notice of the claim was not given, either at the meeting or before it, to the chairman or the convener of the meeting; and (b) where the claim or part is secured: IR 1986, r 1.19(3).
[47] IR 1986, r 1.19(2).
[48] Ibid, r 1.21.
[49] IA 1986, s 4(6); IR 1986, r 1.24. (IA 1986, Sch A1 para 30(3) if there is a moratorium.)
[50] Ibid, s 5(2). (IA 1986, Sch A1 para 37(2) if there is a moratorium.) See also s 4A and Sch A1 para 37.
[51] In the case of a proposal by a liquidator or administrator, IA 1986, ss 4–7 are not specifically modified by the LLP Regulations 2001.
[52] IA 1986, s 4A(2). (IA 1986, Sch A1 para 36(2) if there is a moratorium.)

the members' meeting to have effect instead of the decision of the creditors' meeting, or make such other order as it thinks fit.[53] It is not entirely clear how rr 1.18 and 1.20 of the IR 1986[54] – which govern the voting rights of members and the requisite majority for the passing of a resolution at a members' meeting – are to be applied to LLPs. Rule 1.18, as it applies to companies, provides, inter alia, for members to vote according to the rights attaching to their shares in accordance with the articles of association; r 1.20 provides, inter alia, that subject to any express provision in the articles, a resolution is to be regarded as passed if voted for by more than one half in value of the members present in person or by proxy and voting on the resolution. Regulation 10(1)(b) of the LLP Regulations 2001 provides that the IR 1986 apply to LLPs with such modifications as the context requires for the purpose of giving effect to the provisions of the IA 1986 which are applied by the LLP Regulations 2001. Presumably, therefore, the voting rights and the requisite majority will depend upon the terms of the LLP agreement and, in default of agreement, members will be entitled to votes of equal weight, and a resolution will be passed if supported by a simple majority of members voting.

CHALLENGE TO THE VOLUNTARY ARRANGEMENT

23.22   A voluntary arrangement can be challenged on the grounds that it unfairly prejudices the interests of a creditor, member or contributory of the LLP.[55] Any member of an LLP, any person entitled to vote at the creditors' meeting, and the nominee, can apply to the court under IA 1986, s 6(1).[56] An application cannot be made after the end of the period of 28 days after the nominee has lodged his report.[57] The court has power to revoke or suspend any approval given at the creditors' meeting, or to give a direction for the summoning of a further meeting to consider any revised proposal which the person who made the original proposal may make.[58]

ADMINISTRATION OF THE VOLUNTARY ARRANGEMENT

23.23   The administration of the voluntary arrangement is carried out by the nominee, who is known as the supervisor after approval.[59] Following approval, the members or, where appropriate, the liquidator or the administrator must do all that is required for putting the supervisor into possession of the assets included in the arrangement.[60] The nature of the role to be performed by the supervisor, and the extent to which he will become involved in the day-to-day administration of the LLP, will depend upon the terms of the arrangement. The supervisor is entitled to

---

[53]   IA 1986, s 4A(6). (IA 1986, Sch A1 para 36(5) if there is a moratorium.)
[54]   SI 1986/1925.
[55]   IA 1986, s 6(1). (IA 1986, Sch A1 para 38(1) if there is a moratorium.)
[56]   Ibid, s 6(2). (IA 1986, Sch A1 para 38(2) if there is a moratorium.)
[57]   Ibid, s 6(3). (IA 1986, Sch A1 para 38(3) if there is a moratorium.) The 28-day period cannot be extended: *Tager v Westpac Banking Corp* [1997] 1 BCLC 313
[58]   IA 1986, s 6(5). (IA 1986, Sch A1 para 38(5) if there is a moratorium.)
[59]   Ibid, s 7(2). (IA 1986, Sch A1 para 39(2) if there is a moratorium.)
[60]   IR 1986, r 1.23(1).

apply to the court for directions in relation to any matter arising under the voluntary arrangement.[61] Any of the LLP's creditors or any other person who is dissatisfied by any act, omission or decision of the supervisor may apply to the court. On such an application, the court may confirm, reverse or modify any act or decision of the supervisor, give him directions or make such other orders as it thinks fit.[62] Rules 1.31 to 1.34 make provisions relating to the conversion of a voluntary arrangement into winding-up proceedings, under Art 37 of EC Council Regulation No 1346/2000.[63]

---

[61] IA 1986, s 7(4). (IA 1986, Sch A1 para 39(5) if there is a moratorium.)
[62] Ibid, s 7(3). (IA 1986, Sch A1 para 39(3) and (4) if there is a moratorium.)
[63] See **22.3**.

Chapter 24

ADMINISTRATION

INTRODUCTION

24.1 The administration procedure was introduced for companies in the 1985/86 legislation and for partnerships by the Insolvent Partnerships Order 1994.[1] The administration procedure was applied to LLPs by the LLP Regulations 2001.[2] With effect from 15 September 2003, the procedure as it applies to companies has been substantially amended by the Enterprise Act 2002.[3] The primary feature of the new scheme is that an administrator may be appointed out of court.[4] A new schedule – Sch B1 – has been inserted into the IA 1986 in place of ss 8–27. This new regime has not, however, yet been applied to LLPs (or insolvent partnerships), and Art 3(3) of SI 2003/2093 specifically provides that the former administration provisions continue to apply for the purpose of giving effect to the Insolvent Partnerships Order 1994 and reg 5 of the LLP Regulations. It is anticipated that the new regime will, in due course, be applied to LLPs and partnerships. This chapter is written, however, on the basis of the administration procedure as it continues to apply to LLPs.

24.2 The purpose of an administration order is to give to an LLP in financial difficulties a breathing space to enable attempts to be made by it to trade out of its problems, or to provide an opportunity for its assets to be more advantageously realised than would occur in liquidation.[5] The court may make an administration order in respect of an LLP if it is satisfied that the LLP is or is likely to become unable to pay its debts,[6] and that the making of an order would be likely to achieve one or more of the purposes set out in IA 1986, s 8(3).[7] Those purposes are:

---

[1]   SI 1994/2421, Sch 2, para 6.

[2]   IA 1986, Part II; LLP Regulations 2001, reg 5 and Sch 3.

[3]   Enterprise Act 2002 (Commencement No 4 and Transitional Provisions and Savings) Order 2003, SI 2003/2093.

[4]   See generally Davies, *Insolvency and the Enterprise Act 2002* chapters 6–12.

[5]   See generally Lightman and Moss, *The Law of Receivers and Administrators of Companies* (Sweet & Maxwell, 3rd edn, 2000) chapter 23.

[6]   As defined in IA 1986, s 123. See *Highberry Ltd v Colt Telecom Group Plc (No 2)* [2003] BPIR 324.

[7]   IA 1986, s 8(1). The phrase 'likely to achieve' would, on the balance of current authority, appear to mean 'a real prospect' rather than 'likely, on a balance of probabilities, to be achieved': see *Re Consumer and Industrial Press Ltd* (1988) 4 BCC 68, *Re Harris Simmons Construction Ltd* [1989] 1 WLR 368, *Re Manlon Trading Ltd* (1988) 4 BCC 455, *Re Primlaks (UK) Ltd* (1989) 5 BCC 710, *Re SCL Building Services Ltd* (1989) 5 BCC 746, *Re Rowbotham Baxter Ltd* [1990] BCC 113 and *Three Rivers DC v Bank of England (No 4)* [2002] 4 All ER 881.

(a)   survival of the LLP, and the whole or any part of its undertaking, as a going concern;

(b)   the approval of a voluntary arrangement under Part I of the IA 1986;

(c)   the sanctioning under s 425 of the CA 1985 of a compromise or arrangement;

(d)   a more advantageous realisation of the LLP's assets than would be effected on a winding up.[8]

The order made by the court specifies the purpose or purposes for which it is made.

PROCEDURE

24.3 An application for an administration order can be made by the LLP or by one of the LLP's creditors.[9] Once presented, a petition cannot be withdrawn without the leave of the court.[10] Notice of the petition is to be given to any person who has appointed, or is or may be entitled to appoint, an administrative receiver of the LLP[11] and, if there is a pending petition for the winding up of the LLP, to the petitioner.[12] If an administrative receiver has already been appointed, the petition will be dismissed unless: (a) the person who appointed the receiver consents to the administration order; or (b) if an administration order were made, any security by virtue of which the receiver was appointed would be invalid.[13]

24.4 The court has power, pending a final determination of the petition, to make an interim order or any other order that it thinks fit, including an order restricting the exercise of any powers by any of the members or by the LLP itself.[14]

24.5 The mere presentation of an administration petition operates as an interim moratorium. IA 1986, s 10(1) provides that during the period beginning with the presentation of the petition and ending with the making of an order or the dismissal of the petition:

(i)   no determination may be made or order made for the winding up of the LLP;[15]

(ii)   no landlord or other person to whom rent is payable may exercise any right of forfeiture by peaceable re-entry in relation to premises let to the LLP in respect of a failure by the LLP to comply with any term or condition of its

---

[8]   IA 1986, s 8(3).

[9]   Ibid, s 9(1).

[10]   Ibid, s 9(2)(b).

[11]   Ibid, s 9(2)(a).

[12]   IR 1986, r 2.6(2)(c).

[13]   IA 1986, s 9(3).

[14]   Ibid, ss 9(4) and (5).

[15]   Ibid, s 10(1)(a). See **26.1**.

tenancy of such premises, except with the leave of the court and subject to such terms as the court may impose;[16]

(iii)   no steps may be taken to enforce any security over the LLP's property, or to repossess goods in the LLP's possession under any hire purchase agreement, except with the leave of the court and on such terms as the court may impose;[17]

(iv)   no other proceedings and no execution or other legal process may be commenced or continued, and no distress may be levied, against the LLP or its property except with the leave of the court and subject to such terms as the court may impose.[18]

Section 10(1) does not, however, prevent the presentation of a winding-up petition, the appointment of an administrative receiver or the carrying out by such a receiver of any of his functions.[19]

24.6   If the court is satisfied that one or more of the purposes set out in **24.2** are likely to be achieved, it has a discretion whether to make an administration order. If an order is made, any petition for the winding up of the LLP will be dismissed and any administrative receiver is to vacate his office.[20] During the period in which the administration order is in force, no determination or order may be made for the winding-up of the LLP, no administrative receiver may be appointed, no other steps may be taken to enforce any security over the LLP's property, or to repossess goods in the LLP's possession under any hire purchase agreement, except with the consent of the administrator or the leave of the court, no landlord or other person to whom rent is payable may exercise any right of forfeiture by peaceable re-entry in relation to premises let to the LLP in respect of a failure by the LLP to comply with any term or condition of its tenancy of such premises, except with the consent of the administrator or the leave of the court and subject (where the court gives leave) to such terms as the court may impose, and no other proceedings and no execution or other legal process may be commenced or continued, and no distress may be levied, against the LLP or its property except with the consent of the administrator or the leave of the court.[21]

ROLE OF THE ADMINISTRATOR

24.7   An administrator of an LLP has wide powers of management of the affairs, business and property of the LLP, effectively extending to anything that was within the powers of the members before the administration order was made.[22] The administration order does not itself operate to remove the powers of members of

---

[16]   IA 1986, s 10(1)(aa) (as inserted by s 9(2) of the Insolvency Act 2000 brought into force by the Insolvency Act 2000 (Commencement No 1 and Transitional Provisions) Order 2001, SI 2001/766).

[17]   IA 1986, s 10(1)(b).

[18]   Ibid, s 10(1)(c).

[19]   Ibid, s 10(2).

[20]   Ibid, s 11(1).

[21]   Ibid, s 11(3), as amended by IA 2000, s 9(3).

[22]   IA 1986, s 14(1).

the LLP to carry on and manage the LLP's business. However, the administrator has power to prevent any person from taking part in the management of the business of the LLP, and to appoint any person to be a manager of that business.[23] Further, members cannot exercise powers conferred on them by the IA 1986, the CA 1985 or by any LLP agreement which could be exercised in such a way as to interfere with the exercise by the administrator of his powers except with the consent of the administrator.[24] In exercising his powers the administrator is deemed to act as the LLP's agent.[25]

24.8 Once appointed, the administrator is obliged to obtain possession of the LLP's property, and comes under a duty to manage the affairs, business and property of the LLP.[26] An administrator's term of office effectively falls into two parts: first, the time between the making of the administration order and the putting of proposals to the creditors pursuant to IA 1986, s 23[27] and, secondly, the period after approval by the creditors of the proposals. During the first period the administrator has general powers to manage the affairs and business of the LLP, but must do so in accordance with any directions given by the court.[28] Once his proposals have been approved, he is to manage the affairs and business of the LLP in accordance with the proposals (as may from time to time be revised).[29] It would seem that the administrator has power under s 17 of the IA 1986 to sell the entire undertaking of the LLP prior to the approval of his proposals by the creditors without the leave of the court, but administrators usually seek the court's sanction in these circumstances.[30]

24.9 Before putting his proposals to the LLP's creditors, the administrator will require the preparation of a statement of affairs. The administrator has power to require members and employees of the LLP, or persons who have been in its employment within the period of one year before the date of the administration order and who are in the administrator's opinion capable of giving the information required, to provide statements of affairs. The obligation will ordinarily fall on the members of the LLP and, no doubt, in respect of larger LLPs the administrator will require those members who have had de facto financial control of the LLP to prepare the statement of affairs.[31]

---

[23]　IA 1986, s 14(2)(a).

[24]　Ibid, s 14(4).

[25]　Ibid, s 14(5). Absent a special assumption of responsibility, an administrator does not owe a personal duty of care to creditors: *Kyrris v Oldham* [2004] 1 BCLC 305.

[26]　IA 1986, s 17(1) and (2).

[27]　See further **24.10**.

[28]　IA 1986, s 17(2)(a).

[29]　Ibid, s 17(2)(b).

[30]　See *Re T & D Industries Plc* [2000] BCC 956. See also *Re Charnley Davies Ltd* [1990] BCC 605, *Re NS Distribution Ltd* [1990] BCLC 169, *Re Consumer and Industrial Press Ltd (No 2)* (1988) 4 BCC 72, *Re Osmosis Group Ltd* [2000] BCC 428, *Re Montin Ltd* [1999] 1 BCLC 663 and *Re Harris Bus Co Ltd* [2000] BCC 1151.

[31]　IA 1986, s 22. Section 22(3) refers also to 'officers' but this reference is unlikely to broaden the scope of eligible persons beyond members and employees. See LLP Regulations 2001, reg 5(2)(b), CA 1985, s 744 and IA 1986, s 251. Note also the reference in s 22(3) to those who have taken part in the LLP's formation.

24.10   The administrator is under an obligation, within 3 months after the making of the order, to send a statement of his proposals for achieving the purpose or purposes specified in the order to the Registrar of Companies and (so far as he is aware of their addresses) to all the creditors of the LLP.[32] In addition, the administrator must also send a copy of the statement to all the members of the LLP (so far as he is aware of their addresses) or publishes a notice stating an address to which members of the LLP should write for copies of the statement.[33] The proposals are considered by the creditors of the LLP at a meeting summoned by the administrator for that purpose.[34] The meeting may approve the proposals with modifications, but only where the administrator consents to each modification.[35] After the conclusion of the meeting, the administrator reports the result of the meeting to the court and gives notice of the result to the Registrar of Companies[36] and to every creditor who received notice of the meeting and to any other creditor of whom the administrator has since become aware.[37]

CONDUCT OF THE CREDITORS' MEETING

24.11   A creditor may only vote at the meeting if he has given to the administrator, not later than 12.00 pm on the business day before the meeting, details in writing of his debt, and the claim has been admitted by the administrator and, if the creditor intends to vote by proxy, the creditor lodges the proxy with the administrator.[38] The chairman of the meeting has a discretion to allow a creditor to vote notwithstanding that the creditor has failed to comply with these requirements if the creditor's failure was due to circumstances beyond his control.[39]

24.12   The chairman has power to admit or reject a creditor's claim for the purpose of his entitlement to vote.[40] The decision of the chairman is subject to a right to appeal to the court.[41] A secured creditor is only entitled to vote in respect of the balance (if any) of his debt after deducting the value of his security as estimated by him.[42] A resolution put to a meeting of creditors is passed if a majority (in value) of those present and voting, in person or by proxy, vote in favour.[43] However, any resolution is invalid if those voting against it include more than half the value of the creditors to whom notice of the meeting was sent and

---

[32]   IA 1986, s 23(1).
[33]   Ibid, s 23(2).
[34]   Ibid, s 23(1)(b).
[35]   Ibid, s 24(2).
[36]   Ibid, s 24(4).
[37]   IR 1986, r 2.30(1).
[38]   Ibid, r 2.22(1).
[39]   Ibid, r 2.22(2).
[40]   Ibid, r 2.23(1).
[41]   Ibid, r 2.23(2).
[42]   Ibid, r 2.24.
[43]   Ibid, r 2.28(1).

who are not, to the best of the chairman's belief, persons connected with the company.[44]

24.13   If the administrator reports to the court that the creditors' meeting has declined to approve his proposals, the court may discharge the administration order and make such consequential provisions as it thinks fit, or can adjourn the hearing conditionally or unconditionally, or make an interim order or any other order that it thinks fit.[45] Unless modified proposals are put to the creditors and approved, the consequence will inevitably be that the administration will come to an end. If the creditors' meeting approves the administrator's proposals, the administrator manages the affairs and business of the LLP in accordance with those proposals.[46] During the course of the administration, the administrator can propose revisions to his proposals and can call a meeting of the LLP's creditors for the purpose of considering whether the creditors should approve the revisions.[47]

24.14   A creditor or member of the LLP has a right to apply to the court by petition on the ground that the LLP's affairs, business and property are being or have been managed by the administrator in a manner which is unfairly prejudicial to the interests of its creditors or members generally, or some part of its creditors or members (including himself) or that any actual proposed act or omission of the administrator is or would be so prejudicial.[48] This right is similar to the right given by IA 1986, s 6 to challenge a voluntary arrangement,[49] and has similarities to s 459 of the CA 1985.[50]

---

[44]   IR 1986, r 2.28(1A). See IA 1986, ss 249 and 435 for the meaning of 'connected with'.

[45]   IA 1986, s 24(5).

[46]   Ibid, s 17(2).

[47]   Ibid, s 25. The court has a residual jurisdiction under IA 1986, s 14(3) to allow departure from approved proposals but, ordinarily, if an administrator wishes to act inconsistently with the proposals he should seek revision pursuant to s 25; see *Re Smallman Construction Ltd* (1988) 4 BCC 784.

[48]   IA 1986, s 27(1).

[49]   See **23.22**.

[50]   See chapter 27.

Chapter 25

RECEIVERSHIP

INTRODUCTION

25.1 Until recently, receivers and managers of a company's or an LLP's assets and undertaking have been capable of being appointed in or out of court.[1] The High Court has a general power to appoint a receiver in all cases in which it appears to the court to be just and equitable to do so.[2] This power is used fairly frequently in relation to partnerships in dissolution where the partners are unable to agree the terms on which it should be wound up. The power has, however, rarely been exercised in relation to companies, given the provisions in the IA 1986 for the appointment of administrators and administrative receivers.

25.2 Receivers may be appointed out of court by secured creditors as a method by which they can enforce their security. The powers of a secured creditor will depend upon the terms of the relevant instrument, usually a debenture. The debenture will often require the debenture holder to make a demand for repayment before a receiver can be appointed. The debenture holder does not owe a duty of care to the LLP when deciding whether to exercise the power to appoint a receiver, although the power must be exercised in good faith.[3] A specific mortgagee or chargee has the power to appoint a receiver out of court – a so called 'LPA receiver' – but the powers of an LPA receiver are limited and do not extend to running a business. The preferred course was (prior to the changes referred to in **25.3**) for the holder of a debenture to appoint an administrative receiver over the whole or substantially the whole of a company's or LLP's property. The administrative receiver was the creation of the 1985/86 legislation. The statutory provisions, as amended with effect from September 2003, are applied to LLPs. An administrative receiver is:

(a) a receiver or manager of the whole (or substantially the whole) of an LLP's property appointed by or on behalf of the holders of any debentures of the LLP secured by a charge which, as created, was a floating charge,[4] or by such a charge and one or more other securities; or

---

[1] For the law generally on company receivers, see Lightman and Moss, *The Law of Receivers and Administrators of Companies* (Sweet & Maxwell, 3rd edn, 2000).
[2] Supreme Court Act 1981, s 37.
[3] Lightman and Moss, op cit, para 4-048.
[4] See Lightman and Moss, op cit, paras 3-001–3-090.

(b)   a person who would be such a receiver or manager but for the appointment of some other person as the receiver of part of the LLP's property.[5]

PROHIBITION ON THE APPOINTMENT OF ADMINISTRATIVE RECEIVERS

25.3   The administrative receivership regime has been the subject of substantial criticism. The appointment of an administrative receiver by a secured creditor was often seen simply as a means by which one creditor could extract funds from a failing company without regard to the interests of the other creditors or to whether the company could, in fact, be saved.[6] Subject to a number of exceptions, the right of a holder of a qualifying floating charge to appoint an administrative receiver has been abolished in respect of floating charges created[7] on or after 15 September 2003.[8] The exceptions are appointments of administrative receivers relating to capital market projects,[9] public-private partnerships,[10] utilities projects,[11] urban regeneration projects,[12] project finance,[13] financial markets,[14] registered social landlords[15] and protected railway companies.[16]

25.4   The definition of a holder of a qualifying floating charge is contained in IA 1986, Sch B1 para 14.[17] Schedule B1 contains the new administration regime applicable to companies. Where, as in the case of LLPs, the new administration regime is not applied and the former procedure is preserved,[18] this is slightly odd given that, in such a case, para 14 of Sch B1 is not in force. The definition is presumably to be treated as incorporated by reference. The definition is directed primarily at new style debentures executed in relation to companies and which purport to empower the holder to appoint an administrator out of court pursuant to the new administration regime. The definition does, however, include floating charges that purport to empower the holder to make an appointment which would

---

[5]   IA 1986, s 29(2). An administrative receiver is an 'office holder' and must be qualified to act as an insolvency practitioner in relation to the LLP; see IA 1986, ss 230(2), 388(1), 389 and 390.

[6]   See Davies, *Insolvency and the Enterprise Act 2002* chapter 4.

[7]   The date of creation probably means the date on which it is executed by the LLP: see Davies op cit paras 4.22–4.24.

[8]   IA 1986, s 72A inserted by Enterprise Act 2002 s 250(1). See Insolvency Act 1986 Section 72A (Appointed Date) Order 2003, SI 2003/2095 and Enterprise Act 2002 (Commencement No 4 and Transitional Provisions and Savings) Order 2003, SI 2003/2093.

[9]   IA 1986, s 72B.

[10]   Ibid, s 72C.

[11]   Ibid, s 72D.

[12]   Ibid, s 72DA.

[13]   Ibid, s 72E.

[14]   Ibid, s 72F.

[15]   Ibid, s 72G.

[16]   Ibid, s 72GA.

[17]   Ibid, s 72A(3).

[18]   Enterprise Act 2002 (Commencement No 4 and Transitional Provisions and Savings) Order 2003, SI 2003/2093, Art 3(3). Enterprise Act 2002, s 249 provides that s 248 (which replaces Part II of the IA 1986 dealing with administration) shall have no effect in respect of a number of specific types of company including water and sewage undertakers, protected railway companies and public-private partnerships.

be the appointment of an administrative receiver within the meaning of IA 1986, s 29(2). A floating charge will, therefore, be a qualifying floating charge if it purports to empower the holder to appoint an administrative receiver and it is created on or after 15 September 2003. A floating charge holder remains entitled to appoint an administrative receiver if the charge was created before 15 September 2003 (regardless of whether monies were advanced to the LLP before and/or after 15 September 2003).

25.5 It is not clear why the government decided to apply the new IA 1986, s 72A to LLPs (if a conscious decision was made at all) thereby preventing debenture holders from appointing administrative receivers, but decided not to apply the new administration regime. The two reforms are intrinsically linked: the new administration provisions import many of the benefits that floating charge holders had under the administrative receivership regime.[19] Under the new administration regime applicable to companies, a floating charge holder has the right to appoint an administrator.[20] Assuming that the authors are right that the amendments to the IA 1986 automatically apply to LLPs unless specifically excluded,[21] the holder of a floating charge (created on or after 15 September 2003) over the assets of an LLP will not be able to make an out of court appointment of either an administrator or an administrative receiver.

APPOINTMENT OF RECEIVERS

25.6 The provisions of Chapter I of Part III of the IA 1986 relating to receivership (ie receivers or managers, or administrative receivers or managers, of the property of an LLP) are unchanged.[22] A purported appointment of a receiver is of no effect unless the receiver accepts the appointment before the end of the business day next following that on which the instrument of appointment is received by him or on his behalf and, subject to acceptance, is deemed to be made at the time at which the instrument of appointment is received.[23] If the appointment is discovered to be invalid, the court may order the person by whom or on whose behalf the appointment was made to indemnify the receiver against any liability which arises solely by reason of the invalidity of the appointment.[24] A body corporate is not qualified for appointment as a receiver of the property of an LLP, and any body corporate which acts as such is liable to a fine.[25] An undischarged bankrupt who acts as a receiver or manager of an LLP on behalf of debenture

---

[19] IA 1986, Sch B1 paras 14–21 and see Davies, *Insolvency and the Enterprise Act 2002* para 4.12.
[20] Ibid, Sch B1 para 14.
[21] See **22.2**. This view would seem to be shared by the draftsman of the Enterprise Act 2002 (Commencement No 4 and Transitional Provisions and Savings) Order 2003, SI 2003/2093: Art 3(3)(b) would be superfluous if the amendments would not, in any event, apply automatically to LLPs.
[22] IA 1986, s 31 has been amended to make it an offence for a person to act as a receiver or manager while a bankruptcy restrictions order is in force in respect of him: substituted by Enterprise Act 2002, s 257(3), Sch 21, para 1 with effect from 1 April 2004.
[23] IA 1986, s 33(1).
[24] Ibid, s 34.
[25] Ibid, s 30.

holders is (unless he was appointed by the court) liable to imprisonment or a fine (or both).[26] A receiver appointed out of court, or his appointor, may apply to the court for directions in relation to any particular matter arising in connection with the performance of his functions.[27]

DUTIES AND POWERS

All receivers

25.7 Once a receiver or manager has been appointed, every invoice, order for goods or business letter issued by or on behalf of the LLP, or the receiver or manager or the liquidator of the LLP, being a document on or in which the LLP's name appears, must contain a statement that a receiver or manager has been appointed.[28]

25.8 The powers of an ordinary receiver appointed out of court are contained in the debenture. An administrative receiver's powers are deemed to include (except in so far as they are inconsistent with any of the provisions of the debenture) the powers specified in Sch 1 to the IA 1986.[29] A person dealing with an administrative receiver in good faith and for value is not concerned to inquire whether the receiver is acting within his powers.[30]

Administrative receivers

25.9 On appointment, an administrative receiver (in the limited circumstances where he may be appointed[31]) must forthwith send to the LLP and publish in the prescribed manner a notice of his appointment.[32] Within 28 days of his appointment, the administrative receiver must also (unless the court otherwise directs) send a notice of his appointment to all the creditors of the LLP (so far as he is aware of their addresses).[33]

25.10 An administrative receiver is entitled to apply to the court for an order authorising him to dispose of property which is the subject of security in favour of someone other than the debenture holder (usually a prior fixed chargee) where the disposal would be likely to promote a more advantageous realisation of the LLP's assets than would otherwise be effected.[34] Where such an order is made, the

---

26   IA 1986, s 31.
27   Ibid, s 35.
28   Ibid, s 39(1).
29   Ibid, s 42(1).
30   Ibid, s 42(3).
31   See **25.4**.
32   IA 1986, s 46(1)(a). The matters to be stated in the notice are set out in IR 1986, r 3.2(2). The notice is published by being advertised once in the *London Gazette* and once in such newspaper as the receiver thinks most appropriate for ensuring that it comes to the notice of the LLP's creditors; IR 1986, r 3.2(3).
33   IA 1986, s 46(1)(b).
34   Ibid, s 43(1). See IR 1986, r 3.31.

proceeds of the disposal are applied to discharge the sums secured by the security.[35]

25.11   An administrative receiver is deemed to be the agent of the LLP unless and until the LLP goes into liquidation;[36] is personally liable on any contract entered into by him in the carrying out of his functions (except in so far as the contract otherwise provides);[37] and is entitled in respect of that liability to an indemnity out of the assets of the LLP.[38] Although the receiver's agency comes to an end on a subsequent liquidation, his appointment and powers are unaffected and he remains able to get in and realise the LLP's assets either as agent for the debenture holder or as principal.[39]

STATEMENT OF AFFAIRS IN ADMINISTRATIVE RECEIVERSHIP

25.12   An administrative receiver must require a statement of affairs for the LLP to be prepared by some or all of the persons mentioned in **25.13**.[40] The statement must be verified by affidavit and must show:

(a)   particulars of the LLP's assets, debts and liabilities;

(b)   the names and addresses of its creditors;

(c)   the securities held by them;

(d)   the dates when the securities were given; and

(e)   such other information as may be prescribed.[41]

25.13   The persons who can be required to prepare a statement of affairs are:

(a)   those who are or have been members of the LLP;[42]

(b)   those who have taken part in the LLP's formation at any time within one year before the date of the appointment of the administrative receiver;

---

[35]   IA 1986, s 43(3). Where the proceeds are less than such amount as may be determined by the court to be the amount which would be realised on the sale of the property in the open market by a willing vendor, the deficiency must be made up by the receiver: IA 1986, s 43(3)(b).

[36]   IA 1986, s 44(1)(a).

[37]   Ibid, s 44(1)(b). Liability on contracts includes, to the extent of any 'qualifying liability', any contract of employment adopted by him; see IA 1986, s 44(1)(b), (2)–(2D); *Nicoll v Cutts* (1985) 1 BCC 99, 427; *Re Paramount Airways Ltd (No 3)* [1994] BCC 172 and *Powdrill v Watson* [1995] 2 AC 394.

[38]   IA 1986, s 44(1)(c). A receiver is also likely to have the benefit of a contractual indemnity given by his appointor. The liabilities and right of indemnity of a non-administrative receiver are contained in s 37.

[39]   See Lightman and Moss, *op cit*, paras 11-036–11-043.

[40]   IA 1986, s 47(1). See IR 1986, rr 3.3–3.7.

[41]   IA 1986, s 47(2).

[42]   Section 47(3) also refers to 'officers' but this reference is unlikely to broaden the scope of an eligible person beyond members; see LLP Regulations 2001, reg 5(2)(b), CA 1985, s 744 and IA 1986, s 251.

(c)   those who are employees (or have been within that year) and are in the opinion of the administrative receiver capable of giving the information required;

(d)   those who are or have been within that year members of, or in the employment of, an LLP or company which is, or within that year was, a member of the LLP.[43]

ADMINISTRATIVE RECEIVER'S REPORT

25.14   Within 3 months of appointment (or such longer period as the court may allow) an administrative receiver must send a report[44] to the Registrar of Companies, to any trustees for secured creditors of the LLP and (so far as he is aware of their addresses) to all such creditors.[45] The report must deal with the following matters:

(a)   the events leading up to his appointment;[46]

(b)   the disposal or proposed disposal of any property of the LLP and the carrying on or proposed carrying on by him of any business of the LLP;[47]

(c)   the amounts of principal and interest payable to the debenture holders by whom or on whose behalf he was appointed and the amounts payable to preferential creditors;[48] and

(d)   the amount (if any) likely to be available for other creditors.[49]

The administrative receiver must also either send a copy of the report to all unsecured creditors (so far as he is aware of their addresses) or publish a notice stating an address to which the unsecured creditors can write for copies free of charge.[50] A copy of the report must further be laid before a meeting of the unsecured creditors summoned for that purpose unless the court otherwise directs.[51]

---

[43]   IA 1986, s 47(3). 'Employment' includes employment under a contract for services. The persons required to produce the statement must do so within 21 days of being so required (IA 1986, s 47(4)) provided that the receiver or the court may release such a person or extend the time for compliance (s 47(5)).

[44]   The report must include a summary of the statement of affairs made out and submitted pursuant to s 47 and of the administrative receiver's comments (if any) on it: s 48(5).

[45]   IA 1986, s 48(1). See IR 1986, r 3.8. In addition, administrative and other receivers have statutory and common law obligations to account; see IA 1986, s 38 and IR 1986, r 3.32; *Smith v Middleton* [1979] 3 All ER 842.

[46]   IA 1986, s 48(1)(a).

[47]   Ibid, s 48(1)(b).

[48]   Ibid, s 48(1)(c).

[49]   Ibid, s 48(1)(d).

[50]   Ibid, s 48(2).

[51]   Ibid, s 48(2) and (3). See IR 1986, rr 3.9–3.15. Where a meeting is summoned under s 48, the meeting may, if it thinks fit, establish a creditors' committee to exercise the functions conferred on it by or under IA 1986, s 49(1). The committee can call for the administrative receiver to appear before it or furnish information: s 49(2). See IR 1986, rr 3.16–3.30A.

Chapter 26

COMMENCEMENT OF WINDING UP

VOLUNTARY WINDING UP

26.1 The winding up of an LLP may be either voluntary or by the court.[1] Voluntary winding up is initiated by a determination by the LLP under IA 1986, s 84 that it be wound up. Section 84(1) does not state how an LLP is to determine that it is to be wound up. As applied to companies, s 84(1)(b) provides that a company may be wound up voluntarily if the company resolves by special resolution (ie a three-quarters majority) that it be wound up voluntarily.[2] In the absence of any prior agreement between the members, it would appear that a determination by an LLP that it is to be wound up will require a unanimous resolution of the members.[3] Before an LLP can determine that it be wound up voluntarily, it must give written notice to the holder of any qualifying floating charge to which IA 1986 s 72A applies (unless a petition for an administration order was presented before 15 September 2003).[4] Where a notice is given under s 72A(2A), a determination that the LLP be wound up may only be made (a) after the end of the period of 5 business days beginning on the day on which notice is given or (b) if the person to whom the notice is given has consented in writing to the determination.

26.2 A voluntary winding up is deemed to commence at the time when the LLP determines that it be wound up voluntarily.[5] From the commencement of the winding up, the LLP must cease to carry on its business except so far as may be required for its beneficial winding up, but it does not lose its corporate status or lose its corporate powers until it is dissolved.[6] The interest of a member in the

---

[1] IA 1986, s 73(1).

[2] The difference between a special and an extra-ordinary resolution is that a special resolution normally requires not less than 21 days' notice (see CA 1985, s 378). Section 84 as applied to companies also provides that a company may be wound up (a) when the period fixed for the duration of the company by the articles expires, or (b) the event (if any) occurs, on the occurrence of which the articles provide that the company is to be dissolved, and the company passes an ordinary resolution and (c) if the company passes an extraordinary resolution to the effect that it cannot by reason of its liabilities continue its business and that it is advisable to wind up.

[3] See **23.4**.

[4] IA 1986 s 84(2A) inserted by Enterprise Act 2002 (Insolvency) Order 2003, SI 2003/2096 Arts 4, 6, Sch paras 8 and 10. The authors' view is that this amendment applies automatically to LLPs as its application to LLPs has not specifically been excluded (see **22.2**). It should be noted, however, that this amendment appears to be consequential on the introduction of the new administration regime which does not apply to LLPs: see **24.1**.

[5] IA 1986, s 86.

[6] Ibid, s 87.

property of the LLP cannot be transferred (without the sanction of the liquidator) after the commencement of the winding up.[7]

Types of voluntary winding up

26.3 There are two types of voluntary winding up: members' voluntary winding up and creditors' voluntary winding up. Where the LLP cannot (or will not in the liquidation) be able to pay all its debts, the liquidation is a creditors' voluntary winding up.[8] If a declaration of solvency can be made by the designated members, the liquidation is a members' voluntary winding up. The declaration of solvency must be made within the 5 weeks preceding the determination by the LLP that it be wound up.[9]

Members' voluntary winding up

26.4 In a members' voluntary winding up, the LLP appoints one or more liquidators for the purpose of winding up the LLP's affairs and distributing its assets.[10] Again, the LLP legislation does not provide how the LLP is to make that decision. In the absence of an LLP agreement dealing with this issue (either specifically or in general decision-making provisions), the appointment will presumably have to be made unanimously. If the LLP fails to make an appointment, the court has power to do so.[11] On the appointment of a liquidator, the powers of the members cease except to the extent that a meeting of the members summoned for the purpose, or the liquidator, sanctions their continuance.[12]

26.5 If, during the course of the winding up, the liquidator becomes of the view that the LLP will be unable to pay its debts in full within the period stated in the designated members' declaration under IA 1986, s 89, he must:[13]

(a)　　summon and attend a creditors' meeting; and

(b)　　prepare a statement of affairs and lay it before the creditors' meeting.

As from the day of the creditors' meeting, the liquidation becomes a creditors' voluntary winding up.[14]

---

[7]　　IA 1986, s 88. This is an odd modification: the LLP's property is owned by the LLP not the members. The members have no direct interest in the LLP's property; their shares or interests are in the LLP itself.

[8]　　IA 1986, s 90.

[9]　　Ibid, s 89(2). A designated member who makes a declaration of solvency without having reasonable grounds for the opinion that the LLP will be able to pay its debts in full within the specified period is liable to imprisonment or a fine, or both: s 89(4).

[10]　　IA 1986, s 91(1).

[11]　　Ibid, s 108.

[12]　　Ibid, s 91(2).

[13]　　Ibid, s 95.

[14]　　Ibid, s 96.

Creditors' voluntary winding up[15]

26.6 If the LLP determines that it should be wound up pursuant to IA 1986, s 84, but no declaration of solvency is made by the designated members, the liquidation proceeds as a creditors' winding up. In this event, the LLP summons a creditors' meeting for a day not later than 14 days after the date on which the LLP determines that it be wound up.[16] The normal practice in relation to companies is for the meetings of members and creditors to be held on the same day. In cases where the members of the LLP are to determine that it be wound up at a meeting, a similar practice is likely to develop. The designated members are under an obligation to prepare and lay before the creditors' meeting a statement of affairs for the LLP.[17] The designated members also appoint one of their number to preside at the meeting, and the designated member so appointed is under a duty to attend the meeting and preside over it.[18]

26.7 The creditors at their meeting, and the LLP, are entitled to nominate a person to be the liquidator.[19] If the creditors make a nomination, the person nominated becomes the liquidator; but where they do not make a nomination, the person nominated by the LLP becomes the liquidator.[20] In the event that different liquidators are nominated, a member or creditor may, within 7 days, apply to the court for an order directing that the person nominated by the LLP shall be the liquidator instead of, or jointly with, the person nominated by the creditors, or appointing some other person to be the liquidator instead of the person nominated by the creditors.[21] On appointment, all the powers of the members cease except so far as the liquidation committee (or, in the absence of a liquidation committee, the creditors) sanction.[22] If no liquidator is appointed or nominated by the LLP, the powers of the members shall not be exercised except with the sanction of the court or (in the case of a creditors' voluntary winding up) so far as may be necessary to secure compliance with IA 1986, ss 98 (creditors' meeting) and 99 (statement of affairs) during the period prior to the appointment or nomination.[23] This does not apply to the powers of members to dispose of perishable goods and other goods the value of which is likely to diminish if they are not immediately disposed of, and to do all things that may be necessary for the protection of the LLP's assets.[24]

---

[15] A liquidator in a creditors' voluntary liquidation can apply to the court for an order of confirmation that EC Council Regulation No 1346/2000 on insolvency proceedings applies: IR 1986, r 7.62 inserted by Insolvency (Amendments) Rules 2002, SI 2002/1307, Art 9.

[16] IA 1986, s 98(1).

[17] Ibid, s 99(1)(a) and (b).

[18] Ibid, s 99(1)(c).

[19] Ibid, s 100(1). Section 100(4) (which was inserted by the Enterprise Act 2002 s 248(3), Sch 17 paras 9 and 14 in relation to companies) does not apply to LLPs: see Enterprise Act 2002 (Commencement No 4 and Transitional Provisions and Savings) Order 2003, Art 3.

[20] IA 1986, s 100(2). Again, in the absence of any provision in the LLP agreement providing for such nomination to be made by majority decision the nomination would presumably have to be made unanimously.

[21] IA 1986, s 100(3).

[22] Ibid, s 103.

[23] Ibid, s 114(2).

[24] Ibid, s 114(3).

26.8   At the creditors' meeting referred to in **26.6** or at any subsequent meeting, the creditors may appoint a committee of not more than five persons to act as the liquidation committee.[25] If such a committee is appointed, the LLP also has the right to appoint up to five members.[26] The creditors have the right to veto the appointments unless the court directs otherwise.[27]

COMPULSORY WINDING UP

26.9   The court may order the winding up of an LLP if:[28]

(a)   the LLP has determined that it be wound up by the court;

(b)   the LLP does not commence its business within a year of its incorporation, or suspends its business for a whole year;

(c)   the number of members is reduced below two;

(d)   the LLP is unable to pay its debts;

(e)   the court is of the opinion that it is just and equitable that the LLP should be wound up; or

(f)   at the time at which a moratorium for the LLP under s 1A comes to an end, no voluntary arrangement approved under Part I has effect in relation to the LLP.[29]

We will consider each of these in turn.

Determination by the LLP

26.10   The use of this provision is likely to be extremely rare, given the right of an LLP to determine that it be wound up voluntarily.[30]

Failure to commence business within a year or suspension of business

26.11   In relation to companies, the court has refused to exercise its discretion where there are good reasons for the delay in the commencement of the business and where the majority of members wish the company to continue.[31] Where the carrying on of a company's business has merely been suspended, the court usually requires to be satisfied that the company is unable to carry on that business or has

---

[25]   IA 1986, s 101(1).

[26]   Ibid, s 101(2).

[27]   Ibid, s 101(3).

[28]   Ibid, s 122. But note: an LLP which has its centre of main interests outside the UK and does not have an establishment within the UK is not liable to be wound up by the court in England and Wales: Art 3(1) of EC Council Regulation No 1346/2000 on insolvency proceedings and IA 1986, s 117(7).

[29]   Inserted by the Insolvency Act 2000, s 1, Sch 1, paras 1, 6. (In relation to companies, the new sub-section is number (fa).) Such a winding up petition may only be presented by one or more creditors: IA 1986, s 124(3A).

[30]   A determination pursuant to s 122 would, in the absence of a majority voting provision in an LLP agreement, presumably have to be made unanimously.

[31]   *Re Capital Fire Insurance Association* (1882) 21 Ch D 209.

abandoned it before making an order.[32] Again, the wishes of the majority shareholders are taken into account. It seems likely that the courts will apply the same principles to LLPs.

Inability to pay debts

26.12   An LLP is deemed unable to pay its debts:[33]

(i)   if a creditor (by assignment or otherwise) to whom the LLP is indebted in a sum exceeding £750 then due has served on the LLP, by leaving it at the LLP's registered office, a written demand (in the prescribed form) requiring the LLP to pay the sum so due and the LLP has for 3 weeks thereafter neglected to pay the sum or to secure or compound for it to the reasonable satisfaction of the creditor;

(ii)   if, in England and Wales, execution or other process issued on a judgment, decree or order of any court in favour of a creditor of the LLP is returned unsatisfied in whole or in part; or

(iii)   if it is proved to the satisfaction of the court that the LLP is unable to pay its debts as they fall due.

26.13   IA 1986, s 123(2) provides that an LLP is also deemed unable to pay its debts if it is proved to the satisfaction of the court that the value of the LLP's assets is less than the amount of its liabilities, taking into account its contingent and prospective liabilities.

26.14   Although a creditor can present a petition based upon an unsatisfied statutory demand, or the return of execution on a judgment unsatisfied, the service of a statutory demand is, unlike the position in personal insolvency, unnecessary. Proof by a creditor that his particular debt has not been paid is prima facie evidence that the LLP is unable to pay its debts as they fall due so long as there is no bona fide dispute as to the existence of the debt in question. The court will not make a winding-up order if the petition is based upon a debt which is genuinely disputed.[34] The debt is genuinely disputed for the purpose of winding-up proceedings if the court is satisfied that there is a genuine dispute founded on substantial grounds.[35] The court has an overriding discretion as to whether to make a winding-up order but, in circumstances where the petition debt is not disputed on substantial grounds, the court is almost bound to exercise its discretion by making an order. There are, however, some exceptions. For example:

(a)   where the petitioner's debt is less than £750;
(b)   the winding up is opposed by the majority of the other creditors;
(c)   the LLP is in the process of being wound up voluntarily.[36]

[32]   *Re Thomlin Patent Horseshoe Company* (1887) 55 LT 314.
[33]   IA 1986, s 123(1).
[34]   See *Re Richbell Strategic Holdings Limited* [1997] 2 BCLC 429.
[35]   See *Re a Company No 00685 of 1996* [1997] BCC 830.
[36]   IA 1986, s 116 provides that the voluntary winding up of an LLP does not bar the right of any creditor or contributory to have it wound up by the court, but in the case of an application by a

Just and equitable winding up

26.15   Just and equitable winding up is discussed in chapter 27.

APPLICATION FOR A WINDING-UP ORDER

26.16   An application for a winding-up order is made by petition to the Companies Court.[37] IA 1986, s 124, as applied to companies, permits a petition to be presented by the company, its directors or a contributory or contributories.[38] A petition by the directors is presented in their own names rather than in the name of the company and they must act unanimously unless there is a valid resolution passed by a majority of the directors at a board meeting, in which case any director has authority to present a petition on behalf of them all.[39] As applied to LLPs, s 124 clearly permits a petition to be presented by the LLP itself or by any creditor or creditors (including any contingent or prospective creditor or creditors).[40] How the remainder of s 124(1) is to be applied to LLPs, however, is less clear. By reg 5(2)(b) of the LLP Regulations 2001, references in the IA 1986 to a director or to an officer of a company include references to a member of an LLP. It would seem, therefore, that the reference in s 124(1) to the directors (which is not specifically modified) is to be read as a collective reference to the members. In this regard, the ability of the members, as a class, is unlikely to add anything to the ability of the LLP itself to present a petition. The issue is whether individual members have standing to present a winding-up petition. On an ordinary reading of s 124(1), this would seem to depend on whether members are contributories.

26.17   By s 79(1) of the IA 1986, 'contributory' is defined as: (a) every present member of the LLP and (b) every past member of the LLP liable to contribute to the assets of the LLP in the event of its being wound up, and for the purpose of all proceedings for determining, and all proceedings prior to the final determination of, the persons who are to be deemed contributories, includes any person alleged to be a contributory. The liability of members and past members to contribute to the assets of the LLP on a winding up is set out in s 74. That section provides that when an LLP is wound up every present and past member of the LLP who has agreed with the other members or with the LLP that he will, in circumstances which have arisen, be liable to contribute to the assets of the LLP in the event that the LLP goes into liquidation is liable, to the extent that he has so agreed, to contribute to its assets to any amount sufficient for payment of its debts and liabilities, and the expenses of the winding up, and for the adjustment of the rights of the contributories among themselves. However, a past member is only liable if the obligation arising from the agreement survived his ceasing to be a member.

---

contributory the court must be satisfied that the rights of the contributories will be prejudiced by a voluntary winding up.

[37]   IA 1986, s 124.

[38]   Or by the clerk of a magistrates' court in the exercise of the power conferred by s 87A of the Magistrates' Courts Act 1980.

[39]   *Re Instrumentation Electrical Services Limited* (1988) 4 BBC 301 and *Re Equiticorp International Plc* [1989] 1 WLR 1010.

[40]   IA 1986, s 124(1).

26.18   In the case of companies limited by shares, every present and past member is liable to contribute to the company's assets to any amount sufficient for the payment of its debts and liabilities, and the expenses of the winding up, and for the adjustment of the rights of the contributories amongst themselves, but the liability is limited to the amount unpaid on his shares.[41] A member, or indeed a past member, whose shares are fully paid up is still a contributory even though he can have no liability on a winding up.[42]

26.19   A current or past member of an LLP who is party to an agreement pursuant to which he is liable to contribute to the assets of the LLP in the event of a winding-up (and under which, in the case of a past member, the liability survives the cessation of his membership) is clearly a contributory. The position of a current member who is not party to such an agreement, or a past member who either was never party to such an agreement or was party to such an agreement but under which the liability did not survive the cessation of his membership, is more difficult. Although in company law the courts appear to take a broad view of the meaning of contributory, the status of a contributory would seem to depend on the fact that the current or past member was, at some time, liable on his shares, and a view that this status is unaffected by the fact that he has discharged that liability. It is difficult to see, in the light of the way the modified ss 74 and 79 have been drafted, on what basis a current or past member of an LLP can be regarded as a contributory if he is not, and has never been, party to an agreement under which he would be obliged to contribute to the assets of the LLP on a winding up.

26.20   In other words, whilst the meaning of contributory can extend to someone under a liability on a winding up, or someone who has discharged such liability, it is difficult to see how it can extend to someone who was never under such an obligation or who was under such an obligation but was released from it by the cessation of his membership. Nevertheless, it seems unlikely that it was intended to limit the right to present a winding-up petition to members (or past members) who are or were party to agreements under which they are liable to contribute to the LLP's assets on a winding up. It is to be borne in mind that a winding-up order can be sought where the LLP is solvent, for example, on the just and equitable ground, where no question of the liability of members to contribute to the LLP's assets can arise.

26.21   In the circumstances, it seems possible that the courts will seek to construe IA 1986, s 124(1) so that all members (and past members) have standing to present winding-up petitions. One possibility would be to construe 'contributory' as meaning a member or past member who is liable to contribute to

---

[41]   IA 1986, s 74(2)(d). A past member is not liable to contribute if he ceased to be a member a year or more before the commencement of winding up (s 74(2)(a)) and is not liable for any debt or liability contracted after he ceased to be a member (s 74(2)(b)).

[42]   *Re Anglesea Colliery Company* (1866) LR 1 Ch App 555 and *Re Consolidated Goldfields of New Zealand Ltd* [1953] Ch 689. A petition presented by a past member of a company who has no interest in the winding up (ie because he is not entitled to any sum from the company *qua* member or to share in surplus assets) would presumably be struck out as an abuse of process. See *Re Compania de Electricidad de la Provincia de Buenos Aires* [1980] Ch 146 for a case in which past members had interests as creditors.

the assets of the LLP pursuant to an agreement between the members or who would be liable if he were a party to such an agreement. Such a construction would however effectively equate members and contributories and would probably be regarded as stretching the ordinary meaning of the words in ss 74 and 79 too far. The other possibility would be for the court to treat s 124(1) as having been modified pursuant to reg 5(2)(g) of the LLP Regulations 2001 so that the reference to 'directors' in s 124(1) means the members together or individually, or (less plausibly) so that 'contributory or contributories' means members (and past members) regardless of whether they are contributories. Regulation 5(2)(g) provides for the relevant sections of the IA 1986 to be modified by such further modifications as the context requires for the purpose of giving effect to that legislation as applied by the LLP Regulations 2001.

26.22   As stated above, our view is that it is unlikely to have been intended to prevent members (or past members) who are not contributories from presenting a petition; so that the modification suggested in **26.23** should, in our view, probably be treated as having been made by reg 5(2)(g). The issue as to whether a member is a contributory can, of course, be avoided altogether by including in the LLP agreement an obligation on all members to make a nominal contribution on a winding up.

26.23   It needs to be borne in mind that a petitioner, whether a current or past member, will need to establish that he has a sufficient interest in the winding up. In most cases, this will require the member to show that the LLP is solvent and that he has an interest in the surplus assets or that, by having the LLP wound up, he will avoid a liability. A current member will usually have such an interest. In most cases, however, past members are unlikely to have a sufficient interest. If, as will often be the case, the LLP agreement makes provision for the financial consequences of cessation, a past member's rights will be governed by the agreement, and he may have no interest in the LLP or any surplus assets on a winding up. If there is no LLP agreement (or the agreement does not deal with the financial consequences of cessation) the position is more difficult. The authors suggest in chapter 16[43] that, in this situation, a member's share in the LLP is likely to be determined, with the effect that he will have no interest in any winding up. A past member may, of course, have rights against the LLP in the capacity of creditor, for instance for an ascertained but unpaid profit share, or to enforce cessation rights granted to him in the LLP agreement, in which case he will be able present a petition in that capacity.

26.24   A petition can now be presented by a liquidator (within the meaning of Art 2(b) of the EC Council Regulation[44] on insolvency proceedings) appointed in proceedings by virtue of Art 3(1) of that Regulation, or by a temporary administrator (within the meaning of Art 38 of the EC Council Regulation).[45]

---

[43]   See **16.32–16.41**.

[44]   1346/2000.

[45]   Inserted by the Insolvency Act 1986 (Amendment) (No 2) Regulations 2002, SI 2002/1240, regs 3 and 8.

26.25 A petition may also be presented by the official receiver where an LLP is being wound up voluntarily on the basis that the voluntary winding up cannot be continued with due regard to the interests of the creditors or the members.[46]

26.26 The Secretary of State for Trade and Industry has power pursuant to s 124A(1) to present a petition where it appears to him from:[47]

(a)   any report made or information obtained under Part XIV of the CA 1985;

(b)   any information obtained under s 2 of the Criminal Justice Act 1987;

(c)   any information obtained under s 83 of the Companies Act 1989 (powers exercisable for purpose of assisting overseas regulatory authorities),

that it is expedient in the public interest that the LLP should be wound up.[48]

26.27 The rules relating to the form, presentation, service and advertisement of the petition are contained in rr 4.7–4.13 of the IR 1986. On the hearing of a winding-up petition, the court may dismiss it or adjourn the hearing conditionally or unconditionally or make an interim order, or any other order that it thinks fit.[49]

26.28 A winding-up order relates back to the time of the presentation of the petition, the winding up being deemed to commence on that date.[50] Any disposition of the LLP's property and any transfer by a member of his interest in the property of the LLP, or alteration in the status of the LLP members, made after the commencement of the winding up is void unless the court otherwise orders.[51] Similarly, any attachment, sequestration, distress or execution put in force against the estate or effects of the LLP after commencement of the winding up is void.[52]

---

[46]   IA 1986, s 124(5).

[47]   Ibid, s 124A(1)(b) as it applies to companies was omitted from the IA 1986 as applied to LLPs by the LLP Regulations 2001. Whether, therefore, either or both of the new s 124A(1)(b) and (bb) inserted by SI 2001/3649, Art 305 (which relate to the Financial Services and Markets Act 2000) likewise do not apply to LLPs is unclear.

[48]   A public interest winding-up petition may be the only sanction in the event of continued breaches of the LLP legislation (such as the requirement for filing of annual accounts or changes of members and such like) by the LLP and its members or designated members in circumstances in which the members are all resident overseas.

[49]   IA 1986, s 125(1). See IR 1986, rr 4.14–4.21A.

[50]   IA 1986, s 129(2). Where a winding-up order is made subsequent to a determination by the LLP that it be wound up, the winding up is deemed to have commenced at the time of the determination: s 129(1).

[51]   IA 1986, s 127. This is an odd modification: the LLP's property is owned by the LLP not the members. The members have no direct interest in the LLP's property; their shares or interests are in the LLP itself. *Quaere* whether the reference to property of the LLP is intended to be a reference to an interest in any surplus assets on completion of the winding up (cf s 127 as it applies to companies). *Quaere* also whether the effect of s 127 is to prevent a member from ceasing to be a member after the commencement of winding up (whether pursuant to a right in the LLP agreement or pursuant to s 4(3) of the LLP Act 2000) at least where the cessation involves a transfer of the outgoing member's share or interest in the LLP. See also IA 1986, s 88 in relation to voluntary liquidations.

[52]   IA 1986, s 128(1).

26.29   Once a winding-up order has been made,[53] no action or proceeding is to be proceeded with or commenced against the LLP or its property except by leave of the court and subject to such terms as the court may impose.[54] Between the date of the presentation of a winding-up petition and the making of an order, the LLP or any creditor or member may apply to the court for a stay of existing proceedings.[55]

FUNCTIONS OF OFFICIAL RECEIVER AND APPOINTMENT OF A LIQUIDATOR

26.30   The official receiver becomes the liquidator of the LLP, by virtue of his office, until another person is appointed as liquidator.[56] The official receiver may, at any time when he is the liquidator, summon separate meetings of the LLP's creditors and contributories for the purpose of choosing a liquidator to act in his place;[57] and he must decide within 12 weeks of the making of the winding-up order whether to summon such meetings.[58] If he decides not to do so, he must give notice of his decision to the court and to the LLP's creditors and contributories.[59] He must summon the meetings if requested by one-quarter in value of the LLP's creditors.[60] The official receiver may also at any time when he is the liquidator apply to the Secretary of State for the appointment of a person as liquidator in his place.[61] If meetings are held pursuant to the above provisions but no person is appointed as liquidator, the official receiver must decide whether to refer the need for an appointment to the Secretary of State.[62] If the question is referred to the Secretary of State, the Secretary of State must decide whether to make an appointment.[63] If he decides not to, the official receiver continues to be the liquidator.

26.31   If meetings of the creditors and the contributories are summoned, the creditors and the contributories may at their respective meetings nominate a liquidator.[64] If the creditors make a nomination, the person nominated becomes the liquidator; but where they do not, the person nominated by the LLP becomes the liquidator.[65] In the event that different persons are nominated, any contributory or creditor may, within 7 days, apply to the court for an order either appointing the person nominated by the contributories to be the liquidator instead of or jointly with the person nominated by the creditors or appointing some other person to be

---

[53]   Or a provisional liquidator has been appointed.
[54]   IA 1986, s 130(2).
[55]   Ibid, s 126(1).
[56]   Ibid, s 136(2). The official receiver is also the liquidator during any vacancy: IA 1986, s 136(3).
[57]   IA 1986, s 136(4). As to the meaning of 'contributories', see **26.18–26.23**.
[58]   Ibid, s 136(5)(a).
[59]   Ibid, s 136(5)(b).
[60]   Ibid, s 136(5)(c).
[61]   Ibid, s 137(1).
[62]   Ibid, s 137(2).
[63]   Ibid, s 137(3).
[64]   Ibid, s 139(2).
[65]   Ibid, s 139(3).

the liquidator instead of the person nominated by the creditors.[66] IA 1986, s 141 contains provisions relating to the establishment of a liquidation committee.

26.32 The official receiver may require preparation of a statement of affairs for the LLP.[67] He may make the request of anyone who is or has been a member of the LLP, anyone who has taken part in the formation of the LLP at any time within one year before the date of the winding-up order,[68] anyone who is in the LLP's employment or has been in its employment within the last year and who is in the official receiver's opinion capable of giving the information required, or anyone who is or, within that year, has been a member of or in the employment of an LLP or company which is, or was within that year, a member of the LLP. The request is made in a prescribed form and requires the person so requested to provide information verified by affidavit including details of the LLP's assets, debts and liabilities and the names and addresses of its creditors.[69]

26.33 The official receiver is under a duty pursuant to IA 1986, s 132 to investigate the promotion, formation, business dealings and affairs of the LLP and to make such report (if any) to the court as he thinks fit. Where the LLP has failed (which is presumably determined by its solvency), he is under a further duty to investigate the causes of the failure. In addition, the official receiver is under an obligation, at least once after the making of the winding-up order, to send a report to the creditors and members.

26.34 The official receiver may apply to the court for an order for the public examination of any person who:

(a)   is or has been a member[70] of the LLP;
(b)   has acted as liquidator, administrator or receiver or manager of the LLP; or
(c)   not falling within (a) or (b) above, is or has been concerned, or has taken part, in the promotion, formation or management of the LLP.[71]

26.35 Unless the court orders otherwise, the official receiver must make an application for an order for a public examination if requested to do so by one-half in value of the LLP's creditors or three-quarters in value of the LLP's contributiories.[72] As stated above,[73] it will not necessarily be clear who is a contributory of the LLP.

---

[66]   IA 1986, s 139(4).
[67]   Ibid, s 131.
[68]   Or, where a provisional liquidator is appointed, the date of his appointment.
[69]   IA 1986, s 131(2).
[70]   Section 133 also refers to 'officer' but this reference is unlikely to broaden the scope of eligible person beyond members. See LLP Regulations 2001, reg 5(2)(b), CA 1985, s 744 and IA 1986, s 251.
[71]   IA 1986, s 133.
[72]   Ibid, s 133(2).
[73]   See **26.18–26.23**.

Chapter 27

UNFAIR PREJUDICE AND JUST AND EQUITABLE WINDING UP

INTRODUCTION

27.1 This chapter is concerned with the court's power:

(a)   to grant relief under s 459 of the CA 1985 to a member whose interests have been unfairly prejudiced by the conduct of the LLP's affairs; and

(b)   to order the winding up of an LLP on the just and equitable ground pursuant to s 122(1)(e)[1] of the IA 1986.

27.2 A detailed exposition of these provisions as they apply to companies is beyond the scope of this work.[2] Indeed, as explained below, the significance of these provisions to LLPs is likely to be fairly limited. What follows includes a brief analysis of the relevant law and a discussion as to how it may be applicable to LLPs.

THE LEGISLATIVE PROVISIONS

Companies Act 1985, section 459

27.3 Section 459 provides:

> '...a member of a limited liability partnership may apply to the court by petition for an order under this Part on the ground that the limited liability partnership's affairs are being or have been conducted in a manner which is unfairly prejudicial to the interests of its members generally or of some part of its members (including at least himself) or that any actual or proposed act or omission of the limited liability partnership (including an act or omission on its behalf) is or would be so prejudicial.'

27.4 If the court is satisfied that a petition is well founded, it may make such order as it thinks fit for giving relief in respect of the matters complained of.[3] Without prejudice to these general powers, the court may make an order:

---

[1]   It should be noted that the equivalent provision in the IA 1986 as it applies to companies is s 122(1)(g).

[2]   For a detailed exposition, see Joffe, *Minority Shareholders Law Practice and Procedure* (Butterworths, 2nd edn, 2004) chapters 4 and 5.

[3]   CA 1985, s 461(1). See in relation to the interrelationship between s 459 and derivative actions *Clark v Cutland* [2003] 2 BCLC 393 (CA).

(a)   regulating the conduct of the LLP's affairs in the future;
(b)   requiring the LLP to refrain from doing or continuing an act complained of by the petitioner or to do an act which the petitioner has complained it has omitted to do;
(c)   authorising civil proceedings to be brought in the name and on behalf of the LLP by such person or persons and on such terms as the court may direct;
(d)   providing for the purchase of the shares of any members in the LLP by other members or by the LLP itself.

27.5   The normal order, particularly where the unfairly prejudicial conduct has caused an irretrievable break down in relations, is likely to be that the respondents or the LLP acquire the petitioner's share and interest in the LLP at a valuation to be determined by an independent expert.[4] An order can make alterations to the LLP agreement, and any such alteration has the same effect as if duly agreed by the members of the LLP.[5] Section 461(4) states that if an order requires the LLP not to make any, or any specified, alteration in the LLP agreement, the LLP cannot then make such an alteration without the leave of the court.[6] Although this provision only refers to an order requiring the LLP not to make alterations to the LLP agreement, it seems clear that an order could equally prohibit *members* from making such alterations; and, in such a case, the members would presumably be in the same position as s 461(4) expressly states in relation to the LLP.[7]

Contracting out of section 459

27.6   The members of an LLP may by unanimous agreement exclude the right contained in s 459(1) for such period as shall be agreed. Any such agreement must be recorded in writing,[8] and can clearly be a term of the LLP agreement. The requirement for such an agreement to be recorded in writing will mean that, for the contracting out from s 459 to remain effective, any new member of the LLP must assent in writing to this agreement.

Insolvency Act 1986, section 122

27.7   Section 122(1)(e) of the IA 1986 provides that an LLP may be wound up by the court if the court is of the opinion that it is just and equitable that the LLP should be wound up. Section 125(2) of the IA 1986 provides that if a petition is presented by members of the LLP as contributories[9] on the ground that it is just and equitable that the LLP should be wound up, and the court is of the opinion that the petitioners are entitled to relief by winding up the company or by some other means and that, in the absence of any other remedy, it would be just and equitable

---

[4]   See in relation to the appropriate date of valuation *Profinance Trust SA v Gladstone* [2002] 1 WLR 1024 (CA) at 1041–1042. As to the 'shares' of members, see the discussion at **8.17–8.19** and **16.28–16.42**.
[5]   CA 1985, s 461(4).
[6]   Ibid, s 461(3).
[7]   It would, however, probably be wise, from the members' point of view, for the order to contain an express liberty for the members to apply to the court for leave to make alterations.
[8]   CA 1985, s 459(1A).
[9]   Ie as present or past members of the LLP liable to contribute to the assets of the LLP on a winding up: see further **26.18–26.24**.

that the LLP should be wound up, the court must make a winding-up order. However, the court is not obliged to make a winding-up order if it is of the opinion that some other remedy is available to the petitioners and that they are acting unreasonably in seeking to have the LLP wound up instead of pursuing that other remedy. In relation to companies, the petitioner will often be regarded as having a reasonable alternative remedy if the respondents have offered to purchase his shares at a price fixed by an independent valuation. [10] It is an abuse of process for a petition to be pursued in circumstances where the petitioner has unreasonably rejected an offer of settlement that gives him all that he could reasonably expect if he succeeded at trial. It seems very likely that this approach will be applied to LLPs.

WHO CAN PRESENT A PETITION?

27.8 It is the members of the LLP who have standing to present a petition under s 459. The term 'member' is defined in s 4 of the LLP Act 2000. Section 4(1) provides that, on incorporation, the members of an LLP are the persons who subscribed their names to the incorporation document (other than those who have died or been dissolved). Section 4(2) provides that any other person may become a member of an LLP by and in accordance with an agreement with the existing members. [11] In respect of companies, s 459(2) of the CA 1985 provides that the provisions of ss 459–461 apply to a person who is not a member of a company but to whom shares in the company have been transferred or transmitted by operation of law. This provision is not applied to LLPs. [12]

27.9 One situation in which the court's powers pursuant to ss 459 and 122(1)(e) may be significant is where a member wishes to cease to be a member of the LLP, but no terms have been agreed between the members as to the financial consequences of cessation. A member who finds himself in this situation will obviously seek to negotiate exit terms with his fellow members. If, however, no terms can be agreed, the member will be in a difficult position. Assuming that there is no binding agreement to the contrary, he has the right, pursuant to LLP Act 2000, s 4(3), to cease to be a member by giving reasonable notice. [13] But whether he exercises this statutory right, or a right to retire contained in the LLP agreement, the LLP legislation does not contain any default provisions as to the financial consequences of a cessation in the absence of agreement amongst the members. The view of the authors, expressed in chapter 16, is that, in the event of a member

---

[10] *Re a Company* [1983] BCLC 151 at 157–160; *Re a Company (No 003843 of 1986)* [1987] BCLC 562 at 570; *Re a Company (No 004415)* [1997] 1 BCLC 479 at 485–487. See *Virdi v Abbey Leisure* [1990] BCLC 342 at 345–349, where the Court of Appeal refused to strike out a petition on the basis that, on the facts, the petitioner was not acting unreasonably in rejecting the respondents' offer; and *North Holdings Ltd v Southern Tropics Ltd* [1999] 2 BCLC 625, where the Court of Appeal refused to strike out the petition where the value of the shares depended upon matters of fact and law that would have to be determined by the Court. See also *CVC v Almeida* [2002] 2 BCLC 108.

[11] See **8.2** and **8.5**.

[12] LLP Regulations 2001, reg 4(1), Part I of Sch 2.

[13] See **16.2**.

leaving without there being any agreement as to his financial entitlement, he has no implied or inherent right to payment for the value of his share in the LLP, and that his share is probably determined by the cessation.[14] So long as he continues to be a member, the person wishing to leave clearly has standing to present a petition under s 459 or s 122(1)(e).[15]

27.10 If, however, a member gives notice of retirement and ceases to be a member, the position is less clear. If we are correct in chapter 16 in saying that the 'share' of a member who leaves in these circumstances is determined, no purpose is likely to be served by the now former member presenting a petition. Indeed, a petition presented by a former member in these circumstances is likely to be struck out as an abuse of process on the basis that he does not, in the case of a s 122(1)(e) petition, have a sufficient interest in the winding up or will not, in the case of a s 459 petition, be entitled to any relief.[16]

27.11 If, contrary to the authors' view, an outgoing member's share or interest survives the cessation of his membership, the outgoing member will be concerned to realise its value. On the face of s 459, however, former members do not have standing to present a petition. For the outgoing member to have standing, it would be necessary to read the reference to 'member' in s 459 as including 'former member', or at least 'former member with whom the LLP and the continuing members have reached no agreement as to the financial consequences of his cessation'. In the authors' view, such a reading of s 459 is not justified. 'Member' in the LLP Act 2000 (including s 4(3)) does not include former members. Similarly, the term 'member' as used in the CA 1985 as it applies to companies does not include former members.[17] We discuss the standing of members and former members to present a winding-up petition in chapter 26.

APPLICATION TO LLPs

27.12 Section 459(1A) of the CA 1985 enables the members of an LLP to agree to exclude the operation of s 459(1). Most LLPs which adopt a written LLP agreement are likely to include a provision excluding the operation of the section. The purpose of an LLP agreement is to regulate the rights and obligations of the members between themselves, and between the members and the LLP: members are unlikely to want to give individual members an opportunity to attempt to go behind the terms of the agreement by asserting unfair prejudice. The authors' experience is that, at least in relation to professional service LLPs, the right to petition under s 459 is routinely excluded. Indeed, if the members of the LLP enter into a reasonably comprehensive LLP agreement, then as appears from what

---

[14] See **16.28–16.42**. He will have a right to payment if an agreement to that effect can be inferred from the dealings of the members prior to his cessation: see **9.5**.

[15] A member who presents a petition to have the LLP wound up must have a sufficient interest in the winding up; see Joffe, op cit, paras 4.2–4.9; and French, *Applications to Wind Up Companies*, para 7.5. In most cases, this will require the petitioner to show that the LLP is solvent (at least on a balance sheet basis) and that the petitioner will be entitled to a share of the surplus assets.

[16] See Joffe, op cit, paras 4.2–4.9 and 5.210–5.225; French, op cit, para 7.5.

[17] See CA 1985, s 22.

follows, the scope for the application of the unfair prejudice and just and equitable winding-up principles underlying ss 459 and 122(1)(e) is likely to be limited, even if the operation of s 459 is not excluded.

O'Neill v Phillips

27.13 The leading authority on the court's jurisdiction under s 459 is the House of Lords decision in *O'Neill v Phillips*.[18] The facts were briefly, as follows.[19] Pectel Ltd employed Mr. O'Neill as a manual worker. Mr Phillips, the sole shareholder, gave Mr O'Neill 25 per cent of the shares and appointed him as a director. Mr Phillips indicated that he hoped Mr O'Neill would take over the running of the company and that, if he did, he would be entitled to 50 per cent of the profits. Mr O'Neill duly took over the running of the company and was credited with half the profits. Mr Phillips indicated in negotiations that he was in principle willing to increase Mr O'Neill's shareholding and voting rights to 50 per cent when certain targets were reached. However, Mr Phillips then lost confidence in Mr O'Neill, and took back control. He told Mr O'Neill that he would no longer receive 50 per cent of the profits but only his salary and any dividends payable on his 25 per cent shareholding. The judge dismissed a s 459 petition presented by Mr O'Neill (in which Mr O'Neill sought, inter alia, an order that Mr Phillips or the company purchase his shares at a fair value). The judge's decision was reversed by the Court of Appeal but restored by the House of Lords.

27.14 In his speech, Lord Hoffmann (with whom the other Law Lords agreed) undertook a detailed analysis of what constitutes unfairly prejudicial conduct.[20] His starting point was that the purpose of the s 459 jurisdiction is to give the court power to grant relief in circumstances in which it just to do so, and to free the courts from technical considerations of legal right.[21] However, he stressed that what is fair depends upon the context and background and that, in the case of s 459, the background has two features. First, a company is an association of persons for an economic purpose, the terms of which are contained in the articles of association and, sometimes, in collateral agreements between the shareholders. Secondly, company law has developed from the law of partnership, which was treated by equity as a contract of good faith such that one of the traditional roles of equity was to restrain the exercise of strict legal rights contrary to good faith.[22] Consequently:

> 'The first of these two features leads to the conclusion that a member of a company will not ordinarily be entitled to complain of unfairness unless there has been some breach of the terms on which he agreed that the affairs of the company should be conducted. But the second leads to the conclusion that there will be cases in which equitable considerations make it unfair for those conducting the affairs of the company to rely upon their strict legal powers. Thus unfairness may consist in a breach of the

---

[18]   [1999] 1 WLR 1092.

[19]   Taken from the headnote, ibid at 1092.

[20]   His speech is also instructive in relation to the court's power to order winding up on the just and equitable ground.

[21]   Ibid at 1098.

[22]   Ibid.

rules or in using the rules in a manner which equity would regard as contrary to good faith.

> This approach to the concept of unfairness in s 459 runs parallel to that which your Lordships' House, in *In re Westbourne Galleries Ltd* [1973] AC 360, adopted in giving content to the concept of "just and equitable" as a ground for winding up...

> I would apply the same reasoning to the concept of unfairness in s 459. The Law Commission, in its Report on Shareholder Remedies (1997) (Law Com No 246), p 43, para 4.11, expresses some concern that defining the content of the unfairness concept in the way I have suggested might unduly limit its scope and that "conduct which would appear to be deserving of a remedy may be left unremedied". In my view, a balance has to be struck between the breadth of the discretion given to the court and the principle of legal certainty. Petitions under s 459 are often lengthy and expensive. It is highly desirable that lawyers should be able to advise their clients whether or not a petition is likely to succeed. Lord Wilberforce... said that it would be impossible "and wholly undesirable" to define the circumstances in which the application of equitable principles might make it unjust, or inequitable (or unfair) for a party to insist on legal rights or to exercise them in particular way. This of course is right. But that does not mean that there are no principles by which those circumstances may be identified. The way in which such equitable principles operate is tolerably well settled and in my view it would be wrong to abandon them in favour of some wholly indefinite notion of fairness.'

27.15   There is no reason to think that this analysis will not be treated by the courts as equally applicable to LLPs. Thus if the members of an LLP have entered into a reasonably comprehensive LLP agreement, the scope for the application of the principles underlying s 459 is likely to be limited. A member will not usually be able to appeal to concepts of fairness and good faith if the affairs of the LLP are being conducted in accordance with the terms of the agreement to which he is a party. Where there is no LLP agreement, or the agreement does not deal with particular issues, the statutory default rules will apply.[23] Again, a member is unlikely to be able to complain of unfairness if the affairs of the LLP are governed in accordance with a default rule where no agreement has been made between the members. It has to be borne in mind that an LLP agreement need not be made in writing. An oral agreement, or even understanding with contractual force, will oust the default rules, and can be enforced by the members. Conduct in accordance with the LLP agreement (oral or written) and/or the default rules will only be unfair if there are equitable considerations which make it unfair for the other members to rely upon their strict legal powers.

27.16   In company cases, such unfairness often arises from the fact that the legal framework (ie the CA 1985 and the articles of association) pursuant to which the affairs of the company are conducted does not reflect the true agreement or understanding between the members. In other words (and having regard to the second background matter referred to by Lord Hoffmann), the true agreement or understanding makes it unconscionable for the other members to stand on their strict legal rights. The same principles are likely to be applied to LLPs; but, given

---

[23]   LLP Regulations 2001, regs 7 and 8. See generally on the default rules, **9.6–9.8**.

the comparatively informal way in which LLP agreements may be formed, and the operation of the default rules, the occasions on which the true understanding is not reflected in the operative agreement are likely to be relatively few. The jurisdiction in company cases is often exercised because the reality of the relationship between the shareholders is one of quasi-partnership but their legal rights are defined by reference to their choice of a limited company through which to conduct their business. The ability of the members of an LLP to determine their mutual rights and obligations by agreement, without being constrained by the corporate governance and capital rules of a company, is such that members can (and will usually) give contractual effect to their quasi-partnership relationship.

27.17   Will similar considerations apply to petitions presented on the just and equitable ground under s 122(1)(e) of the IA 1986? In general terms, Lord Hoffmann's analysis will be applicable to petitions presented under s 122(1)(e). It is unclear, however, at least in relation to LLPs, whether the jurisdiction under s 122(1)(e) is broader than that under s 459. So far as the statutory wording is concerned, the jurisdiction under s 122(1)(e) is broader in the sense that it is not statutorily constrained by a need to find unfairly prejudicial conduct. This issue is discussed further below.

27.18   When will a member obtain relief under s 459 or a winding-up order pursuant to s 122(1)(e)? If the petitioner can establish that the conduct of the other members is in breach of the LLP agreement or the default terms, he may be entitled to relief. For example, if the member is excluded from the management of the LLP, or from the carrying on of the LLP's business, contrary to the terms of the LLP agreement or default rule (3).[24] Further, relief may be granted if (notwithstanding what is said above) the member can establish that other members are acting unconscionably or contrary to good faith although in accordance with their strict legal rights. In either case, however, relief is unlikely to be granted if the LLP agreement gives the member an 'exit route', or if the other members make a reasonable offer to purchase the disenchanted member's share.

27.19   A written LLP agreement will usually make detailed provision for the circumstances in which a member can cease to be a member, and the financial consequences of cessation. Where such terms have been agreed, relief is unlikely to be granted under s 459 or s 122(1)(e). It is possible that relief would be granted, even if the member had an exit route, if the compensation payable to an outgoing member pursuant to the LLP agreement is well below the true value of his share[25] and the conduct of the other members is such that he is, in effect, being forced out against his will. In this situation, relief may be granted unless the other members make a reasonable offer to purchase his share at its true value.[26]

---

[24]   Other examples of potentially unfair conduct are given in Joffe, op cit, pp 176–191.

[25]   For example, if an outgoing member is entitled only to payment of his capital and current account balances and the true value of the net assets is substantially in excess of their book value.

[26]   See Joffe, op cit, paras 5.197–5.200.

Breakdown of relationship between members

27.20   Will relief be granted to a member merely because he wishes to leave the LLP in circumstances in which the LLP agreement does not make provision for the financial consequences of cessation and he cannot come to an agreement as to his entitlement with his fellow members? As mentioned in **27.9–27.10**, although a member has a right to cease to be a member by giving reasonable notice to the other members,[27] the LLP Act 2000 and LLP Regulations 2001 do not include any express default provision as to the financial consequences of cessation. Unless an ad hoc agreement is made by the members, the only option available to a member wishing to leave, and to realise his share in the LLP, may be to petition the court pursuant to s 459 for an order that the other members acquire his share or pursuant to s 122(1)(e) for an order that the LLP be wound up.

27.21   In the authors' view, a petition pursuant to s 459 is unlikely to succeed if the member merely wishes to leave, and the majority have refused to purchase his share. A submission was made in *O'Neill v Phillips* that the trust and confidence between the parties had broken down and that because of this there ought to be a parting of the ways, and that the unfairness lay in Mr Phillips not being willing to allow Mr O'Neill to recover his stake in the company. It was argued that, even if Mr Phillips was not at fault in causing the breakdown, it would be unfair to leave Mr O'Neill locked into the company as a minority shareholder. Lord Hoffmann rejected this argument on the basis that, in effect, the jurisdiction under s 459 does not extend to 'no fault divorce'. Lord Hoffmann stated that:[28]

> '[Counsel's] submission comes to saying that, in a "quasi-partnership" company, one partner ought to be entitled at will to require the other partner or partners to buy his shares at a fair value. All he need do is to declare that trust and confidence has broken down. In the present case, trust and confidence broke down, first, because Mr Phillips failed to do certain things which, on the judge's findings, he had never promised to do; secondly, because Mr O'Neill wrongly thought that Mr Phillips had committed various improprieties; and finally because, as the judge said [1997] 2 BCLC 739, 742, he was "inclined to see base motives in everything that Mr Phillips did." Nevertheless it is submitted that fairness requires that Mr Phillips or the company ought to raise the necessary liquid capital to pay Mr O'Neill a fair price for his shares.
>
> I do not think that there is any support in the authorities for such a stark right of unilateral withdrawal. There are cases, such as *In re A Company (No 006834 of 1988), Ex parte Kremer* [1989] BCLC 365, in which it has been said that if a breakdown in relations has caused the majority to remove a shareholder from participation in the management, it is usually a waste of time to try to investigate who caused the breakdown. Such breakdowns often occur (as in this case) without either side having done anything seriously wrong or unfair. It is not fair to the excluded member, who will usually have lost his employment, to keep his assets locked in the company. But that does not mean that a member who has not been dismissed or excluded can demand that his shares be purchased simply because he feels that he has lost trust and confidence in the others. I rather doubt whether even in partnership law a dissolution would be granted on this ground in a case in which it was still possible under the

---

[27]   LLP Act 2000, s 4(3).
[28]   *O'Neill v Phillips* above, at 1104.

articles for the business of the partnership to be continued. And as Lord Wilberforce observed in *In re Westbourne Galleries Ltd* [1973] AC 360, 380, one should not press the quasi-partnership analogy too far: "A company, however small, however domestic, is a company not a partnership or even a quasi-partnership."

The Law Commission Report on Shareholder Remedies to which I have already referred considered whether to recommend the introduction of a statutory remedy "in situations where there is no fault" (paragraph 3.65) so that members of a quasi-partnership could exit at will. They said, at p 39, para 3.66:

"In our view there are strong economic arguments against allowing shareholders to exit at will. Also, as a matter of principle, such a right would fundamentally contravene the sanctity of the contract binding the members and the company which we considered should guide our approach to shareholder remedies."

The Law Commission plainly did not consider that s 459 already provided a right to exit at will and I do not think so either.'

27.22 Despite these words, there are, we suggest, two distinct situations to be considered: first, where a member decides that he wants to leave, and seeks to negotiate terms with the other members, but they refuse to buy him out and this causes a breakdown in relations: and, secondly, where relations between one member and the others break down (without fault on either side) to such an extent that it is not feasible for them to carry on in business together and, at that point, one member wishes to leave. Under s 459, relief cannot be granted in either situation unless there is unfairly prejudicial conduct on the part of the other members. In an ordinary company case, there will not be unfairly prejudicial conduct unless the majority exclude the minority from involvement in the company contrary to a legitimate expectation of involvement on the part of the minority.[29] The authors' view is that, in relation to LLPs, it is almost certain that Lord Hoffmann's analysis will be applied to both situations, so that relief will not be granted under s 459.[30] The position is, however, far less clear in relation to just and equitable winding up petitions. In *Re Guidezone Ltd*[31] Jonathan Parker J held that the just and equitable winding up jurisdiction was no wider than the jurisdiction under s 459 in the sense that, if the conduct of the respondent is not unfair for the purposes of s 459, it cannot support a petition on the just and equitable ground. This finding has been the subject of criticism[32] and is inconsistent with prior authority.[33] In the authors' view, it should not be applied to LLPs. The statutory jurisdiction to wind up an LLP on the just and equitable ground is, prima facie, broader than the jurisdiction under s 459 in the sense that a finding of unfairly prejudicial conduct is not a statutory prerequisite to the making of a winding-up order. A winding-up order can be made if it is just and equitable in all the circumstances; a finding that one party has acted in a way that constitutes unfair

---

[29]   See *Larvin v Phoenix Office Supplies Ltd* [2003] 1 BCLC 76.

[30]   See also *McKee v O'Reilley* [2003] EWHC (Ch) 2008, [2004] 2 BCLC 145.

[31]   [2001] BCC 692.

[32]   'Just and equitable winding up: The strange case of the disappearing jurisdiction', Acton, (2001) 22(5) *Company Lawyer* 134.

[33]   *Re Noble* [1990] BCLC 273; *Vujnovich v. Vujnovich* [1990] BCLC 227 and *Jesner v Jarrad Properties Ltd* [1990] BCC 807.

prejudice is not necessary. Although a court is unlikely to make a winding-up order merely because the petitioner wishes to realise his investment (even if his desire to leave has caused an irretrievable breakdown in relations),[34] there may well be circumstances in which it would be just and equitable to make a winding-up order in the absence of unfairly prejudicial conduct on the part of one member. Suppose, for instance, that an LLP is formed by four members in circumstances in which they agree to carry on business together through the vehicle of an LLP. Relations between one of the members and the other three break down (with no fault on the part of any of them), making it impossible for them to continue business together, and the one wishes to leave. He is willing to be bought out (at a valuation to be fixed by an independent expert), but the others refuse. If no 'exit regime' has been agreed, either in advance or on an ad hoc basis following the break down, it may well, in these circumstances, be just and equitable to wind up the LLP in order to enable the one member to realise the value of his share. If the finding made in *Re Guidezone* is correct, a winding-up order could not be made.

27.23   The approach taken in *Re Guidezone* is to be contrasted with the position in partnership law. In partnership cases, the court has a discretion to order dissolution on the just and equitable ground pursuant to s 35(f) of the Partnership Act 1890 if there has been a complete breakdown in relations between the partners, provided that the breakdown has not been caused (at least exclusively) by the petitioning partner.[35] There are pre-*Guidezone* authorities in which it was held that partnership principles are to be applied to quasi-partnership companies.[36]

27.24   It is not easy to predict how the courts will approach petitions by members of LLPs. The courts will inevitably be influenced strongly by the law relating to companies and partnerships. That said, the courts will, within the s 459 and s 122(1)(e) framework, have to resolve the difficulties arising from the grant to members of a statutory right to cease to be members but the omission from the legislation of provisions dealing with the financial consequences of such retirement. Unless the courts are willing to exercise the powers under ss 459 and 122(1)(e) either to require the other members to purchase the outgoing member's share or to order a winding up, a member who wishes to leave will have a stark choice: either he continues as a member until such time as agreement can be reached[37] or he gives notice and ceases to be a member and thereby possibly forfeits his share.

27.25   The authors' view is that the courts are likely to develop the law on just and equitable winding up so that a member will be entitled to relief if there has been a complete breakdown in relations (for reasons unconnected with his desire to exit the LLP) and the other members unreasonably refuse to acquire his share even in the absence of prior misconduct or bad faith on the part of the non-petitioning

---

[34]   See French, op cit, p 274; *Re Anglo-Continental Produce Co Ltd* [1939] 1 All ER 99 at 102–103.
[35]   See French, op cit, pp 281–283; Blackett-Ord, *Partnership* (Butterworths Tolley, 2nd edn, 2002) pp 310–312.
[36]   *Symington v Symington Quarries Ltd* (1905) 8 F, Ct of Session; *Re Yenidje Tobacco Ltd* [1916] 2 Ch 426; *Re Straw Products* [1942] VLR 222 and *Re Wondoflex* [1951] VLR 458.
[37]   Or the LLP is wound up by a creditor or by determination of the members or he has grounds for a s 459 or a just and equitable winding-up petition.

members. However, it is extremely doubtful, in our view, whether the courts will grant relief under s 459 and s 122(1)(e) in cases in which the petitioner is simply attempting to use the statutory provisions as a means of exiting from the LLP with compensation for the value of his share in a situation where relations had not (prior to his wishing to leave) broken down.

Chapter 28

CONDUCT OF THE LIQUIDATION

GENERAL

28.1 In very general terms, it is the liquidator's duty to get in and realise the LLP's assets and to distribute the assets to the LLP's creditors and, if there is a surplus, to those entitled.[1] The IA 1986 contains provisions relating to the conduct of liquidations, and the powers of liquidators and the court, in respect of both voluntary and compulsory winding up.[2] These provisions are not modified substantially for LLPs and reference should be made to the standard insolvency texts.[3] Particular aspects of the conduct of liquidations are considered below.

STATUS OF MEMBERS' CLAIMS

28.2 One issue that does arise in respect of LLPs is the status of the claims of members in the liquidation. In company law, a sum due to a member, in his capacity of member, by way of dividends, profits or otherwise is not deemed to be a debt of the company payable to that member in a case of competition between that member and any other creditor not a member of the company; but under IA 1986, s 74(2)(f) such sums may be taken into account for the purpose of the final adjustment of the rights of contributories amongst themselves. A member of a company can prove for sums not due to him in his capacity as a member, and such claims rank alongside the creditors. A member of a company is not entitled to any payment in respect of his shares as such but, if there is a surplus, it is distributed, in the case of a voluntary winding up, among the members according to their rights and interests in the company.[4] In the case of a compulsory winding up, the court adjusts the rights of the contributories among themselves and distributes any surplus among the persons entitled to it.[5] Sections 107 and 154 are applied to LLPs. The 'rights and interests' of the members (for the purpose of s 107) and the 'rights of the contributories' (for the purpose of s 154) will be governed by the terms of the LLP agreement. In default of agreement, any surplus will be divisible amongst the members/contributories in equal shares pursuant to default rule (1). The LLP legislation does not impose a capital and share structure for LLPs. The

---

[1] See IA 1986, s 107 (voluntary liquidations) and ss 143(1), 144(1) and 154 (compulsory liquidations). See, in relation to the interaction between receiverships and winding up, *Buchler v Talbot* [2004] 1 All ER 1289. See also the Proceeds of Crime Act 2002 s 426 in relation to property subject to restraint orders.

[2] See IA 1986, ss 107–116; 143–200.

[3] See, for example, *Palmer's Company Law* paras 15.401 et seq; Totty and Moss, *Insolvency* chapters E2 and E3.

[4] IA 1986, s 107.

[5] Ibid, s 154. The issue of who is a 'contributory' is not straightforward: see **26.17–26.22**.

members are free to agree whether, and how much, each of them is to contribute to the assets of the LLP, both in the ordinary course of trading and in the event of winding up. In addition, they are free to agree what rights they will each acquire by reason of their contributions. In default of agreement, members are entitled to share equally in the capital and profits of the LLP.[6]

28.3 The issue which arises is whether a member can prove for sums owed to him by the LLP and, if so, whether his claim ranks alongside ordinary creditors. Presumably, a member will be able (in the same way as in company law) to prove for sums not due to him in his character as a member and such claims will rank alongside the ordinary creditors, for example, if he has made a loan to the LLP.

28.4 Sums due to a member in his capacity as a member are not so straightforward. Rather oddly, s 74(2)(f) of the IA 1986 has not been applied to LLPs, with the result that the legislation does not include an express provision deferring the rights of members in a liquidation. The types of claim that may fall into this category will include claims in respect of capital contributions and accrued, but unpaid, profit share. Although the legislation does not impose a capital or share structure for LLPs, the legislation does recognise the concept of members' 'capital'.[7] It seems likely that LLP agreements will impose on members (or at least on 'equity' members) obligations to contribute 'capital' in the same way as traditional partnership agreements currently do. In our view, it is inherent in a contribution by a member of a sum 'by way of capital' (rather than 'by way of loan') that the member has no implied right to repayment either during the continuance of the LLP's trading or on a winding up. A right to repayment will arise either when he ceases to be a member (if the LLP agreement makes provision in this regard) or otherwise by way of express agreement,[8] or if there are surplus assets on a winding up. It must follow that a member cannot prove for his capital in a winding up; a member's entitlement will be limited to a share in any surplus assets distributable. It remains to be seen whether there will be a move away from the traditional partners' capital, to contributions by members being by way of loan. Militating against this, however, may be the requirements of outside financiers, such as banks, who are likely to look at the capital base of an LLP (notwithstanding the fact that there are no capital maintenance provisions) with the result, it is suggested, that most LLP agreements will in fact require capital contributions from the members.

28.5 As to accrued profit share, a member's entitlement to call for his profit share in respect of any period, and to enforce that entitlement against the LLP as a creditor, will probably depend upon whether or not there has been a division amongst the individual members of their respective shares of the profits of the LLP for that period. The issue of division is discussed at **13.8–13.10**. Where, therefore, there has been a division, and resulting allocation, of profits to the individual members, there would seem no reason, in the absence of any statutory deferral of

---

[6] LLP Regulations 2001, reg 7(1).
[7] See **13.2**. Sums due to a member, otherwise than in his capacity as a member, will presumably include any unpaid salary of an employee member.
[8] See **13.6**.

members' claims, why a member cannot submit a proof in respect of a claim for allocated but unpaid profit share.

DISCLAIMER OF ONEROUS PROPERTY

28.6 A liquidator may, by the giving of a prescribed notice, disclaim onerous property; and may do so notwithstanding that he has taken possession of it, endeavoured to sell it or otherwise exercised rights of ownership in relation to it.[9] Onerous property is any unprofitable contract and any other property of the LLP which is unsaleable or not readily saleable, or is such that it may give rise to a liability to pay money or perform any other onerous act.[10] If a liquidator disclaims onerous property, the effect is to determine, as from the date of the disclaimer, the rights, interests and liabilities of the LLP in or in respect of the property disclaimed.[11] A disclaimer does not, except so far as is necessary for the purpose of releasing the LLP from any liability, affect the rights or liabilities of any other person.[12] Disclaimed property vests in the Crown as bona vacantia. If a freehold is disclaimed, the freehold interest is determined and the land escheats to the Crown, but charges and leaseholds created out of a disclaimed freehold survive.[13] A person interested in any property of the LLP can apply in writing to the liquidator requiring him to decide whether he will disclaim the property.[14] A liquidator cannot disclaim the property after the period of 28 days (or such longer period as the court may allow) from the date of the application has elapsed.[15] Any person sustaining loss or damage as a result of a disclaimer is deemed a creditor of the LLP and may prove for the loss or damage.[16]

28.7 A disclaimer of a leasehold does not take effect unless (a) a copy of the disclaimer has been served (so far as the liquidator is aware of their addresses) on every person claiming under the LLP as underlessee or mortgagee, and (b) no application for a vesting order[17] is made within a period of 14 days beginning on the day on which the last notice is served or, where an application for a vesting order has been made, the court directs that the disclaimer take effect.[18]

28.8 Any person who claims an interest in disclaimed property, or any person who is under any liability in respect of the disclaimed property (not being a liability discharged by the disclaimer), may apply to the court for a vesting order.[19] The court may, on such an application, make an order, on such terms as it thinks fit, vesting the property in, or for its delivery to, a person entitled to it or a person

---

[9]   IA 1986, s 178(2); IR 1986, rr 4.187–4.194.
[10]   IA 1986, s 178(3).
[11]   Ibid, s 178(4)(a).
[12]   Ibid, s 178(4)(b).
[13]   *Scmlla Properties Ltd v Gesso Properties (BVI) Ltd* [1995] BCC 793.
[14]   IA 1986, s 178(5).
[15]   Ibid.
[16]   Ibid, s 178(6); see *Re Park Air Services Plc* [1997] 1 WLR 1376.
[17]   Pursuant to IA 1986, s 181. See further **28.8**.
[18]   IA 1986, s 179.
[19]   Ibid, s 181(2).

subject to an undischarged liability (or a trustee for such a person).[20] Where the disclaimed property is leasehold, there are additional requirements.[21] The court cannot make a vesting order of property of a leasehold nature in favour of any person claiming under the LLP as underlessee or mortgagee except on terms making that person subject to the same liabilities and obligations as the LLP was subject to at the commencement of the winding up or, if the court thinks fit, subject to the same liabilities and obligations as that person would be subject to if the lease had been assigned to him at the commencement of the winding up.[22] If no person claiming under the LLP as underlessee or mortgagee is willing to accept an order on the terms required, the court may vest the LLP's estate or interest in the property in any person who is liable to perform the lessee's covenants in the lease.[23] A person claiming under the LLP as underlessee or mortgagee not willing to accept an order is excluded from all interest in the property.[24]

RESCISSION OF CONTRACTS

28.9   A person who is, as against the liquidator, entitled to the benefit or subject to the burden of a contract made with the LLP may make an application to the court for an order rescinding the contract on such terms as to payment by or to either party of damages for the non-performance of the contract, or otherwise, as the court thinks just.[25] Any damages which the court orders the LLP to pay may be proved as a debt in the winding up.[26]

CROWN PREFERENCE AND TOP SLICING

28.10   In a winding up, a company's, or LLP's, preferential debts are paid in priority to all other debts.[27] Preferential debts rank equally amongst themselves after the expenses of the winding up and are paid in full unless the assets are insufficient in which case they abate in equal proportions.[28] If the assets are insufficient, preferential debts have priority over the claim of a holder of a debenture secured by a floating charge and, accordingly, are paid out of any property comprised in or subject to that charge.[29] The categories of preferential debts are set out in IA 1986, Sch 6. An important aspect of the insolvency law reforms introduced by the Enterprise Act 2002 was the abolition of the preference given to Crown debts (ie unpaid income tax deducted pursuant to the PAYE regulations and unpaid VAT). Crown preference has now been abolished (in

---

[20]   IA 1986, s 181(3).
[21]   Ibid, s 182.
[22]   Ibid, s 182(1). The court may make an order relating to only part of any property comprised in a lease and the requirements of s 182(1) apply to the part: s 182(2).
[23]   IA 1986, s 182(3).
[24]   Ibid, s 182(4).
[25]   Ibid, s 186(1).
[26]   Ibid, s 186(2).
[27]   Ibid, s 175(1).
[28]   Ibid, s 175(2)(a).
[29]   Ibid, s 175(2)(b).

general terms) for insolvency proceedings commenced on or after 15 September 2003.[30] The remaining categories of preferential debt are employees' remuneration and levies on coal and steel production. Transitional provisions are set out in the Enterprise Act 2002 (Commencement No 4 and Transitional Provisions and Savings) Order 2003, Art 4.[31] The abolition does not apply to a winding up where before 15 September 2003:

(a)   a petition for an administration order was presented;
(b)   a voluntary arrangement had effect;
(c)   a receiver was appointed under a floating charge; or
(d)   a petition for winding up was presented.[32]

The abolition also does not apply to a case where:

(e)   an administration order was made before 15 September 2003 and is discharged and, immediately on the discharge, a winding-up order or a determination to wind up is made (whether on or after 15 September 2003);[33] or
(f)   proposals for a voluntary arrangement are made (whether before or after 15 September 2003) by a liquidator in a winding up, and the winding up petition was presented, or determination to wind up was made, before 15 September 2003, or the proposals are made by an administrator appointed where the winding up petition was presented before 15 September 2003.[34]

28.11   Where a company or LLP has given security for its debts by granting a floating charge over its assets, the effect of the abolition of the Crown preference would, in the absence of other reform, have been to pass the entirety of the benefit (of the assets that would otherwise have gone to the Crown) to the holder of the floating charge. One of the purposes of the abolition of the Crown preference was to free up assets for the benefit of creditors generally. Effect has been given to this purpose by the introduction of top slicing provisions.

28.12   The top slicing provisions are contained in IA 1986 section 176A.[35] The top slicing rules apply where there is a floating charge in relation to the property of an LLP:

(a)   which has gone into liquidation; or
(b)   which is in administration; or
(c)   of which there is a provisional liquidator; or
(d)   of which there is a receiver.[36]

---

[30]   IA 1986, Sch 6 paras 1–7 repealed by Enterprise Act 2002, ss 251(1), 278(2), Sch 26.
[31]   SI 2003/2093 (as amended by Enterprise Act 2002 (Transitional Provisions) (Insolvency) Order 2003, SI 2003/2332, Art 2).
[32]   SI 2003/2093, Art 4(1).
[33]   Ibid, Art 4(1A).
[34]   Ibid, Art 4(2).
[35]   Inserted by Enterprise Act 2002, s 252
[36]   IA 1986, s 176A(1).

Where the top slicing rules apply, the liquidator, administrator or receiver is obliged to make a prescribed part of the LLP's net property[37] available for the satisfaction of unsecured debts, and must not distribute that part to the proprietor of a floating charge except in so far as it exceeds the amount required for the satisfaction of unsecured debts.[38] The prescribed part is:

(a)   50 per cent, if the LLP's net property does not exceed £10,000;[39] or

(b)   50 per cent of the first £10,000 in value and 20 per cent of that part of the LLP's property which exceeds £10,000, if the LLP's net property exceeds £10,000,[40]

but the prescribed part cannot exceed £600,000.[41]

28.13   There is no obligation to apply the prescribed part for the benefit of the unsecured creditors if:

(a)   the LLP's net property is less than the prescribed minimum (ie less than £10,000[42]), and the liquidator, administrator or receiver thinks that the cost of making a distribution to unsecured creditors would be disproportionate to the benefits;[43] or

(b)   the obligation is disapplied by a voluntary arrangement in respect of the LLP, or by a compromise or arrangement agreed under s 425 of the Companies Act;[44] or

(c)   the liquidator, administrator or receiver applies to the court for an order on the ground that the cost of making a distribution to unsecured creditors would be disproportionate to the benefits, and the court orders that the obligation shall not apply.[45]

---

[37]   An LLP's net property is the amount of its property which would, but for IA 1986, s 176A, be available for satisfaction of claims of holders of debentures secured by, or holders of, any floating charge created by the LLP: IA 1986, s 176A(6).

[38]   IA 1986, s 176A(2).

[39]   Insolvency Act 1986 (Prescribed Part) Order 2003, SI 2003/2097, Art 3(1)(a).

[40]   SI 2003/2097, Art 3(1)(b).

[41]   Ibid, Art 3(2).

[42]   Ibid, Art 2.

[43]   IA 1986 s 176A(3).

[44]   Ibid, s 176A(4).

[45]   Ibid, s 176A(5).

Chapter 29

MISFEASANCE AND ADJUSTMENT OF PRIOR TRANSACTIONS

MALPRACTICE AND MISFEASANCE

29.1 Sections 206–211 of the IA 1986 create various offences arising out of dishonesty on the part of members of the LLP. Section 212 of the IA 1986 provides a summary civil procedure for obtaining redress in respect of the misapplication and retention of, and accountability for, money and other property of the LLP, and for misfeasance and breach of fiduciary or other duty in relation to the LLP. Section 212 does not impose substantive liabilities, but merely provides a procedure by which, usually, a liquidator can seek relief against a wrongdoing member. The section applies where the LLP is in the course of winding up and applies in relation to any person who is or has been a member of the LLP,[1] has acted as liquidator, administrator or administrative receiver of the LLP[2] or is or has been concerned in the promotion, formation or management of the LLP.[3] The section enables the court to examine into the conduct of the person concerned, and to compel him to repay, restore or account for property of the LLP or to contribute such sum to the LLP's assets by way of compensation as the court thinks just.[4] An application pursuant to the section can be made by the liquidator, by any creditor or, with the leave of the court,[5] any contributory.[6]

FRAUDULENT TRADING

29.2 Where the business of an LLP has been carried on with intent to defraud creditors, or for any fraudulent purpose, under IA 1986, s 213 the court may declare that any persons who were knowingly party to the carrying on of the business (with intent to defraud creditors or for any fraudulent purpose) are liable to make such contribution to the LLP's assets as the court may think proper.[7] An application can only be made by the liquidator.[8] It is not enough for the liquidator to show that the LLP carried on trading at a time when the members knew that it

---

[1] IA 1986, s 212(1)(a).
[2] Ibid, s 212(1)(b).
[3] Ibid, s 212(1)(c).
[4] Ibid, s 212(3). See *Re Simmons Box (Diamonds) Ltd* [2002] BCC 82.
[5] Ibid, s 212(5).
[6] Ibid, s 212(3).
[7] See *Morris v State Bank of India* [2003] BCC 735. See also CA 1985, s 458 which makes 'fraudulent trading' a criminal offence (whether or not the LLP has been, or is in the course of being, wound up).
[8] IA 1986, s 213(2).

was insolvent. Actual dishonesty must be established.[9] The court has a wide discretion as to the amount which the wrongdoer may be ordered to contribute to the assets of the LLP. The principle on which the court's power should be exercised is that the contribution to the assets in which the company's creditors will share in the liquidation should reflect (and compensate for) the loss which has been caused to those creditors by the carrying on of the business in the manner which gives rise to the exercise of the power. There is no power to include in an order a punitive, as well as a compensatory, element.[10] Given the wrongful trading provisions in IA 1986, s 214, which do not require proof of dishonesty, applications to the court under s 213 are not made very often. Proof of fraudulent (rather than simply wrongful) trading may, however, be of significance in the assessment by the court of the amount to be contributed to the LLP's assets on a wrongful trading application under s 214. It is to be noted, however, that orders pursuant to s 214 can only be made against members or former members,[11] shadow members[12] and, probably, de facto members,[13] whereas s 213 applies in relation to any person who was knowingly a party to the fraudulent carrying on of the business.

WRONGFUL TRADING

29.3   A member or former member[14] of an LLP is liable for wrongful trading if:

(a)   the LLP has gone into insolvent liquidation;
(b)   at some time before the commencement of the winding up, he knew or ought to have concluded that there was no reasonable prospect that the LLP would avoid going into insolvent liquidation; and
(c)   he was a member (or shadow member) at that time.[15]

29.4   However, a member will escape liability if he took every step with a view to minimising the potential loss to the LLP's creditors as (assuming him to have known that there was no reasonable prospect that the LLP would avoid insolvent liquidation) he ought to have taken.[16] The conclusions which the member ought to reach, and the steps which he ought to take, are assessed by reference to the conclusions or steps that a reasonably diligent person – having the general knowledge, skill and experience that may reasonably be expected of a person

[9]   *Re Patrick and Lyon Ltd* [1933] Ch 786.
[10]   *Morphitis v Bernasconi* [2003] Ch 552.
[11]   IA 1986, s 214(1).
[12]   Ibid, s 214(7).
[13]   *Re Hydrodan (Corby) Ltd* [1994] BCC 161.
[14]   Or a shadow member and, probably, a *de facto* member. 'Shadow member' means a person in accordance with whose directions or instructions the members of the LLP are accustomed to act (but a person is not deemed to be a shadow member by reason only that the members of the LLP act on advice given by him in a professional capacity); IA 1986, s 251. As to the meaning of 'shadow member', see *Secretary of State for Trade and Industry v Deverell & anor* [2000] Ch 340 esp at para 35 (considering the meaning of 'shadow director').
[15]   IA 1986, s 214(2) and (7).
[16]   Ibid, s 214(3).

carrying out the same functions as are carried out by the member in relation to the LLP and the general knowledge, skill and experience that that member has – would have reached or taken.[17] The functions carried out by the member include any functions which he does not carry out but which have been entrusted to him.[18]

29.5 The test for wrongful trading is, therefore, essentially objective. The objectivity is, however, couched by reference to the general knowledge, skill and experience that may reasonably be expected of a person carrying out the same functions as are carried out by the member and a subjective element is introduced by reference to the general knowledge, skill and experience that the member has. It will be necessary, therefore, for all members (whether or not they are generally involved in the management of the LLP) to keep up to date with the financial position of the LLP. In cases where the LLP is of doubtful solvency, each member will need to be in a position to assess for himself whether the LLP will be able to avoid insolvent liquidation. This is likely to require the production of regular and reliable profit and loss and cash flow forecasts as well as historic management accounts.[19] In some cases, a proper analysis of the position will not be possible without outside professional advice. Clearly, members directly involved in management will be most at risk but it seems unlikely that the courts will be particularly lenient when it comes to 'ordinary' members.

ADJUSTMENT OF WITHDRAWALS

29.6 Section 214A of the IA 1986 is a new section (inserted by the LLP Regulations 2001).[20] The purpose of the section is to enable a liquidator to claw back withdrawals made by members within the 2 years prior to the commencement of the liquidation.

29.7 A member or former member is liable under s 214A to make a contribution to the LLP's assets if:

(a)   within the period of 2 years prior to the commencement of winding up he was a member of the LLP who withdrew property of the LLP whether in the

---

[17]   IA 1986, s 214(4).

[18]   Ibid, s 214(5).

[19]   See *Re Continental Assurance Co of London Plc* [2001] BPIR 733.

[20]   It may be arguable that s 214A is ultra vires the LLP Act 2000, although we consider that such an argument would be likely to fail. Section 14(1) of the LLP Act 2000 provides that regulations shall make provision about the insolvency and winding up of LLPs by applying or incorporating, with such modifications as appear appropriate, Parts I–IV, VI and VII of the IA 1986. LLP Regulations 2001, reg 5(1) provides that, subject to paras (2) and (3), Parts I–IV, VI and VII of the IA 1986 shall apply to LLPs as they apply in relation to companies. LLP Regulations 2001, reg 5(2)(f) provides that the application of the IA 1986 shall be subject to the modifications set out in Sch 3 to the LLP Regulations 2001. Section 214A appears in Sch 3. The issue would be whether s 214A, which is an entirely new substantive provision, is merely a 'modification'. See *R v Secretary of State for the Environment, Transport and the Regions, ex parte Spath Holme Ltd* [2001] 2 AC 349, *R v Secretary of State for the Environment, ex parte Berkshire Royal County Council* (1996) 95 LGR 249, *R v Secretary of State for Social Security, ex parte Britnell* [1991] 1 WLR 198.

form of a share of profits, salary, repayment of or payment of interest on a loan to the LLP or any other withdrawal of property[21] and

(b)   it is proved by the liquidator to the satisfaction of the court that at the time of the withdrawal he knew or had reasonable ground for believing that the LLP:

   (i)   was at the time of the withdrawal unable to pay its debts within the meaning of IA 1986, s 123; or

   (ii)   would become so unable to pay its debts after the assets of the LLP had been depleted by that withdrawal taken together with all other withdrawals (if any) made by any members contemporaneously with that withdrawal or in contemplation when that withdrawal was made;[22] and

(c)   he knew or ought to have concluded that after each withdrawal referred to above there was no reasonable prospect that the LLP would avoid going into insolvent liquidation.[23]

29.8   For the purpose of s 214A, an LLP goes into insolvent liquidation if it goes into liquidation at a time when its assets are insufficient for the payment of its debts and other liabilities and the expenses of the winding up.[24]

29.9   The facts which a member ought to know or ascertain, and the conclusions which he ought to reach, are those which would be known, ascertained or reached by a reasonably diligent person having both (a) the general knowledge, skill and experience that may reasonably be expected of a person carrying out the same functions as are carried out by the member in relation to the LLP, and (b) the general knowledge, skill and experience that that member actually has.[25] The same considerations that apply in relation to s 214[26] will apply to the knowledge of members in respect of s 214A.

29.10   An application can only be made by a liquidator. If a member is found liable, the court may order the member to make such contribution (if any) to the LLP's assets as the court thinks proper.[27] The court cannot, however, make a declaration in relation to any person the amount of which exceeds the aggregate of the amounts or values of all the withdrawals referred to in s 214A(2) made by that person within the period of 2 years referred to in that subsection.[28]

---

[21]   IA 1986, s 214A(2)(a).
[22]   Ibid, s 214A(2)(b).
[23]   Ibid, s 214A(5).
[24]   Ibid, s 214A(7).
[25]   Ibid, s 214A(6).
[26]   See **29.5**.
[27]   IA 1986, s 214A(3).
[28]   Ibid, s 214A(4).

TRANSACTIONS AT AN UNDERVALUE

29.11   An LLP enters into a transaction[29] at an undervalue with a person if it:

(a)   makes a gift to that person or otherwise enters into a transaction on terms that provide for it to receive no consideration; or

(b)   enters into a transaction with that person for a consideration the value of which, in money or money's worth, is significantly less than the value, in money or money's worth, of the consideration provided by the LLP.[30]

29.12   IA 1986, s 238 provides that where the LLP has, at a relevant time,[31] entered into a transaction at an undervalue, and it has subsequently had an administration order made, or has gone into liquidation, the administrator or liquidator may apply to the court for an order restoring the position to what it would have been if the LLP had not entered into the transaction.[32]

29.13   The court is not entitled to make an order if it is satisfied that:

(a)   the LLP entered into the transaction in good faith and for the purpose of carrying on its business; and

(b)   at the time there were reasonable grounds for believing that the transaction would benefit the LLP.[33]

29.14   A transaction is entered into at a 'relevant time' if:

(a)   it is entered into in the period of 2 years ending with the onset of insolvency (or in the case of an administration during the period between the presentation of the administration petition and the making of the order);[34] and

(b)   at the time the LLP enters into the transaction it is unable to pay its debts within the meaning of IA 1986, s 123 or becomes unable to pay its debts in consequence of the transaction.[35]

---

[29]   'Transaction' includes a gift, agreement or arrangement; IA 1986, s 436. See *Re Taylor Sinclair (Capital) Ltd* [2001] 2 BCLC 176.

[30]   IA 1986, s 238(4). See *Re M C Bacon Ltd* [1990] BCC 78, *Philips v Brewin Dolphin Bell Lawrie* [1998] 1 BCLC 7000, *Re Lewis's of Leicester Limited* [1995] BCC 514, *Re Barton Manufacturing Co Ltd* [1998] BCC 827, *Re Shapland Inc* [2000] BCC 106, *Re Mistral Finance Ltd* [2001] BCC 27 and *Re Thoars (decd)* [2003] 1 BCLC 499.

[31]   See **29.14**.

[32]   IA 1986, s 238(1) and (3).

[33]   Ibid, s 238(5).

[34]   Ibid, s 240(1). The onset of insolvency is defined in s 240(3). If the LLP is in administration or has gone into liquidation immediately upon the discharge of an administration order, the onset of insolvency is the date of the presentation of the administration petition. If the LLP went into liquidation at any other time, the onset of insolvency is the date of the commencement of the winding up.

[35]   IA 1986, s 240(2). The requirements of s 240(2) are presumed to be satisfied, unless the contrary is shown, in relation to any transaction at an undervalue which is entered into with a person connected

29.15   If the provisions of ss 238 and 240 are satisfied, the court is to make such order as it thinks fit for restoring the position to what it would have been if the LLP had not entered into that transaction.[36] The court has a broad discretion to determine what order is to be made to restore the position.[37]

29.16   The limitation period for an application to set aside a transaction at an undervalue (or to set aside a preference) is 12 years (the application being an action on a speciality). The period is, however, 6 years if the application is to recover compensation rather than to set aside the transaction.[38]

PREFERENCES

29.17   An LLP gives a preference to a person if:

(a)   that person is one of the LLP's creditors or a surety or a guarantor for any of the LLP's debts or other liabilities; and

(b)   the LLP does anything or suffers anything to be done which (in either case) has the effect of putting that person into a position which, in the event of the LLP going into insolvent liquidation, will be better than the position he would have been in if that thing had not been done.[39]

29.18   IA 1986, s 239 provides that where the LLP has, at a relevant time,[40] given a preference, and it has subsequently had an administration order made, or has gone into liquidation, the administrator or liquidator may apply to the court for an order restoring the position to what it would have been if the LLP had not given the preference.[41] A preference may be given, for example, where the LLP pays a debt owed to one creditor in preference to others, or gives security for an existing debt by creating a fixed or floating charge over its assets, or returns goods delivered but for which payment has not been made.

29.19   The court has no power to make an order in respect of a preference unless the LLP was influenced in deciding to give the preference by a desire to put the creditor in a better position, in the event of the LLP going into insolvent liquidation, than the creditor would have been in had the preference not been

---

to the LLP. For the definition of 'connected person' see ss 249 and 435. Section 240(2) does not apply where the transaction is entered into after the presentation of an administration petition.

36   IA 1986, s 238(3).

37   Ibid, s 241. It would appear that, even if the provisions of ss 238 and 240 are satisfied, the court has a discretion whether or not to make any order: see *Re Paramount Airways Ltd (in administration)* [1993] Ch 223. *Quaere* however whether, in the light of the word 'shall' in s 238(3), the discretion should not be properly regarded as limited to the nature of the order, and as not extending to whether an order should be made at all. See, in relation to the costs of an application under s 238 or 239, *Lewis v IRC* [2001] 3 All ER 499, reversed by IR 1986 r 4.218 as amended by SI 2002/2712.

38   Limitation Act 1980, ss 8, 9; *Priory Garage (Walthamstow) Ltd* [2001] BPIR 144.

39   IA 1986, s 239(4). *Re Thirty-Eight Building Ltd* [1999] BCC 260; *Re Mistral Finance Ltd* [2001] BCC 27.

40   See **29.22**.

41   IA 1986, s 239(1)–(3).

given.[42] This imports a subjective test. A preference will not be set aside unless the LLP positively wished to improve the creditor's position in the event of insolvent liquidation. An LLP can, therefore, act in a way that improves a creditor's position so long as it is motivated by commercial considerations and not by a desire to prefer the creditor. For example, in order to secure the continued provision of necessary supplies from a creditor, the LLP may be forced to pay existing debts or provide security for such debts. The fact that such action inevitably prefers that creditor (and therefore the LLP 'intends' to prefer the creditor) is irrelevant.[43]

29.20　　Where an LLP has given a preference to a person connected with it (otherwise than by reason of that person being its employee) at the time that the preference was given, it is presumed, unless the contrary is shown, that the LLP was influenced by a desire to prefer.[44]

29.21　　The fact that something is done in pursuance of a court order does not, without more, prevent it from constituting a preference.[45]

29.22　　A preference is given at a 'relevant time' if it is given:

(a)　　at a time in the period of 6 months ending with the onset of insolvency or, if the preference is given to a person connected with the LLP (otherwise than by reason only of being its employee), at a time in the period of 2 years ending with the onset of insolvency or, in the case of an administration, during the period between the presentation of the administration petition and the making of the order;[46] and

(b)　　at the time the LLP gave the preference it is unable to pay its debts within the meaning of IA 1986, s 123 or becomes unable to pay its debts in consequence of the preference.[47]

29.23　　If the provisions of ss 239 and 240 are satisfied, the court shall make such order as it thinks fit for restoring the position to what it would have been if the LLP had not entered into that transaction.[48] The court has a broad discretion to determine what order is to be made to restore the position.[49]

---

[42]　IA 1986, s 239(5).

[43]　*Re M C Bacon Ltd* [1990] BCC 78 at 87.

[44]　IA 1986, s 239(6). *Re Shapland Inc* [2000] BCC 106. For the definition of 'connected person', see IA 1986, ss 249 and 435.

[45]　Ibid, s 239(7).

[46]　Ibid, s 240(1). The onset of insolvency is defined in s 240(3). If the LLP is in administration or has gone into liquidation immediately upon the discharge of an administration order, the onset of insolvency is the date of the presentation of the administration petition. If the LLP went into liquidation at any other time, the onset of insolvency is the date of the commencement of the winding up.

[47]　IA 1986, s 240(2). Section 240(2) does not apply where the preference is given after the presentation of an administration petition.

[48]　IA 1986, s 239(3).

[49]　Ibid, s 241. And see footnote 37 above.

EXTORTIONATE CREDIT TRANSACTIONS

29.24   Where the LLP has been party to a transaction for, or involving, the provision of credit to the LLP, and it has subsequently had an administration order made, or has gone into liquidation, the court may, on an application by the administrator or liquidator, make an order in respect of the transaction if the transaction is or was extortionate and was entered into in the period of 3 years ending with the day on which the administration order was made or the LLP went into liquidation.[50]

29.25   A transaction is extortionate if, having regard to the risk accepted by the person providing the credit:

(a)   the terms of it are or were such as to require grossly exorbitant payments to be made (whether conditionally or in certain contingencies) in respect of the provision of credit; or

(b)   it otherwise grossly contravened ordinary principles of fair dealing.[51]

It is presumed, unless the contrary is shown, that a transaction with respect to which an application is made by the administrator or liquidator is (or was) extortionate.[52]

29.26   The court may (concurrently with its powers in respect of transactions at an undervalue[53]) make an order:

(a)   setting aside the whole or part of any obligation created by the transaction;

(b)   varying the terms of the transaction or varying the terms on which any security for the purposes of the transaction is held;

(c)   requiring any party to the transaction to pay to the administrator or liquidator any sums paid to that party, by virtue of the transaction, by the LLP;

(d)   directing accounts to be taken between any persons.[54]

AVOIDANCE OF FLOATING CHARGES

29.27   Under IA 1986, s 245, where an LLP grants a floating charge[55] on its undertaking or property at a relevant time,[56] and the LLP subsequently has an administration order made, or goes into liquidation, the charge is invalid except to the extent of the aggregate of:

---

[50]   IA 1986, s 244.

[51]   Ibid, s 244(3).

[52]   Ibid, s 244(3).

[53]   Ibid, s 244(5). As to transactions at an undervalue, see **29.11–29.16**.

[54]   Ibid, s 244(4).

[55]   'Floating charge' includes a charge which was originally created as a floating charge but which has become a fixed charge: IA 1986, s 251.

[56]   See **29.28**.

(a)   the value of so much of the consideration for the creation of the charge as consists of money paid, or goods or services supplied, to the LLP at the same time as, or after, the creation of the charge;

(b)   the value of so much of the consideration as consists of the discharge or reduction, at the same time as, or after, the creation of the charge, of any debt of the LLP; and

(c)   the amount of such interest (if any) as is payable on the amount falling within paragraph (a) or (b) in pursuance of any agreement under which the money was so paid, the goods or services were so supplied or the debt was so discharged or reduced.[57]

29.28   For the purposes of s 245, the time at which a floating charge is created is a relevant time:

(a)   in the case of a charge created in favour of a person who is connected with the LLP, in the period of 2 years ending with the onset of insolvency; or

(b)   in the case of a charge created in favour of any other person, at a time in the period of 12 months ending with the onset of insolvency; or

(c)   in either case, at a time between the presentation of a petition for the making of an administration order in relation to the LLP and the making of such an order on that petition.[58]

UNENFORCEABILITY OF LIENS

29.29   Where an LLP has gone into administration or liquidation, or a provisional liquidator has been appointed, a lien is unenforceable to the extent that its enforcement would deny possession of any books, papers or other records to the administrator or liquidator or provisional liquidator (as the case may be).[59] This does not apply to a lien on documents which give a title to property and are held as such.[60]

---

[57]   IA 1986, s 245(2). The value of any goods or services supplied by way of consideration for a floating charge is the amount in money which at the time they were supplied could reasonably have been expected to be obtained for supplying the goods or services in the ordinary course of business and on the same terms (apart from consideration) as those on which they were supplied to the LLP: IA 1986, s 245(6).

[58]   IA 1986, s 245(3). Where the LLP creates a floating charge in favour of a person who is not connected with the LLP, the time is not a relevant time unless the LLP is at that time unable to pay its debts within the meaning of IA 1986, s 123 or becomes unable in consequence of the transaction under which the charge is created; IA 1986, s 245(4). The onset of insolvency is, in the case of an LLP in administration, the date of the presentation of the petition on which the order was made and, in the case of an LLP in liquidation, the date of the commencement of the winding up: IA 1986, s 245(5).

[59]   IA 1986, s 246.

[60]   Ibid, s 246(3). See *Re SEIL Trade Finance Ltd* [1992] BCC 538.

TRANSACTIONS DEFRAUDING CREDITORS

29.30   Under IA 1986, s 423, if an LLP enters into a transaction with another at
an undervalue, and has done so for the purpose either of putting assets beyond the
reach of a person who is making or may at some time make a claim against it, or of
otherwise prejudicing the interests of such a person in relation to the claim which
he is making or may make, the court may make such order as it thinks fit for
restoring the position to what it would have been if the transaction had not been
entered into and for protecting the interests of those who are victims of the
transaction. This provision is similar to IA 1986, s 238.[61] The difference is that
s 423 does not impose a time limit in relation to the date of the transaction,[62] and
the LLP need not have gone into administration or liquidation. However, an
application can only succeed under s 423 if the transaction is entered into for the
purpose of putting assets beyond the reach of creditors or otherwise prejudicing the
rights of creditors.[63] This purpose must be a substantial, but need not be the
dominant, purpose.[64]

29.31   An LLP enters into a transaction at an undervalue if:

(i)   it makes a gift to the other person or otherwise enters into a transaction with
         the other on terms that provide for it to receive no consideration;
(ii)   it enters into a transaction with the other for a consideration the value of
         which, in money or money's worth, is significantly less than the value, in
         money or money's worth, of the consideration provided by the LLP.[65]

29.32   An application can be made whether or not the LLP is insolvent, and
whether or not it is in administration or being wound up. If the LLP is in the
process of being wound up, or an administration order is in force in relation to it,
the application is usually made by the liquidator or the administrator.[66] A victim of
the transaction (ie a person who is, or is capable of being, prejudiced by it[67]) can
only make an application with the permission of the court.[68] If a victim of the
transaction is bound by a voluntary arrangement approved under Part I of the IA
1986, the application can be made by the supervisor or by any person who is a
victim whether or not he is bound.[69] In all other situations the application is made
by a victim of the transaction.[70] An application is made on behalf of all the
victims.[71]

---

[61]   See **29.11–29.16**.
[62]   But see *The Law Society v Southall* [2002] BPIR 336.
[63]   IA 1986 s 423(3).
[64]   *Hashmi v IRC* [2002] BCC 943; *Kubiangha v Ekpenyong* [2002] 2 BCLC 597.
[65]   IA 1986, s 423(1).
[66]   Ibid, s 424(1)(a).
[67]   Ibid, s 423(5)
[68]   Ibid, s 424(1)(a).
[69]   Ibid, s 424(1)(b).
[70]   Ibid, s 424(1)(c).
[71]   Ibid, s 424(2).

RE-USE OF LLP NAMES

29.33   IA 1986, s 216 is designed to prevent aspects of the so called 'Phoenix' syndrome, in which those responsible for a failed company buy the assets from the administrator or liquidator at a knock-down price, and then restart the business through the medium of a company using or trading under the name of the failed company.

29.34   Section 216 applies to any person who was, within the 12 months prior to the LLP going into insolvent liquidation, a member or shadow member of the LLP.[72] For the purposes of s 216, a name is prohibited in relation to such a person if:

(a)   it is a name by which the liquidating LLP was known at any time in that period of 12 months; or

(b)   it is a name which is so similar to a name falling within (a) as to suggest an association with that LLP.[73]

29.35   Section 216(3) imposes the prohibition, but it is not entirely clear how it has been modified to apply to LLPs. This has significance in relation to the scope of the civil liability of a person acting contrary to s 216.[74] As it applies to companies, s 216(3) provides that a person to whom it applies shall not, without the leave of the court or in such circumstances as may be prescribed,[75] in the period of 5 years beginning on the day on which the company went into liquidation:

(a)   be a director of any other company that is known by a prohibited name;

(b)   in any way, whether directly or indirectly, be concerned or take part in the promotion, formation or management of any such company;

(c)   in any way, whether directly or indirectly, be concerned or take part in the carrying on of a business carried on (otherwise than by a company) under a prohibited name.

29.36   As section 216(3) applies to companies, (a) and (b) above apply only to impose restrictions in relation to companies. Section 216(3)(c) prevents a person who was a director or shadow director of a company which went into insolvent liquidation from being concerned or taking part in the carrying on of a business in another form, ie as a sole trader or in a partnership. The distinction between (a) and (b) on the one hand and (c) on the other hand is important, because civil liability is only imposed under s 217 in respect of persons acting in contravention of s 216 through the medium of a company. Sections 216 and 217 have not been specifically modified to apply to LLPs, but apply with the general modifications

[72]   IA 1986, s 216(1). An LLP goes into insolvent liquidation for the purpose of s 216 if it goes into liquidation at a time when its assets are insufficient for the payment of its debts and other liabilities and the expenses of winding up: s 216(7).

[73]   IA 1986, s 216(2). References to a name by which an LLP is known are to the name of the LLP at that time or to any name under which the LLP carries on business at that time: s 216(6).

[74]   Civil liability is imposed by IA 1986, s 217.

[75]   IR 1986, rr 4.226–4.230.

set out in reg 5(2) of the LLP Regulations 2001. By reg 5(2)(a), references to a company shall include references to an LLP. In most cases, this necessitates a simple transposition of 'LLP' for 'company'. The question here, however, is whether in ss 216(3) and 217 references to a 'company' ought to be read as references to a company or an LLP. In our view, references to a 'company' ought to be read in this way, with the result that, in (a) and (b) above as applying to a person who was a member or shadow member of an LLP, 'company' should be read as 'company and/or LLP'. Whilst the purpose of the word 'include' in reg 5 is less clear than it might be, it seems to have been intended that, where appropriate, references to a company ought to be read as references to a company and/or LLP. Had the intention been otherwise, no purpose would have been served by the use of the word 'include'. The mischief behind ss 216 and 217 is the misuse of limited liability. Where s 217 applies, the wrongdoer becomes jointly and severally liable for relevant debts. In other words, so far as it applies to companies, personal liability is imposed on the wrongdoer in circumstances in which he would otherwise be able to shelter behind a corporate veil. Prior to the introduction of LLPs, other widely used business entities (which are caught by s 216(3)(c)) did not provide the same limited liability. Now that there are two forms of body corporate providing limited liability, there is no reason why civil liability under s 217 should not apply whether the new entity is a company or an LLP.[76]

29.37   If a person acts in contravention of s 216, he is liable to imprisonment or a fine, or both.[77]

29.38   The court has power to permit use of a name that would otherwise result in a person acting in contravention of s 216.[78] For example, a court may grant permission if the insolvency was not caused by blameworthy conduct on the part of the member.[79] Further, the Insolvency Rules provide for three cases in which s 216(3) does not apply, as follows:

(a)   where a successor LLP or company acquires the whole or substantially the whole of the business of an insolvent LLP under arrangements made by an insolvency practitioner acting as liquidator, administrator or administrative receiver, or as supervisor of a voluntary arrangement, and notice is given to the creditors of the insolvent LLP that the successor LLP or company has assumed, or will assume, a prohibited name (naming a person to whom

---

[76]   However, the modifications to the IA 1986 only apply to LLPs: LLP Regulations 2001, reg 5(1) provides that 'the…provisions of the 1986 Act shall apply in relation to limited liability partnerships as they apply in relation to companies…'. The modifications do not effect general amendments to the IA 1986. As a result, if the original entity which went into insolvent liquidation was a company, references in ss 216(3) and 217 will remain simply to companies with the result that if person subsequently uses a prohibited name in relation to an LLP he will act in contravention of s 216(3)(c) (and thereby commit an offence) but he will not be subject to civil liability under s 217.
[77]   IA 1986, s 216(4).
[78]   Ibid, s 216(3) and IR 1986, rr 4.226–4.230.
[79]   See *Re Bonus Breaks Ltd* [1991] BCC 546, *Penrose v Official Receiver* [1996] 1 WLR 482 and *Re Lighting Electrical Contractors Ltd* [1996] BCC 950.

s 216 applies as having been a member or shadow member of the insolvent LLP);[80]

(b)   where a person applies for leave, he may act contrary to s 216(3) during the period commencing on the day the LLP goes into liquidation and ending on the day falling 6 weeks after that date or on the day on which the court disposes of the application, whichever occurs first;[81] and

(c)   where the successor LLP or company has been known by the name for the whole of the period of 12 months ending on the day the liquidating LLP went into liquidation and has not been dormant at any time in those 12 months within the meaning of s 225 of the CA 1985.[82]

29.39   A person is personally responsible for all the debts[83] of an LLP or company if, at any time, he is involved in the management of the LLP or company in contravention of s 216 or, as a person who is involved in the management[84] of the LLP or company, he acts or is willing to act on instructions given (without the leave of the court) by a person whom he knows at that time to be in contravention of s 216 in relation to the LLP or company.[85] A person personally responsible for debts under s 217 is jointly and severally liable with the LLP or company and any other person who is liable.[86]

---

[80]   IR 1986, r 4.227.

[81]   Ibid, r 4.229.

[82]   Ibid, r 4.230.

[83]   As defined in IA 1986, s 217(3).

[84]   As defined in IA 1986, s 217(4).

[85]   IA 1986 s 217(1) and (5). See *Archer Structures Ltd v Griffiths* [2004] 1 BCLC 201 and *Ricketts v Ad Valorem Factors Ltd* [2004] 1 BCLC 1.

[86]   IA 1986, s 217(2).

Chapter 30

COMPLETION OF THE WINDING UP AND DISSOLUTION

INTRODUCTION

30.1   After completion of the liquidation process, the LLP is dissolved. The dissolution marks the end of the LLP's legal personality.

VOLUNTARY WINDING UP

30.2   In a voluntary winding up, as soon as the LLP's affairs are fully wound up, the liquidator prepares an account of the winding up, showing how it has been conducted and how the LLP's property has been disposed of.[1] Once his account has been prepared, the liquidator calls a meeting of the members and a meeting of the creditors (in the case of a creditors' voluntary liquidation) of the LLP for the purpose of laying the account before the meeting(s), and giving an explanation of it.[2] Within one week after the meeting(s), the liquidator is to send to the Registrar of Companies a copy of the account, and make a return to him of the holding of the meeting(s) and of their dates.[3] If the meeting(s) is (are) not quorate, the liquidator makes a return that the meeting(s) was (were) summoned but was (were) not quorate.[4] The quorum for a meeting of the members of an LLP is the quorum required by the LLP agreement or, if no quorum has been agreed, two members.[5] Once the Registrar has received the liquidator's account and return he registers them and, on the expiration of 3 months from the date of registration, the LLP is deemed dissolved.[6] The court may, on the application of the liquidator or any other interested person, make an order deferring the date of dissolution.[7] It is the duty of the person on whose application an order of the court is made within 7 days to deliver to the Registrar an office copy of the order for registration.[8]

---

[1]   IA 1986, s 94(1) (members' voluntary); IA 1986, s 106(1) (creditors' voluntary).
[2]   IA 1986, s 94(1) (members); IA 1986, s 106(1) (creditors). The meeting(s) are to be called by advertisement in the *Gazette*, specifying its (their) time, place and object and published at least one month before the meeting; s 94(2) (members), s 106(2) (creditors).
[3]   IA 1986, s 94(3) (members), s 106(3) (creditors).
[4]   IA 1986, s 94(5) (members); s 106(5) (creditors).
[5]   IA 1986, s 92(4); s 94(5A); s 106(5A).
[6]   Ibid, s 201(2).
[7]   Ibid, s 201(3).
[8]   Ibid, s 201(4).

COMPULSORY LIQUIDATION

30.3 In a compulsory liquidation, if it appears to the liquidator that the winding up is for practical purposes complete (and the liquidator is not the official receiver), the liquidator summons a final general meeting of the LLP's creditors for the purpose of receiving the liquidator's report of the winding up and determining whether the liquidator should have his release.[9] Where the final meeting has been held the liquidator vacates office as soon as he has given notice to the court and the Registrar that the meeting has been held and of the decisions (if any) of the meeting.[10] Once this notice has been served, or a notice has been given by the official receiver that the winding up by the court is complete, the Registrar registers the notice and, on the expiration of 3 months from the date of registration, the LLP is dissolved.[11] The Secretary of State may, on the application of the official receiver or any other interested person, give a direction deferring the date at which the dissolution of the LLP is to take effect for such period as the Secretary of State thinks fit.[12]

30.4 The official receiver may, if he is liquidator, and it appears to him that the realisable assets of the LLP are insufficient to cover the expenses of the winding up and that the affairs of the LLP do not require any further investigation, apply to the Registrar for the early dissolution of the LLP.[13] Before doing so, however, the official receiver must give 28 days' notice to the LLP's creditors and contributories and, if there is an administrative receiver, to the receiver.[14] Once he has given this notice to the creditors and the contributories, the official receiver ceases (subject to any directions under s 203) to be required to perform any duties imposed on him in relation to the LLP, its creditors or contributories by virtue of any provision of the IA 1986, apart from a duty to make an application for early dissolution as mentioned above.[15] On the receipt of the official receiver's application, the Registrar registers it and, on the expiration of 3 months from the date of registration, the LLP is dissolved.[16] If 28 days' notice is given, the official receiver or any creditor or contributory of the LLP, or (if there is one) the administrative

---

9   IA 1986, s 146(1). Release of the liquidator in a compulsory winding up is governed by IA 1986, ss 172(8) and 174. The liquidator may summon the final general meeting at the same time as giving notice of any final distribution of the company's property but, if summoned for an earlier date, that meeting shall be adjourned (and, if necessary, further adjourned) until a date on which the liquidator is able to report to the meeting that the winding up of the LLP is for practical purposes complete: s 146(2). In the carrying out of his functions in the winding up, it is the duty of the liquidator to retain sufficient sums from the LLP's property to cover the expenses of summoning and holding the final meeting: IA 1986, s 146(3).

10   IA 1986, s 172(8).

11   Ibid, s 205(1) and (2).

12   Ibid, s 205(3). An appeal to the court lies from any decision of the Secretary of State on an application for such a direction; IA 1986, s 205(4). It is the duty of the person on whose application a direction is given or in whose favour an appeal with respect to an application for such a direction is determined within 7 days after the giving of the direction or the determination of the appeal to deliver to the Registrar for registration a copy of the direction or determination as is prescribed; s 205(5).

13   IA 1986, s 202(2).

14   Ibid, s 202(3).

15   Ibid, s 202(4).

16   Ibid, s 202(5).

receiver, may apply to the Secretary of State for directions[17] on the ground that the realisable assets of the LLP are sufficient to cover the expenses of the winding up, or that the affairs of the LLP do require further investigation, or that for any other reason the early dissolution of the LLP is inappropriate.[18] The Secretary of State may give directions making provision for the winding up of the LLP to proceed as if no 28 days' notice had been given, or deferring the date on which the dissolution of the LLP is to take effect for such period as he thinks fit.[19]

RESULTS OF DISSOLUTION

30.5   Upon dissolution, any property still vested in the LLP (other than as trustee) or held on trust for the LLP vests in the Crown bona vacantia.[20] The Crown has power to disclaim property so vesting.[21] If the Crown does disclaim such property, the property is deemed not to have vested in the Crown[22] and s 178(4) and ss 179–182 of the IA 1986 apply as if the property had been disclaimed by the liquidator.[23] The court's power to declare a dissolution void is discussed in chapter 20.[24]

---

[17]   IA 1986, s 203(1).

[18]   Ibid, s 203(2).

[19]   Ibid, s 203(3). An appeal to the court lies from any decision of the Secretary of State on an application for directions under s 203; IA 1986, s 203(4). It is the duty of the person on whose application any directions are given under this section, or in whose favour an appeal with respect to an application for such directions is determined, within 7 days after the giving of the directions or the determination of the appeal, to deliver to the Registrar for registration such a copy of the directions or determination as is prescribed; IA 1986, s 203(5).

[20]   CA 1985, s 654.

[21]   Ibid, s 656.

[22]   Ibid, s 657(1).

[23]   Ibid, s 657(2). See **28.6–28.8**.

[24]   See CA 1985, ss 651–658, especially s 655 which makes provision for the consequence of the LLP's revival after dissolution.

Chapter 31

ARRANGEMENTS AND RECONSTRUCTIONS

INTRODUCTION

31.1 The CA 1985 and the IA 1986 include provisions that enable companies to enter into arrangements and reconstructions with their members and creditors.[1] Compliance with the statutory procedures binds a dissentient member or creditor, enabling a company to put a scheme into effect which, although supported by a substantial majority of the members or creditors, does not command unanimity. The LLP legislation applies these provisions to LLPs.

COMPANIES ACT 1985, SECTION 425

31.2 Section 425 of the CA 1985 lays down a procedure for effecting a compromise or arrangement between an LLP and its creditors or a class of creditors and members or a class of members.[2] The s 425 procedure permits a number of different kinds of scheme. Section 425 schemes may be used by a *company* to effect an internal reorganisation of its share structure, to effect a composition agreement or scheme of arrangement with creditors[3] or to effect a merger with another company. In relation to mergers, a scheme may provide for the business, assets and liabilities of one company to be transferred to another.

31.3   Given the absence of a share structure, the scope for the application of s 425 to the internal organisation of an LLP is likely to be limited, but there is no reason why it should not be used to facilitate mergers. In practice, however, s 425 is unlikely to be of much significance save where the purpose is to bind dissentient creditors. It has been held in relation to companies that a court has no jurisdiction to sanction an arrangement that does not have the approval of the company either by a board resolution or, if appropriate, by resolution of the members in general meeting.[4] The same principle is likely to apply to LLPs. The process by which the LLP determines whether to approve a proposal will be determined by the LLP agreement. In default of agreement, the decision is likely to have to be made by a unanimous resolution of the members.[5] If the purpose of the proposed arrangement

---

[1]   See particularly CA 1985, s 425 and IA 1986, s 110. See *Palmer's Company Law*, chapter 12. Voluntary arrangements under Part I of the IA 1986 are discussed in Chapter 23.

[2]   See generally, *Palmer's Company Law* paras 12.001–12.014 and 12.026–12.034. For an analysis of the s 425 procedure, see *Palmer*, op cit, paras 12.015–12.020 and 12.026–12.034.

[3]   In this regard, see IA 1986, Part I and s 14. See *Lucio Pena v Coyne* 23 July 2004 where the court approved proposals in circumstances in which there had been a transaction at an undervalue pursuant to IA 1986, s 423.

[4]   *Re Savoy Hotel Ltd* [1981] 3 All ER 646; *Palmer*, op cit, para 12.014.

[5]   LLP Regulations 2001, reg 7(6) – default rule (6) – is not likely to be applicable.

is to bind dissentient members, a need to secure the unanimous approval of the arrangement on behalf of the LLP will be fatal. If, on the other hand, the LLP agreement includes an applicable majority voting provision, the proposed arrangement is likely to be capable of being put into effect pursuant to the terms of the LLP agreement without the need for court sanction.

INSOLVENCY ACT 1986, SECTION 110

31.4   The purpose of s 110 of the IA 1986 is to enable a liquidator of an LLP to transfer the assets of the LLP to a new LLP or company in exchange for shares or other interests in the new entity. Section 110 applies where an LLP (known as 'the transferor LLP') is proposed to be, or is being, wound up voluntarily.[6] Section 110 can be invoked where it is proposed that the whole or part of the LLP's business or property should be transferred or sold to another company (whether or not it is a company within the meaning of the CA 1985) (known as 'the transferee company') or to an LLP (known as 'the transferee LLP').

31.5   With the requisite sanction, the liquidator of the transferor LLP may:

(a)   receive, in compensation or part compensation for the transfer or sale, shares, policies or other like interests in the transferee company or LLP for distribution among the members of the transferor LLP;[7] or

(b)   enter into any other arrangement whereby the members of the transferor LLP may, in lieu of receiving cash, shares, policies or other like interests (or in addition thereto), participate in the profits, or receive any other benefit from the transferee company or LLP.[8]

31.6   The requisite sanction is, in the case of a members' voluntary winding up, a determination by the LLP at a meeting of the members conferring either a general authority on the liquidator or an authority in respect of any particular arrangement[9] and, in the case of a creditors' voluntary winding up, that of either the court or the liquidation committee.[10] The process by which the LLP determines whether to confer authority on the liquidator will be determined by the LLP agreement. In default of agreement, the decision is likely to have to be made by a unanimous resolution of the members.[11]

31.7   A sale or arrangement made in pursuance of s 110 is binding on all the members of the LLP.[12] A determination by the LLP is not invalid by reason that it is made before or concurrently with a determination by the LLP that it be wound up voluntarily or for appointing a liquidator; but, if an order is made within a year

---

[6]   Note also that IA 1986, s 110 as it applies to companies is amended generally by para 15 of LLP Regulations 2001, sch 5.
[7]   IA 1986, s 110(2).
[8]   Ibid, s 110(4).
[9]   The LLP agreement and quorum requirements of IA 1986, s 92(3) and (4) apply for this purpose.
[10]   IA 1986, s 110(3).
[11]   LLP Regulations 2001, reg 7(6) (default rule (6)) is not likely to be applicable.
[12]   IA 1986, s 110(5).

for winding up the LLP by the court, the determination by the LLP is not valid unless sanctioned by the court.[13]

31.8   A member who votes against the proposal, and expresses his dissent from it in writing addressed to the liquidator within 7 days after the date on which the sanction was given, may require the liquidator either to abstain from carrying the arrangement into effect or to purchase his interest at a price to be determined by agreement or arbitration.[14] If the liquidator elects to purchase the member's interest, the purchase money must be paid before the LLP is dissolved and must be raised by the liquidator in such manner as may be determined by the LLP.[15]

---

[13]   IA 1986, s 110(6).
[14]   Ibid, s 111(2).
[15]   Ibid, s 111(3).

Chapter 32

DISQUALIFICATION

THE LEGISLATION AND THE SCOPE OF A DISQUALIFICATION ORDER

32.1 The CDDA 1986 is applied to LLPs by the LLP Regulations 2001.[1] The CDDA 1986 empowers the court, in a number of circumstances, to make a disqualification order and, in two circumstances, requires the court to make such an order. A person who is subject to a disqualification order (made pursuant to the CDDA 1986, as applied by the LLP Regulations 2001 to LLPs) must not:

(a)   be a member of an LLP or a director of a company, act as receiver of an LLP's or a company's property or in any way, whether directly or indirectly, be concerned or take part in the promotion, formation or management of an LLP or a company unless (in each case) he has the leave of the court; and

(b)   act as an insolvency practitioner,

for a specified period.[2] As a result of the amendments made by IA 2000, s 6, the Secretary of State now has power to accept a disqualification undertaking rather than make or proceed with a disqualification application.[3] The terms of the undertaking are that the person giving the undertaking will not be a member of an LLP or a director of a company, act as receiver of an LLP's or a company's property or in any way, whether directly or indirectly, be concerned or take part in the promotion, formation or management of an LLP or a company unless (in each case) he has the leave of a court, and will not act as an insolvency practitioner.[4] The Secretary of State has power to accept an undertaking if the conditions in CDDA 1986, s 6(1) are satisfied and it appears to him that it is expedient in the public interest that he should do so (instead of applying, or proceeding with an

---

[1]   LLP Regulations 2001, reg 4(2) and Part II of Sch 2. CDDA 1986 has been amended by IA 2000, ss 5–8 and Sch 4. Sections 5 and 6 and Sch 4 as amended were brought into force for companies on 2 April 2001 by the Insolvency Act 2000 (Commencement No 1 and Transitional Provisions) Order 2001, SI 2001/766. The CDDA 1986 has also been amended by the Enterprise Act 2002, s 204. Specific commencement orders and regulations have not been made in relation to LLPs. The authors' view is that the amendments (other than those relating to the changes to the company administration regime, which have been expressly disapplied) apply automatically to LLPs: see **1.14–1.15**.

[2]   CDDA 1986, s 1(1). See CDDA 1986, s 22(10) in relation to acting as a receiver.

[3]   CDDA 1986, ss 1A, 7(2A), 8(2A), 8A, 9(1A). See *Secretary of State for Trade and Industry v Davies* [2002] 2 BCLC 263. The OFT has power to accept a disqualification undertaking from a person who is a member of an LLP if the OFT thinks that the LLP has committed a breach of competition law and that the conduct of the person as a member makes him unfit to be concerned in the management of an LLP: CDDA 1986 ss 9A and 9B (inserted by Enterprise Act 2002 s 204(1), (2) with effect from 20 June 2003).

[4]   CDDA 1986, s 1A.

application, for a disqualification order).[5] The conditions in s 6(1) are that the person is or has been a member of an LLP which has at any time become insolvent (whether while he was a member or subsequently) and that his conduct as a member of that LLP (either taken alone or taken together with his conduct as a member of any other LLP or as a director of any company or companies) makes him unfit to be concerned in the management of an LLP or a company.[6]

32.2 It is important to note the distinction between an order made pursuant to the CDDA 1986 itself and an order made pursuant to the CDDA 1986 as applied by the LLP Regulations 2001 to LLPs. Regulation 4(2) of the LLP Regulations 2001 provides that the provisions of the CDDA 1986 shall apply to LLPs, except where the context otherwise requires, with a number of general modifications including, pursuant to reg 4(2)(a), that references to a company shall include references to an LLP. The Regulations do not, therefore, purport to effect general amendments to the Act. So far as the CDDA 1986 (as applied to LLPs by the LLP Regulations) is concerned, the reference in s 1(1) of the Act to a company will, presumably, be read in the light of the general modifications, as a reference to an LLP or a company, with the result that (as set out in **32.1**) a person who is subject to a disqualification order as a result of his involvement with an LLP will not be able to be a director of a company or be concerned or take part in the promotion, formation or management of a company as well as an LLP. If, however, a disqualification order is made against a person (by reason of his involvement with a *company*) pursuant to the CDDA 1986 itself, the person against whom the order is made is not, it seems, disqualified from acting in respect of an LLP.[7]

32.3 As set out in **32.1**, a disqualification order made under the CDDA 1986 (as applied by the LLP Regulations 2001 to LLPs) will operate to prevent the person against whom the order is made not only from being a member of an LLP, but also from being a director of a company or being involved in the promotion, formation or management of an LLP or a company. 'Management' connotes an element of decision-making affecting the corporate enterprise as a whole, ie activities involving policy and decision-making related to the affairs of a corporation where the formation of those policies or the making of those decisions may have some significant bearing on the financial standing of the corporation or the conduct of its

---

[5]   CDDA 1986, s 7(2A). See also s 8(2A).
[6]   See **32.5–32.10**.
[7]   The application of the CDDA 1986 to insolvent partnerships (pursuant to the Insolvent Partnerships Order 1994, SI 1994/2421, as amended by the Insolvent Partnerships (Amendment) Order 2001, SI 2001/767) operates in a slightly different way. A disqualification order made against a person by reason of his involvement with an insolvent partnership operates so as to prevent him from being a director of a company or from being involved in the management, etc of a company. It does *not* operate so as to prevent such a person from being a partner in another firm or from being involved in the management, etc of a firm; see Mithani *Directors' Disqualification*, 2nd edn, paras V25–41. The view expressed in Blackett-Ord *Partnership* (Butterworths Tolley, 2nd edn, 2002) para 3.28 that a disqualification order made in respect of conduct as a company director or in respect of conduct as a partner prohibits, in both cases, that person from being a partner in a firm is, the authors consider, wrong.

affairs.[8] That said, management does not require involvement in the 'ultimate control' of the company. Consequently, it is very difficult, in any given case, to draw the line between management and administration. This is particularly so, given that s 1(1) includes the words 'be concerned' as well as 'take part' in management. These considerations are likely to apply in an LLP context.

32.4 One particular issue that may arise is the effect of a disqualification order on a professional. Subject to the grant of leave pursuant to s 17 (which is discussed further below), a disqualified professional will not be able to be a member of an LLP, although he could be a partner in a partnership. Employment of a person as a solicitor or accountant by an LLP will not necessarily involve participation in the management of the LLP within the meaning of s 1(1). Nevertheless, a professional will need to consider extremely carefully the scope of his duties as an employee and whether the carrying out of such duties will result in the breach by him of the order. Where there is any doubt, the professional will not wish to take any risk, given that breach of a disqualification order is a criminal offence[9] and an application for leave to act would be appropriate.

UNFITNESS

32.5 The CDDA 1986 provides for a disqualification order to be made in a number of different circumstances, the most important of which is (pursuant to s 6) that the person has been a member of an insolvent LLP and his conduct as a member makes him unfit to be concerned in the management of an LLP or a company.[10]

32.6 The court is obliged to make a disqualification order against a person in any case where, on an application under s 6, it is satisfied that he is or has been a member of an LLP which has at any time become insolvent (whether while he was a member or subsequently) and that his conduct as a member of that LLP (either taken alone or taken together with his conduct as a member of any other LLP or as a director of any company or companies) makes him unfit to be concerned in the management of an LLP or a company.

32.7 For the purposes of s 6, an LLP or company becomes insolvent if:

(a)   it goes into liquidation at a time when its assets are insufficient for the payment of its debts and other liabilities and the expenses of the winding up;

---

[8]   See *Re Market Wizard Systems (UK) Ltd* [1998] 2 BCLC 282; *CCA v Bracht* (1989) 7 ACLC 40; *Re a Company* [1980] 1 Ch 138; *R v Campbell* [1984] BCLC 83 and *Re Clasper Group Services* (1988) 4 BCC 673; Mithani, op cit, paras V64–66.

[9]   CDDA 1986, s 13. The offence is one of strict liability: a belief that the relevant conduct did not breach the order is irrelevant: *R v Brockley* [1994] 1 BCLC 606. A breach will also make the professional responsible, jointly and severally with the LLP, for the debts and other liabilities of the LLP incurred at a time when he is involved in the management of the LLP; see CDDA 1986, s 15.

[10]   See, in relation to the right of the official receiver to make an application under IA 1986 s 236 to obtain information for the purposes of instituting disqualification proceedings, *Re Pantmaenog Timber Co Ltd* [2004] 1 AC 158.

(b)   an administration order is made in relation to the LLP or company; or

(c)   an administrative receiver of the LLP or company is appointed.[11]

32.8   References to a person's conduct as a member of an LLP or LLPs or as a director of any company or companies include, where that LLP or company or any of those LLPs or companies has become insolvent, that person's conduct in relation to any matter connected with or arising out of the insolvency of that LLP or company.[12]

32.9   It is not entirely clear how s 6 is to be treated as modified for the purpose of its application to LLPs. Regulation 4(2)(a) of the LLP Regulations 2001 provides that references to a company shall include references to an LLP. In relation to companies, a distinction is drawn between the conduct of the director in relation to the 'lead company' (ie the company in respect of which the application is made) which it must be shown has become insolvent, and his conduct in relation to 'collateral companies', which may or may not have become insolvent. In the authors' view, the reference in s 6(1)(a) to 'company' and the reference in s 6(1)(b) to 'that company' (ie to the 'lead company') are modified so that they are to be read solely as references to 'LLP' and 'that LLP' respectively, and the reference in s 6(1)(b) to 'any other company or companies' (ie 'collateral companies') is to be read as 'any other LLP or LLPs or company or companies'. Although reg 4(2) provides for references to a director to include references to a member of an LLP and references to a company to include references to an LLP, the appropriate modification is not 'director or member' or 'company or LLP' where the context requires otherwise. If the reference in s 6(1)(a) to the lead entity (ie the entity which has become insolvent and in respect of which the application is made) is to an 'LLP or company', an application for disqualification could be made pursuant to the CDDA 1986 (as applied to LLPs by the LLP Regulations 2001) even if the entity in respect of which the application is made is a company. This, it is suggested, would be bizarre, and would be to treat the CDDA 1986 as having been amended generally rather than applied to LLPs with modifications.

32.10   If the authors have correctly concluded (in **32.2**) that an order made pursuant to the CDDA 1986 (as applied to LLPs by the LLP Regulations 2001) imposes both LLP and company prohibitions, whereas an order made pursuant to the CDDA 1986 itself only imposes company prohibitions, this point is not merely of academic interest. At the same time, although references to the lead entity are, in our view, to be read as references to an LLP (and not an LLP or company), there would seem no reason why the references in s 6(1)(b) to 'any other company or companies' should not be read as references to 'any other LLP or LLPs or company or companies'.

32.11   In ss 6 and 7, 'the court' means:

(a)   where the LLP in question is being or has been wound up by the court, that court;

---

[11]   CDDA 1986, s 6(2).

[12]   Ibid, s 6(2).

(b)   where the LLP in question is being or has been wound up voluntarily, any court which has or (as the case may be) had jurisdiction to wind it up;

(c)   where neither of the preceding paragraphs applies but an administration order has at any time been made, or an administrative receiver has at any time been appointed, in relation to the LLP in question, any court which has jurisdiction to wind it up.[13]

32.12   In ss 6 and 7, 'member' includes a shadow member.[14] Under s 6, the minimum period of disqualification is 2 years, and the maximum period is 15 years.

32.13   In determining whether a person's conduct as a member or shadow member of a particular LLP or LLPs or as a director or shadow director of any particular company or companies makes him unfit to be concerned in the management of an LLP or company, the court is directed to pay particular regard to the matters set out in Sch 1 to the CDDA 1986. Part I of Sch 1 applies to all the relevant LLPs or companies and Part II applies to those that have become insolvent.[15]

32.14   Part I matters in relation to LLPs are as follows:

(a)   Any misfeasance or breach of any fiduciary or other duty by the member in relation to the LLP.

(b)   Any misapplication or retention by the member of, or any conduct by the member giving rise to an obligation to account for, any money or other property of the LLP.

(c)   The extent of the member's responsibility for the LLP entering into any transaction liable to be set aside under Part XVI of the IA 1986 (provisions against debt avoidance).

(d)   The extent of the member's responsibility for any failure by the LLP to comply with any of the following CA 1985 obligations, namely, keeping of accounting records (ss 221 and 222), register of members (s 288), annual returns (s 363) and charges (ss 399 and 415).

(e)   The extent of the member's responsibility for any failure by the members of the LLP to comply with s 226 or s 227 of the CA 1985 (duty to prepare annual accounts), or s 233 of that Act (approval and signature of accounts).

---

[13]   See CDDA 1986, s 6(3). See Mithani, op cit, paras III 105–123. The entity referred to here is the lead entity such that references to 'company' should, in the authors' view, be read as references to 'LLP'.

[14]   CDDA 1986, s 6(3C). 'Shadow member' means, in relation to an LLP, a person in accordance with whose directions or instructions the members of the LLP are accustomed to act (but so that a person is not deemed a shadow member by reason only that the members act on advice given by him in a professional capacity); CDDA 1986, s 22(5). As to the meaning of 'shadow member', see *Secretary of State for Trade and Industry v Deverell & anor* [2001] Ch 340, esp at para 35 (considering the meaning of 'shadow director').

[15]   Where consideration is being given to the person's conduct in relation to a collateral entity and that entity is a company, references in the Sch 1 matters to 'member' and 'LLP' should be read as 'director' and 'company' respectively. In determining whether to accept a disqualification undertaking, the Secretary of State is to have particular regard to the matters set out in Sch 1: CDDA 1986, s 9(1A).

32.15   Part II matters relating to LLPs are as follows:

(a)   The extent of the member's responsibility for the causes of the LLP becoming insolvent.

(b)   The extent of the member's responsibility for any failure by the LLP to supply any goods or services which have been paid for (in whole or in part).

(c)   The extent of the member's responsibility for the LLP entering into any transaction or giving any preference, being a transaction or preference liable to be set aside under s 127 or ss 238–240 of the IA 1986.

(d)   The extent of the member's responsibility for any failure by the members of the LLP to comply with s 98 of the IA 1986 (duty to call creditors' meeting in creditors' voluntary winding up).

(e)   Any failure by the member to comply with any obligation imposed on him by the following provisions of IA 1986, namely s 22 (LLP's statement of affairs in administration), s 47 (statement of affairs to administrative receiver), s 99 (member's duty to attend meeting; statement of affairs in creditors' voluntary winding up), s 131 (statement of affairs in winding up by the court), s 234 (duty of anyone with LLP property to deliver it up) and s 235 (duty to co-operate with liquidator, etc).

(f)   The extent of the member's and shadow members' responsibility for events leading to a member or shadow member, whether himself or some other member or shadow member, being declared by the court to be liable to make a contribution to the assets of the LLP under s 214A of the IA 1986.[16]

Case-law

32.16   Although the question of unfitness is one for the trial judge on the facts of each case, a substantial body of reported case-law has been developed.[17] It is beyond the scope of this work to undertake an analysis of the case-law as it applies to companies and, indeed, many of the cases, particularly those at first instance, are only helpful (if at all) as examples of conduct which has or has not, in the light of all the relevant circumstances, been regarded as rendering the director concerned unfit. The general function of the court is to: 'decide whether [the conduct of the director], viewed cumulatively and taking into account any extenuating circumstances, has fallen below the standards of probity and competence appropriate for persons fit to be directors of companies'.[18]

32.17   The key issue for members of LLPs will be how the courts apply the existing case-law. Given that the matters identified by the statute as being relevant are essentially the same,[19] and that members of LLPs are in many respects equated with directors, the expected standards of conduct are likely to be very similar. That said, in view of the flexibility of LLPs as business vehicles, the precise roles of members, and the extent of their involvement in management, may vary much more than the roles and involvement of directors. In the case of small LLPs, in

16   Inserted by LLP Regulations 2001, reg 4(2) and Part II of Sch 2.
17   See the cases cited in Mithani, op cit, paras III335–774.
18   *Re Grayan Building Services Ltd* [1995] Ch 241 at 253F per Hoffmann LJ.
19   CDDA 1986, Sch 1.

which all the members are closely involved in the management of the LLP, there may be little difference. For larger professional LLPs, however, there are likely to be members who have little (if any) involvement in the day-to-day management or decision-making of the LLP and whose roles are not readily equated with company directors.

32.18   In *Re Westmid Packing Services Ltd*, Lord Woolf MR made the following comments: [20]

> 'Each individual director owes duties to his company to inform himself about its affairs and to join with his co-directors in supervising and controlling them. A proper degree of delegation and division of responsibility is of course permissible, and often necessary, but total abrogation of responsibility is not... It is of the greatest importance that any individual who undertakes the statutory and fiduciary obligations of being a company director should realise that these are personal responsibilities.'

'LLP member' may be substituted for 'company director' in this statement.

Collegiate responsibility

32.19   The members as a whole have a collegiate or collective responsibility for the conduct of the LLP's affairs as against the outside world, and in particular creditors. In this connection each member owes continuing duties to the LLP to inform himself about its affairs and to join with his co-members in supervising and controlling these affairs. There certainly can be a proper and reasonable degree of delegation, and division of responsibility, in the management of the business. But, on the other hand, like a company director, no individual member can simply abrogate his part of the collegiate responsibility for the LLP's dealings with the outside world and the impact of its financial position on creditors. [21] Delegation of functions to a management committee (of other members and/or non-members) will not, therefore, absolve a member from all responsibility, and from his duty to keep himself informed; nor will it absolve him from his part in the collegiate responsibility of supervising and controlling the carrying out of the delegated functions. [22] In particular, where statutory duties are laid on the members as a whole, each member has, as a general rule, a duty to inform himself properly, and not simply to leave the decision-making to the other members. [23]

32.20   The extent to which, for the purposes of disqualification proceedings, a member may safely leave responsibility for delegated matters [24] to those to whom they have been delegated will need to be worked out through judicial decisions, and in any event, in any particular case will turn largely on how the particular

---

[20]   [1998] 2 All ER 124 at 130 and 131.

[21]   See Lord Woolf MR in *Re Westmid* above at 130a–c.

[22]   See *Re Barings Plc (No 5)* [1999] 1 BCLC 433 at 487e–f and 489b–c (Jonathan Parker J), the second passage being expressly approved by the Court of Appeal in the same case [2000] 1 BCLC 523 at 535, para 36.

[23]   See, for example, *Re Landhurst Leasing Plc* [1999] 1 BCLC 286 at 346e–h and *Re Galeforce Pleating Co Ltd* [1999] 2 BCLC 704 at 716a–d.

[24]   As opposed to matters allocated by statute to the members as a whole.

LLP's business is organised and the part which the member could reasonably be expected to play.[25]

32.21   Those members of the LLP who are members of the management committee (or otherwise take an active part in the management of the LLP's affairs) will have their conduct considered, on any application for disqualification, in the context of the management role which they in fact had.[26]

OTHER GROUNDS FOR DISQUALIFICATION

32.22   Section 2(1) of the CDDA 1986 provides that the court may make a disqualification order against a person if he is convicted of an indictable offence (whether on indictment or summarily) in connection with the promotion, formation, management, liquidation or striking off of an LLP, with the receivership or management of an LLP's property or with his being an administrative receiver of an LLP.[27]

32.23   The 'court' for the purpose of s 2 means any court having jurisdiction to wind up the LLP in relation to which the offence was committed, or the court by or before which the person is convicted of the offence, or in the case of a summary conviction in England and Wales, any other magistrates' court acting for the same petty sessions area.[28] The maximum period of disqualification under s 2 is, where the disqualification order is made by a court of summary jurisdiction, 5 years, and in any other case, 15 years.[29]

32.24   Section 3(1) of the CDDA 1986 provides that the court may make a disqualification order against a person where it appears that he has been persistently in default in relation to provisions of the companies legislation or the LLP Act 2000 or LLP Regulations 2001 requiring any return, account or other document to be filed with, delivered or sent, or notice of any matter to be given, to the Registrar of Companies.[30] On an application under s 3, the fact that a person has been persistently in default in relation to such provisions may (without prejudice to its proof in any other manner) be conclusively proved by showing that

---

[25]   See generally *Re Landhurst Leasing Plc* [1999] 1 BCLC 286 at 345e–346h and *Re Barings Plc (No 5)* in the Court of Appeal above at 536, para 36(iii).

[26]   Ibid: and see Jonathan Parker J in *Re Barings Plc (No 5)* at first instance above at 484b–e.

[27]   This section should not, presumably, be treated as having been modified so that it reads '...striking off of an LLP or company, or...management of an LLP's or a company's property'. If the section is treated as having been modified in this way, an application could be made pursuant to the CDDA 1986 (as applied to LLPs by the LLP Regulations 2001) notwithstanding that the relevant conduct related to a company.

[28]   CDDA 1986, s 2(2).

[29]   Ibid, s 2(3).

[30]   It is not clear whether this section (as applied to LLPs) should be treated as applying to offences in relation to either LLPs or companies. Where at least one of the offences relates to an LLP there would seem no reason why the application could not be made pursuant to the CDDA 1986 (as applied to LLPs by the LLP Regulations 2001) but it would be very odd if an application could be made in this way if all the offences related to companies. This issue is significant because of the wider scope of an order made under the LLP legislation; see **32.2**.

in the 5 years ending with the date of the application he has been adjudged guilty (whether or not on the same occasion) of three or more defaults in relation to those provisions.[31] A person is to be treated under s 3(2) as being adjudged guilty of a default in relation to any provision if either:

(a)   he is convicted (whether on indictment or summarily) of an offence consisting in a contravention of or failure to comply with that provision (whether on his own part or on the part of any company or LLP); or

(b)   a default order is made against him under any of the s 242(4)[32] of the CA 1985 (order requiring delivery of company accounts), s 245B of that Act (order requiring preparation of revised accounts), s 713 of that Act (enforcement of company's duty to make returns), s 41 of the IA 1986 (enforcement of receiver's or manager's duty to make returns), or s 170 of that Act (corresponding provision for liquidator in winding up), in respect of any such contravention of or failure to comply with that provision (whether on his own part or on the part of any LLP or company).[33]

32.25   In s 3 'the court' means any court having jurisdiction to wind up any of the LLPs or companies in relation to which the offence or other default has been or is alleged to have been committed.[34] The maximum period of disqualification under s 3 is 5 years.[35]

32.26   Section 4(1) of the CDDA 1986 provides that the court may make a disqualification order against a person if, in the course of the winding up of an LLP, it appears that he has been guilty of an offence for which he is liable (whether he has been convicted or not) under s 458 of the CA 1985 (fraudulent trading), or has otherwise been guilty, while a member or liquidator of the LLP or receiver of the LLP's property or administrative receiver of the LLP, of any fraud in relation to the LLP or of any breach of his duty as such member, liquidator, receiver or administrative receiver.[36] In s 4 'the court' means any court having jurisdiction to wind up any of the LLPs in relation to which the offence or other default has been or is alleged to have been committed; and 'officer' includes a shadow member.[37] The maximum period of disqualification under s 4 is 15 years.[38]

---

[31]   CDDA 1986, s 3(2).
[32]   It would appear that this ought to be a reference to CA 1985, s 242(3).
[33]   CDDA 1986, s 3(3).
[34]   Ibid, s 3(4).
[35]   Ibid, s 3(5).
[36]   This section should not, presumably, be treated as having been modified so that s 4(1)(b) reads '...while an officer of an LLP or company...of fraud in relation to the LLP or company...'. If the section is treated as having been modified in this way, an application could be made pursuant to the CDDA 1986 (as applied to LLPs by the LLP Regulations 2001) notwithstanding that the relevant conduct related to a company. Similarly, presumably, an offence pursuant to CA 1985, s 458 would have to relate to an LLP so as to fall within CDDA 1986, s 4(1) as applied to LLPs by the LLP Regulations 2001. This issue is significant because of the wider scope of an order made under the LLP legislation; see **32.2**.
[37]   CDDA 1986, s 4(2).
[38]   Ibid, s 4(3).

32.27   Section 5 of the CDDA 1986 provides that where a person is convicted of a relevant summary offence the court by which he is convicted (or, in England and Wales, any other magistrates' court acting for the same petty sessions area) may make a disqualification order against him if during the 5 years ending with the date of the conviction, he has had made against him, or has been convicted of, in total not less than three default orders and relevant offences. [39]

32.28   An offence is relevant for the purposes of s 5(2) if it is a conviction (either on indictment or summarily) in consequence of a contravention of, or failure to comply with, any provision of the companies legislation or the LLP Act 2000 or LLP Regulations 2001 requiring a return, account or other document to be filed with, delivered or sent, or notice of any matter to be given, to the Registrar of Companies (whether the contravention or failure is on the person's own part or on the part of any LLP). [40] The maximum period of disqualification under s 5 is 5 years.

32.29   Section 8(1) of the CDDA 1986 provides that if it appears to the Secretary of State from investigative material that it is expedient in the public interest that a disqualification order should be made against any person who is or has been a member or shadow member of any LLP, he may apply to the court for such a disqualification order. [41] 'Investigative material' means a report made by inspectors under s 437 of the CA 1985, ss 167, 168, 169 or 284 of the Financial Services and Markets Act 2000, or from information or documents obtained under s 447 or s 448 of the CA 1985, s 2 of the Criminal Justice Act 1987, s 83 of the Companies Act 1989 or ss 165, 171, 172, 173 or 175 of the Financial Services and Markets Act 2000. [42] However, the court may only make a disqualification order against a person under s 8 if it is satisfied that his conduct in relation to the LLP makes him unfit to be concerned in the management of an LLP. [43] In s 8 'the court' means the High Court. [44] The maximum period of disqualification under s 8 is 15 years. [45]

32.30   Section 9A of the CDDA 1986 provides that the court must make a disqualification order against a person if an LLP of which he is a member commits a breach of competition law and the court considers that his conduct as a member makes him unfit to be concerned in the management of an LLP. [46]

32.31   Section 10 of the CDDA 1986 provides that where the court makes a declaration under s 213 or s 214 of the IA 1986 that a person is liable to make a contribution to an LLP's assets, then, whether or not an application is made by any

---

[39]   CDDA 1986, s 5(1) and (3). 'Default' means the same as in s 3(3)(b).

[40]   Ibid, s 5(1). This section should not, presumably, be read as modified to apply to offences relating to companies as well as LLPs. See footnote 36 above.

[41]   This section should not, presumably, be read as modified to apply to companies as well as LLPs. See footnote 36 above.

[42]   CDDA 1986, s 8(1A).

[43]   Ibid, s 8(2).

[44]   Ibid, s 8(3).

[45]   Ibid, s 8(4).

[46]   The relevant law is set out in CDDA 1986 s 9A(4). See s 9B in relation to competition undertakings and s 9C in relation to competition investigations.

person, the court may, if it thinks fit, also make a disqualification order against the person to whom the declaration relates.[47] The maximum period of disqualification under s 10 is 15 years.[48]

32.32   Section 11(1) of the CDDA 1986 provides that it is an offence for a person who is an undischarged bankrupt or in respect of whom a bankruptcy restrictions order is in force to act as a member of an LLP or as a director of a company or directly or indirectly to take part in or be concerned in the promotion, formation or management of, an LLP or a company, except with the leave of the court.[49] For the purpose of s 11, 'the court' is the court by which the person was adjudged bankrupt.[50] The leave of the court cannot be given unless the bankrupt gives notice to the official receiver of his intention to apply for it. It is the duty of the official receiver, if he is of opinion that it is contrary to the public interest that the application should be granted, to attend on the hearing of the application and oppose it.[51]

32.33   If a court under s 429 of the IA 1986 revokes an administration order under Part VI of the County Courts Act 1984, the person to whom that section applies by virtue of the order under s 429(2)(b) cannot, except with the leave of the court which made the order, act as a member or liquidator of an LLP, or directly or indirectly take part or be concerned in the promotion, formation or management of, an LLP.[52]

CONSEQUENCES OF CONTRAVENTION

32.34   If a person acts in contravention of a disqualification order or disqualification undertaking, or is guilty of an offence under s 11, he is liable on conviction on indictment, to imprisonment for not more than 2 years or a fine, or both; and on summary conviction, to imprisonment for not more than 6 months or a fine not exceeding the statutory maximum, or both.[53]

---

[47]   This section should not, presumably, be read as modified to apply to companies as well as LLPs. See footnote 36 above. Oddly, a reference to s 214A has not been added to s 10 notwithstanding that it has been added to the matters to be taken into account in determining unfitness set out in Sch 1.

[48]   CDDA 1986, s 10(2).

[49]   It does not matter whether s 11 is treated as modified to refer to companies and LLPs. An undischarged bankrupt will be prevented from acting in relation to a company by s 11 of the CDDA 1986 itself or in relation to an LLP by s 11 of the CDDA 1986 as applied to LLPs by the LLP Regulations 2001.

[50]   CDDA 1986, s 11(2).

[51]   Ibid, s 11(3).

[52]   Ibid, s 12. It does not matter whether s 12 is treated as modified to refer to companies and LLPs. A person affected by the order is prevented from acting in relation to a company by s 12 of the CDDA 1986 itself or in relation to an LLP by s 12 of the CDDA 1986 as applied to LLPs by the LLP Regulations 2001.

[53]   CDDA 1986, s 13. See also CDDA 1986, s 12A in respect of Northern Irish disqualification orders.

32.35   Under CDDA 1986, s 15, a person is personally responsible for all the relevant debts[54] of an LLP or a company if at any time:

(a)   in contravention of a disqualification order or disqualification undertaking or of s 11, he is involved in the management of the LLP or company, or

(b)   as a person who is involved in the management of the LLP or company, he acts or is willing to act on instructions given without the leave of the court by a person whom he knows at that time to be the subject of a disqualification order or disqualification undertaking or to be an undischarged bankrupt.

Where a person is personally responsible under s 15 for the relevant debts of an LLP or company, he is jointly and severally liable in respect of those debts with the LLP or company and any other person who, whether under s 15 or otherwise, is liable.[55]

32.36   For the purposes of s 15, the relevant debts of an LLP or company are:

(i)   in relation to a person who is personally responsible under (a) in **32.35**, such debts and other liabilities of the LLP or company as are incurred at a time when that person was involved in the management of the LLP or company; and

(ii)   in relation to a person who is personally responsible under (b) in **32.35**, such debts and other liabilities of the LLP or company as are incurred at a time when that person was acting or was willing to act on instructions given as mentioned in that paragraph.[56]

32.37   For the purposes of s 15:

(a)   a person is involved in the management of an LLP or company if he is a member of an LLP or director of the company or if he is concerned, whether directly or indirectly, or takes part, in the management of the LLP or company;[57] and

(b)   a person who, as a person involved in the management of an LLP or company, has at any time acted on instructions given without the leave of the court by a person whom he knew at that time to be the subject of a disqualification order or disqualification undertaking or to be an undischarged bankrupt is presumed, unless the contrary is shown, to have been willing at any time thereafter to act on any instructions given by that person.[58]

---

54   See **32.37**.
55   CDDA 1986, s 15(2).
56   Ibid, s 15(3).
57   Ibid, s 15(4).
58   Ibid, s 15(5).

APPLICATIONS FOR LEAVE TO ACT

32.38   A disqualified member can apply to the court for leave to act.[59] Leave can be granted for a disqualified member to be a member of an LLP or a director of a company, or can be limited to permission to act in the management of an LLP or company. On the hearing of an application for leave, the Secretary of State (or the official receiver or the liquidator) must appear and call the attention of the court to any matters which seem relevant, and may give evidence or call witnesses.[60] The discretion to grant leave is unfettered. The suggestion in some authorities that particular factors or circumstances amount to prerequisites for the granting of leave has been rejected.[61] The discretion is to be exercised by the court in the light of all the circumstances which will, of course, vary considerably from case to case. The granting of leave does not require the respondent to show exceptional circumstances.[62] There are several matters which will ordinarily fall to be considered in deciding whether the discretion ought to be exercised. These matters fall, broadly, under two heads. First, whether the granting of the leave sought would undermine the purposes of the disqualification order. Secondly, the reasons the applicant has advanced for the granting of leave.

32.39   In considering whether the purpose of the disqualification order would be undermined, there are a number of factors which may be relevant. The court will inevitably be concerned with the question whether the involvement of the applicant with a limited liability entity would pose a risk to the public if leave is granted. This will involve a consideration of, inter alia:

(a)   the nature of the conduct for which the applicant was disqualified;
(b)   the nature of the role the applicant wishes to undertake and the terms of the leave which are proposed;
(c)   other evidence relevant to the possibility of the applicant repeating the conduct for which he was disqualified including evidence:
  (i)   of the applicant's past employment history;
  (ii)   from the applicant as to whether he has 'learnt his lesson'; and
  (iii)   as to his conduct since the events giving rise to the disqualification proceedings.

32.40   In considering the reasons advanced by the applicant for the granting of leave (referred to in the cases as the 'need' for the order) the court will primarily be concerned with:

---

[59]   See CDDA 1986, ss 1 and 17.
[60]   Ibid, s 17.
[61]   See *Re Barings Plc (No 3)* [1999] 1 All ER 1017 and *Re Dawes & Henderson (Agencies) Ltd (In Liquidation) (No 2)* [1999] 2 BCLC 317.
[62]   See *Secretary of State for Trade and Industry v Rosenfield* [1999] BCC 413 at 414E–F and 415E–G.

(a)   reasons personal to the applicant; and

(b)   reasons relevant to the LLP or company in respect of which leave is sought.

32.41   It is for the judge to decide in the light of all the circumstances whether to exercise his discretion. Courts acting in an appellate capacity are slow to interfere with the exercise by the judge of his discretion, and only interfere if the judge has erred in principle.[63] It appears that the courts may be more inclined to grant leave if the leave sought is for the applicant to be involved in management (in circumstances in which the applicant is supervised and does not have power to make decisions affecting the financial position of the company or LLP) rather than as a director or member.[64]

32.42   A person who is subject to a disqualification undertaking may apply to the court to reduce the period for which the undertaking is to be in force, or for an order that it cease to be in force.[65] On the hearing of an application, the Secretary of State must appear and call the attention of the court to any matters which seem to him to be relevant, and may give evidence or call witnesses.[66]

---

[63]   *Secretary of State v Collins* [2000] 2 BCLC 223.

[64]   Ibid.

[65]   CDDA 1986, s 8A(1).

[66]   Ibid, s 8A(2).

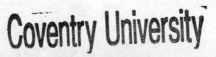

Appendix 1

LIMITED LIABILITY PARTNERSHIPS ACT 2000[1]

ARRANGEMENT OF SECTIONS

Section

---

[1]   Act reference: 2000 c 12.
Royal Assent: 20 July 2000.
Long title: An Act to make provision for limited liability partnerships.
Commencement: Limited Liability Partnerships Act 2000 (Commencement) Order, SI 2000/3316, reg 2, with effect from 6 April 2001

Introductory

1 Limited liability partnerships

(1) There shall be a new form of legal entity to be known as a limited liability partnership.

(2) A limited liability partnership is a body corporate (with legal personality separate from that of its members) which is formed by being incorporated under this Act; and –

(a)   in the following provisions of this Act (except in the phrase 'oversea limited liability partnership'), and

(b)   in any other enactment (except where provision is made to the contrary or the context otherwise requires),

references to a limited liability partnership are to such a body corporate.

(3) A limited liability partnership has unlimited capacity.

(4) The members of a limited liability partnership have such liability to contribute to its assets in the event of its being wound up as is provided for by virtue of this Act.

(5) Accordingly, except as far as otherwise provided by this Act or any other enactment, the law relating to partnerships does not apply to a limited liability partnership.

(6) The Schedule (which makes provision about the names and registered offices of limited liability partnerships) has effect.

Incorporation

2 Incorporation document etc

(1) For a limited liability partnership to be incorporated –

(a)   two or more persons associated for carrying on a lawful business with a view to profit must have subscribed their names to an incorporation document,

(b)   there must have been delivered to the registrar either the incorporation document or a copy authenticated in a manner approved by him, and

(c)   there must have been so delivered a statement in a form approved by the registrar, made by either a solicitor engaged in the formation of the limited liability partnership or anyone who subscribed his name to the incorporation document, that the requirement imposed by paragraph (a) has been complied with.

(2) The incorporation document must –

(a)   be in a form approved by the registrar (or as near to such a form as circumstances allow),

(b)   state the name of the limited liability partnership,

(c)   state whether the registered office of the limited liability partnership is to be situated in England and Wales, in Wales or in Scotland,

(d)   state the address of that registered office,

(e)   state the name and address of each of the persons who are to be members of the limited liability partnership on incorporation, and

(f)   either specify which of those persons are to be designated members or state that every person who from time to time is a member of the limited liability partnership is a designated member.

(2A) Where a confidentiality order, made under section 723B of the Companies Act 1985 as applied to a limited liability partnerships,[1] is in force in respect of any individual named as a member of a limited liability partnership under subsection (2) that subsection shall have effect as if the reference to the address of the individual were a reference to the address for the time being notified by him under the Limited Liability Partnerships (Particulars of Usual Residential Address) (Confidentiality Orders) Regulations 2002 to any limited liability partnership of which he is a member or if he is not such a member either the address specified in his application for a confidentiality order or the address last notified by him under such a confidentiality order as the case may be.

(2B) Where the incorporation document or a copy of such delivered under this section includes an address specified in reliance on subsection (2A) there shall be delivered with it or the copy of it a statement in a form approved by the registrar containing particulars of the usual residential address of the member whose address is so specified.

(3) If a person makes a false statement under subsection (1)(c) which he –

(a)   knows to be false, or
(b)   does not believe to be true,

he commits an offence.

(4) A person guilty of an offence under subsection (3) is liable –

(a)   on summary conviction, to imprisonment for a period not exceeding six months or a fine not exceeding the statutory maximum, or to both, or
(b)   on conviction on indictment, to imprisonment for a period not exceeding two years or a fine, or to both.

Amendments—SI 2002/915.

Note 1—The phrase in line 2 of subsection (2A) 'as applied to a limited liability partnerships' is printed here as it appears in SI 2002/915.

3 Incorporation by registration

(1) When the requirements imposed by paragraphs (b) and (c) of subsection (1) of section 2 have been complied with, the registrar shall retain the incorporation document or copy delivered to him and, unless the requirement imposed by paragraph (a) of that subsection has not been complied with, he shall –

(a)   register the incorporation document or copy, and
(b)   give a certificate that the limited liability partnership is incorporated by the name specified in the incorporation document.

(2) The registrar may accept the statement delivered under paragraph (c) of subsection (1) of section 2 as sufficient evidence that the requirement imposed by paragraph (a) of that subsection has been complied with.

(3) The certificate shall either be signed by the registrar or be authenticated by his official seal.

(4) The certificate is conclusive evidence that the requirements of section 2 are complied with and that the limited liability partnership is incorporated by the name specified in the incorporation document.

Membership

4 Members

(1) On the incorporation of a limited liability partnership its members are the persons who subscribed their names to the incorporation document (other than any who have died or been dissolved).

(2) Any other person may become a member of a limited liability partnership by and in accordance with an agreement with the existing members.

(3) A person may cease to be a member of a limited liability partnership (as well as by death or dissolution) in accordance with an agreement with the other members or, in the absence of agreement with the other members as to cessation of membership, by giving reasonable notice to the other members.

(4) A member of a limited liability partnership shall not be regarded for any purpose as employed by the limited liability partnership unless, if he and the other members were partners in a partnership, he would be regarded for that purpose as employed by the partnership.

5 Relationship of members etc

(1) Except as far as otherwise provided by this Act or any other enactment, the mutual rights and duties of the members of a limited liability partnership, and the mutual rights and duties of a limited liability partnership and its members, shall be governed –

(a)   by agreement between the members, or between the limited liability partnership and its members, or

(b)   in the absence of agreement as to any matter, by any provision made in relation to that matter by regulations under section 15(c).

(2) An agreement made before the incorporation of a limited liability partnership between the persons who subscribe their names to the incorporation document may impose obligations on the limited liability partnership (to take effect at any time after its incorporation).

6 Members as agents

(1) Every member of a limited liability partnership is the agent of the limited liability partnership.

(2) But a limited liability partnership is not bound by anything done by a member in dealing with a person if –

(a)   the member in fact has no authority to act for the limited liability partnership by doing that thing, and

(b)   the person knows that he has no authority or does not know or believe him to be a member of the limited liability partnership.

(3) Where a person has ceased to be a member of a limited liability partnership, the former member is to be regarded (in relation to any person dealing with the limited liability partnership) as still being a member of the limited liability partnership unless –

    (a)   the person has notice that the former member has ceased to be a member of the limited liability partnership, or

    (b)   notice that the former member has ceased to be a member of the limited liability partnership has been delivered to the registrar.

(4) Where a member of a limited liability partnership is liable to any person (other than another member of the limited liability partnership) as a result of a wrongful act or omission of his in the course of the business of the limited liability partnership or with its authority, the limited liability partnership is liable to the same extent as the member.

7 Ex-members

(1) This section applies where a member of a limited liability partnership has either ceased to be a member or –

    (a)   has died,

    (b)   has become bankrupt or had his estate sequestrated or has been wound up,

    (c)   has granted a trust deed for the benefit of his creditors, or

    (d)   has assigned the whole or any part of his share in the limited liability partnership (absolutely or by way of charge or security).

(2) In such an event the former member or –

    (a)   his personal representative,

    (b)   his trustee in bankruptcy or permanent or interim trustee (within the meaning of the Bankruptcy (Scotland) Act 1985) or liquidator,

    (c)   his trustee under the trust deed for the benefit of his creditors, or

    (d)   his assignee,

may not interfere in the management or administration of any business or affairs of the limited liability partnership.

(3) But subsection (2) does not affect any right to receive an amount from the limited liability partnership in that event.

8 Designated members

(1) If the incorporation document specifies who are to be designated members –

    (a)   they are designated members on incorporation, and

    (b)   any member may become a designated member by and in accordance with an agreement with the other members,

and a member may cease to be a designated member in accordance with an agreement with the other members.

(2) But if there would otherwise be no designated members, or only one, every member is a designated member.

(3) If the incorporation document states that every person who from time to time is a member of the limited liability partnership is a designated member, every member is a designated member.

(4) A limited liability partnership may at any time deliver to the registrar –

(a)   notice that specified members are to be designated members, or

(b)   notice that every person who from time to time is a member of the limited liability partnership is a designated member,

and, once it is delivered, subsection (1) (apart from paragraph (a)) and subsection (2), or subsection (3), shall have effect as if that were stated in the incorporation document.

(5) A notice delivered under subsection (4) –

(a)   shall be in a form approved by the registrar, and

(b)   shall be signed by a designated member of the limited liability partnership or authenticated in a manner approved by the registrar.

(6) A person ceases to be a designated member if he ceases to be a member.

9 Registration of membership changes

(1) A limited liability partnership must ensure that –

(a)   where a person becomes or ceases to be a member or designated member, notice is delivered to the registrar within fourteen days, and

(b)   where there is any change in the name or address of a member, notice is delivered to the registrar within 28 days.

(2) Where all the members from time to time of a limited liability partnership are designated members, subsection (1)(a) does not require notice that a person has become or ceased to be a designated member as well as a member.

(3) A notice delivered under subsection (1) –

(a)   shall be in a form approved by the registrar, and

(b)   shall be signed by a designated member of the limited liability partnership or authenticated in a manner approved by the registrar,

and, if it relates to a person becoming a member or designated member, shall contain a statement that he consents to becoming a member or designated member signed by him or authenticated in a manner approved by the registrar.

(3A) Where a confidentiality order under section 723B of the Companies Act 1985 as applied to limited liability partnerships is made in respect of an existing member, the limited liability partnership must ensure that there is delivered within 28 days to the registrar notice in a form approved by the registrar containing the address for the time being notified to it by the member under the Limited Liability Partnerships (Particulars of Usual Residential Address) (Confidentiality Orders) Regulations 2002.

(3B) Where such a confidentiality order is in force in respect of a member the requirement in subsection (1)(b) to notify a change in the address of a member shall be read in relation to that member as a requirement to deliver to the registrar, within 28 days, notice of—

(a)   any change in the usual residential address of that member; and

(b)   any change in the address for the time being notified to the limited liability partnership by the member under the Limited Liability Partnerships (Particulars of Usual Residential Address) (Confidentiality Orders) Regulations 2002

and the registrar may approve different forms for the notification of each kind of address.

(4) If a limited liability partnership fails to comply with subsection (1), the partnership and every designated member commits an offence.

(5) But it is a defence for a designated member charged with an offence under subsection (4) to prove that he took all reasonable steps for securing that subsection (1) was complied with.

(6) A person guilty of an offence under subsection (4) is liable on summary conviction to a fine not exceeding level 5 on the standard scale.

Amendments—SI 2002/915.

Taxation

10 Income tax and chargeable gains

(1) In the Income and Corporation Taxes Act 1988, after section 118 insert –

'Limited liability partnerships

118ZA Treatment of limited liability partnerships

For the purposes of the Tax Acts, a trade, profession or business carried on by a limited liability partnership with a view to profit shall be treated as carried on in partnership by its members (and not by the limited liability partnership as such); and, accordingly, the property of the limited liability partnership shall be treated for those purposes as partnership property.

118ZB Restriction on relief

Sections 117 and 118 have effect in relation to a member of a limited liability partnership as in relation to a limited partner, but subject to sections 118ZC and 118ZD.

118ZC Member's contribution to trade

(1) Subsection (3) of section 117 does not have effect in relation to a member of a limited liability partnership.

(2) But, for the purposes of that section and section 118, such a member's contribution to a trade at any time ('the relevant time') is the greater of –

    (a) the amount subscribed by him, and
    (b) the amount of his liability on a winding up.

(3) The amount subscribed by a member of a limited liability partnership is the amount which he has contributed to the limited liability partnership as capital, less so much of that amount (if any) as –

    (a) he has previously, directly or indirectly, drawn out or received back,
    (b) he so draws out or receives back during the period of five years beginning with the relevant time,
    (c) he is or may be entitled so to draw out or receive back at any time when he is a member of the limited liability partnership, or
    (d) he is or may be entitled to require another person to reimburse to him.

(4) The amount of the liability of a member of a limited liability partnership on a winding up is the amount which –

(a) he is liable to contribute to the assets of the limited liability partnership in the event of its being wound up, and

(b) he remains liable so to contribute for the period of at least five years beginning with the relevant time (or until it is wound up, if that happens before the end of that period).

118ZD Carry forward of unrelieved losses

(1) Where amounts relating to a trade carried on by a member of a limited liability partnership are, in any one or more chargeable periods, prevented from being given or allowed by section 117 or 118 as it applies otherwise than by virtue of this section (his 'total unrelieved loss'), subsection (2) applies in each subsequent chargeable period in which –

(a) he carries on the trade as a member of the limited liability partnership, and

(b) any of his total unrelieved loss remains outstanding.

(2) Sections 380, 381, 393A(1) and 403 (and sections 117 and 118 as they apply in relation to those sections) shall have effect in the subsequent chargeable period as if –

(a) any loss sustained or incurred by the member in the trade in that chargeable period were increased by an amount equal to so much of his total unrelieved loss as remains outstanding in that period, or

(b) (if no loss is so sustained or incurred) a loss of that amount were so sustained or incurred.

(3) To ascertain whether any (and, if so, how much) of a member's total unrelieved loss remains outstanding in the subsequent chargeable period, deduct from the amount of his total unrelieved loss the aggregate of –

(a) any relief given under any provision of the Tax Acts (otherwise than as a result of subsection (2)) in respect of his total unrelieved loss in that or any previous chargeable period, and

(b) any amount given or allowed in respect of his total unrelieved loss as a result of subsection (2) in any previous chargeable period (or which would have been so given or allowed had a claim been made).'

(2) In section 362(2)(a) of that Act (loan to buy into partnership), after 'partner' insert 'in a limited partnership registered under the Limited Partnerships Act 1907'.

(3) In the Taxation of Chargeable Gains Act 1992, after section 59 insert –

'59A Limited liability partnerships

(1) Where a limited liability partnership carries on a trade or business with a view to profit –

(a) assets held by the limited liability partnership shall be treated for the purposes of tax in respect of chargeable gains as held by its members as partners, and

(b) any dealings by the limited liability partnership shall be treated for those purposes as dealings by its members in partnership (and not by the limited liability partnership as such),

and tax in respect of chargeable gains accruing to the members of the limited liability partnership on the disposal of any of its assets shall be assessed and charged on them separately.

(2) Where subsection (1) ceases to apply in relation to a limited liability partnership with the effect that tax is assessed and charged –

    (a) on the limited liability partnership (as a company) in respect of chargeable gains accruing on the disposal of any of its assets, and

    (b) on the members in respect of chargeable gains accruing on the disposal of any of their capital interests in the limited liability partnership,

it shall be assessed and charged on the limited liability partnership as if subsection (1) had never applied in relation to it.

(3) Neither the commencement of the application of subsection (1) nor the cessation of its application in relation to a limited liability partnership is to be taken as giving rise to the disposal of any assets by it or any of its members.'

(4) After section 156 of that Act insert –

'156A Cessation of trade by limited liability partnership

(1) Where, immediately before the time of cessation of trade, a member of a limited liability partnership holds an asset, or an interest in an asset, acquired by him for a consideration treated as reduced under section 152 or 153, he shall be treated as if a chargeable gain equal to the amount of the reduction accrued to him immediately before that time.

(2) Where, as a result of section 154(2), a chargeable gain on the disposal of an asset, or an interest in an asset, by a member of a limited liability partnership has not accrued before the time of cessation of trade, the member shall be treated as if the chargeable gain accrued immediately before that time.

(3) In this section 'the time of cessation of trade', in relation to a limited liability partnership, means the time when section 59A(1) ceases to apply in relation to the limited liability partnership.'

11 Inheritance tax

In the Inheritance Tax Act 1984, after section 267 insert –

'267A Limited liability partnerships

For the purposes of this Act and any other enactments relating to inheritance tax –

    (a) property to which a limited liability partnership is entitled, or which it occupies or uses, shall be treated as property to which its members are entitled, or which they occupy or use, as partners,

    (b) any business carried on by a limited liability partnership shall be treated as carried on in partnership by its members,

    (c) incorporation, change in membership or dissolution of a limited liability partnership shall be treated as formation, alteration or dissolution of a partnership, and

    (d) any transfer of value made by or to a limited liability partnership shall be treated as made by or to its members in partnership (and not by or to the limited liability partnership as such).'

12 Stamp duty

(1) Stamp duty shall not be chargeable on an instrument by which property is conveyed or transferred by a person to a limited liability partnership in connection with its incorporation within the period of one year beginning with the date of incorporation if the following two conditions are satisfied.

(2) The first condition is that at the relevant time the person –

    (a)   is a partner in a partnership comprised of all the persons who are or are to be members of the limited liability partnership (and no-one else), or

    (b)   holds the property conveyed or transferred as nominee or bare trustee for one or more of the partners in such a partnership.

(3) The second condition is that –

    (a)   the proportions of the property conveyed or transferred to which the persons mentioned in subsection (2)(a) are entitled immediately after the conveyance or transfer are the same as those to which they were entitled at the relevant time, or

    (b)   none of the differences in those proportions has arisen as part of a scheme or arrangement of which the main purpose, or one of the main purposes, is avoidance of liability to any duty or tax.

(4) For the purposes of subsection (2) a person holds property as bare trustee for a partner if the partner has the exclusive right (subject only to satisfying any outstanding charge, lien or other right of the trustee to resort to the property for payment of duty, taxes, costs or other outgoings) to direct how the property shall be dealt with.

(5) In this section 'the relevant time' means –

    (a)   if the person who conveyed or transferred the property to the limited liability partnership acquired the property after its incorporation, immediately after he acquired the property, and

    (b)   in any other case, immediately before its incorporation.

(6) An instrument in respect of which stamp duty is not chargeable by virtue of subsection (1) shall not be taken to be duly stamped unless –

    (a)   it has, in accordance with section 12 of the Stamp Act 1891, been stamped with a particular stamp denoting that it is not chargeable with any duty or that it is duly stamped, or

    (b)   it is stamped with the duty to which it would be liable apart from that subsection.

13 Class 4 national insurance contributions

In section 15 of the Social Security Contributions and Benefits Act 1992 and section 15 of the Social Security Contributions and Benefits (Northern Ireland) Act 1992 (Class 4 contributions), after subsection (3) insert –

'(3A) Where income tax is (or would be) charged on a member of a limited liability partnership in respect of profits or gains arising from the carrying on of a trade or profession by the limited liability partnership, Class 4 contributions shall be payable by him if they would be payable were the trade or profession carried on in partnership by the members.'

Regulations

14 Insolvency and winding up

(1) Regulations shall make provision about the insolvency and winding up of limited liability partnerships by applying or incorporating, with such modifications as appear appropriate, Parts I to IV, VI and VII of the Insolvency Act 1986.

(2) Regulations may make other provision about the insolvency and winding up of limited liability partnerships, and provision about the insolvency and winding up of oversea limited liability partnerships, by –

(a) applying or incorporating, with such modifications as appear appropriate, any law relating to the insolvency or winding up of companies or other corporations which would not otherwise have effect in relation to them, or

(b) providing for any law relating to the insolvency or winding up of companies or other corporations which would otherwise have effect in relation to them not to apply to them or to apply to them with such modifications as appear appropriate.

(3) In this Act 'oversea limited liability partnership' means a body incorporated or otherwise established outside Great Britain and having such connection with Great Britain, and such other features, as regulations may prescribe.

15 Application of company law etc

Regulations may make provision about limited liability partnerships and oversea limited liability partnerships (not being provision about insolvency or winding up) by –

(a) applying or incorporating, with such modifications as appear appropriate, any law relating to companies or other corporations which would not otherwise have effect in relation to them,

(b) providing for any law relating to companies or other corporations which would otherwise have effect in relation to them not to apply to them or to apply to them with such modifications as appear appropriate, or

(c) applying or incorporating, with such modifications as appear appropriate, any law relating to partnerships.

16 Consequential amendments

(1) Regulations may make in any enactment such amendments or repeals as appear appropriate in consequence of this Act or regulations made under it.

(2) The regulations may, in particular, make amendments and repeals affecting companies or other corporations or partnerships.

17 General

(1) In this Act 'regulations' means regulations made by the Secretary of State by statutory instrument.

(2) Regulations under this Act may in particular –

(a) make provision for dealing with non-compliance with any of the regulations (including the creation of criminal offences),

(b)   impose fees (which shall be paid into the Consolidated Fund), and

(c)   provide for the exercise of functions by persons prescribed by the regulations.

(3) Regulations under this Act may –

(a)   contain any appropriate consequential, incidental, supplementary or transitional provisions or savings, and

(b)   make different provision for different purposes.

(4) No regulations to which this subsection applies shall be made unless a draft of the statutory instrument containing the regulations (whether or not together with other provisions) has been laid before, and approved by a resolution of, each House of Parliament.

(5) Subsection (4) applies to –

(a)   regulations under section 14(2) not consisting entirely of the application or incorporation (with or without modifications) of provisions contained in or made under the Insolvency Act 1986,

(b)   regulations under section 15 not consisting entirely of the application or incorporation (with or without modifications) of provisions contained in or made under Part I, Chapter VIII of Part V, Part VII, Parts XI to XIII, Parts XVI to XVIII, Part XX or Parts XXIV to XXVI of the Companies Act 1985,

(c)   regulations under section 14 or 15 making provision about oversea limited liability partnerships, and

(d)   regulations under section 16.

(6) A statutory instrument containing regulations under this Act shall (unless a draft of it has been approved by a resolution of each House of Parliament) be subject to annulment in pursuance of a resolution of either House of Parliament.

Supplementary

18 Interpretation

In this Act –

'address', in relation to a member of a limited liability partnership, means –
(a) if an individual, his usual residential address, and
(b) if a corporation or Scottish firm, its registered or principal office,
'business' includes every trade, profession and occupation,
'designated member' shall be construed in accordance with section 8,
'enactment' includes subordinate legislation (within the meaning of the Interpretation Act 1978),
'incorporation document' shall be construed in accordance with section 2,
'limited liability partnership' has the meaning given by section 1(2),
'member' shall be construed in accordance with section 4,
'modifications' includes additions and omissions,
'name', in relation to a member of a limited liability partnership, means –
(a) if an individual, his forename and surname (or, in the case of a peer or other person usually known by a title, his title instead of or in addition to either or both his forename and surname), and
(b) if a corporation or Scottish firm, its corporate or firm name,

'oversea limited liability partnership' has the meaning given by section 14(3),
'the registrar' means –

(a) if the registered office of the limited liability partnership is, or is to be, situated in England and Wales or in Wales, the registrar or other officer performing under the Companies Act 1985 the duty of registration of companies in England and Wales, and

(b) if its registered office is, or is to be, situated in Scotland, the registrar or other officer performing under that Act the duty of registration of companies in Scotland, and

'regulations' has the meaning given by section 17(1).

19 Commencement, extent and short title

(1) The preceding provisions of this Act shall come into force on such day as the Secretary of State may by order made by statutory instrument appoint; and different days may be appointed for different purposes.

(2) The Secretary of State may by order made by statutory instrument make any transitional provisions and savings which appear appropriate in connection with the coming into force of any provision of this Act.

(3) For the purposes of the Scotland Act 1998 this Act shall be taken to be a pre-commencement enactment within the meaning of that Act.

(4) Apart from sections 10 to 13 (and this section), this Act does not extend to Northern Ireland.

(5) This Act may be cited as the Limited Liability Partnerships Act 2000.

SCHEDULE
NAME AND REGISTERED OFFICES

Section 1

PART I
NAMES

1 Index of names

In section 714(1) of the Companies Act 1985 (index of names), after paragraph (d) insert –

'(da) limited liability partnerships incorporated under the Limited Liability Partnerships Act 2000,'.

2 Name to indicate status

(1) The name of a limited liability partnership must end with –

(a)   the expression 'limited liability partnership', or
(b)   the abbreviation 'llp' or 'LLP'.

(2) But if the incorporation document for a limited liability partnership states that the registered office is to be situated in Wales, its name must end with –

(a)   one of the expressions 'limited liability partnership' and 'partneriaeth atebolrwydd cyfyngedig', or

(b)   one of the abbreviations 'llp', 'LLP', 'pac' and 'PAC'.

3 Registration of names

(1) A limited liability partnership shall not be registered by a name –

(a)   which includes, otherwise than at the end of the name, either of the expressions 'limited liability partnership' and 'partneriaeth atebolrwydd cyfyngedig' or any of the abbreviations 'llp', 'LLP', 'pac' and 'PAC',

(b)   which is the same as a name appearing in the index kept under section 714(1) of the Companies Act 1985,

(c)   the use of which by the limited liability partnership would in the opinion of the Secretary of State constitute a criminal offence, or

(d)   which in the opinion of the Secretary of State is offensive.

(2) Except with the approval of the Secretary of State, a limited liability partnership shall not be registered by a name which –

(a)   in the opinion of the Secretary of State would be likely to give the impression that it is connected in any way with Her Majesty's Government or with any local authority, or

(b)   includes any word or expression for the time being specified in regulations under section 29 of the Companies Act 1985 (names needing approval),

and in paragraph (a) 'local authority' means any local authority within the meaning of the Local Government Act 1972 or the Local Government etc. (Scotland) Act 1994, the Common Council of the City of London or the Council of the Isles of Scilly.

4 Change of name

(1) A limited liability partnership may change its name at any time.

(2) Where a limited liability partnership has been registered by a name which –

(a)   is the same as or, in the opinion of the Secretary of State, too like a name appearing at the time of registration in the index kept under section 714(1) of the Companies Act 1985, or

(b)   is the same as or, in the opinion of the Secretary of State, too like a name which should have appeared in the index at that time,

the Secretary of State may within twelve months of that time in writing direct the limited liability partnership to change its name within such period as he may specify.

(3) If it appears to the Secretary of State –

(a)   that misleading information has been given for the purpose of the registration of a limited liability partnership by a particular name, or

(b)   that undertakings or assurances have been given for that purpose and have not been fulfilled,

he may, within five years of the date of its registration by that name, in writing direct the limited liability partnership to change its name within such period as he may specify.

(4) If in the Secretary of State's opinion the name by which a limited liability partnership is registered gives so misleading an indication of the nature of its activities as to be likely to cause harm to the public, he may in writing direct the limited liability partnership to change its name within such period as he may specify.

(5) But the limited liability partnership may, within three weeks from the date of the direction apply to the court to set it aside and the court may set the direction aside or confirm it and, if it confirms it, shall specify the period within which it must be complied with.

(6) In sub-paragraph (5) 'the court' means –

(a)   if the registered office of the limited liability partnership is situated in England and Wales or in Wales, the High Court, and

(b)   if it is situated in Scotland, the Court of Session.

(7) Where a direction has been given under sub-paragraph (2), (3) or (4) specifying a period within which a limited liability partnership is to change its name, the Secretary of State may at any time before that period ends extend it by a further direction in writing.

(8) If a limited liability partnership fails to comply with a direction under this paragraph –

(a)   the limited liability partnership, and

(b)   any designated member in default,

commits an offence.

(9) A person guilty of an offence under sub-paragraph (8) is liable on summary conviction to a fine not exceeding level 3 on the standard scale.

5 Notification of change of name

(1) Where a limited liability partnership changes its name it shall deliver notice of the change to the registrar.

(2) A notice delivered under sub-paragraph (1) –

(a)   shall be in a form approved by the registrar, and

(b)   shall be signed by a designated member of the limited liability partnership or authenticated in a manner approved by the registrar.

(3) Where the registrar receives a notice under sub-paragraph (2) he shall (unless the new name is one by which a limited liability partnership may not be registered) –

(a)   enter the new name in the index kept under section 714(1) of the Companies Act 1985, and

(b)   issue a certificate of the change of name.

(4) The change of name has effect from the date on which the certificate is issued.

6 Effect of change of name

A change of name by a limited liability partnership does not –

(a)   affect any of its rights or duties,

(b)   render defective any legal proceedings by or against it, and any legal proceedings that might have been commenced or continued against it by its former name may be commenced or continued against it by its new name.

7 Improper use of 'limited liability partnership' etc

(1) If any person carries on a business under a name or title which includes as the last words –

    (a)   the expression 'limited liability partnership' or 'partneriaeth atebolrwydd cyfyngedig', or

    (b)   any contraction or imitation of either of those expressions,

that person, unless a limited liability partnership or oversea limited liability partnership, commits an offence.

(2) A person guilty of an offence under sub-paragraph (1) is liable on summary conviction to a fine not exceeding level 3 on the standard scale.

8 Similarity of names

In determining for the purposes of this Part whether one name is the same as another there are to be disregarded –

    (1)   the definite article as the first word of the name,

    (2)   any of the following (or their Welsh equivalents or abbreviations of them or their Welsh equivalents) at the end of the name –

        'limited liability partnership',
        'company',
        'and company',
        'company limited',
        'and company limited',
        'limited',
        'unlimited',
        'public limited company',
        'open-ended investment company', and
        'investment company with variable capital', and

    (3)   type and case of letters, accents, spaces between letters and punctuation marks,

and 'and' and '&' are to be taken as the same.

Amendments—SI 2001/1228.

PART II
REGISTERED OFFICES

9 Situation of registered office

(1) A limited liability partnership shall –

    (a)   at all times have a registered office situated in England and Wales or in Wales, or

    (b)   at all times have a registered office situated in Scotland, to which communications and notices may be addressed.

(2) On the incorporation of a limited liability partnership the situation of its registered office shall be that stated in the incorporation document.

(3) Where the registered office of a limited liability partnership is situated in Wales, but the incorporation document does not state that it is to be situated in Wales (as opposed to England and Wales), the limited liability partnership may deliver notice to the registrar stating that its registered office is to be situated in Wales.

(4) A notice delivered under sub-paragraph (3) –

    (a)   shall be in a form approved by the registrar, and

    (b)   shall be signed by a designated member of the limited liability partnership or authenticated in a manner approved by the registrar.

10 Change of registered office

(1) A limited liability partnership may change its registered office by delivering notice of the change to the registrar.

(2) A notice delivered under sub-paragraph (1) –

    (a)   shall be in a form approved by the registrar, and

    (b)   shall be signed by a designated member of the limited liability partnership or authenticated in a manner approved by the registrar.

Appendix 2

LIMITED LIABILITY PARTNERSHIPS REGULATIONS 2001[1]

SI 2001/1090

ARRANGEMENT OF REGULATIONS

Regulation

---

[1]   Made under: Limited Liability Partnerships Act 2000, ss 14–17.
The Schedules to these Regulations modify or amend existing legislation, or apply to LLPs certain subordinate legislation, and are not set out here. The primary legislation affected is reproduced as amended on the companion CD-ROM. These Regulations are also reproduced with the Schedules on the companion CD-ROM.

PART V
FINANCIAL SERVICES AND MARKETS

6 Application of provisions contained in Parts XV and XXIV of the 2000 Act to limited liability partnerships

PART VI
DEFAULT PROVISION

7 Default provision for limited liability partnerships
8 Expulsion

PART VII
MISCELLANEOUS

9 General and consequential amendments
10 Application of subordinate legislation

PART I
CITATION, COMMENCEMENT AND INTERPRETATION

1 Citation and commencement

These Regulations may be cited as the Limited Liability Partnerships Regulations 2001 and shall come into force on 6 April 2001.

2 Interpretation

In these Regulations –

'the 1985 Act' means the Companies Act 1985;
'the 1986 Act' means the Insolvency Act 1986;
'the 2000 Act' means the Financial Services and Markets Act 2000;
'devolved', in relation to the provisions of the 1986 Act, means the provisions of the 1986 Act which are listed in Schedule 4 and, in their application to Scotland, concern wholly or partly, matters which are set out in Section C.2 of Schedule 5 to the Scotland Act 1998 as being exceptions to the reservations made in that Act in the field of insolvency;
'limited liability partnership agreement', in relation to a limited liability partnership, means any agreement express or implied between the members of the limited liability partnership or between the limited liability partnership and the members of the limited liability partnership which determines the mutual rights and duties of the members, and their rights and duties in relation to the limited liability partnership;
'the principal Act' means the Limited Liability Partnerships Act 2000; and
'shadow member', in relation to limited liability partnerships, means a person in accordance with whose directions or instructions the members of the limited liability partnership are accustomed to act (but so that a person is not deemed a

shadow member by reason only that the members of the limited partnership act on advice given by him in a professional capacity).

PART II
ACCOUNTS AND AUDIT

3 Application of the accounts and audit provisions of the 1985 Act to limited liability partnerships

(1) Subject to paragraph (2), the provisions of Part VII of the 1985 Act (Accounts and Audit) shall apply to limited liability partnerships.

(2) The enactments referred to in paragraph (1) shall apply to limited liability partnerships, except where the context otherwise requires, with the following modifications –

    (a) references to a company shall include references to a limited liability partnership;

    (b) references to a director or to an officer of a company shall include references to a member of a limited liability partnership;

    (c) references to other provisions of the 1985 Act and to provisions of the Insolvency Act 1986 shall include references to those provisions as they apply to limited liability partnerships in accordance with Parts III and IV of these Regulations;

    (d) the modifications set out in Schedule 1 to these Regulations; and

    (e) such further modifications as the context requires for the purpose of giving effect to those provisions as applied by this Part of these Regulations.

PART III
COMPANIES ACT 1985 AND COMPANY DIRECTORS DISQUALIFICATION ACT 1986

4 Application of the remainder of the provisions of the 1985 Act and of the provisions of the Company Directors Disqualification Act 1986 to limited liability partnerships

(1) The provisions of the 1985 Act specified in the first column of Part I of Schedule 2 to these Regulations shall apply to limited liability partnerships, except where the context otherwise requires, with the following modifications –

    (a) references to a company shall include references to a limited liability partnership;

    (b) references to the Companies Acts shall include references to the principal Act and regulations made thereunder;

    (c) references to the Insolvency Act 1986 shall include references to that Act as it applies to limited liability partnerships by virtue of Part IV of these Regulations;

    (d) references in a provision of the 1985 Act to other provisions of that Act shall include references to those other provisions as they apply to limited liability partnerships by virtue of these Regulations;

    (e) references to the memorandum of association of a company shall include references to the incorporation document of a limited liability partnership;

    (f) references to a shadow director shall include references to a shadow member;

(g)   references to a director of a company or to an officer of a company shall include references to a member of a limited liability partnership;

(h)   the modifications, if any, specified in the second column of Part I of Schedule 2 opposite the provision specified in the first column; and

(i)   such further modifications as the context requires for the purpose of giving effect to that legislation as applied by these Regulations.

(2) The provisions of the Company Director Disqualification Act 1986 shall apply to limited liability partnerships, except where the context otherwise requires, with the following modifications –

(a)   references to a company shall include references to a limited liability partnership;

(b)   references to the Companies Acts shall include references to the principal Act and regulations made thereunder and references to the companies legislation shall include references to the principal Act, regulations made thereunder and to any enactment applied by regulations to limited liability partnerships;

(d)   references to the Insolvency Act 1986 shall include references to that Act as it applies to limited liability partnerships by virtue of Part IV of these Regulations;

(e)   references to the memorandum of association of a company shall include references to the incorporation document of a limited liability partnership;

(f)   references to a shadow director shall include references to a shadow member;

(g)   references to a director of a company or to an officer of a company shall include references to a member of a limited liability partnership;

(h)   the modifications, if any, specified in the second column of Part II of Schedule 2 opposite the provision specified in the first column; and

(i)   such further modifications as the context requires for the purpose of giving effect to that legislation as applied by these Regulations.

PART IV
WINDING UP AND INSOLVENCY

5 Application of the 1986 Act to limited liability partnerships

(1) Subject to paragraphs (2) and (3), the following provisions of the 1986 Act, shall apply to limited liability partnerships –

(a)   Parts I, II, III, IV, VI and VII of the First Group of Parts (company insolvency; companies winding up),

(b)   the Third Group of Parts (miscellaneous matters bearing on both company and individual insolvency; general interpretation; final provisions).

(2) The provisions of the 1986 Act referred to in paragraph (1) shall apply to limited liability partnerships, except where the context otherwise requires, with the following modifications –

(a)   references to a company shall include references to a limited liability partnership;

(b)   references to a director or to an officer of a company shall include references to a member of a limited liability partnership;

(c)   references to a shadow director shall include references to a shadow member;

(d)   references to the 1985 Act, the Company Directors Disqualification Act 1986, the Companies Act 1989 or to any provisions of those Acts or to any provisions of the 1986 Act shall include references to those Acts or provisions as they apply to limited liability partnerships by virtue of the principal Act;

(e)   references to the memorandum of association of a company and to the articles of association of a company shall include references to the limited liability partnership agreement of a limited liability partnership;

(f)   the modifications set out in Schedule 3 to these Regulations; and

(g)   such further modifications as the context requires for the purpose of giving effect to that legislation as applied by these Regulations.

(3) In the application of this regulation to Scotland, the provisions of the 1986 Act referred to in paragraph (1) shall not include the provisions listed in Schedule 4 to the extent specified in that Schedule.

PART V
FINANCIAL SERVICES AND MARKETS

6 Application of provisions contained in Parts XV and XXIV of the 2000 Act to limited liability partnerships

(1) Subject to paragraph (2), sections 215(3),(4) and (6), 356, 359(1) to (4), 361 to 365, 367, 370 and 371 of the 2000 Act shall apply to limited liability partnerships.

(2) The provisions of the 2000 Act referred to in paragraph (1) shall apply to limited liability partnerships, except where the context otherwise requires, with the following modifications –

(a)   references to a company shall include references to a limited liability partnership;

(b)   references to body shall include references to a limited liability partnership; and

(c)   references to the 1985 Act, the 1986 Act or to any of the provisions of those Acts shall include references to those Acts or provisions as they apply to limited liability partnerships by virtue of the principal Act.

PART VI
DEFAULT PROVISION

7 Default provision for limited liability partnerships

The mutual rights and duties of the members and the mutual rights and duties of the limited liability partnership and the members shall be determined, subject to the provisions of the general law and to the terms of any limited liability partnership agreement, by the following rules:

(1) All the members of a limited liability partnership are entitled to share equally in the capital and profits of the limited liability partnership.

(2) The limited liability partnership must indemnify each member in respect of payments made and personal liabilities incurred by him –

(a)   in the ordinary and proper conduct of the business of the limited liability partnership; or

(b)   in or about anything necessarily done for the preservation of the business or property of the limited liability partnership.

(3) Every member may take part in the management of the limited liability partnership.

(4) No member shall be entitled to remuneration for acting in the business or management of the limited liability partnership.

(5) No person may be introduced as a member or voluntarily assign an interest in a limited liability partnership without the consent of all existing members.

(6) Any difference arising as to ordinary matters connected with the business of the limited liability partnership may be decided by a majority of the members, but no change may be made in the nature of the business of the limited liability partnership without the consent of all the members.

(7) The books and records of the limited liability partnership are to be made available for inspection at the registered office of the limited liability partnership or at such other place as the members think fit and every member of the limited liability partnership may when he thinks fit have access to and inspect and copy any of them.

(8) Each member shall render true accounts and full information of all things affecting the limited liability partnership to any member or his legal representatives.

(9) If a member, without the consent of the limited liability partnership, carries on any business of the same nature as and competing with the limited liability partnership, he must account for and pay over to the limited liability partnership all profits made by him in that business.

(10) Every member must account to the limited liability partnership for any benefit derived by him without the consent of the limited liability partnership from any transaction concerning the limited liability partnership, or from any use by him of the property of the limited liability partnership, name or business connection.

8 Expulsion

No majority of the members can expel any member unless a power to do so has been conferred by express agreement between the members.

PART VII
MISCELLANEOUS

9 General and consequential amendments

(1) Subject to paragraph (2), the enactments mentioned in Schedule 5 shall have effect subject to the amendments specified in that Schedule.

(2) In the application of this regulation to Scotland –

(a)   paragraph 15 of Schedule 5 which amends section 110 of the 1986 Act shall not extend to Scotland; and

(b)   paragraph 22 of Schedule 5 which applies to limited liability partnerships the culpable officer provisions in existing primary legislation shall not extend to Scotland insofar as it relates to matters which have not been reserved by Schedule 5 to the Scotland Act 1998.

10 Application of subordinate legislation

(1) The subordinate legislation specified in Schedule 6 shall apply as from time to time in force to limited liability partnerships and –

(a) in the case of the subordinate legislation listed in Part I of that Schedule with such modifications as the context requires for the purpose of giving effect to the provisions of the Companies Act 1985 which are applied by these Regulations;

(b) in the case of the subordinate legislation listed in Part II of that Schedule with such modifications as the context requires for the purpose of giving effect to the provisions of the Insolvency Act 1986 which are applied by these Regulations; and

(c) in the case of the subordinate legislation listed in Part III of that Schedule with such modifications as the context requires for the purpose of giving effect to the provisions of the Business Names Act 1985 and the Company Directors Disqualification Act 1986 which are applied by these Regulations.

(2) In the case of any conflict between any provision of the subordinate legislation applied by paragraph (1) and any provision of these Regulations, the latter shall prevail.

****

INDEX